DATE DUE

THE RUMBLE OF
CALIFORNIA POLITICS
1848-1970

ORIGINAL CONTRIBUTORS

ROYCE D. DELMATIER
Chairman, Department of Political Science
Chico State College

JOHN E. BAUR
Associate Professor of History
San Fernando Valley State College

BENJAMIN F. GILBERT
Professor of History
San Jose State College

KENNETH G. GOODE
Assistant to the Executive Vice Chancellor
University of California at Berkeley

JAMES E. GREGG
Professor of Political Science
Chico State College

JUDSON A. GRENIER
Associate Professor of History
California State College at Dominguez Hills

WILLIAM H. HUTCHINSON
Professor of History
Chico State College

CLARENCE F. McINTOSH
Professor of History
Chico State College

FRANK A. MESPLE
Coordinator of Consulting Services
California State Senate

LEONARD ROWE
Division of Social Sciences
Bennington College

DONALD E. WALTERS
Professor of History
San Jose State College

EARL G. WATERS
Chief, State Division of Investigation
Department of Professional and Vocational Standards

THE RUMBLE OF CALIFORNIA POLITICS

1848-1970

GENERAL EDITORS

ROYCE D. DELMATIER
Chairman, Department of Political Science
Chico State College

CLARENCE F. McINTOSH
Professor of History
Chico State College

EARL G. WATERS
Chief, State Division of Investigation
Department of Professional and Vocational Standards

JOHN WILEY & SONS, INC.
New York • London • Sydney • Toronto

Library of Congress Catalog Card Number: 78–126224

ISBN 0–471–20633–4 (cloth)
    0–471–20634–2 (paper)
Printed in the United States of America

10 9 8 7 6 5 4 3 2 1

DEDICATED TO

John, Karl, Denise, Charmaine

and the Student Generation

that hopefully will solve the
problems of peace among men where
the Older Generation has failed

"and the truth will make you free"
John, VIII, 32

⊷PREFACE⊷

The politics of California is a subject of increasing significance in the affairs of today's citizen. The state's phenomenal twentieth century population growth has increased its importance in national politics, and, since the Second World War, its governors and United States Senators have become major politicians on the national scene. The purpose of this volume is to assist the reader in understanding the realities and the uniqueness of the California political scene.

Twelve specialists have contributed chapters to this book. Each author has an in-depth knowledge, established through research or experience, of the political era about which he has written. The specialists are responsible for original drafts of chapters and most of the illustrations and bibliographic references that accompany them. Each of these authors, with one exception, is identified at the foot of the first page of the appropriate chapter. The exception is Kenneth G. Goode, whose contributions are included in Chapters 1, 2, and 13. The general editors assume responsibility for the selection of the original contributors and for the outline of the work. They tried to allow the interpretations of the individual specialists to stand as presented, believing that these contribute to the richness and interest of the volume. Inevitably, the substance of these interpretations has been altered somewhat through the process of editing so that the editors assume final responsibility for interpretation. The editors also supplemented the illustrations and reference notes.

Among the current works available on California's political institutions, none spends more than one chapter describing the history of its politics. This book follows a chronological approach with the exception of Chapters 12 and 13, in which special topics are considered. The result is a coherent history of California politics, 1848–1970, which we hope will have an appeal to college students and general readers alike. This is the only volume that gives a complete coverage of California politics from the signing of the Treaty of Guadalupe Hidalgo on February 2, 1848 in which Mexico ceded California to the United States to the Direct Primary Election of June 2, 1970 in which the candidates were chosen for the thirty-fifth gubernatorial election. We hope our readers, and our colleagues in the fields of history and political science, will find this a valuable and useful volume. We welcome your suggestions and criticisms. We further wish to express our sincerest and most grateful thanks to three

Preface

extraordinary young women with outstanding typing capabilities: Mrs. Connie M. Homesley, Secretary to the Department of Psychology, Chico State College; Mrs. Betty J. Mills, Secretary to the Department of Political Science, Chico State College; and Miss Frances E. Tozier, Private Secretary to the Executive Secretary, State Board of Equalization.

Chico, California   R. D. DELMATIER
August 1970   C. F. MCINTOSH
                                                                       E. G. WATERS

·CONTENTS·

CALIFORNIA COUNTIES
1970

(from *Patterns on the Land*)

THE RUMBLE OF
CALIFORNIA POLITICS
1848-1970

The Origin
of its Species

In the beginning there were the Indians. For thousands of years they lived in El Dorado, a rich land where nature provided an abundance of plant and animal food. Around 20,000 B. C. their ancestors had migrated across the Bering Straits from Asia onto the two great continents which were to become the Americas. They settled in this land which swooped down from the majestic Sierra to the broad, blue Pacific and reached from the giant forests of redwoods and pines to the silent Mojave Desert. Most hunted and fished, some foraged. The stalwart sought game and speared salmon, others snared small game and gathered grasshoppers and caterpillars, clams and mussels. Foragers lived on acorns and piñon nuts, seeds and berries. Only a few dug for roots. It is not, therefore, to the credit of early American settlers that all the California Indians were contemptuously referred to as 'Diggers.' But American settlers were not the first to intrude. The first strangers that we know of were explorers by sea. In their quest for gold, they had dared the unknown Atlantic and found a new world. Others would follow and extend their search till they had reached the vast Pacific. Now, less than fifty years after Columbus cast eyes on this new land, Hernando de Alarcon led the first white men to see the rich soil of California.

An omen of what was to come was in the name these Spaniards gave to this new land. Just who christened it California is not clearly recorded, but by the time discoverer Juan Rodriguez Cabrillo entered San Diego Bay in 1542, the name was well established. To the Spanish, the word described that paradise peopled with beauteous black women with golden arms in the romance, *Las Sergas de Esplandian* (circa 1492–1510). So this was the mythical paradise, the land of gold and fabulous women.

 Royce D. Delmatier and Earl G. Waters were primarily responsible for the original draft of Chapter 1.

1

Whatever the mythical meaning of the word for a place which existed only in dreams, California was to become and remain a kind of paradise—a garden of Eden, a land of gold, of fabulous women, of fabulous everything. And, what is California today? It is the land whose population thinks in superlatives.

It is a land of near-perfect climate, of flowers, of fruits, and nuts. It has twelve hundred miles of shoreline, twenty thousand square miles of desert, mountains whose peaks match the grandeur of the Swiss Alps. It is a country containing productive valleys, giant forests, barren hills. It is a colossal colossus. It is a land of super superlatives. Consequently, it is a land of hope and promise, and a breeding ground of faddists, cultists, and extremists of every stripe.

California is a state full of contradictions. The world's tallest living things are destroyed there to make packing cases for its newest inventions. The most Democratic county helps to send a Republican to Congress while the most Republican county elects a Democrat. A state with unsurpassed scenic beauty, its people work overtime defacing the natural wonders with man-made structures.

California has three of the largest astronomical observatories in the world yet its people cannot see three years ahead in its public planning. It harbors the world's leading scientists, but does not solve its air and water pollution problems. It is a place where people cheer Black athletes, but refuse them membership in the athletic clubs, a place that brags about having the largest Chinese settlement outside of Asia and discriminates against Orientals in its residential areas, a state that struggles for welfare and education funds and squanders millions on a foolish state exposition venture 400 miles from the center of its population. It is a state possessing awesome stands of virgin redwoods and a Governor who dismisses redwood conservation efforts with a flip, "If you've seen one tree, you've seen them all."

A state that turned a fertile valley into a desert and a desert into a fertile valley, California is also a state where a body of fresh water became a great salt sea and yet millions are spent turning the ocean into drinking water.

California, a land spawned on the opportunities for the riches of gold, one hundred twenty-two years later continues to offer unlimited golden opportunities. In this land where spoilers stripped the slopes of Lassen of its forests, the Owens Valley of its waters, the Mother Lode of its soil, the Santa Clara Valley of its orchards and Monterey Bay of its fish, all the while its leaders eulogize the pioneers of progress. This land has an ugly history of violence, depredation, crime, scandal and discrimination which hides behind a fabricated history of romantic nonsense.

This, then, is the Golden State. This, then, is where the paradox is the norm and the norm is always unusual. How did this spectacular wonderland get this way? How does it continue to foster fantastic anachronisms along with its dramatic innovations? Just how good is its government? Is it still the frontier of America? What qualities of leadership does it have?

California's contrasts and constant metamorphisms can be explained in terms of its origins as a state, its geography, and the background of its populace. Physically, the state reaches along the Pacific seaboard a distance equal to that covered on the Atlantic by all of twelve states from Maine to Georgia. It takes ten of these states to equal the square mileage of California. California enjoys a mild climate along most of its coastline, but in the interior it offers a variety from temperatures of 45° below to a blistering 134°. The average annual rainfall ranges from less than 2 inches to more than 109 inches. Some areas have recorded as high as 174 inches in one year and as much as 26 inches in a twenty-four hour period, while others have gone 401 consecutive days without rain. Annual snowfall in parts of the majestic Sierra Nevada Mountains is between 400 and 500 inches. So people freeze in one place and bask in the sun elsewhere. One county may be threatened with a flood while in another county people are irrigating their land.

California's people are either the descendants of invaders from many lands or the invaders themselves. First came the Spaniards. Following Alarcon's exploration of the lower Colorado by way of the Gulf of California in 1540, Cabrillo made extensive explorations along the California coast as far as Monterey Bay. Upon his death in 1543, Bartolome Ferrelo continued the voyage perhaps as far as the Rogue River in Oregon.

Thirty-five years later, in 1579, Francis Drake landed north of San Francisco Bay and took possession for England. This claim was never pursued by settlement, and the Spanish continued for the next 200 years to explore and eventually settle the area. Most notable in the efforts to colonize this portion of the New World was the revered Father Junipero Serra, the Franciscan friar who founded a string of missions starting in San Diego, in 1769, to beyond San Francisco Bay. These stand today, 200 years later.

In 1812, forty-three years after Father Serra founded his first mission, Ivan A. Kuskoff established Fort Ross on the Sonoma Coast. The Russian colonists managed for more than a quarter of a century to pillage the coastal waters of seal, otter and fur-bearing ocean mammals, and voluntarily withdrew in 1841.

Meantime, in 1822, the rest of California exchanged allegiance from Spain to Mexico, which had rebelled to form an independent nation. The transition from Spanish to Mexican rule in Upper California, 1821–1825, was gradual and ran rather smoothly. In light of the growth of discontent among the missionaries, mission Indians, soldiers, and settlers during the privations and hardships caused by the Mexican war of independence, 1808–1821, this was no mean achievement. In spite of this peaceful transition, instability and weakness characterized the two decades of republican rule before conquest by the United States.[1]

Mexico's ownership of California was therefore to be short-lived. In June of 1846 the Bear Flag, standard of the California Republic, was raised at Sonoma; and less than a month later, on July 7, Old Glory flew over Monterey. California has the distinction of having been under more flags than any other state, a distinction which has influenced its culture.

The political influence of the native-born Spanish-speaking Californians (*Californios*) in the affairs of the territory was reduced suddenly from majority to minority status with American conquest and the Gold Rush, 1846–1849, and gradually diminished during the remainder of the nineteenth century. It declined first to the regional base of coastal California south from Monterey and then to local pockets of support, which continued into the twentieth century.

The peak of the *Californio* power in the American period came in the constitutional convention of 1849 in Monterey. *Californios* numbered eight out of the total delegation of forty-eight, a slight over-representation since they made up some thirteen percent of the population and had sixteen percent of the delegates. Included were: Jose Antonio Carrillo, Mariano Guadalupe Vallejo, Pablo de la Guerra, Jose M. Covarrubias, Miguel de Pedrorena, Antonio M. Pico, Jacinto Rodriguez, and Manuel Dominguez. Probably most influential were Carrillo of Los Angeles and Vallejo of Sonoma and de la Guerra of Santa Barbara. The *Californios* sometimes voted as a bloc, as against a proposal to limit the suffrage to white males only, but also divided along sectional lines, as on the issue of creating a state in the north and a territory in the south. The delegation voted unanimously to print all laws in Spanish as well as English, a measure which remained in effect until 1879 during the life of the first Constitution.

Some of the *Californio* leaders took active parts in American political parties in the early 1850's at the local, county, and state levels. Seven served in one or more of the first three Legislatures. Although some supported the Whig Party, a majority entered the Democratic Party ranks where Antonio Coronel was an effective leader for thirty years. A few, like Mariano Vallejo, entered the Republican Party as early as 1856, but more went into it by way of the Union cause during the Civil War. Other important *Californios* in political party activities included: Tomas Sanchez, Joaquin Carrillo, Jose Maria Covarrubias, Pablo de la Guerra, Antonio M. de la Guerra, Andres Pico, Jose G. Estudillo, Reginaldo F. del Valle, and Romualdo Pacheco, Jr. The parties continued to honor the *Californios* and their descendants in the twentieth century by naming them to delegations and committees. Their influence, however, was minimal.[2]

4

Africans and individuals of African descent, as well as Indians and Spaniards, were also important in early California history. As Spanish explorers moved northward through Mexico and into what is now southwestern United States, blacks accompanied them and played a prominent role in the exploration and settlement of this region. By the eighteenth century virtually every description of Spanish towns in the provinces of Chihuahua, Durango and Sonora has reference to the presence of Blacks and mulattos. When the Spanish empire was expanded to include Baja California in the early 1700's, a large number of Blacks and persons of unclassified, mixed ancestry (*castas*) moved across the Gulf of California to that peninsula.

It is not surprising that Blacks played an important role in the exploration and settlement of California. It has been estimated that at least twenty percent of the Spanish-speaking settlers and soldiers in California in the 1790's were of African descent, without whose presence "several Spanish settlements in California could not have been founded. . . ."[3] In 1781, when the city of Los Angeles was founded, twenty-six of the original forty-six settlers were of African descent. Santa Barbara possessed a Spanish-speaking population which was more than one-half non-white, San Jose at least 24.3%, and Monterey 18.5% in 1790; and San Francisco a military garrison of at least 18.1% Black in 1782.[4]

During the first two centuries of Spanish domination in North America Blacks did not figure prominently in the political affairs of the empire. However, between 1769 through 1821, a few persons of African descent were able to rise to offices of political prominence. Francisco Rey, a mulatto rancher, served as mayor of Los Angeles from 1793 to 1795; Jose Bartolome Tapia, a mulatto who owned the scenic Rancho Malibu, served as majordomo (a supervisory position) of San Luis Obispo Mission as did Miguel Pico at Ventura Mission from 1819 through 1821. Although these examples illustrate that persons of African descent during the Spanish period in California held political offices of considerable prestige and power, because it was quite easy for a person of African descent to undergo a "race change", records of contributions that persons of Afro-American descent made in California politics are, for the most part, unavailable.

The Pico family, whose members rose to positions of wealth and political prominence, typifies the "race change" process. Santiago de la Cruz Pico (Spanish-Indian) married Maria de la Bastida (mulatto) and five of their sons (Miguel, Patricio, Francisco Javier, Jose Maria and Jose Dolores) served as soldiers, rising to the rank of *cabo* (corporal) and *alferez* (ensign). In 1860 Miguel's widow died, leaving fifteen children, one hundred sixteen grandchildren and ninety-seven great grandchildren, a total of 116 males and 112 females.

5

Andres Pico, the son of Jose Maria Pico, who had married the mulatto Gertrudis Amezquita in 1791, rose to the rank of captain in the Spanish army, served as an official delegate to Mexico City, represented Californians at the treaty discussions with John C. Frémont in January, 1848, and served as a member of the California State Legislature. His older brother, Pio Pico, after serving in numerous capacities in the government, became governor in 1845, serving until the United States forces overran the province in 1846.

The Pico family, as did most families of African descent who acquired wealth and prominence, tended to marry socially prominent and wealthy lighter-skinned persons and thus changed their race and dispersed their African and Indian ancestry in ever more minute quantities.

One of the most successful Blacks on the California political scene during the late Mexican period was the mulatto William Alexander Leidesdorff. From 1841 to 1845 he operated a trading vessel between San Francisco and Hawaii. With the wealth that he accumulated he purchased extensive property in and about San Francisco. In 1844 he became a Mexican citizen and the following year he became the United States Vice-Consul, serving under Thomas O. Larkin. The eminent California historian, H. H. Bancroft, states that Leidesdorff "was not only one of (San Francisco's) most prominent businessmen, but a member of the council, treasurer, and member of the school committee, taking an active part in local politics. . . ."[5]

The Black polulation of California grew during the 1848 Gold Rush. Initially, Blacks did not suffer from any serious overt discrimination since California was still largely Hispano-Mexican. However, when whites became dominant in the gold region, the intense rivalry for riches led to antipathy between whites and non-whites so that Blacks, along with Indians and Mexicans, suffered from physical assaults and discriminatory practices.

During the 1850's Blacks began to move from the goldfields into the cities and towns. By 1860 one-third of the state's Blacks resided in San Francisco or Sacramento counties and the cities of San Francisco and Sacramento became the early centers of organized activities by Blacks. Between 1852 and 1856 Blacks succeeded in establishing the Baptist, African, Methodist-Episcopal and African Methodist Episcopal Zion churches, the San Francisco Athenaeum (an educational and cultural center), *The Mirror of the Times* newspaper and numerous private schools.

The government of California, from its very beginning, placed persons of African descent under severe legal proscription. In 1849, which marked the end of the Mexican era, the California Constitutional Convention, with the mulatto Antonio M. Pico in attendance as a delegate, voted to disfranchise "Indians, Africans and the descendants of Africans." Furthermore, Blacks generally could not obtain land under the preemption laws, nor because they could not qualify for citizenship, could they obtain land anywhere in federal territories in the West.

The 1849–1850 Legislature continued the establishment of racist policy. Although the Legislature failed to pass a law prohibiting the entry of free Blacks into California, it did limit membership in the militia to "free white males," prohibited non-whites from testifying in court against whites, and adopted vagrancy-peonage laws.

Between 1850 and 1862, the "Chiv Democrats," a pro-southern faction, gained a predominant position in California politics and more laws proscribing the rights of Blacks were passed, including one which made it possible for Blacks who had entered California before 1850 to be seized by anyone who claimed them as ex-slaves without the Blacks having any right to testify on their own behalf. However, the "Chivs" failed in their attempt to pass a law which would have made California a half-slave and half-free state.

Responding to these assaults on their rights, Blacks convened the first Convention of the Colored Citizens of the State of California in 1855. This organization, which lasted until World War I, fought for equal protection under the laws, passed resolutions against discriminatory housing and education and petitioned the State Legislature for legal redress. In 1862 Blacks in San Francisco organized the Franchise League to secure the right to vote and began campaigning for the right to testify in court cases involving whites.

The efforts of these groups, although courageous, were ineffective, for it was not until the Republican party assumed control over California politics that the barriers of discrimination and segregation began to break down. In 1863 Blacks obtained the right to testify in cases where whites were defendants and in 1870 the first Black jury was convened in Sacramento. Although not ratified by California, the Fifteenth Amendment gave Blacks the right to vote, which they began to do in the 1870's. It was not until 1874, when the Legislature decided that non-white children could go to a white school if no colored school existed, that the statewide segregated school system, which was formally established in 1870, began to change its posture. Continuous boycotts, law suits, resolutions by the Colored Citizens Convention and editorials in *The Mirror of the Times* ended the dual school system of education after 1875.

Some of the most outstanding Blacks who were active in civic and political affairs in California during this time were: William Smith, Biddy Mason, Miffin W. Gibbs, Moses Rodgers, George W. Dennis, John A. Barber, Henry Miles and Mammy Pleasant.[6]

It would now take the population of twenty-one states to equal California. Here are the people from every nation and every race in the world. True, the foreign born represent less than a tenth of the population, but their off-spring make California a prism of minority groups. Here, too, are the people who have uprooted themselves from every state in the nation to resettle in the Golden West, and along with their belongings, they have brought their customs and beliefs and their prides and prejudices.

Under the Spanish and the brief Mexican regime, California was being gradually settled by leisure-loving people content to live a pastoral life on the land grants. But their way of life was threatened by foreigners. In addition to the Russians at Fort Ross, British and Yankee traders began to arrive and a few hundred, like William Hartnell and Thomas O. Larkin, had settled among them by 1846. A Swiss, John A. Sutter arrived in 1839 and founded Nueva Helvetia, which was later to be Sacramento, on a 48,839 acre grant.

Fur traders from the east blazed trails overland to California. In 1826, Jedediah Smith set out from Bear Lake in Utah, traveling down the Colorado and along the Mojave River, into San Bernardino and the Mission San Gabriel. From there he went north to the central valley. Other fur traders such as James Ohio Pattie, Ewing Young, William Wolfskill and Joseph Walker, were among the early pathfinders. Famed Kit Carson and John C. Frémont became pathmarkers across the western wilderness.

In 1841 Captain John Bartleson led the first sizeable overland party of settlers to the Golden West. John Bidwell was a member of this group of thirty-four emigrants which became commonly known as the Bidwell Party because Bidwell later wrote about the experience. Bartleson was incompetent and lost the leadership by default.

The westward flow had started and for the next several years the hardy pioneers, coming both overland and around the Horn, settled in the northern part of the state mainly around the Napa, Sonoma and Sacramento Valleys. They set themselves to developing the riches of their new homeland, building grain and saw mills and producing wheat, hides, tallow, soap and lumber. Their migration did not then affect the Spanish-California settlements, which were mostly in the south around San Diego, Los Angeles, Santa Barbara, San Buenaventura and San Luis Obispo, with the principal port and capitol at Monterey.

But friction was to develop between the American settlers and the Californians, albeit some of it was provoked needlessly by Fremont. What Fremont's ambitions might have led to were not to be known for hostilities broke out between the United States and Mexico which resulted in Commodore John D. Sloat's bloodless conquest of Monterey and the rapid acquisition of California. It was not, however, until February 2, 1848, nineteen months after Captain William Mervine had raised the Stars and Stripes over California, that the territory was officially ceded by Mexico under the Treaty of Guadalupe Hidalgo.

Unknown until after the signing was the fact that the week before, on

January 24, James Wilson Marshall had made the discovery that was to alter the course of California, if not American, history. California was after all what Alarcon and Cabrillo had thought it was 300 years earlier, El Dorado! Marshall's discovery of gold in Sutter's millrace at Coloma turned the rumble of the West into a roar that has grown louder each decade for more than one hundred years. The American sources of the flood of migrants begun in 1848 would profoundly influence California politics. New York was the leading contributory state during the nineteenth century. Illinois and surrounding north central states replaced her during the first four decades of this century, and they were, in turn, replaced by the Lone Star State of Texas and her neighbors. These emigrants brought their political views and institutions with them and have shaped and reshaped the political future of the Golden State; in the process, they have bewildered political analysts.[7]

At the end of the Mexican War, California was under the control of military government. This was a situation not to the liking of either the early Californians or the more recent emigrants. Their impatience was marked by growing protestations. Meanwhile, some claimed that President Zachary Taylor favored procrastination because of the inevitable conflict in Congress in the attempt to provide civil government for California.[8] But the rush of the forty-niners by land and sea to this El Dorado brought about chaotic conditions which demanded rapid action. During this period no law existed except for the laws of nature and of the divine.

The clamor for statehood had begun shortly after Mervine's raising of the flag in 1846, but it was not until May of 1849 that actual plans were made for a constitutional convention to meet in August of that year. General Bennett Riley, just appointed military governor in April 1849, concurred and proclaimed the convention would be held on September 1, in California's second oldest military settlement, Monterey. The meeting place was Colton Hall, a two-story adobe built two years earlier by the Reverend Walter Colton as a schoolhouse and public hall. Colton, with Robert Semple, had established the first American newspaper in California in 1846. Becoming the first American Alcalde, Colton used convict labor and sold town lots, taxed liquor stores and fined gamblers to provide the labor and funds for the building.[9]

The convention of forty-eight delegates, many of whom were meeting one another for the first time, proceeded to draw up a constitution with which Congress was to concur a year later on September 9, 1850. It was provided that the newly drafted constitution would be submitted to a vote of the people on November 13 and that a governor and other state officers would be elected at that time. Election day was greeted by torrential rains and approximately 14,000 hardy souls cast their ballots. Less than fourteen percent of the estimated qualified voters adopted the state's new charter and placed in office Peter H.

Peter Burnett (1807–1895), a Democrat, was the first American civil governor of California. (Courtesy of California State Library.)

Burnett as the first Governor. General Riley, by proclamation, recognized the new government on December 20 and resigned as military governor.

All of these procedures were illegal, or at least extralegal, since Congress had given no authority. But the crusty pioneers proceeded to elect the first two United States Senators immediately after the swearing in of Burnett. Frémont was elected on the first ballot and William M. Gwin on the third. The two set out for Washington immediately, arriving in January to camp on the steps of Congress until the following September. They must have spent their time profitably lobbying for statehood since on September 9, 1850, California became one of only two states west of the Appalachian Mountains (outside of those hewn out of the original thirteen) ever admitted without going through territorial status. Two days later, Frémont and Gwin were seated as members of the United States Senate, with Fremont by lot drawing the short term which expired March 4, 1851, while Gwin's initial term was to run to March 4, 1855. Frémont's career as a senator then was to last only 175 days.[10]

California's bumptious entrance into the family of states had broken the precarious balance between the North and South in the United States Senate. The fact it was the first noncontiguous land to become a state, if an issue at all, was dwarfed by the slavery extension question. In this debate the giants of the second generation of American politics were pitted against each other. Clay, Webster, Calhoun were the old guard. Leaders of a new generation were Jefferson Davis, Stephen A. Douglas, William H. Seward and Salmon P. Chase. Calhoun fought bitterly. From his deathbed he sent for Gwin in order to explain his opposition. But Clay's suave peacemaking carried the day and the Compromise of 1850 resulted in California's admission.[11] The plea of Sam Walter Foss in "The Coming American" carved in marble over California's State Office Building No. 1 in Sacramento, seemed to have been answered:

> Bring me men to match my mountains
> Bring me men to match my plains
> Men with empires in their purpose
> And new eras in their brains.

The Democratic Party, for the most part, came to accept the Compromise of 1850 as the final settlement of the slavery problem. The Whigs were unable to unite on the question. Many of their leaders in the North opposed the solution and refused the renomination of Millard Fillmore as the party standard bearer in 1852. Within a few years, many had bolted to the new Republican Party, which supported the halting of slavery expansion ideas initially put forward by the Free Soil Party.

The political transmutations on the national scene were reflected in the early political history of California. Of the sixteen Free Soilers elected to Congress in the late 1840s, one, Frémont, was from California. And when the remnants of the Whigs moved into the "Know-Nothing" (American) Party and ran Fillmore as a third party candidate for President in 1856, California had already the year before elected as governor one of their new party members. This was John Neely Johnson, who later served on the Supreme Court of Nevada.[12]

The office of governor under the first constitution provided a two-year term commencing with the first Monday after the first day in January, the first office holder excepted, for Burnett was sworn in on December 20, 1849, five days after the effective date of the constitution. Constitutional amendments adopted in 1862 changed the term to four years and moved the commencement up to the first Monday after the first day of December. The adoption of the second constitution in 1879, still in force with numerous amendments, retained the four-year term but restored the January date for the term's beginning. This also provided elections would be held in even numbered years and to square things limited the first term of the new governor to be elected under this constitution to three years, thereafter reverting to four.

California has been served by thirty-three governors, thirteen of whom have been Democrats, eighteen Republicans, one Progressive and one American ("Know-Nothing"). Only two of the fourteen governors who have served California in the twentieth century have been Democrats. Both of these, Culbert L. Olson and Edmund G. "Pat" Brown, were soundly defeated in bids for re-election. However, Brown is one of the four ever to be reelected to a second term. John Bigler was the first, although the terms then were two years. Hiram W. Johnson was elected twice, but resigned in the middle of his second term to go to the United States Senate, and Earl Warren resigned during his third term to become the Chief Justice of the United States.

Two governors, Washington Bartlett and James Rolph, died in office while five have resigned—three, Milton S. Latham, Newton Booth and Hiram W. Johnson, to become United States Senators and Warren to become Chief Justice. Through these deaths and resignations, seven lieutenant governors moved up to the governorship. The four who succeeded in the nineteenth century—John McDougal, John G. Downey, Romualdo Pacheco and Robert W. Waterman—did not return in their own right while the three later ones—William D. Stephens, Frank F. Merriam and Goodwin J. Knight—all were successful in winning a full term at the polls.

Five governors held elective office for more than twenty years: Johnson for thirty-five, George C. Perkins for thirty-one, Warren for twenty-seven, Brown for twenty-three and Rolph for twenty-two. The latter three climaxed their elective office careers with the governorship, while Johnson and Perkins (both of whom had previously held elective office) went on to the national Senate. Warren served his entire career in public office, while Ronald Reagan became governor without previously holding any public office.

Six men have been both governor and United States Senator, although no Democrat has accomplished this feat in more than a century. One Democrat, John B. Weller, who had earlier served three terms in Congress from Ohio, served one term as Senator from California and then sought the governorship. He was inaugurated January 8, 1858. Just one hundred years later, Senator William F. Knowland, the Republican leader in Congress, viewing the governorship as a stepping stone to the presidency, tried the same trick and was roundly defeated. The other five, Latham, Leland Stanford, Booth, Perkins and Johnson, all held the chief executive job before going to Washington.

Eight California governors also served in the House of Representatives, but all except Pacheco had been to Washington before becoming governor. Pacheco was the only one of Spanish descent and also the first native son to serve.[13] His mother was the beautiful Ramona Carrillo, described in California history by Richard Henry Dana, Jr. California was not to have another native son governor until George C. Pardee, first born in the state, was elected in 1902.

Pacheco, having been lieutenant governor, governor and congressman, rounded out his career serving as Minister to the Central American States. Other California governors who served in diplomatic positions for the United States were Bigler as Minister to Chile, John B. Weller as Minister to Mexico, Frederick F. Low as Minister to China and Henry T. Gage as Minister to Portugal.

From the start, the central figures in California politics were and continue to be exceptional personalities. For the independent spirit which moved these early citizens to leave behind their homes and families to be pioneers and pathfinders was ordained to make them leaders. And most of those who have followed have also been natives of other lands who left behind them family and friends to find a new way of life in the Golden State. Some have carved distinguished careers, some in both public and private life, some have been more notorious than glorious, but all have been stamped of a different mold and many have been most colorful.

Burnett's abrupt resignation, in the middle of his term as first governor, provides for California political history the first of many intriguing stories which remain shrouded in mystery. He had been a typical pioneer, moving from state to state in search of new adventures and a better life. Born in Tennessee, he went to Missouri where he became a district attorney. Going to Oregon in 1843, he became a moving spirit in their legislative committee and subsequently a Supreme Court Justice. Learning of the gold rush, he set out for the mines only to become enmeshed in the plans for civil government which his legal background made imperative in his mind.[14]

His abilities attracted the attention of Military Governor Riley, who appointed him a superior judge on August 13, 1849. Although not a member of the Constitutional Convention, he attended the sessions in Monterey in September, and at its conclusion announced his candidacy for governor. Out of an estimated population of 107,000, of which 76,000 were Americans, only 14,199 voted. Burnett received 6,783 and was sworn in December 20.[15]

When he resigned January 9, 1851, his only explanation was: "My only regret is that my feeble abilities have allowed me to accomplish so little for the state."[16] Personal, financial and business problems weighed heavily in his decision. Bancroft concludes that Burnett's character was "too slow in action, too wordy in speech, too conservative for the period, and too prejudiced for the rapid changes taking place." Six years later, Governor Johnson named him to the State Supreme Court.[17]

Burnett was succeeded by Lieutenant Governor John McDougal, described by his contemporaries as "that gentlemanly drunkard." McDougal's self-description was that he stood in awe of only two persons, God Almighty and Mrs. McDougal.

The Democratic Party held its first organizational meeting in San Francisco on October 25, 1849, on the heels of the Constitutional Convention. Meeting

ALTA CALIFORNIA.

SAN FRANCISCO, THURSDAY NOV. 1, 1849.

Mass Meeting.

At a meeting of the Democratic citizens of the town of San Francisco, called at Dennison's Exchange, on Thursday Evening, October 25th, 1849,

On motion of James L. Freaner, Esq. the Hon. JOHN W. GEARY was called to the chair.

On motion of W. V. Voorhies, Esq. the following named gentlemen were then chosen as Vice Presidents:

Messrs. O. P. SUTTON, Dr. McMILLAN,
E. V. JOYCE, THOS. J. AGNEW,
— McVICKAR, — MERRILL,
and W. H. JONES; and

Messrs. JOS. T. DOWNEY, J. ROSS BROWN, DAN'L CRONIN and JOHN A. McGLYNN were, on motion, appointed Secretaries.

Immediately after the meeting had been organized, it was ascertained that the room in which it was convened, would not hold one quarter of the people who had assembled to participate in its proceedings. It was therefore moved that the meeting adjourn to the Square, in front of the Exchange, which motion was carried.

Upon the re-organization of the meeting, the objects thereof, were explained in a short and pertinent address by the Chairman.

Mr. W. V. Voorhies then came forward and introduced the address and resolutions which he had been solicited by the committee of arrangements to prepare for the occasion, by a short, eloquent and forcible speech, in which he briefly stated the present political condition of California—her many diversified interests, and the necessity of her being properly represented in our National Councils. He totally repudiated the idea of "partyism merely for the sake of party," but at the same time, he earnestly contended that the measures and policy of the Democratic Party, embrace those principles which are essential and necessary to the future welfare and prosperity of the country. He then read the following Address, Preamble and Resolutions, which were unanimously adopted, and

On motion, 20.000 copies of the same were ordered to be printed for circulation.

[A press of other matter precludes the appearance of the address.]

PREAMBLE AND RESOLUTIONS.

The *Alta California*, a San Francisco newspaper, reported the first California Democratic Party meeting. (Courtesy of California State Library.)

in Portsmouth Square with John W. Geary, last American Alcalde and first Mayor of San Francisco, acting as chairman, its purpose was to select candidates for the upcoming election on November 13. Geary later became territorial governor of Kansas and governor of Pennsylvania, but his name has been preserved in San Francisco as the name of the city's longest boulevard.

State-wide party organization developed and grew rapidly after the first Legislature established counties. The first state convention of the Party was held at Benicia on May 19, 1851, with 176 delegates present. They endorsed their state and congressional ticket and elected the first state central committee. McDougal, seeking to retain the governorship inherited from Burnett, became locked in a contest with John Bigler, Speaker of the Assembly. Bigler was victorious on the sixth ballot and became the third consecutive Democratic governor winning the 1851 election easily along with the entire ticket. The only county in the state which he lost to the Whig Party candidate was San Francisco. Reelected in 1853, he was the only governor to be accorded that honor until Hiram Johnson, sixty-one years later.[18]

The Democratic Party, with the election of Burnett of 1849 and its overwhelming victory in 1851, maintained control over California government until the Civil War. Of the governors from 1849 to 1879, only Johnson of the American Party, and Stanford, Low and Booth of the Republicans were elected over Democratic candidates. In terms of years, the Democrats held the office for eighteen of the first thirty years. Of the first seven United States Senators, only Free Soiler Frémont was not of the Party.

While the 1851 Legislature became embroiled in a battle over the United States Senate seat, it was more an intraparty tussle since Frémont never had a chance. The hero of the Bear Flag was nearly ignored, receiving but eight votes on the first ballot. Ten days and 142 ballots later, there was no one in sight with a majority, and the session adjourned leaving California for 330 days with only Senator Gwin in Washington. On the following January, the two houses met in convention and on the eighth ballot Weller emerged the victor.

The most powerful leaders in the early Democratic Party were David Colbreth Broderick and Gwin even though Burnett, McDougal and Bigler were to be the first governors. These two early independent spirits who had migrated to the land of gold had been "professional" politicians, and their influence, along with that of others, was to be rapidly felt. In fact, so great was their impact upon the new state that the *New York Herald* suggested:

When President Taylor was elected, all the democratic politicians of the United States were thrown out of employment and, gold being discovered simultaneously in California, they went off there. . . . They introduced the New York system of politics in San Francisco.[19]

15

The *Herald* should have added the Southern system to that of New York. Historian Robert Glass Cleland succinctly put it:

> The struggle for supremacy among these self-constituted leaders furnished the chief element of excitement in state politics until the Civil War, and culminated in the bitter feud between Broderick and Gwin which disrupted the Democratic Party and prepared the way for Republican control.[20]

Broderick was born February 4, 1820 in Washington, D.C. His father had been brought from Ireland by the government to do the decorative stonework interior of the national Capitol. His father's death caused his widowed mother to move to New York where David apprenticed as a stonecutter to help support

David C. Broderick (1820–1859), leader of a Democratic Party faction in the 1850's. (Courtesy of California State Library.)

her and his younger brother. By 1840 he was foreman of Fire Engine Company 34, a position of eminence in New York City politics. At the same time William Marcy Tweed held a similar position with Company 6. The Tammany of the time was mired in the sanctimonious grandiloquence of the forties. The "ward heelers" were closer to the immigrants and, to the consternation of the Sachems of Tammany, began the take over which was to climax in the rule of "Boss" Tweed.

In 1848, after two unsuccessful bids for Congress as a Tammany candidate, Broderick took off for the west. His parting shot to his good friend and fellow Tammany dandy, General Daniel E. Sickles, later to be a hero of Gettysburg, was that if he ever returned to the east it would be as the United States Senator from California.[21]

In San Francisco he set up business in smelting and assaying gold and became a delegate to the Constitutional Convention. In 1850, when one of the State Senators from San Francisco resigned, Broderick was the successful candidate in a special election to fill the vacancy. The following year he was elected President of the Senate. Not having lost sight of his goal of becoming a United States Senator, Broderick worked behind the scenes but lost in January 1852 to John B. Weller. It would not be Broderick's turn until 1857. During these early years the lessons that he had learned with Tammany were to prove invaluable.

William M. Gwin, the second principal in this legend of early politics, was born in Tennessee October 9, 1805. Graduating in medicine from Transylvania University in Kentucky, he commenced his practice in Clinton, Mississippi. Judging from his subsequent career, medicine did not appeal to him as much as politics. Soon after his arrival in Mississippi he accepted appointment as United States Marshal in 1833, and in 1840 was the successful Democratic candidate for Congress. While watching the inaugural parade of General Taylor on March 5, 1849, Gwin told Senator Stephen A. Douglas he was going to California and would be back within the year as the United States Senator from the new state, a promise he was to keep.[22] Gwin arrived in California in June 1849 and, like Broderick, was a delegate to the Constitutional Convention, and shortly thereafter realized his ambition.

The lines between Broderick and Gwin in their struggles for control of the Democratic Party were clearly drawn by 1854. In the party convention that year the Gwin forces were led by David S. Terry.

Terry was born in Kentucky March 8, 1823. His family moved to Mississippi the next year and on to Texas when he was twelve. By the time Terry arrived in California with the forty-niners he was a giant of a man, standing six foot three inches and weighing 220 pounds.

Within five years he had formed a strong political alliance with Gwin and in 1854 led the latter's supporters at the convention. But despite Terry's forceful

Leader of the pro-slavery California Democrats, William M. Gwin (1805–1885) who represented the state in the United States Senate for nine years before the outbreak of the Civil War. (Courtesy of California State Library.)

David S. Terry (1823–1889), quick tempered pro-Southern Democrat who gained a seat on the California Supreme Court by switching to the American Party. (Courtesy of California State Library.)

leadership the Gwin faction was no match for the superb convention maneuvering of Broderick whose candidates were victorious. Following this defeat Terry joined the Know-Nothings and was quick to reap reward for that switch. For when that Party swept the 1855 elections carrying ex-Whig John Neely Johnson to the governorship, ex-Democrat Terry was elected Associate Justice of the State Supreme Court and became Chief Justice two years later.

The Democratic Party Convention of 1854 was easily one of the two most riotous ever held. Convening at the First Baptist Church in Sacramento on July 18, their conduct won them a *persona non grata* vote of the church trustees. Broderick, using the same tactics employed later at the Republican Convention in Chicago by David Davis and Abraham Lincoln, packed the church with his supporters hours ahead of the stated meeting time and then had the fire marshal order the doors closed. Then the Broderick faction nominated and elected Edward McGowan permanent chairman. Gwin's forces refused to recognize this action and elected ex-governor John McDougal permanent chairman. The convention then tried to proceed with two sets of officers on the platform, but in this stormy situation the trustees invited the two factions to meet elsewhere the following day. This they did, with the McGowan group at Carpenter's Hall and the McDougal followers at Musical Hall. Gwin's forces put forth Milton S. Latham and James A. McDougall for Congress but shortly after the convention spokesman for both withdrew their names and the Broderick forces swept the September elections.[23]

With this victory over Gwin, Broderick had now achieved the control of the Democratic Party which he had been aiming for since his 1851 election as President of the Senate, and since the election of John S. Bigler as Governor that same year and reelection two years later. Bigler's reelection was to place him as the only Democrat ever to be reelected governor until "Pat" Brown performed the same feat 109 years later. But these successes still fell short of Broderick's ultimate goal, the United States Senate. To gain this objective Broderick is reputedly to have said, "I am going to that Senate. I'll go if I have to march over a thousand corpses and every corpse a friend."[24]

Federal patronage today plays an important role in party politics but in the state's early history it was of even greater moment, particularly with the slavery issue dominating the national scene. And while by 1855 Broderick had gained virtual control over the party within the state, Gwin remained the unquestioned California party leader in Washington, D. C. During this period only one federal appointment was refused him—Judah P. Benjamin of Louisiana as federal district judge for the southern California district. Benjamin was a typical southern pro-slavery Democrat who was afterward to be Secretary of State in the Southern Confederacy.[25]

Both California seats in 1855 were held by pro-slavery Democrats, Gwin

19

and Weller. Gwin's term was to expire that year while Weller's ran until 1857. Broderick, unable to muster the strength to gain the seat for himself, managed to block Gwin's reelection and held the seat vacant for two years until Weller's term also expired. Then, in 1857, Broderick brought into play some of the Tammany tactics. He reversed the order of nominations so that the full six-year term would be voted first. In this maneuver he enlisted the support of the erstwhile Gwin supporter, Latham, who had withdrawn as Gwin's candidate for Congress in the face of Broderick's formidable strength in 1854. Gwin paid Latham off for his efforts with the federal appointment to Port Collector of San Francisco, a reward made easier to secure by reason of the impression Latham had made on President Franklin Pierce during his one term in Congress.[26]

Latham, later to become Governor and United States Senator, has been described as "A northerner by birth, a southerner by training and a Californian by choice." He was born in Ohio on May 23, 1827. Some twenty years later he moved to Alabama and studied law in the offices of Solomon Heydenfeldt. Together they moved to California in 1849 and in 1851 Heydenfeldt became the first elected justice of the State Supreme Court and the following year Latham went to Congress. It was at this time that Latham incurred the wrath of Joseph W. McCorkle, not alone by defeating him in his bid for reelection but by stealing his girl, Miss Sophia Birdsall, whom he wedded while she was supposedly waiting for McCorkle's return from Washington.

The Broderick–Latham coalition worked successfully for Broderick and he gained the long-term nomination, defeating the Gwin–Weller forces led by Heydenfeldt. Latham, now confident he would be the nominee for the short term, was rudely awakened to the tremendous power he had helped secure for Broderick. Confronted with the demand for full control over federal patronage Latham balked and was immediately dumped by Broderick who blocked the nominations of Gwin, Latham, McCorkle, and Stephen J. Field for fourteen ballots. Meantime, Gwin signed a secret agreement with Broderick surrendering patronage and won the retention of his seat on the fifteenth ballot while Latham's only honor to take home was his own. Weller turned around and ran for Governor successfully.[27]

Ironically, Broderick's victory he had so long sought was to prove a hollow one. Aligned with the Anti-Lecomptonite wing of the Democratic Party he arrived in Washington to be confronted with the doughface President, James Buchanan. The Anti-Lecomptonites had gained their name by their opposition to the pro-slavery constitution framed at Lecompton, Kansas. The pro-southern Democrats in California were known at that time as Chivalry Democrats or "Chivs", of which Gwin was one. Buchanan refused to honor the Broderick–Gwin agreement on patronage and the breach which had been temporarily healed on the surface was again split wide open. It was to grow in intensity and bitterness and end in violent deaths.

Broderick naturally blamed Gwin for Buchanan's frigid treatment. State Senator William I. Ferguson, supposedly keeper of the all important secret patronage agreement, was called out by a pro-southerner and lost his life in a duel on September 14, 1858. The night of his death his desk was rifled. These incidents were to figure prominently in the blistering campaign of 1859. But worse was to follow and Broderick would not live to enjoy the fruits of the elections.

On the morning of June 26, 1859 Broderick was reading the paper at breakfast in the International Hotel in San Francisco. Becoming incensed at the disparaging and caustic remarks about him attributed to Gwin's close friend and political ally, Supreme Court Chief Justice Terry, Broderick indignantly called Terry "a damned miserable wretch." This was dutifully reported to Terry by on-lookers. Terry immediately resigned from the court, a job he was about to lose anyway since he had failed to win renomination at the Democratic Convention earlier that year, and demanded a retraction or satisfaction.

In the cold gray dawn of September 13 the two men met behind the barn of the Lake House Ranch on the foggy shores of Lake Merced just south of the San Francisco County line. Two shots rang out. Broderick's was low, striking the ground at Terry's feet about the same time as a well aimed bullet hit Broderick's chest and he fell mortally wounded.

So ended, in his thirty-ninth year, the political career of Senator Broderick. But it was also the beginning of the end of the political careers of both Terry as well as Gwin, for whom he undoubtedly had provoked the duel. The seeds of their political demises were sown by the funeral oration delivered for Broderick by Colonel E. D. Baker, later to die a hero leading Union troops at the battle of Ball's Bluff, Virginia. His eulogy, which portrayed Broderick as an anti-slavery martyr, is regarded as a classic of its kind.[28]

It was perhaps inevitable that the big, quick tempered Terry would also die a violent death. From the time of his arrival in California his sharp tongue, big fists, Bowie knife and pistol had earned him a reputation as a firebrand. Although one writer has stated that "No man ever found David S. Terry hob-nobbing with criminals or working in the slimy depths of political sewers in order to reach official position."[29]

While as Chief Justice, Terry demonstrated a respect for law and order, he often failed to apply this to his personal conduct. In 1856, having urged Governor Johnson to suppress the Second Committee on Vigilance as a lawless mob, Terry, still on the Supreme Court, used his Bowie knife on Sterling A. Hopkins, a Committee policeman who was trying to effect an arrest. For this

21

A cartoon opposing David S. Terry (1823–1889) following the fatal duel with David Broderick. (Courtesy of California State Library.)

Terry was confined at Fort Gunnybags, the barricaded headquarters of the Committee on Sacramento Street in San Francisco, for twenty-five days until Hopkins was out of danger.[30]

With the advent of the Civil War Terry and Gwin obtained commissions in the Confederate Army. After Appomattox the pair went to Mexico where Gwin became associated with the Mexican Imperial Government of Maximilian. Terry later returned to California and took up the practice of law in Stockton. In 1886 he married the beautiful fiery-haired Sarah Althea Hill who had a temper that possibly matched his own. She had been the mistress of millionaire banker William Sharon, owner of the Palace Hotel in San Francisco, and United States Senator from Nevada. Following this affair she sued widower

Sharon for alimony claiming to have been his common law wife and won a judgment in the superior court, later upheld by the Supreme Court. Sharon then took the case to the United States Circuit Court. By the time the decision was handed down by Justice Stephen J. Field, Sharon had died, his son continuing the action, and Sarah had found her new romance with Terry.

Field was another of the forty-niners from New York. He was elected first Alcalde of Marysville, sat in the second Legislature where he became Broderick's supporter and in 1857 was elected to the State Supreme Court where he served with Terry for two years, becoming Chief Justice when Terry resigned prior to his tragic duel. In 1863 he was appointed by Abraham Lincoln as the first Californian to the United States Supreme Court, where he served for thirty-four years as a great defender of corporate wealth. Field's service on the Court was longer than any other man before or since.[31]

Following the federal court reversals of Sarah's suit, the hot-headed Terry made such dire threats against Field that the Attorney General of the United States, W. H. H. Miller, appointed David S. Neagle, a United States Deputy Marshal, as Field's personal bodyguard.

On the morning of August 14, 1889, Field, en route to San Francisco under the protection of Neagle, left the train at Lathrop just outside of Stockton and entered the station for breakfast. Moments later Terry, with his pretty red-haired wife, entered the same restaurant. Unknowingly they had been traveling the same train as Field. Spotting the Federal Justice the giant Terry rushed over and smashed him twice in the face before his bodyguard could interfere. Neagle, obviously frightened, drew his .44 calibre revolver and fired twice, hitting Terry both times in the chest. When he hit the floor he was dead, thirty years lacking a month to the day he had shot Broderick.

The tempestuous Sarah, who it was rumored could hit a four-bit piece twice in the air before it fell, rushed to her satchel which contained a revolver but someone seized her before she got hold of the gun. So great was her grief that she was to spend the rest of her days in the Stockton Asylum where she died in 1937, forty-eight years later. The bitterness over Terry's conduct was evidenced by the State Supreme Court's failure to adjourn for Terry's funeral, a custom of the Court in honoring former Chief Justices.[32]

Bitterness stemming from the Broderick–Gwin conflict remains unmatched in its scope and consequences in California politics. But other struggles over the prize of United States Senator continued. This early contest left California with only one United States Senator for the better part of two years. Again in 1899, the Legislature bogged down in naming a senator to succeed Stephen M. White, and Thomas R. Bard was not sworn in until 1900. Altogether, then, the state was short one senator for a total of four years during the nineteenth century.

Through 1969 there have been thirty-seven senators from California with nineteen Democrats and, except for Frémont, the others Republicans. Six, Broderick, John F. Miller, Stanford, George Hearst, Johnson and Clair Engle, have died in office. Four have resigned: Eugene Casserly for personal reasons; William G. McAdoo defeated for renomination; Sheridan Downey who chose not to stand for reelection and subsequently resigned to give the new Senator elect, Republican Richard Nixon, a month's seniority; and Nixon to become Vice President. Thus, twelve senators have come to office through vacancies by death or resignation. Three were appointed by the governor but never confirmed by the Legislature. These were Henry P. Haun, George Hearst, and Thomas L. Storke, the Santa Barbara publisher who was appointed to succeed McAdoo even though he had not been a candidate for the office. Five others were never elected in their own right: Latham, John S. Hager, Abram Pease Williams, Charles Felton and Pierre Salinger. The remaining four, George Hearst, George Perkins, Knowland and Thomas Kuchel, successfully stood for election after their appointment.[33]

The 1860 Legislature was the last to be dominated by the Lecomptonite and pro-slavery wing of the Democratic Party. Latham had aligned himself with this wing and won election as Governor in 1859. Had Broderick's death occurred before instead of six days after the election, perhaps the returns would have been different. Meanwhile, lameduck Governor Weller had the task of appointing a successor to Broderick. He chose an innocuous pro-slavery man named Henry P. Haun of Marysville, probably having in mind that he would seek the job himself when the Legislature convened in January. But when it did meet both Haun and Weller were passed over for Latham. So Latham became the United States Senator just five days after he had been inaugurated Governor. Some said the Legislature did this to get rid of Latham as Governor. This time Latham returned to San Francisco with the honor that had been denied him by Broderick three years earlier.

Lieutenant Governor John G. Downey took the oath of office replacing Latham on January 14, 1860, giving California three governors in one week. Downey was born in County Roscommon, Ireland in 1827 and arrived in America at the age of fifteen. Working in drugstores in the nation's capital, Vicksburg and Cincinnati, he migrated west and opened his own store in Los Angeles in 1850 to become the only druggist between San Francisco and San Diego. The proceeds of this business were invested in land and part of the profit from his real estate investments were to begin the University of Southern California. For Downey, himself a Catholic, donated the initial land to start that Methodist school of higher learning. His selection as a running mate for Latham was a combination of giving the Lecomptonite Democratic ticket both the balance of a southern California candidate, and one to offset Broderick's

24

man John Conness among the Irish voters supporting the Anti-Lecomptonite ticket.

Downey distinguished himself in his first year as governor by his forthright veto of the heavily lobbied "Bulkhead Bill," a scheme to give the San Francisco Dock and Wharf Company a gigantic monopoly of the San Francisco waterfront. Hailed by the *San Francisco Bulletin* as the "Andrew Jackson of California" he was greeted in the bay city by elated throngs in a torchlight parade, but popularity was not enough to win him a second term. By the following year Civil War had broken out and while Downey declared he had no sympathy for the secessionists, he did believe every section of the country had constitutional rights to decide the slavery question individually. The Union Democrats nominated Conness over Downey on the fourteenth ballot. The Breckenridge Democrats nominated John R. McConnell of Nevada City. In the three-way race Republican Leland Stanford was the victor.

Two years later in 1863 Downey won the Democratic nomination for Governor but was defeated by Republican Frederick F. Low. In the same year Congressman Aaron A. Sargent and Timothy G. Phelps, both Republicans, sought to succeed Latham in the United States Senate, but the vigor of their efforts served to destroy each other and the Legislature elected Conness as the compromise candidate. Sargent was to wait until 1872 before going to the United States Senate. Downey returned to Los Angeles where he became president of the first railroad south of the Tehachapis, the Los Angeles and San Pedro Railroad Company, and also founded the city of Downey.[34]

In the presidential election of 1860, Downey and McDougall supported Douglas while Weller, Gwin and Latham supported Breckenridge. McDougall was rewarded the following year by being sent to the United States Senate, replacing Gwin, for one term. Gwin, who had counselled Buchanan against any warlike measures against the seceding states and particularly against reinforcing Fort Sumter, was "rewarded" by Secretary of State William H. Seward by being arrested for treason and held in military prison for a few months. At the same time, Charles L. Weller, brother of former Governor Weller, was imprisoned on Alcatraz for "treasonable expressions."[35]

During these years the major issue besides the sectional split was the transcontinental railroad bill favored by candidates of both parties. While the Democratic Party was torn asunder by the rivalries of its leaders as well as the sectional issue, the Republican Party minimized the slavery question and certainly did not champion the cause of the blacks as did the Radical Republicans of the east and middle west.

The two major parties throughout California's history have been the Democrats and Republicans. The Republicans, because they did not form on the national level until 1854, were off to a slow start in the Golden State. The

Republican Party's first candidate for President in 1856 was the dashing path-marker, General Frémont. Abraham Lincoln was proposed as a running mate, but in a series of maneuvers he lost to William L. Dayton of New Jersey. Fate had saved Lincoln for another day, as the Frémont-Dayton ticket went down to defeat and Lincoln emerged at the 1860 convention to become the first successful Republican candidate for president.

In California the Republican Party also met with success, helped immeasurably by the Democrats intraparty squabbling and personal ambitions of its leadership. Internal dissention continues to plague the party to this day, and the stronger the control the Democrats have over the Legislature, the more prone they are to bicker away amongst themselves to their own destruction. In the years 1858 through 1861 they enjoyed their most lopsided control in the state's history, numbering 93, 102, 111 and 90 out of a possible 115 seats. In 1858 and 1859 they were split into the Lecompton and Anti-Lecompton Democrats, in the next two years they were divided into the Union and Breckenridge Democrats.

Excepting the 1856 session the Democrats controlled all of the first thirteen sessions. The Americans had won control in the election of 1855 with their gubernatorial candidate John Neely Johnson's victory. Earlier Johnson had been Resolutions Committee chairman of the first Whig convention and president of the fourth Whig convention. The Whigs were never close to control of the Legislature but they counted 42 out of 115 members in 1854 and in 1855 they held the balance of power between the Broderick and the Gwin factions. The last session in which there were Whigs was in 1856, and the first session in which there were Republicans was in 1857. The Legislature reached its present membership of 120 in 1862 and the Republicans gained control for the first time in 1863.

While Leland Stanford was to become the first Republican governor in 1862, it was not until 1867 that a Republican, Cornelius Cole, was elected to the United States Senate.

In these early years partisanship was based solely upon the political parties and the splits within them, and the national issues, principally slavery and secession. But there was to creep into the California political arena its own brand of sectionalism, northern versus southern California. This has grown and continues to be a major political division. Generally speaking, the south means south of the Tehachapi Mountains; more specifically, those ten counties below the straight line formed by the northern boundaries of San Luis Obispo, Kern, and San Bernardino Counties. The forty-eight counties above this line comprise the north.[36]

While Downey was to be the first governor from southern California he came into office only by stepping up from the office of lieutenant governor,

26

Table I

Sectionalism in California Politics 1849–1969

Number of years northerners and southerners have held the governorship
and two United States senatorships

	North	South	North Controlled All Three Offices	South Controlled All Three Offices	
1849 1879	Governor 27 U.S. Senator 29 Seat "A" U.S. Senator 28 Seat "B" TOTAL 84	Governor 3 U.S. Senator 0 Seat "A" U.S. Senator 0 Seat "B" TOTAL 3	25	0	Vacant 3
1879 1909	Governor 15 U.S. Senator 14 Seat "A" U.S. Senator 30 Seat "B" TOTAL 59	Governor 15 U.S. Senator 15 Seat "A" U.S. Senator 0 Seat "B" TOTAL 30	5	0	Vacant 1
1909 1939	Governor 19 U.S. Senator 22 Seat "A" U.S. Senator 24 Seat "B" TOTAL 65	Governor 11 U.S. Senator 8 Seat "A" U.S. Senator 6 Seat "B" TOTAL 25	10	0	
1939 1969	Governor 19 U.S. Senator 26 Seat "A" U.S. Senator 6 Seat "B" TOTAL 51	Governor 11 U.S. Senator 4 Seat "A" U.S. Senator 24 Seat "B" TOTAL 39	2	2	
TOTALS	259 73%	97 26%	42	2	4

and he was not reelected. In 1875 Romualdo Pacheco and in 1887 Robert Waterman were southern inheritors of the governorship but it was not until George Stoneman selection in 1882 that the south was to place a Governor directly in office.

The first United States Senator from southern California was Stephen M. White in 1892. With the election of George Murphy in 1964 the state for the first time sent two southern Californians to the United States Senate. In 1966 the election of celluloid personality Ronald Reagan gave the ten southern counties both United States Senate seats and the governorship to boot for the first time in the state's history.

Only ten of California's seventy governors and United States Senators have come from nonmetropolitan areas. Nine of these were in the state's first sixty years up to 1909 and none in the second sixty excepting Clair Engle of Red Bluff. The nine from earlier years were: Bard from Hueneme, Budd from Stockton, Farley from Jackson, Gillett from Eureka, Haun from Marysville, Irwin from Yreka, Pacheco from San Luis Obispo, Perkins from Oroville, and Sargent from Nevada City. Of the ten only five were elected by popular vote.

The northern counties have contributed fifty-one of the seventy United States Senators and governors, with San Francisco alone being responsible for twenty-three or thirty-three percent of them. San Francisco was for many years the political capital of the state. While the north has produced twenty-three of the thirty-three governors and twenty-eight of the thirty-seven senators, Los Angeles, the second largest metropolitan area in the nation, has contributed only fifteen senators and governors.

Numerically the split between Republicans and Democrats holding the offices of governor and United States Senator has been fairly even, being thirty-five and thirty-two respectively, but in years of tenure the Republicans have a far greater margin. One explanation is that of the twelve governors and senators who served more than one and one-half terms, eight were Republicans and only four were Democrats. The four Democrats ran up only thirty-four years among them, while the eight Republicans served one hundred thirty-four. Johnson and Knowland together controlled one Senate seat for forty-two years, eight years longer than the four Democrats combined. Two out of the four Democrats were reelected in the first decade, and the second two in the last quarter of the state's political history, so no Democrat was reelected for a period of eighty-eight years. Downey is the only Democrat to serve two full six-year terms as United States Senator and Brown is the only one to serve two full four-year terms as Governor.

Not until recent years has the governorship been looked upon as the state's most prized political office and even today, despite Knowland's ill-fated effort to trade a United States Senate seat for the corner office, there are divided views

28

Table II
Partisanship in California Politics 1849–1969
Number of years Democrats, Republicans, and minor parties have held the
governorship and two United States senatorships

	Democrats	Republicans	Democrats Controlled All Three Offices	Republicans Controlled All Three Offices	
1849 1879	Governor 18 U.S. Senator 23 Seat "A" U.S. Senator 16 Seat "B" TOTAL 57	Governor 10 U.S. Senator 4 Seat "A" U.S. Senator 12 Seat "B" TOTAL 26	7	1	Free Soilers 2 Americans 2 Vacant 3
1879 1909	Governor 10 U.S. Senator 11 Seat "A" U.S. Senator 6 Seat "B" TOTAL 27	Governor 20 U.S. Senator 18 Seat "A" U.S. Senator 24 Seat "B" TOTAL 62	0	11	Vacant 1
1909 1939	Governor 0 U.S. Senator 0 Seat "A" U.S. Senator 12 Seat "B" TOTAL 12	Governor 28 U.S. Senator 30 Seat "A" U.S. Senator 18 Seat "B" TOTAL 76	0	18	Progressives 2
1939 1969	Governor 12 U.S. Senator 6 Seat "A" U.S. Senator 12 Seat "B" TOTAL 30	Governor 18 U.S. Senator 24 Seat "A" U.S. Senator 18 Seat "B" TOTAL 60	0	10	
TOTALS	126 35%	224 62%	7	40	10

as to which offers the greater reward. But in the early years there was little doubt as to which wielded the most power. As a small state California had little to offer by way of patronage, and the real political plum appointments were those at the federal level handed out by the President on the advice of the United States senators. This patronage largely determined the party control over California.

The year 1863 was the first year for the Republicans to gain control over the Legislature and in the same year Frederick F. Low defeated former Governor Downey to become the state's first four-year governor. Those defeats for the Democrats were brought about by their continued bickering. Gwin, the pro-southerner, had left the state but the wounds were still unhealed. Lincoln had defeated Douglas in 1860 by some 734 votes and secured California's four electoral votes. The Democratic delegation was led that year by John Bidwell of Chico. In Charleston, South Carolina, it voted for Daniel S. Dickinson on the first ballot and then followed the lead of the ultra southern pro-slavery faction by a 7-1 vote. Bidwell, who cast the single California vote against the delegation majority, then went to Baltimore where he supported Douglas. It was also that year of 1860 that Douglas, professed friend of Broderick, voted for confirmation of Calhoun Benham as United States Attorney for California. Benham had been one of Terry's seconds in the fatal duel and this action by Douglas alienated many who felt he was untrue to Broderick. Four years later Bidwell was a delegate again to Baltimore but this time to the Union Party convention.

By 1864 Benham, along with Gwin and Terry and some other high state officials, was serving in the Confederate Army. At the state Democratic convention four ex-governors, all named John—Bigler, McDougall, Weller and Downey—were named delegates to the national convention along with six others. Earlier that year the State Legislature had adopted a pocketful of resolutions declaring uncompromising loyalty to the Union cause, endorsement of President Lincoln for reelection, and repudiation of all state supremacy doctrines as political heresy. The Democrats had been taking abuse since the start of the Civil War because of the activities of many in the party like Benham, Gwin and Terry who were avid pro-southerners. As a consequence the word Democrat had almost become synonimous with disloyalty. Once again Lincoln received the five electoral votes of California, this time by some 18,302 votes.[37]

The Democratic Party in 1865 was faced with the opposition of two of the most influential newspapers of the day, the *Sacramento Union* and the *San Francisco Bulletin*. Of the two the *Union* was by far the more bitter in its attacks on the Democrats. The Democratic Party, its editor charged, was composed of three elements:

For who constitutes the "Democracy" of California? As a basis, we have some fifteen thousand thoroughbred Secessionists, born in the South, educated in the political school of Calhoun and Yancey. . . . To these may be added ten thousand renegade "Yankees" . . . . The remainder of the party is of foreign origin, and having sinned against the Government simply through ignorance, is the only section of it which is likely to be converted by the logic of events.[38]

A San Francisco correspondent of the *Union* branded the Democrats as both traitors and cowards. The Democrats were . . .

Believers in bondage, they never backed their faith with bayonets. . . . Born on the soil which they sought to betray, they have availed themselves of the security guaranteed them to deal the deadliest blows against the very heart which sheltered them. They shrunk from the open front where cannon spoke to cannon and saber crossed with saber in un-answerable argument, to hiss their hate in the bushes and impregnate the free air with the blasting venom of their breaths.[39]

With the fall of Richmond and Lee's surrender and the assassination of Lincoln came the first serious division in the Union Party. Two factions which came to be known as the "long-hairs" and the "short-hairs" developed.

The short-hairs were in large part Democratic followers of Senator Conness who had united during the Civil War on the issue of preservation of the Union. They supported Governor Low as a candidate to succeed Senator McDougall when his term expired in 1867. Conness had helped control the Union Party convention in 1863 to gain the gubernatorial nomination for Low and was now supporting him for the senatorship. The short-hairs also were playing another game, that of districting San Francisco into wards which they hoped would help them control the next election. Determined opposition to Low's candidacy caused Conness to withdraw his support and seek some other candidate, resulting in the acrid resentment of the Low faction.

The bitter feud came to a head in July of 1865 when the Sacramento County Union Party delegates met in convention and the chairman announced the long-hair candidate for convention secretary after a voice vote which many believed indecisive. When the short-hair demand for a count of the votes was denied, pandemonium broke loose. Canes, spittoons, inkstands, clubs and chairs flew in all directions in the wildest donnybrook ever seen at a state political convention.

On August 2, Low withdrew from the contest but this move did not serve to heal the breach in the Union Party; and while the short-hairs did succeed in carrying the primaries in San Francisco that year and switched their support to John B. Felton for the United States Senate, he did not win. For the following year the Legislature chose another forty-niner, Cornelius B. Cole. Ten years

31

later Felton made another try for the Senate but it was not until another fifteen years had passed that another Felton, Charles N., achieved this ambition and was selected to fill out the two years remaining of the term when George Hearst died in office.

The 1866 Legislature preoccupied itself with futile attempts to serve as the self-appointed advisor to the Federal government on the immediate post-war issues. Five different joint resolutions, together with amendments, were introduced that year dealing with the policies of President Andrew Johnson and the relationship of the Federal government with the southern states and Confederate leaders. These resolutions serve only to point up the spectroscopic opinions held by the legislators by reason of their states of origin which continue to this day to divide and influence California government. The first three were offered in the State Senate and the last two in the Assembly.

(1) Democrat John S. Hager proposed support for President Johnson's stand that the question of the franchise for the freedmen of the south should be decided by the individual states.

(2) Democrat James Johnson's resolution simply made the not so profound observation that the Confederate states were not out of the Union, to which Union Party member Joseph Kutz pungently suggested the additional wording "but are emphatically out in the cold."

(3) Union Party member Horace Hawes also not so profoundly offered a resolution declaring the right of secession to be repugnant to the Constitution and rejoiced that reason and force of arms had reestablished the authority of the Federal Constitution over all the states and territories forever. The Hawes resolution was adopted by the Senate twenty-six to five, but the Assembly amended in that portion of the Declaration of Independence relating to the right of revolution before adopting it forty-seven to seven. When it was returned to the Senate for concurrence, it died.

(4) Meantime, Democrat R. P. Mace proposed that reason and humanity dictate a course of forgiveness toward those recently in armed rebellion and recommended unconditional pardon for Jefferson Davis.

(5) Union Party member Thomas J. Sherwood promptly offered and had passed a resolution by a fifty-eight to twenty vote, calling for a speedy trial for Davis and the full measure of punishment if convicted. In the Senate Democrat James Johnson amended the resolution to leave the Davis question to the courts and to President Johnson, after which that resolution died.

In the party conventions that year President Johnson was hailed as the hero of the Democratic Party for his veto of the Freedmen's Bureau Bill while the Union Party declared open war against him for the rest of his term.[40]

Although Conness himself was possibly in favor of Black suffrage, the short-

32

hairs were generally opposed and since the Democrats adopted a party plank in opposition it seems too coincidental that the short-hairs just happened to take a similar stand. The evidence suggests this "me-too" stand was a deliberate appeal to the Democratic voters. The result was that in many counties the Democrats adjourned their conventions without nominations and supported the short-hair ticket.

A typical example of the resolutions adopted by the short-hairs was that of Yuba County, which read:

> RESOLVED, that while we are willing to extend to the African or black race upon the continent all their rights, we still believe this to be a white man's government, and that allowing or permitting the black to vote would be unnatural, impolitic and degrading.[41]

This type of resolution served to assure the continuance of the term "Copperhead" to the Democrats and short-hairs in California.

In 1867 Democrat Senator Conness continued his efforts to control the Union Party and advanced George C. Gorham for Governor in the belief that this would help him in his bid for reelection the following year. But Gorham's popularity had faded due to his stand on the discredited "Bulkhead Bill" and the leading press vigorously protested his nomination by the Union Party.

The election of 1867 was the first to use the Porter Primary Election Law, passed during the 1866 legislative session, and the first primary election law passed in the United States. The law was optional—a party could elect to operate under it if it wished to. In San Francisco the pro-Gorham faction decided to adopt it, but used such a liberal test to determine who could vote in the Union Party primaries in that city that many Democrats apparently took part and voted for Gorham delegates to go to the Union Party convention.[42]

A second convention was held in July by a seceding group of long-hairs, formerly Republicans. They aligned themselves with the National Republican Party. They nominated John Bidwell who promptly declined, and Caleb T. Fay, former San Francisco Assemblyman, was substituted.

The Democratic candidate for governor was Henry Huntley Haight, a San Francisco lawyer-politician who enjoyed an excellent reputation and practiced in association with his father. He had been a Whig when he arrived in California in 1850 but during the decade he gravitated to the Republican Party. During the next decade he became dissatisfied and became a Democrat.

The anti-Chinese Coolie Association emerged as a major campaign issue, Bidwell stood opposed to slavery in any form and Gorham expressed opposition to Chinese immigration. With the Union Party split and the Democrats advancing an outstanding candidate, Haight won by 9,546 votes and the Democrats were back in the governor's office for the first time since the outbreak of war. They

33

also captured the Assembly, seventy to ten. Their success in San Francisco stemmed from the solid backing of the Irish and German population. The Union party retained control of the State Senate by four seats.[43]

In 1868 the Legislature elected Irish-born Eugene Casserly, a lawyer and Democrat, to succeed Conness as the United States Senator. Following Casserly's election a wild celebration was held at the Magnolia Hotel in Sacramento where the bourbon flowed freely to all. Throughout his term in office charges were heard that he had bribed his way to the Senate.[44]

Despite losing the state elections the previous year the Republicans did carry the state in 1868 for General Ulysses S. Grant over Horatio Seymour by 502 votes out of 108,670 cast. "Waving the bloody shirt," an expression said to be from a speech by Benjamin F. Butler when he waved a bloodstained shirt in the House of Representatives claiming it to be the nightshirt of a carpetbagger flogged by the KKK, figured in the campaign, as did such slogans as "Scratch a Democrat and you'll find a rebel." Grant's victory was the third of five straight Republican national victories in California. For that matter, the Democrats were to carry only five of the first twenty presidential elections voted upon in California.

Governor Haight opposed the Fifteenth Amendment giving the Blacks the right to vote, and the preponderantly controlled Democratic Legislature refused ratification. This was not corrected until Senator Albert S. Rodda sponsored a measure which prompted the Democratic Legislature of 1962 to ratify the Amendment, ninety-two years after it had become part of the United States Constitution.

In February 1874 Senator Casserly resigned with another year to serve, and the Legislature selected Democrat John S. Hager of San Francisco to complete the term. He had previously served in the State Senate and had sat with distinction on the Fourth District Court for seven years. For the new full term the following year the Legislature elected Governor Newton Booth, and Lieutenant Governor Pacheco completed the gubernatorial term.

In the elections of 1875 four candidates sought the governorship: William Irwin, Democrat; Timothy G. Phelps, Republican; John Bidwell, Independent; and William E. Lovett, Taxpayer. As the latter two were offshoots of the Republican Party, Irwin won easily, with the combined vote of the other three failing to equal Irwin's total vote. Coming from Ohio where he had been a professor at Marietta College, Irwin was at the time of his election the editor of the *Yreka Union*, and President Pro Tempore of the State Senate.

Pacheco, who had served as governor after Booth resigned to become United States Senator, had been passed over at the Republican convention in favor of Phelps. He ran again for Lieutenant Governor on the Independent ticket with Bidwell. In 1876 he ran for Congress on the Republican ticket from the Fourth

District. It was a close vote and the Secretary of State refused to certify the election until the Supreme Court ordered a canvas of the vote which showed Pacheco had defeated Peter D. Wigginton by one vote! All this had taken much time and Pacheco was not sworn in until December 3, 1877. But Wigginton was not one to give up easily. Carrying his fight to the House of Representatives, the Committee on Elections split with a majority favoring him. The majority report was thereupon adopted by the House 137 to 126, with Wigginton being sworn in on February 7, 1878. Pacheco had served 285 days as governor and sixty-five days as congressman, fifteen days less than a full year in both jobs combined.[45]

Thus, politics in California have been and continue to be unique and often unintelligible. Although parties are not mentioned in the Federal Constitution, their importance in elections is undisputed. Likewise, the role of the states in conducting elections to fill various offices at all levels of government is of extreme importance. The closed partisan Direct Primary election in this state is an outstanding example of the weight of these influences. Political parties in the United States have usually been loosely disciplined organizations, and the Democratic Party in California has been exceptionally weak along these lines. Notwithstanding this fact, political parties in California must still be an object of intensive study, because "that's all there is."[46]

FOOTNOTES

1 The older studies are essential in viewing the subject; see Hubert Howe Bancroft, *History of California*, (San Francisco: The History Company, 1886–1890), II, 450–538; Theodore H. Hittell, *History of California* (San Francisco: N. J. Stone & Company, 1897–1898), I, 648–667, and II, 43–106; Zephyrin Engelhardt, *The Missions and Missionaries of California* (San Francisco: The James H. Barry Company, 1913), III, 58–421; and Irving Berdine Richman, *California Under Spain and Mexico, 1535–1847* (Boston: Houghton Mifflin Co., 1911), pp. 210–244. Of the recent surveys, three present the main outlines: John Walton Caughey, *California* (Second ed.; New York: Prentice-Hall, Inc., 1953), pp. 157–159; Andrew F. Rolle, *California: A History* (New York: Thomas Y. Crowell Company, 1963), pp. 129–132; and Ralph J. Roske, *Everyman's Eden: a History of California* (New York: The Macmillan Company, 1968), pp. 145–162.

2 Leonard Pitt, *The Decline of the Californios: A Social History of the Spanish-Speaking Californians, 1846–1890* (Berkeley: University of California Press, 1966), pp. 42–47, 130–147, 195–213, 229–244, and 269–276; and Walton Bean, *California: An Interpretive History* (New York: McGraw-Hill Book Company, 1968), pp. 128–133 and 176–177.

3 Jack D. Forbes, *Afro-Americans in the Far West* (Berkeley: Far West Laboratory for Educational Research and Development, 1966), p. 12.

4 *Loc. cit.*

5 Bancroft, *op. cit.*, V, 455, 648, 652–6.

6 See Delilah L. Beasley, *The Negro Trail Blazers of California* (Los Angeles: Times Mirror Printing and Binding House, 1919), 317 pp.

7 Warren S. Thompson and others, *Growth and Changes in California's Population* (Los Angeles: Haynes Foundation, 1955), p. 68.

8 Bancroft *op. cit.*, VI, 261 ff. The leaders in this early movement were Sam Brannan, owner of the *California Star,* and Dr. Robert Semple, later to be President of the Constitutional Convention.

9 The office of Alcalde is treated in Benjamin Franklin Gilbert, "Mexican Alcaldes of San Francisco, 1835–1846," *Journal of the West*, II (July, 1963), 245–256.

10 For the complete details of these historic events in California's early history, see Cardinal Goodwin, *The Establishment of State Government in California, 1846–1850* (New York: The Macmillan Company, 1914), 359 pp.; William Henry Ellison, *A Self-governing Dominion: California, 1849–1860* (Berkeley: University of California Press, 1950), 335 pp.; and Joseph Ellison, *California and the Nation, 1850–1869*, University of California Publications in History, Vol. 16 (Berkeley: University of California Press, 1927), 258 pp.

11 Bancroft, *op. cit.*, 342–343; and Charles M. Wiltse, *John C. Calhoun: Sectionalist, 1840–1850* (Indianapolis: The Bobbs-Merrill Company, Inc., 1951), Chap. XXX.

12 Peyton Hurt, "The Rise and Fall of the 'Know Nothings' in California," *California Historical Society Quarterly*, IX (March, 1930), 16–49.

13 Although if one counts the thirty-three Spanish and Mexican and Military governors, the honor belongs to Luis Antonio Arguello who served from 1822 to 1825. With California celebrating her bicentennial in 1969–1970, we find that her sixty-six governors each served an average of three years and twenty days. Much of the material on the governors was taken from H. Brett Melendy and Benjamin F. Gilbert, *The Governors of California: Peter H. Burnett to Edmund G. Brown* (Georgetown, California: The Talisman Press, 1965), 482 pp. Another important resource is: Secretary of State, *California Blue Book* (Sacramento: State Printing Office, 1881–1967). Biennial until 1919, quadrennial thereafter, none issued in 1897, 1901, 1905, 1936. 29 vols.

14 Peter H. Burnett, *Recollections and Opinions of an Old Pioneer*. (New York: D. Appleton and Company, 1880), p. 252 ff. The works of William E. Franklin concerning Burnett are authoritative: *The Governorship of Peter Hardeman Burnett, First Governor of the State of California* (Unpublished Ph.D. dissertation, Stanford University, 1954); and "The Religious Ardor of Peter H. Burnett: California's First American Governor," *California Historical Society Quarterly*, XLV (June, 1966), 125–132.

15 Bancroft, *op. cit.*, p. 305.

16 Burnett, *op. cit.*, p. 377.

17 Bancroft, *op. cit.*, pp. 643–645. Bancroft states that John McDougal later became a United States Senator. This is not true. The United States Senator was James McDougall,

who was Attorney General under Burnett. See also H. Brett Melendy, "Who Was John McDougal?", *Pacific Historical Review*, XXIX (August, 1960), 231–244.

18 Bancroft, *op. cit.*, p. 304 and p. 648; Winfield J. Davis, *History of Political Conventions in California, 1849–1892* (Sacramento: California State Library, 1893), pp. 11–12.

19 Quoted in *Daily Alta California*, July 16, 1856, p. 1; and in Earl Pomeroy, "California, 1846–1860: Politics of a Representative Frontier State," *California Historical Society Quarterly*, XXXII (December, 1953), 291–302. The latter provides excellent perspective on the politics of the era.

20 *A History of California: The American Period* (New York: The Macmillan Company, 1930), p. 350.

21 Jeremiah Lynch, *A Senator of the Fifties: David C. Broderick of California* (San Francisco: A. M. Robertson, 1911), p. 34. See also L. E. Fredman, "Broderick: A Reassessment," *Pacific Historical Review*, XXX (February, 1961), 39–46.

22 William McKendree Gwin, *Memoirs on History of the United States, Mexico, and California* (Unpublished MSS, University of California at Berkeley, Bancroft Library, 1878), p. 5. Excellent studies on Gwin include: Hallie Mae McPherson, *William McKendree Gwin, Expansionist* (Unpublished Ph.D. dissertation, University of California at Berkeley, 1931), 358 pp.; Helen Blattner, *The Political Career of William McKendree Gwin*, (Unpublished M.A. thesis, University of California at Berkeley, 1914); and Earl Ramey, *The Political Career of Wm. M. Gwin, 1833–1855* (Unpublished M.A. thesis, Stanford University, 1930).

23 Davis, *op. cit.*, p. 29 ff. A full study on Terry is A. Russell Buchanan, *David S. Terry of California: Dueling Judge* (San Marino: The Huntington Library, 1956), 238 pp.

24 James O'Meara, *Broderick and Gwin* (San Francisco: Bacon & Co., 1881), p. 131.

25 Bancroft, *op. cit.*, p. 663.

26 William F. Thompson, Jr., "M. S. Latham and the Senatorial Controversy of 1857," *California Historical Society Quarterly*, XXXII (June, 1953), 145–159. Also useful is William F. Thompson, Jr., *The Political Career of Milton Slocum Latham of California* (Unpublished M.A. thesis, Stanford University, 1952).

27 Bancroft, *op. cit.*, p. 691 ff.; and Lynch, *op. cit.*, pp. 156–157.

28 The Terry–Broderick duel is fully treated in Carroll Douglas Hall, *The Terry–Broderick Duel* (San Francisco: The Colt Press, 1939), 89 pp. See also O'Meara, *op. cit.*, pp. 218–246. For a discussion of the issues involved, see Donald E. Hargis, "The Issues in the Broderick–Gwin Debates of 1859," *California Historical Society Quarterly*, XXXII (December, 1953), 313–325. For a recent biography of Broderick which stresses his anti-slavery position see: David A. Williams, *David C. Broderick, A Political Portrait* (San Marino, California: The Huntington Library, 1969), 254 pp.

29 A. E. Wagstaff, comp. and ed., *Life of David S. Terry* (San Francisco: Continental Publishing Company, 1892), p. 19.

30 The role of Governor Johnson, and that of Major General William Tecumseh Sherman, commanding the California State Militia, during this trying period is well

documented in Herbert G. Florcken, "The Law and Order View of the San Francisco Vigilance Committee of 1856," taken from the Correspondence of Governor J. Neely Johnson, *California Historical Society Quarterly*, XIV and XV (December, 1935; March, 1936; June, 1936; and September, 1936), 350–374, 70–87, 143–162, and 247–265.

31   Stephen J. Field, *Personal Reminiscences of Early Days in California* (San Francisco: Privately Printed, 1893), pp. 2, 21, 61, 81–87, 143–162, and 247–265. Available at The Bancroft Library, University of California, Berkeley.

32   The Terry–Field duel and the United States Supreme Court decision, *In re Neagle*, are fully treated in David Farrelly and Ivan Hinderaker, *The Politics of California* (New York: The Ronald Press Company, 1951), pp. 24–31. Other sources include: Field, *op. cit.*, pp. 279–472; Wagstaff, *op. cit.*, 526 pp.; and Donald Wheaton, *The Career of David S. Terry* (Unpublished M.A. thesis, University of California at Berkeley, 1921). A slightly different version of Terry's attack is presented by Robert H. Kroninger, *Sarah and the Senator* (Berkeley: Howell-North, 1964), 253 pp.

33   Much of the material on the United States Senators was taken from the Eighty-First Congress, Second Session, *Biographical Directory of the American Congress, 1774–1949*, compiled by James L. Harrison, (Washington, D. C.: U.S.G.P.O., 1950), 2057 pp.

34   Julia H. Macleod, "John G. Downey as one of the 'Kings'," *California Historical Society Quarterly*, XXXVI (December, 1957), 327–331. The "Bulkhead Bill" story is told in Hubert Howe Bancroft, *Chronicles of the Builders of the Commonwealth* (San Francisco: The History Company, 1892), II, Chap. IV. See also Elizabeth Bergstrom, *The Life and Activities of John Gately Downey, with a Short Sketch of the City of Downey* (Unpublished M.A. thesis, University of Southern California, 1930); and Mary Purdy, *The Governorship of John Gately Downey of California, 1860–1862* (Unpublished M.A. thesis, Stanford University, 1933).

35   See Bancroft, *History of California*, VI, 731 ff. and VII, 251 ff. For twentieth century views of the complexities surrounding the 1860 election, see Philip G. Auchampaugh, "James Buchanan and Some Far Western Leaders, 1860–1861," *Pacific Historical Review*, XII (June, 1943), 169–180; A. Russell Buchanan, "James A. McDougall—A Forgotten Senator," *California Historical Society Quarterly*, XV (September, 1936), 199–212; and William Lawrence Shaw, "McDougall in California," *California Historical Society Quarterly*, XLIII, (June, 1964), 119–134.

36   Winston W. Crouch, John C. Bollens, Stanley Scott, and Dean E. McHenry, *California Government and Politics* (4th ed.; Englewood Cliffs, N.J.: Prentice-Hall, Inc., 1967). p. 93. Carey McWilliams says this is too far north, as he would not include San Luis Obispo, Kern, and Imperial Counties in southern California. See his *Southern California Country: An Island on the Land* (New York: Duell, Sloan, and Pearce, 1946), pp. 4–5.

37   Davis, *op. cit.*, pp. 201–212.

38   *Sacramento Union*, August 2, 1865.

39   *Ibid.*, September 15, 1865.

40   Davis, *op. cit.*, pp. 213–219.

41   Davis, *op. cit.*, pp. 219–240; and Thomas E. Malone, *The Democratic Party in California, 1865–1868* (Unpublished M.A. thesis, Stanford University, 1949), Chap. 1.

42   Malone, *op. cit.*, pp. 55–56.

43   Davis, *op. cit.*, pp. 241–268. Other works to be consulted are: A. Russell Buchanan, "H. H. Haight on National Politics, May 1861," *California Historical Society Quarterly*, XXXI (September, 1952), 193–204; and Cora Cody, *John Bidwell: His Early Career in California* (Unpublished M.A. thesis, University of California at Berkeley, 1927).

44   Malone, *loc. cit.*

45   Davis, *op. cit.*, pp. 335–365.

46   Outstanding articles on California politics are few and far between. One such is by Dean E. McHenry, "The Pattern of California Politics," *The Western Political Quarterly*, I (March, 1948), 44–53.

The Beginnings of
the Republican Party

On March 12, 1856, the editor of Sacramento's allegedly neutral *Spirit of the Age* offered his readers in California's most politically-alert town a prophecy for that presidential year:

> In the approaching election, it is highly probable that we may witness the appearance of a new party in the political field—a party as yet unknown in the history of California, and one of the principles of which it has been the determined effort of all politicians to suppress and avoid.

He referred to the Republican Party, founded two years earlier in Ripon, Wisconsin, named for Jefferson's old Democratic Republican faction, and primarily created to resist the Kansas-Nebraska Act of 1854 which reopened the further expansion of slavery. To this journalist, slavery was an especially dangerous issue in California, because its "citizens from all sections of the Union" might easily succumb to division. A Republican movement would force every politician to declare himself on the subject when westerners ought to remain free of controversies pertaining solely to the east. He reported that preliminary steps were under way to establish a free-soil faction on the Pacific coast. Here was evidence that such sentiment was stronger in California than political experts had believed.

Even before 1856, Californians had influenced the new party. John C. Frémont, who had tied in his colorful destiny with California's by several overland expeditions, military exploits during the Mexican War, a short term as United States Senator, and various economic interests in the gold rush, had been suggested in the fall of 1855 as the party's first presidential candidate. His wealthy

 John E. Baur was primarily responsible for the original draft of Chapter 2.

40

banker friend, Joseph Palmer of San Francisco, was in the East urging Frémont's selection.[1]

Since California's admission to the Union in 1850, the Democratic Party had dominated state politics. In 1855, however, a Democratic split allowed the American Party to fill the power vacuum, elect a governor, and win control of the state Legislature's lower house. In California, the Native Americans, or "Know-Nothings," had remained relatively quiet on the anti-Catholic and anti-foreign issues. Rather, they emphasized in a cosmopolitan society their adherence to the Union against all sectional issues, while naturally praising the federal Constitution's separation of church and state. Their following came mainly from the defunct Whig Party and some frustrated Democrats as well as those miners who resented foreigners in the diggings. "Know-Nothing" victories helped cement a temporary alliance of rival northern and southern factions among California Democrats.

Now entered the Republicans, a third force, but certainly not in the role of moderators! Early in 1856, Cornelius Cole, who had studied law with William H. Seward, set up on his Sacramento press a form of "birth certificate" for the party. He dated it March 8, 1856.[2] On April 19, in the same city, the first Republican mass meeting took place. All was quiet until the speaker was introduced. Then a general disturbance began, and because of the small number of pioneer Republicans present, the hecklers won out. From the beginning the party was unfortunate in its almost unanimously bad press. Wrote the strongly Democratic *Butte Record* of this conclave: "The Nigger worshippers made a grand fizzle of their meeting on Saturday evening, at Sacramento. The whole affair is so truly ludicrous it is hardly mentioned." But it *was* mentioned—vehemently. The *Shasta Republican*, now bearing an anachronistic title, called the Black Republican effort a "decided failure." A more sympathetic account depicted bullies mouthing "all sorts of hideous yells, in order to drown out the speaker's voice. . . . The stand was overturned and the meeting broken up. . . . The thing was a species of low rowdyism."[3] Rotten eggs flew and firecrackers popped in many Republican gatherings throughout that spring and summer.

A broadside of extreme bitterness was printed in conspicuous type and posted throughout Sacramento. It boldly declared:

TO ARMS!

TO ALL TRUE AND PATRIOTIC AMERICANS! WHEREAS SUNDRY PERSONS IN THIS COMMUNITY HAVE COMMENCED THE AGITATION OF SUBJECTS WHICH ARE TREASONABLE, AND WHICH HAVE A TENDENCY TO EXCITE AND DISTURB GOOD CITIZENS AND DESTROY THAT AMITY WHICH EXISTS AMONG US AS BRETHREN, AND TO WEAKEN OUR LOVE FOR THE GLORIOUS CONSTITUTION AND LAWS

OF THE LAND: AND WHEREAS, SAID AGITATORS ARE TRAITORS. NOW, THEREFORE, ALL GOOD CITIZENS ARE CALLED ON TO ATTEND A PUBLIC MASS MEETING, TO BE HELD AT THE ORLEANS HOTEL ON SATURDAY, TO DEVISE MEANS TO PROTECT THE PUBLIC WELFARE, BY APPOINTING A COMMITTEE TO HANG ALL THE LEADERS, AND AS MANY OF THE ATTACHES OF SAID TRAITORS AS MAY BE DEEMED NECESSARY TO RESTORE THE PUBLIC QUIET AND TO PUT A STOP TO SUCH TREASONABLE PRACTICES. ALL GOOD CITIZENS ARE REQUESTED TO ATTEND.

No Republicans were hanged, but there were numerous Californians who would have liked to have knotted nooses for them. Meanwhile, the Sacramento *Tribune* declared that the mere fact that public discussion on the slavery issue had been permitted proved the sincere tolerance and high ethics of Sacramentans![4]

In San Francisco, the earliest Republicans frequently met in the shop of George H. Blake, a hatter. Their deliberations to thwart overwhelming Democratic odds were dubbed "the Hat-Store Convention," while up the street confident Democrats meeting at the Cosmopolitan Saloon labelled their opponents' gathering "the Forlorn Hope."[5]

Nevertheless, formal party organization proceeded. The first state convention met in Sacramento's Congregational church on April 30. Only 125 delegates were present, for the number of Republicans, as contemporary informants agree, was exceptionally small. To be a party member took moral and physical courage. Representation was lopsided. More than half the delegates came from San Francisco and Sacramento, centers of population and power, while only thirteen counties mustered any delegates at all. Much of the platform they adopted reflected the party nationally. Slavery must be prohibited in the territories. Most emphasized was the call for "speedy construction of a national railroad by the most central and eligible route, from the Missouri River to the bay of San Francisco." Two years earlier there had been a movement in California to create a party solely to seek the coveted Pacific Railroad. The homestead bill, popular throughout the West, was also championed. And for miners' votes, the party favored improvement in the "present system of free mining established in our state." By acclamation, delegates to the first large congregation of Republicans, at San Francisco's Music Hall, July 19, ratified the national convention's choice of Frémont.[6]

The nascent party's quality was far more impressive than its quantity. The leadership was remarkable for so new and despised a group. All major movements begin with small, dedicated minorities, usually fairly homogeneous in sentiment, and this was classically true of California's pioneer Republicans,

John C. Fremont (1813–1890), son-in-law of Senator Thomas Hart Benton of Missouri, Far Western explorer, and controversial participant in the Mexican and Civil Wars, briefly served as Senator. This photograph was probably taken during his 1856 campaign for the Presidency. (Courtesy of California State Library.)

possessed of the crusader's spirit with his usual virtues and vices. Friends and antagonists profiled the party's heads, praising or attacking top men as political advantage ordered. The American Party insisted that most Republicans had been former Democrats, naming Joseph A. Nunes, Wilson Flint, Judge Frederick P. Tracy, and General C. H. S. Williams as recent Democratic turncoats. Of course, Democrats featured the fact that several Republican organizers had been "Know-Nothings." Truth would say that both parties lost to the new one, and that a large body of Whigs now followed Frémont. Affluent businessmen were especially notable in the leadership. Even opponents indirectly complimented the Republicans, for although professing to believe that their principles were maniacal, they admitted that almost no drunkenness or disorder existed among the Republican stalwarts at their mission-like meetings.

Oratorical plusses blessed the party. One of these was charismatic Edward D. Baker, former Illinoisan, friend of Lincoln, and since 1852 a California resident, dedicated to fighting the state's Chivs by giving leadership to the free-soil forces. By 1856, Baker's forensic talents were well known and appreciated. Even the hardest foes of Republicanism gave grudging recognition to his speaking prowess and occasionally to his logic. One of these wrote:

> Although he was talking Republicanism [in Butte County], to our nation the very quintessence of sectionalism—his speech was more national and less of party, than that of the Union-saving and Union-loving [Democratic Senator Henry S.] Foote. It was a source of regret, that a man capable of accomplishing so much, should be exerting his talents in behalf of a party, organized upon sectional issues alone. . . . His doctrines are abominable and unworthy of his eloquence. It was painting the devil in a beautiful frame.[7]

43

Another waxing giant of the party was Cornelius Cole, who would remain in Republican affairs until he became a centenarian. Cole had spoken against slavery in his native New York, although like virtually all responsible Californians, he was never an abolitionist. In 1854, Cole, then a Democrat, was defeated as candidate for Sacramento County District Attorney by the Native Americans. Gradually, he gathered free soilers into the nucleus of a party. Among his friends were merchants such as Collis P. Huntington, Mark Hopkins, Edwin B. Crocker and his brother Charles, whose later fortunes would then have seemed unbelievable. Huntington and Hopkins were named delegates to the National Republican Convention of 1856. As Cole later reminisced, these men were "all personal as well as political friends of mine. There were not, for some time, besides these, as many [Republicans] as could be counted on one's fingers. Our meetings, held in some private office, were earnest, if not enthusiastic." While additions came slowly, Cole noted that there were no desertions. The future leaders "enlisted for the war, so to speak"—not realizing how literal that phrase would become for America! It was this same Cole, with his usual insight into the problems of the day, who remarked in 1922, "Mr. Harding measures up very well in the company of American Presidents."[8]

Leland Stanford, another Sacramento colleague of Cole, was a likely figure for the party. From youth he had despised slavery, and like many Republicans, began his political interest as a Whig. Charles Crocker made the acquaintance of both Stanford and Huntington through their work for the cause years before these men would become business associates and three of the Central Pacific's Big Four.

In an era of roaring personal journalism when voters looked to the leadership of their favorite paper, Republicans could at first count on only one, the *San Francisco Journal*, but with surprising rapidity, often through temporary financing, party papers multiplied. Several of these were short-lived, founded merely for the Frémont campaign. The *Sacramento Age* noted that "So far as newspaperdom is concerned, in point of numbers the Democrats and Americans have the ascendancy, but in diligence, quiet, hard work, without parade, the Republican party is unceasingly watchful." Sometimes this was a painful chore, as a *San Francisco Chronicle* employee learned when his partisan head was broken! By election day, Republicans boasted eighteen newspapers throughout the state, particularly in San Francisco, San Jose, Sacramento, and Stockton. Even two French-language journals and a German one were included.[9]

By necessity, the election canvass of California Republicans differed from that of their eastern colleagues. For example, though a hard core felt strongly about slavery, the average voter, isolated by geography and economic interests from the Northeast, in 1856 showed little concern for the problem. Inevitably, the chief campaign issue remained the Pacific Railroad, a technological blessing desired by nearly all Californians regardless of party. Since the federal railroad surveys of 1853, California had eagerly watched Congress' handling of this question. Dixie wanted the eastern terminus to be in the South, while northerners sought to establish Chicago as the eastern end. Southern Democrats prevented the passage of any railroad bill which would have required federal loans and land grants to support construction by one of the possible northern routes the 1853 survey had indicated. Republicans insisted that there was no constitutional question involved, and Frémont publicly echoed them. Their partisans repeated the charge that California delegates to the Democratic national convention that year had refused to back Buchanan for the presidency because of his reputed coolness to the railroad bill.[10]

In California, all three parties officially and genuinely supported the railroad. "Know-Nothings" declared that the Republican Party, a sectional grouping, could not win, so the only way California could get her railroad would be by electing their candidate, Millard Fillmore. Meanwhile, Democrats stole Republican glory by favoring the federal use of lands and moneys to construct the line. This unanimity of purpose among the quarreling trio did not remove the railroad as the prime campaign issue. Republicans insisted that the 1856 Democratic platform merely stated that everything "constitutionally possible" would be done by that party to get the railroad, while Republicans flatly guaranteed to build it. To the Democratic press, their talk was irresponsible demagoguery:

> The Constitution is no barrier to them. They even say, "let the Union slide," when their national doctrines jeopardize its safety. . . . Here in California, they seek to hide their sectional deformity by manifesting infinite zeal for the Pacific Railroad, and exalting that national project above all other measures and considerations.[11]

The Democrats insisted that a Republican victory actually would prevent the building of the line, for such a project would require united national energy, which no sectional party could ever achieve.

Possessing a large and still prestigious minority of native Spanish-speaking residents, the state offered Republicans a challenge to win this supposed bloc vote. The campaign had both advantages and disadvantages. Among the latter was the fact that southern California, still largely Spanish-speaking and pastoral, was a hotbed of Southern Democrats, due to the influx of Texans and other proslavery men. *Californios* in the past had generally supported their politics. On the other hand, Frémont had been popular among *Californios* because of his role in the eminently just Capitulation of Cahuenga, at which California insurgents surrendered to him in January, 1847, ending the Mexican War on the Pacific coast. A friendship had developed between Frémont and Andres Pico, signer of the capitulation. Many *Californios*, opposing current American filibustering in Central America with California as a base, and advocating the Pacific Railroad, joined the young Angeleno journalist, Francisco P. Ramírez, in supporting the Republicans. Frémont was even depicted as a sort of precursor of the Good Neighbor Policy who would prevent the use of United States soil to attack the "weak and undefended republics of this continent."[12]

Appealing to the German, Irish, and French communities, the Republican Sacramento platform had:

> Resolved, that we heartily welcome to our country, the honest and in-dustrious emigrants who seek our shores to escape from European des-potism, and we deprecate all attempts to embitter their feelings against our free institutions by political persecution, on account of their foreign birth.

Their stand set Republicans at odds with "Know-Nothings." Generally, they bracketed together minority groups and free labor, as did Joseph A. Nunes, a Jew, who declared that slavery tyrannized the white race as well as the black, for it was inimical to free labor.[13]

Although James Buchanan himself had once said that Frémont's achievements in the Mexican War were notable, Democrats did not hesitate to rip to pieces his reputation as soldier and explorer. It was charged, not without some validity, that he had discovered nothing new and had been virtually led by the hand by the old scouts, Kit Carson and Joseph R. Walker. Republicans probably lost more votes from the well-publicized connection of Frémont with the tarnished banking house of Palmer, Cook and Company, although he had never been a partner. Poor timing hurt, too, for during the campaign the courts confirmed title to Frémont's Mariposa estate, where poor miners were reported being driven from his lands.

No one denied the Republicans' persistence and energy. They seemed to campaign everywhere. "Frémont clubs" sprouted throughout the state, even in isolated and hostile regions, facilitating communication with other Republican groups and circulating election propaganda. Their zealots were admonished to "hold meetings frequently—enlist your own members in the work. Many a swarthy miner can make a good speech—especially upon the merits of Repub-licanism," this though Frémont was exceedingly unpopular in virtually all mining districts![14]

John Carr of Trinity County could exclaim, "No young ordained missionary to the heathen ever accepted his calling with more zeal to convert the heathen, than I did to spread the doctrine of free soil and free men." Meanwhile, B. F. Converse, who spoke seven languages, was eloquent enough to win two con-verts in the diggings near Yreka, and this determined trio remained for weeks the only Republicans out of three hundred miners, but they "made one or two speeches that were marvels of eloquence, logic, and patriotism. When the polls closed we found there were forty voters for Frémont." And there was also the dedicated schoolmaster of Diamond Springs who publicly proclaimed the Republican platform. Next day, he found the textbooks thrown out of his school and the building boarded up, while parents took their children out of his class. Later, while "speechifying," the same mentor barely missed tar and feathering. One Republican pioneer told the ruffians at his mass meeting that from each of the hen-laid missiles they were throwing would hatch "a Republican chicken."[15]

Parades and barbeques were frequent, supplying about equal portions of victuals, vigor, and vituperation. If special effects alone could have won votes, Republicans would have garnered many more than the polls recorded. Prominently featured were huge cloth banners with locomotives in full steam, Frémont's image looming nearby, or sometimes sitting squarely atop the boiler! On election eve in San Francisco, a mammoth Republican parade was held: there was the ubiquitous locomotive, made of canvas and paint; a printing press rode through the streets, operating all the while; behind it a blacksmith's forge was in noisy action. Together they symbolized Republican free labor and speech.

Humor and violence mixed easily during this infamous "Rotten Eggs Campaign." For years to come the career of William Aldridge, Fresno County's "Lone Republican," would spur legends. This inoffensive clerk of a general store in Fine Gold Gulch had announced his intention to vote for the "Pathfinder," though a couple of local bullies wanted to deny his use of the polls. Solidly demanding fair play, the Southern Democratic citizenry saw that the unique dissenter officially expressed his preference, and so the results stood at: Buchanan, 218; Fillmore, 123; and Frémont, 1. Years later a Republican governor sent him a fine new hat. In 1859, he was honored by having his portrait framed in the Millerton Hotel, "that the passerby may look upon the Lone Republican."

Another anecdotal figure was Joseph Francis of Rattlesnake, who was known only as a name when he went to the Republican convention at Auburn. Without debate, he was selected as delegate to the state convention, but because the California constitution denied citizenship to Negroes, Francis was removed when his race was discovered. Democratic papers generally in 1856 used this incident to taunt the "Negrophile party."[16]

A campaign technique of questionable virtue but long lineage which some Republicans employed for prestige purposes was that of publishing lists of prominent citizens as eager new supporters of their party. These were probably unethically used with hopes that no retractions would be asked, or perhaps overzealous party members did not check their data!

Silk badge of the 1856 Republican campaign in California. Note the misspelling of "Pathfinder," Fremont's nickname which recent historians reduce to "Pathmarker." (Courtesy of California State Library.)

In contrast to the violent previous weeks election day, November 4, 1856, arrived without untoward incident. When all votes had been counted and confirmed, Buchanan had 53,365; Fillmore, 36,165; and Frémont was a poor third with only 20,693. Frémont carried by a plurality only San Luis Obispo, Santa Barbara, and Santa Clara counties, and did reasonably well in Alameda, Monterey, San Francisco, and San Mateo counties. In Mariposa, where his mining interests were famous, the "Pathfinder" made a pathetic showing of 165 votes against Buchanan's 1,254.[17]

In the California Legislature, however, Republicans were not so handily defeated. "Know-Nothings" were swept from power, replaced by Democrats. The State Senate lineup stood at eighteen Democrats, eleven Americans, and three Republicans, while the Assembly numbered sixty Democrats, eight Americans, and eleven Republicans.

Republicans immediately assessed the meaning of these results. The *North Californian*, a Republican journal of Oroville, suggested that, "If we could have had two months longer in which to have combatted prejudice and error, we believe we could have doubled our numbers in the State." As early as July, the *Democratic State Journal* had agreed that far:

> It must be confessed that the Republicans are gaining strength. As we prophecied would be the case, long ago, Black Republicanism is rising out of the ashes of know Nothingism, and is fast becoming *the* opposition party of the day, but its start occurred too late for it to be dangerous. It cannot inspire sufficient confidence by the month of November to enlist the support of that class of the community which possess no positive views upon any political subject.

Party leaders felt that Democratic unity had spelled triumph and noted that, although the devoted inner circle of their own fold had remained strong, they had not always been able to keep newer converts as faithful. Looking ahead, some were pleased that with their own rise and the rapid decline and moral bankruptcy of the "Know-Nothings," the days were numbered for the Chivalry hegemony in state politics. They referred, too, to the fact that David C. Broderick, opposed to the Chivs, was the choice for United States Senator of most influential Republicans, still too weak to name their own man. Public assertion that Broderick was a crypto-Republican had not hurt him. A moderate paper, the *Telegraph*, concluded that "Republicanism is not very horrible on close inspection—its principles bear a close scrutiny, and seem to grow brighter." The party organization was barely seven months old that November. Seldom had a political group with so many amateur leaders achieved so much in so short a time.[18]

In 1857, Republicans had their first chance to run a gubernatorial candidate. They chose Edward Stanly, a former Whig congressman from North Carolina. Although Stanly had no hope of winning, the Grand New Party wanted to make a good showing in voter turnout. Stanly was as much image as action. A lifelong opponent of Democrats, he had always passionately despised the principle of secession. In 1853, he moved to California and in 1856 supported Frémont. Though nominated by the Republicans, Stanly had not affiliated with them and disagreed with the party's stand on territorial slavery. He proved to be a sarcastic speaker of rather irritable temper, not very familiar with state issues, which, fortunately for him, were deemphasized in this campaign. Stanly opposed the pro-slavery Dred Scott decision of the United States Supreme Court, favored the Pacific Railroad, and supported foreign immigration, while strongly denouncing nativists for their bigotry against the foreign-born. No American-Republican axis thus would be possible against the Democrats. Even after a year of existence, the party still did not present full tickets in all California's counties, particularly not in the far north. Yet, those men who were nominated possessed good qualities. One fair-minded but somewhat sour observer noted that, "A party in a hopeless minority can always select good men for office." Once more, Democrats swept the state with 53,122 votes for John Weller, while Stanly gained only 21,040.[19]

By 1857, the Broderick and Gwin forces had split on the issues of federal patronage and Kansas statehood. Broderick's attack on President Buchanan at last led California Democrats to demand the Senator's resignation, since they felt he no longer represented the state. Twice Broderick refused to quit. In 1859, the Anti-Lecompton Democrats nominated Republican-leaning John Curry. The Republicans themselves chose for their gubernatorial candidate Leland Stanford, who had run for State Treasurer in 1857. Arriving in California that July, Horace Greeley, the powerful journalist and a leading eastern Republican, advised his California counterparts to join the Anti-Lecompton Democrats, but Stanford refused to withdraw in favor of a fusion ticket. Meanwhile, Frank Pixley, a journalist rising fast in the party, denounced both Gwin and Broderick, urging Republicans to remain distinct and separate. In that year's acrid campaign, Curry and the Chiv Latham challenged each other, and debated throughout the state, although Gwin and Broderick, having become exceedingly abusive, as we have seen, received more public attention. Latham won with a larger vote than that of Curry and Stanford combined. Indeed, Leland Stanford gained fewer votes than Stanly had two years earlier!

The pro-Southern faction seemed victorious until the violent death of Broderick. At the end of his life Broderick functioned almost as a Republican, having favored Stanford for governor and Baker for Congress. Had he lived he might well have become a Republican. Edward D. Baker, an unsuccessful California candidate for Congress but soon to become United States Senator from Oregon, delivered Broderick's funeral oration with such eloquence that he helped widen the Democratic schism and boost Republicanism. The Republicans adopted Broderick as their martyr to liberty.

The next year, 1860, ushered in America's most crucial presidential contest, the only one in which the minority refused to accept the majority decision. Now, Democrats both nationally and statewide were split. John G. Downey supported Douglas, the Union Democrat, while Weller favored the southerner, Breckinridge. California's Republicans had their chance and knew it. On May 16, when the party met in Chicago, the California delegation was still uninstructed. Some of its members favored Seward, but Lincoln's stock was rising. When he won nomination, "Wide Awake clubs" organized throughout California to campaign for the "Railsplitter." Lincoln's friend, Baker, was on hand, now possessing the added aura of a senator. His oratory and charm pepped up the dullness of other party figures, such as Stanford. The highlight of the 1860 campaign on the coast was probably Baker's speech of October 26 in San

Francisco. When the assemblage "caught sight of his silver locks, cheer rose upon cheer in discernible enthusiasm." Baker, as he had a year previously, praised the martyred Broderick, and concluded, "Oh, how long, shall the hopes of Freedom and her Champion be crushed forever and forever?" And these words, we are told, accompanied by his "eye of fire," noble brow and chin to match, created a sensation![20]

Republicans were already experts in political hoopla. One of their popular campaign songs for Lincoln went: "We split our throats and cast our votes for Abe of Illinois." And these votes made a difference. As he did nationally, Lincoln carried California and its four electoral votes, but not by a majority. The outcome showed: Lincoln, 38,733; Douglas, 37,999; and Breckinridge,

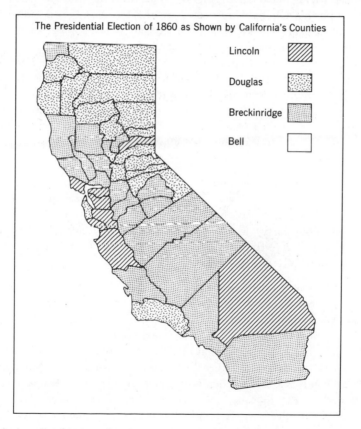

The Presidential Election of 1860 as Shown by California's Counties

Lincoln

Douglas

Breckinridge

Bell

Lincoln had a plurality in only nine counties as they existed in 1860, but carried the state's four electoral votes because of the large vote for him in the big counties of San Francisco and Marin and Santa Clara.

33,969. In Los Angeles, a center of secessionist talk, Lincoln got only 20% of the total. So hostile was the majority in Ventura, for example, that a Republican club had to meet behind closed doors in an adobe house near the aging mission, members being admitted only by signals and a password.[21]

After the firing on Fort Sumter, Republicans endorsed the bold stand of Lincoln. State sentiment rapidly shifted. From San Francisco's clergy, significant molders of opinion, the party won strong Union support. Many who had been lukewarm, or even apolitical, now looked upon Chivs as treacherous and Republicans more as prophets of patriotism than of radicalism.

Leland Stanford was a logical candidate for governor in 1861. He had served the party devotedly since its founding and had run enthusiastically for Governor in 1859, sacrificing personal interests when he knew he could not win. Now, he was a prospering merchant, respected by the business world, and still well liked by Californians who knew him. Earlier that year he had been sent to confer with Lincoln on federal appointments for California.

The gubernatorial campaign meant for Stanford canvassing on hot trails and dusty roads through semi-frontier counties. Even the opposition press found his speeches mild and courteous, though never splendid oratory. By then, uniformed marching clubs with their glazed caps and capes, typified California campaigns as they drilled, marched and carried torches through the streets of any good-sized town. Cornelius Cole, who accompanied Stanford at this time, remembered:

> Our audiences were large, and though made up in a great number of our political opponents, we were accorded a respectful hearing on all occasions. . . . It may be said that while we presented the most advanced doctrines of our party, they seldom, if ever, met with open dissent; on the contrary, they were frequently greeted with cordial approval and sometimes when wholly unexpected.[22]

By July, California's Union Democrats, following the stand of the late Senator Douglas, declared secession a dangerous heresy, though for a time they opposed the use of force against the seceding states. Now, however, Union Democracy seemed the "me-too" faction, and in the September election Stanford won by 56,036 votes, or almost double that of either opponent. The Union Democrat, John Conness, got 30,944, and Breckinridge Democrat John R. McConnell had 32,751. This outcome was particularly remarkable, partly because until a few months earlier Republicans had claimed only seven newspapers while Douglasites controlled twenty-four and Breckinridge men twenty-two. The Republicans also elected three Congressmen, Aaron A. Sargent, Timothy G. Phelps, and Frederick F. Low. With little violence and few arrests, California had definitely pledged herself to the federal cause.

Among the new Republican faces in Washington was Sargent, an Argonaut and a party founder. He would work diligently, helping to write the Pacific Railroad bill and getting it passed.

As governor, Stanford proved capable, though hardly a great executive. He revealed common sense and usually worked in harmony with the Legislature. Only five times did he veto a bill. In 1863, he was not renominated. The story went out that his expanding involvement in railroad matters would require all his time. At best this was only partly true. Actually, forces against him prevented renomination. Stanford was criticized for continuing his partisanship in favor of the original Republicans, when *Zeitgeist* seemed to call for harmony with the Douglas–Broderick–Anti-Lecompton Democrats in the newly renamed Union Party.[23]

Stanford's nemesis was John Conness, who was building a formidable political machine. Here was a remarkable figure, an Irish-born immigrant to New York at twelve and later a forty-niner, who succeeded in the mercantile business and better yet in politics. Conness had served twice in the state Legislature as a Douglas Democrat, learning well under the tutelage of Broderick. He had been defeated for governor in 1861, and then was elected the next year as a Union Democrat to the United States Senate, serving 1863–69. Conness' rise to the Senate was probably due to the desire for that exalted seat by Congressmen Sargent and Phelps. One of Sargent's supporters had accused Phelps' men of

Leland Stanford (1824–1893), as he looked when he became California's first Republican governor in 1862 when his railroad empire was still in the future. (Courtesy of California State Library.)

trying to bribe him to help Phelps' cause, and when the charge became public, Sargent's and Phelps' resulting enmity cancelled both their senatorial bids. Thus Conness succeeded Latham in Washington. Shortly after this, Conness, feeling the two wings of California Democracy could never reunite, became a Union Republican. Conness seemed to be everywhere, organizing Union leagues in California towns and fitting them into his evolving machine. He efficiently got his candidates nominated, and, for a time, elected, often by means which his opponents considered corrupt and ruthless even in that age. Conness opposed Stanford's renomination in the latter's home town, Sacramento, and saw that he was defeated in the Unionist convention. This infuriated Stanford's champion, Frank M. Pixley, and the Conness-Pixley feud was both long-lived and colorful.

Meanwhile, the spirit of the times also called for attempts to remove legal restrictions against Blacks. The first bills of this nature were introduced in 1863, but it was not until more than a decade and three federal amendments later that legal measures were enacted to provide equal rights for Blacks. Now, Republicans in their heyday could win with the issue of defending the Union and by equating their opponents with rebellion and slavery. Once triumph was theirs, they won many adherents. A cynical Sacramento writer observed "with what rapidity the numbers of a party are increased in the flush of victory, and when there are spoils of office almost within grasp."[24]

Reflecting in 1863 the national Northern Democratic policy, California Democrats nominated John G. Downey for governor, called the costly war a failure, opposed Black equality, and attacked Lincoln's recent Emancipation Proclamation. Realizing their own victories, the Unionists, as Republicans called themselves, emphasized national rather than party issues and ran a candidate whose broad views symbolized the interparty suggestion of their new label. He was Congressman Low, who seemed to stand for progress in transportation and education. Low won by 68,482 votes against fusionist independents and the Union Democrat, Downey, who garnered 44,632 votes.

The next year, Lincoln again carried California, but this time by 18,302 votes, or 59.2% against McClellan's 40.8%. Cornelius Cole, another wartime Republican-Unionist winner, went to Congress in 1863, there to secure the establishment of mail steamship service between San Francisco and the Orient. In 1865, Cole got a law allowing railroads to issue their own first mortgage bonds to the amount equal to bonds issued them by the government. This virtually doubled the Pacific Railroad subsidies. In 1867, Cole entered the United States Senate.

With the end of the Civil War, a "speedy split" occurred within the Unionist fold. Although this schism did not exactly follow the old party lines of prewar

Republicans and Northern Democrats, many former Democrats did return to their earlier allegiance and tried to hinder or modify the national administration's Reconstruction policies. The classic Republicans, now dubbed "Long-hairs," opposed the "Short-hairs," supposedly a rougher element strong in San Francisco and composed of former Democrats still within the disunited Unionist camp. These epithets may have originated during a California Assembly debate in 1865 over redistricting the supervisorial wards of San Francisco. Friends of John Conness were accused of gerrymandering the city so its politics could be controlled by the "roughs" or "Short-hair boys." Soon, the expression was generally used throughout California, while foes of "Short-hairs" naturally became "Long-hairs."[25]

Leader of the "Short-hairs" was Conness, genius of manipulation, whom a San Francisco paper called the "Great Senatorial Prestidigitator." Conness worked in a quieter manner than his mentor, Broderick, did during his days of power. Meanwhile, Low's appointees labored with him to win the counties. They often allowed Democrats to vote at Unionist primaries and won their support by opposing votes for Negroes and favoring the Democrats' eight-hour day campaign.

Reactions were violent! The Sacramento County Union convention of July 25, 1865, was surely the most memorably vicious evidence of this split. There were 106 delegates present, "Long-hair" and "Short-hair" forces about equal in number. When W. H. Barton, a "Long-hair," was elected temporary secretary by voice vote, the Low delegates insisted on polling the voters. Then trouble began:

> So sudden was the outbreak that it is hard to describe the scene that followed and that has never before or since been witnessed in any political convention in this state. Barton was intercepted by his opponents before he could reach the secretary's table and was told that he should not serve in that position. . . . The delegates on the long-hair side of the house hastened to his support, while the Low men presented a solid front to bar his way to the desk, and instantly the battle was on. . . . Weapons for the combatants appeared as if by magic, and solid hickory canes, which appeared to be abundant on both sides, were vigorously used. . . . Spittoons were numerous and flew through the air like bombshells. Inkstands supplied the place of cannon balls and the artillery was in full action. Pistols were drawn and used freely as clubs, but no firearms were discharged or knives used. The principal weapons of warfare on both sides were the chairs, which had not been furnished with the idea of their being applied to the heads of the delegates, and which were not very well

adapted for that purpose, but were swung in the air by vigorous arms and used with telling effect, being broken over the heads of the contending parties.

Legs were broken off chairs to be used as bludgeons. The battle lasted about five minutes. Then "Long-hairs" abandoned the field, some jumping through windows. Later, the "Long-hairs" organized their wounded legion in another hall while the victorious "Shorts" proceeded with business. Each convention nominated a full ticket and delegates to the state convention. Five or six men had been severely wounded. From one victim's head several pieces of an earthenware spittoon had to be removed. No wonder this conclave is known as the "Spittoon Convention."[26]

Bloodied faces did not delay politicking. The "Long-hairs" nominated Newton Booth for state senator, while "Short-hairs" favored E. H. Heaton. The "Shorts" supported Low for United States Senator, although he afterwards declined the honor, probably, as has been suggested, because he disliked the blatant way it had been procured. When Low withdrew, the schism narrowed a bit, for Cornelius Cole was elected United States Senator as candidate of both factions of the tormented party.

The gubernatorial election of 1867 brought more intraparty crises. There were four candidates in the field for governor: Fay, Pixley and Gorham from San Francisco and Bidwell from Chico. On March 17, 1867, *The Elevator*, a weekly journal published in San Francisco by colored men, and organ of the colored population of the state, prophesied that a nomination by the Union convention would be equivalent to election, and expressed its preference for George C. Gorham for governor. It could not support Frank M. Pixley because of his record on the suffrage question. John Conness' "Short-hairs" pushed for George C. Gorham. They prevented the seating of other "Short-hairs" from San Francisco's and Sacramento's determining delegations and thus secured Gorham's nomination. Gorham promised labor an eight-hour day law and gained some support in rural areas, but most "Long-hairs" believed that he was too strongly tied to the Central Pacific. They preferred the wholesomeness of the "Honest Farmer," John Bidwell, whom thirty-six key newspapers championed. So these dissident "Long-hairs" got up a new faction, the National Republican Party, eschewing the Unionist label. Many of them were old-time Republicans.

John Bidwell was considered a "Long-hair." He announced that he would make no deals. One admiring writer exclaimed that Bidwell was too good to be governor of "such a wicked people as the people of California," while other journalists depicted him as a victim of Conness' trickery of foisting Gorham on the Unionists.

Caleb T. Fay had called for Bidwell's unanimous nomination for governor at the secessionist Republican convention at Sacramento, July 16, but Bidwell had not been consulted, and four days later he telegraphed the National Republicans that he would not accept the honor. Thus Caleb T. Fay, as second-best, became the standard-bearer. Fay was an able and an honest man, who as a Yankee youth, like so many other later politicians, had come to California in 1849 and become a successful businessman. He first gained public attention in 1851, when he bought a slave in Sacramento in order to free him. This well-reported event gave Fay an indelible reputation as an abolitionist. During the 'sixties he rose in the State Assembly, and was so well thought of by San Francisco's wealthy merchants that in 1867 two hundred of them supported him for governor. He had been defeated twice for Mayor of the Bay City, but had made many friends as a hard-working reformer who favored Negro testimony in criminal cases and was incensed by Conness' reign.[27]

Although both Fay and the public generally knew that he had no chance of victory, the candidate campaigned vigorously, cheerfully, and, according to most reports, with great dignity. He faced one of the nastiest and most exciting political canvasses in early California history. Perhaps his campaign stance is best summarized in an excerpt from one of his speeches: "I hold that since slavery is destroyed, there is no form of usurpation now so dangerous to American liberty as plottings of unscrupulous demagogues to foist themselves into power against the manifest will of the masses."[28]

As the season progressed, the canny Sacramento *Union* surmised that of California's approximately 100,000 voters, 57,500 were Unionists and 42,500 Democrats. Gorham, the "Short-hair" Unionist, probably represented little more than a third of all Unionists and had come into the convention with only about that many votes, but by "trading" gained a majority. Conness was a gambling genius, and counted on cohesion of the party this time. He lost. Most powerful newspapers, hitherto Unionist for six years, attacked both Conness and Gorham and demanded that the latter withdraw.

On the stump, Gorham proved to be an eloquent and rapid talker with a fund of sarcasm as his campaign stock. He, too, had been a forty-niner and a clerk under Stephen J. Field when the latter was Alcalde of Marysville. Like Conness, he had made an easy transition from Douglas Democrat to Unionist, and had even written a biography of Edwin M. Stanton, who, characteristically, had served in both Buchanan's and Lincoln's cabinets!

In 1867, the Democrats were about as united as the Unionists had been half a dozen years earlier. They chose as candidate the San Francisco attorney, Henry H. Haight, who had campaigned for McClellan for President in 1864. Despite this and the fact that Unionists could boast that financially California was in good shape, Haight was virtually assured victory. The Democrats made a clean sweep of California's highest elective offices. Haight had 49,905 votes, Gorham 40,359, and Fay came in a very poor third with only 2,088. John P. Jones, popular Trinity County ex-sheriff, forty-niner, and State Assemblyman, had been added to Gorham's ticket in order to gain rural and mining votes. As candidate for lieutenant governor, he ran 4,225 votes ahead of Gorham. This 1867 defeat turned Jones to Virginia City's silver mines where he would soon become a millionaire and Nevada's United States Senator for thirty years.

Election postmortems revealed that in still another way Unionists might have been their own worst enemies. Considering the Conness–Gorham axis dishonest, many "Long-hairs" had refused to vote at all; probably twenty thousand of them, uninspired by Fay, had stayed home in San Francisco, Sacramento, and Nevada counties and several other areas which showed a very poor voter turnout. But the Unionists still controlled the State Senate.

One of the best summations of the Unionist debacle came from San Francisco's prestigious *Alta California*:

> The Union party has not displayed superior generalship during the campaign. From the firing of the first gun at the Primaries until now, there has been a painful lack of discretion and wisdom. . . . The first mistake made by the managers was in planning a canvass which seemed to leave popular sentiment altogether out of sight. Party usages were conformed to, and political machinery was legitimately applied, but more effort was made to capture the politicians than to captivate the people. It is a fatal error to believe that Conventions can elect any man. The canvass being opened, the enemy, with great dexterity, used against the Union party several issues which good generalship would have kept out of the fight, or turned to better advantage. The Chinese Question, the Eight-hour Law, and a skilful handling of Congressional legislation, have been potential in the hands of the Democracy, who have conducted their canvass with dignity, astuteness, and ability, especially as they were able to make points against the honest opinions of the head of the Union State ticket, which could not be made against the Union party.
>
> Still, no small share of the defeat is chargable [sic] to the fact that the Union party of California has never closely cohered. The original Republicans have been jealous and suspicious of those liberal Democrats who, with them, formed the Union party at the beginning of the war. The original Republicans have never forgotten that they were "originals," and have kept up the clannish divisions of former times, with a few noble exceptions, in the distribution of National, State and local patronage, with scrupulous exactness. Nothing but a great National exigency had kept those discordant elements together, and, as soon as that binding pressure was over, men,

who never disagreed as to principles, but continually quarreled about personal advancement, fell out of the ranks, and were no longer useful against the enemy.[29]

Postwar conditions had posed new problems which several founders of California Republicanism-Unionism were now too old or rigid to accept. The frayed shibboleths of Union, nonextension of slavery, states rights, and the Pacific Railroad no longer worked magic. Now, organized labor, the anti-Chinese cause, the farmers' dilemma, and concern over the expanding roles of the Central Pacific were far more relevant. Could a shredded party survive the disappearance of the prime reasons for its birth? Obviously, disguised as all-things-to-all-men Unionism, it could not. Yet, diehards fought against leaving what had once been so good a thing. Democrats were still called traitors, and as late as 1867, the *Alta California* insisted that the foe's triumph would strengthen the "party of anarchy," because "these men have not been on probation long enough, and we do not believe that the loyal State of California is yet ready to invite them to seats in the Government." It dubbed the bolting "Long-hairs," who had made a Democratic victory probable, the "Soreheads."[30]

Yet, the Bloody Shirt never proved so effective a banner in Reconstruction-Era California as it did in the Middle West. California, as Carey McWilliams has sagely explained, had its own unique postwar problems and politics, all quite different from the mainstream of national issues in the tarnishing Gilded Age.

When postwar prosperity began to lag, racism moved ahead, and the Chinese were cavalierly blamed for the job shortages. Angry men formed anti-Chinese clubs, demanding to know the stand of each candidate on this issue. Ironically, many California Unionists, who felt that the Civil War had solved the states' rights issue, now found a states' rights matter on their own doorstep as they protested the federal government's Burlingame Treaty of 1868, which allowed Chinese immigration. Unionists vaguely agreed that Chinese labor—in excess—was economically injurious to the west, but felt that since the treaty was binding, it must be upheld. Privately, many party leaders favored cheap Oriental labor, convinced that the railroad could not be completed nor San Francisco's inchoate industry developed without it.

When the Democrats gained control of the Legislature in 1868, they passed the eight-hour workday bill, but exempted from it agricultural and domestic labor—major forms of employment in largely pre-industrial California. They also passed in 1870 some initial anti-Chinese legislation, but this was not nearly as extensive as pressure groups demanded.

During this period, political corruption was especially rife, one exception to California's isolation from contemporary national political phenomena!

Republicans, Democrats, and minor parties printed their own ballots usually in distinctive colors and designs so that their henchmen at the polls could tell immediately in that pre-secret ballot age the preference of each voter. Designs contained patriotic slogans, flambuoyant eagles or floral formats on both front and back. Party leaders wanted to discourage ticket-splitting so they made it exceedingly difficult to do. To select someone on the opposition ticket, one had to paste over the name of the regular candidate a gummed slip bearing the substitute's name. These "stickers" were furnished by the opposition. To discourage this, regular tickets were printed in extremely small type, close together, or in irregular shape, so if a voter tried to glue his protest name over the party favorite, he would almost certainly cover up part of another name, and the ballot would be declared invalid! Most famous example of the abuse was the bizarre ballot put out by Republicans in a Vallejo election in 1871. It was five inches long and half an inch wide, with the names of thirty-six candidates in the smallest type possible. Since this ballot was striped green, it was called the "Tapeworm Ballot." Democrats followed this stratagem, and reformers within a couple of years had got an election law by which the California Secretary of State provided uniform paper ballots to all parties.

In 1871, the now-renamed Republican Party effectively estimated the new political issues of railroads and Orientals. Scholarly and analytical Newton Booth became the party's gubernatorial candidate by acclamation. He possessed as vivid an anti-railroad image as Gorham's had been "pro" four years earlier. The *Sacramento Union* somewhat simplistically claimed prime credit for defeating Gorham in 1867, and now editorially asserted that it had compelled the Republican convention to nominate Booth or again suffer defeat. While he was in the State Senate, Booth had attacked Governor Haight's objections to the Fifteenth Amendment, and this move brought him the attention needed by a potential candidate. During Booth's campaign, Black clubs organized in the larger towns and called for a Republican victory. Their impact, of course, was psychological rather than vote-rich, since barely one per cent of Californians were Black. Opposition to Booth by the Central Pacific proved a boon, gaining him reformers' votes. Booth announced his concern over Chinese immigration, but pledged protection of the rights of those Orientals already in California, a broad enough stand to win most Republicans. Both he and Haight were anti-monopolists, and the election returns were reasonably close—63,581 votes for Booth against 57,520 for Haight. Booth carried along with him three Republican congressmen. His party, which had lost control of both houses in Sacramento in 1869, now held the lower house again. Interestingly, Republicans, nominally opposing unrestrained railroad practices, chose for United States Senator Aaron A. Sargent, a friend of the Central Pacific, who would be defeated later for a second term because of his alliance with the railroad.[31]

For Justices of the Supreme Court, Long Term, A. L. Rhodes; Short Term, Addison C. Niles; For Superintendent of Public Instruction, H. N. Bolander; For Justices of the Peace, C. W. Riley, O. A. Munn.

Republican State Ticket.—For Governor, Newton Booth. For Lieutenant Governor, Romualdo Pacheco. For Secretary of State, Drury Melone. For Controller, James J. Green. For State Treasurer, Ferdinand Baehr. For Surveyor-General, Robert Gardner. For Attorney-General, John L. Love. For Clerk of the Supreme Court, Grant I Taggart. For State Printer. Thomas A Springer. For Harbor Commisioner, John A. McGlynn. For Amend. to Art. 1 of the Const.—Yes. Refund Debt—No. For Congressman—Third District, John M. Coghlan. For Assemblyman, M. J. Wright. For Sheriff, Joseph Jacobs. For Treasurer, E. D. Perkins. For Recorder, Geo. C. McKinley. For Clerk, Chas. A. Kidder. For District Attorney, J. F. Wendell. For Assessor, Joseph Hoyt. For Surveyor, Wm. W. Fitch. For Supt. of Schools; Wm. H. Fry. For Pub. Administrator, Hazen Hoyt. For Coroner, C. E. Holbrook. For Supervisor, 1st Dist., A. D. Starr. For Constables, Ed Longan and W. Markey. For Roadmaster, A. E. Thurber.

THE FAMOUS VALLEJO TAPEWORM BALLOT
Presented by Benj. Shurtleff

For State Printer.
EDWARD G. JEFFERIS.

61

Back and front of the Vallejo Tapeworm Ballot of September, 1871. (Courtesy of California State Library.)

Hated symbol of the railroad monopoly was the free pass, against which reformers then ranted. According to Jackson A. Graves, an unnamed young Republican liberal of Los Angeles denounced the free pass during a campaign in the 'seventies, and confessed that in a moment of weakness he had accepted one. Pulling the paper from his pocket, he tore it to tiny shreds before the eyes of his enthusiastic audience, and exclaimed that "By this act I denounce the monopoly and I pledge myself to do everything that I can to rescue our fair land from the strangle-hold it has upon us." The crowd cheered, but it did not know that his pass was about to expire, or that he had the renewal for it safely in another pocket.[32]

Newton Booth loomed as a hero in a generally lackluster period of California politics. Champion of farmers and foe of the machine, he created a new machine to beat the old one. This vehicle was the People's Independent Party. The faction adopted an anti-monopoly platform and enlisted both disenchanted Republicans and Democrats. On the contemporary scene were the Patrons of Husbandry, a farmers' organization offering serious opposition to the entrenched older parties. The Patrons vociferously attacked monopolies, extravagance and corruption in government and excessive freight rates, and favored cooperative banks, strict government control of railroads, steamships, and urban public utilities. They also championed an honest primary law. Their leaders, like Populists of a few years later, had little political experience and their program, though moralistic, was not extensive enough to win a majority of California's electorate. At best they hoped to serve as the balance of power.

Although he denied it when the opposition faced him with the issue, Newton Booth wanted to climb from governorship to the United States Senate. In his reform campaign he was backed by the powerful *Sacramento Union*. Noting the lack of uniformity in their membership, critics of the Independents called them "Dolly Vardens," after the multicolored calico dress patterns just then the rage of American fashion. Elsewhere in the nation, their counterparts, the Liberal Republicans, were also being dubbed "Dollies." Like many other short-lived third-party movements in California, the "Dolly Vardens," despite their heterogeneous origins, gained sudden and considerable strength because the older parties' programs were uninspiring and intraparty loyalty and discipline were weak. By 1873, the Independent tickets were in the field in most counties. That year, they made impressive gains in local elections at the expense of the regular Republicans, and made it possible for Newton Booth, by the barest of margins, to take his senate seat in 1875. Booth's broken promise not to seek the senatorship while governor resulted in a law making a governor ineligible for senator while he held office. It was not repealed until the twentieth century. Booth was also criticized for signing the several temperance bills that the anti-liquor "Dollies" presented during their brief moment of glory.

Another oddly-shaped ballot of 1871, depicting the Republican gubernatorial candidate and victor, Newton Booth (1825–1892). (Courtesy of California State Library.)

Booth, it was said, was too deeply involved in the liquor business not to be hypocritical![33]

In 1875, the "Dolly Vardens" nominated John Bidwell for governor and the incumbent Republican governor, Romualdo Pacheco, for lieutenant governor. Pacheco temporarily left the regular Republicans to join them. He was the only *Californio* to be a governor after the Mexican War, though his term was brief, completing Booth's who had gone on to Washington. The regular Republicans countered with Timothy G. Phelps, while Democrats presented William Irwin. Now there were four parties in the field, three of them weakening the Republicans, since the Independent and Taxpayers' parties drew largely from their ranks.

John Bidwell this time accepted the call. His biographer, Rockwell D. Hunt, said that Bidwell probably received more abuse during the 1875 campaign than in all his other political activities combined. Yet, he remained calm to the point of aloofness. Bidwell was assailed as a landgrabber because of the vastness of his prospering pioneer Rancho Chico, which, it was claimed, had been acquired through improper land titles. Bidwell categorically denied this. Then the *Alta California* charged that as a naturalized Mexican citizen in early California he had not been granted American citizenship by the Treaty of

Romualdo Pacheco (1831–1899). Native Californian and Republican governor, February—December, 1875, completed Booth's term, and that year left the regular party to run for lieutenant governor on the Dolly Varden ticket. (Courtesy of California State Library.)

Guadalupe Hidalgo, and thus was still a foreigner, ineligible for candidacy! Actually, Bidwell was an antimonopolist and a temperance man. He was certainly no spellbinder. His lecture-like speeches left good impressions, but they drew few votes. In them, Bidwell, owner of some twenty thousand acres, attacked Republican Phelps as a land baron.[34]

The "Dolly Vardens'" only chance in this, their last campaign, was in winning over Republicans. They did not emphasize the Chinese issue as much as the Democrats had so they gained little attention from the urban workers. As a result, their schism only assured one more Republican defeat and the quick demise of "Dolly Vardenism." The election returns showed Phelps with 31,322 votes, Irwin had an enormous majority with 61,509, and Bidwell trailed with 29,752. Democrats regained the State Legislature and won two seats in the House of Representatives.

Monotonously, recrimination followed the closing of the polls. Some Republicans blamed their failure on the Gorham faction. Others called Senator Booth the sorehead who had destroyed their rising hopes, saying that this treacherous man had "twice defeated his own party," and so would hold his senate seat

John Bidwell (1819–1900), the "Honest Farmer." Overland leader of the Bidwell–Bartleson party in 1841, he later built a ranching empire and participated in reform politics as Dolly Varden candidate for governor in 1875, and Prohibitionist Presidential candidate in 1892. (Courtesy of California State Library.)

with no Republicans behind him. The angry *Alta* called Booth's Independent Party "a mushroom which grew in a night on a dunghill of aspersion, slander, and prejudice."[35] Yet, this "dunghill party" had made a dedicated attempt to carry the popular will to victory, and it had urged the writing of a new, more just state constitution, a move for which regular Republicans still showed considerable reluctance.

Now, with the campaign over, California, feeling the effects of the Panic of 1873, the close of the mining bonanza, deflation of bloated hopes for the Pacific Railroad as California's panacea, and noting with alarm the landing of more Chinese every month, could see that neither great party had solved or resolved issues unique to the Pacific coast. The "Discontented Seventies" soon looked to newer groupings, programs, and slogans.

Perhaps it was surprising that the Republican Party had managed to survive. It had had several advantages: the incumbent national party gave it patronage and psychological support; it could be argued, too, that, the Democrats had seldom offered much better alternatives than the Republicans. With the completion of the railroad, Midwesterners with their Republican views were beginning to add their votes, even in the once pro-southern "Cow Counties." Presidential election returns showed that Californians were almost evenly divided in their loyalties to the two major parties, and that on the national level they were usually slanted a bit more toward Republicanism.

What California Republicans of the late 'seventies needed to find was a precise balance of idealism and pragmatism to save their party in this new age of tumult which was not unlike the age that had seen their spectacular rise only two decades before.

FOOTNOTES

1   Jeter Allen Isely, *Horace Greeley and the Republican Party, 1853–1861* (Princeton: Princeton University Press, 1947), p. 162. See also, Allan Nevins, *Frémont: Pathmarker of the West* (New York: D. Appleton and Company, 1939), p. 426.

2   Edward A. Dickson, "Lincoln and Baker: The Story of a Great Friendship," *Historical Society of Southern California Quarterly,* XXXIV (September, 1952), 233. For Cole's political career, see, Cornelius Cole, *Memoirs* (New York: McLoughlin Brothers, 1908) and "Cornelius Cole," in Alonzo Phelps, *Contemporary Biography of California's Representative Men* (San Francisco: A. L. Bancroft and Company, 1882), II, 225–226.

3   *Spirit of the Age* (Sacramento), April 21, 1856.

4   Quoted in Cole, *op. cit.,* p. 114. See also Walter R. Bacon, "Fifty Years of California Politics," Historical Society of Southern California *Publications,* V (1900), 36.

5   George E. Barnes, "A Hat-Store Convention," *San Francisco Bulletin,* October 31, 1896.

6   Winfield J. Davis, *History of Political Conventions in California, 1849–1892* (Sacramento: California State Library, 1893), p. 51.

7   *Butte Record* (Oroville), September 5, 1856. See also Harry C. Blair and Rebecca Tarshish, *The Life of Col. Edward D. Baker* (Portland: Oregon Historical Society, 1960), pp. 65–76, and Milton H. Shutes, *Colonel E. D. Baker* (San Francisco: California Historical Society, 1938), pp. 7–9.

8   Cole, *op. cit.*, p. 113. For the last quote, see Rockwell D. Hunt, *California in the Making: Essays and Papers in California History* (Caldwell, Idaho: The Caxton Printers, Ltd., 1953), p. 99. See also Mrs. Catherine Coffin Phillips, *Cornelius Cole: A California Pioneer and United States Senator* (San Francisco: John Henry Nash, 1929), 379 pp.

9   *Spirit of the Age* (Sacramento), October 14, 1856. Ruhl Jacob Bartlett in his *John C. Frémont and the Republican Party* (Columbus: Ohio State University Press, 1930), p. 37, emphasizes Cole's Sacramento *Times'* influence as the "campaign organ" of the Republicans in 1856. See also, "Early Republican Newspapers in California," *Overland Monthly*, XIII (November, 1874), 483–484.

10   On September 4, 1856, Frémont, in replying to the *San Francisco Bulletin's* questioning on the railroad unequivocally supported it. His responses were widely published. See *Sacramento Union*, October 2, 1856. Consult also Joseph Ellison, *California and the Nation, 1850–1869* (Berkeley: University of California Press, 1927), 258 pp.

11   *Butte Record* (Oroville), August 2, 1856.

12   See particularly *El Clamor Público* (Los Angeles), October 11, 1856. An excellent study of affairs in Los Angeles at the time is William B. Rice, *The Los Angeles Star, 1851–1864* (Berkeley and Los Angeles: University of California Press, 1947), pp. 148–150.

13   See, *Speech of Joseph A. Nunes, Esq., Delivered Before the 11th District Republican Club, September, 1856* (Sacramento: State Central Committee of the Republican Party, 1856), p. 8. Some "Know-Nothings" and Republicans did actively seek union; see, *Democratic State Journal* (Sacramento), November 10, 1856, and *Placer Press* (Auburn), July 19, 1856.

14   Isaac Cox, *The Annals of Trinity County* (San Francisco: Commercial Book and Job Printing, 1858), p. 136, and *Marysville Herald*, September 27, 1856, and Columbia *Weekly Columbian*, August 23, 1856, for similar accounts of zealous Republican converts and their missionary progress.

15   John Carr, *Pioneer Days in California* (Eureka: Times Publishing Company, 1891), pp. 329–331, 336–338; Burton B. Porter, *One of the People* (Colton: privately printed, 1907), p. 62; and T. E. Jones, "Some Reminiscences of Early Trinity," *Overland Monthly*, X (January, 1887), 24–25, as well as W. A. Croffut, "Early California Politics: General Frémont's Campaign," *The Argonaut*, XVII (October 24, 1885), 5.

16   For the details of this anecdote, see Paul E. Vandor, *History of Fresno County, California, With Biographical Sketches* (Los Angeles: Historic Record Company, 1919), p. 94; *Memorial and Biographical History of the Counties of Fresno, Tulare, and Kern, California* (Chicago: The Lewis Company, c. 1890), p. 60; and Eugene L. Menefee and Fred A. Dodge, *History of Tulare and Kings Counties, California* (Los Angeles: Historic

The Rumble of California Politics

Record Company, 1913), p. 103. Joseph Francis' plight is chronicled in Auburn's *Placer Press*, July 26, 1856, and with slight variations in practically every non-Republican journal in California that year.

17   Peyton Hurt, "The Rise and Fall of the Know-Nothings in California," *California Historical Society Quarterly,* IX (June, 1930), 107, and Davis, *op. cit.,* p. 74. The *Humboldt Times* (Union) reported that Republicans won more than double the votes that optimistic opponents allowed them in Humboldt County. Bartlett, *op. cit.,* p. 40, believes Frémont lost some votes because California Republicans failed to stress the free-soil issue where it was considered of minor interest. For the comments of a cautious San Francisco banker against Frémont during the campaign, see: Dwight L. Clarke, *William Tecumseh Sherman: Gold Rush Banker* (San Francisco: California Historical Society, 1969), pp. 249, 263.

18   *San Jose Telegraph,* January 13, 1857.

19   A good recent account of the campaign is Norman D. Brown, "Edward Stanly: First Republican Candidate for Governor of California," *California Historical Society Quarterly,* XLVII (September, 1968), 251–272. See also, J. G. De R. Hamilton, "Edward Stanly," in *Dictionary of American Biography* (New York: Charles Scribner's Sons, 1935), XVII, 515–516. Stanly is lengthily sketched in the *Alta California* (San Francisco), August 5, 1857, and the *Sacramento Union,* July 18, 1857, contains a telling analysis of his speechmaking.

20   See, *Speech of Hon. Edw. D. Baker, U.S. Senator from Oregon, Delivered at a Republican Mass Meeting . . . in the city of San Francisco, October 26th, 1860* (San Francisco: Privately Printed, 1860). Available at Henry E. Huntington Library, San Marino, California.

21   An interesting survey is Edward A. Dickson, "How the Republican Party Was Organized in California," *Historical Society of Southern California Quarterly,* XXX (September, 1948), particularly pp. 200–202. Elijah R. Kennedy *The Contest for California in 1861: How Colonel E. D. Baker Saved the Pacific States to the Union* (Boston and New York: Houghton Mifflin Company, 1912), pp. 144–146, is as enthusiastic as the title denotes and is, perhaps, a delayed reaction to Baker's charm. The Spanish-speaking *Californios,* such as the Carrillos and de la Guerras, supported Lincoln as they had Frémont. See Cameron Rogers, ed., *A County Judge in Arcady: Selected Private Papers of Charles Fernald* (Glendale: Arthur H. Clark Company, 1954), p. 41.

22   Cole, *op. cit.,* p. 135.

23   George T. Clark, *Leland Stanford* (Stanford: Stanford University Press, 1931), pp. 85–144, discusses his political career of this period. California Republicanism during the Civil War is covered in Milton H. Shutes, *Lincoln and California* (Stanford: Stanford University Press, 1943).

24   "Letter from Sacramento," in *Weekly Alta California* (San Francisco), June 22, 1861.

25   Davis, *op. cit.,* p. 213. Lincoln's second victory in California is treated in William Zornow, "California Sidelights on the Presidential Election of 1864," *California Historical Society Quarterly,* XXXIV (March, 1955), 49–64.

The Beginnings of the Republican Party

26   See William L. Willis, *History of Sacramento County, California* (Los Angeles: Historic Record Company, 1913), pp. 84–85, and the *Sacramento Daily Bee* and *Sacramento Daily Union*, both of July 26, 1865.

27   Gorham and Conness are severely criticized in Hubert Howe Bancroft, *History of California* (San Francisco: The History Company, 1890), VII, 323–329. Several unfriendly articles on Gorham are found in the *Sacramento Union* during the campaign summer of 1867. Particularly informative is that of August 29, 1867. For Conness, see *Biographical Directory of the American Congress* (Washington: Government Printing Office, 1961), p. 730.

28   Davis, *op. cit.*, pp. 247–252, presents a calm appraisal of the heated 1867 campaign, as he does of most political events of the period. On the forgotten Caleb T. Fay, see Oscar T. Shuck, ed., *Representative and Leading Men of the Pacific* (San Francisco: Bacon and Company, 1870), pp. 303–317, well-balanced for a "mugbook." Sketchier is Phelps, *op. cit.*, II, 327–330.

29   *Alta California* (San Francisco), September 6, 1867.

30   *Ibid.*, September 7, 1867.

31   See, "Booth's Long Career," in *San Francisco Examiner*, July 15, 1892, and Theodore H. Hittell, *History of California* (San Francisco: N. J. Stone and Company, 1898), IV, 498–500, 517–518. Booth's oratory is illustrated in Lauren E. Crane, ed., *Newton Booth of California: His Speeches and Addresses* (New York: G. P. Putnam's Sons, 1894); we learn he opposed capital punishment in 1873. George H. Tinkham, *California Men and Events, 1769–1890* (Stockton: Record Publishing Company, 1915), pp. 217–222, covers Booth's rise, with his own slant apparent. Consult again the reliable Davis, *op. cit.*, pp. 310–311.

32   Jackson A. Graves, *My Seventy Years in California, 1857–1927* (Los Angeles: Times-Mirror Press, 1927), p. 252. Graves also notes the common practice of buying votes in Los Angeles of the "sunny seventies." In an alley near the Temple Block voters were herded, then taken to the courthouse to cast their ballots, and finally paid off in a saloon, p. 255. For ballot-box stuffing and the Tapeworm Ballot, see Marguerite Hunt, *History of Solano County, California* (Chicago: S. J. Clarke Company, 1926), I, 68–69.

33   Hittell, *op. cit.*, IV, 519–520, and Bancroft, *op. cit.*, VII, 364–367. The California press, 1873–75, is filled with critiques and satires on the Dolly Vardens. For the origin of this term, see Hans Sperber and Travis Trittschuh, *American Political Terms: An Historical Dictionary* (Detroit: Wayne State University Press, 1962), pp. 129–130.

34   On John Bidwell, see the two factual but highly laudatory biographies, Rockwell D. Hunt, *John Bidwell: Prince of California Pioneers* (Caldwell: Caxton Printers, Ltd., 1942), pp. 300–319, and Marcus Benjamin, *John Bidwell, Pioneer* (Washington: Privately Printed, 1907), p. 36. Available at Chico Public Library, Chico, California.

35   *Daily Alta California* (San Francisco), September 6, 1875. For a longer view, consult Bancroft, *op. cit.*, VII, 367.

The Period of the
Workingmen's Party

The Workingmen's Party of California arose in the decade of the terrible
seventies. Several conservative San Francisco newspapers compared the movement with the horrible actions of incendiaries and levelers in the Paris Com-
mune insurrection and massacres of 1792 and 1871. The depression after the
Panic of 1873 reached its apex in 1877, generating much economic and political
radicalism. Although the panic did not reach California until 1875, economic
decline set in as early as 1865 when output of the gold mines began to diminish.

The foundries and machine shops of San Francisco reduced their production
of mining machinery and real estate values in the city depreciated as wages
and prices fell. When the transcontinental railroad was completed in 1869,
California markets became overstocked and the Central Pacific Railroad dis-
charged thousands of unskilled workers. By January 1870, San Francisco alone
had 7,000 unemployed.[1]

In 1873 California farmers organized the Peoples' Independent Party to
protest high freight rates and discriminatory practices of the Central Pacific,
unjust taxes, and control of water supplies by large landowners. On August 25,
1875, the Bank of California in San Francisco, considered the financial giant
on the Pacific Coast, temporarily closed its doors. The bank was closely associated with development of Nevada mines whose shares had recently dropped
over $100,000,000 in value. Two other San Francisco banks and several in the
interior also closed. And the mysterious death of William C. Ralston, cashier
of the Bank of California and a civic leader of San Francisco, created more of a
sensation than the closing of his bank. Whereas the Panic of 1875 was sym-

Benjamin F. Gilbert was primarily responsible for the original draft
of Chapter 3.

bolized in northern California by the closing of the Bank of California, it was symbolized in Los Angeles by the Temple and Workman Bank failure.[2]

Although the Bank of California soon reopened along with San Francisco's closed stock exchanges, economic troubles spread throughout the state. The winter of 1876–77 brought slight rainfall curtailing normal agricultural production. Henry George in his classic, *Progress and Poverty,* described the agrarian distress:

> . . . in the purely agricultural districts of Southern California there was in 1877 a total failure of the crop, and of millions of sheep nothing remained but their bones. In the great San Joaquin Valley were many farmers without food enough to support their families until the next harvest time, let alone to support any laborers.[3]

In the Sacramento Valley wheat dropped in price and sheep sold for one dollar each. In January 1877, another panic occurred in mining stock when the Consolidated Virginia Mines of the Comstock Lode announced the usual monthly dividend would not be paid. The stock market collapse amounted to one thousand dollars for each adult male in San Francisco while during the year there were 451 business failures in the state and destitution became widespread. Workingmen, farmers, and businessmen suffered and blamed the Chinese for their plight. Walter M. Fisher, a British visitor to California in 1876, remarked: "To the Irish or English-born peasant, to the German *Bauer,* to the native American teamster and miner—in short, to all those who make up the proletarian class in the Great West, the Chinese is not a man but an infernal puzzle and portent."[4]

Anti-Chinese politics and legislation quickly gained popularity in California. Various foreign miners' license taxes enacted by successive legislative sessions were imposed primarily upon the Chinese, who were also denied citizenship and suffrage and restricted in the use of courts and schools. Anti-coolie unions tried to stop Chinese immigration, but the Burlingame Treaty of 1868 allowed unrestricted entry and the number of new arrivals increased rapidly until 1876. By that year San Francisco manufacturers employed about 14,000 Chinese, and many worked elsewhere in either industry or agriculture and on irrigation and reclamation projects.

A brutal Chinese massacre rocked Los Angeles in 1871, when a frenzied mob lynched nineteen Chinese in the Calle de Los Negros section. The nation was shocked, and Los Angeles appeared in the headlines of Eastern newspapers for the first time. A grand jury indicted 150 men, but only six rioters were sentenced to short jail terms. In February 1877, several employers of Chinese labor at Chico in Butte County were threatened and a portion of their properties was burned. The next month five men attacked Chinese workers on the Lemm

71

Ranch, shooting or burning five to death in their cabin. After the murderers were arrested, they claimed to be under orders of a Workingmen's Protective Association.[5]

The United States census of 1870 listed 49,277 Chinese in California. The number increased to 75,132 by 1880. Over one-half of the Chinese were concentrated in San Francisco. In response to demands of anti-coolie associations and labor organizations the Board of Supervisors enacted a series of anti-Chinese ordinances. For example, the "Queue Ordinance" required a male prisoner to have his hair clipped to within one inch of his scalp. A "Laundry Ordinance" imposed a license of fifteen dollars a quarter upon laundries having no horse-drawn vehicle. Since most Chinese laundries were without animal power, the law discriminated against them. Many state and municipal laws directed against the Chinese were ineffective, since they conflicted either with the Burlingame Treaty, the Fourteenth Amendment, or the Civil Rights Act, or because enforcement proved impracticable.[6]

In 1875 Andrew Jackson Bryant was elected Mayor of San Francisco by anti-Chinese and labor groups. The next year Bryant recommended that the Board of Supervisors should send a committee of prominent citizens to Washington to urge restriction of Chinese immigration. He also suggested that the Supervisors call an anti-Chinese meeting. The Board unanimously endorsed both proposals. At the mass meeting, held on April 6, 1876, Governor William Irwin served as chairman and as keynote speaker, claiming that the Chinese were the enemy of American civilization.[7]

Meanwhile, Senator Creed Haymond proposed that the State Senate form a special committee to investigate Chinese immigration into California. The Senate approved and a committee of seven Senators held sessions in San Francisco and Sacramento to hear testimony on the subject. The committee envisioned California as a potential "lesser Asia," memorialized Congress to end Chinese immigration, and claimed white labor could not compete with coolies.[8]

Theodore H. Hittell, a major California historian, later remarked that the State Senate Committee's special object was: ". . . to manufacture anti-Chinese thunder and furnish pabulum for the future demagogues of the San Francisco 'sand-lots.' "[9] In 1876 the Joint Special Committee of Congress to investigate Chinese Immigration also met in San Francisco and Sacramento to hear witnesses. Although Senator Oliver P. Morton of Indiana chaired the committee, its actual working members were Senator Aaron A. Sargent, Congressman W. A. Piper of California and Congressman Henry Cooper of Tennessee. Both Sargent and Piper were honorary officials of the Anti-Coolie Union of San Francisco. Senator Sargent wrote the majority report repeating charges against the Chinese that had been made by the State Senate Committee.

Frank M. Pixley, a former State Attorney General and a Regent of the Univer-

Frank M. Pixley (1825–1895), who served as a San Francisco assemblyman in 1859, as attorney general from 1862 to 1863, as a regent of the University of California from 1875 to 1880, and in other city and state offices. (Courtesy of California State Library.)

sity of California, represented the City of San Francisco before the Congressional Committee. Assuming the role of a prosecuting attorney, he acted in apparent collusion with Senator Sargent in insulting pro-Chinese witnesses and flattering anti-Chinese witnesses. Dr. Charles C. O'Donnell, one of his star witnesses, was to become a prominent sand-lot demagogue the next year. He falsely testified that 150 Chinese lepers roamed San Francisco streets.[10]

In July 1877 the nation's first major labor uprising occurred as the result of a series of railroad strikes protesting wage cuts. Initial riots broke out in West Virginia, Maryland, and Pennsylvania. The strike eventually spread to eleven other states from New York to Texas. After strikers in Pittsburgh took possession of railway property, a pitched battle developed between federal troops and workers.

When news of the strike reached San Francisco, local officials of the Workingmen's Party of the United States called a mass meeting, on the evening of July 23rd, to express sympathy with fellow workers in the East. It was held at the triangular sand-lot bound by Market and McAllister Streets and the fence of the new City Hall. Here several thousand workers stood ankle-deep in sand. They passed resolutions condemning wage cuts, graft, watered stocks, and subsidies. Although speakers tried to avoid the Chinese issue, anti-coolie agitators were present in the crowd. After the meeting, a group of hoodlums began a march toward Chinatown. Although the police held most back, a few penetrated into the quarter. Before reaching the outskirts of Chinatown, the mob smashed windows of several Chinese stores, burned a Chinese laundry at Leavenworth and Turk Streets, and destroyed fifteen wash houses.

The next day concerned property owners and merchants assembled at the Chamber of Commerce to organize a Committee of Safety. Headed by William Tell Coleman, the "Lion of the Vigilantes of 1856," the committee had the backing of Mayor Bryant and the Chief of Police. General McComb, commanding 1,200 soldiers at the Presidio, promised aid as did Governor William Irwin, who came down from Sacramento. At Irwin's request the Secretary of the Navy dispatched three warships to San Francisco from Mare Island Navy Yard. For a week the *Lackawanna, Monterey,* and *Pensacola* were anchored off the Embarcadero with a force of bluejackets and marines ready to assist Coleman if necessary.

Coleman armed and drilled 5,438 volunteers. He then purchased 6,000 hickory pick-handles, and had his volunteers whittle them into billies. To prevent killings, these were substituted for firearms. Hence the Committee of Safety became known as the Pick Handle Brigade. Its ranks were increased to 6,500 members while posses of special police and of the Grand Army of the Republic were mustered. Archbishop Joseph Sadoc Alemany issued a pastoral letter asking all reliable citizens, particularly Catholics, to support authority. Moreover, even labor leaders and some anti-Chinese groups repudiated the riotous element.

During the emergency rioters threatened to destroy the Pacific Mail Steamship Company wharves where Chinese immigrants were landed. On the afternoon of July 27, the *City of Tokio* put ashore 138 Chinese, who were protected by Coleman's forces and the police. That evening hoodlums set fire to the Pacific Mail lumber yards at the foot of Brannan Street near the wharves. When firemen and police arrived on the scene, 1,500 rioters holding a bluff situated just above the blaze hurled rocks and other missiles upon them. Coleman at once ordered 700 members of his Pick Handle Brigade to charge up the bluff. After a two-hour battle, the rioters were dispersed.

The next day the three warships returned to Mare Island. On July 30, the Pick Handle Brigade disbanded. The lawless element was completely demoralized, and the local crisis stemming from the great railroad strike of 1877 ended.[11]

The "July riots" caused much excitement in the East Bay. But a show of force by authorities persuaded Oakland workingmen to postpone a planned mass meeting, and civic leaders felt a possible riot had been averted.[12]

Ironically, Denis Kearney, a member of the Pick Handle Brigade, arose as the idol of the San Francisco sand-lot mobocracy. He became the heart and soul of the Workingmen's Party, a significant third party that profoundly stirred California politics for four frantic years. Kearney was born in Oakmount, Ireland in 1847. Orphaned at the age of eleven, he went to sea as a cabin boy, sailing mostly on American ships. When he first arrived in San Francisco in 1868, he was serving as first officer of the *Shooting Star*. For the next four years he sailed on coastal steamers, and then in 1872 he left his seafaring life to purchase a draying business in San Francisco. He married Mary Leary in 1870, reared children, and was naturalized in 1876. Kearney's draying business prospered and he accumulated some property. Thrifty and industrious, he advocated temperance in the use of liquor and tobacco. During the Presidential campaign of 1876 he marched in torchlight processions as a "Hayes Invincible."[13]

Although Kearney lacked a formal education, he assiduously read history, political tracts, and the writings of Darwin and Spencer. He purposely trained himself in public speaking. For two years he regularly attended the Lyceum of Self-Culture, a debating club meeting on Sunday afternoons. He attacked religion, condemned the working classes, and initially defended the Chinese and even capitalists. His audiences usually considered him a conceited bore whose remarks were emotional and illogical. With his thick Irish brogue Kearney powerfully bellowed his words, but gradually developed into a voluble speaker. The official contemporary historians of the Workingmen's Party wrote: ". . . he attacks his subject without circumlocution, and goes to the very gist of a matter at once, and without any preparatory skirmishing."[14]

Suddenly Kearney reversed his pro-Chinese and pro-capitalist views. Whether he changed because of stock market losses, or since he foresaw a role as a demagogue, is not clear. Kearney lacked originality as a thinker and even his rallying cry, "The Chinese Must Go," was allegedly suggested to him by Chester Hull, a *San Francisco Chronicle* reporter. After Kearney became an agitator, Henry George remarked that ". . . the temperance which he had practiced and preached as to liquor and tobacco did not extend to opinions or their expression."[15] In describing Kearney's appearance, Hubert Howe Bancroft, the historian, wrote: ". . . he was below medium height, compactly built, with a broad head, slight mustache, quick but lowering blue eyes, and nervous temperament."[16]

Political action quickly followed the July unrest. At a meeting on August 22, 1877, the Workingmen's Trade and Labor Union of San Francisco was organized with John G. Day as chairman, Kearney as secretary, and J. J. Hickey as treasurer. Kearney forcibly asserted that ". . . all other parties are breeders of

75

Denis Kearney (1847–1907), the sand-lot orator and leader of the Workingmen's Party. (Courtesy of Bancroft Library.)

thieving broadcloth and enemies of the workingmen." This local organization met only once again to nominate a ticket for the forthcoming municipal election, but failing in the attempt it disintegrated.

Kearney then visualized himself leading a state-wide party of the unemployed and discontented masses. On the evening of September 21, about 2,500 unemployed men and women gathered at Union Hall. Former Senator Philip A. Roach, the first and principal speaker, criticized the Legislature for curtailing appropriations for public works and recommended construction of a bulkhead for San Francisco harbor to provide jobs. Kearney spoke next urging every workingman to buy a musket, and predicted that within a year 20,000 laborers in San Francisco would be armed. Moreover, he proposed "a little judicious hanging" to stop capitalists and "stock sharps" from robbing the people. In an editorial, entitled the "Communistic Fury," the *Daily Alta California* exclaimed:

A few Communists, so lacking in ability, discretion and knowledge, that they are not likely to ever have much influence, have combined to hold themselves out as representative workingmen of San Francisco, though there is nothing that they dislike more than manual labor, and nothing that could gratify them more than to be entrusted with some office in which they could get large pay for small effort.[17]

As the new party took shape a division occurred within its ranks. On October 5, 1877, the Kearney faction was organized into the Workingmen's Party of California. Elected officials included Kearney as President, John G. Day as Vice President, and H. L. Knight as Secretary. A committee drafted a platform pledging to unite all workingmen and their allies into one political party for defense against "the dangerous encroachments of capital." Moreover, the party proposed to rid the country of "cheap Chinese labor" and to destroy the land monopoly in California.[18] On October 8, some 1,200 Kearneyites met on the steps of the United States Branch Mint and organized a club in the tenth ward. At subsequent meetings in different parts of the city other clubs were formed. On October 16, Kearney issued a manifesto, appearing in the *San Francisco Chronicle*, that declared: "To an American, death is preferable to life on a par with the Chinaman." After stating that Congress ". . . has often been manipulated by thieves, peculators, land grabbers, bloated bondholders, railroad magnates, and shoddy aristocrats—a golden lobby dictating its proceedings," he added: "Our own legislature is little better." Kearney concluded that the workers should control politics and must ". . . meet fraud with force."

On the evening of October 29, several thousand persons climbed to the top of Nob Hill to attend a mass meeting. Near the palatial residences of such nabobs as Charles Crocker, Mark Hopkins, and Leland Stanford, Kearney harangued: "The Central Pacific Railroad men are thieves and will soon feel the power of workingmen. When I have thoroughly organized my party, we will march through the city and compel the thieves to give up their plunder." Kearney also threatened to tear down the Crocker "spite fence." Charles Crocker had purchased most of the entire block bounded by California, Sacramento, Taylor, and Mason Streets to build his mansion. When an undertaker named Yung refused to sell his modest home and garden on this square, Crocker fenced it in forty feet high on three sides. Kearney allegedly said: "I will give Crocker until November 29th to take down the fence around Jung's [sic] house, and if he doesn't do it, I will lead the workingmen up there and tear it down, and give Crocker the worst beating with the sticks that a man ever got."

The next night Kearney addressed a meeting of the Tenth Ward Workingmen's Club held in Irish-American Hall, and proposed mobilizing 50,000 workers to drive the Chinese either out of the country or into San Francisco Bay. On the evening of November 2, Kearneyites assembled at Columbia and 24th Streets to organize the Eleventh Ward Club. After a bonfire was lighted on the corner, John G. Day announced that Kearney could not appear since his youngest

Denis Kearney addressing the Workingmen atop Nob Hill on the night of October 29, 1877. (Courtesy of Bancroft Library.)

child had just died. Mounting a hay wagon, Dr. Charles C. O'Donnell then told the crowd that a monster procession was to be held on Thanksgiving Day. He stated that the workers would march to the Pacific Mail Steamship Company's dock and warn its agent not to allow any more Chinese to land.

The next evening, the Kearneyites crowded in front of Dr. O'Donnell's office on Kearny Street near Washington Street. When Denis Kearney appeared on the balcony, he excitedly said: "Fellow Workingmen: I expect to be arrested before tomorrow morning. If I am, I don't want any of you men to commit any overt act." Immediately a squad of police officers approached the stairs to O'Donnell's office. One policeman climbed to the balcony asking Kearney to come down. He was then charged with two misdemeanors. The following day other party leaders were arrested at Horticultural Hall. All were charged with committing "acts injurious to public morals and safety," but in a trial before the City Criminal Court the complaints were dismissed. The leaders were then re-arrested on warrants charging the incitement of riot at the earlier Nob Hill meeting. Again the court dismissed the charges, but the arrests only tended to strengthen the Workingmen's Party. Meanwhile, in South San Francisco the Potrero Workingmen's Union was organized at the Union House near the Tubbs Ropewalk to encourage support for the San Francisco Workingmen.

In the gigantic Thanksgiving Day parade of November 29, some 7,000 to 10,000 workers marched celebrating both the holiday and the release of their liberated heroes. Although the police and National Guard were alerted to circumvent any pillage, property owners and the denizens of Chinatown trembled. In the line of march, from Fourth and Brannan Streets to the City Hall sand-lot, were cigarmakers, piledrivers, and other San Francisco unions as well as a mixed delegation of Oakland workers. The paraders carried placards with such slogans as "Patronize White Labor" and "Labor Shall Be King." No

Dr. Charles C. O'Donnell (1834–1912), who served one term as San Francisco coroner and as a Workingmen's delegate to the Constitutional Convention. (Courtesy of Bancroft Library.)

Denis Kearney being drawn on his own dray in a Workingmen's procession upon his release from jail. (Courtesy of Bancroft Library.)

incidents occurred and the Chinese were not assailed on the streets. The *San Francisco Chronicle* described the parade as creditable and law-abiding.[19]

At the sand-lot meeting William Wellock, the Vice President of the Kearney faction, was principal orator. In part he said:

> I am proud of being able to hurl back, in the presence of such a vast assembly, all the lies of the press and the pulpit; and proud that working-

men have marched through the streets of the city in such a peaceable manner that not the slightest disturbance has been created, nor the smallest spark permitted to fall anywhere.[20]

Dr. O'Donnell then gave a brief address and Frank C. Filley read a poem. In his speech Kearney praised the *Chronicle* and denounced the *Call*, but denied the frequent charge that the *Chronicle* wrote his speeches.

That evening a meeting was held in Charter Oak Hall to discuss a proposed state convention of the Workingmen's Party at which delegates were to be nominated to a forthcoming convention to draft a new California Constitution. After discord broke out among party leaders, the Sacramento representatives withdrew, refusing to accept Kearney's dictatorial tactics. Toward the end of 1877, intraparty dissension grew, and to restore harmony Kearney and Knight attended party meetings in the interior and as far south as Los Angeles.

At a San Jose meeting, on December 22, Kearney and Knight addressed a crowd in front of the Auzerais House. Standing on an old gravel wagon, Kearney

The fourth San Francisco City Hall with the edge of the sandlot to the right. (Courtesy of Bancroft Library.)

81

blasted the San Jose press and local politicians such as Caius T. Ryland, a Trustee of the State Normal School, and State Senator Bernard D. Murphy. He claimed to command 40,000 San Francisco workingmen, who were ready to shoulder muskets and to burn any building on his order. When Knight spoke, he charged that the Chinese were forcing California boys to be hoodlums and girls to be prostitutes. In an article about the San Jose meeting the *Daily Alta California* commented: "The speaking was a repetition of the blasphemy, contradictions and poor grammar reported as being used in San Francisco."[21]

Meanwhile, an initial meeting of the Workingmen's Party of Los Angeles was held on August 3, 1877. It convened in front of the courthouse, a location later called the Los Angeles "sand lots." In contrast to San Francisco the party was more conservative, less torn by factionalism, virtually non-violent, and not based largely on the unemployed. Among early participants in the south-land movement were Alfred Moore, Judge John S. Thompson, and Judge W. C. Wiseman. When Kearney appeared in Los Angeles at the end of the year, L. E. Page, a carriage manufacturer, had gained control of the local party. Page served as President of the first Los Angeles Workingmen's Club. By the fall of 1878 seven Los Angeles clubs were organized. Branches of the Workingmen's Party were also established in Colusa, Sacramento, and other interior cities as well as in cities on or near the coast such as Gilroy, Watsonville, San Luis Obispo, and Santa Barbara.

On January 3, 1878, Kearney led a march of about 1,500 unemployed to the San Francisco City Hall. A committee demanded that Mayor Bryant give them either jobs, food, or a place in the city jail. Bryant replied that he could not comply with the demands. Two days later Kearney and other party leaders were indicted on charges of conspiracy and attempts to incite riots. Although freed on bail, Kearney was rearrested several times, but finally acquitted. To suppress the Kearneyites, Mayor Bryant issued a proclamation forbidding assemblies. He and the Board of Supervisors also persuaded the State Legislature to enact a "gag law," empowering the police to arrest persons gathered on the streets in numbers of three or more. As a result of these threats and to prevent any revival of vigilantism the Workingmen's Party organized military companies.

The first state convention of the Workingmen's Party met in San Francisco for several days beginning January 21st. Kearney was elected "permanent" President, and resolutions were adopted condemning his recent imprisonment and Mayor Bryant's betrayal of the workers. The party's platform opposed Chinese labor and monopolies, favored an eight-hour day, recommended vesting the pardoning power in commissions, and demanded direct election of the President, Vice President, and United States Senators.[22]

The Workingmen's Party won its first victory in a special election, held on

January 22, 1878, to fill the office left vacant by the death of the Republican Senator of Alameda County, Nathan Porter. "Barebones" John W. Bones polled 2,747 votes to defeat his nearest rival, William W. Crane, Jr. In another special election, on February 19, the Workingmen's Party elected J. E. Clark as a Santa Clara County assemblyman to replace the late Clarence W. Upton. Clark won by a majority of 158 votes, but the party's candidate for the local senatorial seat was defeated by 21 votes.[23]

The next month the Workingmen's Party gained victories in the Oakland and Sacramento municipal elections. In Oakland the Workingmen allied themselves with Democrats to elect Washburne R. Andrus, a carpenter, as the mayor. Workingmen's candidates were also elected police judge and city attorney, and two were elected to the City Council. In April and May the Workingmen won elections in Berkeley, San Leandro, Hayward, Redwood City, Santa Cruz, and Nevada City. In the Los Angeles municipal election of December 2, 1878, the Workingmen won twelve of the fifteen City Council seats, two vacancies on the Board of Education, and other city offices.

Meanwhile, on March 30, 1878, the Legislature passed an enabling act for an election in mid-June of delegates to frame a new California Constitution. The measure, signed the next day by Governor William Irwin, apportioned the 152 convention delegates in a complex manner whereby one delegate was to be elected from each Assembly and Senatorial district for a total of 120 district delegates. Additionally, 32 delegates were to be elected at large with the stipulation that eight should be residents of each of the four congressional districts in California. It should be noted that the Legislature of 1876 had authorized a vote on the proposed constitutional convention. In an election, held September 5, 1877, the people approved with 73,460 in favor to 44,200 against.[24]

Despite the Workingmen's Party gain of initial political muscle, another rupture occurred within its official ranks at a crucial moment. Frank Roney, author of the party's platform, differed with Kearney on several matters. Roney opposed Kearney's battle against the *Call* in favor of the *Chronicle*. The two adversaries also fought over the role of labor unions in party's affairs. Moreover, Roney objected to Kearney's assumption of the title of "Lieutenant General" of the military units.[25] The struggle between the two contenders culminated on April 27, 1878, when the party's State Central Committee met. Kearney introduced a resolution making party officers ineligible as nominees for any public office, but Roney felt that ward club officials should be considered as potential delegates to the Constitutional Convention. A majority of the central committee refuted Kearney's resolution. When Kearney appealed directly to the workers, he was first removed from the committee and then as the party's president. As a result Roney was elected chairman of the central committee.

Neither Democrats nor Republicans wanted the Workingmen to frame the new Constitution. When their respective central committees met in different rooms at the Palace Hotel in San Francisco during April, each committee tried to fuse Democrat and Republican parties in nominating their delegates. Although the fusion attempts failed, the Democrats and Republicans were able to put Non-Partisan tickets on the ballot in most areas of the state.

Two separate Workingmen's state conventions met in San Francisco on May 16, to nominate delegates. The Kearney faction met at Charter Oak Hall and the Roney faction met at Tittle's Hall. Since Kearney attracted more rural support than Roney, his convention was able to nominate delegates-at-large from all four Congressional districts while Roney's only nominated a slate to represent the First Congressional District, comprising the City and County of San Francisco. Moreover, Kearney controlled all Assembly and Senatorial district Workingmen's delegates nominated from San Francisco. Besides Roney, the Kearneyites were also opposed in labor circles by the National Labor Party's slate of candidates affiliated with the National Workingmen's Party. Henry George, who was writing his *Progress and Poverty*, refused to be a Workingmen's Party nominee and lost his chance to try putting his ideas for taxation of land values into the new Constitution.[26]

A total of 506 candidates was nominated as delegates throughout the state, but eight declined to run. In an exciting campaign the various factions and political parties held many mass meetings. On election day, June 19th, early returns appeared to favor the Workingmen's Party. At a sand-lot meeting Kearney boasted that Workingmen would frame the Constitution. When returns from the interior showed a victory for Non-Partisans, Kearney charged that the voting was fraudulent.[27] In the final count Non-Partisans mustered seventy-eight delegates while Workingmen had only fifty-one. Eleven Republicans, ten Democrats, and two Independents were also elected. Workingmen's strength centered in San Francisco and in several northern coastal and mountain counties. The Non-Partisan party, comprising both Democrats and Republicans, elected its entire ticket for delegates-at-large as well as forty-six district delegates. Representing primarily agricultural interests, Non-Partisans controlled the Constitutional Convention.[28]

A month after the election, Kearney traveled East to visit his elderly mother in Boston and to attempt organizing a national party of workers. He assisted Benjamin F. Butler in his unsuccessful campaign for the governorship of Massachusetts. In an interview with a Boston journalist Kearney threatened that if Butler were not elected, Beacon Street and Back Bay would run with blood. After Kearney gave a few fiery speeches, Butler disclaimed him, and Kearney returned to San Francisco. Yet while Kearney was East it was proposed

"The Peoples' Money" or a propaganda banknote with portraits of Denis Kearney (1847–1907) and Benjamin F. Butler (1818–1893). (Courtesy of Bancroft Library.)

that he should be a candidate for Vice President on a ticket with Butler for President.[29]

California's second constitutional convention met in the Assembly Chamber of the Capitol at Sacramento for 157 days from September 28, 1878 until March 3, 1879. Governor Irwin presided the first three days while the convention organized itself. The Workingmen's delegates initially supported Henry Larkin as their candidate to preside, but then switched to W. J. Tinnin, a Democrat elected on the Non-Partisan ticket, in an effort to defeat Joseph P. Hoge, a corporation lawyer. On the fifth ballot Hoge was elected President, defeating Tinnin by the narrow vote of 74 to 73. In vain the Workingmen protested that two delegates, Eugene Fawcett and David S. Terry, voting for Hoge were not qualified as members. They argued that since Fawcett was a judge, he was not eligible to hold another elective office, and since Terry had participated in a duel, he was disqualified. However, the convention ignored two provisions of the Constitution of 1849 in allowing Fawcett and Terry to retain their seats.

Most delegates were either lawyers or farmers and others were physicians, teachers, journalists, merchants, miners, and carpenters. Their average age was forty-eight. Hubert H. Bancroft in his *History of California* implied that foreign-born delegates exercised much influence at the convention, asserting that 35 members and almost one-half the San Francisco delegates were so classified. Actually, only 28 of the 152 were foreign-born, but 18 or more than half of the 30 San Francisco district delegates, all Workingmen, were foreign-born. Only two delegates were native Californians compared to seven of the 48 delegates

85

at the Convention of 1849. These were Bernard F. Kenny and John C. Stedman, two San Francisco Workingmen delegates; the former died during the session, and the convention elected his brother, John J. Kenny, to fill the vacancy.[30]

Although the Sacramento convention delegates were not as colorful as the members of the Monterey Convention of 1849, many had fascinating personalities. President Joseph P. Hoge, a native of Pennsylvania, was a graduate of Jefferson College. After practicing law in Ohio and Illinois, he served two terms in Congress from 1843 to 1847. He then resumed his law practice at Galena, Illinois in partnership with Samuel M. Wilson. During the Gold Rush the two partners settled in San Francisco. Hoge became active in Democratic state conventions, and was elected as a Non-Partisan delegate from the First Congressional District. A skilled parliamentarian, he performed his task well as presiding officer. Isaac S. Belcher of Marysville, a Non-Partisan, served as President Pro Tem.[31]

Besides Hoge, there were several other prominent delegates from the First Congressional District. Both Eugene Casserly and John S. Hager had served in the United States Senate. Morris M. Estee had been Speaker of the Assembly in 1873 and 1874. John F. Miller, a former Union general, had served as Collector of the Port of San Francisco in the Johnson administration, and later became President of the Alaska Commercial Company. Among notable Workingmen's San Francisco district delegates were two lawyers, Clitus Barbour and Charles J. Beerstecher. Barbour had defended his party's leaders at the time of their arrests while Beerstecher had been active in the local German Club, in labor reforms, and in the socialistic Workingmen's Party of the United States.

David S. Terry of Stockton, a Democrat elected on the Non-Partisan ticket for San Joaquin County, chaired the committee drafting provisions of the Constitution for the legislative branch. The controversial aspects of his earlier career and as the slayer of David C. Broderick were partially mitigated by his solid work at the Convention.[32] James J. Ayers, a Non-Partisan from Los Angeles, viewed Terry as helpful, courteous, and efficient.[33] Ayers considered Volney E. Howard, a Democrat and a district delegate of Los Angeles, the greatest intellectual on the Convention floor. He stated that Howard's analytical mind probed every issue to the core and that his sympathies ". . . embraced the whole range of human aspirations and human rights."[34]

Conservatives and liberals were about equally divided in the convention, but the conservatives with a larger proportion of lawyers possessed more political skill. Both the Workingmen and the farmers lacked parliamentary experience, and neither group would cooperate with the other to solve adequately the pressing economic and social problems. While Non-Partisans controlled a majority on twenty-one of the thirty committees, the Workingmen had a majority on only two.

The agrarians were more responsible for drafting the new constitution than any other interest group. The Constitution created an elected Railroad Commission of three members to regulate railroads and other public utilities and a State Board of Equalization to equalize the valuation of taxable properties and to assess properties of railroads operating in more than one county. Corporations were to be formed only under general laws, and each stockholder was made liable for his proportion of all debts of a corporation. Moreover, corporation directors were made liable to creditors for all money embezzled or misappropriated.

Legislative powers were considerably restricted while special legislation was forbidden in many cases. Appropriations to benefit any religious school or hospital and gifts of public money were prohibited. Lobbying was made a felony. Few changes were made in the executive branch, but the governor's pardoning power was limited. One judicial reform increased Supreme Court membership from five to seven. Unlike the first Constitution, all Supreme Court decisions were required to be written and explained.

The minimum school year was increased from three to six months. The state school fund and state school tax were to support only primary and grammar schools. This provision tended to hinder the growth of high schools and other public schools. The University of California acquired status as a public trust independent of political or sectarian influence.

The Legislature could not create cities by special laws, but could incorporate, organize, and classify cities and towns according to population by general laws. A city with a population over 100,000 was allowed to frame its own charter. These provisions ended the tight control over cities by the Legislature, and an amendment of 1890 permitted home rule for a city with a population over 3,500.

One concession to the Workingmen was the provision for an eight-hour day on all public works. The Workingmen and other groups alike welcomed the vicious anti-Chinese article authorizing the Legislature to protect the state from "dangerous or detrimental aliens" and to remove them under certain conditions. Chinese were not to be employed on public works or by corporations. The Legislature was to discourage immigration of aliens ineligible as United States citizens. The Constitution described "Asiatic coolieism" as a form of slavery to be forever prohibited. Moreover, the Legislature was to delegate power to cities and towns to remove Chinese or to locate them within prescribed areas.

The completed Constitution, initially of 16,000 words, was adopted by the delegates with 120 in its favor and 15 against. A few delegates abstained and some were absent. Several voting against the Constitution signed it. The Convention then adopted an address to the people explaining major differences between the Constitution of 1849 and the new proposed one. Governor Irwin proclaimed an election for May 7, 1879, to allow voters either to ratify or reject the document.

A vigorous campaign against the Constitution was launched by banks, railroads, manufacturing firms, mining companies, and water and gas companies. Most major California newspapers, except the *San Francisco Chronicle*, opposed ratification. Kearney stumped the state supporting it, while H. L. Knight, former Secretary of the Workingmen's Party, opposed it. The Constitution was approved by a vote of 77,959 to 67,134. San Francisco rejected it by 1,592 out of a total of 38,034 votes. Alameda County voted 4,054 in favor to 6,054 against while Santa Clara County voted 2,500 in favor to 3,261 against. Mining and lumbering areas rejected it by small majorities. The agricultural counties of Colusa, Lake, Mendocino, Monterey, Placer, San Joaquin, Santa Cruz, Sonoma, and Tulare voted heavily in the affirmative.[35]

The Constitution became effective with regard to state officers and their terms on July 4, 1879, and as the state's fundamental law on January 1, 1880. Henry George commented: "The resulting instrument is a sort of mixture of constitution, code, stump-speech, and mandamus."[36] James Bryce viewed the document as a "horrible example" of democracy in the American West.[37] Hubert H. Bancroft called it a "Child of the workingmen's party" whose approval was an agrarian achievement.[38] John P. Young, who wrote in 1915 about the *Chronicle's* campaign for the constitution, emphasized that it was not a "sandlot instrument," stating: "There probably never was a more misrepresented and misunderstood political instrument. . . ."[39]

While the convention was still in session, the Workingmen's Party had reached the zenith of its power early in 1879. By January the party was organized in forty counties and planned branches in the remaining twelve counties. Two months later Mayor Andrus of Oakland was reelected and the party won in San Luis Obispo, but was defeated in Sacramento.

Once the Constitution was ratified, the *Chronicle* sponsored a new political party to implement its provisions. On May 10, the New Constitution Party held its first meeting in Stockton. A week later its supporters convened in San Francisco with Cornelius Cole in the chair. Several leaders of the Democratic, Republican, and Workingmen's parties joined the movement. David S. Terry became an important organizer of the New Constitution Party. Among others present at the San Francisco meeting were Nathaniel Bennett, Alexander Campbell, Volney E. Howard, and Oliver M. Wozencraft representing the two major parties, and Clitus Barbour and Charles J. Beerstecher representing the Workingmen.

Meanwhile, the Workingmen met in San Francisco and decided not to fuse with the New Constitution Party. At the Workingmen's state convention, held on June 3, Kearney was reelected as President. The party nominated William F. White of Santa Cruz for Governor and Mayor Washburne R. Andrus of Oakland for Lieutenant Governor. A comprehensive platform was adopted with a plank pledging: "The letter and spirit of the new constitution must be enforced."

Both the New Constitution Party and the Democratic Party nominated Dr. Hugh J. Glenn, a Colusa wheat rancher, for Governor, but they had different nominees for Lieutenant Governor. The Republican Party nominated George C. Perkins for Governor with John Mansfield as his running-mate. All four party platforms supported the Constitution of 1879. On election day, September 3, the Republican Party won all major state offices, except Justices of the Supreme Court, who were elected on several tickets. Perkins was elected Governor polling 67,965 votes to 47,647 for Glenn and 44,482 for White. Workingmen's candidates elected to state office included Robert F. Morrison as Chief Justice, five of the six Associate Justices, one Railroad Commissioner, eleven Senators, and sixteen Assemblymen.

In the San Francisco municipal election, held on the same day, Workingmen were elected mayor, sheriff, auditor, public administrator, surveyor, and attorney; moreover, three of the twelve supervisors and four of the twelve school directors won on the Workingmen's ticket. Mayor Isaac S. Kalloch was an ordained Baptist minister. Although Kalloch had initially opposed Kearney, the two became political allies. During the campaign Charles de Young, editor of the *Chronicle*, printed scandals about Kalloch's private life. In retaliation from his pulpit at Metropolitan Temple, Kalloch denounced de Young and his family. On August 23, de Young drove in a carriage to the Temple sending a message to Kalloch that someone wanted to see him. When Kalloch approached the carriage, de Young fired shots from a derringer wounding the candidate. Kalloch's political managers kept him in bed at the Temple during the remainder of the campaign. On election day many voted for Kalloch out of sympathy, and he had 20,069 votes to 19,550 for B. P. Flint, his Republican rival.

After the 1879 election, the Workingmen's Party declined in popularity. When Kearney tried to influence the assemblymen belonging to his party during the session of the 1880 Legislature, his abusive behavior resulted in a resolution barring him from the chamber. Charles Beerstecher, the Workingman on the Railroad Commission, became a pawn of railroad interests. Mayor Kalloch constantly fought with the Board of Supervisors during his two-year term. As the feud between Kalloch and Charles de Young grew more intense, the mayor's son and clerk, Milton Kalloch, entered the *Chronicle's* business office, on April 23, 1880, where he fatally shot de Young. The son blamed de Young for the publication of a pamphlet denouncing his father as an adulterer and grafter. At his murder trial Milton Kalloch was acquitted.[40]

Meanwhile, on May 3, the Supervisors instigated the first of several un-

DE·YOUNG FIRING UPON KALLOCH FROM THE CARRIAGE

An illustration from Frank Leslies's Illustrated Newspaper of September 13, 1879, showing Charles de Young (1847–1880) firing at Kalloch. (Courtesy of Bancroft Library.)

successful efforts to impeach Mayor Kalloch. In revenge Kalloch denounced the Supervisors from his pulpit. Later in the year, when President Rutherford B. Hayes visited the city, the Supervisors refused to include Kalloch on the official welcoming committee. Hayes was the first President ever to visit California while in office. The Ebell Society in Oakland entertained Lucy Hayes, and she was lauded by the Women's Christian Temperance Union at San Jose for bringing temperance to the White House. President Hayes gave a political speech on the capitol steps at Sacramento, on September 22, after a welcome by Governor George C. Perkins. In October the President's party visited Yosemite and then southern California.[41]

In the close election of 1876 Hayes had carried California by less than 2,800 votes. In 1880 Hayes's nomination for Collector of the Port of San Francisco was rejected by the Senate. Senators Newton Booth and James F. Farley of California opposed the nominee under the doctrine of senatorial courtesy and rallied a majority of both parties against him. The object was evidently to re-establish the usage so that the next President would not venture to question it. However, by the close of his term Hayes, a Civil Service reformer and an opponent of Congressional usurpation of executive powers, felt that he had stopped senatorial patronage and stated: "No member of either house now attempts even to dictate appointments."[42]

Although the Republican Party won the California governorship in 1879, only one of its six Presidential electors was elected in 1880. During the Presidential campaign both Republicans and Democrats favored strict regulation of Chinese immigration. The Democrats attacked with the forged "Morey Letter," supposedly written by James A. Garfield to an employer, defending mass importation of cheap Chinese labor. Since Republicans could not prove that the letter was a fake, it cost Garfield many votes, particularly in California. Winfield S. Hancock narrowly carried the state. All Democratic electors, except David S. Terry, won. Henry Edgerton defeated Terry by a vote of 80,348 to 79,858. Hence five California electoral votes went to Hancock and one to the victorious Garfield. It was the first of four times that California has cast its electoral votes for the loser.[43]

By 1881 the Workingmen's Party was no longer a power in California politics; only three of its Assemblymen were reelected, but they won on the Democratic ticket. Republicans won all except two minor offices in the San Francisco municipal election of 1881, and Kalloch was replaced by Mayor Maurice C. Blake. Out-of-town newspapers congratulated the city upon emancipation from the rule of ruffian Kalloch and his "Hoodlum" party.[44]

The Workingmen had already weakened the Democrats in San Francisco. After the Republican victory of 1881, the Democrats were demoralized. As a result "Blind Boss" Chris Buckley, co-proprietor of a Bush Street saloon, arose as the "Caesar of the local Democracy." Buckley gained control over smaller Democratic bosses, and in 1882 he divided the city into forty-seven districts or clubs. His chief lieutenant, Sam Rainey, welded the Fire Department into a compact political arm commanding an estimated 3,000 votes. Fung Jing Toy or "Little Pete," the principal tong chieftain of Chinatown, allied himself with Buckley whom he called the "Blind White Devil."[45]

Buckley took the San Francisco delegation to the Democratic convention at San Jose in 1882. He backed George Hearst for the governorship, but General George Stoneman was nominated. The Democratic Party made a strong comeback with Stoneman defeating Republican Morris M. Estee by a vote of 90,694 to 67,175. Two minor candidates, Dr. R. H. McDonald of the Prohibition Party and Thomas J. McQuiddy of the Greenback Labor Party, polled respectively 5,572 and 1,020 votes. Stoneman had a clear majority of over 55% of the total vote, and served as governor from 1883 to 1887.[46]

In 1882 Buckley selected Washington Bartlett as Democratic candidate to run against Mayor Blake of San Francisco. Bartlett won and the Democrats also captured the Board of Supervisors. Although Bartlett gave the Democratic ticket respectability because of his partial independence from Buckley, the "Blind Boss" was able to control the Supervisors until he sold out to the Republicans in 1884. Two years later Buckley recaptured the Board of Supervisors enabling him to rule San Francisco.

In the 1884 presidential election California's eight electoral votes were cast for Republican James G. Blaine. While each Democratic Cleveland elector carried over 89,000 votes, each Blaine elector carried over 102,000. Evidently there were not many renegade Republicans or Mugwumps in California. The term was derisively applied to those Republicans who bolted the party to support Grover Cleveland. It was jocularly stated that a Mugwump was a person with his mug on one side of the fence and his wump on the other. In the national election the Mugwumps were credited with being a strong factor in Cleveland's victory.

Bartlett was reelected to a second term in 1884. When the Democratic State Convention met in San Francisco on August 31, 1886, the gubernatorial nomination was an open race. Buckley at first opposed Bartlett, but then supported him upon realizing that the rural delegates would accept the San Francisco Mayor. Bartlett defeated his Republican rival, John F. Swift, by 84,970 to 84,316 or a margin of only 654 votes. Swift had mistakenly rejected the nomination of the anti-foreign American Party whose candidate, Peter D. Wigginton, polled 7,347 votes. Robert W. Waterman, a Republican, who had also accepted the American Party nomination, was elected Lieutenant Governor by mustering 94,969 votes. For the first time California had a Governor and a Lieutenant Governor of different parties. (This would occur again in 1894 when the governorship was won by Democrat James H. Budd and the lieutenant governorship by Republican Spencer G. Maillard.) Bartlett died in office on September 12, 1887, and the next day Waterman succeeded him. Bartlett's administration had lasted only eight months, and he was the first California Governor to die in office.[47]

From 1886 to 1890 Buckley retained his power as a major political boss in San Francisco. Jeremiah Lynch, a Democratic State Senator representing the city, exposed him in a pamphlet of 1889 entitled, *Buckleyism: The Government of A State*. He charged that Buckley took bribes from both parties in the last Legislature.[48]

Meanwhile, Buckley supported George Hearst in his election to the United States Senate in 1887 to succeed Senator Abram Pease Williams, a Republican.

Hearst, a Democrat, had served in the Senate four months the previous year after Governor Stoneman had appointed him to the seat vacated by the death of Senator John F. Miller. The Legislature of 1885 had elected Leland Stanford as California's other Senator. In 1890 Buckley sold out his party to the Republicans to assure Stanford's reelection the next year. In return Stanford assisted in providing a Democratic Legislature to reelect Hearst in 1893. However, Hearst died in office in 1891, and was succeeded by a Republican, Charles N. Felton.

A grand jury, appointed by Judge William T. Wallace in 1891, investigated both Buckley and the corrupt Republican State Legislature. When Buckley was indicted, he traveled to Europe and Canada. Upon returning to San Francisco in 1894, he was again indicted, but the grand jury was invalidated on a technicality. For the next six years Buckley played a minor role in San Francisco politics. After the Australian ballot and a new primary law were adopted in 1900, he vanished from the political scene.

Despite the disappearance of the Workingmen's Party, Denis Kearney continued in politics for a time. In 1881 he spoke for the Anti-Monopoly Party and during the next year for the Democrats. After failing to reorganize the Workingmen in 1883, he retired from politics. He became a real estate broker and then operated an employment office, and he informed Lord Bryce that the new Constitution and the anti-Chinese restriction bills of 1879 and 1882 had started a boom in California. Furthermore, he told Bryce that his only crime was opposing the Mongolization of California. Kearney spent the winter of 1887–88 in New York and Washington, D.C. agitating for total exclusion of the Chinese.[49]

In the early nineties an uncle left Kearney a fortune in real estate, mostly in Fresno. In 1899 Kearney while conversing with Wells Drury, stated: "Watching the wheat game is harder work than excluding the Chinese." Drury described Kearney as a capitalist, saying: "The canvas overalls and jumper had disappeared. Gone was the drayman's leather apron, fastened by copper rivets. . . ." Kearney's San Francisco residence was destroyed in the earthquake and fire of 1906. The former sand-lot chieftain joined a mass exodus to the East Bay, settling in Alameda where he died on April 24, 1907. Few remembered the man who was once the overbearing autocrat responsible for swaying the hungry and the unemployed. Shortly before his death, novelist Gertrude Atherton asked Kearney how he reconciled his wealth with his previous radical principles, and he lightly replied: "Oh, you know, somebody has to do the work."

The Workingmen's Party was a significant third party that influenced both local and state politics and to a degree the national political scene. Despite its short duration, it had a marked impact on the two major parties and on other contemporary minor parties. Although it partially mitigated a few economic and social ills, it fostered a long lasting racial prejudice as did other parties. The Constitution it helped to draft has endured by means of several hundred amendments. Provisions of the anti-Chinese article, partly contrived by the Workingmen's Party, were deleted over the years with its last item repealed on November 4, 1952. By 1960 the California Constitution grew to almost 80,000 words, making it the second longest among the States and trailing only that of Louisiana, but after a 1962 amendment removed obsolete items, the document was reduced to about 70,000 words.[50]

FOOTNOTES

1 For details of the economic distress in California during the seventies, see William C. Fankhauser, *A Financial History of California* (Berkeley: University of California Press, 1913), pp. 228–273 and Ira B. Cross, *Financing An Empire: History of Banking in California* (Chicago: The S. J. Clarke Publishing Company, 1927), I, 363–447.

2 The suspension of the Bank of California is discussed in Cecil G. Tilton, *William Chapman Ralston: Courageous Builder* (Boston: The Christopher Publishing House, 1935), pp. 324–424; data concerning the failure of the Temple and Workman Bank may be found in Maurice H. and Marco R. Newmark, eds., *Sixty Years in Southern California* (New York: The Knickerbocker Press, 2nd ed., 1926), pp. 477–479; also see: Robert G. Cleland and Frank B. Putnam, *Isaias W. Hellman and the Farmers and Merchant Bank* (San Marino: The Huntington Library, 1965), pp. 31–42.

3 Henry George, *Progress and Poverty* (New York: Robert Schalkenbach Foundation, 1946), p. 79.

4 Walter M. Fisher, *The Californians* (London: Macmillan and Company, 1876), p. 54.

5 Chester P. Dorland, "The Chinese Massacre in Los Angeles in 1871," *Annual Publications* (Los Angeles: Historical Society of Southern California, 1894), III, Part II, 22–26; Mary R. Coolidge, *Chinese Immigration* (New York: Henry Holt and Company, 1909), p. 263.

6 A few significant books about the Chinese in California are Elmer C. Sandmeyer, *The Anti-Chinese Movement in California* (Urbana: The University of Illinois Press, 1939); Ping Chiu, *Chinese Labor in California, 1850–1880: An Economic Study* (Madison: The State Historical Society of Wisconsin, 1963); and Gunther Barth, *Bitter Strength: A History of the Chinese in the United States, 1850–1870* (Cambridge: Harvard University Press, 1964).

7 Sandmeyer, *op. cit.*, pp. 58–59.

8 *Chinese Immigration; Its Social, Moral, and Political Effect: Report to the California State Senate* (Sacramento: F. P. Thompson, Supt. State Printing, 1878), p. 64.

9 Theodore H. Hittell, *History of California* (San Francisco: N. J. Stone & Company, 1897–98), IV, 575.

10 Coolidge, *op. cit.*, pp. 96–108; Sandmeyer, *op. cit.*, pp. 82–89; a pro-Chinese

account is George F. Seward, *Chinese Immigration* (New York: Charles Scribner's Sons, 1881), 420 pp.

11   The July unrest and the Pick Handle Brigade are treated in James A. B. Scherer, *"The Lion of the Vigilantes": William T. Coleman and the Life of Old San Francisco* (Indianapolis: The Bobbs-Merrill Company, 1939), pp. 265–282; the naval role is covered in Arnold S. Lott, *A Long Line of Ships: Mare Island's Century of Naval Activity in California* (Annapolis: United States Naval Institute, 1954), pp. 110–112.

12   Edgar J. Hinkel and William E. McCann, eds., *Oakland, 1852–1938: Some Phases of the Social, Political and Economic History of Oakland, California* (Oakland: The Oakland Public Library, 1939), II, 745–746; J. P. Munro–Fraser, *History of Alameda County* (Oakland: M. W. Wood, Publisher, 1883), pp. 694–696.

13   A comprehensive study on Kearney is Frank Fahey, *Denis Kearney: A Study in Demogoguery* (Unpublished Ph.D. dissertation, Stanford University, 1956); one short sketch is in Miriam A. deFord, *They Were San Franciscans* (Caldwell: The Caxton Printers, Ltd., 1947), pp. 195–211.

14   J. C. Stedman and R. A. Leonard, *The Workingmen's Party of California: An Epitome of Its Rise and Progress* (San Francisco: Bacon & Company, 1878), p. 96.

15   Henry George, "The Kearney Agitation in California," *Popular Science Monthly*, XVII (August, 1880), 438.

16   Hubert H. Bancroft, *History of California* (San Francisco: The History Company, 1886–1890), VII, 358.

17   *Daily Alta California*, September 23, 1877.

18   Winfield J. Davis, *History of Political Conventions in California, 1849–1892* (Sacramento: California State Library, 1893), p. 366.

19   *San Francisco Chronicle*, November 30, 1877.

20   Stedman and Leonard, *op. cit.*, p. 38.

21   *Daily Alta California*, December 23, 1877.

22   An excellent treatment of the Workingmen's Party in Los Angeles is Grace H. Stimson, *Rise of the Labor Movement in Los Angeles* (Berkeley and Los Angeles: University of California Press, 1955), pp. 13–31; the party's activities in the Sacramento Valley are covered in Joseph A. McGowan, *History of the Sacramento Valley* (New York and West Palm Beach: Lewis Historical Publishing Company), I, 337–338; for a competent summary of the Chinese problem, the Workingmen's party, the agricultural revolution, and the constitution of 1879 see: Lawrence Kinnaird, *History of the Greater San Francisco Bay Region* (New York and West Palm Beach: Lewis Historical Publishing Company), II, 50–84; the first Workingmen's party platform is in Davis, *op. cit.*, pp. 379–381.

23   Theodore H. Hittell, *History of California* (San Francisco: N. J. Stone & Company, 1897–1898), IV, 610; Stedman and Leonard, *op. cit.*, p. 66.

24   For the enabling act and proceedings see E. B. Willis and P. K. Stockton, *Debates and Proceedings of the Constitutional Convention* (3 vols., Sacramento: J. D. Young, Supt. State Printing, 1880).

25 Ira B. Cross, ed., *Frank Roney, Irish Rebel and California Labor Leader: An Autobiography* (Berkeley: University of California Press, 1931), p. 295.

26 Davis, *op. cit.*, pp. 383–389; a concise account of the Workingmen's Party based upon a master's thesis completed at Stanford University in 1940 is Ralph Kauer, "The Workingmen's Party of California," *Pacific Historical Review*, XIII (September, 1944), 278–291; a chapter on the Workingmen's party appears in Oliver Carlson, *A Mirror for Californians* (Indianapolis: The Bobbs-Merrill Company, 1941), pp. 238–262; for Henry George's campaign as a delegate see: Don C. Shoemaker, ed., *Henry George: Citizen of the World* by Anna George de Mille (Chapel Hill: The University of North Carolina Press, 1950), pp. 80–81 and Charles A. Barker, *Henry George* (New York: Oxford University Press, 1955), pp. 243–252.

27 *Daily Alta California*, June 24, 1878.

28 The most detailed published account of the convention and its background is Carl B. Swisher, *Motivation and Political Technique in the California Constitutional Convention, 1878–79* (Claremont: Pomona College, 1930); another excellent account is Dudley T. Moorhead, *Sectionalism and the California Constitution of 1879* (Unpublished Ph.D. dissertation, Stanford University, 1941), which is abstracted by the author under the same title in the *Pacific Historical Review*, XII (September, 1943), 287–293. It should be noted that the actual count of delegates according to party affiliation is difficult to determine since various sources give different figures. The convention elected five delegates to replace those who died either before or during the session and to replace one who was disqualified for not being a citizen. The figure of 51 Workingmen's delegates includes two from Los Angeles County, who were jointly nominated by both farmers and Workingmen. The convention delegates are listed in Davis, *op. cit.*, pp. 390–392; in the *California Blue Book or State Roster, 1907* (Sacramento: State Printing Office, 1907), pp. 530–532; and in Bancroft, *History of California*, VII, 402–406.

29 Ira B. Cross, *History of the Labor Movement in California* (Berkeley: University of California Press, 1935), p. 117; Hubert H. Bancroft in *Popular Tribunals* (San Francisco: The History Company, 1887), II, 714, stated: "The New York *Graphic* elevated the name of Ben Butler for United States president and Denis Kearney for vice-president, the latter scarcely detecting the covert irony."

30 Bancroft, *History of California*, VII, 407.

31 For brief biographies of most delegates see: T. J. Vivian and D. G. Waldron, *Biographical Sketches of the Delegates to the Convention* (San Francisco: Francis & Valentine, 1878).

32 Terry's role as a constitution-maker is in A. Russell Buchanan, *David S. Terry of California: Dueling Judge* (San Marino: The Huntington Library, 1956), pp. 170–190.

33 James J. Ayers, *Gold and Sunshine: Reminiscences of Early California* (Boston: The Gorham Press, 1922), p. 312.

34 *Ibid.*, p. 309.

35 Swisher, *op. cit.*, p. 109; for the *Chronicle's* role in supporting ratification see: *The San Francisco Chronicle and Its History* (San Francisco, 1879), pp. 17–18; and John

P. Young, *Journalism in California* (San Francisco: Chronicle Publishing Company, 1915), pp. 91–96.

36   George, "The Kearney Agitation in California," 445–446.

37   James Bryce, *The American Commonwealth* (London: Macmillan and Company, 2nd rev. ed., 1891), II, 396–402.

38   Bancroft, *History of California*, VII, 399–400.

39   Young, *op. cit.*, pp. 91–93.

40   A complete study of Mayor Kalloch's life is M. M. Marberry, *The Golden Voice: A Biography of Isaac Kalloch* (New York: Farrar, Straus and Company, 1947); also see: Irving McKee, "The Shooting of Charles De Young," *Pacific Historical Review*, XVI (August, 1947), 271–284; two contemporary pamphlets of interest are J. H. Shimmons, *The Shame and Scourge of San Francisco, Or, An Expose of the Rev.* Isaac S. Kalloch (n.p., 1880) and *Chinatown Declared a Nuisance!* (San Francisco, 1880).

41   The visit of President Hayes to the Pacific Coast is covered in Charles R. Williams, *The Life of Rutherford Birchard Hayes* (Columbus: Ohio State Archaeological and Historical Society, 1914), II, 286–298; and in John E. Baur, "A President Visits Los Angeles," *Historical Society of Southern California Quarterly*, XXXVII (March, 1955), 33–47.

42   Leonard D. White, *The Republican Era: 1869–1901, A Study in Administrative History* (New York: The Macmillan Company, 1958), p. 33.

43   Davis, *op. cit.*, pp. 430–431; Sandmeyer, *op. cit.*, p. 92.

44   Kauer, "The Workingmen's Party of California," 289.

45   Alexander Callow, Jr., "San Francisco's Blind Boss," *Pacific Historical Review*, XXV (August, 1956), 261–279; "Little Pete" is discussed by Richard H. Dillon, *The Hatchet Men: The Story of Tong Wars in San Francisco's Chinatown* (New York: Coward-McCann, Inc., 1962), pp. 303–340; for Sol Bloom's relations in his youth with Buckley see: *The Autobiography of Sol Bloom* (New York: G. P. Putnam's Sons, 1948), pp. 86 89.

46   Data about the 1882 Democratic convention at San Jose may be found in Mr. and Mrs. Fremont Older, *George Hearst: California Pioneer* (Los Angeles: Westernlore, 1966), pp. 187–193; and in Edith Dobie, *The Political Career of Stephen Mallory White* (Stanford University Press, 1927), pp. 32–36. The 1882 election returns are given in Davis, *op. cit.*, p. 453.

47   There has always been confusion between Washington A. Bartlett, who was the first American Alcalde of Yerba Buena and who changed its name to San Francisco, and Washington Bartlett, who was Mayor of San Francisco and who became governor. This confusion is admirably clarified in H. Brett Melendy, "California's Washington Bartletts," *Pacific Historical Review*, XXXI (May, 1962), 139–142 and in Melendy and Benjamin F. Gilbert, *The Governors of California* (Georgetown: The Talisman Press, 1965), pp. 219–225; also see: Robert W. Righter, *The Life and Public Career of Washington Bartlett* (Unpublished M.A. thesis, San Jose State College, 1963) and his article, "Washington Bartlett: Mayor of San Francisco, 1883–1887," *Journal of the West*, III (January, 1964), 102–114.

48 Jeremiah Lynch, *Buckleyism: The Government of A State* (San Francisco, 1889), pp. 12–13.

49 Bryce, *op. cit.*, II, 745–750.

50 Paul Mason, comp., *Constitution of the State of California: Annotated* (Sacramento: California State Printing Office, 1946); Winston W. Crouch, *et. al.*, *California Government and Politics* (Englewood Cliffs: Prentice-Hall, Inc., 4th ed., 1967), p. 39.

The Period of
the Populist Party

California Populism arose during a confusing period of senate change which reflected the political instability of the times. The period 1886 to 1896 saw seven different men represent California in the United States Senate. Leland Stanford, elected on January 28, 1885 and reelected in 1890, died in office on June 21, 1893. Governor Henry H. Markham appointed George C. Perkins on July 22, 1893 to serve until the election of Stanford's successor. On January 23, 1895 the Legislature confirmed Markham's selection by electing Perkins who then continued to serve for twenty-two years, a period exceeded only by Hiram W. Johnson in later years. The other senate seat was occupied in 1886 by John F. Miller, elected in 1880. Miller died in office on March 8, 1886 and George Hearst, father of William Randolph Hearst, was appointed on March 23, 1886 by Governor George Stoneman. Hearst had been Stoneman's opponent for the Democratic nomination for Governor in 1882. He took his seat in the Senate on April 9, 1886 and had been in Washington with his family less than four months when the Legislature on August 4, 1886 elected Abram Pease Williams, founder and first president of the San Francisco Board of Trade, to fill out the balance of Miller's term which would expire on March 3, 1887. Williams took his seat on December 6, 1886, but the new Legislature which convened the next month had a majority of Democrats who promptly elected Hearst to the full new term and Hearst was back in the Senate on March 4, 1887. Four years later on February 28, 1891 Hearst was dead, and on March 19, 1891 Charles N. Felton was elected to fill out the term. He did not take his seat, however, until December 7, 1891 and the next Legislature elected Stephen M. White to the full term. White was seated on March 4, 1893. This seat, then, changed hands six

Donald E. Walters was primarily responsible for the original draft of Chapter 4.

99

times within a seven year period, and it alternated each time between Republicans and Democrats.[1]

Since the Populist (or "People's") Party where it appeared in any strength in various parts of the nation was almost always preceded by the "non-partisan" Farmers' Alliance, it became the common practice of historians to think of the Alliance as the first organizational form of Populism. California had not only this Farmers' Alliance stage of Populism but also a still earlier movement whose members and leadership soon very largely transferred their allegiance to the People's Party.[2] This movement was Nationalism, the short-lived socialist evangelism inspired by Edward Bellamy's utopian novel, *Looking Backward*, published in 1888. The Nationalists were far more numerous in California than in any other state. The rapid growth of Nationalism in California and its assimilation by the Farmers' Alliance and People's Party were unique to California Populism.

The first California Nationalist Club appeared in Oakland in April 1889 where the moving spirit was a local labor leader, Eugene Hough. The man chiefly responsible for the rapid growth of Nationalism in the Bay Area was Burnette Haskell, a strange personality who figured prominently in the labor and radical movements of San Francisco and the West from the early eighties until near the end of the century.[3] Soon after, in the summer of 1889, Nationalism took root in southern California where it spread in remarkably rapid fashion.[4] Of the fifty-five clubs in California, thirty-three were organized out of Los Angeles. Many small towns in the Los Angeles area and south to San Diego soon had clubs. By the time the Nationalists reached their peak of activity in southern California the Farmers' Alliance appeared and within a short time the Nationalist clubs were virtually forgotten. The leading organizers of the Nationalists recruited for the Farmers' Alliance and the most faithful members of the Nationalist clubs outside the city became charter members of the Alliance.

The prime movers among the Nationalists in southern California were usually labor leaders or spiritualists, or in some cases both. One of the notable figures in the spread of the Nationalist gospel, and, later, Populism, was a woman, a rugged veteran fighter of the labor movement, Mrs. Anna Ferry Smith. Mrs. Smith in the summer of 1889 began organizing Nationalist clubs in the southern part of the state. Another leader was Herbert Guy Wilshire, the eccentric, wealthy real-estate promoter whose socialist magazines of a later decade enjoyed national circulation and influence, and whose name has been perpetuated by the famous Los Angeles boulevard. Wilshire, in addition to serving as speaker, chairman of meetings, and campaigner, was also a financial "angel" who paid some of the bills incurred in organizing the Nationalist clubs.[5] Arthur Vinette, probably the most prominent Los Angeles labor leader of the day, was a tireless Nationalist organizer. Another active Nationalist leader was

Burnette Haskell (1857–1907), eccentric, colorful San Francisco radical prominent in Nationalism, Populism, the labor movement, and other causes during the eighties and nineties. (California Historical Society.)

Mrs. Clara Foltz, member of a distinguished California family, sister of Republican Samuel Shortridge who later became a United States Senator, the first California woman to be admitted to the bar, a redoubtable public speaker and exponent of woman suffrage.

Both in the north and in the south Nationalism increased its membership and activity during the latter half of 1889 and 1890. Haskell thought by the spring of the latter year that the movement had grown to the point where a state convention was desirable in order to bring the rather loosely joined and uncoordinated local groups into a unified state organization. But an anti-Haskell faction had developed within the San Francisco Bellamyites and this state convention instead of bringing unity actually split the Nationalists into two opposing camps and presumably thereby hastened the subsequent early demise of the whole fad.

Important opposition to Haskell came from the single-tax editor of the San Francisco *Star*, James H. Barry, who publicized Haskell's record as an anarchist and sponsor of numerous discredited radical or labor projects, and charged that Haskell was trying to boss the Nationalists through a clique of old "labor cronies" and the use of unscrupulous tactics. Barry gave his support to a newcomer both to San Francisco and the Nationalist movement who became the leader of the anti-Haskell forces and thereby rose to prominence as a reform leader. This was Thomas V. Cator later to be the most prominent leader of California Populism. When Haskell's following appeared to be winning control of the convention, Cator led bolting delegates (perhaps in the majority) to a meeting in the Palace Hotel where they formed a new convention and promptly claimed to be the only legal one. The two rival conventions adopted very similar programs including such proposals as government ownership of transportation, communication, and postal banks; direct election of senators; municipal ownership of utilities; Australian ballot; initiative; referendum; and "scientific money."

J. W. Hines of San Jose, "a man of influence among farmers," a former Green-backer who published the San Francisco *Pacific Union*, was elected state chairman of the Cator-led Nationalists and his paper was made their official organ. This fitted well with the intention of the Nationalist leaders announced at the convention to assist in the founding of a California Farmers' Alliance. The strategy of building some kind of farmer-labor political party on the basis of a unity between the prospective farmer organization and the city Nationalists was quite visible.

Nationalists, both in northern and southern California, entered politics in 1890. Wilshire ran for Congress in the south as an avowed Nationalist, and votes for him totalled about 1,100.[6]

In northern California Cator ran for Congress in the Fourth Congressional District on a "reform Democratic" ticket. Cator was no doubt encouraged by his Nationalist associates but his most important sponsor was James Barry whose weekly, the *Star*, had the greatest influence and circulation of reform papers in California. A fellow Single Taxer and Democrat and frequent close associate of Barry, James Maguire, expressed disapproval of Barry's endorsement. This was the first episode of an evolving Cator–Barry–Maguire relationship which colored much of the association between the California Democratic and Populist parties. Cator got 1,492 votes which was enough to produce a victory for Cutting, the Republican candidate, who received 13,196 votes while the regular Democrat, Ferral, only received 12,091.

The "Nationalist phase" of California Populism was very brief. No state organization ever materialized following the bitterly divided state convention and the whole Nationalist fad began to flicker out by the end of 1890. Nationalism had brought to the fore Cator and others who were to dominate the urban leadership of the Populists. It had made clear the intention of city reformers to try to employ the Farmers' Alliance for their own political ends even before the Alliance was organized.

Organization of the Farmers' Alliance in California began in the Spring of 1890 when the first sub-Alliance was formed in Santa Barbara County with eight members on April 11. Here also, on May 3, was formed the first county Alliance comprising eight sub-Alliances and 200 members, in a convention in the city of Santa Barbara.[7] Once the Alliance program reached the California farmers it took root and became, for a brief period, a real force. But it was not farmers, as such, who planted the seeds of the Alliance in California. The movement in California was inaugurated under the auspices of the state's radicals: a group small in number, articulate, preponderantly urban in outlook, and, for the most part, rootless and mobile. Such people were to be found in and near Santa Barbara, especially in the nearby spiritualist colony of Summerland. Mrs. Anna Smith had come to Summerland in February 1890 and set up a Nationalist club.

In spite of the overtones of impractical radicalism which characterized its beginning, the Alliance speedily grew in numbers. The development of greatest strength took place in the more markedly rural, more isolated back country. Gradually many of the recent Nationalist converts assisted in setting up sub-Alliances. Organization gained momentum, and so rapid was the growth of the Alliance that by November there were 173 sub-Alliances. Some Grange leaders provided valuable help in the organizing drive. Best known of those who became active in the Alliance was J. V. Webster of Creston, near Paso Robles. He represented, better than any other man, the tradition of the Grange as a serious political force. Webster had been in the second California constitutional convention, had cooperated with the Workingmen delegates, had since that time participated in several short-lived political movements, and was accepted in these as the very personification of the embattled farmer in political dress.

The first state convention of the Alliance opened at San Jose on November 20, with thirty-eight delegates present from thirteen counties. It is remarkable how many of the Populist leaders of succeeding years were present. One of the Los Angeles delegates was E. M. Wardall, a shrewd and able leader, who was before long to become the foremost director of Alliance and People's Party policy. Dore and Gilbert from Fresno County were to occupy positions of leadership in the state Populist organization throughout its history. From Ventura County came Marion Cannon, the greatest Alliance leader in California, whose brief association with the People's Party constituted a major chapter in its history.

Cannon, at first chosen temporary chairman, then permanent chairman, and finally the first state president of the order, brought a businesslike steadiness to the course of the Alliance. Cannon was "a man of great force of character, a good speaker, and of pronounced executive ability."

The state constitution which the convention adopted was largely an adaptation of the parent order. It fixed an initiation fee of one dollar, quarterly dues

103

Marion Cannon (1834–1920), President of the California Farmer's Alliance which he led into the People's Party in 1891; in 1892 he was the first California Populist to be elected to Congress. (Courtesy of Mrs. Harold F. Taggart.)

of fifty cents with membership free to women. The platform however, although naturally in harmony with the national one, was essentially a freshly wrought document.

Grievances had been taken in vain to the lawmakers. To meet these abuses resolutions called for: 1. Abolition of National Banks and the replacement of their notes by sufficient legal tender notes; 2. Government ownership of public transportation and its operation at actual cost; 3. Restoration of unearned land grants to the government and regulations to prevent monopolistic land speculations; 4. Australian ballot; 5. Direct election of President, Vice President and Senators; and 6. Free silver.[8]

By the end of 1891 the Farmers' Alliance in California was reputed to have some 30,000 members with over 500 sub-Alliances and 34 county Alliances. The appeal of the Alliance which made it attract so large a following was primarily a promise of economic improvement. The two-fold program was comprised of political demands and a formula of economic cooperation.

It will be recalled that at a time when not a single sub-Alliance had yet appeared in California the Nationalists had announced their intention to join hands with the Alliance in order to promote political action. Marion Cannon insisted a month after the first state convention of the Alliance, at which he had been elected president, that the Alliance was not forming a new party and

Stephen M. White (1853–1901), Democratic leader of the eighties and nineties, who promoted fusion with the Populists, was elected to United States Senate in 1893. (California Historical Society.)

would work only through existing parties. But he qualified this by asserting that where no acceptable candidate was offered the Alliance would put up its own man. He announced that the main interest of the Alliance was in Congress and that state and local offices of an executive nature from governor on down would be ignored. The Alliance was seeking measures, not men, and the first measure was that in four years the government would assume ownership of the

Central Pacific and Union Pacific roads for debts owed.[9] Cannon would later boast of his own part in leading the Alliance into a third party. As early as May, 1891, Stephen M. White, the astute Democratic lawyer of Los Angeles, who was shortly to bring to successful conclusion his long campaign to win a seat in the United States Senate, saw the strength of the Alliance and concluded that it would become political.[10]

The 1891 session of the Legislature was marked by a series of sordid scandals of bribery and corruption which greatly stimulated thought of a new, cleaner party. There were numerous bills to "cinch" the·railroad, and the public had begun to realize that some of the proponents of such bills, professedly anti-monopolists, were often merely blackmailers. One assemblyman was exposed in the act of selling San Francisco police jobs. The climax came with the so-called "waste-paper scandal" when pay-off money wrappers were discovered in the Assembly library. Up and down the state the righteous indignation of the citizenry was set forth in resolutions by the local Alliances.

In August the call was issued for the organization of a California People's Party at a convention to meet in Los Angeles, October 22. It was addressed to the Farmers' Alliance, the Colored Farmers' Alliance, Patrons of Husbandry, Knights of Labor, Federated Trades, Citizens' Alliance (just recently and very weakly organized as an urban counterpart of the Farmers' Alliance), and "all other reform organizations in the State of California in sympathy with this call." The practice of convening the Farmers' Alliance and related orders and the People's Party at about the same date and same place was followed generally throughout the life of the Populist movement in California and the personnel of the several conventions was virtually the same for few local units could afford to send more than one delegation.

The People's Party convention as it met on October 21 was comprised so largely of members of the Farmers' Alliance that it was referred to in the press as a joint meeting of the Alliance and the People's Party. The platform adopted by the new party included planks calling for government ownership of communication and transportation, women suffrage, and outlawing of saloons. Planks aimed at labor demanded the eight-hour day on all public works (with only American citizens to be eligible for such work) and "the abolition of all private armed bodies of men such as the Pinkerton police force."[11]

At the local level the organization of the new party amounted to little more than a metamorphosis of the Farmers' Alliance in the rural areas; and in San Francisco party gatherings probably included few who were not formerly members of Nationalist clubs. Some of the Populist leaders realized that the party would not become effective unless it attracted city workers. The problem was partially faced, a few gestures made, but San Francisco election returns showed that these efforts had failed. Where the new party had possibilities or in other words where the Alliance was strong, namely, in the south and the interior, the Democratic leadership was early on the ground to cultivate the good will of the Populists. It happened that these areas were predominantly Republican, a factor not overlooked by the Democrats. From this time a strange association of Populists and Democrats began which brought both groups considerable success at the polls. This success, however, was soon transformed into disaster.

Chief interest in the campaign of 1892 revolves around the failure of the new party to line up labor, and the partial fusion, its workings and its consequences, with the Democrats. The Populist campaign of 1892 in California opened in San Francisco at a large theater July 16 with speeches by Cator and J. A. Johnson, editor of the San Francisco *People's Press*. Cator spoke for two hours; he denounced monopoly control of business and dwelt upon what he called the public's insistence on free coinage of silver. Cator rose rapidly to the leadership of the California Populists. Cator obtained his ascendancy, amounting to "party boss," through his great oratorical talent, his legal expertise so often needed to rescue the new party from technical obstacles, and his ability to provide desperately needed funds.[12]

County conventions, beginning with San Luis Obispo, July 28, were held to nominate candidates for the Legislature and county offices and to draw up local demands. The momentary strength of the movement was evidenced by the fact that Hiram Johnson, later Governor of California, appeared at the

Thomas V. Cator (1851–1920), California's leading Populist, was a talented attorney and orator whose personal political ambitions fatefully influenced the course of Populist party policy. (Courtesy of Mrs. Harold F. Taggart.)

Populist Party Sacramento County convention to ask the party's nomination as sheriff.[13] The Populists gave him their nomination but he later failed to get his own Republican Party's nomination and withdrew from the race.

In the campaign Democratic candidates denounced the McKinley tariff act as a measure to benefit trusts and the Sherman Silver Act as a feeble compromise; the Republicans pointed with pride to tariff, trust and money legislation. Populists lambasted both parties for failure to legalize silver. Republican newspapers, growing apprehensive about the possibility of a Populist-Democratic fusion for it was apparent that Populism was strongest in Republican counties of the south, began to bombard Populism as radicalism.

Meanwhile, however, Populists and Democrats were sounding out possibilities of combining forces. Stephen M. White promoted fusion in the Sixth Congressional District to improve his senatorial prospects.[14] He realized that Populism had made greater inroads upon the Republican Party than upon the Democratic in the southern counties where, normally, since 1886, Republicans polled majorities. Against some opposition White managed to engineer endorsement of Cannon, Populist candidate for Congress (and former Democrat), at the Democratic convention in Los Angeles, September 10. The whole Ventura Populist organization, headed by Cannon, seems to have been friendly to White and the Democrats. In Los Angeles the key man in the "fusion" plans was Henry C. Dillon. Dillon was the Populist candidate for District Attorney of Los Angeles County; he also received the endorsement of the Democrats. He had only recently been prominent in Democratic ranks and was ready to support White. The Democrats named several others on the Populist ticket as their party choices for office. In the Seventy-second Assembly District, south of Los Angeles, White's influence was sufficient to induce the Populists to withdraw their announced candidate in favor of Thomas J. Kearns, a Populist who was a personal friend of White.

In San Francisco the lack of any real mass following of Populism was disguised somewhat by the enthusiasm of the loyal few and the activities of many of the state Populist leaders who made the city their headquarters. The party's municipal and legislative nominating convention assembled August 20 and continued for more than a week. Cator apparently directed affairs from behind the scenes. One woman was placed on the ticket, Mrs. Clara (Shortridge) Foltz, for City and County Attorney. The platform included proposals for municipal ownership of water, light and street railways, free public baths, free employment offices, initiative and referendum. A plank on schools sternly warned against the diversion of public money to benefit any religious group.

More important than the resolutions, was the nomination of the party candidate for congressman, Fourth District. The Democratic nominee, a man who had acquired a wide reputation as a friend of labor, was James G. Maguire who

108

had feuded with Cator since 1890. The Populists, at the behest of Cator who withdrew his own name, nominated E. P. Burman to run against Maguire. This campaign in many ways resembled the campaign of 1890. But John Barry this time enthusiastically supported the Democrat, Maguire, and Maguire won. The Republican candidate, Charles Alexander, was widely regarded as pledged to the Southern Pacific. The Populist decision to run Burman as an effort to enlist mass labor support to the new party was a costly one. All of San Francisco's labor papers backed Maguire and disapproved of Burman's candidacy.[15] Closely related to the Burman candidacy was Cator's intention to become the Populist choice for United States Senator.

In the California election of 1892 the Populist ticket attracted Republicans in greater number than Democrats. There were two major reasons for this: first, the Populist Party was better organized and the Farmers' Alliance was more powerful in those agricultural areas in which recent migration had brought proportionately more Republicans; second, the McKinley tariff and the Republican evasiveness on the money question had alienated many Republican farmers, whose products continued to bring decreasing prices.

In 1888 Republican presidential electors and in 1890 a Republican governor had been chosen by comfortable majorities, showing the tendency even then toward a one-party dominance, a tendency interrupted by the Populist "agrarian revolt." Now in 1892 eight Democratic and one Republican electors were chosen. General James B. Weaver, the Populist Party candidate for president in 1892, polled around 25,000 votes.

The figures on congressional elections show the source of Populist strength. The last banner year for the Democrats was 1882 when all six congressmen elected were Democrats. In succeeding years Democrats could elect at most only two congressmen. In 1892 four Democrats (plus Cannon) were chosen. The Sixth District of the eighties became with some variations the Sixth and Seventh of the nineties. The re-apportionment on the basis of the 1890 census, reflected the great immigration of 1885–1890 into the southern counties of the state. In the presidential election of 1888 and the gubernatorial contest of 1890 the Republican majorities of the Sixth District (before re-apportionment) just about accounted for the state victories for Harrison in 1888 and Markham in 1890. There was a different story in 1892. In the Sixth Cannon received 20,676 votes (10,861 Democrat and 9,815 Populist) to Lindley, the Republican, who received 14,271. W. W. Bowers, a more ardent silver advocate than any Democrat or Populist, and extremely popular with the farmers, had been elected in 1890 with a majority of over four thousand; now in 1892 he was elected in the Seventh by a slim margin of 987 votes (Bower 15,856 to Wellron, Democrat, 14,869). Hiram Hamilton, Populist, polled 5,578 votes.[16]

The Populists did not win a senatorial seat in the Legislature, but did elect eight to the Assembly: the five endorsed by the Democrats, two endorsed by Republicans, and one Charles A. Barlow, from San Luis Obispo County, the only candidate elected on a "straight" Populist appeal. Dillon won his race for District Attorney of Los Angeles County, again a fusionist victory.

The attempt of Stephen White to secure some of the eight Populist votes in the Assembly for his candidacy for the Senate led to a sensational episode early in 1893 which hurt the prestige of the young People's Party.[17] There were fifty-nine Democrats in the new Legislature, eight Populists, one Non-Partisan, one Independent, and fifty-one Republicans. After White won the Democratic caucus and assured himself of the solid fifty-nine votes of his own party he got a pledge of support from the Independent. He could then count on sixty votes, one short of the majority needed when both houses, comprising a total of 120 members, were polled. Cannon and several other prominent Populists who worked with White during the campaign had sought to help him get pledges of support from Populist candidates for the Assembly. When the November election was over, however, a strong drive developed within the Populists to keep the vote of the "Big Eight" solid for a Populist senatorial candidate, i.e. the acknowledged leader, Cator.

Much publicity was accorded the "Big Eight" as the day neared for the opening of the Legislature and the election of a senator. From Populist national headquarters and from many local alliances and People's Party organizations came letters and telegrams to the assemblymen, urging "Stand firm". The metropolitan press, at times possibly animated by Republican hopes for a deadlock, paid the eight great attention, now respectful of their integrity, now speculating as to who might give way. Much of the attitude of the Populist press was summed up in a *Western Watchman* editorial: "The Eight can engrave their names in lasting honor, or enshroud them in unending infamy."[18]

On January 18, 1893 balloting began in a joint session of the Legislature and Populist Thomas Kerns on the very first ballot voted for White who was elected. It was generally overlooked at the time that Kerns' vote was less decisive than might have been expected because White had persuaded one Republican to be absent so that White's pledged 60 votes would constitute a majority of the 119 cast.

A scene of tumult followed Kerns' vote. Arnold Bretz, Oakland People's Party Assemblyman, rose to charge that Kerns' vote had been bought and that Cannon had negotiated the purchase. The Assembly voted to investigate the charge; the outcome was exoneration of White and Cannon and brief suspension of Bretz. The welter of charges and counter-charges which followed the Kerns-Bretz affair probably amounted to an indictment of the low moral tone of the legislators in general. Irate Populists expelled Cannon from the party, yet they

The "Big Eight," Populist members of the State Assembly in 1893. Starting on the left they are, in the first row, Massey Thomas (Santa Clara County), P. R. Adams (Santa Cruz County), C. F. Bennett (Orange County), and C. A. Barlow (San Luis Obispo County); and, in the second row, W. A. Van (Colusa County), H. J. T. Jacobsen (Fresno County), and Arnold Bretz (Alameda County). (Courtesy of Mrs. Harold F. Taggart.)

were measurably discredited as a new force for obtaining "purity in government."

It is practically impossible to assess the harm which the Cannon–Kerns–Cator
episode inflicted upon California Populism. The loss of Cannon meant the party's
loss of its best known and most popular figure who had provided the leadership
in the building of the Alliance. Cannon's excommunication was felt especially
in the agrarian and southern wing of the party. After the senatorial fight Cator
was accepted as the logical leader and dominated every action of the party until
May 1898. Fusion with the older parties had been a blunder that had brought
only misfortune.

The years 1893 and 1894 encouraged California Populists to greater effort to
enlist labor support. The panic and the onset of depression in '93, the turbulent
manifestations of widespread unemployment culminating in the tragi-comedy
of the Coxey Armies in '94 and the great railway strike of '94, reviving and
renewing the deep California hatred against the "Octupus", all fostered the
conviction that a strong farmer-labor party would become a major power in the
state.

An immediate response to the "panic" was a renewed agitation for unlimited
coinage of silver. President Grover Cleveland found the limited silver coinage
of the Sherman Silver Purchase Act a deterrent to recovery and a threat to
governmental solvency and in an August message successfully demanded its
repeal. This was the first of a series of events which antagonized Californians
against the Cleveland administration and the Democratic Party. Populist
speakers were in great demand at a series of silver rallies in Los Angeles while
repeal was before Congress and Cator was especially in demand for similar
meetings in San Francisco. While the issue of free silver seemed to be so useful a
means of reaching the public, numerous Populists became alarmed that it was
threatening to eclipse the rest of their program and to create again the harmful
prospect of fusion.

Meanwhile the parties were organizing for the campaign of 1894. The county
conventions of the People's Party were held in May and generally instructed
their delegates to oppose fusion. The delegates gathered in Sacramento May 21
for the state convention. The proceedings were carried on the front pages of the
metropolitan dailies and flattering estimates of the party's strength were
frequent. One side of the reformer character was demonstrated at the convention
when a delegate from Pasadena rose to protest that he smelled tobacco smoke
and that ladies were present. This breach of the code was soon corrected and, in
the same vein, the convention declined a local brewer's offer to supply it with
free beer.

The platform was long and involved.[19] It included an endorsement of the
Omaha platform and the thirteen demands prepared on February 22 by the

Labor Congress. Women's suffrage was one of the main planks. Others were reduction of the state budget by 25% including the scaling down of official salaries to correspond with fallen prices, a graduated inheritance tax, prohibition of all oriental immigration and restriction of all other immigration as necessary, government-built and owned Nicaraguan canal, and maintenance of a non-sectarian school system. The ninth plank called for free coinage of silver at sixteen to one and the eighteenth plank opposed fusion with any other party.

In the makeup of the state ticket realistic recognition of the greater Populist strength in the rural areas compelled the choice of a farm representative for the gubernatorial nominee who turned out to be J. V. Webster of San Luis Obispo County. Southern California was represented on the ticket only by Louis Luckel who was nominated for Attorney General. A. J. Gregg, Oakland "labor candidate," was chosen for Lieutenant Governor.

The outstanding nomination of the San Francisco County convention was Adolph Sutro for mayor. A Swiss mining engineer who had accumulated a fortune in San Francisco real estate, Sutro was generally well liked and had received a great deal of newspaper publicity through his Cliff House where he entertained notable people. He became a Populist nominee clearly because of his hatred of the Southern Pacific. He had sought a reduced trolley fare from downtown to his Cliff House; and the Southern Pacific, which allegedly controlled the street railways, had ignored his demands. So Sutro began to build his own line, which, although not completed until 1896, compelled the Southern Pacific to grant a nickel fare.[20] Consequently, Sutro, a lovable old philanthropist-eccentric, became a public hero. He appeared at several Populist campaign meetings on both sides of the bay and was a considerable asset to the party.

The Republican Party under the pressure of the leading dailies, such as the *San Francisco Chronicle* and the *Call*, the *Los Angeles Express*, the *Fresno Republican* and the *Sacramento Bee* and also pressured by many leaders who were personally for free silver, adopted a platform in state convention, which included a plank favoring free silver at 16 to 1. Morris M. Estee was nominated a second time for Governor at Sacramento in June of 1894.

Senator White, the leader of California Democrats, believed that his party must swing to silver. His cohorts controlled the machinery of the state convention at San Francisco in August. But after an endorsement of the Cleveland administration (strongly "gold standard") the money plank of the platform, after many hours of struggle, could only be "evasive." T. W. H. Shanahan, Shasta County State Senator, who exercised great influence throughout the state especially among farmers, denounced the straddling and closing of debate on the money issue and announced his departure from the party to go over to the Populists.

The Populist campaign throughout the state far surpassed the campaign of

Adolph Sutro (1830–1898), mining engineer of Comstock Lode fame who was elected mayor of San Francisco in 1894 on the Populist ticket. (California Historical Society.)

1892. Cator, the most active of Populist orators, made much of the silver issue. Webster concentrated on the economy plank and pledged to reduce expenses by 25%.

The leading issues of 1894 are not easy to determine. The silver question was hardly an issue, for most of the speakers of all three parties advocated free silver. Estee at rallies denounced Wall Street as vehemently as Cator did in the campaign and as Bowers had done in Congress. Spencer A. Maillard, who spoke sixty consecutive nights from the Siskiyou to San Diego, W. W. Bowers and Grove Johnson and other Republicans made tariff and free silver the bases for their speeches. Whenever White spoke, and it was often, he argued as did Estee on the money question.

All the parties poured out anti-railroad sentiment. The Democratic candidate, James H. Budd, was on record for government ownership of railroads. Estee announced that he favored social ownership of telegraph and telephone and, by implication of railroads. Estee was hurt by the wide-spread belief that he was the choice of Colonel Dan Burns, Republican boss allegedly in league with the Southern Pacific. Much of the explanation of the outcome on election day is quite simple: many voters voted not for someone or something but against something or someone. So in 1894 thousands of Democrats voted against the administration, because of the panic and depression, because of the injunctions, or because of the repeal of the Sherman Act. Many Democrats voted Populist.

James H. Budd (1851–1908), governor 1895–1899 who was the last Democrat to hold this office for forty years. (California Historical Society.)

   The Populists scored great gains, doubling their vote of 1892.[21] Of the Democrats only Budd, who won over Estee 111,944 to 110,738, and Maguire, who again carried the Fourth Congressional District, withstood the Republican avalanche. Six of the seven congressional seats, an overwhelming majority of both houses of the Legislature, and the entire executive slate from the Lieutenant Governor down, went to the Republicans. The vote for Webster was 51,304, which was double Weaver's vote of 1892, and constituted 18% of the total vote. There was not a single state or congressional race in which the Populist vote did not constitute a comfortable balance of power, a fact that Democrats and some ambitious Populists certainly noted.
   Webster ran ahead of both Estee and Budd in Humboldt and Shasta counties (with 33% and 35% of total vote). Webster ran second in Del Norte, San Diego, Merced, San Luis Obispo, and Tulare counties, with votes of 27% to 33%, and a strong third in Alameda, Fresno, Monterey, Nevada, and Santa Cruz counties.
   The election of but one assemblyman, J. L. Barker of Santa Barbara, on a straight Populist ticket and two on fusion with independent Republican tickets, Calvin Ewing of San Francisco, and A. J. Bledsoe of Eureka, was disturbing to many Populists, some of whom, looking to office, could see real advantages in fusion. But neither Ewing nor Bledsoe were bona fide Populists.

Yet in local contests Populists made a better showing. Sutro was elected Mayor but this was more a personal endorsement than an endorsement of the Populist Party which failed to elect a single Populist candidate to any other San Francisco office. In their first contest, 1892, only thirteen men were elected to county offices, and then with the help of Democrats; but in 1894 the Populists elected from one to seven men on straight Populist tickets in twenty-four counties, for a total of sixty-two winners. To the devout Populists the election of 1894 was a great milestone; they had the Democrats on the run, next would be the Republicans. To the party's politicians, however, fusion held new appeal as they measured the scant rewards their great campaign effort had yielded. Thus in the Assembly the Populists would have but one authentic representative compared to eight in 1893. In the entire state outside of San Francisco the Republicans had with a popular vote of 93,433 a total of fifty-three Assembly seats; the Democrats with a vote of 59,663, seven seats; and the Populists with 53,122 votes, only *one* seat.

Populist leadership experienced many trials during 1895. Populist newspapers encountered severe financial difficulties and many suspended publication. The urban equivalent to the Farmers' Alliance, the Industrial Legion, which had never really been successful, collapsed completely. Socialist competition threatened more seriously and was especially alarming to party leaders in Los Angeles. Finally, even the Farmers' Alliance which had furnished so much of the strength of the party was beginning to disintegrate.

In the field of politics California Populists were made uneasy by the agitation for free silver in 1895 by leaders of the old parties.[22] To some Populists this threatened to deprive the party of its most important political appeal, cheaper money. The most noteworthy project of the silver promoters in California in 1895 took the form of a Silver Convention which met in San Francisco in August. This idea was conceived by Timothy Guy Phelps, known as the "grand old man" of the G. O. P., a leader since 1858, and it won the support of John P. Young, editor of the *San Francisco Chronicle*. In attendance at the convention were 547 delegates including leading politicians, editors, and businessmen some from as far south as Orange County. George W. Baker, Republican and Southern Pacific lawyer, presided. The convention and similar silver agitation not only caused consternation to Populists fearful of losing either a vote-getting issue or their party identity; it also served to persuade both Democrats and Republicans that the victory of their parties in 1896 would depend upon their endorsement of free silver.

Much of the leadership of the Democratic Party, including the so-called "Federal Brigade" of office-holders identified with President Cleveland's anti-silver policies, was out of touch with the rank and file of their party. William J. Bryan, on a silver lecture campaign in the West in September, at times received more courtesy from Silver Republican leaders than he did from his own party's leaders in California. John P. Irish, California Democratic congressman, defended the gold standard in a series of debates with Cator. The latter appeared by this time to have become a paid agent of the silver promoters headed by George Baker who became California Chairman of the Silver Party.[23] The provincialism of both of the major parties in California, often evident during this period, was never more pronounced than in regard to the silver question. The California Republicans were plumping for free silver, misinterpreting the positions of national leaders and placing themselves in a position requiring almost every last one of their state leaders to do an embarrassing flip-flop in 1896. Some Populists saw this coming and unwisely counted on a similar failure of Democratic national leadership to gratify popular sentiment for free silver. The pressure of the silver agitation in California was indicated when both California senators, White (Dem.) and Perkins (Rep.) voted "aye" on the free silver amendment which passed the Senate January 21, 1896; also, in February when the measure was defeated in the House, all of California's congressmen (six Republicans, one Democrat) voted for free silver at 16 to 1. Little wonder that some Populists cooperated with the silver men, confident that the major party national conventions would disappoint the silver-minded voters who would then turn to the Populist Party.

The strength of silver sentiment was further demonstrated at the major parties' state conventions in California. The Republicans in May endorsed free silver, elected delegates to the national convention who were pledged to McKinley and then instructed them to vote for a silver plank! The Democrats, June 17–18, endorsed silver over the bitter opposition of Pond, Daggett, Irish, J. D. Phelan and others of the party's top command.

The state convention of the People's Party drew much attention from the public. Would the party adopt the one-issue idea to enlarge its immediate voter appeal? Or would the middle-of-the-roaders carry the day for retention of the entire Omaha platform, emphasizing such planks as government ownership of railroads and anti-monopoly, which many silver supporters thought "cranky socialism"? The fight expected at this convention never materialized. A proposal for a "union of reform forces" was adopted without serious opposition. This proposal authorized consultation with the Silver Party in order to arrive at a mutually acceptable presidential candidate at St. Louis. It was stipulated, however, that the candidate must be pledged to the Populist platform. The convention reaffirmed the Omaha platform but the mood to capitalize on the silver issue was strong. Apparently few in attendance saw much chance of either of the old parties adopting silver so that the question of fusion received little attention.

On the eve of the Democratic convention in Chicago in 1896 there was no

George C. Perkins (1893–1923), a Republican, California's first governor under the new constitution of 1879, United States Senator 1893–1915. (California Historical Society.)

question of the overwhelming sentiment among California Populists against fusion with the Democrats. Many Populists were little enamored of silver and hostile to both old parties. Wardall was quoted in the *Call* on June 23 as saying: "I don't think there is any possibility of union except with the silver men." The Populists, according to Wardall, would not accept Teller, the silver Senator from Colorado who had just bolted the Republican convention, unless he came out openly for the People's Party:

The Democratic party may adopt a radical free-silver plank, but that is only one of our demands. We are the anti-monopoly party and free silver is only part of our financial policy, though it is the most important one. . . . To combine with the Democrats now would be throwing away the party.

But the endorsement of free silver and the nomination of Bryan on July 10 by the Democrats created consternation among California Populists.

The later arrivals in the party, those drawn by a single issue, silver, who climbed on the band-wagon, were immediately favorable to the endorsement of Bryan. The big and little politicians who had retained some tie with the Democratic Party, such as Dillon and many others of the Los Angeles leadership, unhesitatingly hailed the nomination of Bryan. The ex-Republicans who retained a trace of partisan animosity against the Democrats opposed Bryan. The state executive commitee, controlled by the anti-fusionists, issued a statement on July 11, criticizing the press for misrepresenting the party's position, and saying:

We will not support the Democrat nominee for President under any circumstances . . . The Democratic party is a party of conservatism . . . antagonistic to the principles of Populism . . . [it] has been discredited by the people and an endorsement of its nominee by us would be taken as an endorsement of its record. This we will never give.[24]

The California delegation to the national convention, followed all along the way by the San Francisco press as public interest was great, began to weaken as it made its way toward St. Louis.

The convention was one of the most turbulent in American political history. Several California delegates were of some importance in the proceedings. The second day, July 23, Wardall as chairman of the Committee on Credentials, presented a report that was favorable to the Bryan men. Cator was the first to second the nomination of Bryan, who received a large majority over Norton ("middle-of-the-road") on the first ballot. California gave Bryan twenty-four votes and Norton thirteen.

Upon the return of the delegates there began an active usually behind-the-scene campaign on the part of Cator, Wardall and others to capitalize on the bright fusion prospects. Their task was two-fold: to pacify and reconcile the dissident elements within the party leadership and to bargain with the Democrats and silver Republicans over the projected joint ticket.

The division of fusion candidates between the Democrats and Populists caused a great many headaches on both sides. White again pulled most of the ropes on the Democratic side and Cator and Wardall strove to coordinate the Populists. Cator, who now saw a real chance of winning a seat in the United States Senate, had a working agreement with White in which the Populists would run candidates for the Assembly and the Democrats seek candidates for the Senate.[25] Although the rumor was current that White would not be a candidate in 1899, he had his eye to the legislature of that year in case he should seek to succeed himself.

By the third week in August candidates had been nominated by both the Democrats and the Populists in all of the state's seven congressional districts. A joint conference committee met in San Francisco August 22 which recommended an identical list of electoral candidates and a fusion slate for congressmen of four Democrats and three Populists. Resignations were asked from all the congressional candidates already named so that fusion choices could be smoothly made. Democrats were chosen for the First, Second, Third and Fourth, and Populists for the Fifth, Sixth and Seventh. But fusion proved unobtainable in two districts, the First, where the Populist refused to withdraw, and the Fifth (comprising part of San Francisco, San Mateo and Santa Clara counties) where the Democratic nominee (a Catholic) persisted in the race because of the nativist ties of the San Francisco Populists.

In the Sixth District (comprising coastal counties from Santa Cruz to Los Angeles) the Los Angeles Populist candidates competed so vigorously among themselves as to permit a San Luis Obispo man, C. A. Barlow, a Populist assemblyman in 1893, to win the nomination.[26] There was little contest for the Seventh District (twelve counties extending from Stanislaus to San Diego). The Democrats were not very eager to get the nomination in this strongly Republican district. The nomination of the Populists went to Dr. Curtis H. Castle, Merced physician.

Outside of Thomas Cator the People's Party played a minor part in the campaign. Cator's senatorial candidacy constituted a serious obstacle to acceptance of fusion by many Democrats whose resentment was naturally encouraged by the Republican press. Barry of the *Star* warmly supported Bryan but savagely attacked Cator. The Democratic *Examiner*, presumably at last convinced that Cator was too much of a liability, on October 25 repudiated him, denied he was the Democratic senatorial nominee and condemned his "anarchistic views."

It was a spirited and exciting campaign. There were many rallies, marching bands, parades, a flood of pamphlet material. In the "battle of the standards" nearly all of the big Republican dailies as well as most of the party leaders were obliged to eat crow as they engaged in heavy attacks on free silver.[27] Republican leaders were pessimistic in August, but as the "campaign of fear" against Bryan grew, and employer intimidation of workers increased, their hopes mounted in October. Senator Redfield Proctor, treasurer of the Republican National Committee, brought a "sack" of $35,000 to San Francisco October 17 to be matched by California Republicans.[28] This sudden flood of money made possible a spectacular grand finale to the G. O. P. campaign in the Bay Area where it was most needed. The Democrats' and Populists' campaign was embarrassed by lack of funds and would have been completely submerged by the flood of Republican oratory and literature if it had not been for the assistance of their silver allies.

Despite the angry temper of editorials and oratory, election day saw un-precedentedly large numbers of California voters cast their ballots without disorder. Examination of the results indicates that San Francisco provided the key to the Republican victory, a victory so narrow that the McKinley elector with the lowest vote was edged out by the fusionist with the highest so that the state's electoral vote went eight to McKinley and one to Bryan. The San Francisco Democratic plurality in 1892 had been 6,596 which by adding the Weaver vote of 2,508 provided a margin of 9,104; in the gubernatorial election of 1894 the Democratic plurality was 11,454 and the Webster vote 6,459, giving a margin over the Republicans of 17,913—and the entire Republican vote had been only 20,615. Now in 1896 the Republicans actually carried the city for McKinley, by the thin margin of 457 votes.[29] In Alameda County the Republican vote was likewise greatly increased. Strangely the city of Los Angeles gave a majority to Bryan, the only sizable urban center to do so; Los Angeles County remained in the G. O. P. column however.[30]

In the congressional races the fusionists fared better, winning four of the seven seats; Maguire as usual winning the Fourth easily in spite of the drift to McKinley in San Francisco; Marion DeVries defeating the incumbent Republican, embarrassed by support of free silver in Congress, Grove Johnson; Populist Barlow winning in the Sixth by a scant 663 votes; and most astonishing of fusionist victories Populist Castle in the Seventh nosing out Republican Congress-man Bowers, regarded as a great favorite and safe winner, by 244 votes.

The Republicans won most decisively in the contests for the Legislature even if by comparison with 1894 they actually lost ground. While the outgoing Assembly comprised sixty-three Republicans, fourteen Democrats, one Populist, two Independents, the new Assembly would include forty-seven Republicans, twenty-two Democrats, and eleven Populists. In the Senate elected in 1894 the Republicans outnumbered the Democrats twenty-five to fifteen; in 1897 twenty-eight to twelve. This legislative outcome ensured the election of the Republican choice for United States Senator, George Perkins. Cator received eleven Assembly votes for senator from as many Populists; ten Democratic votes, purely complimentary, went to Maguire.

Although their party had elected two congressmen, almost a dozen Assembly-men and a goodly number of local officials in 1896, there was little rejoicing in the hearts of most California Populists. They had sacrificed most of their party platform for the sake of victory on the silver issue and this victory had not been won. The disintegration of the party which had begun with the entrance into fusion so opposed by the more socialistic minded elements now proceeded rapidly. The Farmers' Alliance was wholly dead; two or three local cooperatives bore the Alliance name but operated on an independent basis.[31] Middle-of-the-road Populists expressed their resentment toward fusionist party leaders, many of whom were now holding public offices. Populist morale suffered further with reports of alleged corruption or questionable behavior on the part of Populist legislators.[32] Some of the prominent San Francisco Populists took the lead in 1897 in the organizing of local chapters of Eugene Debs' new "Social Democracy of America" which soon evolved into the Socialist Party.[33] When Populist leaders once more attempted to effect fusion with the Democrats in the elections of 1898 the weakened Populist Party was fatally split in two; after the 1898 election little more was heard of Populism in California. A rather bizarre episode in the final collapse of the movement was the 1898 announcement by Thomas Cator, leader of Nationalists and Populists, that he was joining the Republican Party.[34]

The patent similarity of so much of the Populist program to the legislative achievements of the Progressive-Republican administration of Governor Hiram Johnson makes it unnecessary to insist upon the reality of the Populist heritage. Populist proposals such as ballot reform, initiative, referendum, recall, direct primaries, income tax, unemployment relief, and farm benefit programs have long since been enacted into law.

Populist attitudes towards the political party also seem to anticipate those of the Progressives. Populists very generally distrusted politics and political leadership and staked fundamental reform on transference of political power to the people. Hence the appeal of direct legislation (initiative and referendum). Moreover, Populists emphasized national, society-wide issues and were slow to accept a party quest for state offices and slower still in regard to local offices. They talked of fitness of the man as the essential criterion for local office and deprecated attention to party affiliation. Along these lines the Populist stance contributed, as the Progressive would, to the weakening of the responsible role of the political party. One of the notable characteristics of California politics during much of the present century has been this emphasis on the candidate as an individual.[35]

FOOTNOTES

1 Hubert Howe Bancroft, *History of California* (San Francisco: The History Company, (1886–1890), vol. VII. Chap. XVI.

2 Donald E. Walters, "Populism in California" (Unpublished Ph.D. thesis, University of California, 1952) 398 pp.

3 Nationalist activities in northern California may be followed in abundant news-

paper clippings in the Burnette Haskell Notebooks, V. 7 and 8, Bancroft Library, University of California at Berkeley.

4 *Nationalist*, I (November 1889), 266.

5 Wilshire's political activities are briefly described in Ralph Hancock, *Fabulous Boulevard* (New York: Prentice-Hall, Inc., 1949), pp. 86–112.

6 Howard H. Quint, "Gaylord Wilshire and Socialism's First Congressional Campaign," *Pacific Historical Review*, XXVI (Nov., 1957), 327–340.

7 Santa Barbara *Press*, May 4, 1890.

8 The constitution appears in the weekly *Pacific Rural Press*, X (Nov. 29, 1890), 450 ff.

9 *San Francisco Examiner*, Nov. 29, 1890.

10 White to T. W. H. Shanahan, May 10, 1891, White Letters, Stanford University Library.

11 The platform appears in Winfield J. Davis, *History of Political Conventions in California, 1849–1892* (Sacramento: California State Library, 1893), pp. 587–588.

12 Harold F. Taggart, "Thomas Vincent Cator, Populist Leader of California," *California Historical Society Quarterly*, XXVII (1948), 311–318, and XXVIII (1949), 47–55.

13 *Sacramento Union*, August 11, 1892; *Sacramento Weekly Bee*, August 10, 1892.

14 On White's dealings with the Populists in addition to the White Letters, see Edith Dobie, *The Political Career of Stephen Mallory White* (Stanford University Press, 1927), p. 103 ff.

15 For a full account see Donald E. Walters, "The Feud Between California Populist T. V. Cator and Democrats James Maguire and James Barry," *Pacific Historical Review*, XXVII (1958), 281–298.

16 Secretary of State, *California Blue Book 1893* (Sacramento: State Printing Office), p. 122.

17 For the entire episode see Harold F. Taggart, "The Senatorial Election in California in 1893," *California Historical Society Quarterly*, XXII (March, 1940) 59–73; and Dobie, *op. cit.*, p. 146 ff.

18 Eureka *Western Watchman*, December 31, 1892.

19 It appeared in full in the San Francisco *Call*, May 24, 1894.

20 San Francisco *Weekly Star*, February 8, 1896.

21 For election results see *California Blue Book 1895*, pp. 254–274.

22 Harold F. Taggart, "California and the Silver Question in 1895," *Pacific Historical Review*, VI (September, 1937), 249–269.

23 Several letters in the Cator Papers, Stanford University Library, ask Cator's assistance in getting money from Baker. For example, Kenney to Cator, April 15, 1896, "Please see Baker again. I am busted flat."

24 Los Angeles *Civic Review*, July 11, 1896.

25 One San Francisco Populist leader later recalled, "Anything from poundmaster to

Judge of the Supreme Court was traded off for the legislative ticket in order to send Mr. Cator to the Senate." San Francisco *Call*, August 18, 1898.

26 Los Angeles *Civic Review*, August 22, 1896.

27 The *Sacramento Bee* remained consistent in its advocacy of free silver and supported Bryan. All of the Democratic papers, including those that had disliked free coinage, supported Bryan.

28 See Harold F. Taggart, "The Party Realignment of 1896 in California," *Pacific Historical Review*, VI (1937), 249–269.

29 Yet San Francisco elected a Democrat, James Phelan, Mayor, and a majority of Democrats to seats in the Legislature.

30 See *California Blue Book*, 1899.

31 The minutes of the still surviving Paso Robles Farmers' Alliance Business Association show that this organization amended its constitution at this time to delete the requirement that its members belong to the Alliance.

32 See White Letters; San Francisco *Call*, March 7, October 15, 16, November 2, 1897; San Luis Obispo *Reasoner*, March 11, 1897; San Luis Obispo *Breeze*, March 9, 1897.

33 San Francisco *Call*, July 16, August 1, 1897.

34 Cator's lengthy statement appears in San Francisco *Call*, December 28, 1898.

35 See Dean E. McHenry, "The Pattern of California Politics," *The Western Political Quarterly*, I (1948), 44–53.

The Mechanics
of Reform

Growing prosperity in California was not affected measurably by the short-lived "panics" of 1903 and 1907. The economic climate was more favorable to the reform movement than it had been for the rise of the Populists. Prosperity sparked population growth which began to polarize political power between the urban centers of north and south.[1]

The fastest growing section during this period was the true trans-Tehachapi: the Los Angeles Lowlands, Imperial Valley, and San Diego. The immigrants who made up this influx came largely from areas of Republican persuasion; a similar Republican influx began changing the political climate of Fresno and contiguous counties around 1900.

Population growth also established Republican hegemony, which coincided with the founding of the Southern Pacific (Espee) Company's Political Bureau. This bureau was established by William F. Herrin, brilliant corporation lawyer, devout Catholic, practicing Democrat, when he was named the Espee's General Counsel in 1893.

Prior to this time, the Espee's *modus operandi* had been to act as honest broker between factions of whichever major party could serve it best. C. P. Huntington's political janizary, W. W. Stow, had pursued this method as an intuitive art, using local "bosses" and "machines," and keeping the name, Espee, out of it as much as possible.[2]

Herrin made the Political Bureau a more open and persuasive tool for measuring political returns against favors and funds dispensed. His way of operating made the Espee highly visible, Republican ascendancy made the Republican party the Espee's major object and the combination established the political monolith image in California politics.

 William H. Hutchinson was primarily responsible for the original draft of Chapter 5.

Table I
California Vote
1894–1910

Election and Year		R	D[1]	Prohibition	Other[2]	Total
Gov. 1894		110738	111944	10561	51304	284547
Pres. 1896		146753	144766	3620	3617	298756
Gov. 1898		148354	129261	4297	5143	287064
Pres. 1900		164755	124985	6562	7572	303874
Gov. 1902		146332	143783	4766	9592	304473[5]
Pres. 1904		205226	89404	7380	29535	331545
Gov. 1906		125887	162653[3]	7355	16036	312030
Pres. 1908		214398	131770	11770	28659	386597
Gov. 1910	Primary	215605	47369[4]	1682	4554	269210
	General	177191	154835	5807	47819	385713

[1] Includes Populist Fusion Vote, 1896; Populist and Silver Republican Fusion Vote, 1898; 45,008 Independence League votes, 1906; 4,278 Independence League votes, 1908.

[2] Populist vote, 1894, 1896; Socialist Labor, 1898; Socialist Democrat, 1900, 1902; Socialist, 1904, 1906, 1908, 1910.

[3] As this vote was divided between T. A. Bell, Democrat, and W. H. Langdon, Independence League, the Republican candidate, J. N. Gillett, won.

[4] T. A. Bell was unopposed in the Democratic primary.

[5] 316,198 votes were cast; the figure shown is those counted.

Note: H. T. Gage, 1898, was the only gubernatorial candidate to receive a majority. William McKinley, 1896, was the only Presidential candidate *not* to receive a majority.

Table II
How California Counties Voted
1898–1910
(Alpine County Omitted)

Year and Candidate[1]	Gov. or Pres. R	Gov. or Pres. D	Cong. R	Cong. D	Senate R	Senate D	Assm. R	Assm. D	Even split of multiple seats
1898 Gage	36	20	28	28[2]	22	11	38	17[3]	1 (Assembly)
1900 McKinley	39	17	41[4]	15[5]	20	7	36	16	4 (Assembly)
1902 Pardee	28	28[6]	32	24[7]	13	18	35	20	1 (Assembly)
						1 Ind.			
1904 Roosevelt	54	2	46	10	28	1	45[8]	11[9]	
1906 Gillett	22[10]	34	44	12	20	17	43[11]	13	1 (Senate)
1908 Taft	51	6	50	7	20	5	41[12]	13	3 (Assembly)
1910 Johnson	35	22	35	22	17	18	43[13]	12	2 (Assembly)

[1] Data for 1894 and 1896 could not be procured without more labor than seemed justified in the premises.

[2] Fusion support in 27 counties.

[3] Fusion support in 6 counties; won 4 others by less than 1% of vote cast.

[4] Won 8 of these by less than 1% of vote cast.

[5] Won 4 of these by less than 1% of vote cast.

[6] Won 5 of these by less than 3% of vote cast.

[7] Fusion support in 3 counties.

[8] Won 2 of these by less than 1% of vote cast.

[9] Won 2 of these by less than 1% of vote cast.

[10] In 12 of these, total D-Ind. League vote exceeded R.

[11] Won 2 of these by less than 1% of vote cast.

[12] Won 4 of these by less than 1% of vote cast.

[13] Fusion support in 7 counties.

Note: Theodore Roosevelt's "rape" of the California electorate accentuates California's conformity to national patterns in Presidential elections, and highlights its fluidity in local matters. TR's impact carried over to Taft and gives significance to the inclusion of his name in the Lincoln–Roosevelt League.

When it is said today that Herrin dictated political life from county road district to United States Senator, it is well to savor this shibboleth *cum grano salis*. The Espee did not have to concern itself overly with "cow counties," which in its biased view included most of the south, as long as northern urban centers provided the necessary power base. For example: the Republican state convention of 1902 boasted 830 delegates, of which San Francisco County sent 177; Alameda 71; Santa Clara 37; Sacramento 28; Sonoma 22, and Los Angeles 96, an increase of eleven over its 1898 delegation. By contrast, Amador County sent 5; Butte 12; Kings 4; Shasta 8; Ventura 9; Lassen 2, and Mono 1. This same leverage applied to the other party conventions—congressional, state senatorial, assembly, judicial, and the like—at which party business was conducted. The small delegations, however, had a not unimportant role. They served as "trade-offs" for local candidates who, because their political aspirations exceeded their resources, needed Espee support. Republican delegates from irretrievably Democratic counties, such as Colusa, Lake, Tulare and Yolo, carried this kind of convention weight.

The normal apathy of the electorate, enhanced in this period by the economic climate, was vital to Espee control of the urban blocs. Too few voters bothered to participate consistently in the crucial ward and precinct caucuses where delegates to "superior" conventions were selected.[3] Alert machine politicians saw to it that *their* supporters were always present in adequate numbers. Another political gambit gave the Espee working control of the Republican State Central Committee during Herrin's heyday.

Statewide campaigns were directed by the Executive Committee of the State Central Committee, but Executive Committee members were not required to be members of the State Central Committee—they were chosen by the chairman of the State Convention, or by the gubernatorial candidate. Here again, the northern urban centers held control, as exemplified by the twenty-one member Executive Committee for 1896, which included Abe Ruef and twelve others from San Francisco and its satellites.

Urban legislators from the north—San Francisco alone electing twenty-seven of the 120 total—made another lever. Legislators with bills for the folks back home had to come to the Espee for support. In the Legislature, too, the Lieutenant Governor's importance was substantial. By courtesy, not right, he named the Senate's committees that could provide interment for undesired bills.[4] The history of this period in California politics was written by the laborious struggles of diverse reform groups to master the mechanics of political power.

McKinley's first presidential victory appears to have established the image of Herrin's monolith. California's Republicans had departed for their national convention in a special train which flaunted a banner proclaiming their un-

128

Table III

Composition of California Legislature
1894–1910

Session and Year	Senate			Assembly		
	R	D	Other[1]	R	D	Other[1]
31st 1895	25	15		64	14	2 Pop. Party
32rd 1897	28	12		47	8	16 Fusion
33rd 1899	26	14		59	20	7 D-PP 2 PP
34th 1901	34	6		60	20	1 Ind.
35th 1903	33	5	1 D-UL 1 Ind. R.	60	13	6 D-UL 1 UL
36th 1905	33	3	3 R-UL 1 D-UL	71	4	4 R-UL
37th 1907	27	6	1 R-D-UL 5 R-UL 1 D-NP	56	5	3 R-D-UL 12 R-UL 2 R-D 2 D-IL
38th 1909	24	7	1 R-D-UL 5 R-UL 1 D-UL 2 D & Others	46	17	12 R-UL 2 R-IL 3 D-UL-IL
39th 1911	28	8	4 R-UL	69	11	

[1]Symbol UL represents Union Labor Party; its combinations largely in Alameda and San Francisco counties. Symbol IL represents Independence League which also confined to two largest Bay Area Counties.

Note: Republican domination of the legislature is shown clearly above. It has not been possible to determine accurately the number of legislators from both parties who espoused the Lincoln–Roosevelt League's program in the 1909 session.

129

dying allegiance to the free and unlimited coinage of silver. They returned with banner furled and with political egg on their face, after being "Hanna-ized" into "gold bugs." The Republican national convention, dominated by Mark Hanna of Ohio, had repudiated them on the monetary issue.

This produced great Democratic rejoicing. Their party was committed to the sacred doctrine of 16 to 1, as were the Populists. With both parties in agreement on the proposed coinage ratio between silver and gold, which would have placed an artificially high value on silver, any Democrat who could see through a ladder simply fused the Democratic-Populist vote in 1894 and felt the warm glow of virtue triumphant. If outraged cries from rejected Free Silver Republicans meant votes as well, then California was triply safe for Bryan. Bryan supporters' optimism turned out to be delusion, however, which was shattered when McKinley took the state by 1,987 votes without even visiting it. Bryan Bryan lost San Francisco, Santa Clara, and San Joaquin counties by 2,178, and these counties gave Budd a handsome 12,546 vote margin. This dramatic shift brought anguished cries about the omnipotent Espee which had practised free and unlimited expenditures in McKinley's behalf.

These cries reflected the arrant provincialism of the north's political wise-acres. The state-wide vote in 1896 increased by 14,208, a scant 5% over 1894. The five major southern counties showed a whopping 31.2% increase, with each party making almost identical percentage gains, which netted the Republicans a tidy 2,896. Population origins explain most of this Republican edge, because the Espee, except to some extent in Los Angeles city politics, was not yet a southland power. These results portended the urban polarization of political power between northern and southern sections. Local reform movements at the poles were germane to the ultimately successful cleansing of state politics through its dominant Republican party.

Los Angeles's glacial growth ended with the Espee's construction into the town in 1876. An era of comparative good feelings between Angelenos and Espee ended when Espee efforts to dominate the rail-waterfront linkage at Los Angeles triggered the protracted "Free Harbor" fight. This forced the Espee into Los Angeles city politics during the 1890's on a continuing basis, which provided its opponents with the focus of oppression that every reform movement needs for self-justification. It also enabled the Espee's adversaries to link it with the city's saloons, gambling houses, and brothels. Neither Espee nor its officials were involved in these institutions, but the exigencies of urban politics forced the Espee to use those who were.

Towards the close of the Free Harbor fight, the city sought municipal control of the water facilities so vital to a community surrounded by desert. These ultimately successful contests, far more than ideologies or rhetoric, taught the basic lessons of practical, non-partisan political effort to a welter of disparate reform elements.[5] Reformers fell into two broad categories, political-moral and social-economic, which were less miscible than oil and water. Adhesion did evolve, however, out of the realization that political democracy had to precede social democracy that would abolish urban turpitude.

A non-partisan Direct Legislation League (DLL) arose in 1895, with the primary aim of city charter reform. In 1902, it gained voter approval of amendments, which included the initiative, referendum, and recall. The Legislature had to approve all city charter changes, and in 1903 it begrudgingly approved the amendments: "The voice of the people is not the voice of God," cried Assemblyman Grove L. Johnson,[6] "for the voice of the people sent Jesus to the Cross."

The Good Government League (GGL) then used these amendments to recall a city councilman in 1904. Two years later, the Non-Partisan City Central Committee of One Hundred, "overwhelmingly Republican and conservative,"[7] scored substantial gains in the municipal elections. In 1909, many from this group surfaced again as a Recall Campaign Committee, which revived the GGL and received support from a separate Good Government Fund. Reform control of city government came in this year's elections, thanks to an assist from the Espee which backed the Socialist candidate for Mayor in an effort to thwart the non-partisan strength of the reformers.[8] The linkage between these persistent champions of civic reform and the later Lincoln–Roosevelt League is seen clearly in the latter's support by them.

Partisan reform of San Francisco's political quagmire also sprang from a desire to "conserve the constitutional forms which [conservatives] thought were in jeopardy from corrupt manipulation."[9] In keeping with city sophistication, these conservative reformers were not above manipulation themselves. For example, "good boss" Gavin McNab (Dem.), played an important role in the reform mayoralty of James D. Phelan, 1897–1901.

Phelan, who properly belongs in the state's roster of "millionaire progressives," was above temptation while in office. He was Irish and Catholic, two prominent hues in his city's political spectrum. During his time in office Phelan accomplished essential charter reforms, instituted civil service reforms, and gave political prominence to Franklin K. Lane as his reform City Attorney. Utility rates were reduced, studies were begun for a municipally-owned water supply from Hetch Hetchy, and wage and hour laws for city employment were passed. Political corruption was reduced to the petty vice level, for which the city had a tolerance sanctified by tradition and use. Given Phelan's "friend of labor" actions, it is ironic that his reforms and his political future were affected by labor strife.

The Employers Council and labor's City Front Federation met head-on early in 1901, when organized teamsters refused to join a non-union drayage firm in delivering the baggage of an Epworth League convention. This snowballed into a militant confrontation in the "general strike" pattern. Phelan finally ordered police protection for the non-union drivers, and labor responded angrily. Concurrently, Phelan lost conservative support for allegedly dilatory tactics in dealing with what conservatives viewed as civil insurrection. The end result was Phelan's retirement from major personal political activity for many years. No direct carryover can be traced from the Phelanites to the later successful drive to "kick the Espee out of politics."

The Espee, however, felt the aftermath of Phelan's mayoralty in the resulting political vacuum. The vacuum was filled by Abe Ruef and his Union Labor party which boasted the union label but nothing else. Ruef's rise to power weakened the keystone in Herrin's political arch—the San Francisco legislators and delegates—between 1902–06, because Ruef's ambitions made him an undependable ally. His strength was enhanced by alliance with a "Good Government (Rep.)" movement in Santa Clara County which wrested control away from the existing Republican "machine." This movement was led by E. A. and J. O. Hayes, whose nicknames "Red" and "Black" derived from the colors of their cough-drop advertisement beards. The brothers may have espoused "Good Government" out of civic morality; however; their alliance with Ruef dimmed their moral image.

Two other urban reform movements chipped away at Herrin's monolith during Phelan's administrations. Sacramento elected a reform mayor in 1900 and again in 1902 on a platform which had enjoyed carpenter work by Hiram W. Johnson, and his brother Albert M.[10] "Holy Hiram," as Franklin Hichborn later dubbed him, then became corporation counsel for the city. The brothers were opposed by their father, Grove Johnson, who once described his sons as filled with "bile" and "booze." This reform movement may explain why Sacramento continued Republican in presidential contests, but went solidly Democratic in the gubernatorial elections of 1902, 1906, and 1910, while gaining more civic reform in 1907.

Fresno acquired a new city charter in 1899, thanks to support by its leading conservative citizens and the *Fresno Morning Republican* whose editor, Chester H. Rowell, ran for Mayor in 1900 on a reform platform. He was defeated, along with most of the reformers seeking civic office, but the reformer candidates did force the local Espee "push" to run capable and honest men.

These urban reform movements have obscured an agrarian, conservative, anti-Espee Republicanism of long standing which contributed to two Espee defeats in 1898–1902, and whose alliance with veterans of the Los Angeles reform fights enhanced the Lincoln–Roosevelt League's success in 1910. While this anti-Espee Republicanism was dispersed throughout the state, its most visible figures were T. R. Bard, Ventura County, Thomas Flint, Jr.,[11] San Benito County, and Dr. Chester Rowell, Fresno. Bard's political career has been described adequately elsewhere.[12]

Dartmouth student, prominent Mason, active Native Son of the Golden West, Thomas Flint was the scion of one of the state's first great agrarian Anglo families. He had won the first of four consecutive terms in the state senate in 1888, and served that body as President Pro Tempore for five straight sessions, 1895–1903. His district of Monterey and San Benito counties went Democratic more often than not in state and national elections, but his appeal crossed party boundaries.

Dr. Chester Rowell has been overshadowed by his namesake nephew and protégé, Chester H. Rowell, in the annals of California politics.[13] A Civil War veteran who completed his medical education in San Francisco, he removed to "Fresno Station" in 1874. He found it to be hot, wicked, arid and Democratic; he left it hot, temperance-minded, irrigated and Republican. He founded the *Fresno Morning Republican* in 1876, to bring the light to the heathen during the Hayes-Tilden contest, and kept the paper alive thereafter at personal sacrifice. Later edited by his brilliant nephew, the *Morning Republican* became the leading newspaper of the middle San Joaquin Valley by 1900. Rowell added to his record of distinguished public service by gaining election to the State Senate in 1898 in the normally Democratic counties of Fresno and Madera.

The rural anti-Espee Republicanism these men represented surfaced at the state convention of 1898, in support of the gubernatorial aspirations of Dr. George C. Pardee, who had given his native Oakland an anti-Espee mayoralty in 1893–95. Pardee did not have enough strength to make a floor fight or to attract "trading" delegations, however, and he withdrew in favor of the Espee's choice, Henry T. Gage of Los Angeles.[14]

Pardee's support then closed ranks behind their party's choice, after the fashion of "Civil War orthodoxy." This demanded allegiance to a Republican in preference to a candidate of the Secession-tainted, fiscally irresponsible Democratic party. The top of the Republican ticket was completed by the choice of J. H. "Uncle Jake" Neff, the Republican patriarch of Placer County, who had proved his political power among the Mother Lode's miners.

Solidarity and state-wide support from the Republican press more than offset the Espee label the Democrats pinned on Gage. His opponent, Congressman James G. McGuire of San Francisco, was a "single taxer," a Catholic, and the Populist nominee as well. His party regarded him as the man most likely to accomplish the successful fusion of Democrats, Populists, and dwindling Free Silver Republicans, but he suffered a resounding defeat by Gage.[15] Five northern urban counties gave Gage a 12,437-vote edge; seven southland counties sup-

133

Table IV

Congressional Vote: 1896–1910

(*California Blue Book* for each election)

	1st Dist.			2nd Dist.			3rd Dist.			4th Dist.		
	R	non-R[1]	Elected	R	non-R	Elected	R	non-R	Elected	R	non-R	Elected
1896	17826	17825	R	18613	24434	D-PP	19788	16119	R	10940	19074	D
1898	19598	18244	R	20400	25196	D-PP	20592	14051	R	13695	12084	R
1900	21227	16869	R	23019	22253	R	22109	15404	R	17111	13827	R
(1901)[2]	(21365)	(19201)		(21954)	(20394)		(19046)	(11127)		(18904)	(13263)	
1902	21268	20506	R	21181	22267	D	20532	10130	R	16005	16762[3]	D-UL
1904	21602	17903	R	22873	23171	R	24637	10827	R	20012	15079	R
1906	18954	15720	R	23411	21786	R	21510	13844[6]	R	5678[7]	3415	R
1908	20624	16929	R	28627[8]	21196	R	27857[9]	14864	R	9202	8196	R
1910	16570	19935[12]	D	25346	24876	R	34291[13]	6653	R	10188	7814	R

	5th Dist.			6th Dist.			7th Dist.			8th Dist.		
	R	non-R	Elected	R	non-R	Elected	R	non-R	Elected	R	non-R	Elected
1896	19351	19319	R	23494	24157	D-PP	18939	19183	D-PP			
1898	20254	17352	R	24050	20499	R	20793	20680	R			
1900	23443	18307	R	27081	23467	R	23450	20366	R			
(1901)[2]	(21651)	(17769)		(15822)	(15108)		(18260)	(14760)		(20439)	(17759)	
1902	16577	23332[3]	D-UL	17268	14547	R	19407	8336[4]	R	20135	17910	R
1904	23701	20288	R	18828	14611	R	31091[5]	14853	R	23683	17497	R
1906	22530	20268	R	18928	14171	R	22338	14838	R	22548	17995	R
1908	28127	28171[10]	R	21323	18156	R	37244[11]	30568	R	29305	23270	R
1910	33265	22397	R	19717	20976	R	36435	23645	R	28202	26260	R

[1] Includes all non-Republican votes except Prohibition which are not included in this tabulation.

[2] These figures reflect the 1900 county vote as applied to the new districts created in 1901.

[3] Rise of Union Labor party in San Francisco explains this upsurge in non-Republican vote; both districts elected Democratic-Union Labor candidates this year.

[4] This sharp decline probably due to lack of strong non-Republican organizations or candidates, with a strong Republican candidate profitting by fact this first Congressional election after re-districting.

[5] This increase probably stemmed from "machine" success in organizing the Los Angeles city and county party machinery. The "coat-tail" effect of Theodore Roosevelt's candidacy cannot be overlooked.

[6] Independence League explains increase in non-Republican vote and supports premise of some migration to Independence League from Republican ranks.

[7] Earthquake of April, 1906 explains this decline in vote.

[8] The sharp increase in Republican vote over 1906 seems due to Taft's polling power; each District had same Republican candidate as in 1906.

[9] An exodus from San Francisco to Alameda County and the East Bay generally accounts for some of this sharp increase.

[10] A shift in residence from quake-ravaged sections of San Francisco into that city's 5th district sections explains part of this increase.

[11] This phenomenal spurt in votes cast stems from complex factors which defy succinct footnoting

[12] John Raker's personal appeal and reputation explain this Democratic victory.

[13] Successful candidate had both Republican and Democratic nominations; non-Republican vote is Socialist only.

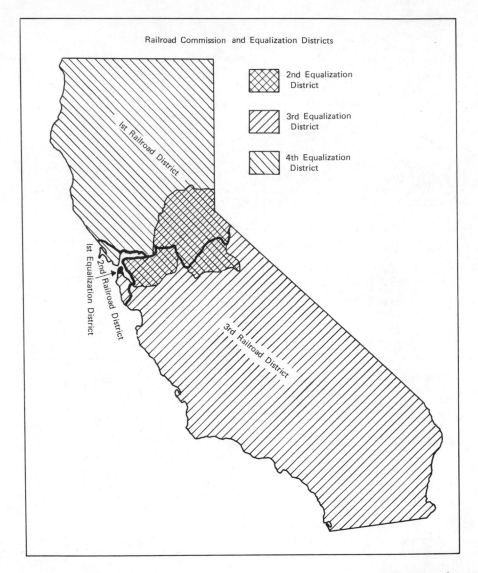

Railroad Commission and Equalization Districts

2nd Equalization District

3rd Equalization District

4th Equalization District

The Railroad Commission and Equalization Districts remained unchanged during the period of this chapter. Heavy black line marks the state's division into only three Railroad Commission districts.

plied 4,781 more, and irrevocably Republican Humboldt County added almost 1,000.[16] The vote in the other forty-four counties was approximately evenly divided.

Gage's victory was accompanied by continued Republican control of the legislature which made it certain that Senator S. M. White (Dem.) of Los Angeles would not be returned to Washington. The Espee had sought to assuage the southland's sense of loss in advance by nominating Gage, also an Angeleno, for governor. Herrin's faith in the leverage of San Francisco's bloc on the Republican majority makes the most reasonable explanation for his choice of Daniel M. Burns as White's successor as Senator in Washington. He could not have found a man better able to re-ignite the sectional fires and to inflame the anti-Espee Republican champions of political morality.[17] It must be added, too, that in a day when serious aspirants for the Senate contributed to legislators' campaign expenses as a matter of course, the Espee simply failed to do its homework in 1898. This became apparent when the legislature convened on January 2, 1899.[18]

Five anti-Burns candidates who were also anti-Espee, held fifty-five of the eighty-five Republican votes. Three of these contenders, including T. R. Bard, were from the south, while two were San Franciscans. The fragmented opposition to Burns continued down the ballots and the days until simple exhaustion, coupled with depletion of the legislators' expense allowances for the session, brought adjournment on March 19. This left the state with but one Senator, George C. Perkins,[19] and left the anti-Burns forces with a moral victory.

Dr. Rowell and Flint then began to unite the opposition behind Bard, despite the latter's disinclination to assist them. Their fruits were harvested when the legislature, pursuant to a call by Governor Gage, met in extraordinary session on January 29, 1900, with the Espee's choice still D. M. Burns. A Republican caucus to decide the Senatorial matter showed that Burns had gained nothing while Bard had gained much. A subsequent rump caucus resulted in fifty-two pledges for Bard. This was nine short of the majority necessary to elect, but after a period of presumably agonizing re-appraisal, Herrin made his decision: an anti-Espee Senator was preferable to the continued onus of depriving California of its due representation in Washington. On February 6, 1900, Bard was elected, after seconding speeches which included an expression of undying party loyalty by Grove Johnson.[20]

Population growth reflected in the 1900 census entitled the state to another congressman, and required re-districting of the Legislature. This was done quite happily in 1901 by the Republicans, who used their urban strength to neutralize Democratic counties in most districts. Sectional polarization was advanced by Los Angeles County's gain of a congressman all its own, and by the gain of five legislative seats to fourteen total, most of which were held by the city.

McKinley's second victory climaxed political events for 1900, and it appears

that he could have won "going away" in California without Espee support.
Increased commercial activity with the new Pacific possessions, burgeoning
petroleum production, and general agricultural prosperity contributed to the
appeal of "McKinley and Protection." His party swept all seven congressional
seats and added nine to its commanding majority in the Legislature. The total
vote increased only 5,116 over 1896, but McKinley's vote increased by 18,000,
Bryan's declining even more numerically, and he carried nine more counties

than the thirty won in 1896. Had McKinley lived out his second term, political reform in California well might have taken a different turn.

As United States Senator, Bard was a hard-working member in the basic committee business of preparing legislation. He was not a political animal, nor politically sapient, and he was remarkably unadept at dipping into the pork barrel. He did attempt to break the unholy alliance between federal patronage and the Espee in California, and McKinley tacitly supported his initial efforts. He got nothing from President Roosevelt but a political waltz of "one step forward, one step backward, hesitate and sidestep."

Roosevelt was too concerned with being elected in his own right in 1904 to take sides in the Republican infighting in California. He was abetted by Bard's colleague, "Slippery George" Perkins, who faced re-election in 1903 and was adjusting his relations with the Espee accordingly. Roosevelt's equivocal stand blunted the Bardians' next move to cleanse their party. Their chosen vehicle was Thomas Flint; their goal was the governorship.

It has been said that Flint's quest was the result of circumstance, which seems inaccurate.[21] Flint formally announced his candidacy in May, 1901, making it the longest *open* quest for high office then known to the state's political history, and Bard publicly expressed his support of Flint shortly thereafter.[22] Significantly enough, Flint's announcement was made in Los Angeles, and the southland in general witnessed sustained efforts in his behalf. This emphasis brought Flint 40% of his hardcore support, whose members detrained at Sacramento for the 1902 convention flaunting lapel badges reading "South of Tehachapi—ANTI GAGE."

State-wide support for Flint centered largely in rural areas, and was directed by prominent local legislators who had been anti-Burns, then pro-Bard in 1900, including James N. Gillett of Eureka, who now was running for Congress from the Humboldt County-dominated First District. Republican League clubs sprang up in the San Joaquin Valley in Flint's behalf, and "Uncle Jake" Neff added Mother Lode support when he broke openly with Gage in 1901. Two of the "Big Three" of Republican journalism, H. G. Otis's *Times* and J. D. Spreckels' *Call*,[23] supported Flint, as did the Rowell paper and other rural journals.

This alliance between southern California reformers and agrarian anti-Espee Republicans foreshadowed their later coalition in the Lincoln–Roosevelt League. Lack of a central focus and concerted action plagued Flint's quest just as it would plague the anti-Espee forces until Hiram Johnson.

Gage was the Espee's choice to succeed himself, probably because he had so alienated every Republican of any consequence that he had no organization of his own.[24] Flint's challenge induced three other candidates to enter the field in the hope of profiting from the major contest. The strongest of these, because of his Alameda County delegation numbering seventy-one, was Dr. Pardee, whom Flint and Rowell had supported in 1898. J. O. "Black" Hayes held his county's thirty-seven delegates and Abe Ruef could deliver at least twenty more in his behalf. E. B. Edson, who represented the lava-scarred lands against the Oregon line, was the third contender and one with easily eroded support.

When the convention assembled, Flint had 250 unwavering delegates out of the 416 necessary. The other anti-Gage forces held enough votes to nominate Flint if they could be united behind him. The situation thus paralleled the 1899 Legislature, and this similarity was heightened by D. M. Burns' role as Gage's floor manager, which moved the *Call* to acidulous comment.[25]

Even before the convention opened, the possibility of a deadlock that could be swayed to Flint had caused Herrin to hedge his bet on Gage. Herrin viewed Pardee as infinitely less dangerous and more local than Flint and the state-wide opposition he represented. Details of his deal with Pardee remain unclear, but its existence became apparent with the convention's first order of business, the election of its permanent chairman.

Flint and Pardee previously had agreed to support Neff for this post and Flint accordingly nominated him. He was dismayed and angered when Pardee nominated Congressman Victor H. Metcalf, his fellow Alamedan, in an effort to split the anti-Gage forces into such segments as would permit Espee organization of the Convention. Flint's forces "bowed their necks" and stood firm for Neff. Metcalf held a slender margin when only San Diego County remained to be polled. U. S. Grant, Jr., cast its nineteen votes to give Neff the victory, $423\frac{1}{2}$ to $406\frac{1}{2}$, and the *Call* trumpeted the victory with a blaring headline STATE CONVENTION REPUDIATES GAGEISM.[26] What went unnoticed apparently was Abe Ruef's twenty votes for Neff. This may have been done for Herrin's edification, as a part of Ruef's consistent support of Hayes for the gubernatorial nomination.

The balloting on this matter brought Herrin small comfort.[27]

	1st	2nd	3rd	4th	5th
Gage	322	325	$322\frac{1}{2}$	$339\frac{1}{2}$	$335\frac{1}{2}$
Flint	$251\frac{1}{2}$	$269\frac{1}{2}$	279	274	280
Pardee	$119\frac{1}{2}$	$123\frac{1}{2}$	$121\frac{1}{2}$	$142\frac{1}{2}$	$142\frac{1}{2}$
Edson	74	52	39	14	14
Hayes	62	60	57	58	58

Herrin abandoned Gage on the next ballot, making George C. Pardee the Republican nominee for governor. Alden Anderson, who had been a studiously impartial Speaker of the Assembly during the senatorial deadlock in 1899, completed the top of the ticket.

Disappointed as they were, Flint and the Bardians knew as well as "Billy" Herrin that it was fear of them, not love of Pardee, that had brought the latter

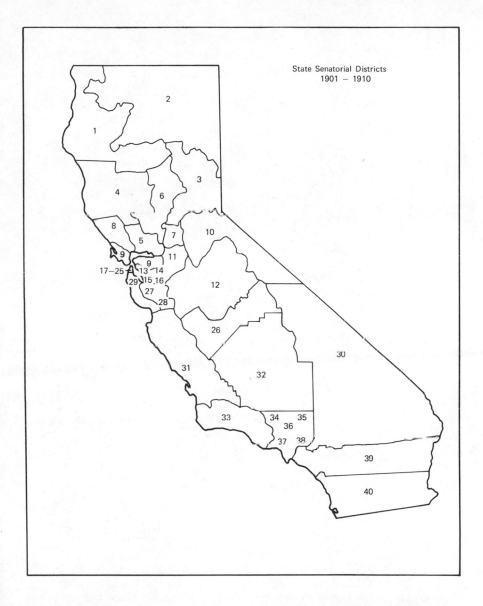

State Senatorial Districts
1901 – 1910

the prize.[28] However, in Pardee their party had a respectable candidate and they closed ranks behind him. Neff named Flint and twelve of his supporters to the Executive Committee, and W. M. Cutter, another Bardian, served as treasurer of Pardee's campaign, to which Bard was among the largest individual contributors. Every facet of the political prism showed the Bardians that

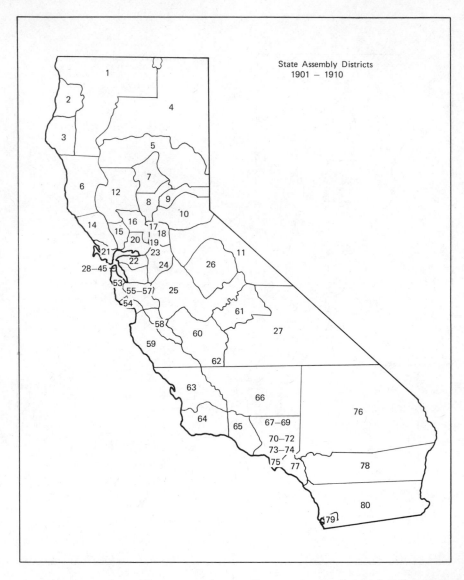

State Assembly Districts
1901 — 1910

Pardee was in their debt most substantially. To the Bardians, this debt was compounded by Pardee's election.

Franklin K. Lane (Dem.) linked the Espee with Pardee's nomination, and exploited the antilabor label that was pinned on Pardee in San Francisco. Herrin employed Ruef and his ostensibly Union Labor Party to offset this label, but their effectiveness remains moot. San Francisco had gone solidly for Gage

142

in 1898; it gave Lane almost the precise margin, 9,637 votes, it had given McKinley in 1900. This barely was offset by Pardee's margins in Los Angeles and Alameda counties, but these margins were clouded by charges of fraud.[29] Sacramento County gave Gage a 2,275 margin in 1898 and McKinley almost 1,200; it went for Lane by 493 votes. Without support from the counties that had formed Flint's delegate strength, Pardee's margin of 2,549 would not have existed. As it was, he suffered the ignominy of trailing his running mate, although not as badly as would Gillett in 1906.[30]

Herrin's enforced support of Pardee was his second major setback in two years and placed him in an invidious position, both politically and personally. These defeats had shown that an alliance between southern California and the northern rural counties could be effective, even under fragmented direction. Herrin had not seen this in time, and his San Francisco bastion now was tottering from Ruef's emergence as its political power. Ruef could be bargained with, even purchased, but the burning question always was would he "stay bought." Compounding Herrin's problems was E. H. Harriman's assumption of control of the Espee. A more urbane predator than Huntington, Harriman publicly eschewed political power but privately wanted results.

To regain the control necessary to the Espee's needs, Herrin had to increase and consolidate his strength in Los Angeles, and had to organize and control the political apparatus of hitherto neglected "cow counties." The results of this drive appear to have made Herrin's lieutenant in Los Angeles, the magnificently-mustachioed Walter F. X. Parker, virtually an independent agent. The first fruits of this drive were harvested within two years.

While Pardee's election marked the nadir of Republican appeal, his party retained commanding control of the legislature. Its anti-Espee members joined the "push" to return G. C. Perkins to the Senate, which makes another "bead upon the string of confusions."[31] The party's rebound in 1904 was as dramatic as "Teddy" Roosevelt himself, and raises an unresolvable question as to the relative importance of Herrin's organizing drive and Roosevelt's personality in this resurgence.

The Espee dominated both Republican state conventions in 1904, that for delegates to the national convention and the usual state convention in August. The delegate primary in Los Angeles, for example, saw a clean sweep for Espee candidates. This seems due to Walter Parker's control of the party test for primary voting, which required only a declaration of "present intention" to vote the Republican ticket at the next general election. H. G. Otis railed that Parker had voted innumerable Democrats and Socialists by this device. Tom Flint was defeated roundly for chairman of the state convention in August and decided to retire from political life. These gains partially offset the growing power of the Ruef–Hayes alliance. The "Boodling Boss" and the bearded

143

Table V

Population Growth and Presidential Vote in
Selected Economic Areas[1]
1890–1910

County	Population			Vote					
				1892		1900		1908	
	1890	1900	1910	R	D	R	D	R	D
SAN FRANCISCO AREA									
Economic Area A									
Alameda	93864	130197	246131	8792	7121	14324	6677	21380	7110
Contra Costa	13515	18046	31674	1631	1332	2165	1549	3336	1610
Marin	13072	15702	25114	1187	950	1681	904	2732	983
San Francisco	298997	342782	416912	24416	31022	35208	25212	33184	21260
San Mateo	10087	12094	26585	1089	1020	1645	926	2865	1314
Solano	20946	24143	27559	2403	2174	3114	2262	3136	2033
Total	450481	542964	773975	39518	43619	58137	37530	66633	34310
% Increase		20.4	42.5			47.1	(13.9)	14.6	(8.5)
SAN JOSE AREA									
Economic Area B									
Santa Clara	48005	60216	83539	4621	4169	7110	4672	7988	3836
% Increase		25.4	38.7			53.8	12.1	12.4	(18)
NORTH CENTRAL COASTAL AREA									
Economic Area 2									
Napa	16411	16451	19800	1769	1478	2017	1432	2405	1336
Sonoma	32721	38480	48394	3016	3451	4381	3517	5427	3168
Total	49132	54931	68194	4785	4929	6398	4949	7832	4504
% Increase		11.8	24.1			33.7		22.4	

SACRAMENTO AREA									
Economic Area C									
Sacramento	40339	45915	67806	4362	3503	5506	4325	6519	4533
STOCKTON AREA									
Economic Area D									
San Joaquin	28629	35452	50731	2958	3110	3564	3162	4470	3331
Total: C and D	68968	81367	118537	7320	6613	9070	7487	10989	7864
% Increase		18.0	45.7			23.9	13.2	21.2	5.0
FRESNO AREA									
Economic Area E									
Fresno	32026	37862	75657	3031	3455	3585	3590	6384	4743
LOWER SAN JOAQUIN VALLEY AREA									
Economic Area 5									
Merced	8085	9215	15148	782	998	811	1106	1107	1100
Stanislaus	10040	9550	22522	1063	1369	1078	1318	1663	1390
Total	50151	56627	113327	4876	5822	5474	6014	9154	7233
% Increase		12.9	100.0			12.3	3.3	67.2	20.3
UPPER SAN JOAQUIN VALLEY AREA									
Economic Area 6									
Kern	9808	16480	37715	992	1266	1692	1960	2270	2215
Kings	(in Tulare)	9871	16230			1032	879	1201	879
Madera	(in Fresno)	6364	8368			764	737	598	574
Tulare	24574	18375	35440	1984	2640	1755	2246	2742	2329
Total	34382	51090	97753	2976	3906	5243	5822	6811	5997
% Increase		48.6	91.3			76.2	49.0	30.0	3.0

145

[1]The economic area classification of California counties is based upon Warren S. Thompson, *Growth and Change in California's Population* (Los Angeles: The Haynes Foundation, 1955), pp. 1–5. Metropolitan areas are designated with capital letters and nonmetropolitan areas by numbers.

brothers nominated "Red" Hayes in the Republican Fifth District (San Francisco) congressional convention over Espee opposition, and posed the threat of a substantial bargaining bloc of legislators at the next session.

Internal maneuvering changed to effective unanimity at the polls, which made 1904 the ebb tide of Democratic strength until 1920. Roosevelt took fifty-four counties, while the hapless Alton B. Parker carried but two, Colusa and Mariposa, and these by truly wafer-thin margins. Forty-six counties produced a Republican sweep of the now eight Congressional seats, and gave the party 104 of the 120 legislative seats. Roosevelt's "halo effect" enhanced Taft's vote in 1908, but it did not visibly affect the gubernatorial vote of either James N. Gillett or Hiram W. Johnson.

What did assist Gillett was the manner of Bard's defeat for re-election by Frank P. Flint of Los Angeles.[32] That the Espee had defeated Bard, by whatever means, paled beside the Bardians' view that Pardee had been guilty of gross ingratitude in not vigorously supporting Bard's re-election, and, far worse, that he had been guilty of complicity in accomplishing Bard's defeat. None can deny Pardee's surface neutrality. His adherents then and a later student of his administration deny his complicity.[33] The operative fact is simply that the Bardians believed both charges. They took their political revenge in 1906.

In retrospect, Pardee was not a malleable ingot in the Espee's political forge,[34] which he proved by his support of the Western Pacific Railroad's entry into northern California. His proposed manifesto of independence from the Espee and all its works was a casualty of the disaster of April, 1906.[35] He is known as the "father of conservation" in California with good reason, and his support of a state highway system was farseeing. Additionally, unlike many of his predecessors, he made "his residence in Sacramento as the law requires, and . . . put in his time in the office, attending to its duties."[36] By any standards, other than Bardian, he merited re-election.

The Bardians' first choice for the Republican gubernatorial nomination in 1906 was C. M. Belshaw, a pro-Bard legislator in 1899 and pro-Flint in 1902, but property losses consequent to the 1906 disaster forced Belshaw to renounce his aspirations. This disaster, it should be noted, left San Francisco with the most over-represented legislative districts in the state which made the Espee's task that much easier after Ruef was removed from power. With Belshaw unavailable, the next best anti-Pardee Republican available was James N. Gillett. If this seems paradoxical, such is nothing new to politics.

Gillett has been described as an Espee puppet.[37] However, as a State Senator, Gillett had supported Bard in 1899 and had held twenty delegates for Tom Flint in 1902. Moreover, he had not been an Espee congressman in Bard's eyes during their association in Washington. What impelled Gillett first to seek the governorship remains unclear, but he had requested Bard's support on March 11, 1906, and had campaigned statewide thereafter.

Population Growth and Presidential Vote in
Selected Economic Areas
1890–1910

County	Population			Vote					
	1890	1900	1910	1892 R	1892 D	1900 R	1900 D	1908 R	1908 D
LOS ANGELES AREA *Economic Area F*									
Los Angeles	101454	170298	504131	10226	8119	19200	13172	41483	22076
Orange	13589	19696	34436	1153	1000	2157	1780	3244	1911
SAN DIEGO AREA *Economic Area G*									
San Diego	34987	35090	61665	3525	2334	3800	2678	5412	2393
SAN BERNARDINO AREA *Economic Area H*									
San Bernardino	25497	27929	56706	3686	2548	3135	2348	4729	2685
IMPERIAL VALLEY AREA *Economic Area 8*									
Imperial (in San Diego)			13591					909	675
Riverside (in S.D. & S.B.)		17897	34696			2360	1143	3229	1374
Sub-Total	175527	270910	691634	18590	14001	30652	21121	59006	31114
% Increase		54.4	155.3			64.9	50.9	92.5	47.3
SOUTH COASTAL AREA *Economic Area 7*									
Santa Barbara	15754	18934	27738	1485	1230	1988	1616	2713	1995
Ventura	10071	14367	18347	1283	960	1710	1449	1864	1545
PART SOUTH CENTRAL COASTAL AREA[1] *Part Economic Area 3*									
San Luis Obispo	16072	16637	19383	1433	1210	1564	1713	2008	1381
Total: Southern California	217424	320848	757102	22791	17401	35914	25899	65591	36035
% Increase		47.6	136.0			57.6	48.8	82.6	39.1

[1]Included in this tabulation because today it is commonly lumped with the other counties as part of southern California.

The delegate primaries encouraged Pardee by seemingly bringing him 350 of the 413 necessary for nomination. Pardee was whistling past the graveyard in this calculation, because his first and only ballot strength was almost thirty per cent less than this estimate. Some of this erosion was due to elected delegates being *instructed* by their Central Committee. Some was due to uninstructed delegations, designed for trading purposes, in which Pardee felt he had friends. In Chester H. Rowell's view, the only speculation about delegates concerned those from the country, because Los Angeles and San Francisco belonged to Parker and Ruef, who in turn belonged to Herrin, who was owned by Harriman. By this reasoning, California's government could be no better than what the country could force the urban poles to accept.[38] The flaw in this reasoning was the assumption that Ruef belonged to Herrin. On the eve of the convention, Rowell saw it this way: "Pardee or Gillett it is then, and either of them is fit for the place and worthy to be elected to it."[39]

The Bardians' delegate strength was intertwined with Espee efforts for Gillett. A Roosevelt Republican Club was organized in San Diego to gain an anti-Pardee delegation because of his treatment of Bard in 1905 but was defeated by the "regulars," who sent a Gillett delegation for the same result. Ventura County's contingent was comprised of three Bard members and five Espee choices, all pledged to Gillett. Tom Flint's influence was given to Warren R. Porter, who went to the convention with thirty-six anti-Pardee delegates and wound up as Gillett's running mate. Flint thereafter was finance chairman of Gillett's campaign. In the Fresno delegation, fifteen of seventeen were for Gillett, and "the whole San Joaquin Valley, except Tulare and three votes from Merced was solid for Gillett."[40]

This strength enabled the Espee to organize the convention without dealing with Ruef. It then plumbed the possibility of nominating Gillett without Ruef's help: 156 of San Francisco's 159, bound by "unit rule" and committed, perhaps for revenue only, to "Black" Hayes. Success would have saved Herrin considerable cash and Gillett and his supporters considerable campaign embarrassment.

Herrin remained aloof from Santa Cruz and left field direction to Walter Parker. Buttressed by the knowledge that Pardee had no chance, and secure in the knowledge that Ruef's bloc was a purchasable commodity, Parker selected and rejected candidates for state and local offices, bullying delegates and candidates with the delicacy and finesse of a hog butcher. His deals and trades were not too dissimilar from any political convention's transactions. What made them malodorous was his blatant display of raw power, which sent a wave of revulsion rippling across the state. When it became absolutely clear that no one could be nominated without Ruef, his bloc was purchased for $20,000.[41] On September 6, 1906, Gillett was nominated on the first ballot,

$591\frac{1}{2}$ to $233\frac{1}{2}$, to bring the last Republican nominating convention in California to an end.

Following their usual practice, the Democrats held their state convention after the Republicans. The choice of its 732 delegates was Theodore A. Bell, a thirty-four-year old attorney from Napa, who had been elected to Congress in 1902 and defeated in the Roosevelt landslide of 1904. Throughout August, 1906, Bell had been engrossed in the Milwaukee national convention of the Fraternal Order of Eagles, emerging as Grand Worthy Vice President.[42] What political noises he had made before his nomination had been congressional in tone, and the assumption is that he had waited to see whom the Republicans would select.[43] He enjoyed the support of the McNab-Phelan faction in San Francisco, and received Union Labor Party support there even though he repudiated Ruef. Young, vigorous, politically magnetic and militantly anti-Espee, his prospects of victory were excellent until W. R. Hearst clouded them.

It has been said that Hearst's political asininity and ambition coincided in this year because he wished to drape the mantle of William Jennings Bryan about himself.[44] Whatever his reasons, he severed his long and strong Democratic ties and formed the Independence League. The League nominated Hearst's choice for Governor, W. H. Langdon, civic-reform minded District Attorney of San Francisco,[45] who ran on a pro-labor, anti-Espee platform.

Both Bell and Langdon made capital of Parker's conduct at Santa Cruz, and spared no chance to rivet the Herrin-Ruef-Gillett link in the public mind. They made capital, too, of the President's refusal to endorse Gillett, and both took gleeful note of Samuel Gompers' antilabor branding of Gillett. It was not enough to deny Gillett a plurality victory, in which he trailed his running mate by a crisp 8,103 votes.

Gillett's total (125,887) made a deep trough between the twin peaks of Roosevelt's and Taft's impressive sweeps, which has obscured the fact that twenty-six more counties went Republican in congressional and legislative elections in 1906 than in 1902. This local level recovery can be attributed in part to Espee success in gaining control of Republican machinery in many "cow counties." While the Republicans lost twenty-one straight party-label legislative seats, their fusion gains virtually offset this loss and they kept solid control of the Legislature.

So Gillett's narrow margin was not a repudiation of his party but of Gillett as symbol of the Espee's manhandling of the Santa Cruz convention. It often has been said that the Hearstian rift in San Francisco alone deprived Bell of more than 10,000 votes and ensured his defeat. The traditionally Democratic mountain and valley counties and Los Angeles county also gave Langdon enough votes to defeat Bell.

A few weeks too late to affect the election, the Oliver Grand Jury in San

Table VII

The Nature of Republican Control by Economic Areas
1898–1910

	Total Elections[1]	R	R²	R-Fusion	D	D²	D-Fusion	Joint DR Candidates, 1910	Other
SAN FRANCISCO AREA									
Economic Area A									
Alameda	75	66	1	4	—	—	—	4	—
Contra Costa	24	20	1	1	1	—	—	1	—
Marin	24	21	2	—	1	—	—	—	—
San Francisco	172	93	4	37	12	—	22	4	—
San Mateo	24	22	1	—	—	—	1	—	—
Solano	24	20	—	—	3	1	—	—	0
Total	343	242	9	42	17	1	23	9	0
% of Total		85.42			11.95			2.62	
SAN JOSE AREA									
Economic Area B									
Santa Clara	43	39	1	—	—	2	—	—	1 Ind
% of Total		93.0			4.65				2.33
NORTH CENTRAL COASTAL AREA									
Economic Area 2									
Napa	24	20	—	—	3	1	—	—	—
Sonoma	32	20	2	—	7	1	2	—	—
Total	56	40	2	0	10	2	2	0	0
% of Total		75.0			25.0				

150

	Total							
Economic Area C								
Sacramento	38	25	3	—	5	1	1	3
STOCKTON AREA								
Economic Area D								
San Joaquin	31	22	2	—	5	1	1	—
Total	69	47	5	—	10	2	2	3
% of Total		75.4			20.3			4.3
FRESNO AREA								
Economic Area E								
Fresno	31	20	2	—	8	—	1	—
LOWER SAN JOAQUIN AREA								
Economic Area 5								
Merced	25	3	2	—	17	1	2	—
Stanislaus	25	11	0	0	11	2	1	—
Total	81	34	4	—	36	3	4	—
% of Total		46.9			53.1			
UPPER SAN JOAQUIN AREA								
Economic Area 6								
Kern	25	6	2	—	15	1	1	—
Kings	25	15	4	—	—	3	3	—
Madera	26	9	1	—	11	2	3	—
Tulare	25	7	2	—	13	—	3	—
Total	101	37	9	—	39	6	10	—
% of Total		45.54			54.46			

151

[1] Total elections comprise Presidential, gubernatorial, congressional and legislative for the period shown. It should be remembered that one-half, or twenty, Senate seats were contested biennially.

[2] Indicates margin of less than 3% of vote cast.

Table VIII

The Nature of Republican Control by Economic Areas (cont.)
1898–1910

	Total Elections	R	R^2	R-Fusion	D	D^2	D-Fusion	Joint DR Candidates, 1910	Other
LOS ANGELES AREA									
Economic Area F									
Los Angeles	87	81	1	2	—	1	2	—	—
Orange	24	22	—	—	2	—	—	—	—
SAN DIEGO AREA									
Economic Area G									
San Diego	30	29	—	—	—	1	—	—	—
SAN BERANRDINO AREA									
Economic Area H									
San Bernardino	26	25	—	—	—	—	1	—	—
IMPERIAL VALLEY AREA									
Economic Area 8									
Imperial	7	6	—	—	1	—	—	—	—
Riverside	24	24	—	—	—	—	—	—	—
SOUTH COASTAL AREA									
Economic Area 7									
Santa Barbara	24	21	3	—	—	—	—	—	—
Ventura	24	23	1	—	—	—	—	—	—
Total	246	231	5	2	3	2	3	0	0
% of Total		96.75			3.25			0	0

South Central Coastal Area
Economic Area 3

San Luis Obispo	24	13	—	—	7	1	3	—	
Monterey	24	14	3	1	2	3	1	—	
San Benito	24	9	4	—	9	—	1	1	
Santa Cruz	24	18	—	—	4	2	—	—	
Total	96	54	7	1	22	6	5	1 }	1.0
% of Total		64.6			34.4				

Sacramento Valley Area
Economic Area 4

Butte	25	18	3	0	2	1	1	—	
Colusa	25	2	—	—	21	—	1	1	
Glenn	25	2	1	—	19	1	1	1	
Sutter	25	18	3	—	2	1	1	—	
Tehama	25	12	4	—	8	1	—	—	
Yolo	25	4	3	—	17	1	1	—	
Yuba	25	18	2	—	4	—	1	—	
Total	175	74	16	—	73	5	5	2 }	1.14
% of Total		51.4			47.4				

North Coastal Area
Economic Area 1

Del Norte	25	22	—	—	2	1	—	—	
Humboldt	32	32	—	—	—	—	—	—	
Lake	25	2	—	—	20	1	1	1	
Mendocino	25	12	3	—	7	2	1	—	
Total	107	68	3	—	29	4	2	1 }	0.9
% of Total		66.4			32.7				

Table VIII (*continued*)

	Total Elections	R	R[2]	R-Fusion	D	D[2]	D-Fusion	Joint DR Candidates, 1910	Other
SIERRA AREA									
Economic Area 9[1]									
Amador	25	13	3	—	5	2	2	—	—
Calaveras	25	16	4	—	3	1	1	—	—
El Dorado	25	5	1	—	12	6	1	—	—
Inyo	26	13	4	—	6	2	1	—	—
Lassen	25	22	—	—	3	—	—	—	—
Mariposo	25	1	2	—	19	1	2	—	—
Modoc	25	9	1	—	12	2	1	—	—
Mono	25	18	4	—	—	2	1	—	—
Nevada	24	16	2	—	3	2	1	—	—
Placer	24	16	2	—	4	1	1	—	—
Plumas	24	22	—	—	1	1	—	—	—
Shasta	25	10	2	—	10	2	1	—	—
Sierra	24	21	—	—	3	—	—	—	—
Siskiyou	24	10	2	—	5	7	—	—	—
Trinity	25	21	2	—	1	1	—	—	—
Tuolumne	25	5	2	—	15	1	2	—	—
Total	396	218	31	—	102	31	14	—	—
% of Total		62.9			37.1				

[1]Alpine County omitted.
[2]Indicates margin of less than 3% of vote cast.

Francisco handed down indictments against Ruef and Mayor Eugene Schmitz. Thereafter, the protracted graft trials catapulted Hiram Johnson into the statewide prominence vital to his success in 1910. These trials also fissioned political allegiances in San Francisco with pro- and anti-graft prosecution sentiments, which compounded an already unstable situation of Democratic, Republican, and now leaderless Union Labor factions and "bosses."

The immediate effect of the graft trials was to give San Francisco a short-lived reform government, which adopted the recall in 1907. This same year saw Sacramento obtain a new charter and employ the initiative to grant the Western Pacific Railroad a franchise, a matter long opposed by the Espee. Sacramento also elected Clinton L. White as a reform Mayor.

A counterpoint to reform was provided by the 1907 legislature. Walter F. X. Parker personally directed its blatant manipulation by the Espee, whereby it visibly became "the people of California." Despite this brazen domination and then because of it, two handmaidens of reform were born.

In 1906, both major parties had pledged themselves to some form of candidate primary. As he left office, Governor Pardee described the direct primary as a "thorough-going remedy for the admitted evils of conventions and county (*central*) committees."[46] Senator C. M. Belshaw introduced a primary measure on January 17, 1907, and the Senate finally passed it on March 5; it cleared the Assembly after modification. Innocuous as it was, it gave the Legislature power to make laws for both delegate and candidate primary elections if the people approved. They did approve in 1908 by 76.6% (152,853) to 23.4% (46,772). Forty per cent of the negative vote came from six southland counties; the balance largely came from the smaller mountain and valley counties. The Bay Area counties endorsed it by margins up to 90% in San Francisco. Lincoln–Roosevelt League strength in the 1909 Legislature produced a measure which permitted Hiram Johnson to win the first and perhaps the most important primary election in the state's history.

The genesis of the Lincoln–Roosevelt League itself came from the "pens of dishonor" into which the 1907 Legislature was herded by the Espee's minions. Chester H. Rowell covered this session for his paper, and was moved to an editorial calling for statewide political reform within the Republican Party.[47] His sentiments were shared by E. A. Dickson, a young reporter who was covering the session for the *Los Angeles Express*, and who had carte blanche from his publisher, E. T. Earl,[48] to practice crusading reform journalism. Rowell had come to the realization that individuals were powerless to combat the Espee, and he was seeking a Republican nucleus of opposition. Dickson suggested the civic reform group in Los Angeles, and the result was a meeting there at Levy's Cafe on May 21, 1907, which was dominated by newspapermen and lawyers.

155

This group adopted a "Platform of Principles," in which the foremost plank was to free the Republican Party of Espee domination. They adopted the name, "Lincoln-Republican Clubs." A second larger gathering assembled at Oakland's Hotel Metropole on August 1, 1907, at which the "Platform of Principles" and a new official title, "The League of Lincoln–Roosevelt Republican Clubs of California," were adopted. Six of the eight officers elected at this meeting, including its president, Frank H. Devlin of Vallejo, and Chester H. Rowell, one of its four vice presidents, came from north of the Tehachapi. This indicates the League's secure base in southern California, and its awareness that its great fight against Espee influence in the Republican party would be to add northern interior California to this base while besieging San Francisco.

The Lincoln–Roosevelt League was aided in its cause by its state-wide newspaper support. Powerful journals at each of the urban poles supported it fervently, while its press allies in the Great Valley ranged from Modesto to Chico. This support came close to realizing a plan advanced in 1898 by A. J. Pillsbury, then editor of the *Tulare Register*, for a league of Republican newspapers to support a league of Republican clubs to bring about reform. Not content with this favorable press support, the League founded its own journals— the *Pacific Outlook* in Los Angeles, and the *California Weekly* in San Francisco.

San Francisco became League headquarters and Chester H. Rowell took extended leave of his Fresno editorial duties to direct its operations. The witches' cauldron of factional and graft prosecution politics was complicated even more by strong San Francisco sentiment, including union labor's, for the Hetch Hetchy water project. The League espoused the John Muir—Sierra Club stand of esthetic preservation, perhaps because the San Joaquin Valley feared that Hetch Hetchy presaged diminution of its available irrigation water supply.

This political pot boiled over in the municipal election of 1907, when a basically Democratic reform government was elected at the expense of whatever Republican unity Rowell had achieved. By March, 1908, however, he had assembled a group which provided necessary organization at the Assembly District level. The result was to enhance League strength in both the delegate primary and legislative elections of 1908.

The first test of League strength came at the state convention (May 14, 1908) to choose delegates to the national gathering. The League was committed to Taft-for-President, and charged the Espee with seeking an "open" delegation that E. H. Harriman, now overlord of the Espee, could manipulate to his own end. For several weeks before the convention, the *Fresno Republican* heralded League victories in the delegate primaries which would give it control of the convention. The "puffery" in these claims became apparent when *instructed* delegates among the 629 attending gave the Espee the "clout" it needed.[49] The League did gain a Taft-instructed delegation, and elected one of its slate of four delegates-at-large,[50] defeating Harrison Gray Otis. This was a doubly sweet victory to Rowell, who characterized the *Angeleno* publisher as Harrison *Bray* Otis. Otis reciprocated by dubbing Rowell a "little windy nincompoop of Fresno village." In contrast with the Republican convention, the Democrats were like cooing doves when they gathered in Fresno this year, and sent a delegation pledged to W. J. Bryan, their party's quadrennial sacrifice, to the national assemblage.

The League gained minority representation on the State Central Committee appointed at the delegate convention. This minority then challenged the chairman's actions time and time again, and each time was overruled. This seemingly futile tactic appears to have been deliberate on the Leaguers' part. Their newspaper support gave widespread publicity to their suppression by the chair, and reinforced the image created by the Espee's tactics at Santa Cruz in 1906 and in the Legislature of 1907.

The second Republican state convention in 1908 was to select nominees for judicial and other posts. From Rowell's own accounts,[51] the League had no real hope of controlling this convention, but did good work at the local level in nominating legislators who favored it. At convention's end, Rowell summarized the League's accomplishments during its first year.

> . . . at the recent Republican primaries the League cast over 50,000 votes; was directly instrumental in bringing out the votes of more than 50,000 other Republicans; carried [sic] the banner Republican counties of California; secured control of a third of the legislature and improved the quality of the other two-thirds; and laid the foundations of an assured victory two years hence.[52]

Roosevelt's mantle proved ample enough to encompass the portly figure of William H. Taft in the general election. In the legislative elections, the Democrats gained seventeen seats over 1906, six of which were fusionist victories, for a total of thirty. This was a remarkable increase over 1904, when only eight Democrats had been elected, and moved C. H. Rowell to remark that Herrin was back in Democratic Party affairs.[53] The gain was not enough to affect Republican control of both houses, however, which ensured G. C. Perkins of another term in the Senate.[54]

A thirty-four member press corps covered the 1909 Legislature and represented all the state's major newspapers as well as the two major wire services. The League was expected to make this session a newsworthy one. Additionally, the League mailed weekly articles and legislative summaries to almost 200 newspapers throughout the state, so that this session stands as the best reported in California's political history to date. What was reported, by and large, were temporizings between the Espee and the reformers.

On January 29, 1909, the *California Weekly* proclaimed that the anti-machine element was in definite control of the Assembly and nearly in control of the Senate. Looking back across his years, Franklin Hichborn would remember that the anti-Espee group had a slight majority on paper in both houses.[55] What becomes apparent is that League strength depended upon anti-Espee Democrats. This dependence was made clear in the defeat of proposed Assembly rules, which placed no time limit for reporting bills from committee and required a two-thirds vote of elected legislators, rather than two-thirds of those present and voting, to refer bills to or get them out of committee. Assemblyman A. M. Drew, of Fresno, led the fight against these stifling proposals; he had twenty-two other Republicans on his side and gained eighteen Democrats to defeat them forty-one to thirty-two. If the League and its allies had any such strength in the Senate, it is not visible from this distance. In neither House could reform strength prevents its organization by the Espee.

Adroit use of this organization enabled the Espee to fight its delaying actions against reform measures. It was aided by the fact that the reformers lacked a strategic battle plan, a manual of tactics, and a central command. They did get a watered-down railroad rate regulation bill, but lost proposals to incorporate the initiative, referendum, and recall into state political life, and they got only an advisory vote for United States Senator, rather than the "Oregon plan" of making the popular vote binding upon legislators. They did get an Anti-Race-track Gambling Bill, which represented a victory over the "vice" elements, and after a long deadlock in the Senate, they got a candidate primary law that would prove sufficient unto the task ahead in 1910.

Before this task could be accomplished, the League had to find a candidate for the primary. Its progressive faction favored F. J. Heney, who was anathema to the conservative brethren for many reasons, including his acceptance of the Democratic nomination for district attorney of San Francisco in 1909. The conservatives were not averse to F. K. Mott, thrice Mayor of Oakland, or W. H. Davis, a former Mayor of Oakland, or C. M. Belshaw, or Harris Weinstock of Sacramento. Neither League faction sought a nominating convention, for fear of disrupting the movement beyond repair.

Just who was responsible for persuading Hiram Johnson to become the League's candidate, or for first persuading Mrs. Johnson to agree to it, still provokes folklorish disputation. There are about as many claimants of this honor as there are light beams in the Milky Way. It is considered here that Chester H. Rowell deserves the accolade, not for his persistence alone but also for his skillful handling of the League's oligarchial meetings.[56] A. J. Wallace of Los Angeles, the millionaire state president of the Anti-Saloon League, was chosen for Lieutenant Governor. Wallace's appointment was a sop to the south and a shock to the "wet" north, and John Downey Works, another "dry" from the southland with a distinguished judicial record, was selected to seek the advisory vote for United States Senator.

Where the League solved its candidate crisis, the Espee did not. Alden Anderson, mentioned previously and now State Superintendent of Banks under Gillett, was its choice. Charles F. Curry, Secretary of State since 1898, entered the fray, and there is a Borgia-like premise that he did so at the urging of D. M. Burns,[57] who was seeking revenge for his abandonment by Herrin in 1900. Philip A. Stanton, who entered the Assembly from Los Angeles in 1903 and had served as its Speaker in 1909, also joined the fray. Stanton's reputation and record qualified him as an Espee legislator, which led to speculation that he was Walter Parker's personal choice, and indicated a breach with Herrin. The final contestant was Nathaniel Ellery, then State Engineer, who probably ran for the pleasure of hearing his own speeches.

Anderson and Curry split the northern urban vote, where the League was held correctly to be antilabor, and Stanton took the southland's urban "machine" vote. Johnson was elected by his reform strength in the south, despite labor strife in Los Angeles, and by the northern rural counties, where it often has been said erroneously that he ran poorly.[58] The total Republican gubernatorial vote, 215,605, was the party's highest to this point, and it evaporated between primary and general, in which Johnson polled only 177,191 votes for a decline of 17.8%.

The significance of this primary was simply that with a field of five, the old convention system would have enabled Espee manipulation to nominate Anderson. This primary was a political curiosity because it polled more partisan votes than the subsequent general election. Another unusual aspect of this first primary was that four State Senators and twenty-five Assemblymen each received two or more nominations, thus presaging crossfiling,[59] and that not one of these was defeated in the general election.

After Johnson's victory, the Republican state convention contained only 428 delegates, of whom a minority were "machine" representatives. It endorsed women's suffrage and a national income tax, among other measures, which made California Republicans for the first time since the 1860's "more radical" than the Democrats. Johnson, however, did not undertake an educational campaign offensive against his Democratic opponent. During the primary campaign, Johnson had uttered one simple clarion call, "kick the Southern Pacific out of politics." He saw no need to change his tactics, and it well could be that Johnson, or his advisors, realized that a single simple theme was the best way to avoid campaign blunders by "Holy Hiram," a notably thin-skinned warrior in the heat of battle.

The 1910 Democratic state convention met in Los Angeles for the first time in that party's history. T. A. Bell's loss to Gillett in 1906 was no barrier to his second nomination, as he was unopposed, and the tradition that Americans do not like a loser was not supported by his state-wide vote which was the highest percentage for any Democratic gubernatorial candidate to that point in the state's history. This fact belies the theory that James D. Phelan's fortuitous absence in Europe was Phelan's way of helping Johnson without offending his fellow Democrats.[60] The same source alleges that Phelan and other Democrats felt that Bell was not as anti-Espee as he proclaimed. What did hurt Bell was his educational campaign on a wide range of reform issues, which left the simple, gut issue of the Espee to Johnson.

Bell was hurt even more when the Espee threw its support to him; he did not want the support of these sinister politicians. But he received it publicly when Walter Parker worked openly for him in Los Angeles, and an assortment of known Espee factotums did the same in northern California. Johnson made the most of this unexpected good fortune, and together with the bombing of the *Los Angeles Times*, October 1, 1910, it offset some of the antilabor label with which the League was branded. The *Times* bombing, perhaps, prevented the Socialist vote, which reached the highest of any third party since the Populists in 1894, from going higher. When the returns were tallied, Johnson became another plurality governor. More than 90% of his margin (22,356) came from the southern counties, Alameda and Humboldt, and three San Joaquin Valley counties, Fresno, Stanislaus, Tulare, which went Republican for the first time in a gubernatorial election.

Johnson carried more counties than any Republican candidate for governor since Gage, and while his party's roster of counties in congressional and legislative elections declined substantially from the 1906–1908 level, their distribution reduced the Democratic seats in the legislature from thirty to nineteen. With this victory, the League briefly became *the* Republican party in California, until its metamorphosis into the Progressive camp.

Victory had not destroyed a political monolith, the record of Herrin's previous defeats refutes this premise, but it had overcome urban-based "boss" control of the state's political destiny. Victory did not usher in the era of mob rule feared by the anti-Espee conservative agrarians who had helped to fashion it; neither did it produce the millenium craved by reformers. It did produce Hiram W. Johnson's legacy to California politics, and this seems accomplishment enough.

FOOTNOTES

1   Several available works bear directly upon the period, 1896–1910; see Walton Bean, *Boss Ruef's San Francisco* (Los Angeles and Berkeley: University of California Press, 1952); C. Raymond Clar, *California Government and Forestry* (Sacramento: State

Printing Office, 1959); W. H. Hutchinson, *Oil, Land, and Politics: The California Career of Thomas Robert Bard* (Norman, Oklahoma: University of Oklahoma Press, 1965) 2 vols.; George E. Mowry, *The California Progressives* (Los Angeles and Berkeley: University of California Press, 1951); W. W. Robinson, *Lawyers of Los Angeles* (Los Angeles: Los Angeles Bar Association, 1959); and Gerald T. White, *Formative Years in the Far West* (New York: Appleton-Century-Crofts, 1962) which treats of petroleum's rise to prominence in California and the emergence of the Standard Oil Company of California. Basic material on the governors of this period is to be found in H. Brett Melendy and Benjamin G. Gilbert, *The Governors of California: Peter H. Burnett to Edmund G. Brown* (Georgetown, California: The Talisman Press, 1965), as indexed. Five unpublished Ph.D. dissertations have been useful in preparing this chapter: Albert Howard Clodius, *The Quest for Good Government in Los Angeles 1890–1910* (Claremont Graduate School, 1953); Miles Chapman Everett, *Chester Harvey Rowell, Pragmatic Humanist and California Progressive* (University of California at Berkeley, 1966); Robert Edward Hennings, *James D. Phelan and the Wilson Progressives of California* (University of California at Berkeley, 1961); Alice M. Rose, *The Rise of California Insurgency: Origins of the League of Lincoln-Roosevelt Republican Clubs, 1900–1907* (Stanford University, 1942); and Edward F. Staniford, *Governor in the Middle: The Administration of George C. Pardee . . . , 1903–1907* (University of California at Berkeley, 1955). The unpublished typescript of Franklin Hichborn's "California Politics, 1891–1939" (University of California at Los Angeles Library, 1949) has been used as well in preparing this chapter. Population growth and voting statistics are taken from Warren S. Thompson, *Growth and Change in California's Population* (Los Angeles: Haynes Foundation, 1955) and Secretary of State, *California Blue Book* (Sacramento: State Printing Office, 1881–1967), for 1897, 1899, 1903, 1907, 1909. Four recent surveys present an outline of this period: Walton Bean, *California: An Imperative History* (New York: McGraw-Hill Book Company, 1968); John W. Caughey, *California* (Second Ed.; New York: Prentice-Hall, Inc., 1953); Andrew F. Rolle, *California: A History* (Second Ed.; New York: Thomas Y. Crowell Company, 1969); and Ralph J. Roske, *Everyman's Eden: A History of California* (New York: The Macmillan Company, 1968).

2   David Lavender, *The Great Persuader* (New York: Doubleday & Company, 1970), pp. 363–364, presents a different view of Stow's relations with Huntington.

3   The Direct Primary Law of March 23, 1901, made delegate primary elections "obligatory and mandatory" only in the City and County of San Francisco and in the cities of Los Angeles, Oakland, Sacramento, San Jose, San Diego, Stockton, Alameda, Berkeley, Fresno, Pasadena and Vallejo (Stats., 1901; Ch.198). It was repealed in 1911 (Stats., 1911; Ch.713).

4   James H. Budd suffered the removal of this courtesy from his appointed Lieutenant Governor by the Republican-controlled Senate.

5   Clodius, *op. cit.*, treats of the reform movements and personalities in almost excruciating detail.

6   In dress and deportment, Grove Johnson was a punctilious gentleman of the old school. In the Assembly, he was the Espee's servant.

7   Clodius, *op. cit.*, p. 127.

8   Clodius, *op. cit.*, p. 209. This fund was the creation of Meyer Lissner, and was designed to provide a continuing flow of financial support to reform movements.

9   Hennings, *op. cit.*, p. iii.

10   Albert Johnson was a "single taxer," and addicted to intoxicating liquor, often to excess.

11   Flint is mentioned hereinafter without the "Jr."

12   Hutchinson, *op. cit.*, as indexed.

13   Everett, *op. cit.*, treats extensively the relationship between uncle and nephew in the conduct of the *Fresno Morning Republican.*

14   Melendy and Gilbert, *op. cit.*, pp. 259–271, for the basic details of this administration.

15   Hichborn, *op. cit.*, pp. 347–355, *passim.*

16   The agrarian anti-Espee faction in this election won two of the three Railroad Commission seats with Nehemiah Blackstock, Ventura County, representing the Third District, and E. B. Edson, Siskiyou County, representing the Second. Their effectiveness remains undetermined.

17   Burns' term as Secretary of State (1880–1883) had produced a shortage of funds for which he was indicted but never tried. During his tenure as "boss" of San Francisco (1891–1894) and as a Police Commissioner, these rumors had spread enough so that it was expedient for him to leave the state briefly after his acquittal on graft charges. Also, in a mining venture in Mexico, he allegedly bilked his associates to his own profit. Burns long had been identified with northern California's horse-racing and saloon elements, and he had been prominently active in several Republican state conventions, as an Espee "programmer".

18   Hutchison, *op. cit.*, II, as indexed.

19   George C. Perkins generally has been regarded as an unalloyed Espee servant. Such an unqualified categorization does an injustice to his ability to keep a foot in every political camp that seemed necessary to his survival, and to change his stances with grace and agility.

20   Hichborn, *op. cit.*, p. 430, presents his case for Burns' enduring animus towards Herrin as a result of this election.

21   Rose, *op. cit.*, p. 41.

22   San Francisco *Evening Call*, July 27, 1901, p. 6.

23   M. H. DeYoung's *San Francisco Chronicle* was the other member of the "Big Three" at this point in time.

24   The theory has been advanced that the Espee supported its gubernatorial choices for a single term only, lest they achieve an organization of their own. In this context, the choice of Gage to succeed himself may have been due to his alienation of every substantial segment of his party.

25   The *Call's* anti-Espee attitude in this period may have been due as much to John D. Spreckel's personal animus toward Herrin as to a commitment to political reform.

26   August 26, 1902, p. 1.

27   *Sacramento Bee,* August 26, 1902, p. 5. In this period. the *Bee* was anti-Espee and pro-Democrat with almost equal virulence.

28   Mowry, *op. cit.*, p. 16, indicates that Pardee's campaign platform was constructed in Herrin's office.

29   Of the 316,198 votes cast statewide, only 304,473 were counted. The charges against Pardee's supporters revolved around some 5,000 ballots in Alameda and Los Angeles counties.

30   Melendy and Gilbert, *op. cit.*, pp. 273–287, for the details of this administration.

31   Bean, *Boss Ruef,* p. 35, says that Ruef was the key to Perkin's re-election in this year. The fact remains that the anti-Espee Republicans who had backed Flint's bid for the gubernatorial nomination stood by Perkins, probably because they knew him and were afraid they might get someone more subservient to Herrin.

32   Hutchinson, *op. cit.*, II, 265–268, treats of Frank Flint's relations with Bard. He is not to be confused with the aforementioned Thomas Flint, and there was no family linkage between the two.

33   Staniford, *op. cit.*, pp. 287–296, does not subscribe to Pardee's complicity in Bard's defeat, and documents his case very well.

34   Melendy and Gilbert, *op. cit.*, pp. 274 *et seq.*

35   Chester H. Rowell to Mark Sullivan, May 27, 1910; letter in Rowell Papers, Bancroft Library, University of California at Berkeley. Sullivan was editor of *Collier's Magazine.*

36   *Fresno Morning Republican,* September 2, 1906, p. 4.

37   Mowry, *op. cit.,* p. 58

38   *Fresno Morning Republican,* August 19, 1906, p. 4.

39   *Ibid.*, September 2, 1906, p. 4.

40   *Ibid.*, September 7, 1906, p. 1.

41   San Francisco *Evening Call,* September 11, 1906, pp. 1, 2. There are other figures given for the amount paid Ruef in this matter.

42   *Sacramento Bee,* August 18, 1906, p. 5.

43   Some evidence exists that no ambitious Democrat wished to run against Pardee, and that Gillett's nomination made the contest attractive to Bell.

44   Hennings, *op. cit.*, pp. 44–45.

45   The first major error of Ruef's political "boss" career was placing Langdon on his municipal ticket.

46   State of California, *Journal of the Senate,* 1907, p. 18.

47   *Fresno Morning Republican,* February 20, 1907, p. 4.

48   E. T. Earl's role as publisher of the *Express* entitles him to as much credit certainly as that given Dickson. He has not yet received it.

49   It has been said that the Lincoln–Roosevelt League came within forty votes of controlling this convention. This appears to be questionable, in the light of research for *Oil, Land, and Politics* (fn. 1, *supra*) and research for this chapter.

50   This slate was composed of T. R. Bard, Dr. Chester Rowell, Col. E. A. Forbes, and J. H. Neff; the last named being elected.

51   *Fresno Morning Republican*, August 2–30, 1908.

52   *Ibid.*, August 30, 1908, p. 4.

53   *Ibid.*, August 13, 1908, p. 4.

54   Here again, Lincoln–Roosevelt League support went to G. C. Perkins; perhaps because they had no acceptable candidate of their own, or because Perkins was preferable to any other candidate they might espouse.

55   Hichborn, *op. cit.*, p. 758.

56   Everett, *op. cit.*, p. 331, agrees with this view.

57   Hichborn, *op. cit.*, p. 937.

58   Wallace and Works also gained plurality victories in multi-candidate races. Wallace polled almost 35,000 votes less than Johnson, while Works ran 2,000 votes behind Wallace. The total vote for Lieutenant Governor declined 16,790 from the gubernatorial contest; for United States Senator, 34,990. Works was sent to the Senate by the League-controlled Legislature of 1911.

59   It is germane to note here that fusion nominations were a political practice of long standing in California.

60   Hennings, *op. cit.*, p. 83; fn. 87.

Hiram Johnson and
the Progressive Years

Early in January, 1911, a new era began in California politics. Hiram Johnson, age forty-five, returned to the town of his birth to take the oath of office as the state's twenty-third Governor, deliver his inaugural address, and launch a career that would re-write the political record books. He was the first Governor to be re-elected since John Bigler in 1853, and the first to be re-elected to a four-year term. His accomplishments would include a thirty-five year career as governor and senator, achievement of national stature, and initiation of the only massive revisions of the Constitution of 1879 and the statute books of the state. In his inaugural, Johnson repeated the theme of his election campaign: special interests and vested privilege stood between the people and progress. "The rights of men and the absolute sovereignty of the people" must be established, he maintained, by eliminating the "interests" from positions of influence in government. Once this was accomplished, he asked the legislature, "How best can we arm the people to protect themselves thereafter?" Then followed, for the first time in a major political speech by Johnson, a long list of specific reform proposals based upon the Republican platform, including a direct primary amendment, the initiative, referendum and recall, employers' liability legislation, a short ballot, and laws regulating railroad rates and the civil service. The high-powered session of 1911 was underway.

Johnson was the dominating figure of the Progressive years in California. The peculiar nature, success and longevity of the movement in the state are largely due to Johnson's leadership and the political organization he developed, and they, in turn, are the product of an unusual background and character.

Johnson was born into a political family. His father, Grove Johnson, was a

 Judson A. Grenier was primarily responsible for the original draft of Chapter 6.

Hiram Johnson (1866–1945) takes oath of office to become twenty-third governor of California. (Courtesy of Bancroft Library.)

successful lawyer and politician in Sacramento, who had ties with the Southern Pacific Railroad. Johnson graduated from the local public high school at the age of sixteen and entered the University of California in 1884. In the midst of his junior year, he withdrew from college to marry and study law in his father's office. Admitted to the California bar in 1888, he joined in partnership with his father and elder brother, Albert M. Johnson, who was brilliant but moody and who later became an alcoholic. The Johnson brothers managed their father's successful campaign for Congress in 1894 but urged him not to run for re-election in 1896, partly because of his Southern Pacific connections. Father and sons split bitterly on the question and remained political enemies the rest of their lives. The elder Johnson became a power in the state Assembly as leader of the conservatives; the two brothers associated themselves with reformers in Sacramento and in San Francisco, where they moved in 1902 to open a law office. Charting an independent course, Hiram established a reputation as trial lawyer and reform politician and a professional association with William H. Langdon, District Attorney. After Francis J. Heney was shot during the San Francisco graft trials, Johnson was appointed chief prosecutor. In this role and in his speeches as a member of the San Francisco Lincoln-Roosevelt League, he attracted the attention of the reformers and was offered the League's backing for the governorship. At first he declined, hesitating to return to Sacramento, fearing financial losses, and privately indicating a preference to run for the Senate. Nevertheless, he reconsidered, and swept to victory in the first statewide nominating primary and the general election by his single-minded, slashing attack on the railroad. The bright red Locomobile, driven by his son, in which he toured the state, became a symbol both of Johnson's progressive outlook and his independence of the Southern Pacific. He would continue to use the automobile in his successive campaigns for Governor and Senator; roaring over unpaved roads, Johnson's political caravans would reach a small town or crossroads, loudly ring a bell to draw listeners, and deliver the message.

Physically, Johnson was short and stocky, with a round, rather pink face; the high celluloid collar he always wore in public gave him the appearance of a bulldog. His behavior enhanced the image. His platform stance was grave, jerky, thrusting, his favorite gesture a pounding of his left hand with his right fist in the Roosevelt manner, as if, according to one observer, "to hammer his talk into his hearers." A fighter, once he determined upon a course of action he rarely changed his mind; just as rarely did he forgive or forget opposition. Believing himself to be a leader of the righteous struggling against the forces of evil, he persuaded the voters of the fact. George Mowry has characterized Johnson as nervous, moody, insecure, pessimistic, self-centered, egotistical, and jealous of potential rivals. His behavior toward Francis Heney and, later, William D. Stephens and Edward A. Dickson, would seem to confirm this impression. On the other hand, Spencer Olin, Jr., has corrected the picture somewhat by showing Johnson in private life as warm, pleasant and loyal to his friends and associates, pursuing his public career at a financial sacrifice to himself.[1]

Johnson's occasional irascibility was matched only by his invective, examples of which are legion. Of *Times* publisher Harrison Gray Otis, he once said:

"Here he sits in senile dementia, with gangrened heart and rotting brain, grimacing at every reform and chattering in impotent rage against decency and morality, while he is going down to his grave in snarling infamy." During the debate over recall of judges, he characterized the American judiciary as "the last stand of corporate aggression." The nature of the campaign run by his Republican opponent for the governorship in 1914, Captain John D. Fredericks, was compared by Johnson to that of a Texas politician who, after promising the moon, concluded, "Those are my sentiments. But if you don't like them, Ladies and Gentlemen, I can damn soon change them." Johnson liked to meet his enemies head on, he tolerated no pussy-footing.[2]

As Governor, Johnson proved honest and courageous; his administration is perhaps the most incorruptible in the history of the state. He held firm personal control of the reins of government. Final decisions in all matters were his, and colleagues were expected to acquiesce. Appointments to state offices also were his; government jobs went only to those who could provide the most efficient service and whose political attitudes were similar to his. Entire allegiance was demanded. If an opponent held an important position, the Governor found a means of dismissing him or of abolishing the position. Records were kept of every member of both houses of the legislature in order to apply pressure for passage of particular pieces of legislation or to reward supporters; it proved effective politics. He and his lieutenants directed legislative activity in a manner his predecessors would have considered unseemly, if not unconstitutional. According to veteran Senate Secretary Joseph A. Beek, during the Johnson administration ". . . subservience to the executive went so far that even the appointment of legislative committees, the awarding of important chairmanships, and the selection of legislative officers were decided in the Governor's office." If necessary, Johnson would intervene in a legislative struggle with a summons. For example. E. A. Dickson recalls that when the fight for women suffrage seemed lost, "Governor Johnson asked the recalcitrant legislators to meet in his office. He then read the sufferage [sic] platform plank on which every one of them had been elected. Bringing his hand down firmly on his desk, the Governor said, 'Gentlemen, you pledged yourself to that plank and you cannot repudiate it now.' That ended the opposition."[3]

Characteristic of the new emphasis on positive leadership was Johnson's creation of a State Board of Control and his request that it prepare for submission to the Legislature "the first budget in the history of California or of any other state in the union." Completed two weeks prior to the convening of the 1913 legislative session, the unified budget proposal contained recommended appropriations for every department in the state government. Johnson and his successor, Governor Stephens, continued the practice of submitting an annual budget until a constitutional amendment wrote it into law. In the first six months of its existence the State Board of Control was called by critics the "wrecking crew," composed of "pseudo friends of the governor." Johnson's answer was that that sort of "wrecking" would be done with his hearty approval.[4]

Through his power of appointment, Johnson helped determine the shape of politics for many years to come. For example, to head the newly-created Industrial Welfare Commission, the Governor named prominent Katherine Philips Edson, president of the California Federation of Women's Clubs. Harris Weinstock, Sacramento businessman who would have been the Lincoln-Roosevelt League's candidate for governor in 1910 had Johnson not accepted, was appointed to a variety of positions, including special commissioner to investigate the Industrial Workers of the World and State Market Director. Former Governor George C. Pardee was chosen chairman of the State Conservation Commission. John Francis Neylan, a twenty-six-year-old legislative reporter for the *San Francisco Bulletin* (Fremont Older's paper), was named first chairman of an agency he had helped create, the State Board of Control. In 1911 Johnson appointed to the office of Superintendent of State Printing the publisher of the *Berkeley Gazette*, Friend Richardson. Richardson reorganized the office and supervised admirably the printing of free school textbooks; in 1914, though registered as a Progressive, he won the nomination for State Treasurer from all three parties and was elected to the first of two terms. In general, the new heads of departments brought a new vigor, honesty and efficiency to the administrative units under their supervision.

The man who merits particular attention as a Johnson protege died before he could fulfill the promise of his early career. John Morton Eshleman of El Centro, Berkeley graduate and lawyer, had been elected to the Assembly in 1907 from Berkeley on an anti-race track platform. His legislative experience made him an indignant foe of the Southern Pacific machine. One of the original members of the Lincoln-Roosevelt League, he ran as the League's candidate for Railroad Commissioner in 1910, and served as chairman of the commission from 1911 to 1914. Johnson, never too happy with Albert J. Wallace as Lieutenant Governor, personally chose Eshleman to be his running-mate in 1914. Holding the second office in the state for more than a year, Eshleman displayed leadership qualities and moral courage. For example, he cast a tie-breaking vote in a 1915 roll call on a "dry zone bill," which would have had the effect of making much of San Francisco dry. Eshleman's vote lost him friends, but he pointed out that San Francisco had recently voted itself wet and that worthy ends do not justify unworthy means. Johnson fully intended Eshleman to be his successor as governor, but the untimely death of the Lieutenant Governor at age thirty-nine in the spring of 1916 put an end to those plans.

The Legislature itself underwent certain changes during the Johnson years.

169

After 1915, party caucuses to name house leaders were discontinued. Passage of a constitutional amendment in October, 1911, established the so-called "bifurcated session," splitting the legislative session into two parts. The first session ran for thirty days, following which the Legislature adjourned for at least thirty days; in the reconvened second session no new bills could be introduced without consent of three-fourths of the legislators and no member could introduce more than two new bills. Evidence suggests that the bifurcated session was the brainchild of Democratic Senator Anthony Caminetti, a progressive who hated the influence of "corporate interests" and hoped that bifurcation would prevent bills being passed with undue speed, recklessness and secrecy. Another 1911 legislative task was the decennial reapportionment; urban areas and southern California were seriously underrepresented in both houses. A deadlock over changes forced calling of a special legislative session. (The controversy produced public debate about secession in the south.) Legislators from rural areas fearing big city, union domination and desiring to protect farming, mining and lumbering interests, finally pushed through a reapportionment measure which again left San Francisco and Los Angeles underrepresented. The struggle was a harbinger of yet more serious rural-urban and north-south quarrels to come. Among the leaders of the Legislature during the Progressive years was C. C. Young of Berkeley, elected in 1913 Speaker of the Assembly, a position he retained until he became Lieutenant Governor in 1918.[6]

The accomplishments of the 1911 California Legislature have become legendary; Theodore Roosevelt called the measures passed "the most comprehensive legislation ever passed at a single session of any American legislature." Foremost among them were statutes and constitutional amendments carrying out Johnson's pledges to lessen the influence of the railroads and provide the people a greater degree of democracy. Two laws and three constitutional amendments gave the state Railroad Commission effective powers to regulate rates charged by the Southern Pacific and other public utilities. In its first year of existence the new Railroad Commission heard and decided more cases than were filed with previous commissions in twenty-five years.

The 1911 Legislature submitted twenty-three constitutional amendments to the voters, many of which were a spur to bi-partisanship and direct democracy. Among them were the initiative, which permitted voters to amend the constitution or enact new laws; the referendum, which placed on the ballot measures already passed by the legislature; the recall, which forced officials into an electoral test of their public support prior to the normal expiration of their terms of office. To generate an initiative, 8% of the number of qualified voters who voted for governor in the last general election was required; only 5% were needed for a referendum. The recall issue generated the most heat prior to the fall election, chiefly because it included recall of judges. The Republican

Party seriously split on the matter; for example, Senator-elect John D. Works branded recall of the judiciary "reform run mad." Making support of recall a matter of party loyalty, Johnson campaigned vigorously for two months for its adoption. His efforts were rewarded at the polls when the voters approved all but one of the amendments, and ratified recall by a three-to-one margin. Also passed in 1911 were woman suffrage, "restoration of the true Australian ballot without party circle or column," non-partisan election of all judges and educational officials, the right of cities to adopt a commission form of government, and a "complete system of direct primary elections, including presidential preference and election of convention delegates."[7]

Additional legislation aimed at political reform was introduced by the Progressives in later years. In 1913 non-partisanship was extended to include city and county officials other than judges. Rationale for local non-partisanship was that there were no "Democratic" or "Republican" techniques for fighting crime, teaching school or picking-up trash; in concerns of city government, supporters argued, party politics actually was an intrusion. The Progressives attempted to bring state elections under the non-partisan blanket in 1915, but Republicans blocked enforcement of the law by filing a petition for referendum. In the subsequent election, state non-partisanship was defeated. But the Progressives had discovered another device, crossfiling, which would serve much the same function. In 1913, anticipating formation of a new political party, they revised the direct primary law to eliminate the requirement that a man be a registered voter in the party whose nomination he seeks. This measure, drawn up by C. C. Young and enacted with little fanfare, altered the makeup of politics in California for nearly a half century. Candidates could file for nomination in the primaries of any and all political parties; party registrations would not appear on the ballot. The immediate purpose of crossfiling was to enable the progressives to retain the Republican label while assuming as well that of the new Progressive Party. In 1914 and 1916, Johnson men could challenge regular Republicans in their primary and, failing to capture enough votes, have another round as Progressives in the general election. In practice, the Johnsonites frequently won both nominations.

The effect, *in toto*, of the progressive political reforms was to seriously undermine traditional politics in the state. The number of partisan offices was reduced from several thousand to about one hundred and fifty. Party leadership was cut off from the grassroots, labels were non-existent or misleading, incumbents or famous-names were given an additional advantage, and party responsibility within and without state government was obliterated. In their idealism, the progressives sought to transfer responsibility for government from the machine to the people: freed of party allegiance, voters would seek out and elect the best men available. But, as Raymond Moley has remarked, the "independent" voter is a myth. "With the parties shackled by law, other forms of collective action were free to invade the political field and claim the loyalty of voters." Long after the Progressive Party faded into the pages of history, its political legacy, improvised and opportunistic, remained.[8]

Until December, 1913, the California Progressives operated within the traditional structure of the Republican Party. But when, on January 23, 1911, the National Progressive Republican League was founded in the Washington home of Senator Robert M. LaFollette of Wisconsin, three Californians, Johnson, Heney, and William Kent, were amongst the charter members. The purpose of the new organization was to garner the GOP nomination for a Progressive in 1912. The California Progressives soon became involved in the three-way struggle between the forces of LaFollette, President Taft and former President Roosevelt for the nomination. Taft made a speaking tour to California in early autumn, 1911, but surrounded himself with conservatives and declined John-son's invitation to stay at the governor's home in Sacramento, thus alienating Progressives already dubious about his record. LaFollette won early support from William Kent and Rudolph Spreckels and, later in 1911, the backing of Heney, Older, Dickson and Rowell, but clearly most of these men, along with Johnson, would have preferred Roosevelt. The former President visited Cali-fornia in March, 1911, spent long hours cementing his friendship with John-son, and toured the state. A luncheon thrown for Roosevelt by Publisher Edwin Earl in Los Angeles attracted all the Progressives in southern California, on whom TR heaped fulsome praise for their recent successes.

On January 14, 1912, Roosevelt asked Johnson to come East for political discussions. In the course of that trip the Governor became convinced of the hopelessness of the LaFollette candidacy and the seriousness of Roosevelt. When a postcard poll of local party workers showed a six-to-one preference for Roosevelt, Rowell called a Roosevelt organizational meeting for late February, 1912. That month, too, E. T. Earl began a publicity campaign intended to produce a Roosevelt-Johnson Republican ticket; his Los Angeles *Express* carried a front-page cartoon showing the two men in a fraternal bond linking east and west with the slogan, "Hands Across the Continent." Under the leadership of Dickson thus began what one student has called "the most extensive campaign in history to secure the nomination of a man for second place on the national ticket." (Ironically, when the ticket finally was forged, the two men wore the colors of another party.) Johnson's candidacy for the vice-presidential spot was enhanced when the Roosevelt slate polled more than the votes of Taft and LaFollette combined in the May primary in California.[9]

From beginning to end of the fateful Republican convention in Chicago in June of 1912, the California Progressives were in the thick of the fight to nominate Roosevelt at any cost. When the Republican National Committee awarded to Taft delegates two disputed positions from San Francisco districts, Committeeman Heney became so livid and volatile that he accused the committee of "crookedness" and had to be restrained from physical violence. In a train on the way to Chicago, the California delegation passed a resolution empowering Johnson to agree to any plan which would place Roosevelt's name on the ballot. While in Chicago, the Governor twice led his delegation out of the convention hall in righteous indignation and, when Taft was nominated by the regulars, took part in the birth of a new Progressive Party. Johnson was given interim charge of the party until its formal convention opened on August 5. Two days thereafter the Governor agreed to run as Progressive candidate for Vice President on a slate headed by Roosevelt.

Formation of a national Progressive Party provoked doubts as to proper party allegiance of the Progressives on the state level. But traditional and practical considerations prevailed, and the Californians decided to campaign nationally as Progressives and locally as Republicans. In spite of vehement Old Guard protests, the Progressives swept the Republican primary on September 3, and, by nominating at least eighty of one hundred delegates to the state convention, assured that Roosevelt's name rather than Taft's would appear on the November ballot as the Republican candidate. Only by writing in Taft's name could a Californian cast a vote for the national nominee. As vice-presidential candidate, Johnson did most of his campaigning out of the state; he delivered 500 speeches in a major cross-country tour. In November, although the nation elected Woodrow Wilson, California was one of six states to be carried by the Roosevelt-Johnson team.

The 1912 campaign was something of a political catharsis, producing both emotional exhaustion and factionalism in the California progressive movement. When the Legislature met in Sacramento for the 1913 session, it clearly lacked the unity of 1911. Within the party structure, men like Spreckels had been alienated and others nursed grievances. For example in the south, E. T. Earl and Meyer Lissner, never very friendly, no longer were working together by 1913. Earl also broke with Rowell and, in 1916, with Governor Johnson himself. In the north, the strongest party members tended to gather around Heney, Congressman Kent and newspaper editor Fremont Older, all of whom had minor disagreements with Johnson which were exacerbated by 1914.

Nevertheless, in 1913 the Progressives, with Johnson's blessing, moved at last to withdraw from the Republican Party. Under continual pressure to do so from regulars, urged on by their own moral convictions, and protected from the most severe consequences by the device of crossfiling, they acted late in the year. Lissner and Rowell carried the argument, and, on December 6, the California Progressive Party was formally organized. Emerging at the very time progressivism nationally was on the wane, it would have a brief and checkered career.

Meanwhile, in the summer of 1913, Heney informed Johnson that he intended to run for either the Senate or the governorship in 1914. Receiving no counsel, in the fall Heney publicly declared for the Senate. The Governor, by this time noticeably cool to the former prosecutor, remarked that he, too, was considering a senate race; if so, countered Heney, he would run for Governor instead. As a way out of the dilemma, Johnson determined to seek re-election as Governor, but with his eye on the senate seat which would become vacant two years hence. To block Heney, Johnson convinced Rowell to compete for the senate nomination in the 1914 Progressive primary. But Heney defeated Rowell easily, enhancing his own prestige and hurting the Governor's. Johnson, undaunted, ran a campaign independent of Heney, forming non-partisan "Johnson-Eshleman clubs" to support his candidacy.

Both men ran as Progressives and both had opposition from regulars in the other two major parties, but the caliber of opposition varied greatly, Heney's being considerably more formidable. The Republicans nominated veteran congressman and publisher Joseph R. Knowland of Oakland, the Democrats former San Francisco Mayor James D. Phelan. Phelan, wealthy. liberal and imbued with a sense of *noblesse oblige*, afforded a striking contrast with the outspoken Heney. Since 1911, he had identified himself closely with the career of Woodrow Wilson. After the 1912 election, the new President appointed Phelan special commissioner to Britain, Germany and Spain. When Wilson offered to name him ambassador to a large European country, Phelan declined, but promised the President to run for the Senate. In the primary and general election, he argued that, given a Democratic President and Congress, a Democratic senator could best serve California. Delivering an average of six speeches daily, Phelan also campaigned for a low tariff, repeal of canal tolls, and Oriental exclusion. It proved successful in making Phelan California's first popularly elected Senator.[10] Results of the 1914 balloting were Phelan, 279,000, Heney, 255,000, Knowland, 254,000, Johnson, 460,000, Fredericks (Rep.), 271,000, Curtin (Dem.), 116,000.

After studying the returns, Heney charged that he was the victim of a Johnson-Phelan plot to exchange support, particularly in the San Francisco area. Scholars who have investigated the charge disagree as to its validity. Olin points out that Heney's accusation against Johnson in 1914 is essentially the same as that made about the Governor by Hughes' forces two years later.

In general, the 1914 election was not a success for Progressives nationally or within California. Of the seventeen initiative measures submitted to state voters, only six were adopted. Among the most important to be rejected were a

Hitting a dusty campaign trail in central California is the Johnson–Eshleman automobile caravan during the election of 1914. The Governor is in the foreground. (Courtesy of Bancroft Library.)

compulsory eight-hour law and statewide prohibition of alcohol. Although Oregon, Washington and Arizona went dry that month, California remained wet by some 130,000 votes; *Sunset* magazine attributed the result to "California's wine industry and San Francisco's robust thirst."[11]

When studying the Johnson years, it is natural to concentrate upon the Progressives, for not only were they in control of the state's administrative machinery, but the newly-introduced constitutional reforms and alterations in the structure of party committees so muddied the political waters that only the Progressive Movement appears to have recognizable shape and thrust. Other political forces, however, were active during the Johnson years.

Republican conservatives, including many of the more wealthy and powerful men in the state, endured the 1911–1912 years, when reform sentiment was at its peak, by bemoaning the takeover of the party by the progressives and attacking "radicals" within and without the party. Led by the triumvirate of conservative newspapers, the *Los Angeles Times*, *San Francisco Chronicle* and *Oakland Tribune*, they compared the Johnson administration to a cowbird in a nest which others had feathered. On the municipal level, particularly in southern California where city government often read like the roster of the local chamber of commerce, regular Republicans remained strong. United States Senator George C. Perkins represented conservative interests nationally until his retirement in 1915, and John D. Works, although elected to the Senate by a Progressive-dominated Legislature, refused to support third-party movements or candidates.

From 1911 to 1913, Progressives dominated the Republican State Central Committee. But at the Republican convention at Sacramento in 1912, thirteen

But There Is!

"HUMPH! THERE AINT NO SICH ANIMAL!"

REPUBLICAN ELEPHANT

PROGRESSIVE BAGMEN'S DUPE

GALE

Old Guard Republicans resented progressives campaigning for both Progressive and Republican Party nominations. In this 1914 cartoon, the *Los Angeles Times*, principal southern California spokesman for the regulars, criticizes progressive perversity. (Courtesy of UCLA Special Collections.)

delegates who favored Taft's candidacy walked out and formed a rival state central committee. Although the rival body was not appointed in conformance with state election laws, the national party gave it official sanction. When, on December 5 and 6, 1913, the Progressives dissolved the legal Republican State Central Committee and formed a new party, Republican regulars were quick to move to regain control. Gustav Grenner and Francis V. Keesling, chairman and vice-chairman of the new central committee, and national committeemen Philip Stanton and, later, William H. Crocker, aided in revitalizing the conservative wing, which dominated the party from 1914 until the state Republican convention of 1916, when the Progressives again captured party machinery.[12]

During the Johnson years, conservative Republicans remained in the minority in the Legislature and retained about half the seats in Congress. "Regulars" made a comeback in 1914–1916, particularly in the south. Movement of rural Midwesterners into southern California, the influence of the anti-Johnson *Los Angeles Times,* aversion of the middle-class voters to the violence displayed in the *Times* bombing and San Diego "free speech" fight, all contributed to growing conservatism in that area. By 1916 the Republican Party clearly was claiming greater support in southern California than it had in 1910; both pro-Hughes and anti-Johnson sentiment concentrated in the south. The conservative majorities run up below the Tehachapis would give southerners greater voice and influence in the Republican Party in the years ahead.[13]

In spite of Woodrow Wilson's victories in California in 1912 and 1916, James D. Phelan's successful campaign for the Senate, and the election of Democratic congressmen from communities as diverse as Santa Rosa, Fresno and San Diego, the Democratic Party was dormant in California. Historian Robert Glass Cleland's judgment that the Democrats "went into a prolonged eclipse in state politics" during the early twentieth century appears valid. Democratic voter registration vis-à-vis the other parties declined; many registered Democrats, such as Francis J. Heney, became Progressives. Traditional sources of Democratic support, rural voters of southern background and city workingmen, were attracted, respectively, by conservative Republican and liberal Progressive candidates. Crossfiling dealt another blow to political machinery already rusty from lack of success in state elections; many a Democratic nomination went to members of other parties. As early as 1911 when visiting California, Wilson remarked: "I can't, for the life of me, in this place be certain that I can tell a Democrat from a Republican." Non-partisanship election reform further blurred party lines, injuring the Democrats in areas where party recognition afforded clues to voting.[14]

Leadership was weak within the Democratic Party; its successful politicians campaigned chiefly as individuals. Phelan ran on his record as Mayor of San Francisco and what he could accomplish for the entire state. Although his warm

Senator James Duval Phelan (with moustache) plays host at his home, Villa Montalvo, near Saratoga, while guests, including Congressman William Kent, Secretary of the Treasury William Gibbs McAdoo, and two prominent liberal poets, George Sterling, and Edwin Markham, demonstrate "flower power." (Courtesy of Bancroft Library.)

hospitality drew many visitors to his Senate office in Washington and his spacious home near San Francisco, party connections were seldom a factor. After he entered the Senate, Phelan's campaigning in California was devoted largely to seeing Wilson returned to office and the Japanese to their homeland. Another progressive Democrat who provided leadership during the first decade of the century, Franklin K. Lane, also was siphoned off to Washington. Lane was serving as chairman of the Interstate Commerce Commission when Wilson selected him in 1913 to be Secretary of the Interior, a position he held until 1920. The party's two-time candidate for Governor, Theodore Bell, had taken on the aura of a loser, and the two men who ran against Johnson in 1914 and 1916, John B. Curtin and George S. Patton, were and remain forgotten men.

Something of the inconstant quality of the party is illustrated by the fact that among the state's most widely-read and influential newspapers were some which were nominally Democratic. A biographer of William Randolph Hearst asserts that by the end of the decade, "with his three great newspapers in California, he virtually controlled the state." But the Hearst press continued to play the maverick, an independent role pursued by the publisher himself in his quest for political power. Hearst claimed to control the delegation to the Democratic convention in 1912, but clearly he was more interested in national politics than in providing leadership on the state level.[15]

The Democratic Party remained progressive in spirit during the Johnson years; party platforms were as liberal as those of the opposition and more so in matters affecting labor. Under Wilson's leadership, the national party pressed for legislation creating an eight-hour day for railway workers, abolishing child labor and exempting unions from anti-trust prosecution. This record won Wilson official support of organized labor in California; wherever unions were strong the national Democratic ticket did exceptionally well. However, these same areas went heavily for Johnson, so state Democrats generally were unable to ride the President's coattails.[16]

Two additional political parties, the Prohibitionists and Socialists, held state conventions, wrote platforms and ran candidates for most offices, polling between ten to thirty percent of the votes each. Often a ballot contained five names, although after crossfiling became common, it was not unusual for a candidate to bear the colors of more than one party. (In the 1914 primary a legislator won the nomination of all five.) Prohibitionist Assembly candidates ran most strongly in southern California, notably Orange County; the party seldom won an election on its own but frequently placed second in votes received.[17]

The Progressive years marked high water for the Socialist Party in the state. With political success came a more temperate attitude and demeanor, and it was often difficult to tell a Socialist from a Progressive by reading a platform or speech. (Conservatives, of course, attempted to link the two.) The party's candidate for President, Eugene V. Debs, received one out of every eight votes cast in California in 1912. That year a Socialist was elected to the Assembly from Los Angeles County; he probably would have won re-election in 1914 had not the Progressives determined to run a candidate in his district. One Socialist senator and two assemblymen were elected in 1914 but lost their seats in 1916. The Socialist assemblymen concentrated upon legislation they deemed beneficial to labor, such as the eight-hour day, a guaranteed job and workmen's compensation.

With the exception of author Jack London, the two best-known Socialists in the state were associated with local politics. The Reverend J. Stitt Wilson, a Methodist minister with a strong sense of the social gospel, won the mayoralty of Berkeley in 1911 with the support of many of the wealthy, middle-class elements in the community. His two-year administration was moderate and efficient, much like that of Milwaukee. Wilson polled 40% of the vote when he ran for Congress in 1912 against prominent conservative Joseph R. Knowland. Perennial candidate for Mayor of Los Angeles was union attorney Job Harriman. On two occasions, in 1911 and 1913, Harriman nearly was elected, the latter year losing by less than a thousand votes. He campaigned in 1911 with the support of the American Federation of Labor and a platform which one historian avows "corresponded to the purposes of the Los Angeles Chamber of Commerce, emphasizing the development of a municipal seaport and a municipal water supply." Harriman won a plurality of the votes in the 1911 primary. Although the major parties concentrated their forces against him, most observers conceded him the election. But four days before the election, the Socialist-backed Mc-Namara brothers confessed to bombing the *Los Angeles Times,* and public outrage contributed to Harriman's defeat.[18]

Decline of the Socialist Party in California after the middle years of the decade may be attributed to many factors: a conservative trend nationally, popular revulsion at the violent tactics of the IWW, which was unjustly linked with the Socialists, "law and order" agitation by business elements, the Mooney trial, and the coming of World War I. Not least important was dissension and dis-agreement within the party itself, particularly over support for arrested radicals and American entrance into the war.

The struggle of labor for better working conditions and effective unionism had political overtones during the Progressive years. The State Federation of Labor and the San Francisco Labor Council were two particularly strong pressure groups with pipelines to the Governor and the Legislature. Many of the reforms enacted by the Progressives originally were proposed by labor spokesmen. In 1911, thirty-nine out of forty-nine labor measures put before the Legislature

Socialist Party headquarters in the Canadian building on Main Street in Los Angeles during the 1911 mayoralty campaign. The man wearing a hat is Job Harriman. (Courtesy of Security-Pacific National Bank.)

were adopted; they included an eight-hour day for women, employers' liability, workmen's compensation, free school textbooks, and restrictions on child labor. In 1913, the Legislature created commissions to examine and control housing, industrial accidents and industrial welfare, and a state labor bureau. Labor also benefited from laws involving old age insurance and pensions for mothers and teachers. Johnson had once been lawyer for several San Francisco unions and was himself sympathetic to unionism, as were most Progressives from northern California, although none of them were drawn from the ranks of unions. The same cannot be said for the Los Angeles Progressives, who tended to be biased against organized labor for fear of the closed shop and labor bossism. Nonetheless, labor leaders throughout the state supported the Progressive Movement and Johnson personally.[19]

Not all workingmen in California were willing to resort to traditional politics to ameliorate their lot. The Johnson years began and ended with well-publicized trials of disaffected radicals, the McNamaras in Los Angeles, and Mooney and Billings in San Francisco, and politics throughout the period was marked by concern over business-labor disputation and violence. Central to the controversy was a fight for and against the open shop.

Judged by its long-range effects, the bombing of the *Los Angeles Times* and subsequent trial is the most important manifestation of the struggle. Whereas San Francisco had long since adjusted to organized labor, Los Angeles in 1910 was strongly anti-union. To labor it was known as a "scab" city; to business, however, as the secretary of the tightly-knit Merchants and Manufacturers' Association testified in 1914, "the open shop is Los Angeles' greatest asset as a creator of a high and consistent level of prosperity." The most effective foe of unionism was Harrison Gray Otis, whose lifelong war against organized labor began in a dispute with *Times* printers in 1890. Labor, in turn, identified the *Times* as its principal antagonist. In 1910 a series of strikes in street railways, breweries and metal trades heightened tensions in the city; and the council passed an ordinance against picketing. San Francisco unions supported the strikers out of fear that the open shop, if maintained indefinitely in Los Angeles, would spread to their city. Early in the morning of October 1, 1910, a blast ripped through the *Times*, setting secondary explosions which destroyed the building and killed twenty men; many more were injured. Promptly Otis and the Merchants and Manufacturers' Association blamed "Unionite murderers" for the blast and dispatched private investigators to track down those responsible. Six months later, three members of the Bridge and Structural Iron Workers Union, Ortie McManigal and James B. and John J. McNamara, were arrested in the East and illegally extradited to California. The McNamara trial began on October 11, 1911, three weeks before the city's primary election, and ended suddenly on December 1, when, at the urging of their lawyer Clarence Darrow and the muckraker Lincoln Steffens, the McNamaras confessed responsibility for the bombing. In addition to its effects upon the election, the confession so demoralized labor that the strikes were crushed, the organizing drive ended, and the open shop maintained in Los Angeles for another three decades. The entire affair encouraged San Francisco merchants to press for the open shop and thus, indirectly, led to the Mooney case. The national shock effect of the *Times* bombing ultimately resulted in creation by Congress in August, 1912, of a Commission on Industrial Relations.[20]

California agricultural and waterfront regions also suffered from labor turmoil during these years, much of it involving the Industrial Workers of the World. IWW organizers usually addressed itinerant farm or dock workers on vacant lots or street corners; if meetings were interrupted by police, they would claim abridgement of free speech. Should city officials throw them in jail for violating ordinances against street meetings, a call would go out to IWW supporters from all over the west to descend upon the area, taxing it beyond limits. These "free speech" fights affected politics wherever they occurred and helped determine results of local elections in Fresno, Oakland, Porterville, and other communities. The most serious incidents took place in San Diego in the spring of 1912. After

Los Angeles Times building on October 1, 1910, after bomb had killed twenty men, destroyed the building, and set off the chain of events leading to the McNamara trial with its far-reaching political consequences. (Courtesy of Security-Pacific National Bank.)

hearing a speech against the IWW delivered by Otis, the city council prohibited street meetings in the downtown section. Inevitably, hundreds of wobblies descended upon San Diego to fill the jails and clog the arteries of the city. Private vigilante groups and the police responded violently, and many workers and radicals, as well as a few bystanders, were brutally beaten. The anarchist Ben Reitman was subjected to mob torture. Governor Johnson dispatched Harris Weinstock to San Diego to investigate, and the commissioner held hearings in mid-April. Weinstock's report condemned actions of all sides in the dispute, but was particularly critical of city officials, the press and the mob.[21]

Most vexing to state authorities of the many incidents involving the IWW was the famous "Wheatland Riot," which occurred on August 3, 1913, on the ranch of a hopgrower named Ralph Durst near Marysville in Yuba County. The largest single employer of agricultural labor in the state, Durst, by circulating alluring advertisements in California, Oregon and Nevada, had attracted 2,800 workers to do the labor of 1,500. Most were poor farmers from nearby, but about one-third were migratory workers. Some twenty-seven languages were spoken. Men, women and children milled about the ranch without adequate food, water, sanitation, toilet facilities or living quarters. About thirty workers formed an IWW local and sponsored a mass protest meeting. IWW member Richard Ford was chosen to demand from the owner such amenities as drinking water and separate toilets for men and women. During the ensuing argument, Ford was slapped by Durst. The following day, while another mass meeting was in progress, a posse arrived from Marysville to arrest Ford and disperse the crowd. After a deputy fired a shot in the air to "sober the mob," a melee broke out, killing the District Attorney, a deputy sheriff and two workers. Governor Johnson dispatched five companies of the National Guard to Wheatland, but the farm workers had scattered before they arrived. State officials employed detectives to arrest numerous suspects around the state. Four men eventually were taken to Marysville for trial, which began in January, 1914. Ford and Herman Suhr, another member of the IWW, were convicted of second-degree murder and sentenced to life imprisonment. The IWW attempted, unsuccessfully, to apply pressure for release of the men by organizing a boycott of California fruit. They then presented new evidence on the case to Hiram Johnson. The Governor agreed that mitigation of the sentence might be justified, but refused to take any steps while "the threats of injury and sabotage continue." Effects of the Wheatland episode were many: it confirmed the public image of the IWW as violent, stimulated middle-class fear of the organization, and led to calls for "law and order" from business associations; it made the IWW chief spokesman for the farm laborer for a decade; it focused attention on the problem of the migrant worker and lent impetus to the work of the new state Commission on Immigration and Housing.

Two years later the city of San Francisco became the focus of violence. A

Preparedness Day Parade, one of many to be held across the nation, was scheduled for July 22, 1916. Among the sponsors of the parade was the local chamber of commerce "Law and Order" committee formed a few days earlier to curtail union activity. Organized labor, believing the parade to be a demonstration for the open shop, denounced it. During the parade a bomb exploded on Market Street, killing ten and injuring fifty others. A few days later, police arrested a left-wing socialist and minor figure in San Francisco labor, Thomas J. Mooney, and four associates, including Warren Billings. In the investigations and trial which followed, some of the individuals connected with the Boss Ruef trials of the previous decade were again involved, and political questions outweighed the pursuit of justice. District Attorney Charles M. Fickert, who originally had been elected to office on his promise to end the Ruef graft prosecutions, sought to convict Mooney and Billings. Fremont Older, editor of the *Bulletin*, who had crusaded against Ruef and later against Ruef's continued incarceration, severely criticized the arrest and trial. Fickert turned preparation of the case over to a private detective for the United Railroads who had been investigating Mooney prior to his arrest. No attempt was made to pursue aspects of the case which did not point to Mooney's guilt; furthermore, Fickert relied upon very dubious testimony, some of it apparently perjured. Walton Bean avers that the District Attorney prosecuted not in good faith but because to convict the widely-hated radicals might make him Governor of California.[22]

Mooney was tried in January, 1917, and sentenced to hang; Billings was given life imprisonment. Many individuals, including Woodrow Wilson's special investigator, believed they were unjustly convicted, victims to the continuing struggle for the open shop. But the specter of the McNamara confessions hung over Mooney; the parallels between the two cases were striking. Older asked Johnson to mitigate the sentences, but the Governor refused. When international protests over the forthcoming execution reached the ears of Woodrow Wilson, the President asked the new Governor, William Stephens, to consider commutation. Mooney was granted a reprieve and, in November, 1918, following both the general election of that year and the armistice, Stephens commuted the sentence to life imprisonment. But most Californians continued to believe in his guilt and not until 1939, twenty-two years after conviction, was Mooney pardoned.

Anti-Japanese sentiment in California still ran strong in 1913. For example, beginning in 1911, a variety of proposals to exclude Japanese immigrants had been introduced by Californians to Congress. In 1912, the *Los Angeles Examiner* set off a wave of hysteria by revealing that a Japanese syndicate was about to buy land fronting Magdalena Bay in Baja California. Other newspapers carried headlines such as "Jap Puts on Airs" or "Yellow Peril in College Town" when Orientals sought to buy urban real estate. Agricultural interests were even more concerned. Ignoring the fact that Japanese farmers had been first to cultivate large areas of the Sacramento-San Joaquin valleys, they charged that a lower standard of living and exploitive techniques were responsible for Japanese economic success. Politicians Chester Rowell, Hiram Johnson, and James Phelan echoed these sentiments. "The problem," as Thomas A. Bailey has written, "was basically one of prejudice against the Japanese as a race."[23]

Thirty-four bills curbing Japanese rights were introduced into the 1913 Legislature; clearly members were bent upon passing some sort of restrictive legislation. In 1911 Governor Johnson had sidetracked such bills in response to requests from Republican Secretary of State Philander C. Knox, who had been angered by Democratic criticism. Now the shoe was on the other foot; Wilson was President, and California Democrats were under pressure to move slowly. About April 1, Johnson switched from an attitude of opposition to alien land legislation to one of support; it must be assumed that his decision was political. The move would be popular with the voters and furthermore, as he later chortled to Roosevelt, would embarrass Wilson. When the usual recess ended, both the Senate and the Assembly passed bills excluding from land ownership aliens ineligible for citizenship (namely Japanese as there had been no legal immigration from China since 1882), but differences between the bills remained to be adjusted. In mid-April both Secretary of State William Jennings Bryan, and President Wilson telegraphed Johnson and the Legislature, asking that Orientals not be discriminated against. On April 23 the President wired the Governor and Legislature requesting leave to send Bryan to California for discussions. The Legislature voted to receive the Secretary, and Johnson invited him to be his guest, but remarked that he doubted the value of the visit because the matter was solely a California concern.

Bryan's mission was doomed from the outset. Before he arrived, Johnson asked Attorney General Ulysses S. Webb and Heney to draft a new bill prohibiting aliens ineligible for citizenship from owning land or leasing it for more than three years. Secretary Bryan arrived on April 28, held long conferences with Johnson, Lieutenant Governor Wallace, President Pro Tem Albert Boynton, Speaker C. C. Young and leaders of all parties, and spoke to a formal meeting of both houses. All the while the Webb bill was working its way through the Legislature. Bryan argued that discrimination against the Japanese would offend Japan and violate a 1911 treaty with that nation. Johnson countered that offense was unjustified and that federal law, by declaring Japanese ineligible for citizenship, had done the discrimination. Senator Lee Gates of Los Angeles thanked the Secretary on behalf of the Legislature for concerning himself with state matters, and, as Bryan left the capital, the Webb bill passed the Senate, 35 to 2, and the Assembly, 72 to 3. Although urged by Bryan to veto the measure, Johnson signed it into law with a statement of support.

Wilsonites considered mounting a referendum, but wary of the fate of issues with racial overtones, decided against it. The San Francisco *Argonaut* estimated that voters would have sustained the law by a margin of five or ten-to-one. Although challenged repeatedly in the courts, the Alien Land Law remained in effect until declared invalid by the California Supreme Court in 1952.

Meanwhile, Johnson's career in state government was drawing to a close. In his 1915 inaugural he proposed little that was new, urging his listeners rather "to perfect, preserve and perpetuate" the various measures already enacted. Much less legislation emerged; significantly, as the 1915 Legislature adjourned, Commissioner Harris Weinstock opened a campaign in San Francisco to nominate Johnson for the Senate.[24]

When the election year 1916 began, the future looked bleak for the Progressives. Nationally, the movement had fallen apart as Progressives returned to the Republican fold. The California Progressives therefore determined to make an attempt at unity. Lissner and Rowell backed a plan to hold the national Progressive Party convention at the same time as the Republican, with a view toward eventually combining forces in a ticket of Justice Charles Evans Hughes for President and Johnson for Vice President. Additionally, negotiations began for a re-combination of forces within California, a movement opposed vitriolically by the Old Guard press. On February 27, Progressive leaders met in San Francisco with a group of Republicans of "forward-looking tendencies" and formed a new group called "United Republicans." The Johnsonites, as Mowry phrases it, "had at least a foot in the door of the Republican party again." In a May primary to choose Republican convention delegates, however, the United slate was soundly beaten by conservatives, leading the Old Guard to assume that Johnson was no longer a force in California politics. This attitude, wishful thinking more than reality, led regulars to make a series of blunders which may have cost their party the presidency.

When both conventions met in Chicago in June, Johnson worked diligently behind the scenes to have Roosevelt nominated by both parties. When the Republicans rejected him for Charles Evans Hughes, and Roosevelt himself rejected the proferred Progressive nomination, Johnson returned to California beaten and discouraged, his friendship with Roosevelt at an end. To help soothe the disappointment, the national Republican steering committee promised Rowell to help clear the path in California for Johnson's election to the Senate, and named Rowell, together with regular Republican, William H. Crocker, as the two national committeemen. Old Guard Republicans in California did not approve, but Johnson publicly announced his support of Hughes.[25]

On July 8, 1916, the last official meeting of the Progressive Party of California was held in San Francisco. The Governor explained to the nearly one thousand delegates the course of events in Chicago, declared that he would support Hughes but did not demand it of them, and asked that they organize within the party of their choice so that the Progressive Movement would endure. He, Johnson, would run for the Senate on both the Progressive and Republican tickets. Delegates then divided into two meetings to organize for Hughes and for Wilson, but both groups endorsed Johnson for the Senate. Republican regulars, meanwhile, had determined to nominate Willis H. Booth of Los Angeles and refused to honor the agreement made by Rowell. The fateful primary would take place only ten days after presidential candidate Hughes made a speaking tour of the state.

Governor Hiram W Johnson

The People's Candidate

for

United States Senator

Born—At Sacramento, Cal., 1866. Educated—Public Schools and University of California. Lawyer—Admitted to practice 1888. Republican Governor—Elected 1910. Candidate for Vice-President on ticket with Theodore Roosevelt in 1912. Re-elected Governor in 1914 by plurality of 189,000—greatest plurality ever given a Governor since the Civil War.

"If I am elected United States Senator, with such vision as I have governmentally, I shall endeavor to represent all our people. I shall be from no locality, nor for any particular locality. I shall be a Californian for California."

Hiram W. Johnson.

With Hiram W. Johnson in the Senate, California will be represented by an experienced executive, an able lawyer, a giant in debate—such a champion as the United States Senate has not seen since Webster.

Campaign literature in 1916 displays Hiram Johnson striking his favorite pose. (Courtesy of UCLA Special Collections.)

The Rumble of California Politics

The Hughes trip to California in August, 1916, has been the subject of more recrimination, debate and analysis than any other political tour in the state's history; that it eventually led to the loss of the state for Wilson and thus, the presidency, is clear. The debate concerns which specific event or individual is responsible for the mistakes and misunderstandings.

Republican conservatives, tasting victory over the Progressives at last, isolated Hughes from Johnson and his supporters. At a public meeting in the Civic Auditorium in San Francisco, Hughes, after being introduced by Crocker, saluted the banker as "San Francisco's favorite son," unwittingly, perhaps, snubbing Johnson. During his two days in the Bay city, Hughes also alienated labor by crossing a picket line (erected by the Central Labor Council) to enter a restaurant displaying a large "Open Shop" sign, and there addressed the Chamber of Commerce, thus apparently aligning himself with anti-union forces in that bitter struggle over the open shop which had disrupted California for a decade. Finally, the following Sunday morning, Hughes and Johnson actually checked into the same Long Beach hotel, the Virginia, without knowing of each other's presence and without meeting. Democrats later circulated the story that the two men met in the lobby and refused to shake hands, but this allegation was untrue. Not until later in the day, after their candidate had left for Los Angeles, did the Hughes men recognize the slight and attempt to arrange a hasty meeting of the two. But by then Johnson was miffed at the behavior of Keesling, whom he considered guilty of a deliberate affront, and rebuffed the offer. Hughes left California without seeing the Governor.[26]

On August 29 it was clear that conservative strategy had backfired. Johnson defeated Booth by 20,000 votes to win the GOP primary; progressives regained control of Republican Party machinery, and at the state Republican convention in September, Rowell was elected to succeed Keesling as chairman of the Republican State Central Committee. In the remaining months before the general election the progressives campaigned for Johnson with greater fervor and conviction than they did for Hughes; the Old Guard Republican press took just the opposite course, not endorsing the Governor, in some cases, until the day before the election. In November, early returns from southern California seemed to favor both Johnson and Hughes, but as the counting dragged on, the Republican presidential candidate's lead dwindled and then disappeared. Wilson had carried San Francisco by more than 15,000 votes, enough to give him victory in the state as a whole by only 3,420 out of a total of 1,045,858. For the first election in the state's history where one million votes were cast, it was a scant margin. But with it went the presidency.

Because Johnson had won by 300,000 votes (carrying fifty-six of fifty-eight counties), regulars charged that he had sabotaged Hughes by failing to campaign adequately for him and by mis-spending party funds. The *Times* called it an "unparalleled political crime." But Johnson had always been something of a "loner"; there is no evidence that he was less active for Hughes than he had been for cohorts in previous elections. Rather, Wilson's victory should be attributed to a combination of factors: his own strength, particularly among women and workingmen; the "peace" vote; the support of San Francisco and the northern counties (he carried forty-two); Hughes' rather cold personality; the Old Guard's overconfidence and snubbing of the progressives; and, finally, less-than-enthusiastic progressive campaigning for Hughes.[27]

For Hiram Johnson to step down from a position of political power—even to assume another—was an onerous task. In July of 1916, he had rather reluctantly appointed Congressman William D. Stephens of Los Angeles Lieutenant Governor; Stephens would succeed him. The south was given the governorship in part because Johnson, like Senator Phelan, was from the northern part of the state. Stephens and his friends were certain the Governor would resign within a month. But when Stephens visited Johnson in December and asked his advice in preparing the annual message to the Legislature, Johnson responded that he intended to remain in office, at least through the first legislative session. Hard words followed, and the two men did not again communicate. January passed, the 1917 Legislature had organized, but Stephens had done nothing but preside; Johnson lingered on. When the Lieutenant Governor's supporters suggested politely that the Governor should live up to his agreement, they were rebuked; when they suggested taking legal proceedings, they received profanity. Johnson told his friends that Stephens was "a Taft" who belonged "body and soul" to E. T. Earl and Dickson.[28]

For two weeks in March, 1917, Johnson served as both Governor and Senator. How long he would have remained in two positions, as he had become accustomed to representing two parties, is difficult to judge. But war with Germany loomed on the horizon, and President Wilson called a special session of Congress to deal with the crisis. Addressing the Legislature for the last time. the Governor said his farewells, paid a final tribute to Eshleman, and relegated the burdens of office to his successor (without mentioning him by name). On March 15, Hiram Johnson did "the most difficult thing of my life." He resigned. A vibrant and colorful era in California politics had come to a close.

FOOTNOTES

1 Chief sources of material about Hiram Johnson and progressive politics are the Hiram Johnson papers in the Bancroft Library at the University of California (Berkeley), the Edward A. Dickson papers at University of California, Los Angeles, and George E. Mowry's *California Progressives* (Chicago: Quadrangle Books, 1963), 344 pp. Also utilized were quotations from Samuel G. Blythe, "Putting the Rollers Under the S.P.,"

The Saturday Evening Post, 183 (Jan. 7, 1911), 6–7; Spencer Olin, Jr., *California's Prodigal Sons* (Berkeley: University of California Press, 1968), 241 pp.; Ralph J. Roske, *Everyman's Eden* (New York: Macmillan, 1968), 598 pp.; and H. Brett Melendy and Benjamin F. Gilbert, *The Governors of California: Peter H. Burnett to Edmund G. Brown* (Georgetown, California: The Talisman Press, 1965), 482 pp.

2   Mowry, *op. cit.*, pp. 126, 149, 213.

3   Joseph Allen Beek, *The California Legislature* (Sacramento: California State Printing Office, 1960), pp. 193–194; E. A. Dickson, "Susan B. Anthony," Dickson MSS.

4   *California Progressive Campaign Book for 1914:* Three Years of Progressive Administration in California Under Governor Hiram W. Johnson (San Francisco: 1914), pp. 15–17.

5   Beek, *op. cit.*, pp. 113–114.

6   Thomas S. Barclay, "The Split Session of the California Legislature," (1931), reprinted in David Farrelly and Ivan Hinderaker, *The Politics of California* (New York: The Ronald Press Co., 1951), pp. 148–149; George W. Bemis, "Sectionalism in State Politics," *The Annals* of the American Academy of Political and Social Science, 248 (November, 1946), 233–234.

7   Joseph P. Harris, *California Politics* (San Francisco: Chandler Publishing Company, 1967), p. 113; *Progressive Campaign Book*, pp. 9–10; *San Francisco Examiner*, February 11, 1911; Letter, John Works to E. A. Dickson, March 6, 1911, Dickson MSS.

8   Dean E. McHenry, "Pattern of California Politics," *The Western Political Quarterly*, I (March, 1948), 51–52; Harris, *op. cit.*, p. 8; Raymond Moley "27 Masters of Politics," (1949), reprinted in Farrelly, *op. cit.*, pp. 225–227.

9   A. Lincoln, "Theodore Roosevelt, Hiram Johnson, and the Vice-Presidential Nomination of 1912," *Pacific Historical Review*, XXVIII (August, 1959), 282.

10   Jean Tully, *The Public Life and Achievements of James Duval Phelan* (Unpublished M.A. thesis, College of the Pacific, 1935), pp. 47–50; Frances A. Groff, "The Senator from California," *Sunset*, 35 (July, 1915), 156–159; Noel Sullivan, "Tribute to James D. Phelan," *Overland Monthly*, 88 (November, 1930), 326.

11   Olin, *op. cit.*, p. 103; Zoeth Skinner Eldredge, ed., *History of California* (New York: The Century History Co., 1915), vol. 4, pp. 462–463; "A Knockout Blow for Booze," *Sunset*, 33 (December, 1914), 1083–1084.

12   Olin, *op. cit.*, p. 94.

13   In "Progressivism and the California Electorate," *The Journal of American History*, LV (September, 1968), 297–314, Michael Rogin compares election returns for 1908 and 1916 and concludes that by the latter year, ". . . the Republican party became more exclusively southern than it had been before the rise of progressivism."

14   Robert Glass Cleland, *California in Our Time* (New York: Alfred A. Knopf, 1947), p. 28; *California Outlook*, X (May 20, 1911), 7.

15   W. A. Swanberg, *Citizen Hearst* (New York: Charles Scribner's Sons, 1961), pp. 276, 337. Also see Robert E. Hennings, "California Democratic Politics in the Period of Republican Ascendancy," *Pacific Historical Review*, XXXI (August, 1962), 267–280.

16   Rogin, *op. cit.*, 310.

17   For details on the Prohibitionists, see Gilman M. Ostrander, *The Prohibition Movement in California, 1848–1933* (Berkeley: The University of California Press, 1957), 241 pp.

18   Ralph E. Shaffer, *A History of the Socialist Party of California* (Unpublished M.A. thesis, University of California at Berkeley, 1955); Earl S. Pomeroy, *The Pacific Slope* (New York: Alfred A. Knopf, 1965), pp. 182–185; see also Ira Kipnis, *The American Socialist Movement, 1897–1912* (New York: Columbia University Press, 1952), 496 pp.

19   *Progressive Campaign Book,* pp. 23–24.

20   Cleland, *op. cit.,* pp. 67–87; Pomeroy, *op. cit.,* pp. 180–182; James Weinstein, *The Corporate Ideal in the Liberal State* (Boston: Beacon Press, 1968), pp. 173–182.

21   On the I.W.W., *San Francisco Call,* February 10 and 19, 1912; Hyman Weintraub, *The I.W.W. in California: 1905–1931* (Unpublished M.A. thesis, UCLA, 1947), pp. 23–49. On Wheatland, Weintraub, *op. cit.,* pp. 66–82; "The Case of Ford and Suhr," *Sunset,* 35 (November, 1915), 853; Woodrow C. Whitten, "The Wheatland Episode," *Pacific Historical Review,* XVII (February, 1948), 37–42; and Walton Bean, *California* (New York: McGraw-Hill Book Company, 1968), p. 296.

22   Bean, *op. cit.,* p. 358; Pomeroy, *op. cit.,* pp. 217–223; see also Richard H. Frost, *The Mooney Case* (Stanford: Stanford University Press, 1968), 563 pp. and Curt Gentry *Frame-Up: The Incredible Case of Tom Mooney and Warren Billings* (New York: W. W. Norton and Company, 1967), 496 pp.

23   On anti-Japanese sentiment, James D. Phelan, "The Japanese Question from a Californian Standpoint," *Independent,* 74 (June 26, 1913), 1439–1440; Kiyoshi Kawakami, "How California Treats the Japanese," *Independent,* 74 (May 8, 1913), 1019–1022; Carey McWilliams, *California: the Great Exception* (New York: A. A. Wyn, 1949), p. 180. On the Webb Act, Thomas A. Bailey, "California, Japan, and the Alien Land Legislation of 1913," *Pacific Historical Review,* I (1932), 37–59; *San Francisco Argonaut,* May 10, 1913, p. 297; and Beek, *op. cit.,* pp. 132–137. Phelan's conviction that "where two races are endeavoring to live side by side, one must take the inferior place, or an irrepressible conflict is precipitated," is a typical attitude.

24   Thomas G. Paterson, "California Progressives and Foreign Policy," *California Historical Society Quarterly* XLVII (December, 1968), 329–342.

25   Gladwin Hill, *Dancing Bear: an Inside Look at California Politics,* (Cleveland and New York: The World Publishing Company, 1968), pp. 67–68; Mowry, *op. cit.,* pp. 219–220.

26   Mowry, *op. cit.,* pp. 222–244.

27   See, for example, the respective Mowry and Olin versions, as well as Cleland, *op. cit.,* 59–66. A. Holman, "The Case of Hiram Johnson: Guilty," *North American Review,* CCV (1917), 186–202, gives a contemporary version, and, somewhat later, F. M. Davenport, "Did Hughes Snub Johnson," *American Political Science Review,* XLIII (April, 1949), 321–332.

28   *Los Angeles Times,* November 16, 1916; Frank Jordan, comp., "Statement of Vote at General Election held on November 7, 1916," (Sacramento: California State Printing Office, 1916), 36 pp.; Bean, *op. cit.,* p. 339; Melendy, *op. cit.,* pp. 319–320.

The Republican Party's California

Governor Hiram W. Johnson resigned on March 15, 1917 to become United States Senator. His successor, William Dennison Stephens, assumed the governorship without either having been elected to it or to the office of lieutenant governor. Born in Ohio, he had served as Mayor of Los Angeles and in 1910, 1912 and 1914 had been elected to Congress from the Tenth District. While in Washington, D.C. he had obtained continued federal support for the San Pedro Harbor development.

John M. Eshleman, who had been elected Lieutenant Governor in 1914, was Johnson's personal choice as his successor should he be successful in his projected Senate race. His death on February 28, 1916 forced Johnson to choose a new lieutenant governor to fill the unexpired term and to succeed him as governor should he win the senate seat.

In announcing his appointment of Stephens on July 18, 1916, the day he qualified for the Senate race, Johnson said:

"After long and earnest consideration, I selected Mr. Stephens because he possesses these sterling qualities so well known to the people of Los Angeles, which will enable him, if he should become Governor, to preserve and perpetuate California's governmental advance."

There is no doubt he gave "long and earnest consideration" to the problem but it remained that Stephens was a bitter pill which had to be swallowed in order to secure the southern Progressive support for his senatorial candidacy. Johnson had preferred H. L. Carnahan of Riverside but southern pressure forced him to accept the decision of forty prominent Progressives who voted 37 for Stephens and 3 for Carnahan. Twelve years later Carnahan finally became

 Royce D. Delmatier was primarily responsible for the original draft of Chapter 7.

Lieutenant Governor—this time being appointed to the post by Governor C. C. Young when Fitts resigned.

A 1948 constitutional amendment provided that when the lieutenant governor succeeded the governor, the President Pro Tempore of the Senate became lieutenant governor. This provision enabled Harold J. "Butch" Powers to become Lieutenant Governor in 1953 when Goodwin J. Knight succeeded Earl Warren as Governor upon the latter's appointment as Chief Justice of the United States.

With Johnson in Washington, Stephens set about preparing to win a term as Governor in his own right in 1918. But Johnson was prompt to demonstrate the control he intended to retain over California politics for years to come. Calling a conference of fifty Progressives loyal to him in November of 1917 he proposed they notify Stephens of their opposition and then announce their support for Chester Rowell. The plan fell through due to Rowell's inability to make up his mind.[1]

The Direct Primary Law of 1909 had made possible the nomination of Hiram Johnson the following year. Sweeping into office in 1911 with large majorities in both legislative houses Johnson quickly made nonpartisan the judicial and public school offices and in 1913 extended this to all county officials. In the same year the Legislature devised that unique California law known as cross-filing, which was to remain until 1959 when the first Democratic Legislature of the twentieth century wiped it out. This law permitted a candidate to file on all party primary tickets, regardless of his own affiliation, which, in fact, was not disclosed. Thus by winning a plurality on the party ticket or tickets other than his own he could win election in the primary providing he also won his own party nomination. If he failed to win his own party nomination he was disqualified regardless of what other party nominations he may have won. This last provision had been written into the law in 1917. Prior to the complete eradication of crossfiling, an amendment in 1952 voted by the electorate required the candidate at least to state his own party affiliation.

The espousing of liberal causes by the progressives effectively stole the thunder from the Democrats during the first two decades of the twentieth century. For while the leadership of the Democratic Party was growing stronger under Theodore Bell, Francis J. Heney, Franklin K. Lane and James D. Phelan, the progressive leaders in statewide rebellion decided to use the Republican Party as their vehicle. Heney joined them but was betrayed by Johnson in the United States Senate race of 1914. In 1918 Heney ran for Governor on both the Democratic and Progressive tickets with Stephens crossfiling for Governor on the Republican, Prohibition and Progressive tickets. On July 16, 1918, San Francisco's Republican Mayor James Rolph, Jr., "Sunny Jim" who had been born and lived in the Mission district "south of the slot", crossfiled on the

193

Republican and Democratic tickets. He became the first gubernatorial candidate to run on the primary tickets of the two major parties. Heney was again the victim since Democratic San Francisco would vote for its popular Mayor in preference to him.

In December, 1917, Congress submitted to the states the National Prohibition Amendment that became an issue in the California gubernatorial elections the following year. During the latter years of the decade the California Anti-Saloon League was headed by the Reverend Daniel M. Gandier, a Presbyterian minister who bore the title of "State Superintendent" of the League. Progressives Dr. John Randolph Haynes, Marshall Stimson and Chester Rowell all served as officers. In 1918 Gandier sought to unite the drys behind a governor and lieutenant governor who were pledged to ratification of the Eighteenth Amendment. Stephens, an out and out dry, received the League's endorsement for governor while Speaker of the Assembly Clement Calhoun Young of Berkeley got the nod for lieutenant governor. The popular Rolph was a wet.

A second issue in the campaign was the scheduled execution of the supposed

Mayor James Rolph, Jr. (1869–1934) handling the trowel in the laying of the cornerstone for the San Francisco City Hall in 1913. The City Hall had collapsed when the devastating earthquake and fire of 1906 had left most of San Francisco in ruins. It was the only major building destroyed by the quake—not by the fire that followed. Thanks to style-loving Rolph, European stonemasons and craftsmen were brought over to embellish the new building and give it the finishing touches that distinguish Europe's public buildings and palaces. (Courtesy of *San Francisco Examiner*.)

Governors also lay cornerstones. Here is Governor C. C. Young (1869–1947) performing the feat some fifteen years later than Rolph. (Courtesy of *San Francisco Examiner*.)

Preparedness Day bomber, Tom Mooney. Stephens stayed the execution until December 13, well after the elections, claiming more time was needed to study the case. Rolph charged that this action was a cheap political trick to avoid an unpopular decision. Stephens later commuted Mooney's sentence to life imprisonment.

Stephens won the Republican, Prohibition and Progressive nominations beating Rolph by 21,952 in the former and Heney by 1,724 in the latter. Heney was beaten by Rolph in the Democratic primary 74,955 to 60,662 with San Francisco voting for Rolph 17,469 to Heney's 6,870. But Rolph, having failed to win his own party nomination, was disqualified as the Democratic Party nominee.

A fight developed within the Democratic Party between Rolph and Heney supporters. Even though the Democratic voters had shown their preference for the San Francisco Mayor, the Democratic State Central Committee, despite the efforts of powerful San Francisco Democrat Gavin McNab, endorsed Heney. This squabble proved to be much ado about nothing since the Secretary of State Frank C. Jordan ruled that neither could stand in the general election having been defeated in the primary. Rolph and Heney appealed this ruling to the Supreme Court which decided unanimously that the statutes were constitutional. The star of the Democratic Party had sunk so low that it failed to qualify a candidate for governor in the 1918 general election. From this time through 1930 California belonged to the Republican Party.

Rolph took his defeat hard. Although his 39% was far from a majority he had won pluralities over the others having beaten Stephens in total votes by 35,008 and Heney by 157,865. Theodore Bell of Napa, attorney for the California Wine-growers Association and Democratic nominee for Governor in 1906 and 1910, rounded up enough signatures of registered voters not voting in the primary to qualify him as an Independent. But even with the Democratic State Central Committee endorsement he was beaten by Stephens and polled only 39% of the vote in the general election.[2] It was under these circumstances that Stephens became the first gubernatorial candidate since 1898 to win by a majority vote in the general election. Beginning in 1918, and continuing to the present, only Merriam in 1934 has not gained a majority vote in the general election.

The 1918 campaign had its effects on the Democratic Party organization in 1920. Since election of the various county central committees is based upon the vote cast for the party nominee for governor, the failure of the party to put forth a candidate left the county clerks in a quandry.

The Anti-Saloon League had not stopped at electing a governor and lieutenant governor but had extended its campaigns to the Legislature where it succeeded in electing a clear majority pledged to ratification. In 1919 Stephens and Young battled vigorously for the Prohibition Amendment and gained Senate approval 24 to 15, and won 48 to 28 in the lower house. Frederick M. Roberts, Republican of Los Angeles, the first Black ever elected to the California Legislature where he served from 1919 to 1933, cast his first legislative vote in favor of ratification. A victim of the flu epidemic that was sweeping the country, he had been carried in on a stretcher to record his vote even though it was not a deciding one.

Thus the California Legislature buckled under the pressure of a militant minority despite the fact that the electorate in 1914, 1916 and 1918 had refused passage of Prohibition propositions. Its action, however, was not nationally significant since within three days twelve more states had voted ratification and Prohibition was part of the United States Constitution. The Prohibitionists gained their strength by linking with the Progressives and reached their peak of power in California during 1918–1919. By the end of 1920 Gandier had died and the whole crusade was crumbling. Enforcement, in what had been the wettest state in the Union, was, to say the least, not enthusiastic and California became a bootlegger's paradise. The main sources of supply during the early 1920's were Canada and illicit stills.[3]

Liquor even flowed freely at the 1920 Democratic National Convention that opened in San Francisco June 28, 1920, the first of three major party nominating conventions to be held in that city. Only five of a total of seventy national conventions have been held west of the Mississippi.

The California delegation to the Democratic National Convention in 1920 was led by Edward L. Doheny, later to be involved in the Teapot Dome scandal.

John B. Elliott, who was Collector of the Port of Los Angeles under the Wilson administration, led the fight for William Gibbs McAdoo, Wilson's Secretary of the Treasury. On the forty-fourth ballot James M. Cox, wealthy Ohio publisher and Governor of that state, secured the nomination. The California delegation, still battling over their "Crown Prince," split thirteen for McAdoo and thirteen for Cox. Doheney and six others were nominated for vice president but when Cox suggested Franklin Delano Roosevelt, then Assistant Secretary of the Navy, the other six withdrew.

The progressives reentering the Republican fold in 1916 signalled the start of a bitter intraparty fight between the regulars and the deserters. While Johnson won the Senate seat that year Hughes lost the state. The years following were downhill for the progressives although Stephens lasted until 1922 and Young was able to win in 1926.

The split over the League of Nations and over Johnson's new supporters were merely symptoms of a much deeper antagonism. In the Legislature the old conservative forces were creeping back into control where they would remain until 1959.[4]

The major split in state politics during the years 1910 to 1930 was between the conservatives and the progressives in the Republican Party. Overcome during the 1910's by the avalanche of Johnson Progressives the conservatives were finding their way back to power aided by the complacency which stemmed from prosperous times. By 1923 Friend W. Richardson had become Governor

Governor Friend W. Richardson (1865–1943) strolling through Capitol Park in Sacramento. (Courtesy of *San Francisco Examiner*.)

and Frank F. Merriam was presiding as Speaker although the Senate remained in progressive control. A veteran reporter commented: "It looks like old times around the corridors and hotel lobbies. No legislator needs to pay for meals anymore. The old guard has come out of its hole at last."[5]

Californians exhibited the same attitude toward state government that Americans showed toward their national government. One writer observed: "Legislatures met with calendrical regularity but enacted few measures of much moment." The conservative wing of the Republican Party grew in strength as the split between the Johnson-Stephens progressives widened. The old-guard Republicans numbered among their leaders William H. Crocker, son of Charles Crocker, and a leader of the San Francisco aristocracy; Joseph R. Knowland, publisher of the *Oakland Tribune*; Herbert Fleishhacker, prominent San Francisco banker; and Michael H. deYoung, publisher of the *San Francisco Chronicle*.

In 1920 Johnson went so far as to endorse Samuel M. Shortridge for the United States Senate because both opposed the League of Nations. On August 2, 1923 President Warren Gamaliel Harding died at the Palace Hotel in San Francisco. The Progressive Voters League was set up as an anti-Richardson group and was involved in 1924 in a bitter fight for control of the Assembly. In 1925 Merriam was reelected Speaker by a vote of 40-39. It could not have been closer. The progressives were on the way back. Chester Rowell, Rudolph Spreckels, and Franklin Hichborn were all prominently identified with the new League. With C. C. Young's victory over Richardson in 1926 the progressives took new hope. The 1926 triumph was a solid achievement, since it was the only time in the twenty years between 1922 and 1942 that a liberal Republican won the Republican gubernatorial nomination in the primary elections. Rolph's 1930 victory pointed to the demise of the progressives although people did not realize it at the time.[6] Johnson personally weathered all changes and remained in the Senate until his death but in other elections in the 1930's the Democrats gradually unseated both conservative and progressive Republicans.

The 1920 United States Senate race proved to be a debacle for both the progressives and Prohibitionists. A. J. Wallace, William R. Kent and Shortridge were the Republican candidates. Wallace, a former Los Angeles councilman, had served as lieutenant governor during Johnson's first term and was an ardent prohibitionist. Kent had served as a Progressive congressman and campaigned on a prohibition enforcement platform. Shortridge, both conservative and wet, won the primary with a plurality of 22,000 over Kent running second to the dismay of both the drys and the progressives for the combined votes of Wallace and Kent would have swamped Shortridge. The latter went on to defeat incumbent Senator Phelan, the one statewide Democratic victor of the 1914 elections. Phelan had been supported by William Randolph Hearst; Daniel C. Murphy,

United States Senator Hiram W. Johnson (1866–1945) participated in the Harding campaign for the presidency in 1920 which one columnist called "an army of pompous phrases marching across the landscape in search of an idea." (The cartoon is by John Knott in the *Dallas News*, October 2, 1920.)

President of the California State Federation of Labor; Chester Rowell, former chairman of the Republican State Central Committee; Dr. Aurelia Reinhardt, President of Mills College; and John Francis Neylan, publisher of the *San Francisco Call*. Phelan was considered the liberal in the race although he was against Japanese immigration and against any Oriental owning land.[7]

Five straight Republican one term governors were to be elected during these years of fractious discord among the conservatives and progressives. The first three, Stephens, Richardson and Young, were defeated in their own party primaries. In 1922, Johnson was seeking his second term in the Senate while Stephens was seeking a second term as Governor. Johnson won easily but Stephens lost the party nomination by 25,000 votes to Friend William Richardson, publisher of the *Berkeley Gazette* and State Treasurer since 1914. His victory with the backing of the *Los Angeles Times–San Francisco Chronicle–Oakland Tribune* axis, coupled with Shortridge's election to the Senate two years earlier, placed the conservatives back in strong control of the Republican Party.

During the nineteen-twenties the governor received additional budgetary powers which gave him a powerful tool in his relationships with the Legislature. In 1911 the Legislature created the State Board of Control which supervised the business actions of all state departments. The Legislature in 1921 created five new state departments among which was the Department of Finance. The State Board of Control constituted the governing body of this new department. Prior to the year 1911 there were no California state budgets. With the creation of the Board of Control in 1911 and continuing through the year 1921, came a period of informal budgets. In 1922 certain organizations led by the Commonwealth Club of San Francisco secured the adoption of an initiative measure providing for an official state biennial budget which the governor had to submit to the Legislature. The first two such budgets were incomplete, covering a little more than half of the actual expenditures of the state. The budget of 1923 submitted by the Governor totalled less than $79,000,000 for the biennium whereas the total of state expenditures exceeded $142,000,000. The budget submitted in 1925 totalled over $103,000,000 while expenditures actually totalled over $180,000,000. Governor Richardson in submitting these two budgets did not want the complete state expenditures to be known. He had run as an economy candidate, and claimed he was cutting everything to the bone, much as another economy minded Governor some forty-four years later. Richardson, in fact, vetoed forty-nine increases in the budgets that had been voted by the Legislature. In his first budget message of 1923, Richardson declared that extravagance in educational matters had run riot during the Stephens administration, and he urged that two state colleges at San Luis Obispo and at Humboldt be closed. They were not.

It was not until 1927 that Governor Young submitted to the Legislature a complete budget covering every state expenditure. Also in that year, on July 27th, the creation of the office of the State Director of Finance was provided for by the Legislature. The State Board of Control was no longer to be the governing body of that Department. Since that time the State Board of Control has handled the payment of just claims against the state. The 1929 budget established a new precedent in the presentation of the state's budgets. Each state agency had to send its requests for expenditures for the coming budget period to the Department of Finance. This placed in the hands of the governor control over budget requests so that proposed expenditures did not depend upon political influence being exerted upon the Legislature.[8]

In the forty-eight years beginning in 1922 the *Times–Chronicle–Tribune* axis, sometimes known as the Chandler–Cameron–Knowland axis after the publishers of the three giants of the state's Republican press, lost only four gubernatorial elections. Harry Chandler relied heavily on the advice of Kyle Palmer, the paper's political editor who engineered the 1922 coup which defeated Stephens. The stand-pat conservatism of the axis was later tempered to a degree by Paul C. Smith (1935–1952), Executive Editor and General Manager of the *Chronicle*, who exercised a great deal of influence on George T. Cameron (1925–1955), son-in-law of de Young.[9]

The *Los Angeles Times* is now in its fourth generation. Founded on December 4, 1881, its editor the next year was Colonel Harrison Gray Otis, from Iowa and a veteran of the Union Army. By 1886, he owned the paper. Bull-voiced, with a fluttering goatee and a quivering walrus mustache, Otis never left anyone in doubt as to where he stood:

> Los Angeles wants no dudes, loafers and paupers, people who have no means and trust to luck, cheap politicians, failures, bummers, scrubs, impecunious clerks, bookkeepers, lawyers, doctors. We need workers! hustlers! Men of brains, brawn and guts! Men who have a little capital and a great deal of energy—first class men![10]

Otis fought to make San Pedro a free harbor for Los Angeles in order to beat Southern Pacific. Followed by his son-in-law, Harry Chandler in 1917, the *Times* took an even stronger role in state politics. During his regime Los Angeles, as rich and as make believe as the movie industry which was a large part of it, experienced its dramatic and gaudy growth. Other industries which would boom included oil and aircraft. To provide water for these industries and the people who would migrate to the southern part of the state to become part of it all, Chandler and the *Times* assisted in engineering one of the greatest water "steals" in history, the Owens Valley project.[11]

Chandler was succeeded in 1945 by his son Norman whose wife Dorothy "Buffie" Chandler played a dominant role in both the political management of the paper and in civic affairs. Norman became a most active supporter of Republican personalities, and he was largely responsible for finding and developing Richard Nixon into national Republican prominence. Meanwhile "Buffie" was developing the culture of Los Angeles with civic auditorium and music center projects totalling $55 million.

The fourth generation brought great grandson Otis Chandler to the helm of the *Times* in 1960. A champion shot putter at Stanford in 1949 and 1950, Otis Chandler began to chart a new course for the Far West's most financially success-ful newspaper. It has become crystal clear, since the advent of Ronald Reagan, that the paper does not necessarily endorse Republicans nor does it necessarily continue support after endorsement. The *Times* has not been hesitant in its criticism but has reacted with caustic comment on various Reagan policies.

While the Republican Party was enjoying forty years of naming California's governors, the Democrats had lapsed into a feeble and somewhat silent minority. Many workers were afraid to let their employers know of their affiliation. At the state level it was the most unsuccessful Democratic Party in the country. And despite the fact that for the last thirty-six years it has held a three to two edge in registration over the Republicans, it has only elected two governors in the seventy-six years since James H. Budd was elected in 1894.

It is easier to relate these facts than to explain them. Seldom does a glimmer of understanding penetrate the gloom that most Democrats in the state believe is their special kind of purgatory. Churchill once observed that "Russian policy is a riddle wrapped in a mystery inside an enigma."[12] There are many who feel this diagnosis might well apply to the Democratic Party of California. Raymond Moley commented "No one can control the Democratic Party of California because no one knows what it is."[13] Will Rogers, whose humor achieved greatness because of the accuracy of his barbs, once said "I am a member of no organized political party, I am a California Democrat." He also observed about the National Democratic Party that:

> Everybody is always asking, "What's the matter with the Democratic Party?" There ain't nothing wrong with it. The only thing wrong with it is the law killed it. It won't let a man vote but once, and there just ain't enough voters at one vote each to get it anywhere.[14]

During the entire decade of the 1920's the Democrats held no United States Senate seat and were able to elect only two congressmen and six state senators and twenty-two assemblymen. Of 703 national and state partisan elections in those years they won only 57 or 8%. In 1930 the entire Republican state-wide ticket headed by Mayor Rolph of San Francisco was elected. Out of 121 partisan offices up for election in the state that year only ten Democrats, one congress-man, three state senators and six assemblymen, were elected. California was virtually a one party state.

The ten elected were all from northern and rural counties. Clarence F. Lea of the First Congressional District was in 1932 halfway to accumulating a Cali-fornia record for congressmen of sixteen consecutive terms in the House. His home county of Sonoma also continued to send Democrat Herbert W. Slater, blind journalist, to the State Senate repeatedly while Siskiyou maintained

Partisan Election in California 1920–1930 Democratic Party Candidates Won 57 of 703

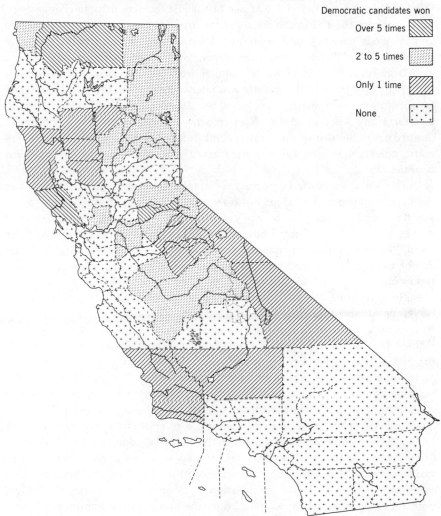

Democratic candidates won

Over 5 times

2 to 5 times

Only 1 time

None

Democratic State Senator James M. Allen for many years. These two counties also sent Democratic assemblymen to Sacramento three times during the decade, and as a result accounted for eighteen of the total fifty-seven Democratic electoral victories or 32% during the decade. Political success of these Democrats was due to their personal popularity rather than their party affiliation which they apparently played down since neither of these counties showed anything near a Democratic majority in registration after its introduction in

1922. In fact no county was Democratic until 1932. Sonoma did not become Democratic until 1942, and it was one of the last four counties to change over.

Throughout the 1920's the metropolitan areas of Los Angeles, San Francisco and Alameda counties sent solid Republican delegations to both legislative houses, and the House of Representatives, with three exceptions. One was a lone Democratic State Senator, the popular Irish Catholic Daniel C. Murphy of San Francisco's Mission District. He was later to become Sheriff and a candidate for Governor. San Francisco also elected two Democratic Assemblymen, John B. Badaracco and Joseph F. Burns. No Democrat had been elected in Los Angeles County since the turn of the century, and during the 1920's only three Democratic one-term assemblymen were elected from any of the ten southern counties.[15]

During these years the Democrats were split asunder by factionalism. True the Republicans had their splits but they managed to solidify sufficiently a few months each alternate year to win the elections. The liberal Democrats were unable to unify behind any leadership for they had no real liberals to unite them. Phelan was anti-Oriental and McAdoo was a dry. It was observed that during these years a liberal was ashamed to be a Republican and afraid to be a Democrat.

Nativism became a political issue once again following the First World War. Governor Stephens jumped on the bandwagon provided by the McClatchy Newspapers, the Native Sons and Daughters of the Golden West, the State Grange, the American Legion and the California State Federation of Labor and urged anti-Oriental legislation. Stephens, while disclaiming any pretensions of racial superiority, still was upset at the spectacle of white children acquiring their education in classrooms crowded with Japanese. The Alien Land Acts of 1913 and 1921 made it impossible for aliens ineligible for citizenship to acquire land by lease or purchase. This was designed to restrict the Japanese. Also in 1921 a Senate Joint Resolution passed the State Legislature and was sent to Congress saying that both Americans and Japanese had agreed upon the unassimilability of the two races and that continued friction between the two races made it imperative that immigration be stopped. Johnson and Shortridge, with the support of Henry Cabot Lodge, the conservative Republican leader of the United States Senate, were able to secure exclusion with the passage of the Immigration Act of 1924.[16]

One of the two groups jockeying for power within the Democratic Party of California during the nineteen-twenties was the southern Democrats in the state. This group was led by McAdoo who was originally from Georgia, and was Woodrow Wilson's son-in-law. Associated in the New York City law firm of McAdoo, Cotton and Franklin he left there in March, 1922, and moved to Los Angeles where he established the firm of McAdoo, Neblett and O'Connor. His

Governor William D. Stephens (1859–1944) delivering a patriotic message during the First World War. (Courtesy of *San Francisco Examiner*.)

decision to migrate stemmed from the realization that to compete with the rising star of Governor Alfred E. Smith of New York would be the height of foolishness. Accordingly he set out to put together a political group that would enable him to lead a delegation to the 1924 Democratic National Convention. Hamilton H. Cotton, originally from Illinois, George Creel, originally from Missouri, John B. Elliott, originally from Kansas, Colonel William H. Neblett, originally from Virginia, and James F. T. "Jefty" O'Connor, originally from North Dakota, joined him.

In the presidential preference primary of 1924 the list of delegates pledged to McAdoo was headed by former Senator Phelan and included the Santa Barbara publisher Thomas M. Storke and Cotton, now a power in Los Angeles County Democratic Party politics. The McAdoo slate won by 112,000 to 19,000 over an unpledged delegation. This set the stage for the famous 103 ballot marathon at Madison Square Garden.

Humorist and Democrat Will Rogers commented on two sets of delegates for McAdoo, the Texans and Californians:

The Texas delegation arrived on burros headed by that fearless old states-
man, Amon G. Carter, the genial dirt farmer of Shady Oaks, Texas (whose
forty acres is on the principal street of downtown Dallas). Amon is National
Committeeman, delegate, alternate, steering wheel, banker, receiver, and
wet nurse for the Texas delegation. They have taken over the Sherman
Hotel and have generously allowed the California delegation to spread their
bed rolls out in the halls, so that they can stand guard over the Texas
delegation.[17]

At the convention McAdoo at one point had within twenty-one votes a
clear majority of the delegates but was still 204 votes short of the necessary two-
thirds. The deadlock that eventually cost him the nomination was due in part
to the so-called "Smith lie," or at least so most McAdoo supporters contended,
that McAdoo was the candidate of the Ku Klux Klan. This in face of the fact
that he was strongly endorsed by Bernard M. Baruch, a Jew, and Phelan, a
Roman Catholic. But McAdoo refused to make a strong anti-Klan statement.

Certainly McAdoo's candidacy was not helped by the disclosure that he had
accepted substantial retainers from Edward L. Doheney, one of the oil magnates
mired in the Harding scandals. Doheney, a benefactor of the University of
Southern California, was a businessman who dabbled in politics, playing both

United States Senator James D.
Phelan (1861–1944) being intro-
duced by United States Senator
Thomas J. Walsh of Montana
(1859–1933) at the Democratic
National Nominating Convention
of 1924 in order to nominate
William Gibbs McAdoo (1863–
1941). (Courtesy of United Press
International.)

sides, for economic advantage. In 1916 he headed the electors for Wilson. In 1920 he headed the California delegation to the Democratic National Convention. During the early 1920's his association with the Harding administration was well known. When the Teapot Dome and Elk Hills oil scandals broke in 1923 the main participants were Harry F. Sinclair and Doheney. Also involved were Secretary of the Interior Albert B. Fall and Secretary of the Navy Edwin Denby. During the Senate hearings in the spring of 1924 it was testified that McAdoo had an annual $25,000 retainer from Doheney who was serving as vice chairman of the Democratic State Central Committee. At the National Convention Smith supporters in the balcony constantly jeered "Oil, oil, oil" at every mention of McAdoo.[18]

The *Springfield Republican* insisted that had it not been for oil McAdoo would have received the nomination. Mark Sullivan was of the same opinion. Historian Kenneth C. McKay later wrote:

> Although from a legal point of view, and perhaps as well, from an ethical point of view, McAdoo was justified in accepting a fee for his legal services, the effect upon the public, failing to distinguish between the service that McAdoo performed for Doheney, and the "service" that men like Albert B. Fall had been performing, was instantaneous.[19]

The Smith–McAdoo deadlock not only resulted in the nomination of John W. Davis but also the hatred McAdoo felt for Smith which was not redressed until another Democratic convention eight years later. As one reporter in 1924 quipped, McAdoo went to his father-in-law's funeral and then to his own. Wilson had died twenty-one weeks before.

Returning to California, the McAdoo group rallied sufficiently to elect the chairman of the State Central Committee in 1924, State Senator Claude F. Purkitt of Willows. This was to be their last major triumph within the party until 1932 when they again swept into power. As for John W. Davis, he was overwhelmingly trounced in the Golden State. Coolidge received 733,000 while LaFollette, running on the Socialist ticket, polled 425,000 and Davis was a poor third receiving only 106,000, or 8%.

The defeat of the national ticket in California in 1924 is a stellar example of the inability of the Democrats to unify and rally behind a single candidate. The dissension among various groups of leaders not only marked defeat in this election but has been the downfall of the party in numerous elections before and since.

In the 1924 election many leading Democrats, some to become even more prominent, deserted the party entirely to support LaFollette. Among these were Rudolph Spreckels, San Francisco banker and progressive leader; Frank R. Havenner, later to serve as Congressman from San Francisco; Franklin Hichborn, newspaper writer and progressive leader from Santa Clara; Culbert L. Olson, later to be State Senator from Los Angeles and Governor; Sheridan Downey, who was to become United States Senator in 1938; Jesse W. Carter, who would become State Senator from Redding and Associate Justice of the State Supreme Court; and Seth Millington, Jr., and Chester Gannon, who would later become members of the ten man Economy Bloc of the Assembly during the 1939–1942 Olson administration.

California was one of eleven states where LaFollette won over Davis. In California LaFollette even beat Coolidge in fifteen northern counties including Sacramento.

Justus S. Wardell, native San Francisco stock broker, and Surveyor of Customs for San Francisco and then Collector of Internal Revenue for the northern district under Wilson, headed the second main faction within the Democratic Party during this decade. Bitterly opposed to the first group, it was composed principally of native Roman Catholics centered in the north. Wardell had been an early supporter of Phelan backing him for Mayor and United States Senator and also was a leading supporter of Alfred E. Smith.

Wardell's group was aligned with a southern group headed by Isidore B. Dockweiler, also a Catholic and an elderly attorney for the Southern Pacific, who led the campaign for Davis.

Dockweiler served as Democratic National Committeeman for sixteen years beating back challenges by McAdoo in both 1924 and 1928. Throughout these years prohibition was to be a troublesome and emotional issue interwoven through the whole fabric of California politics. The wets in the Democratic Party were led by Wardell and Dockweiler while McAdoo and John B. Elliot espoused the dry cause. Southern California, in contrast to the north, generally supported prohibition and in 1928 Elliott forced a dry plank through the state convention even though Smith had won the presidential primary.

The Wardell group had been dominant in the party during the 1926, 1928 and 1930 elections. Wardell had run for governor in the 1926 primary eliminating McAdoo-sponsored Carl Alexander Johnson by 8,000 votes only to be soundly trounced by C. C. Young in the general election. Dockweiler, running a campaign independent of Wardell, sought the nomination for United States Senate and lost to Elliott who then failed to unseat the Republican incumbent. Phelan, who in 1924 had nominated McAdoo, supported Dockweiler. During these six years the Wardell group maintained control of the State Central Committee electing Henry H. McPike of Alameda in 1926 and 1928 and Dr. Zachary T. Malaby, Pasadena physician, in 1930.

In the presidential primary of 1928 the Wardell group pledged to Smith swamped a McAdoo group pledged to Senator Thomas J. Walsh of Montana by 134,000 to 47,000, with the Senator James A. Reed of Missouri group coming

United States Senator Samuel M. Shortridge (1861–1952) campaigning for reelection in 1926. (Courtesy of *San Francisco Examiner*.)

in second with 60,000. Walsh had supported McAdoo to the bitter end in 1920 and 1924. The Walsh delegates had also included Elliott, Creel, and famous California novelist, Kathleen Norris, while the Reed group had been led by Milton K. Young, Los Angeles attorney, and William P. Hubbard of San Francisco, chairman of the Executive Committee of the Democratic State Central Committee. Walsh, one of the heroes of the Teapot Dome exposé, died in 1933 at the age of 73 while on a train in South Carolina enroute from Cuba to Washington, D.C. to accept the appointment as Attorney General in Franklin Delano Roosevelt's cabinet. He had just married a young Cuban bride.

The 1928 Republican convention at Kansas City pitted Secretary of Commerce Herbert C. Hoover against the field. The list of the California Republican delegation pledged to Hoover was headed by Marshal Hale, San Francisco merchant, as northern chairman, and Charles C. Teague, agriculturist from Santa Paula, as southern chairman. Heading the list of delegates was Governor C. C. Young. Other prominent Republicans on the delegation were: Lieutenant Governor Buron R. Fitts; Will C. Wood, State Superintendent of Banks; Frank P. Flint, former United States Senator; John R. Quinn, former national and state commander of the American Legion; Richard E. Collins, chairman of the State Board of Equalization; Charles L. Neumiller, chairman of the Republican State Central Committee; Mayor James Rolph, Jr. of San Francisco; Joseph R. Knowland; Chester H. Rowell; and Louis B. Mayer, motion picture magnate. The majority of the delegation was also pledged to support Hiram W. Johnson in his bid for reelection to a third term. Heading that list was Governor Young, who time and time again had publicly declared his affection for Johnson. The formation of the Hoover ticket was the result of numerous conferences throughout the state that united all factions of the party behind Hoover. But through these conferences the friends of Johnson were able to keep off the ticket some of the more vindictive Johnson antagonists who had been anxious to be selected as delegates: former Governor Richardson; Edward A. Dickson and Harry Chandler, both publishers from Los Angeles; J. O. Hayes of San Jose; and William H. Crocker. Crocker was going anyway as Republican National Committeeman. Hoover's candidacy got a big boost when William Randolph Hearst, usually a Democrat, noted that Hoover was the best man for the job. Hoover was nominated by John L. McNab of Palo Alto, California. Senator Charles Curtis of Kansas was ratified for the second spot on the ticket which gave the team two firsts: Curtis was the first Indian candidate for such high office, and Hoover and Curtis made up the first and only western ticket in history. In the same year Hiram Johnson won his third smashing victory to the United States Senate.[20]

At the 1928 Democratic convention at Houston, Franklin Delano Roosevelt nominated Al Smith, "the Happy Warrior," and the convention took Smith's choice for Vice President, Senator Joseph Robinson of Arkansas. Robinson was the first from one of the seventeen Southern and border states to be nominated by one of the two major political parties since 1864. Phelan, Malaby, Dockweiler, and historian and novelist Gertrude Atherton had joined Wardell in supporting Smith.

Wardell was to hand McAdoo one final setback before the tide turned in 1932 and Wardell would be crushed by the McAdoo forces. To do this, however, the Wardell group in 1930 deserted the Democratic party to support the Republican candidate, Mayor Rolph, against McAdoo's candidate for governor Milton K. Young.

In the sixteen intraparty battles from 1924 to 1932, nominations for governor and United States Senator, delegations in the presidential primaries, national committeeman, and chairmanship of the State Central Committee, Wardell forces won eight out of twelve through 1930. In 1932, however, McAdoo carried the day, personally capturing the nomination for the Senate, as well as the designation of National Committeeman, leading the victorious presidential delegation, and securing as state chairman the election of Maurice F. Harrison.

California politics confuses even the professional political scientists. One of the most significant contributors to the instability of the political winds is the steady and massive migrations which have taken place since the state entered the Union. The tremendous population growth throughout various areas of the state defies all efforts to solidify interests and unify political thinking.

The first tidal wave of migrants following the discovery of gold merely foreshadowed things to come. One boom has followed another. Agriculture, oil, motion pictures, aircraft, manufacturing and tourism are a few of the major contributors to the booms which have made the state the most populated in the nation.[21]

Primarily these people moved to the cities. But, as in Orange County, when they did not move to the city they created urban areas out of what had been rural. So that even though California stands as the leading agricultural state its politics have a distinctly urban flavor.

Sectional cleavages in California politics have been of two kinds; north versus south and urban versus rural. The north, centering around San Francisco and Alameda counties, dominated state politics from 1849 to 1929. It maintained this control, even after southern California population outstripped the north, by obstructing reapportionment of congressional and legislative districts, and by establishing the federal plan of representation in the State Senate. After 1930 the south, growing continually in population, also grew stronger and stronger politically, and with the aid of the Supreme Court's "one-man, one-vote" decision (1962) which forced reapportionment of the State Senate, now dominates state politics.

Originally representation in both houses had been based upon equal population districts. But the Legislature in 1921, 1923 and 1925 failed to reapportion based upon the 1920 census. The Farm Bureau, Grange and San Francisco Chamber of Commerce, representing northern and rural interests, sponsored at the 1926 general election an initiative measure which embodied the federal plan of representation. Under this proposal the state would be divided into eighty equally populated assembly districts and forty senate districts formed on the basis of counties, with no county having more than one senator and no senator representing more than three counties. This proposal carried in all fifty-eight counties excepting Los Angeles while another proposal on the same ballot, which would have simply created a reapportionment commission, was defeated.

Following the mandate of the people the Legislature in 1927 drew up a reapportionment bill based upon the federal plan but a referendum was circulated in a last ditch effort to prevent this plan from being put into effect. At the general election in 1928 the voters repeated even more substantially their support for the federal plan. Soon thereafter the 1931 Legislature was called upon to make a reapportionment based upon the 1930 census and this time the south benefitted greatly by winning representation in both the Assembly and Congress on a strict population basis. Los Angeles County gained eight assembly seats and Orange County gained one. Forty-two of the eighty assembly districts were now south of the Tehachapi Mountains.[22]

The 1920's in California was a period of extravagance, wild speculation, shoddy promotions, and phony real estate developments. The make believe of the movie world seemed to be contagious to epidemic proportions throughout the business world, particularly in southern California.

Notwithstanding the sham and flim flam which was to surround land development and enterprise, this period was to see the establishment of many solid industries which have contributed to the continued growth and prosperity of the state. Not the least of these was the oil industry. Located for the most part in the southern counties of Orange, Los Angeles and Ventura, it extended north into Kern, Kings, Tulare and Fresno counties. From the Kettleman Hills fields to Santa Fe Springs the total oil production and the wealth it created was almost beyond conception. And its wealth stimulated wealth in dozens of different directions among them the railroad, trucking and automobile industries.[23]

During this same period the motion picture industry had descended upon southern California with its flamboyant spending and seemingly inexhaustible opportunities for fabulous fortunes. It employed not only producers, directors, writers, cameramen, actors and extras but also thousands upon thousands of electricians and painters and carpenters to build and maintain movie sets.[24]

The oil and motion picture industries alone sparked a tremendous housing boom which called for many more workers and an acceleration of the lumber industry. California forests produced an annual two billion board feet but this was only a third of its needs so that the neighboring states of Oregon and Washington were able to bask in some of the sunshine of California's new found prosperity.

Meanwhile, agriculture was also prospering. California farm products' annual value increased ninefold in the first four decades of the twentieth century and doubled that in the fifth decade. Even during the 1920's while the farmers throughout the nation were experiencing a terrific slump, California agriculture generally was prosperous. The buxom girls of the gay nineties were now the slim flappers of the jazz age. The popular definition of a flapper was a young lady who went out and sowed her wild oats on Saturday night and went to church on Sunday morning and prayed for crop failure. Throughout the nation potatoes, corn, bread and desserts were forsaken for oranges, lettuce, melons and celery.

From the winter gardenland of Imperial Valley through the Orange groves of San Bernardino and Orange counties to the great lettuce bowl of the Salinas Valley, California was supplying the nation. As one writer observed, California was "America's natural hothouse" with growing conditions that could not be duplicated elsewhere in the country. Its varied climate, soil and weather conditions had no counterpart. Within the state farmers engaged in 118 distinct types of farming producing 214 different agricultural products. Its vegetable crops of lettuce, celery and tomatoes, its citrus crops of oranges, lemons and grapefruit, its vineyards producing grapes and raisins, its specialties of olives and nuts, avocadoes and artichokes, to say nothing of cotton and wool, ranked at the top or near the top in the nation. Diversified and specialized were the two key words, so specialized in fact that many Easterners had to be taught to eat the foods California produced.[25]

Two factors which assisted this agricultural growth and without which it would not have been possible were the technological improvements in shipping such as the refrigerated cars, faster freight schedules, trucking made possible by the development of paved highways, and the development of irrigation. In 1900 only 35% of the farms were under irrigation but by 1930 the figure had risen to 63%.

With all this activity banking and finance of necessity had to grow.

Already during the 1920's the motion picture industry had suffered from the lack of financing for expansion available to it within the state. Forced to seek out eastern banking interests much of the industry eventually ended up in the hands of the Morgan and Rockefeller groups. In the process the bankers, in order to protect their investments, stepped into the picture business demanding improvements in procedures and drastic cuts in production costs. The movie magnates although bitterly resenting the dictation of the eastern financial interests found themselves squeezed into producer-distributor mergers which were to lead to the gigantic chain theater operations.

Other industries, perhaps fortunately, did not find eastern money as readily as the film industry did. Principal among these was agriculture. Here, California financiers were to provide the answer. Chief among these financiers was A. P. Giannini who had come out of retirement as a successful produce merchant to establish the Bank of Italy. He, more than any other single individual, was responsible for the growth of branch banking in California which contributed greatly to the state's position in the world of finance that it enjoys today.

With the decentralization of capital promoted by the Federal Reserve System, which made more money available at lower interest in agricultural areas, and with the willingness of California banks to lend this money to California farms, the way for branch banking was paved. Giannini was quick to see the opportunity. In 1920 the Bank of Italy had twenty-four out of the 179 branch banks in the state or 13% of the total. By 1930 there were 853 and the Bank of Italy had 353 or 41%, three times the number of its nearest competitor. One of Giannini's methods was the establishment of regular savings by school children. Each week money was collected in the classrooms throughout the state to be deposited in the individual savings accounts of each pupil.

In 1928 Giannini founded the Bank of America and by 1930 he had merged into the new bank the old Bank of Italy. By that time he held mortgages on one out of eleven of all farms in the state, in addition to widespread cooperative and seasonal loans to farmers. He had reached the plateau from which his bank would grow to be the nation's and the world's largest. But it had not been all honey and roses. And, as distasteful as it was for him, he was forced to dabble in politics to achieve his goals.

Under the progressive administration of Johnson and his successor, Stephens, things had not been too bad for Giannini. But the restrictions placed upon him by the Richardson administration forced him to seek an alliance with the progressive Republicans. Giannini had also had some problems with the Federal Reserve Board in 1921–1922 which was attempting to control the Bank's growth. He engaged McAdoo as the Bank's special counsel at an annual retainer of $75,000 to work out peacefully solutions with the federal officials. So repressive were the rulings of Richardson's State Superintendent of Banks, John Franklin Johnson, that Giannini sought relief through the Legislature. The issue became so heated that during a hearing of the Assembly Banking Committee legislators had to break up a fist fight between the Superintendent's attorney and Giannini's representative.

High officials of the Bank of Italy now decided to back some candidate to oppose Governor Richardson's bid for reelection in 1926, in order to remove his appointed Superintendent from office. The *Los Angeles Times* headlined, "Bank of Italy goes into politics to back Young." Young had served as Lieutenant Governor under both Stephens and Richardson. Franklin Hichborn, the discerning political analyst, had prophesied in a letter to Senator Hiram Johnson:

> The Bank of Italy crowd would unquestionably like to get the Banking Commissioner and I do not think the deduction is unreasonable that the Bank of Italy crowd will spend money to elect a governor who will have a Banking Commissioner satisfactory to them. Just what a Banking Commissioner would be worth to the Bank of Italy I am not prepared to say but a campaign contribution in six figures would not be unreasonable with such a stake at issue.

Young beat Richardson in the Republican primary by some 16,000 votes.[26]

Will C. Wood, political ally of Young, former Superintendent of Schools for Alameda County, and Superintendent of Public Instruction for the State of California, became the new Superintendent of Banks under Young. Following his service in this post, he became a Vice President of the Bank of America.

With the election of 1920, a trend began which would continue throughout the 1920's. In the presidential preference primary that year, Johnson bested Hoover by 161,207, but lost Los Angeles for the first time in his career by 511 votes. Although he carried the ten southern counties as a whole by 8,301 votes, for the rest of the decade, northern California was to provide the bulk of progressive support while southern California usually returned majorities against the progressive candidates. This was true even in 1922 when Stephens who was from Los Angeles lost the ten southern counties, but carried the north. Johnson refused to even speak to those erstwhile supporters who had backed Hoover, and began an antagonism between Johnson and Hoover that culminated in Johnson's endorsement of Roosevelt in 1932.

Ironically, just as Giannini was achieving the peak for the Bank of Italy, which would become merely the launching plateau for his new Bank of America, the economic bubble of the 1920's was inflating to bursting. It would be foolish to contend that the 1929 Wall Street crash did not affect the California economy. But its effect was delayed. Still the motion picture industry, lax in financial management because of the fabulous revenues it was enjoying, and hampered by lack of funds for expansion into new sound-production techniques, had already experienced setbacks endangering the once seemingly secure jobs of thousands of workers.

By 1930 the forces that would bring about the great depression which would hit bottom by the winter of 1932–1933 were all in motion and the handwriting was beginning to appear on the wall. Although 36% of the banks failed in the United States as a whole during the 1920's, in California the figure was only 8%.

But California did experience severe cutbacks in industry. In 1929 the automobile industry had produced 5,350,000 cars. This was to drop to less than half in five years. In the petroleum industry price wars broke out as the companies attempted to corner the fast diminishing market. Union Oil Company's sales dropped from $89 million to $61 million in 1931 and to $51 million by 1933. Such drastic setbacks in sales brought about cutbacks in production. In 1930 California's oil wells produced 875,000 barrels a day with a market which could only absorb 675,000. Curtailments and retrenchments threw thousands out of work. Explorations ceased. Union Oil reduced its drilling crews from forty-six to six. Companies were squeezed out, bought out, and merged out.

While these reversals in the film and oil industries were serious enough in themselves, the real backbone of the state's economy also commenced to crumble. While the market price for California's specialty crops did not fall comparatively as low as others in the United States, farmers found it hard to meet their total operating costs and, eventually, many found it impossible.

California agriculture had developed apart from the customary American farm tradition and had always lacked a "satisfactory relationship between the land and the families who labor upon it." There was much more land suitable for agricultural development than there were people to farm as compared with the smaller farms of the east and midwest. While some scholars have attributed this to the early Spanish and Mexican land grants, actually the greater size of California farms was influenced more by the peculiar suitability of the soil and climate, the specialization of crops, and the necessity for irrigation. The great expense of irrigation required large areas to make this burden pay through high value crops. The large farms and irrigation costs made it essential to obtain a maximum return from the land, a policy which often resulted in available labor lying idle for months at a time.

Migratory farm labor was as peculiar to California as slavery was to the old South. It was both advantageous to the farmer and malignant to the worker. Harvesting was both seasonal and specialized. Lettuce was harvested in the Imperial Valley before March and in the Salinas Valley after March. Grapes were harvested in the Coachella Valley before July and after that time in the Central Valley. Laborers in these crops migrated from one area to the other. And thousands of migratory workers were required for the diverse harvesting.[27]

These migrant workers have been in turn Indians, Chinese, Japanese, Hindu, Filipino and Mexican and the growers have played upon racial intolerance to maintain their labor forces in sub-standard conditions. By combining the sweatshop tactics of the North with the stoop labor operations of the Southern plantations, California growers sponsored such poor working conditions that California farms were described as "Factories in the Field."

As the large growers increased efficiency with the help of mechanization, they learned to control labor as they had production and prices. As some small growers were liquidated in the immediate post World War I recession, the large exchanges speedily consolidated their position. In this they were helped immeasurably during the "prosperity decade" by the cooperative movement which the party in power chose to encourage. "Sunkist" and "Sun-Maid" became not only household terms but also symbolic of wage rates which were based entirely on insuring large profits with complete disregard for the living conditions of the workers. By the end of the decade, thanks in part to the automobile which enabled migratory labor to move from one harvest to another, California agriculture was prosperous enough, except for the workers.[28]

Most farmers accepted migrant labor as the only profitable way to organize the state's agriculture. But the social and economic problems which arose from the situation were complex. It brought about social stratification, instability, disease and malnutrition, and the necessity for welfare relief expenditures. Only 44% of the workers resided on the farm as contrasted with Iowa's 77%. Thousands literally lived on wheels, roving the state from job to job, their children bouncing from one school to another if, indeed, they were fortunate enough to attend any school.

By the middle 1930's 10% of the farms accounted for 53% of the total acreage and produced 68% of the total value of the farm products. Actually farming had grown so large-scale that 2% of the farms produced 29% of the total value.[29]

Underlying every social, economic and political problem during these years was the inescapable fact of the Great Depression. While California agriculture was stuck with certain high fixed costs the farmers in the Golden State could exercise some control over one cost item. That item was labor. Farm organizations such as the Associated Farmers and the Farm Bureau encouraged holding the workers down and industrial leaders backed their play. Even when prices improved, the farmers were reluctant to increase wages. Concluding that other farm organizations such as the California Farm Bureau represented primarily the large farmers and packers whose interests were inimical to the small farmer, the California State Grange began to disassociate from the programs and activities of the other farm organizations.

While agricultural areas throughout the United States, excluding the deep South, had been relatively free of the class conflict which existed in the industrialized areas, this was not true of California. The types of farming as well as the farm structure within the state have resulted in social, economic and cultural conditions different from anywhere else in the Union. Because of race and nationality differences, because of the migrations and because of the insecurity which caused extremely high turnover, organization was almost impossible. Even so there were revolts due in no small part to chronic low wages and intolerable living conditions aggravated by the depression. Out of twenty-three farm strikes in the United States in 1930–1932, twelve occurred in California. In 1933 thirty-one of the sixty-one farm strikes in the nation took place in the state. California accounted for 180 of the decade's grand total of 275 strikes. The farmers finding Mexicans to be more docile and subservient favored them during the 1920's, but the increased job competition resulting from the depression and the migration of large numbers from the dustbowl led to racial strife which proved to be a great advantage to the large-scale farmers.

These economic stresses were not apparent in California by 1930 and the campaigns followed more traditional lines. The election of 1930 was a bitter blow to the progressives. They had hoped to reelect Young for another four years but former Governor Richardson induced Los Angeles County's crusading District Attorney Buron Fitts to seek the Republican nomination. Fitts had been elected Lieutenant Governor in 1926 along with Young and had resigned in 1928 to take the prosecutor post. He received strong support during the campaign from the *Los Angeles Times*, which made a sectional fight of the election. Its publisher, Harry Chandler, editorialized that: "A vote for either Rolph or Young would perpetuate as iniquitous a system of organized injustice as ever threatened the unity of a state."[30] Perhaps secretly Richardson wanted Mayor Rolph to win and took this means of assuring his victory as a revenge against Young who had unseated him in 1926. If this was Richardson's strategy, it worked. Young and Rolph divided the votes in the north while Fitts, the darling

217

of the Anti-Saloon League, carried the south with votes which would have otherwise gone to Young. Rolph, edging Young 377,000 to 357,000, was the beneficiary. Fitts received 293,000 votes, mostly (182,000) in Los Angeles County where Young ran third. In the general election Rolph trounced Democrat Milton K. Young 999,000 to 334,000.

Young had made several powerful enemies who helped cut short his career. One of these was Tom Finn, San Francisco's powerful political boss during the bootlegging era, whom Young ignored on patronage matters which he had enjoyed since his original deal with Johnson. Finn retaliated in the 1930 election by joining forces with the *Los Angeles Times* to defeat Young. Rolph as a "wet" found slim pickings in the southland but among his supporters was a rising star in Los Angeles politics, Robert W. Kenny. Although Rolph did not campaign as a "wet," he was well known as such. As Kenny put it, he stood out like a neon sign spelling "WET." Frank F. Merriam, former Speaker of the Assembly

While Young and Fitts engaged in hurling verbal invectives, Mayor James Rolph, Jr. (1869–1934) headed the covered wagon parade in the rodeo at Livermore, rode a pinto and wore a ten gallon hat at the rodeo at Salinas, entered a milking contest at Markleeville, crowned queens throughout the state, and wore the costume of a Spanish don at the "La Fiesta" at Santa Barbara. (Wide World Photos.)

who had been defeated by Fitts for the Republican nomination for Lieutenant Governor in 1926, was elected along with Rolph.

Following the election of Rolph, the progressives were inclined to refrain from criticisms and give the new Governor a chance to make good. But the old order conservatives having regained control were imbued with no such tolerant attitude. It was "turn the rascals out" the "rascals" being the progressives.

The first reaction to the Rolph administration was engendered with the "tomfoolery" of the inaugural parade and inaugural ball. The progressives were dismayed that these frivolous affairs should be put ahead of serious state business. When it appeared to them that the new governor was more interested in repealing the Eighteenth Amendment than in the state's serious financial crisis, they were even more disconcerted.

During the next two years the issues of tax equalization, public school support, water conservation and race track betting widened the breach between the two groups. On the water and race track issues, ironically, Rolph stood with

Governor C. C. Young (1869–1947) and Mayor James Rolph, Jr. (1869–1934) in the Contra Costa County booth at the State Fair in Sacramento after Rolph had beaten Young for the Republican nomination for governor. (Courtesy of *San Francisco Examiner*.)

219

the progressives. Supporting race track betting were two of Rolph's strong supporters, San Francisco banker Herbert Fleishhacker and Hollywood producer Joseph Schenck. Schenck had been a Young supporter in 1926.[31]

While the growth of southern California from 1870 to 1900 had been uncommonly rapid, growth in the 1920's was fantastic. During this decade the population in Los Angeles County increased 135% as contrasted to the overall increase in the state as a whole of 66% and in the nation of 16%. The growth was described in wonderment: "Like a swarm of invading locusts, migrants crept in over all the roads . . . . they camped on the outskirts of town, and their camps became new suburbs."[32] By 1930 the ten southern counties contained 54% of the state's population contrasted with the 42% of 1920. This great inpouring of people had a tremendous influence on the state's development.

In 1920 native Californians constituted 20% of the residents of Los Angeles. In 1930 the percentage was the same. Where had the 80% come from? After 1900 the tide of immigrants to the southland was largely made up of persons of moderate means seeking to escape the harsh winters of the East and find retirement in this temperate land. They were mostly from the Middle West. In 1910 the principal states from which they came in the order of numbers were: Illinois, Ohio, New York, Missouri, Pennsylvania, Iowa and Kansas; in 1920 it was Illinois, New York, Ohio, Missouri, Iowa, Pennsylvania and Kansas; and in 1930 it was Illinois, Missouri, New York, Ohio, Iowa, Kansas and Pennsylvania. In each of the three decades the influx was from the same five midwestern and two eastern states.[33]

For the most part they were small town businessmen and farmers, churchgoing Protestants, moralists, drys and Republicans. They had worked hard and lived frugally and now they sought to enjoy the fruits of their labors away from the cold winters and the hot summers. For the "big businessman" these immigrants seeking a haven were to make southern California a "heaven." Here was the ready-made opportunity for the taking, an ideal spot for a local "Great Barbecue" as Parrington put it. "The big boys, the businessmen, the Babbitts, the promoters, the speculators, these were the high priests of Sunkist and of the Chamber of Commerce whose religion was Climate and Profits." They saw a tremendous opportunity to enrich themselves, and trailing after them were the minor promoters and speculators, the salesmen, the preachers, and the bunko-artists. And they were supported by the people they exploited, also midwesterners.[34]

In the minds of the average Angeleno, the businessman, the Chamber of Commerce, the engineers and the City of Los Angeles achieved results with free enterprise and individual initiative and the people applauded. The absence of water resources was the basic weakness of the region: no rivers, no lakes, no creeks, and no harbors. But the Owens Valley Aqueduct, the Colorado River Aqueduct and the deep water harbor of San Pedro, regardless of the tactics employed, helped to alleviate the pressing need.

These enterprises all required imagination, foresight, initiative and political power. So also did the orgy of the real estate boom and the speculation of the black gold fields. During the first half of the decade, real estate valued at two and three-quarter billion dollars changed hands while building took place at a cost of three-quarters of a billion. Three new oilfields at Huntington Beach, Signal Hill and Santa Fe Springs helped to triple petroleum production. During the 1920's Los Angeles was extremely ripe for business and financial adventure. The mood of the community welcomed it. The new citizens wanted to contribute and share in the material progress. "The magic carpet had been ceremoniously laid."[35] There were those, however, whose thirst for power and money caused them to reach too far. One such was Chauncey C. Julian of the Julian Petroleum Corporation.[36]

Julian was a Canadian who had drifted to Texas where he worked as a rigger. Moving on to the California oil fields near Los Angeles he began to invest, in a small way, in oil leases. His entrance into California oil adventures coincided with a general mood of the populace which came to be known as "oil madness," a willingness to invest in anything that smelled of oil. In this atmosphere, the Julian Petroleum Corporation was born. Julian had obtained a ten acre lease a short distance from the discovery well at Santa Fe Springs, and commenced drilling. In a grandiose scheme designed to let the investing public make him rich even if the oil did not, his newly organized corporation, chartered in Delaware, took over the third floor of the Loew's State Building in downtown Los Angeles, and secured a permit from the California Corporations Commissioner to issue 600,000 shares of preferred stock at $50 a share and 600,000 shares of common stock.

Playing on the emotions of the oil-dizzy public and using corny country-folk type of slogans designed to appeal to the midwesterners he launched a gigantic advertising campaign. "I'll tell you, folks, you'll never make a thin dime just lookin' on" . . . "I've got a surefire winner this time" . . . "Come on in, folks, the water's just fine."

"Good Night Nurse"
"Just one day left" and I will have "kissed you goodnight" for evermore on my 100,000 for one lease in the heart of the 4,000 barrel wells at Santa Fe Springs . . .
   Do you realize that my offer to you is nothing short of the "Old Cat's Tonsils?" . . .
Folks, if ever a clean and square offer was submitted to you, surely to

goodness I have placed it before you . . . and the day I betray that royal confidence that you are placing in me my earnest hope is that I fall head first into the deepest well in Santa Fe Springs.

Mail that old check or run in and meet me personally.

C. C. Julian

Suite 321–24 Loew's State Theater Bldg.[37]

Within a few months, $11,000,000 worth of stock had been sold, a figure that would reach $150,000,000 in the next five years. A more discerning group began to question the operation but a financial statement by the nationally known and reputable public auditing firm of Price, Waterhouse and Company indicated only that Julian might be spread a little too far. While some charged that the stock was "watered" it appeared that Julian was using the money to invest in oil producing territory and in equipment. In 1924, two years after the formation of the corporation, Julian turned over its control to S. C. Lewis and Jacob Berman, alias Jack Bennett, for $500,000 which Julian claimed the corporation owed him. Lewis and Berman proved to be as slippery a pair of stock manipulators as could be found, although Julian always claimed he was unaware of this. By 1927, they had issued in excess of 6,000,000 shares or 5,000,000 more than authorized. Lewis was a tireless worker, supervising drilling, planning sales, directing purchases and, most important, manipulating stock pools. By 1926 the shrewd investors were beginning to realize that the market was being flooded with unauthorized stock. Meanwhile, Julian had become involved in two other stock promotion schemes, Western Lead and Monte Cristo Mines.

In 1926 the Julian market suffered a minor crash dropping from $30 to $15 but the big crash came on May 5, 1927, the day the Los Angeles Stock Exchange ordered a halt to the trading of Julian Petroleum shares. In the weeks previous Lewis and Bennett had been busily selling all the stock they could and then fled. Both were later apprehended, tried and acquitted for fraud, but subsequently they were convicted in Federal Court for using the United States mails to defraud and each was sentenced to seven years. In their wake they had caused financial ruin to investors and at least one suicide, the former manager of the Los Angeles Stock Exchange who could not face the revelation.

The inside details of how these men had worked their way into the inner circles of the more respectable business and financial community were never brought to light. There was some claim of a double hi-jacking, and that while Lewis and Company were bilking the investing public, their gains were being siphoned off by the bankers, politicians and civic leaders who permitted them to exist.[38]

It cannot be presumed that sane men of big affairs, bankers, merchant princes and realty financiers, would attempt to install a dummy printing press and print and issue stock of untold millions of shares and peddle it out to the public on the open board of the Stock Exchange unless a cleverly planned system of political protection had been laid to insure their criminal act's immunity from punishment.[39]

Were the banks part of the swindle or merely dupes? Either interpretation stripped them of honesty or intelligence. When former United States Senator Frank P. Flint remained an earnest defender of S. C. Lewis almost to the last, the people were given cause to wonder.

Motley H. Flint, brother of the former United States Senator and prominent civic leader, and Henry M. Robinson, President of the Pacific Southwest Trust and Savings Bank and friend and backer of Charles G. Dawes, Herbert Hoover and C. C. Young, were both named as confederates of Lewis. Through sinking pools, the bankers and the heavy investors, including the motion picture producers, apparently were milking Lewis dry.[40] Just before the suspension of the Julian stock on the Los Angeles and San Francisco exchanges, the California Eastern Oil Company, whose directors and officers were all men of high standing in financial circles, had acquired practically one hundred percent of the assets of the Julian Petroleum Corporation. The corporation offices had already been moved into the Pacific Southwest Bank Building where Robinson could keep a close watch on its activities, nefarious or otherwise.

The Julian crash brought disappointment and disillusionment to thousands who had believed so wholeheartedly in laissez faire. Whether the small investors had suffered more than the large ones was not as important in the overall as was the fact that the confidence of the investing public had been shattered. How could one lose his investment, perhaps part or all of his savings, under this system in which he had grown to believe so wholeheartedly? As Pascal said, "We do not like others to deceive us." And this was no small deception and the headlines were alarming. Despite soothing statements of confidence issued by prominent financial leaders, the day following the stock suspension saw police reserves called out to preserve order in the financial district where crowds of small investors had collected. In the ensuing months startling disclosures rocked the entire state as the officials probed through the Julian transactions. State Superintendent of Banks Will C. Woods exposed huge profits pocketed by pool members through the manipulation of stock over-issuances.

During this period the public was also reading about bank frauds in Nevada, and the embezzlement of $100,000 by an "honest" San Francisco businessman from the firm of which he was president. The atmosphere of respect for the business community was fast changing to bewilderment if not outright distrust.

Within the next few years two more huge scandals were to rock southern California. On the night of December 11–12, 1930, Gilbert H. Beesemyer was indicted for the wrecking of the Guaranty Building and Loan Association, of which he was secretary manager. By his own admission he had converted $8 million of the firm's money into his own personal account. A Grand Jury investigation was called. Beesemyer had made little effort to conceal his looting. "In fact," he stated, "if the State Building and Loan Commissioner had thoroughly and adequately done his duty, instead of accepting as correct the company figures and totals, I would never have been able to get away with this money."[41]

Only a month previous, Charles Whitmore, the commissioner, had resigned and been reappointed for a new four year term by Governor Young. Following the Beesemyer statement, Governor-elect Rolph announced that as soon as he took office he would ask the Legislature to oust Whitmore. Rolph further said the blame in the Beesemyer case had to be placed on Whitmore since the thefts all took place during the years Whitmore held office. Actually, the discovery of the defalcations took place because of a transfer of bank examiners and the new examiner proceeded with an audit. And an astounding audit it was to the new examiner who could not believe such glaring discrepancies could have been overlooked. Beesemyer had kept a separate ledger which chronicled all of the misappropriations he had used on expenditures for property, oil wells and other personal investments.

If the Julian scandal did not frighten off all of the investing public, Beesemyer's activities went far to gather up the remainder. Many had lost their life savings. Their mood was reflected in the multitude of threats made against Whitmore which caused him to vacate his home and ask for police protection.

But even before the Beesemyer story moved off the front pages a new scandal struck. Richfield Oil Company of California was organized in 1923 and began its great expansion program in 1926. By 1930 it was the third largest distributor in California and ranked among the largest in the nation. In 1928 the company had entered into a number of three and five year contracts to buy crude oil at the then prevailing rates in order to keep pace with its rapid sales growth. These had jumped from $38 million in 1927 to $83 million in 1929. This vast expansion took place in the path of declining prices. In 1930, it was still buying 30,000 barrels of crude oil daily at ten cents above current prices. In May of 1932, when payments on the first mortgage failed, the company went into receivership.

Spokesmen for the company blamed the contracts. But the failure of the company was not to shake the public nearly as much as the discrepancies which the receiver reported in the company's reported assets. Where the company had reported $132 million in assets the receiver found only $85 million. He found a deficit of $41 million instead of a surplus of $15 million. When he looked for 361 million barrels of oil reserves he found only 63 million. While the company had paid three and a half million in dividends during the previous year the receiver found an operating deficit of sixteen and a half million for the same period.[42]

Two years later, on April 11, 1932, three former Richfield officials, James A. Talbot, chairman of the board, Clarence M. Fuller, president, and Raymond W. McKee, auditor, went on trial for grand theft and conspiracy charges. The trial became one of the bitterest in Los Angeles court history. The prosecution contended the three juggled the books and drew advances totalling $383,000 with which they bought cars, yachts and other extravagant gifts for themselves while the company was heading for the rocks.

Throughout the months of April and May, during the height of the presidential primary fight, the Richfield trial, a second Julian trial, and a Supreme Court decision on Beesemyer were all front page stories. Also, constantly in the Los Angeles papers during this period were the continuing stories of the receivership scandal, indictments and trials. Meanwhile the people were deciding whether to stay Republican or vote Democratic.

The economic and social discontent during this time was not confined to California and perhaps, despite the ordeals public investors had experienced, particularly in southern California, not as aggravated as in other parts of the country. For certainly there was bewilderment, fear, and a distrust of the business world as exemplified by the ruling Republicans. In 1929, about nine million persons in the United States were holders of stock, a fifth of whom had incomes of less than five thousand dollars. With the October crash and the disaster it wrought, followed by continuing scandalous revelations concerning the fraudulent activities of the Van Sweringen brothers and Samuel Insull on the national scene and the Julian, Lewis, Beesemyer and Richfield disclosures locally, the political effects were as certain as doom.

While spokesmen for the current order continued to preach good times, the preservation of free enterprise and the abolition of poverty, economic conditions for the majority continued to deteriorate. The constant harping on prosperity being just around the corner by the Republican leaders in business and politics only served to further discredit the conservative cause. Utopia had not arrived but the Great Depression had, and this the Republican leaders refused to see or believe.

Had there been some semblance of integrity prevailing in the system, the little people might have at least retained their faith. But faith had received more blows than a punching bag and by 1932 the people were no longer quite as bewildered. They had determined to rid themselves of these leaders who had destroyed their faith, shaken their confidence, frightened and even destroyed them by refusing to obey the moral tenets of honesty, justice and decency.

The incredible era of Republican rule and scandal had opened in the 1920's with the election of Warren G. Harding and ended with the defeat of Herbert

Hoover. It was a decade that historians like to describe in their lectures but never quite seem to explain. It was a period that many of the state's aged pensioners dream about in a misty sort of way but wonder if it really happened. It was a time when a beer baron built during prohibition a ball park for an orphan named Ruth; when an organization based upon bigotry and hatred paraded in glory down the streets of the nation's capital; when a lone pilot flew the Atlantic to become a national, yes, even a world hero; and a time that was to bring about the worst depression the nation and the world has known which was to be the undoing of the Republican Party's supremacy not only in California but in the entire country.

FOOTNOTES

1   George E. Mowry, *The California Progressives* (Berkeley: University of California Press, 1951), pp. 278–285.

2   By far the clearest explanation of this confused election is H. Brett Melendy "California's Cross-Filing Nightmare: The 1918 Gubernatorial Election," *Pacific Historical Review*, XXXIII (August, 1964), 317–330.

3   The story of the campaign from the viewpoint of the drys is presented in Gilman M. Ostrander, *The Prohibition Movement in California, 1848–1933* (Berkeley: University of California Press, 1957) pp. 264–294, and Wendell E. Harmon, *A History of the Prohibition Movement in California* (Unpublished Ph.D. dissertation, University of California at Los Angeles, 1955), pp. 155–200.

4   For the split between the progressives and conservatives, read Mowry, *op. cit.*, Chapter XI, entitled "The Downhill Years." On Johnson's drift away from progressivism, see Richard D. Batman, *The Road to the Presidency: Hoover, Johnson, and the California Republican Party, 1920–1924* (Unpublished Ph.D. dissertation, University of Southern California, 1965), 336 pages.

5   Franklin Hichborn, "California Politics, 1891–1939" (Unpublished MSS: University of California at Los Angeles Library, 1949), V, 2603–2604. The most complete political history of California for the period from 1891 to 1939, has been written by Franklin Hichborn who is an eminent authority on California government and California politics; the work is entitled "California Politics 1891–1939," and is a five-volume set totaling 2,860 pages.

6   Jackson K. Putnam, "The Persistence of Progressivism in the 1920's: The Case of California," *Pacific Historical Review*, XXXV (November, 1966), 395–412, and Russell M. Posner, "The Progressive Voters League, 1923–1926," *California Historical Society Quarterly*, XXXVI (September, 1957), 251–261.

7   Freda K. Walker, *James D. Phelan, Democratic Senator from California, 1915–1921* (Unpublished M.S. thesis, University of California at Berkeley, 1947), 94 pages.

8   State of California, Department of Finance. *Report of the Director of Finance to the Governor,* covering the period January 1, 1927 to January 31, 1930 (Sacramento: California State Printing Office, 1930), pp. 47–51.

9   Robert S. Allen, Ed., *Our Sovereign State* (New York: The Vanguard Press, Inc., 1949), pp. 382–387.

10   *Time* (July 15, 1957), pp. 20–31.

11   Remi G. Nadeau, *The Water Seekers* (Garden City: New York. Doubleday, 1950), 309 pp.

12   Quoted in David J. Dallin, *Soviet Russia's Foreign Policy, 1939–1942*, translated by Leon Dennen (New Haven: Yale University Press, 1942), p. xv.

13   "Chaos in California," *Newsweek* (April 15, 1940), p. 72.

14   Will Rogers, *How We Elect Our Presidents*, Selected and Edited by Donald Day (Boston: Little, Brown and Company, 1952), p. 53.

15   Much of the material in this section has been derived from Robert J. Pitchell, *Unpublished Tables*, compiled by and in the possession of the author, and may be checked by consulting the Secretary of State for *Statement of Vote* (issued after each presidential primary, direct primary, general, and special state election). (Sacramento: State Printing Office), and Hon. Don A. Allen, Sr., *Legislative Sourcebook* (Sacramento: Assembly of the State of California, 1965), 487 pp.

16   Gladys H. Waldron, *Antiforeign Movements in California, 1919–1929* (Unpublished Ph.D. dissertation, University of California at Berkeley, 1956), pp. 41 and 42.

17   Will Rogers, *op. cit.*, p. 118.

18   Ronald E. Chinn, *Democratic Party Politics in California, 1920–1956* (Unpublished Ph.D. dissertation, University of California at Berkeley, 1958), p. 22. For another view on the Democratic Party in California during this period, see: Robert E. Hennings, "California Democratic Politics in the Period of Republican Ascendency." *Pacific Historical Review*, XXXI (August 1962), 267–280.

19   *The Progressive Movement of 1924* (New York: Columbia University Press, 1947), pp. 102–104, and Mark Sullivan, *Our Times* (New York: Charles Scribner's Sons, 1935), VI, 335–337.

20   *Sacramento Bee*, March 14, 1928, p. 1. For an account of the political buildup of Hoover during the 1920's by an important participant, see: Ralph Arnold, "Laying Foundation Stones," *Historical Society of Southern California Quarterly*, XXXVII (1955), 99–124, 243–260, 297–319.

21   There are two very interesting articles by Earl Warren and Carey McWilliams in Farrelly and Hinderaker, *The Politics of California: A Book of Readings*, Chapter 1 entitled "Population and Politics," (New York: The Ronald Press Company, 1951) 320 pp.

22   Francis N. Ahl, "Reapportionment in California," *American Political Science Review*, XXII (November, 1928), 977–981; George W. Bemis, *Sectionalism and Representation in the California State Legislature, 1911–1931* (Unpublished Ph.D. dissertation, University of California, 1934), 228 pp.; Joseph P. Chamberlain, *Legislative Processes: National and State* (New York: Appleton Century-Crofts Company, 1936), Chapt. III; Thomas S. Barclay, "Reapportionment in California," *Pacific Historical Review* V (June, 1936), 93–126; Bureau of Public Administration, *Legislative Appointment* (Berkeley: University of California, 1941), 46 pp.; Joseph A. Beek, *The California Legislature* (Sacramento: State Printing Office, 1942), 223 pp.; and C. C. Young, Ed. *The Legislature of*

The Rumble of California Politics

California (San Francisco: Commonwealth Club of California, 1943), Chapter II. On re-apportionment, the best discussions are to be found in Gordon E. Baker, *The Reapportionment Revolution* (New York: Random House, 1966) 209 pp. and Winston W. Crouch, John C. Bollens, Stanley Scott, Dean E. McHenry, *California Government and Politics* (Englewood Cliffs, N. J.: Prentice-Hall, Inc., 1967), Fourth Edition, 318 pp.

23 Marquis James, *The Texaco Story* (New York: The Texas Company, 1953), 118 pp.; Frank J. Taylor and Earl M. Welty, *Black Bonanza* (New York: McGraw-Hill Book Company, Inc., Whittlesey House, 1950), 280 pp.; Frank F. Latta, *Black Gold in the Joaquin* (Caldwell, Idaho: The Caxton Printers, Ltd., 1949), 344 pp.; and Gerald T. White, *Formative Years in the Far West: A History of Standard Oil Company of California and Predecessors through 1919* (New York: Appleton-Century-Crofts, 1962), 694 pp.

24 See Lewis Jacobs, *The Rise of the American Film* (New York: Harcourt, Brace and Company, 1939), 585 pp.; Howard T. Lewis, *The Motion Picture Industry* (New York: D. Van Nostrand Company, Inc., 1933), 454 pp.; and Leo C. Rosten, *Hollywood: The Movie Colony and the Movie Makers* (New York: Harcourt, Brace and Company, 1941), 436 pp.

25 A strong chapter entitled "The Mosaic of California's Agriculture" may be found in Carey McWilliams, *California: The Great Exception* (New York: A. A. Wyn, 1949), 377 pp.

26 The quotes and the Bank of Italy story have been taken from: Russell M. Posner, *State Politics and the Bank of America, 1920–1934* (Unpublished Ph.D. dissertation, University of California at Berkeley, 1956), p. 126–127; Posner, "The Bank of Italy and the 1926 Campaign in California," *California Historical Society Quarterly*, XXXVII (September 1958 and December 1958), 267–275 and 347–358; see also Marquis James and Bessie Rowland James, *Biography of a Bank: The Story of Bank of America National Trust and Savings Association* (New York: Harper and Brothers, 1954), Chapters XI, XII, XIII, XIV, entitled "A Rift With the Federal Reserve Board," "The Santa Maria Episode and Its Consequences," "The Winning of Southern California," "The Liberty Bank and the Elections of 1926," and Chapter XIX entitled, "Financing Agriculture in the Twenties"; Ira B. Cross, *Financing An Empire: Banking in California* (Chicago: The S. J. Clarke Publishing Co., 1927), Vol. II, Chapters XXV and XXVI entitled "Branch Banking" and "The Federal Farm Loan System in California"; Interview by the author with Colonel William H. Neblett, February 21, 1955.

27 One should read the chapter in McWilliams, *op. cit.*, entitled "California's Peculiar Institution."

28 The story of migratory farm labor in California is presented in Carey McWilliams, *Factories in the Field* (Boston: Little, Brown and Company, 1940), 334 pp. For another authoritative view, see United States Department of Labor, Bureau of Labor Statistics, *Labor Unionism in American Agriculture* (Washington: United States Government Printing Office, 1945), Bulletin No. 836, Chapters V-XI of this work, written by Stuart Marshall Jamieson, cover farm labor in California.

29 The ugly picture of the migratory laborer is graphically painted in Carey McWilliams, *Ill Fares the Land* (Boston: Little, Brown and Company, 1942), 419 pp.

30   *Los Angeles Times*, August 13, 1930, editorial page.

31   Hichborn, *op. cit.*, V, 2603–2604 and 2657. See also Herman G. Goldbeck, *The Political Career of James Rolph, Jr.: A Preliminary Study* (Unpublished M.A. thesis, University of California at Berkeley, 1936), 181 pp.

32   Mildred Adams, as quoted in Carey McWilliams, *Southern California Country: An Island on the Land* (New York: Duell, Sloan and Pearce, 1946), p. 135.

33   For the origins and the characteristics of the Angelenos, see, *ibid.*, Chapters I and VIII and IX.

34   Louis Adamic, as quoted in *ibid.*, p. 160.

35   Guy W. Finney, *The Great Los Angeles Bubble: A Present Day Story of Colossal Financial Jugglery and of Penalties Paid* (Los Angeles: The Milton Forbes Company, 1929), p. 9.

36   The outstanding story of the Julian scandal, and vividly told, is in *ibid.*, 203 pp. See also Lorin L. Baker, *That Imperiled Freedom* (Los Angeles: Graphic Press Publishing Co., 1932), 448 pp; Morrow Mayo, *Los Angeles* (New York: Alfred A. Knopf, 1933), 356 pp.; Luther Whiteman and Samuel L. Lewis. *Glory Roads: The Psychological State of California* (New York: Thomas Y. Crowell Company, 1936), 267 pp.

37   Finney, *op. cit.*, pp. 27–39, and Robert Glass Cleland, *California In Our Time: 1900–1940* (New York: Alfred A. Knopf, 1947), pp. 133–135.

38   See especially Finney, *op. cit.*, Chapter 3 which portrays a clear picture of their business dealings.

39   Baker, *op. cit.*, pp. 24–25.

40   *Ibid.*, Chapters III through XII.

41   *Los Angeles Times*, December 11, 1930.

42   "Richfield Was Victim of Forced Feeding," *Business Week* (May 13, 1931), pp. 33–34.

The Rebirth of
the Democratic Party

The 1932 national election was one of the most important in the history of the country and one of the most significant in California's history. Americans, for the first time in eighty years, gave the Democratic presidential candidate a majority of the popular vote. The shift in California voting was even more dramatic. The state had moved from overwhelmingly Democratic in the first quarter of its history to all but exclusively Republican in the third quarter. The 1932 election marked a rebirth of the Democratic Party.

The United States is basically a two-party country and California has been no exception. From 1860 to 1932, however, the Republican Party had the national government tucked under its wing so that the Democrats had elected only two presidents in all those seventy-two years. California had paralleled the trend with Democratic Governor Budd serving in the 1890's along with Democratic President Cleveland. But while the Democrats nationally were able to capitalize on the Progressive Movement in 1912 and elect Wilson, the California reform was stolen by Johnson with the result the Democratic Party was by the 1920's practically dead.

By 1932 only two Johnson Progressives, besides Johnson himself, still held important state offices. Congressmen Joe Crail of Los Angeles and Phil D. Swing of El Centro, both "drys," decided to forsake the House and make a run for the United States Senate against "standpatter" Shortridge. Swing, probably the best Progressive after Johnson, subsequently withdrew in favor of Crail.

Crail, born in Iowa, had moved to California in 1913 and eventually formed the law firm of Crail, Shutt and Crail. His twin brother Charles became a Superior Court Judge and finally the dean of the Los Angeles Superior Court. Joe Crail

Royce D. Delmatier was primarily responsible for the original draft of Chapter 8.

became financially successful by collecting fees in oil stocks, and interested himself in Republican politics. He served as southern chairman of the State Central Committee from 1918 to 1920, and in 1926 he was elected one of Los Angeles County's two congressmen to represent the most heavily populated district in the United States. He had particular appeal among the "Iowa picnic circuit" crowd in southern California, and bid for the "dry" vote. He received great support from the old Johnson Progressives. Crail's campaign manager was Ross Marshall, political editor of the *Los Angeles Herald Express*. Edward A. Dickson, the editor of the *Express* had first pushed Crail for Congress six years previously. Crail had supported the bills in Congress for the development of the All American Canal and for municipal power. Following this, Chandler and the southern California utility interests fought Crail.

The incumbent senator, Samuel M. Shortridge, had also been born in Iowa. He had migrated to northern California where he practiced law and had been at one time an attorney for Abe Ruef in the San Francisco graft prosecution trials. He had been active in politics and had been, in keeping with his conservatism, a presidential elector for Harrison, McKinley and Taft. First elected to the United States Senate in 1920 he was re-elected in 1926. Originally a "wet" in 1920 he had weaseled on the issue and by 1932 was considered a "dry" although he was "wetter" than Johnson. Representing the "standpat" conservative wing of the Republican Party he had been picked in 1920 by William H. Crocker as the candidate in his "all-out" campaign to defeat Democrat Phelan even though Crocker thought Shortridge to be "the most despicable man in California."

But despite Swing's withdrawal Crail found himself mixed up in a real donnybrook. It was to end with eleven candidates under five different party labels seeking nomination at the August 30 primaries. Six of the eleven each polled over 100,000 votes, the only time in the state's history this has happened, and three gained nomination. Crail did not.

Competing with Crail for the Republican nomination and the elimination of Shortridge was Tallant Tubbs, State Senator from San Francisco. Both of his grandparents, A. L. Tubbs and D. J. Tallant, were early distinguished San Francisco business pioneers. Under the new Federal plan of reapportionment Tubbs was slated to lose his state senate seat in 1932 to which he had been elected in 1924 at the age of twenty-seven, one of the youngest to serve in the state's august body. Tubbs was a "wet." In 1930 he had sought the Republican nomination for Lieutenant Governor as Rolph's running mate but was defeated by "dry" Merriam by 17,000 votes. Now he decided to seek the United States Senate seat, and in this he was backed by Judge Robert W. Kenny of Los Angeles, who was the southern California commander of the Crusaders, a young men's "wet" organization. Kenny became Tubbs' southern California campaign manager. The WONAPERS (Womens Organization for National Prohibition

231

Repeal) also came out for Tubbs, although its Los Angeles County Chairman, Mrs. John C. McFarland, supported McAdoo. Tubbs, a GOP liberal for his times, besides favoring the repeal of prohibition, endorsed passage of laws to establish the thirty-hour work week.

Three other candidates were to jump into the primary race. Two Democrats, William Gibbs McAdoo and Justus S. Wardell, and Prohibitionist Robert P. "Bob" Shuler, became major contenders. Candidates of the Socialist and Liberty parties seeking their parties' nominations rounded out the race.

Of the entire group McAdoo was by far the most prominent nationally. He gained wide recognition for his part in the development of a system of rapid transit tunnels under the Hudson River before President Wilson appointed him Secretary of the Treasury. He later served as Director General of the Railroads of the United States. In 1932 he was chairman of the California delegation to the Democratic National Convention. This was the Garner delegation which McAdoo had led to victory with Hearst's support and now he was to receive the Hearst support in his bid for the Senate.

Wardell, the other Democrat, was a long-time party leader in the north. A native of San Francisco, he operated from a base of power as editor and publisher of the *Daily Journal of Commerce*. He had served one term in the Legislature and had been a delegate to the national conventions in 1904, 1908 and 1928, the last time as chairman of the delegation. He also sought the party nomination for Governor in 1926. He had been a supporter of Smith's but the two had a falling out when Wardell led the 1932 Roosevelt delegation. But now in the Senate race Wardell would receive support from the Smith forces.

Shuler was a fire eating "hell and damnation" Methodist minister who had been born in Virginia, had migrated to religious-minded Los Angeles and in 1920 had become pastor of Trinity Church. In addition to having such a powerful podium as the pulpit of a church which rivaled Aimee Semple McPherson's Angelus Temple, Shuler was editor of the Anti-Saloon organ as well as *Bob Shuler's Magazine*, and owned Radio Station KGEF. Radio broadcasts were not only a wonderful new way to spread the Gospel, but also an effective way to make public the reasons he should be elected to political office. He was one of the first politicians in the nation to discover and utilize the radio as a campaign tool. He was as interested in ending corruption in government as in keeping prohibition. Following his charges of corruption against Robinson and Mayer during the Julian scandals, his radio station license was revoked, and he entered the Senate race on a free speech platform. Knowing that he could not win a major primary, he ran as a Prohibitionist in order to get into the general election. Crail was exceedingly disappointed and shocked over Shuler's entry into the race, because he foresaw that they would split the "dry" moral vote. The feelings of the two men were further complicated by the fact that when Shuler's son had

232

achieved football fame at California Institute of Technology, Crail had appointed him to West Point, where he later became captain of the football team. On the Saturday night before the primary, Shuler sent a memo to the Protestant ministers saying that as the "dry" vote would be split they should vote for Crail, but by then it was too late.[1]

The six main candidates polled 93% of the vote. But Shuler winning the Prohibition Party nomination had pulled some 199,000 Republican votes and 86,000 Democratic and although he ran third in each of these two latter parties his combined vote was greater than that of any other candidate. He had been the first senatorial candidate in the state's history to crossfile and he received votes under all five labels. He was to receive the fewest votes in the general election.

Tubbs was the Republican victor over Shortridge and Crail with 217,000 votes while McAdoo snowed Wardell under for the Democratic nomination. The combined total of the other five candidates regardless of party was less than 102,000.

Shuler (Pro.)	290,862
McAdoo (Dem.)	269,746
Tubbs (Rep.)	217,047
Shortridge (Rep.)	206,450
Crail (Rep.)	187,999
Wardell (Dem.)	116,845
All others	101,762
TOTAL	1,390,711

Every major newspaper in the country hailed the victories of Tubbs and McAdoo as "one for the wets." However, this was not entirely accurate. True, Tubbs was a "wet" and had won the split primary by 11,000 votes. But the three "drys" running in the Republican primary, incumbent Shortridge, challenger Crail and crossfiler Shuler, ran up a combined vote 376,000 greater than Tubbs received. Shuler's entry into the race had been a godsend to Tubbs. McAdoo, who won the Democratic primary, was a pseudo "wet" having been a "dry" all the while until he reluctantly switched after the Chicago convention. The real "wet" in the campaign was Wardell who had been well identified as such for years.

Throughout the 1920's the Republicans held a three to one registration margin. By 1932 it was only three to two and by 1936 it had switched to a three to two Democratic margin. These, then, are the crucial years in analyzing the switchover from Republican to Democratic. The total registration in 1932 was 2,889,000 and in 1936 it had grown to 3,254,000.

1932 Direct Primary: United States Senate Seat

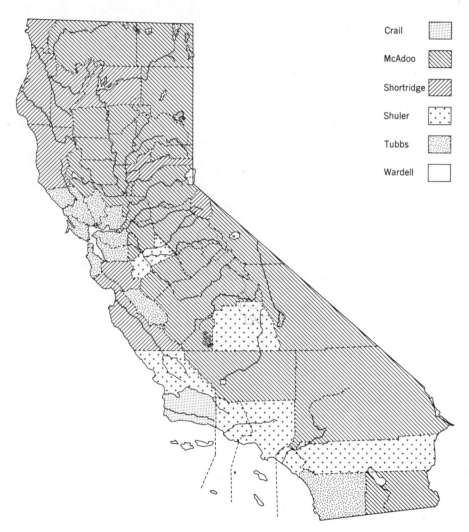

Crail

McAdoo

Shortridge

Shuler

Tubbs

Wardell

Some observers attribute this Democratic transition to the influx of "Okies" and "Arkies" into the state during the depression years. This was not the case for had every single one of the 365,000 new registrants during these four years been from the Democratic South it still would not have been enough to make the change. Furthermore, the vast majority of the "Okies" and the "Arkies" came later in the decade and helped swell the Democratic totals but after the change had already occurred. The fact that the Republican registration decreased by 356,000 while Democratic totals increased by 721,000 refutes any contention that the switch was brought about by the migrants. By the primary elections of 1934 the two parties were even and at the time of the 1934 general election the Democrats had gained a sound majority. The change then was brought by the Great Depression, the popularity of the New Deal and the outstanding campaign of Upton Sinclair.

Sometimes overlooked as a contributing factor to the big switch was the social violence of the times, highlighted by the San Francisco waterfront and general strike of 1934 and the Salinas lettuce strike of 1936. Of course this is understandable because social violence has been prominent in California's history. Starting with the abuse of the Indians and Chinese in the mining camps and the lawless retaliations of the early Californians against the miners, most notorious of which were those led by Joaquin Murietta, the state has literally been a giant arena of combat. The Vigilantes added to California's reputation of unruly behavior as did the Broderick-Terry duel and the subsequent killing of Terry, the burning out of the Chinese at Hunter's Point in 1871, the use of special police to break the waterfront strike in 1901, the Japanese school riots of 1906, the Mussel Slough Tragedy, the bombing of the *Los Angeles Times* in 1910, the Wheatland Riots of 1913, the Preparedness Day bombing of 1916, the Filipino race riots of the 1930's, the Shaw investigations and bombing of 1938, the "Zoot-suiters" and Pachuco riots of 1943 right up to the most recent Watts Riot and other civil disorders and university uprisings.

Reviewing that which was transpiring among the people's representatives during the twelve year period 1926 to 1938 an even clearer picture of the switch emerges. The Republican high point was reached in 1930 with a significant change in 1932 and the Democratic high was reached in 1936. The Republicans held ten of the eleven seats in the House through 1930. In 1932 with the addition of nine new seats the Democrats won eleven of the twenty and in 1936 won sixteen of them. In the Assembly in 1930 Republicans held seventy-four of the eighty seats! Following the 1936 elections the Democrats had control of forty-seven having reduced the Republicans to thirty-three! In the 1932 elections, the Democrats picked up ten of their gain of fifteen in the congressional delegation, and nineteen of their gain of forty-one in the Assembly. In the State Senate in 1930 the Republicans held the same ratio of control as they did in the Assembly with only three Democratic senators out of the total of forty. By 1938 the Democrats had wrested fourteen senate seats for a total of seventeen but were not to win control of the Senate until 1957.

The contrariness of California politics was never more apparent than during these turbulent years. While the people were switching their party affiliations from Republican to Democratic, voting for the national Democratic ticket, and electing Democratic representatives, they were still electing Republicans for governor and United States senator. The control of these two top offices throughout the state's history has been with the Republicans for 62% of the time.

From 1900 through 1930 no Democratic candidate for governor ever came close to winning and only one Democrat, Phelan through a freak election, became United States Senator. Only one Democrat, Wilson in 1916, received the state's electoral vote. Truly, by 1930 the Republicans were running at high tide with only one Democratic congressman, six assemblymen and three state senators elected that year giving the Republicans 133 of the 143 elective offices available. Republican registration that year was 73% of the total, holding the margin, as they had since 1922, in all fifty-eight counties.

In the first half of California's political history to 1909 there had been thirty-four political parties seeking support with one-half of them achieving at least one elective office. As for the United States Senate seats since 1900 one has been in Republican hands for its entirety excepting for the victory of Clair Engle in 1958. The other was won by Democrats in 1914, 1932, 1938, 1944 and 1968. During this period since 1900 only two Democrats, Culbert L. Olson and Edmund G. "Pat" Brown were elected Governor, and only two, Ellis Patterson and Glenn Anderson, Lieutenant Governor. None has been elected Secretary of State although Paul Peek held the office temporarily by appointment. And only once have the Democrats captured the offices of Controller and Treasurer, Alan Cranston and Bert Betts, respectively, both in 1958 along with the big sweep of Engle, Brown and Anderson. The only measurable Democratic success in seeking state office has been the Attorney General post won by Robert W. Kenny in 1942, "Pat" Brown in 1950 and 1954, Stanley Mosk in 1958 and 1962, and Thomas Lynch in 1966.[2]

The year 1932 dawned cold and forbidding and it was not just the weather. The nation's millions were confronted with a frightening economic situation which had seen the national income dwindle to $41 billion, one-half of its total of three years previous. The Bonus Expeditionary Force was to march on the nation's capital and be greeted by machine guns manned by the Army led by General Douglas MacArthur. Whether or not the Bonus march was Communist incited is moot since people all over the country driven to desperation, were ready to march. The farmers, in woeful economic straits, were blockading the roads, and before the end of 1932 some fourteen million people were unemployed. The United States was mired in the worst economic depression in history. In this same year another group of people on the other side of the Atlantic turned to Adolph Hitler. Most Americans, however, found the ballot an adequate means by which to bring about a change in 1932.

For Hoover, 1932 would be different from his first three years in office. It was an election year. And this edition of the quadrennial American super

236

circus was to be one of the most important of all. The tragedies and dejection of unemployment, stock market crashes, and bank and business failures had developed a frustration and resentment that could be forcefully expressed at the polls. A majority of people had lost faith in the magician of the engineering world so they turned him out of office.

In California, Hoover faced no opposition within the Republican Party in the presidential primary. The Democratic Party, however, faced a contest. This was not unusual in California political history, for in seventeen of its thirty presidential primaries (Democratic and Republican 1912–1968) competing slates were entered. Probably six of the bitterest fights occurred in the 1912, 1924 and 1952 Republican and the 1932, 1952 and 1968 Democratic primaries. In 1932 Democrats were offered the choice of John N. Garner, Franklin D. Roosevelt, and Alfred E. Smith, while the Republicans were united on Hoover.[3]

Governor Rolph led the Hoover delegation composed mostly of conservative Republicans but sprinkled with a few progressives. Some of the prominent delegates were Joseph R. Knowland, John F. Hassler and Earl Warren of Oakland; Marshall Hale and Hugh McKevitt of San Francisco; William H. Crocker of Burlingame; Charles C. Teague of Santa Paula; Louis B. Mayer of Santa Monica and Ed Fletcher of San Diego.

Franklin Hichborn analyzed it thusly:

> Progressive Republicans found themselves without organization or influence. At the Republican presidential primaries, the Crocker Teague–Knowland faction took over. They put out a presidential primary ticket for the nomination of Hoover. The Progressives offered no opposition; they left the primary field to their old-time antagonists. This deadly calm within the Republican party forecast the overthrow to come.[4]

The main strategy of the Republican leaders in the California primary was to roll up a large vote for Hoover. Since his renomination was already assured the California vote would neither help nor hinder the Convention outcome but his supporters believed a strong endorsement from this state would greatly assist his reelection in November. In an effort to secure this vote Republican leaders stressed "party unity" while the Republican press bombarded the voters with such headlines as "Republican Veterans to Back Hoover," "Republican Women Back Hoover Vote," "Republicans Prepare for Big Showing for Hoover" and "Get Out a Rousing Vote of Confidence for Hoover."[5] The last week of the campaign was climaxed by a "get out the vote" drive led by Marshall Hale, Republican State Chairman. The Republican leaders were all out to make May 3 a demonstration of loyalty to Hoover.

The Democratic primary of 1932 ranks with the 1912 Republican primary as one of the most interesting in the state's history. California's primary was the only one of the seventeen state primaries where all three major candidates were entered. Having a choice of the nation's three leading candidates for president, they also had a hot contest in the United States Senate race in which a former presidential contender, McAdoo, was now involved.

The Garner ticket in the primary was backed by William Randolph Hearst and McAdoo. Hearst had come a long way since the days when he was a Jeffersonian Democrat and a rabid patriot in support of the Spanish-American War. By 1932 Hearst had perfected his own brand of "Americanism" which, among other things, had no place for Orientals. Nor did it have any place for Tammany Hall, Al Smith or the late Boss Charles F. Murphy, the trio he had feuded savagely with in New York for the past thirty years.

Hearst's importance on the California scene stemmed from his domination of the press. Of the thirteen California newspapers with circulations in excess of 50,000 the five Hearst papers had over 815,000 or 51% of the combined total. His papers ranked one, two, three, five and twelve in order of circulation.[6]

Table I
1931 Circulation of Leading California
Daily Newspapers.

L.A. Herald (evening) (Hearst)	232,587
L.A. Examiner (morning) (Hearst)	214,733
S.F. Examiner (morning) (Hearst)	185,975
L.A. Times (morning)	174,518
S.F. Call Bulletin (evening) (Hearst)	126,102
L.A. Express (evening)	117,427
S.F. Chronicle (morning)	99,378
L.A. Daily News (morning)	99,355
S.F. News (evening)	93,725
Oakland Tribune (evening)	81,611
L.A. Record (evening)	66,137
Oakland Post Enquirer (evening) (Hearst)	56,262
Sacramento Bee (evening)	50,951

The idea of placing a Garner slate in the field is generally credited to Hearst. Garner was his old friend from the 58th and 59th Congresses and both men saw eye-to-eye on public works programs to alleviate unemployment. On January 2, 1932, over a nationwide radio broadcast from Los Angeles, Hearst "nominated" Garner. All of the other candidates, according to Hearst, were tainted with "Wilsonian internationalism" especially Newton D. Baker, Wilson's

Secretary of War. McAdoo, Wilson's Secretary of the Treasury, John B. Elliott, and George Creel, head of the Office of Public Information during the First World War, met at San Simeon to pursue the project.

McAdoo became the California Garner campaign manager and would receive the full support of the Hearst newspapers in his race for the United States Senate. The Roosevelt slate was headed by Justus F. Wardell also running for the Senate.[7]

The prohibition issue was a major one throughout the year 1932. The Smith forces working through John J. Raskob, Chairman of the Democratic National Committee, and Jouett Shouse, Chairman of its Executive Committee, all favored repeal. McAdoo, convinced that an anti-prohibition stand would ruin the Democratic Party's chances in California tried to side-step by advocating a national referendum on the question, a position that satisfied neither side. He refused to attend the annual Jefferson–Jackson Day dinner in Los Angeles in 1931 at which Shouse was the principal speaker. In July of 1931 James A. Farley came to California to work with Wardell, Dockweiler and others of the "wet" group in building up Roosevelt support. Wardell went to Washington, D.C., in January of 1932 to convince the Democratic National Committee to hold its National Nominating Convention in San Francisco. Farley had said earlier that he favored the city as the site, but Chicago guaranteed $200,000 and San Francisco only $150,000, and the Committee awarded the convention to Chicago.[8]

The Garner delegation, boosted by the elaborate build-up of the Hearst newspapers commenced in January, contained more of the leading Democrats than the two opposing tickets. John B. Elliott led the campaign in the south while the former State Chairman Henry H. McPike did the same in the north. They were joined by Milton K. Young, Dr. Zachary T. Malaby, the current State Chairman, Thomas M. Storke, Charles B. Murphy, Mrs. Grace Hargeaves (daughter of William Jennings Bryan), Hamilton H. Cotton, Jesse W. Carter, and National Committeewoman Mrs. Nellie Donohoe.

Returning from the east coast early in April, McAdoo embarked on a speaking trip which took him into every section of the state. He constantly reiterated that he had found growing Garner strength at all stops.

> The fact that Garner is both a western and southern man and that he knows the problems of agriculture as well as governmental finance and adminis-tration commends him strongly to the people.[9]

The *Santa Barbara Daily News*, published by Garner-backer Storke, pounded the same theme:

> Sentiment for Garner is growing everywhere, Garner is regarded as con-servative but fearless. . . . California is interested in neither Republican

239

nor Democratic victory, but it is deeply concerned with lending its efforts to the nomination and election of the best qualified to lift this nation out of the depression. . . . And of all the men who are seeking or have been suggested for the nomination, John N. Garner is the one with the most outstanding ability. Garner is of the west for the west and undoubtedly will be the choice of the west.[10]

Democratic registration in the ten southern counties since the 1930 general election had increased 243,000 while the Republicans had lost 39,000. Spurred on by these gains John B. Elliott who had supported Hoover during the general election campaign of 1928, proclaimed a widespread dissatisfaction with Republican rule and predicted Garner would be the nominee and the victor in November. Sensing Garner strength in the southland, and pointing out that both his opponents were from New York, the final drive to elect the Garner slate was launched April 11 in Los Angeles over a statewide radio hookup during which McAdoo declared:

> Speaker Garner possesses brains, courage, integrity, dependability, and freedom from those sordid and selfish influences which have dominated the government for the past twelve years. . . . Tammany government in New York and Wall Street in New York are under investigation. . . . New York's political, financial, and business leadership has been discredited. . . . We need a change of leadership in Washington, but it is not enough to swap Washington for New York. We must put the mace of power into the hands of a man like Garner, who has the Jacksonian courage to drive the crooks and money changers from the temple of government, and demonstrate that a strong, clean and economical administration can be secured for the people.[11]

The New York, Tammany and Wall Street leadership arguments were constantly hammered home for the next three weeks by the Hearst papers. Headlines such as "Tammany Blamed for Gang Rule" and "Democratic Chief Raskob in Stock Pool" were seen every few days in the Hearst press. That the Hearst newspapers were extremely influential is not to be denied and the whirlwind campaign put on by the Garner forces has seldom been equalled before or since.[12]

The Roosevelt and Smith votes, meanwhile, seemed hopelessly split between the two New Yorkers. Thus, while the Republicans were united behind one candidate, the Democrats were dissipating their strength among the three rivals, a seemingly frequent trait of the Democrats before and since 1932.

Almost unnoticed in 1932 was another group of workers within the Democratic Party, a faction that was to struggle with conservative Democrats for power throughout the 1930's and beyond as the Roman Catholic group gradually faded away and merged with new factions. This new group was basically a liberal one and came to include such men as Upton Sinclair, candidate for governor in 1934; Manchester Boddy of the *Los Angeles Daily News*; Fremont Older of the *San Francisco Call*; Sheridan Downey, to be elected United States Senator in 1938; Culbert L. Olson, to become governor in 1938; and Dr. John Randolph Haynes. For the first time in twenty years, since Hiram Johnson hijacked their program, the liberal Democrats were finding a haven.

Following Roosevelt's overwhelming 725,000 majority vote for reelection as Governor of New York in 1930, a small inner group commenced building him for the presidency. Among these were Louis Howe, Col. E. M. House and James A. Farley who busied themselves selecting key men in every state to support Roosevelt. National Committeeman Isidore B. Dockweiler was mentioned for southern California, but the question of a leader for northern California was more difficult.[13]

Farley's active participation in the Elks had kept him traveling about New York state constantly and afforded him an excellent opportunity to judge political sentiment. Now the 1931 National Convention of Elks was to be held in Seattle and it was decided to use this trip to sound out Roosevelt prospects among the western Democratic state organizations. The journey covered eighteen states and Farley was able to report a growing demand among Democrats for a winner and a willingness to back Roosevelt. He was also able to find the answer in their quest for a northern California leader, for by December 22, 1931, Roosevelt wrote to Justus Wardell, Democratic Party wheelhorse in San Francisco:

> This is just a line to tell you how grateful I am for the fine way you are handling things. I hear from several people who have come here from California that our friend McAdoo is still hoping to get into the game some way. I have a note from Dockweiler in which he says that he is doing everything possible. Keep me in touch with things because, as you know, I greatly value your judgment.[14]

On January 23, 1932 Alaska became the first to instruct its delegates for Roosevelt. On the same day Roosevelt authorized the North Dakota Central Committee to enter his name in the presidential primary. Garner's hat had already been tossed into the ring by Hearst and on February 6 Al Smith announced that he would be available for nomination but would not set up an organization to secure delegates.

Nationally, Roosevelt's strength was also his vulnerability. The years of careful planning which made him the leading candidate also made him a target for a stop-Roosevelt movement if such a coalition could be developed. In

California this was an impossibility. The idea that the Garner and Smith factions might join was ludicrous. Ed Flynn saw this most clearly:

> Conditions in California were very confused. My assignment to smooth the way was not an easy one. There was no real Democratic organization in the state. In and around San Francisco there was a suggestion of one, but in southern California things were so divided that there were almost as many factions as there were democrats. Each claimed it represented the Democracy of California. Before meeting Roosevelt I went to Los Angeles to arrange for a meeting and to endeavor to bring some semblance of unity into the party. The day following my arrival, after meeting many people, I realized the hopelessness of my task. As I saw one group, it would warn me vehemently about the group just arriving. Everywhere I was told not to trust anyone. I decided the political mess in that city was insoluble. There was only one thing to do, and that was to let it stew in its own juice, hoping that there would be some unity behind the Presidential candidate at least. I left the city glad to have escaped with my life.[15]

As finally organized, the Roosevelt ticket in California was headed by Wardell with J. F. T. O'Connor running the campaign in the south and William H. McCarthy as campaign manager for northern California. O'Connor later became Comptroller of Currency and McCarthy became Postmaster of San Francisco. Along with Wardell on the slate were Clara Hellman Heller, later to be National Committeewoman; Robert M. Fitzgerald, dean of the Eastbay Democrats; and Chauncey Tramutolo, noted Democratic lawyer from San Francisco. Notably absent from the slate were the prominent Democrats of southern California who all seemed to be on the Garner ticket.

Smith was even worse off. No big name Democrat was listed anywhere. Why did Smith decide to run? Perhaps Ed Flynn provides the best answer:

> With the approach of 1932 . . . I had committed myself to Roosevelt without consulting Smith largely because I had relied on Smith's public statement that he would not run again for office having been made in good faith. I continued to believe this, and in all fairness to Smith, I believe that he himself held to this position until 1932 . . . Smith gave it to me in a very forceful way. He told me that he was completely through with politics and that no one could induce him to enter the political arena again. . . . No doubt many considerations entered into his subsequent change of plans. President Hoover's loss of prestige and the deepening of the depression changed the outlook considerably. It began to look clearer and clearer that the candidate on the Democratic ticket would stand an excellent chance of being elected. Smith's immediate friends began to bring great pressure on him. If he yielded, it was due to human weakness.[16]

The ticket for Smith got off to a late start but was able to command considerable attention by its attacks upon the Roosevelt leaders in the state, especially Wardell. For a number of years Wardell had headed the Catholic faction of Democrats and as such had supported Smith in 1928. He had joined Roosevelt after apparently having the same disavowal of intention from Smith that Flynn and Lehman had been given. When events proved otherwise Wardell on March 11 telegrammed Smith to the effect that entering the California primary at such a late date would be ill-advised and urged him to reconsider. Smith not only disregarded the advice but resented it and so informed Wardell by return wire.

On April 14, Parson M. Abbott, Smith's leader in California, made a demand that Wardell make public the contents of the telegram. Wardell, feeling that the Smith group was simply using the correspondence to attract eleventh hour attention, left on a campaign trip without bothering to answer Abbott. On April 23, Mrs. Grace Montgomery, wife of the outstanding University of California Shakespearean scholar, who had just returned from a New York conference with Smith, read Smith's reply to a meeting of the Berkeley Democratic Women's Club but this too was ignored by Wardell, despite the efforts of the Garner forces to egg on the controversy.[17]

The last Tuesday in April and the first Tuesday in May were the dates for the three primaries most important to Smith. April 26 was the showdown between Roosevelt and Smith in Massachusetts and Pennsylvania. If Roosevelt won those two states he would have so strong a lead in the race for delegates that he could not be stopped in June. But if Smith could hold the line he would then still be a contender at the convention. Smith was strongest in Massachusetts, one of the two northern states he had carried in 1928. Many felt he was stronger there than in his own state. The dominant faction in the Democratic state organization was led by Governor Joseph B. Ely and was supporting Smith. The Roosevelt forces were led by Mayor James B. Curley of Boston who was also fighting for state control. Because the situation was involved and confused Roosevelt had very little to lose and much to gain. In the Pennsylvania fight much the same condition existed. The regular state organization favored Smith but a splinter group headed by Senator Joseph F. Guffey supported Roosevelt and also was trying to capture the state organization.

Roosevelt's rush for the Democratic presidential nomination received its first direct check when Massachusetts voted to pledge its entire thirty-six convention votes to Smith. In Pennsylvania, the results were inconclusive, with both sides claiming victory.

Now the scene shifted to California for the May 3 primary. On election eve, the director of the Garner campaign in the south, Elliott, correctly prophesied:

Our polls in every county in California show an astounding gain for Garner

243

in the past few days. In this section I think the victory will be complete. The progressive ticket headed by William Gibbs McAdoo, pledged to Mr. Garner, will receive a huge plurality in Los Angeles city and county, where the great Democratic vote of the state is registered.[18]

When the votes were counted Garner had 222,000, Roosevelt received 175,000 and Smith ran third with 142,000. The single Republican slate headed by Governor Rolph and pledged to Hoover tallied 657,000. Roosevelt had captured thirty-four of the forty-eight northern counties and two of the ten southern counties but he had split the total popular vote with Smith who had carried the Catholic Bay Area. Garner had received 74% of his total vote in the ten southern counties so while Roosevelt had a more popular and widespread appeal Garner had captured a narrower but more populous area. Roosevelt's lead of 43,000 in the forty-eight northern counties was offset by Garner in Los Angeles County alone with his 79,000 margin over Roosevelt.

It is impossible to see how any other result could have been expected. Roosevelt had a minimum of publicity in Los Angeles. He was up against a rising McAdoo organization which was using the campaign for Garner as a vehicle for McAdoo's political comeback. The former Secretary of the Treasury was still leading the "drys," and leading the fight against the Sharkey oil bill, both being popular stands in Los Angeles, and campaigning for a Senate seat. The Sharkey bill was a fight between the major oil companies and the independents. Its principal foe was John B. Elliott, chairman of the Executive Committee of the Independent Petroleum Association of California. A close associate of McAdoo's he was also heading the Garner campaign in southern California.[19]

The bungling leadership of the Smith group in California was typified by the statement of Mrs. Grace Montgomery following Garner's victory:

> I look at the situation wholly from the national viewpoint. It is, when so regarded, a signal victory for Smith. He has sounded the death knell of the forces of expediency, and as to the Hearst-McAdoo end of it, New England and New York will make short work of them.[20]

California Republicans claimed they were elated over the great endorsement vote given to Hoover. Marshall Hale, chairman of the Republican State Central Committee, declared:

> The voice of the President's home state carries across the nation today to say 'Well Done' to the Californian in the White House. It sounds as the signal to the Republicans of the nation that California is ready to do battle for President Hoover and march on unitedly to victory in November.[21]

1932 Democratic Presidential Preference Primary

Garner

Roosevelt

Smith

A calmer analysis of the figures hardly justifies this claim of endorsement. While Hoover received 90,000 more votes in the 1932 primary than he had four years earlier the turnout of 46% was exactly the same in both elections. The Democratic turnout of 64% exhibited more interest which cannot be explained away by the fact there were three competing slates in the Democratic

Just after the May primary William Gibbs McAdoo (1863–1941) made the plea, "Let us unite against the common enemy," at a Democratic dinner in San Francisco. Also shown are Mrs. Nellie G. Donohoe, Henry H. McPike, and Dr. Z. T. Malaby. (Courtesy of *San Francisco Examiner.*)

primary for the same situation had existed in 1928 but only 52% of the Democrats voted then. A better explanation is the fact that discontent caused by the Great Depression and coinciding scandals were bringing about a revolt at the polls throughout the country.

With the certain knowledge that Hoover would be renominated many Republican progressives, liberals and dissenters were in a bewildering and homeless position, not only in California but elsewhere in the nation. Such Senators as Hiram Johnson of California, George Norris of Nebraska, Bronson Cutting of New Mexico, Gerald Nye of North Dakota and Robert LaFollette of Wisconsin were among these. While there was no sign of open revolt within the Republican Party it was becoming likely that these progressives might not be able to go along with Hoover. Should Roosevelt be nominated and live up to the progressive tradition of his cousin, he might well receive the support of these leaders.[22]

As the time for the Democratic convention approached, last minute activities in behalf of the three major candidates reached a feverish pitch. The two big questions were: would the opposition to Roosevelt be able to unite on a single candidate and would Roosevelt be able to hold the states already committed to him?

Smith had solidly behind him New York, Massachusetts, New Jersey, Connecticut and Rhode Island. Garner had Texas and California. Roosevelt, with well over half of the delegates, still lacked the needed two thirds. The remaining states were tied to favorite sons. The four key states were Illinois, Indiana, Texas and California. California was to play at this convention a role of importance it has failed to do in subsequent conventions. Illinois was pledged to its favorite son, Senator James H. Lewis, and Indiana was to follow Illinois. Two days before the convention opened Lewis withdrew, whereupon the Illinois delegation immediately selected a Chicago banker, Melvin G. Traylor. It is very seldom that a state is fortunate enough to have two favorite sons qualified for the Presidency, but the Nash–Kelly machine in Chicago was equal to the occasion.

Four big battles between the pro and anti Roosevelt forces marked the opening days of the convention: the two-thirds rule; the seating of the contesting delegates; the selection of the permanent chairman; and the "dripping wet" plank of the platform. The high point for the anti Roosevelts in the balloting came in the fight over the permanent chairmanship between Senator Thomas J. Walsh of Montana supported by Roosevelt, and Jouett Shouse. Walsh won 626 to 528, the highest number of votes the opposition was ever to muster. And when the convention adopted the outright repeal plank in contrast to the Republicans' weak stand, the country was electrified by their bold action.

The sixth session convened on Thursday evening but balloting on the presidential nominee did not commence until 4:28 a.m. the following morning. On the first ballot Roosevelt was far in front with 666 but short of the 770 needed for the two-thirds rule. On the second ballot he picked up only twelve votes and on the third he gained only five more. By then it was 9:15 a.m. Friday and the delegates had reached the limit of physical endurance so the convention recessed until that night.

The hoped for break on the part of Illinois or Indiana or Ohio or Virginia after the first or second ballots had not materialized. The next ballot on Friday evening would be decisive. As Jim Farley theorized: "It is an old axiom in politics that no matter how strong the leading candidate may be, a decline in strength on succeeding ballots is fatal. The arrow must go up and not down." It was decided by Farley, Roosevelt and Howe to concentrate on the Garner delegates from Texas and California. The ninety votes of these two states would give Roosevelt 773 or three more than needed. The delegates from these two states and Illinois could not change without a caucus and this was not possible while balloting was in progress. The caucuses were to be held at 7 p.m. Friday

Table II
Democratic National Convention Presidential Ballots, 1932.

Rank in Convention	State	Votes	On First Three Ballots
1	New York	94	66–28 Smith
2	Pennsylvania	76	46–30 Roosevelt
3	Illinois	58	40–18 Traylor
4	Ohio	52	52–0 White
5	Texas	46	46–0 Garner
6	California	44	44–0 Garner
8	Massachusetts	36	36–0 Smith
11	Indiana	30	14–11 Roosevelt
20	Mississippi	20	10–9 Roosevelt

	Votes	Percentage
Total Votes in Convention:	1154	100%
Majority:	577	50%
Two-Thirds:	770	67%
Roosevelt, First Ballot:	666	58%
Roosevelt, Second Ballot:	678	59%
Roosevelt, Third Ballot:	683	60%
Roosevelt, Fourth Ballot:	945	82%

evening so the ensuing time between the convention recess that morning was one of feverish activity for the campaign managers.[23]

The Garner campaign was being run by Congressman Sam Rayburn of Texas, an astute and honest politician. A meeting between Farley and Rayburn was arranged by Rayburn's longtime friend Senator Pat Harrison of Mississippi. These were three realists who knew that Roosevelt must have the Garner delegation to ensure victory and that no one else could win within a reasonable time to avoid a convention deadlock. As Rayburn stood up to go, he said, "We'll see what can be done."

Meanwhile, pressure was being brought on the Garner-pledged California delegation whose victory in the primaries was due in no small part to the support given by William Randolph Hearst. The delegation chairman, McAdoo, still needed Hearst's support in his bid for the Senate in the upcoming November general election. Hearst's enmity to Al Smith was well known but the man who inflamed his wrath even more was Newton D. Baker, ardent advocate of the League of Nations.

So commenced a series of phone calls to Hearst by Joseph P. Kennedy, a Hearst business associate; Damon Runyan, a noted Hearst writer; Joseph Willicombe, Hearst's secretary; and Farley. All pointed out the danger of a swing to Baker as a dark horse if Roosevelt slipped on the next ballot. Hearst consulted his attorney and political advisor John Francis Neylan and decided the Baker threat must be prevented. Hearst reportedly then gave the word to the California delegation and also called George Rothwell Brown in Washington, D.C., after which Brown made a call on Garner.

But the story that Hearst brought about a switch in the California delegation in a deal to secure the second spot for Garner is refuted by no less an authority than Jesse W. Carter, later to become the "Great Dissenter" of the California Supreme Court. The idea of a swing to Roosevelt on the fourth ballot in return for Garner's nomination as vice president was discussed openly and freely at the caucus and the delegation voted to authorize McAdoo and a steering committee of four to submit the proposition to Roosevelt. According to Carter "There was not a word of truth in the claim that William Randolph Hearst personally engineered the switch because there was no Hearst influence at all with the majority of the delegates." In fact the decision to switch was made before McAdoo came back with the word that Hearst had called.[24]

In Washington Garner, a shrewd politician, had analyzed the three ballots and realized that Smith's bloc of votes were standing firm along with the minor candidates hoping for the deadlock. He was also aware that before anyone of them could possibly capture the nomination another 1924 deadlock would ensue. Realizing that Roosevelt with his majority of the votes was the convention's choice and that only two persons, Van Buren and Champ Clark, had ever received a convention majority only to be denied the nomination, he agreed with Hearst that something had to be done. Placing the party above his candidacy he called Rayburn and McAdoo in Chicago. "Sam," Garner said, "I think it is time to break this thing up. We don't want to be responsible for wrecking the party's chances. The nomination ought to be made on the next roll call."

Garner did not want to be vice president and his decision was not based on any deal but solely for the purpose of breaking the log jam. This feeling on the part of Garner to remain as Speaker led McAdoo to the belief that by assisting in the switch he would get the vice presidential nod. Some of the promises that Roosevelt's floor leaders were making during those hectic hours during the day to the McAdoo and Garner forces were that Garner could have the vice-presidency and McAdoo could control the federal patronage in California.[25]

The caucuses that night were emotional. Just before attending the California meeting McAdoo told Rayburn "California will vote for Garner until hell freezes over, if you say so." This of course, was before Hearst, Garner and Rayburn had given him the word. In the Texas caucus bedlam reigned for its forty-six votes were divided among 184 delegates. In the bitterest fight of the whole convention the delegation voted fifty-four to fifty-one to go with Roosevelt as only 105 were present at the caucus. Contributing to the muleishness of the bitter enders was the bait held out by Illinois and New Jersey of switching to Garner on the next ballot. But Garner and Rayburn saw this for the political flim flam that it was.

California's offer to yield to Texas on the next roll call was refused by Rayburn who wished to avoid any further ill feeling in his delegation after the terrific fight which had occurred in the Lone Star State caucus. Thus, when the convention assembled at 9:00 p.m. Friday, July 1, 1932, California, fourth on the roll, was to have the honor of starring in this dramatic moment of history. For McAdoo the opportunity to cut down his bitter opponent of 1924, the chance to stun the convention with his portentous announcement, must have been the thrill of a lifetime.

> California came here to nominate a President of the United States. She did not come here to deadlock this convention or to engage in another disastrous contest like that of 1924. We came here for that great Texan, John N. Garner. We have not lost one whit of the love and respect in which we hold that great statesman. He is worthy of the highest place you could give him, but he hasn't as many votes as Mr. Roosevelt. When any man is this close to the two thirds, he is entitled to the nomination. Mr. Garner himself is in accord with the position I now take. And so my friends, California therefore switches and casts forty-four votes for Roosevelt.[26]

All but one of the other candidates had fought the hardest they knew how and now, in the spirit of sportsmanship they switched their votes to Roosevelt in the usual custom of making the nomination unanimous. All but one, Al Smith. He refused to the very end to release his votes so the official record shows Roosevelt 945 to 190 for Smith.

The following morning Speaker Garner was nominated for Vice President and that afternoon Governor Roosevelt closed the convention in person with the ringing words: "I pledge you—I pledge myself to a new deal for the American People." The 1932 Democratic Convention was now history but it stands out as one of the most excitingly dramatic and the one in which California played its most important role.

When Governor Budd and United States Senator Stephen M. White were defeated in 1898 thirty-four years were to pass before another Democrat would win a statewide office with the exception of one "flukey" election. This was in 1914 when James D. Phelan sneaked down the middle of a fight between

William Gibbs McAdoo (1863–1941) (at extreme right on platform) announces the swing of his state of California and of Texas to the support of Franklin Delano Roosevelt as the Democratic presidential nominee. (Courtesy of *San Francisco Examiner*, UPI.)

Progressive Francis J. Heney and Republican Joseph R. Knowland. Progressive leader Hiram Johnson's opposition to Heney, the fracturing of the Republicans, and President Wilson's support of Phelan combined to permit the Democratic victory with a minority of the votes.

Commencing with McAdoo's victory in 1932, however, the tide turned and Downey was elected in 1938 and 1944, Clair Engle in 1958 and Alan Cranston in 1968. One Senate seat had only two occupants in forty-two years while the other had nine in sixty years.

The reapportionment of the assembly and congressional seats by the Legislature following the 1930 census was complicated by the increase of congressional seats from eleven to twenty as well as a shift in the center of population from north to south. The north's struggle to retain the balance of power commenced with an Assembly tussle over the Speakership in which the northern candidate Edgar C. Levey of San Francisco defeated Walter J. Little of Santa Monica by a vote of forty-one to thirty-nine.

Levey stacked the committees to favor his reapportionment plan which would have assigned the seats in both the Assembly and Congress evenly between the north and south. State Senator J. W. McKinley of Los Angeles proposed a reapportionment more in tune with the census figures alloting nine Congressional and thirty-eight assembly seats to the north. Despite having lost the speakership battle, Little was successful in getting Assembly support for McKinley's plan and it was this plan which eventually prevailed after bitter

251

fighting. Los Angeles, and indeed the entire southland, regarded this as a great victory for themselves and incidentally for justice.[27]

Through 1930 the eleven congressional seats had been unevenly divided with eight in the north. This gave the north 73% of the seats with 46% of the population. One northern district, the second, had a population of 157,680 while the ninth district in the south had 1,169,495. The new distribution now gave the south 55% of the seats to match their 54% of the population. Of the nine new seats Alameda in the north was given one and the south was given eight of which six went to Los Angeles alone.[28]

In 1930 Republicans held all but one of the eleven seats. In 1932 the Democrats captured eleven of the twenty. But the Democrats did not gain the majority of the seats by winning all nine of the new seats. The total of eleven was achieved by successfully retaining one seat, winning seven of the nine new ones, and unseating three Republicans. Of interest is the fact that in the one district retained by the Democratic incumbent (the only seat they had) and in four of the five seats retained by Republican incumbents, the candidates successfully crossfiled. But in the three instances where incumbents lost, all Republican, and in all nine of the new districts no one escaped the general election runoff. This was in marked contrast to the 1930 elections when nine out of eleven were decided at the primary by virtue of crossfiling.

Actually ten of the eleven in 1930 had been won at the primary but Charles F. Curry of the Third District died and it became necessary to pick a successor at the general election. This was won by his son, Charles F. Curry, Jr., who ran as a write-in candidate. The only race then not won in the 1930 primary was in the Tenth District where Joe Crail was the only one of the eleven winners who had not crossfiled.

Going back to the five congressional election years before 1932, the Republicans had won forty-eight out of fifty-five contests and only two Democrats had ever won. In forty-five of the fifty-five the races were decided at the primaries with only ten contested at the general elections and the Republicans won all ten. But in 1932 the Democrats won ten of the fifteen runoffs.[29]

State senate seats through 1928 had been apportioned primarily on the basis of population. With the adoption of the Federal plan of senate representation the new seating would take place in 1930 and 1932 with the even-numbered seats first in the gubernatorial election years, and the odd-numbered districts holding their elections in the presidential election years. Of the twenty odd-numbered districts the Democrats had won three in 1916 but the Republicans captured all in 1920, 1924 and 1928. In 1930 the Republicans picked up three of the five seats held by Democrats but lost one of their own making the total of thirty-seven Republicans and three Democrats as the 1932 elections opened.

But even with the national victories of 1932 the Democrats only picked off

1932 General Election: Congressional Districts

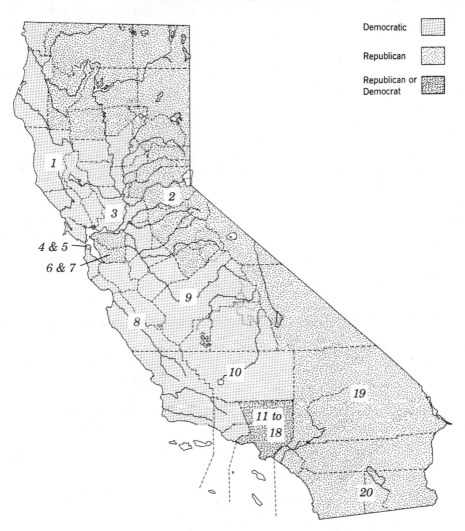

Democratic

Republican

Republican or
Democrat

two of the twenty odd-numbered senate seats. In 1936, however, they increased their hold to nine. Meanwhile in 1934 they had increased their three even numbered seats to six and upped it to eight in 1938 for a total of seventeen, the highest number they were to achieve until 1956 when they held twenty.

Of the forty state senators before the big switchover began in 1930, only thirteen survived the elections of 1930 and 1932; Allen of Siskiyou, Breed of

Alameda, Duval of Ventura, Edwards of Orange, Fellom of San Francisco, Inman of Sacramento, Jones of Santa Clara, McCormick of Solano, McKinley of Los Angeles, Sharkey of Contra Costa, Slater of Sonoma, Swing of San Bernardino and Wagy of Kern. Of these thirteen, eight won in 1930 and five won in 1932. Of the thirteen seven had already served two or more terms and nine were defeated the next time they came up for reelection. Only four went on to serve more than two terms after their 1930–1932 reelections.

The senate reapportionment that went into effect in the 1930–1932 elections left southern California with only ten of the forty senate seats, four in the even-numbered districts and six in the odd. Five of the ten remained solidly Republican throughout the entire decade: San Luis Obispo, Riverside, Kern, San Bernardino and San Diego. The other five changed in the elections of 1934–1936 and remained changed for varying periods. Santa Barbara, one term; Ventura, five terms; Orange, one term; Imperial, two terms; and Los Angeles, three terms. But in the 1932 elections the southland sent a solid Republican delegation to the senate defying the trend in the congressional and assembly representatives.

Because of the delayed reapportionment in 1929 which should have taken place after the 1920 census and the necessity to reapportion immediately in 1931 based on the 1930 census continuity in the Assembly was shot. The result was drastic and confusing changes which failed to follow any previous patterns.

This was particularly true of the 1932 direct primary. In the congressional races, only five were elected at the primary, the lowest number in the thirty years from 1918 through 1948. In the state senate races, only eleven were settled at the primary, which was 55% as compared to the average of 70% for the period 1914–1948. (During the 1920's every Democrat who won a state senate seat did so through crossfiling, as each run-off was won by a Republican.) During this same period, 1914–1948, there were 1,440 elections to the Assembly of which 908 had been decided at the primary, an average of fifty each election year. The general election contests numbered 532 for an average of thirty. 644 assembly candidates had successfully crossfiled for an average of thirty-six. In 1932 only twenty-three of the eighty successfully crossfiled compared to the normal of thirty-six, and there were fifty contests at the general election compared to the normal of thirty. Fifteen of the candidates were disqualified at the primary by losing their own party nomination. In each case it was a Republican capturing the Democratic Party nomination while losing his own. The highest number ever disqualified in any other election had been eight. Only seven Democrats were nominated to fill these vacancies and only four were successful in the general election. In 1932, nominations were vacated for 10% of the congressional, 10% of the state senate, and 18% of the assembly seats.[30]

The ten southern counties in 1930 now had 54% of the population and should have been apportioned forty-three seats in the Assembly but were given only

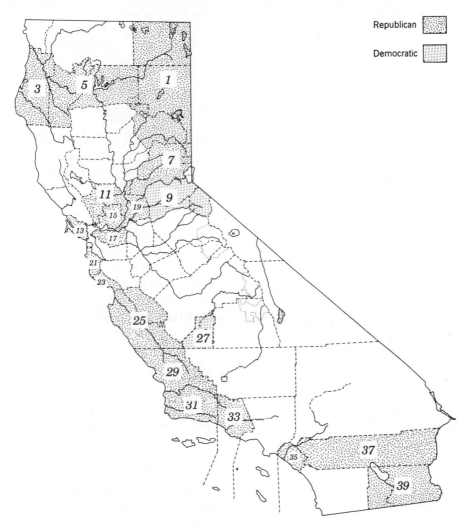

1932 General Election: State Senate Districts

Republican

Democratic

forty-two, an increase of nine over the 1929 reapportionment and a total gain of sixteen over the number of seats in 1928. The south apparently was willing to give up its claim for an additional assembly seat in order to insure its receiving eleven of the highly prized congressional seats instead of the 10–10 even split of Speaker Levey's program. In this reapportionment controversy the San Joaquin Valley delegation represented the balance of power between Los Angeles and San Francisco. Senator McKinley of Los Angeles, chairman of the

255

Senate Reapportionment Committee which drafted the bill as finally passed, explained that "Los Angeles, by surrendering one representative, gives definite proof to the rural counties that they may expect fair treatment."

From 1893 to 1959 with the exception of the years 1937 through 1943 the Republicans held a majority of the assembly seats and from 1889 to 1957 they maintained a majority in the Senate. The domination of the Republican Party had made California virtually a one-party state since the turn of the century but in 1932 the Democrats made a net gain of nineteen seats giving them a total of twenty-five.

Of the twenty-five Democrats elected to the Assembly in 1932 four successfully crossfiled, and twenty-one won in the general election. Of the fifty contested seats at the general election the Republicans won twenty-nine or 58% as compared to the fifty-nine out of sixty-six they had won in five previous elections or an average of 89%.

The loss of continuity in the Assembly was shattering. Of the original eighty assemblymen elected in 1928 only twenty-five remained in 1932. Thirty had dropped out or were defeated in 1930 and twenty-five more were no longer members after the 1932 elections. Of the new thirty elected in 1930 only eleven were reelected in 1932 which brought forty-four newly elected assemblymen to Sacramento in 1933. Actually there were only forty-two new faces since two were members who made comebacks after their 1930 defeats. Of the forty-two the Democrats had picked up nineteen or 45%. This was a startling contrast to the 1930 elections when the Republicans won thirty out of thirty new seats.

Beginning with 1932, Franklin Delano Roosevelt swept the state in four consecutive elections and Harry S. Truman squeaked through to win in 1948, even though popular Governor Earl Warren was the Republican nominee for vice president and Henry A. Wallace secured nearly 200,000 votes. This was not too remarkable for of the eleven Democrats elected to the presidency since the admission of the state, California voted for each of them except Kennedy, and Wilson in his first election.

The political activities following the 1932 direct primary election attracted national interest. The Democrats, in contrast to the unity of the Republicans, had been split asunder not only by the Garner–Smith–Roosevelt campaigns but by the involvement of their leaders in the McAdoo–Wardell contest for the United States Senate nomination.

The party conventions were to be held in Sacramento on September 25 to organize for the general election campaigns, elect new state central committee officers, adopt party platforms and select presidential electors. Because of the bitterness of the presidential preference primary and the senatorial battle in the direct primary it seemed dubious that the opposing factions could be brought together. The breach had been further complicated when Dr. Z. T. Malaby of

1932 General Election: Assembly Districts

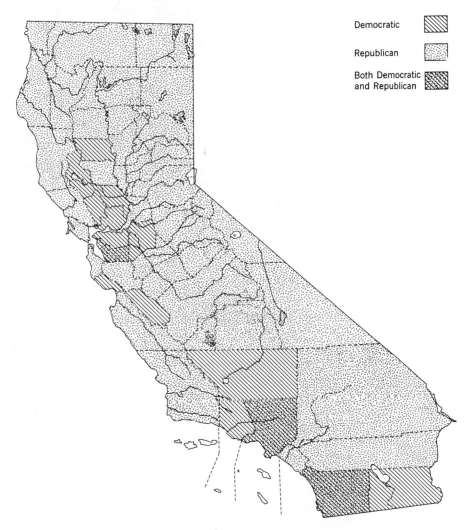

Democratic

Republican

Both Democratic
and Republican

Pasadena, who had been elected chairman of the state central committee by the Wardell forces, deserted to the McAdoo camp during the presidential primary to support Garner while Wardell was campaigning for Roosevelt.

As if to emphasize the importance, in the forthcoming general elections, of California, the state which had broken the national convention deadlock in Roosevelt's favor, two nationally known Democrats, both early Roosevelt sup-

257

porters, Josephus Daniels, Wilson's Secretary of the Navy, and Mayor James Curley of Boston, were scheduled to address the state convention.

In what must stand as one of the all time masterpieces of political maneuvering within the Democratic Party of California, harmony, at least on the surface, among the warring factions was achieved! Exactly what prices were extracted to attain this unity are not all in evidence for Wardell and McAdoo were both now supporting Roosevelt but with the announcement of Frank H. Buck of Vacaville, Democratic nominee for Congress from the Third District, as their candidate for convention chairman and Maurice E. Harrison of San Francisco as their candidate for chairman of the new state committee, it would seem that McAdoo surrendered some party control to the north in return for the unity necessary for him to win the Senate seat in November.

In any case Wardell signalled the unification of the party with his pre-convention statement:

McAdoo, myself, and others have been in friendly conference for several days, looking forward to the success of the party in November. There could be no objection raised to Maurice E. Harrison for state chairman. He is a high grade gentleman, a sound leader in the state organization. McAdoo and myself have linked arms along with our entire party in this contest to win California for Roosevelt and Garner. There is no division in the party.[31]

In the Republican Party, Congressman Harry Englebright of Nevada City, assistant Republican Whip of the House of Representatives, in accordance with previous arrangements, was elected convention chairman. However, a fight developed over the chairmanship of the state central committee. Louis B. Mayer, the Hollywood producer, was vice chairman and the logical choice to succeed Marshall Hale of San Francisco. But some of the southern leaders were unwilling to accept him wanting instead Colonel Eric Fowler, chairman of the Los Angeles County Central Committee. The Hoover campaign leaders and most of the elective state officials including the Governor supported Mayer. When the newly formed state central committee met on September 24 these forces brushed aside the dissident southerners and promptly installed Mayer.[32]

Two days previous Roosevelt had commenced a highly gratifying whistle stop campaign through California entering from Oregon with five minute stops in Redding, Gerber, Woodland and Davis before being greeted in Sacramento by what was described as the largest outpouring of people in the history of the city. Buck, and especially McAdoo, appeared with him throughout the trip which, events proved, did not hurt McAdoo in the least, or for that matter, Buck either.

Following Roosevelt's nomination, the President had summarized the forthcoming election: "This campaign is more than a contest between two men. It is more than a contest between two parties. It is a contest between two philosophies of government."[33]

There were few in the country who would quarrel with that statement, certainly not Roosevelt. In fact, Hoover had handed the New York Governor the perfect distinction all wrapped up in a neat little package. And Roosevelt played it to the hilt. In California he called upon all progressive Americans, regardless of party, to join him as they had Theodore Roosevelt and Hiram Johnson in 1912. Nor did the call go unheeded. On October 14 Senator Johnson dispatched a letter to seventy southern California newspaper editors:

> I am a Progressive Republican. . . . The Progressive believes this government belongs to all its people, not to a favored few, and that it should be administered equally and impartially for all, high and low, rich and poor alike. . . . The Progressive thinks in terms of human beings . . . you stress loyalty and regularity. In this crisis, I stress loyalty to the American people. . . . I cannot and will not support Mr. Hoover.

Other progressive leaders joined Johnson in support of Roosevelt and many rallied to the McAdoo standard. William Green of the American Federation of Labor, as well as the Railroad Brotherhoods, endorsed McAdoo and betting odds were two to one against Tubbs and ten to seven against Shuler running either first or second. By the end of the campaign McAdoo was linked with Johnson as a progressive.

The morning newspapers of Wednesday, November 9 dutifully reported the Roosevelt landslide, which could hardly have been a surprise to the California voters. For the registered Republicans outstripped the Democrats 1,565,264 to 1,161,482 while the Roosevelt ticket won by 476,000 votes. For this to happen meant that at least 717,000 Republicans did not vote for Hoover. Such a phenomenon could not have taken place in the dark.

McAdoo's victory was not as pronounced, in fact he did not get a majority of the votes cast although he carried forty-six counties, but was the beneficiary of the three cornered race. His opponents, Tubbs, the Republican "wet," and Shuler, the Prohibitionist, were such diametrical opposites, that neither would have gotten the other's vote if only one of them had been running. Of course, on the "wet-dry" issue McAdoo had attempted to straddle but whereas the voters had apparently voted "dry" in the primary, by the time the general rolled around they were more concerned with "progressivism" versus "reaction," and had even changed their views on the "wet" issue voting two to one to repeal the Wright Prohibition Enforcement Act. Tubbs had further been deserted by the Republican "drys" who had flocked to Shuler.

It is obvious that the Roosevelt landslide contributed greatly to California

1932 Presidential Election by California Counties

Roosevelt

Hoover

sending the second Democrat of the twentieth century to the United States Senate. Also of no slight help was the fact that for the first time in the century a Democratic candidate received the support of ten of the then thirteen major newspapers of the state. The pattern usually had been the *Los Angeles Daily News* standing alone in support of the Democratic candidate and the *San Francisco News* and the McClatchy *Bees* backing the progressives who were more often

1932 General Election by Counties for United States Senate Seat

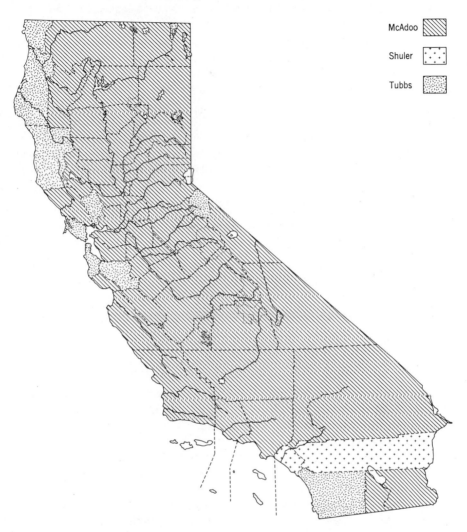

McAdoo

Shuler

Tubbs

Republican while the *Times–Tribune–Chronicle* axis backed the conservatives, leaving the five giant Hearst papers in a position to swing the balance. In the 1932 campaign, because of their affinity for Garner, the Hearst papers backed the Democrats as did the *San Francisco News* and the McClatchy *Bees*, and the axis newspapers stood by themselves. The *Los Angeles Record*, a liberal Scripps–Howard paper, had supported McAdoo in the primary, but its new owner switched to Shuler in the general. Henry Briggs, the editor and a strong McAdoo man, resigned. He was later made postmaster of Los Angeles, following the Roosevelt–McAdoo victories.

Senator Johnson called the election "a ballot revolution by the common people who wanted a greater share in their government."[34] Samuel Lubell agrees that it was a revolution but, unlike the political war that elevated Jackson to the White House, that it represented a break with the past. Between 1900 and 1914 thirteen million immigrants had poured into the United States with children who would reach voting age between 1925 and 1939. Having faced hardships and discrimination in their youth, they were seeking better things for their children when the Great Depression struck. Roosevelt's appearance on the scene in quest of the presidency coincided with this segment of the population's desire for a "new deal."

> The big city masses furnished the vote which elected Roosevelt again and again . . . and, in the process, ended the traditional Republican majority in this country. . . . Between 1920 and 1930, more than 6,500,000 persons were drawn off the farms and hills; 4,500,000 came into New York, Chicago, Detroit and Los Angeles alone. . . . During the last years of Republican rule, from 1920 to 1928, roughly 17,000,000 potential new voters passed the age of twenty-one. . . . By 1928 the urban areas were becoming Democratic and stayed that way.[35]

But even though the Great Depression had not yet hit the state as hard as other regions, it was still forceful enough to cause California voters to vote Democratic for the presidency, a United States Senate seat, the congressional delegation, and bring about a large upsurge in the Assembly, the shift pointed to by Lubell had not quite taken place in the Golden State. California had barely gone Democratic eight to seven. Part of the gains in the Assembly made by the Democrats are more attributable to reapportionment than to switch in party affiliation as the fact that practically no change took place in the state senate and the Legislature remained Republican as did the top state offices. California was still basically a Republican state in 1932.

Furthermore, the Democratic gains in the three metropolitan counties of San Francisco, Alameda and Los Angeles which accounted for 62% of the registered voters, were all made in Los Angeles! San Francisco and Alameda elected no Democratic congressmen, no Democratic state senator, and only one Democratic assemblyman out of a total of eleven. In fact, San Francisco voted Republican for the United States Senate but this was understandable since Tubbs was old family and a popular local figure. On the other hand the scandals, bank, and business failures in the Los Angeles area tremendously influenced the vote there. So the metropolitan areas of the state did not fall into the pattern etched by

Voting Record by County in 1932

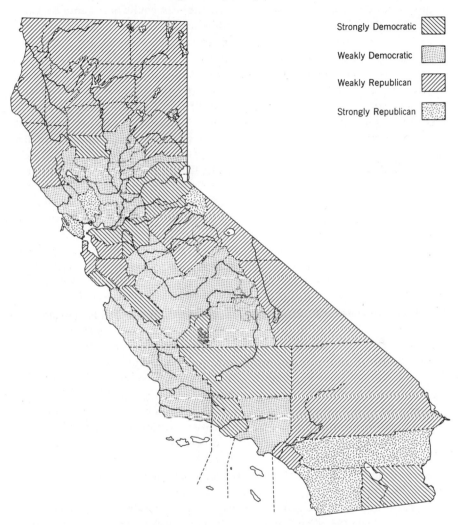

Strongly Democratic

Weakly Democratic

Weakly Republican

Strongly Republican

Lubell, not because his thesis was incorrect, but because the circumstances in those areas differed greatly from the large cities of the east.

In the presidential race the counties went Democratic fifty-seven to one and voted Democratic for the United States Senator forty-six to twelve while they went Republican for the Assembly forty-seven to eleven and for the Senate fifty-four to four. In the previous legislative elections of 1930 they had gone

263

Republican for thirty out of the thirty new seats. Now the Democrats were beginning to win. Such previously solid Republican counties as Santa Barbara, Santa Cruz, Sutter and Lake were found to be supporting Democratic candidates practically across the board. But then Lassen, Plumas, Siskiyou and San Francisco, generally Democratic, were in the Republican column in 1932 for other than the presidential race. If this is confusing it is no more so than all other contradictions which exist in a state whose people are at least provincially individualistic. It is also interesting to note that Robert Whitaker, father of Clem Whitaker of the public relations firm of Whitaker and Baxter which has played a prominent part in Republican politics, was an elector on the Socialist ticket.

The game of politics plays its cruel hoax from time to time and quite frequently in California. Certainly the 1932 California elections must be one of the all time political ironies. The budding politician has impressed upon him the principle that party loyalty and political loyalty to his friends is an absolute must. Wardell was of that school. A native San Franciscan he was a lifelong Democrat. He had labored in the vineyards of party politics for more than thirty years, served in the Legislature and as a national delegate three times. Personally, and through his newspaper the *Daily Journal of Commerce*, he worked tirelessly in support of Democrats all through the lean years. He was well established in the state, particularly in the north, as a party leader and he, better than any other leader, had the ability to unify the regular Democrats and the new liberals. He was a long time friend of Al Smith's and other nationally prominent Democratic regulars and became an early supporter of Roosevelt's only after Smith had released him with his statement that he was through with seeking political office.

Compared with Wardell, McAdoo in California politics was a dilettante, an upstart, and an opportunist. True, he had been nationally prominent before coming to California but his home base had been New York. Unwilling to buck the political machine of Al Smith and Tammany in the pursuit of his political aspirations he had moved to Los Angeles in 1922 where he found a following among the "drys" and the conservative southern Democrats. As the 1932 presidential aspirants emerged he was quick to jump on the Garner bandwagon and thereby form the alliance with Hearst which was to gain him the support of the state's five leading newspapers in his bid for the United States Senate. This was not to be his only demonstration of the fact that opportunism not principle dictated his political course. His switch to Roosevelt at the national convention was followed by his wavering on the issue of prohibition which he straddled all through the general election campaign. So it was that McAdoo, the erstwhile "dry," defeated Wardell the "wet" in the direct primary and badly for Wardell failed to carry a single county. And then following the national

264

convention, McAdoo who had backed Garner successfully in the presidential preference primary, became the staunch supporter of Roosevelt. When both Roosevelt and McAdoo came through victorious in the general election, McAdoo became the new leader of the California Democrats and the loyal Wardell, along with the new liberal group which had been the early supporters of Roosevelt against Garner, was out.

As the new leader and the Democratic United States Senator, McAdoo controlled most of the patronage with Hiram Johnson getting a minor share. In 1933 and 1934 the Democrats had many jobs to reward the faithful, especially in California where no state jobs had been available to Democrats for thirty-four years. Because of his duties in Washington the actual handling of patronage was carried out by his law partner, Colonel William H. Neblett, although in the north he permitted either Maurice Harrison or George Creel to make recommendations.

One of the first big political plums to be handed to a Californian went to McAdoo's other former law partner, J. F. T. O'Connor who was named United States Comptroller of Currency. This was a post which was of great interest to A. P. Giannini and O'Connor had become a close associate of the banker. O'Connor's senate confirmation came only after a struggle which pitted Giannini against the Mellon interests who objected to O'Connor's lack of banking experience.

Meanwhile the deposed party leader and longtime party faithful Wardell had become one of the army of job hunters. Wardell wanted to be appointed to the Federal Reserve Board in San Francisco and in May 1933 he went directly to the President and was sent to Secretary of the Treasury Woodin and O'Connor. After three luncheon engagements with O'Connor the latter promised to see McAdoo about it. Despite O'Connor's strong support McAdoo turned thumbs down.[36] Two months later Wardell was back, this time seeking appointment as Tri-State Administrator of Public Works and again McAdoo said no. Wardell was later given the job in California, and although he made a feeble attempt to run for Governor the following year, the man who had kept the California Democrats together through the long lean years had reached the end of the trail.[37]

The year 1934 was one of high hopes for the Democrats: the Roosevelt and McAdoo victories along with other Democratic successes in 1932, the untimely death of the popular Governor Jimmy Rolph in 1934, and the fact that the Great Depression had finally hit California with full force made victory seem promising. Rolph had been succeeded by the sanctimonious Lieutenant Governor Frank Finley Merriam. He had hardly taken office when he created widespread disagreement over the manner in which he handled the general strike in San Francisco. Then an exciting phenomenon took place in American political history—the Sinclair campaign.

As early as May 1933, Santa Barbara publisher Thomas Storke had sounded out O'Connor on the subject of becoming a candidate for Governor. O'Connor, who bore the full name of James Francis Thaddeus O'Connor, was born in North Dakota and had served as a congressman from that state. Defeated in 1920 for Governor and in 1922 for United States Senator, he had moved to California and formed a law partnership with McAdoo. He had led the Roosevelt slate in southern California, yet he had maintained his alliance with McAdoo, but was friendly with Creel, Harrison and Wardell in the north. He appeared to be the man who could unite all factions, and throughout 1933 and into 1934 his friends urged him to enter the race. Colonel John P. Carter, whom Roosevelt had appointed Collector of Internal Revenue in Los Angeles, traveled to Washington in January to enlist him as a candidate. In February, Storke and Franklin K. Lane, son of Wilson's Secretary of the Interior, made a determined effort to recruit him. In April the California Young Democrats endorsed him.

O'Connor's apparent obliviousness to these beckonings resulted in George Creel jumping into the race obviously encouraged by Storke, Harrison and Cotton who were desperately engaged in heading off Upton Sinclair. Wardell also announced his candidacy. In May Giannini called O'Connor saying he could get Wardell to withdraw if he would run. Joseph Schenk, president of United Artists, also urged him to change his mind, while Dockweiler pleaded with him pointing out he was the unanimous choice of the California Congressional Delegation. On June 20, President Roosevelt told O'Connor he would make a speech in California for him. Three days later the last day for filing had come and gone and O'Connor was now definitely out of a race he himself had never been in. While O'Connor was the most important New Dealer in California, he was having too good a time in Washington to run for Governor in 1934.[38]

This frantic scrambling to recruit a candidate of O'Connor's stature had been occasioned by the fact that the perennial Socialist candidate Upton Sinclair had, in September, 1933, registered Democratic as a prelude to his entry into the gubernatorial race. This move had apparently been prompted by Gilbert F. Stevenson, dispossessed owner of the Santa Monica Miramar Hotel and Los Angeles County committeeman. To launch his campaign, Sinclair sat down and wrote another book, this one entitled: *I, Governor of California and How I Ended Poverty*. In it he proposed radical remedies for unemployment, inequitable taxes, social security and agriculture problems. Now all that was left to do was to get himself elected and then he could put his EPIC (End Poverty in California) program into effect. His book, his candidacy, and his campaign astounded the Democratic politicians.

An indefatigable speaker as well as a prolific writer, Sinclair moved around the state speaking to any group of willing listeners. EPIC clubs sprang up everywhere in the state. By 1934 there were nearly 300 of them and by the end of

March there were 200 more. Starting with one room and one secretary the EPIC headquarters by campaign's end occupied thirty-two offices and had scores of volunteer workers. The depression had created an army seeking a crusade and it had found one.

Sinclair's campaign was aided and abetted by the Democrats once again splitting into factions and putting forth their own favorites as candidates. In addition to Creel and Wardell there were Milton K. Young, Dr. Z. T. Malaby and four other minor personalities, nine in all running for the Democratic nomination.[39]

Whatever else Sinclair's campaign may have done to or for the Democratic Party in California he made one great contribution, a tremendous increase in Democratic registration. Never before had the Democrats outnumbered the Republicans. But with the tremendous drive launched by Sinclair—"Register Now As a Democrat to Nominate Upton Sinclair"—from January to July nearly 350,000 new Democrats registered. By the time of the primary the Democrats had a lead of 75,000 and in Los Angeles County 138,000. Creel, horrified by the change in Los Angeles, wrote:

> Northern California offered no problems, for hardworking, hardheaded native sons and daughters were in a majority, but when I crossed the Tehachapi into Southern California, it was like plunging into darkest Africa without gun bearers.[40]

By August 28, the day of the primary election, it was clear to most neutral observers, like Farley and O'Connor, that Sinclair was winning in a breeze. In the nine-man race Sinclair captured a 52% majority of the 842,000 Democratic votes cast so that he had a total of 436,000 votes against his nearest rival Creel who had 288,000. Wardell and Young each got less than 50,000 and the other five were also-rans. Farley privately advocated that the party now get solidly behind Sinclair, but this was not to be the case.[41]

Merriam, now running for election in his own right, easily captured the Republican nomination 346,000 to 231,000 for former Governor C. C. Young. Young was obviously hurt in his comeback try by the candidacy of the popular John R. Quinn of Los Angeles who had strong backing from the American Legion, was supported by the McClatchy *Bees* and polled 153,000, and by Raymond L. Haight, whose proclivity for splitting campaign votes was to reach even greater heights in later elections. The three progressives had polled 123,000 more votes than old standpat conservative Merriam, and, like the Democrats, blown the election because of their inability to unite.

The 1934 Democratic primary did provide one signal lesson in politics on the bright side in contrast to the already well-established axiom that elections cannot be won without unity. Party leaders were treated to a demonstration that the enemy is not always the fellow wearing the opposite party label and that there is such a thing as loyalty in politics. For the old progressive war horse Hiram Johnson was up for re-election to his fourth term in the United States Senate. He had endeared himself to the President with his dramatic break away from Hoover in 1932 to support Roosevelt. Now, Roosevelt wanted to repay him for that endorsement without being obvious and particularly without Johnson knowing it. Johnson, the father of crossfiling, had always hoped to be the first to capture successfully the nomination of both major parties for one of the two highest state offices. Working through McAdoo and Neblett they effectively blocked out the possibility of any strong Democratic candidate entering the race against Johnson. Giannini helped out with a campaign contribution of $150,000 which in those days was an abundant one, and Johnson became the first candidate for United States Senator to win in the primaries, beating two insignificant Democratic candidates in that primary 656,000 to 50,000 and 45,000.[42]

FOOTNOTES

1   For biographical information on these candidates, see Secretary of State, *California Blue Book, 1932*; Albert Nelson Marquis, ed., *Who's Who in America*, 17th ed., vol. 17, 1932–1933 (Chicago: The A. N. Marquis Company, 1932), 2,671 pp., 30,545 sketches; Justus B. Detweiler, ed., *Who's Who in California, 1928–1929* (San Francisco: Who's Who Publishing Company, 1929), 720 pp.; and V. E. Thurman, comp. and ed., *Who's Who in the New Deal*, California Edition (Los Angeles: The New Deal Historical Society, Inc., 1938), 472 pp. Additional information on the candidates and the United States Senatorial campaign of 1932 in California is based upon interviews by the author with: Joe Crail (nephew of the Congressman), February 19, 1955; Robert W. Kenny, December 29, 1954; Gwen Powers (Secretary to both Joe Crails), February 21, 1955, and the Rev. Robert P. "Bob" Schuler, Sr. February 21, 1955.

2   Robert J. Pitchell, *Twentieth Century California Voting Behavior* (Unpublished Ph.D. dissertation, University of California at Berkeley, 1955), 369 pp. Three dissertations that cover some of the party squabbles of this period are Ronald E. Chinn, *Democratic Party Politics in California, 1920–1956* (Unpublished Ph.D. dissertation, University of California at Berkeley, 1958), 369 pp. and Royce D. Delmatier, *The Rebirth of the Democratic Party in California, 1928–1938* (Unpublished Ph.D. dissertation, University of California at Berkeley, 1955), 333 pp., and Charles W. Noah, *California Politics During the Roosevelt Era, 1932–1939* (Unpublished M. A. thesis, University of Southern California, 1950), 83 pp.

3   This history of the national delegations from California is discussed in Dean R. Cresap, *Party Politics in the Golden State* (Los Angeles: The Haynes Foundation, 1954), pp. 68–76. An excellent study is Marilyn E. McCurtain, *Political Ecology of Three Metropolitan Areas of California: San Francisco, Los Angeles, San Diego, 1850–1950* (Unpublished M.A. thesis, University of California at Berkeley, 1955), 133 pp.

4   Franklin Hichborn, "California Politics, 1891–1939" (unpublished MSS: University of California at Los Angeles Library, 1949) V, 2679.

5   *Oakland Tribune,* April 1, 1932, p. 2, and April 6, 1932, p. 3, and April 17, 1932, p. 2, and May 1, 1932, p. 1.

6   N. W. Ayer and Son's, *Directory of Newspapers and Periodicals, 1932* (Philadelphia: N. W. Ayer and Son, Inc., 1932), pp. 68–115.

7   McAdoo's deal with Hearst in which the former agreed to head the Garner delegation in exchange for Hearst's support for the United States Senate is discussed in George Creel, *Rebel At Large* (New York: G. P. Putnam's Sons, 1947), p. 270. Hearst has commanded an unusually long list of biographies: John K. Winkler, *W. R. Hearst: An American Phenomenon* (London: Jonathan Cape, 1928), 319 pp.; Raymond Gram Swing, *Forerunners of American Fascism* (Coughlin, Long, Bilbo, Townsend, Hearst) (New York: Julian Messner, Inc., 1935), 168 pp.; Oliver Carlson and Ernest Sutherland Bates, *Hearst: Lord of San Simeon* (New York: The Viking Press, 1936), 332 pp.; Ferdinand Lundberg, *Imperial Hearst: A Social Biography* (New York: Equinox Cooperative Press, 1936), 406 pp.; Mrs. Fremont Older, *William Randolph Hearst: American* (New York: D. Appleton-Century Company, 1936), 581 pp.; Edmond D. Coblentz, ed. *William Randolph Hearst: A Portrait in His Own Words* (New York: Simon and Schuster, 1952), 309 pp.; *The Life and Good Times of William Randolph Hearst* (New York: E. P. Dutton and Co., Inc. 1952), 386 pp.; and W. A. Swanberg, *Citizen Hearst: A Biography of William Randolph Hearst* (New York: Charles Scribners Sons, 1961), 653 pp. McAdoo and Garner have had fewer biographers: William Gibbs McAdoo, *Crowded Years: The Reminiscences of William Gibbs McAdoo* (Boston: Houghton Mifflin Company, 1931), 542 pp.; George Rothwell Brown, *The Speaker of the House: The Romantic Story of John N. Garner* (New York: Brewer, Warren and Putnam, 1932), 162 pp.; Marquis James, *Mr. Garner of Texas* (Indianapolis: The Bobbs-Merrill Company, 1939), 158 pp., and Bascum N. Timmons, *Garner of Texas: A Personal History* (New York: Harper and Brothers, 1948), 294 pp.

8   Eugene Edgar Kerrick, Jr., *California and the Presidential Election of 1932* (Unpublished M.A. thesis, University of California at Berkeley, 1956), pp. 10–16.

9   *Los Angeles Herald Express,* April 1, 1932, p. 14.

10   *Santa Barbara Daily News,* April 2, 1932.

11   *Los Angeles Herald Express,* April 5, 1932, p. 11; *ibid.,* April 12, 1932, p. 5.

12   *Ibid.,* April 25, 1932, p. 11; *ibid.,* April 23, 1932, p. 1.

13   Elliott Roosevelt, ed., *F.D.R.: His Personal Letters* (New York: Duell, Sloan and Pearce, 1947–1950), III, 198–202.

14   James A. Farley, *Behind the Ballots* (New York: Harcourt, Brace and Company, 1938), pp. 108–109.

15   *You're the Boss* (New York: The Viking Press, 1947), pp. 119–120.

16   *Ibid.,* pp. 85–87.

17   On the Wardell–Smith–Roosevelt quarrels, see *Los Angeles Times,* April 15, 1932, p. 7; *Oakland Tribune,* April 18, 1932, p. 2; *ibid.,* April 19, 1932, p. 2; *ibid.,* April 24, 1932, pp. A1 and B1; *ibid.,* April 25, 1932, p. 2; and *ibid.,* April 27, 1932, p. 2.

18   *Los Angeles Herald Express,* May 2, 1932, p. 1.

19   One should look at the analyses of the election by Wesley M. Barr, political writer for the *Los Angeles Herald Express,* May 4 and 5, 1932, p. 1; and Walter P. Jones, *Sacramento Bee,* May 4, 1932, p. 1.

20   *Oakland Tribune,* May 4, 1932, p. 2.

21   *Ibid.,* May 4, 1932, p. 2.

22   *Oakland Tribune,* April 3, 1932, p. 1.

23   The best analyses of the convention are: Farley, *op. cit.,* pp. 109–153; *New York Times,* June and July, 1932; *Los Angeles Herald Express, loc. cit.; Chicago Tribune, loc. cit.; San Francisco Chronicle, loc. cit.*

24   *California Supreme Court Justice Jesse Washington Carter,* an interview conducted by the Regional Cultural Oral History Project (University of California at Berkeley, 1959), pp. 144–145. For a short biographical sketch of Carter, one may look at Corinne Lathrop Gilb, "Justice Jesse E. Carter, An American Individualist," *Pacific Historical Review,* XXIX (May, 1960), 145–147.

25   California's role in the Garner switch is discussed in Russell M. Posner, "California's Role in the Nomination of Franklin D. Roosevelt," *California Historical Society Quarterly,* XXXIX (June, 1960), 121–139; and Arthur Mullen, *Western Democrat* (New York: Wilfred Funk, 1940), pp. 275–276; and James A. Farley, *Jim Farley's Story* (New York: McGraw-Hill, 1948), p. 23; and Daniel C. Roper, *Fifty Years of Public Life* (Durham: Duke University Press, 1941), p. 259; and Thomas M. Storke, *California Editor* (Los Angeles: Westernlore Press, 1958), pp. 318–319.

26   The Garner switch is also discussed in: Timmons, *op. cit.,* Chapter X; Farley, *op. cit.,* pp. 144–151; Older, *op. cit.,* pp. 151–153; Coblentz, ed., *op. cit.,* Chapter 13; and Lela Stiles, *The Man Behind Roosevelt: The Story of Louis McHenry Howe* (Cleveland: The World Publishing Company, 1954), p. 166 ff.

27   Elmer Patterson, Jr., *Congressional Reapportionment in California, 1849–1931* (Unpublished M.A. thesis, University of California at Berkeley, 1935), pp. 52–68.

28   The standard authority is Barclay, "Reapportionment in California," *Pacific Historical Review,* V (June, 1936), 93–129.

29   Robert J. Pitchell, "The Electoral System and Voting Behavior: The Case of California's Cross-Filing," *Western Political Quarterly,* XII (June, 1959), 459–484.

30   Robert E. Burke, *Cross-Filing in California Elections, 1914–1946* (Unpublished M.A. thesis, University of California at Berkeley, 1947), pp. 51–94, and Dean E. McHenry "Cross-Filing of Political Candidates in California," *Annals of the American Academy of Political and Social Science,* CCXLVIII (November, 1946), 226–231.

31   *Sacramento Bee,* September 14, 1932, pp. 1–2.

32   *Ibid.,* September 24, 1932, p. 1. Bosley Crowther, *Hollywood Rajah: The Life and Times of Louis B. Mayer* (New York: Holt, Rinehart and Winston, 1960), 399 pp., includes a minimum of information on the political activities of this important figure.

33   William S. Myers and Walter H. Newton, *The Hoover Administration: A Documented Narrative* (New York: Scribner's, 1935), p. 516.

34 *Sacramento Bee*, November 9, 1932, p. 1.

35 *The Future of American Politics* (New York: Harper and Brothers, 1952), pp. 29–34.

36 J. F. T. O'Connor, Year Book Diaries, in possession of the Bancroft Library, University of California, Berkeley, May 8, 1933 ff.

37 *Ibid.*, July 20, 1933, ff.

38 *Ibid.*, May 7, 1933; *ibid.*, January 15 and 20, 1934; *ibid.*, February 6 and 13 and 19, 1934; *ibid.*, April 23, 1934; *ibid.*, May 9 and 29; *ibid.*, June 5 and 20, 1934.

39 The Sinclair campaign is covered in three books by Sinclair himself, and is also the subject of three theses: Upton Sinclair, *I, Governor of California and How I Ended Poverty* (Los Angeles: Upton Sinclair, 1934), 64 pp.; *ibid.*, *The Epic Plan for California* (Los Angeles: Upton Sinclair, 1934), 195 pp.; *ibid.*, *I, Candidate for Governor and How I Got Licked* (New York: Farrar and Rinehart, 1934), 224 pp.; Ronald E. Chinn, *The Sinclair Campaign of 1934* (M.A. thesis, Stanford University, 1937), 132 pp.; Charles E. Larsen, *The Epic Movement in California Politics* (M.A. thesis, University of California, 1945), 64 pp.; George R. Ashton, *Upton Sinclair* (M.A. thesis, University of California, 1951), 176 pp.

40 Creel, *op. cit.*, p. 285.

41 O'Connor, *op. cit.*, August 28 and 29, 1934.

42 Interview by the author with Colonel William H. Neblett, February 21, 1955. Four of the standard books on California politics list 1940 and 1952 as the only elections in which a candidate for United States Senator crossfiled successfully, each neglecting to mention the election of 1934, the first time it was done. See Winston W. Crouch and Dean E. McHenry, *California Government: Politics and Administration*, Revised Edition (Berkeley: University of California Press, 1949), p. 35; Cresap, *op. cit.*, p. 78; David Farrelly and Ivan Hinderaker, *The Politics of California: A Book of Readings* (New York: The Ronald Press Company, 1951), p. 76; Bernard L. Hyink, Seyom Brown, Ernest W. Thacker, *Politics and Government in California*, Sixth Edition (New York: Thomas Y. Crowell Company, 1969), p. 50. Two other books commenting on the 1934 Sinclair campaign are Rosten, *Hollywood: The Movie Colony and the Movie Makers*, Chapter 6; and Roosevelt, *F. D. R.: His Personal Letters*, III, 426–427.

Panaceas and
California Politics

The outcome of the August primary elections in 1934 sent shock waves throughout California political party circles. The gubernatorial primaries were the focus of attention. A three-way race for the governorship was in the offing between Governor Frank F. Merriam, a relatively unpopular conservative Republican candidate; Raymond Haight, a former Republican, victor in both the Commonwealth and Progressive Party primaries; and Democrat Upton Sinclair, an internationally prominent writer and former Socialist Party member who had been registered in the Democratic Party for only twelve months.[1]

Had it not been for Sinclair, August 29 would have been a day of joy and congratulations among Democratic Party workers. The prospects for a Democratic victory in November would have been bright. Both party registration and the overwhelming popularity of the New Deal administration of Franklin Roosevelt were in their favor. How would the party and the electorate react to Sinclair?

The future seemed quite uncertain to the regulars of the two parties, both of which were badly divided, poorly organized, and ineffectively led, for events which they had tried to shape in the past appeared to be beyond their control. California, except in party registration and national politics, was close to being a no-party rather than a two-party state during the turbulent 1930's as political panaceas strongly influenced the course of politics.[2]

When Upton Sinclair announced his gubernatorial candidacy in September, 1933, he had perceived that the weakness of the Democratic Party organization made it vulnerable. Best known for his writings, especially the novel *The Jungle*, the fifty-six year old author had been a Socialist Party candidate in California

 Clarence F. McIntosh was primarily responsible for the original draft of Chapter 9.

272

three times before as nominee for the Tenth District congressional seat in 1920 and gubernatorial nominee in 1926 and 1930. In these races he had not tested either his campaigning or his vote-getting ability for he had not campaigned actively. He merely allowed his name and reputation to be used to help the Socialist Party. A believer in socialism, which he defined as the social ownership and democratic control of the means of production, and a Socialist Party member of long standing, Sinclair had remained a propagandist rather than a party worker since his conversion to the cause in 1904. His experience in propaganda and its techniques was his major asset in the campaign, which he had begun in earnest late in November, 1933.

His first step, after changing his party registration to Democrat, was to prepare his program which he published in a pamphlet, *I, Governor of California; And How I Ended Poverty: A True Story of the Future.* From the phrase "End Poverty In California" came the name EPIC plan. Outwardly it was a program to end unemployment but Sinclair's intention was radical. Unemployment in his view was the result of the profit system. As wealth was concentrated in few hands, workers were unable to buy what they had produced and want in the midst of plenty was the social result. Unemployment, he maintained, was a permanent condition in a profit system society so a more drastic measure than public relief was needed.

He proposed to establish with state aid a "production for use" program which would be a self-sufficient system of land colonies and factories for the unemployed. Within this, he planned that the unemployed would produce goods for their own consumption; that surplus produce from the colonies and factories would be exchanged between them; and that a separate medium of exchange for its use would be created. The system would become self-governing and independent of the capitalist system and would take the unemployed off the backs of the taxpayers. The remaining portions of his plan included a tax program frankly designed to redistribute the income and social welfare measures such as pensions. To put the plan into effect, he needed first to win control of the Democratic Party and, second, of the government in the general election.[3]

Sinclair had been campaigning for five months before his major opponents, George Creel and Justus Wardell, became candidates in April, 1934, and never lost his lead. How his movement became the major faction of the Democratic Party of California within a few months with 436,220 votes out of a total of 844,117 cast for Democratic gubernatorial candidates is one of the amazing stories in the history of California politics.

In brief, Sinclair developed an effective organization and attracted massive grass-roots support. The End Poverty League, established as the official organization of the EPIC movement independent of the Democratic Party, directed the campaign. Although most EPIC workers were politically in-

273

experienced, many of the more important workers had previous experience in other radical and reformist groups, particularly the Socialist Party. From the latter came Richard Otto, campaign manager; J. Stitt Wilson, an effective campaigner who was former Socialist Mayor of Berkeley; H. Jerry Voorhis, a member of the Executive Committee of the Socialist Party of California; and Reuben Boroughs, an experienced journalist who became editor of the campaign newspaper.[4]

To finance the campaign, the League sold copies of *I, Governor of California* and subsequent pamphlets written by Sinclair. It also took up collections at meetings. It published a weekly tabloid newspaper, first entitled *Upton Sinclair's End Poverty Paper* and renamed *Upton Sinclair's EPIC News*, which was either sold or distributed. Early issues numbered 20,000 but the last issue before the primary election totaled 1,450,000. Members of the League paid dues. EPIC-sponsored radio broadcasts, which began in April, 1934, and continued throughout the campaign, appealed to listeners for funds.

Local clubs, directed by the League, became the basis of the mass movement. California chapters of the League for Independent Political Action, a national group which advocated a radical third party, provided the initial core of statewide clubs. These were in Los Angeles, Long Beach, San Diego, Sacramento, and Chico.[5] Attracted to the movement were the unemployed and under-employed. Support also came from revived Bellamy Clubs, technocratic groups, and the Utopian Society of America—all of which advocated, like EPIC, production for use and abolition of the profit system. By October, 1934, an estimated 400,000 southern Californians had been members of the latter, at least for a brief time. Centering mainly in southern California where unemployment was greatest, EPIC clubs numbered 1,000 by late August and 2,000 by the time of the general election. Many members were new registrants in the Democratic Party.

The End Poverty League also attracted supporters and extended its organization by putting together a nearly complete EPIC ticket which included candidates for statewide offices and state senatorial and assembly districts. Most important was the addition of Sheridan Downey, a Sacramento attorney, as the EPIC candidate for the office of lieutenant governor. Downey had announced on October 20, 1933, that he was a Democratic candidate for the office of governor. He had gained some following as chief counsel for a legislative committee investigating the Rolph administration. Downey and Sinclair began a series of correspondence and conferences in early March, 1934. The two men finally ironed out their differences and Downey became Sinclair's running mate in May. His presence gave geographical balance to the ticket, it added an effective campaigner, and it attracted some farmer support. Newspapers immediately dubbed the team "Uppie and Downey." Other candidates for state offices and a legislative slate became part of the EPIC ticket. Of special interest

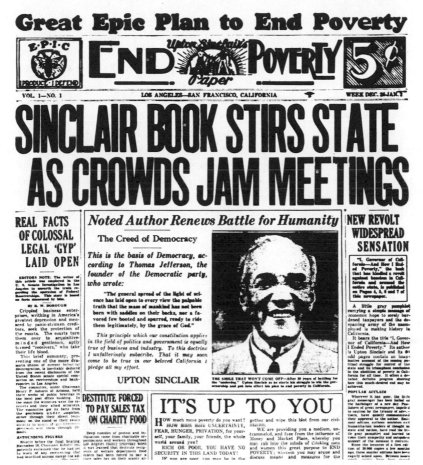

Page one of the first issue of the *End Poverty Paper*. Along with its successor, the *EPIC News*, it was the voice of the End Poverty League. Tabloid-size newspapers were important propaganda vehicles of California political groups during the 1930's and 1940's. (Courtesy of Clarence F. McIntosh.)

was EPIC endorsement of Ellis Patterson, a Republican, for the race in the Thirty-fifty Assembly District, and of Culbert L. Olson, a Democrat, for the Los Angeles County state senatorial seat. Both would become important in California political life. All of the endorsed candidates, except Olson, became, as required, members of the End Poverty League. Olson, who believed that the Democratic Party was the only appropriate instrument by which to bring about reform, promised instead to support EPIC legislative measures. This compromise foreshadowed conflict between the League and the Democratic Party.[6]

Sinclair led the entire EPIC ticket in the primary. The southern California vote was significant in his victory. He received nearly 69% of his vote from the ten southern counties. Downey, the other successful EPIC candidate for nomination to a state-wide office, won handily over nine competitors but trailed the gubernatorial nominee by 100,000 votes. In the nine out of twenty races for State Senate nominations where EPIC-endorsed candidates ran, only three won. Significantly Culbert Olson carried Los Angeles County. In the eighty contests for assembly seats, EPIC candidates won thirty-nine out of the sixty-three races where endorsements were made. Twenty-seven of these were in Los Angeles County and four in Alameda County. Although EPIC forces could not control either house of the Legislature regardless of the general election, there was jubilation in EPIC circles. The editor of the *EPIC News* informed EPIC workers that they were now the Democratic Party in California, "the recognized fighting vanguard of President Roosevelt's New Deal Army."[7]

Sinclair maintained the momentum of his campaign to the general election on November 6. His first move was dramatically executed. He went east for a two-hour appointment with President Roosevelt and afterward held a press conference in which he was lavish in his praise of Roosevelt. He did not disclose what was discussed, but privately he believed that Roosevelt would endorse the principle of production for use in a speech around October 25. Sinclair evidently mistook courtesy and friendliness for approval of his views. He consulted with others in the administration and gained national publicity. The irrepressible candidate capped his journey with the announcement that hence-forth EPIC would mean "End Poverty In Civilization." (His opponents would shortly give it other meanings.) Back in California, his second move was to gain endorsement of the California State Federation of Labor. His third was to reach apparent agreement with McAdoo and Creel on arrangements for the Democratic state convention, contents of the platform, and the naming of Culbert Olson as State Chairman.[8] The Sacramento convention went off as planned and at its conclusion, Sinclair, Creel, McAdoo and Downey affirmed their "complete harmony." Momentarily Sinclair succeeded in identifying himself with the New Deal and gained support from both organized labor and the second largest Democratic Party faction.

Then Sinclair's campaign suffered a set-back. Within eleven days he had a disagreement with Creel over the interpretation of the platform and on October 26, the latter repudiated the Democratic gubernatorial candidate for breaking the Sacramento agreement. Some Wardell and Creel primary backers mean-while vigorously organized special committees to defeat the Democratic heretic. The majority of Democratic federal office-holders, including McAdoo, main-tained public support of Sinclair although they did not work for his victory.

Governor Merriam and the Republican Party attempted unsuccessfully to mount a constructive campaign in September. The party platform pointed to its

Imitation currency which was widely circulated by opponents to Sinclair. (Courtesy of Clarence F. McIntosh.)

progressive record under Hiram Johnson; it endorsed expanded unemployment relief; it supported collective bargaining for labor; it requested national endorsement of the thirty-hour week and six-hour day; it favored enlargement of the state's old-age pension system; and it recommended study of the Townsend plan by the federal government.

The Townsend plan was a pension proposal advocated by Dr. Francis E. Townsend, a retired Long Beach physician, which called for pensions of $200 a month for every person over sixty with a record of good citizenship. The recipients would be required to refrain from remunerative work and to spend their pensions within thirty days. Townsend proposed to finance this by levying a federal sales tax. The plan, he believed, would foster national prosperity. Sinclair had called this "a mere money scheme" that would not bring about the needed reconstruction of society. The move by the Republicans to endorse the Townsend plan was politically practical but fiscally irresponsible.[9]

The Republican platform did stress, however, that the campaign was a nonpartisan affair between Americanism and radicalism rather than between Republicans and Democrats, and it invited Democrats to join in the salvation of the state. This, rather than the other endorsements, set the tone of the campaign. Sinclair became the leading issue in what political scientist Totten J. Anderson, has called "a classic exhibition of political vilification."[10]

The Republican Party was almost lost sight of in the midst of special anti-Sinclair committees—the California League Against Sinclairism, Nonpartisan Merriam for Governor Club, United for California League, and the League Against Religious Intolerance, to name only a few. These groups issued thousands of pieces of scurrilous campaign literature against Sinclair labelling him pro-Communist and anti-religious. The *San Francisco Chronicle* and the *Los Angeles Times* led the attacks of the press as each issue became an anti-Sinclair document. The Hearst press joined them in the attack after mid-October. The pulpit joined the press in the attack as pastors of some leading Los Angeles churches made anti-Sinclair statements on Sunday in order to be featured in the Monday *Times*. Business associations joined the fight. Motion-picture industry leaders put their facilities to work in the campaign to discredit Sinclair as they manufactured "newsreels."

Opponents of EPIC matched Sinclair's followers emotionalism born of frustration with their own emotionalism born of fear that Sinclair might be elected. Fear became widespread among the business interests of the state. No doubt the presence of Raymond Haight, who would draw Republican votes, on the ballot contributed to this fear as it increased the unpredictability of the election's outcome. The relative unpopularity of Merriam was another factor. But its major causes stemmed from the challenge to the depression-weakened economic order brought about by the rising influence of organized labor and increasing acceptance of radical alternatives by a segment of the electorate.

Sinclair was vulnerable to attack. He had been a follower of cults and fads for much of his adult life. He had been a member of Communist-front organizations. His book *The Profits of Religion* was a sharp attack upon aspects of institutionalized religion, and in it, he had made remarks offensive to the major denominations. His claims to harmony with the New Deal were thin. Largely ignored in the campaign was the fact that both the miniscule Communist and Socialist parties, noisy but ineffective, attacked Sinclair respectively as a social fascist and working class traitor.

Crucial to EPIC campaign plans was securing New Deal endorsement of "production for use." But the national administration, originally tolerant of Sinclair, became antagonistic toward him by October 23.

National party leaders, at this point, fell in with a scheme to get Sinclair to

A widely circulated anti-Sinclair leaflet during the 1934 campaign. (Courtesy of Clarence F. McIntosh.)

SINCLAIR

SLANDERER
OF
ALL CHURCHES
AND
ALL CHRISTIAN INSTITUTIONS

ACTIVE OFFICIAL
OF
COMMUNIST ORGANIZATIONS

COMMUNIST WRITER

COMMUNIST AGITATOR

Issued by
THE LEAGUE AGAINST RELIGIOUS
INTOLERANCE

CORDES BUILDING
Room 201
126 POST STREET   SAN FRANCISCO

withdraw from the campaign in favor of Haight. Raymond Haight first suggested the proposal to Sinclair in order to avoid the election of a reactionary. Sinclair declined, but Haight took the matter to Washington using A. P. Giannini, head of the Bank of America, as the intermediary. The banker, a Roosevelt supporter in 1932, feared the consequences that might flow from the election of either Merriam or Sinclair. J. F. T. O'Connor and Farley agreed to cooperate, believing that weakening Merriam in 1934 would guarantee the state to Roosevelt in 1936. Members of Roosevelt's White House staff agreed to the scheme, providing it did not appear that they were directly involved. O'Connor, after learning that the President wanted him to go, flew to Los Angeles ostensibly to consider speaking for the EPIC cause but actually to suggest, if the conditions seemed proper, to Sinclair that he withdraw in Haight's favor.

O'Connor met with Sinclair in Los Angeles on October 30. He suggested to Sinclair that "some arrangements should be made" if he were doubtful about victory. Sinclair, however, offered O'Connor radio time to speak in support of his candidacy. The Comptroller delayed his reply saying he needed time to do some consulting on the matter. He then met with Sinclair's opponents. From Merriam he got the promise that the Governor would announce that his re-election was not a repudiation of the New Deal and that it was brought about with the assistance of many Roosevelt leaders in California.[11] Merriam, who had found that his most direct support was from dissident Democrats, had in effect been saying as much and agreed readily.

Voters turned out in record numbers on November 6. The total votes cast was 2,330,132, some 31,000 above the number cast in the 1932 presidential election. The results brought a defeat to the EPIC movement. Sinclair received 879,537 votes or 37.3% of the total cast for governor. Merriam led him by 259,083 votes, a total of 1,138,620. He received 48.9% of the total. Haight received 320,519 or 12.9% of the vote. George Hatfield, the Republican candidate for Lieutenant Governor, won over Sheridan Downey, 1,220,515 to 1,002,832. In the state assembly races, twenty-four EPIC candidates won. Fifteen of these in Los Angeles County were new Democratic candidates. Three EPIC supporters in the state senate races, including Culbert Olson, also won. Sinclair, although he lost, nearly doubled his total primary vote, mainly in Los Angeles and the San Francisco Bay counties. Democratic defection was strong; he actually polled fewer votes than the combined total of the Democratic vote for primary gubernatorial candidates in fifty out of fifty-eight counties.[12] This would be the first of many statewide elections in which Democratic voters, while outnumbering Republicans, would help elect Republican candidates.

Republican politicians in future elections would frequently charge that the Democratic Party was left-wing or radical, referring to the socialist background of some of the party leaders who emerged in the election of 1934. On the other hand, the EPIC movement transformed the Democratic Party of California into a reformist party. Sinclair quipped in his concession of defeat, "If we had had a better candidate, we might have won!" The election of 1938 would prove him correct.

Factionalism continued to dominate the Democratic Party between 1934 and 1938. The struggle for control of the party was between two major factions, McAdoo and his supporters and the new "liberal" group over which Culbert Olson gradually assumed leadership. Olson was fifty-eight years of age the year he became Democratic State Chairman in California. Having supported reform measures as a legislator in Utah from 1916 to 1920 he had a record in politics that marked him as a reformer. He had been a delegate to the 1920 Democratic National Convention but later that year dropped out of politics because of the limited opportunity for reform in the 1920's. Moving to Los Angeles where he entered private law practice, he shunned politics until 1932 except for a brief re-entry in 1924. In 1932, he helped organize the Los Angeles Democratic Club and became a Roosevelt supporter. Both his appointment as State Chairman and his victory in the state senate race in Los Angeles County in 1934 placed him in a position of influence in the Democratic Party.[13]

Olson strengthened himself by his effective legislative leadership for reform in 1935. He introduced a bill in the State Senate for every plank of the Democratic platform and forced discussion of these bills. He was aided in this, on the one hand, with the virtual retirement by Sinclair from politics. Sinclair had a book to write and a lecture tour to make in an attempt to raise money to pay off debts accumulated during his campaign. Olson made some progress in getting EPIC clubs, over the opposition of the End Poverty League, to convert themselves into Democratic clubs. On the other hand, he gained some assistance from the New Deal administration which wished to improve relations with the EPIC Democrats as the 1936 election approached. As one skilled observer reported to the President, McAdoo was too weak a reed to depend upon in California.

Both Roosevelt and Farley hoped to bolster the President's position by uniting the pro-Roosevelt groups in California on one slate of delegates to the 1936 Democratic National Convention. Olson, after conferences with both national leaders, agreed to work out a compromise list of delegates with the understanding that the national administration would aid him with patronage. One result of this was Olson's appointment as special assistant to the United States Attorney General to give advice on matters relating to California oil. Roosevelt and Farley dealt with the McAdoo faction through the Senator himself.

Olson found himself frustrated at every turn in his effort to get a compromise delegation. He found that the End Poverty League directors were more interested in principle than in the prospect of patronage. They wanted a slate for Roosevelt but pledged to a platform of "production for use." McAdoo took advantage of the circumstances and in a speech at San Francisco took a strong stand against having the delegation pledged to anyone but Roosevelt. Roosevelt eventually selected the slate, and each faction was represented. Since some Democrats who had campaigned against Sinclair in 1934 were included, the State Chairman found his position impossible and withdrew from the delegation.[14]

The End Poverty League then revolted. Sinclair returned to politics again briefly to head a slate pledged to the EPIC program with the understanding that it would vote for Roosevelt on the second ballot at the convention. A dissident Townsend plan faction operating independently of Townsend also formed a slate of delegates pledged to Congressman John S. McGroaty. Thus the Roosevelt slate faced two opponents in the presidential primary on May 18, 1936. Because of the President's popularity, his list of delegates won overwhelmingly, and the factions went on to back him in the presidential campaign.

In 1936 the Republicans faced a more serious presidential primary contest than the Democrats. There were three principals: former President Herbert Hoover, Governor Frank Merriam, and publisher William Randolph Hearst, as well as minor figures like Earl Warren, Republican State Chairman and District Attorney of Alameda County. Some politicians viewed Hoover's political activities in 1935 as an attempt of the Hoover wing of the party to capture control; others viewed them as the beginning of a Hoover bid for renomination. As Hoover's activities continued, it became apparent that he at least had as an objective a California delegation in which he would have considerable influence. Meanwhile, the favorite son candidacy of Merriam also became a possibility. This would assist the Governor in controlling the party. At this point, the interests of anti-Merriam Republicans coincided with Hoover's interests and they persuaded Warren to appoint a state-wide committee to select an unpledged delegation. Two friends of Merriam refused to serve on the committee.

Merriam himself refused a place on the delegation and became head of his own delegation pledged to Governor Alfred Landon of Kansas and backed by William Randolph Hearst. In substance the fight was reduced to a conflict over local control of the party. Neither Hoover nor Landon were mentioned very often in the brief, sharp campaign. The Warren "harmony" slate promoters campaigned against the possibility of Hearst influencing the Republican Party as he had the Democratic. The Merriam–Hearst supporters argued against bossism. The Warren slate defeated the Merriam slate by 90,000 votes, and at the Cleveland convention supported Landon.[15]

The results had the effect of reducing popular belief in the power of the Hearst press in California politics. Observers regarded the election results as a defeat for Hearst rather than for Merriam or Landon. When Landon, with Hearst's support, was defeated by Roosevelt by over 900,000 votes in California alone, Hearst no longer appeared invincible.[16]

With the Roosevelt sweep of all fifty-eight counties, Democrats made gains at other levels. They picked up three congressional seats to hold a total of sixteen out of twenty. In the State Senate, six were added to the ten Democrats already there, and for the first time in the twentieth century, a majority of forty-seven out of eighty seats went to Democrats in the Assembly. Relative strength remained strongest in mountain and valley counties of the north but numerical strength was in the urban counties. The election generally strengthened the liberal bloc of Democrats.

Meanwhile the Depression and the New Deal, in addition to local political conditions, shaped the Merriam administration. Merriam was Iowa-born and educated. After an eight-year career in politics there, he had moved first to Oklahoma Territory in 1901 and then to Long Beach, California, in 1910 where he joined the *Long Beach Press* staff. First elected to the State Assembly in 1916, he became Speaker in 1923. After being defeated as a candidate for the lieutenant governorship in 1926, he won a seat in the State Senate in 1928; that same year as Republican State Chairman he managed the Hoover campaign in California. Elected as Lieutenant Governor in 1930, and as Governor in his own right in 1934, he became the only Governor who has served in both houses of the Legislature and has presided over both of them as well. His opponents thought he was an economy-minded, right-wing reactionary, a view that appeared to be confirmed by his appointment of former Governor Friend Richardson as Superintendent of Banks in 1934. Yet Merriam was an experienced politician and was not doctrinaire. Influenced by the temper of the times and the need for support, his administration was "an exercise in moderation," as Jackson Putnam described it, "in which the Governor sought to alleviate some of the sufferings of the underprivileged without disturbing too deeply the privileges and perquisites of those with a heavy stake in the status quo."[17] During his term, he opposed the New Deal in his speeches but cooperated with it in his legislative proposals and day-to-day administration.

Finances and tax problems, on the one hand, and relief and aged welfare programs, on the other, dominated his administration. In 1935 he submitted a $400,000,000 budget and a tax increase proposal of $155,000,000. He included increased taxes on banks, corporations, insurance companies, and liquor as well as new taxes on income and amusements. Most of his tax proposals passed the Legislature with some compromises and much sound and fury from the EPIC Democrats. Two years later he coupled a larger budget with no new taxes and held the Legislature in line. His State Emergency Relief Administration cooperated with the national administration in its programs for the unemployed.

Six Presidential Elections from 1916 to 1936

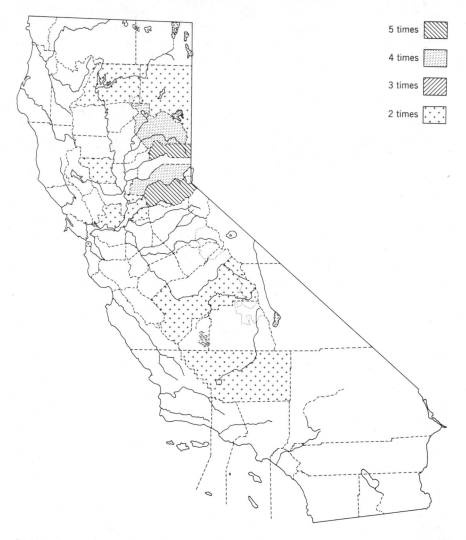

The map shows the centers of Democratic strength by indicating the frequency with which counties appeared among the top ten having the highest percent Democratic vote in each of the six elections.

Expansion of the welfare program for the aged, 1934–1938, was remarkable. California had been the first state to pass a mandatory pension act. This had occurred in 1929. Pension politics, though not depression-born, became greatly intensified by the economic hardships of the 1930's. With the active support of Merriam, pensions were increased from $20.00 per month to a maximum grant of $35.00 and an average grant of $32.43, the highest in the nation by 1938. In addition, under the enabling California legislation which made the state eligible to receive anticipated federal social security funds, California adopted liberalized residence requirements and placed the minimum age of eligibility at sixty-five a full five years before this became national policy. Pension coverage expanded from 17,000 persons in 1934 to more than 125,000 in 1938. These and other improvements, however, were inadequate, and pressures for change continued.

Far more controversial was Merriam's advocacy of a legislative resolution to be sent to Washington endorsing the Townsend plan. The resolution passed the Legislature after considerable controversy in March, 1935. This was the high tide of Townsend influence in California politics. Although most legislators gave into the pressures, Culbert Olson added to his reputation by his fearless opposition to the proposal. The measure, which had no effect in Washington, offended people from a wide political spectrum. Hiram Johnson observed from Washington:

> If anything were wanting to demonstrate the hysteria and utter insanity of these times I think you had it here presented. Just think of the old Tory Republican Party, the party of Harry Chandler, oily Joe Knowland, and the Universities of California and Stanford, and Rowell, and Cameron, and of the Chambers of Commerce generally being for the Townsend plan! With such evidence before us, who can blame a longshoreman communist or a stark mad bolshevik for any intellectual gymnastics. Here are con- servative politics and ultra-respectability literally running riot.[18]

The Republicans had to pay their political debts. A Gallup Poll in 1936 disclosed that 13.7% of the Californians favored the $200 per month pension plan. The Townsendites with 1,200 clubs in California potentially held the balance of power between the two major parties. Merriam continued to espouse the Townsend plan until his defeat in 1938. But worse economic heresy than the Townsend plan was yet to come!

Pension plans rained on California in 1937–1938, as Jackson Putnam, scholar of California pension politics, observed. Some eighty "old age welfare schemes" appeared on the scene.[19] The most important of these came to be known as Ham and Eggs. Its southern California promoters initiated the proposal and it was placed on the November ballot in 1938 by nearly a million signatures.

United States Senator Hiram Johnson (1866–1945) with his friend and staunch political ally, C. K. McClatchy, editor and publisher of the *Sacramento Bee*, in April, 1936. (Courtesy of California State Library.)

By this complex measure, unemployed Californians over fifty years of age would receive thirty one-dollar pieces of scrip each Thursday, thus the slogan "Thirty Dollars Every Thursday." On the back of each warrant was space for fifty-two stamps, and one two-cent stamp bought from the state was to be added to the warrant each week by the holder. This feature would guarantee rapid circulation and four cents per warrant for administrative costs at the end of each year when the state was obligated to redeem the scrip.

286

The Republican politicians who rejected the Ham and Eggs proposal almost to a man, fought among themselves in the primary campaign in 1938 and contributed to their own defeat. Merriam remained a relatively unpopular Governor among Republican factions because of his program of taxes, his cooperation with the New Deal, advocacy of the Townsend plan, and alliance with Hearst in 1936. His severance tax proposal in 1935, which had been defeated, had made him doubly unpopular with oil interests. The raising of liquor taxes led the liquor lobbyist, Arthur H. Samish, to accuse him of being a traitor after the support he had received in 1934. The California Farm Bureau and a new organization, Associated Farmers of California, considered him unreliable on the labor question. The anti-Merriam Republicans backed Lieutenant Governor George J. Hatfield of San Francisco to oppose him. Merriam, however, fought back effectively by cooperating with the Sacramento Grand Jury investigation of lobbying, which discredited many legislators and legislative leaders like Hatfield. He kept newspaper editorial support behind him. He won the primary nomination but the bitterness of the campaign came back to haunt Merriam and the other leading Republicans in the general election campaign. In another contest, Philip Bancroft, old-time progressive Republican, farmer, and son of historian H. H. Bancroft, won the United States Senate nomination.[20]

Merriam and Bancroft, respectively, opposed Culbert Olson and Sheridan Downey in the general election. Olson, who announced his candidacy on September 4, 1937, had never lost the initiative during the primary campaign of eight Democratic candidates. Olson ran on a platform of production for use for the unemployed, public ownership of public utilities, protection of organized labor, an affirmation of civil rights, and a vague endorsement of the Ham and Eggs proposal. (Months later Olson would deny endorsement of the pension panacea but his repudiation in 1939 of messages sent in 1938 did not ring true.)[21] In addition to some Ham and Eggs backing, he received important support from the liberal Democrats and the Communist-influenced "united front" California Federation for Political Unity. His campaign was well financed and managed. He won the primary by a plurality of 42%, carrying fifty-three of the state's fifty-eight counties.

Downey's primary victory was more dramatic for he decisively defeated William Gibbs McAdoo, the incumbent, 511,952 to 375,930. McAdoo had been endorsed by Roosevelt and the President had ridden with the Senator through southern California. Anti-McAdoo sentiment was evident during the tour in the thousands of cards displayed which read "FDR, we love you, but not McAdoo." Roosevelt had joined McAdoo in condemnation of Ham and Eggs, but this had little impact in southern California. Downey since 1934 had moved from movement to movement in a quest for votes and a display of lack of strong political conviction. He was a supporter of Ham and Eggs, was endorsed by Townsend, and had a following among liberal Democrats stemming from the

EPIC campaign. His lead in Los Angeles County (some 173,000 votes) was impressive.

Ellis E. Patterson, who since 1934 had moved from Republican assemblyman endorsed by EPIC into the Democratic Party, won the Democratic nomination for Lieutenant Governor. The Democratic ticket pro-organized labor, anti-big business and reformist was distinctly "liberal" in the context of the times.

In contrast to 1934, most major Democratic factions and leaders united for the general election campaign. Both Olson and Downey received the endorsement of the national administration. The Republican candidates, Merriam and Bancroft, ran independent campaigns with the Governor making frequent informal talks. The Republicans used charges and techniques of the 1934 campaign, but Olson and Downey were not as vulnerable, except on Ham and Eggs, as Sinclair had been. As in 1934, the Democrats gained support from organized labor, but it was a greatly expanded, more influential labor backing than had been available in the previous campaign. An anti-labor initiative measure, Proposition 1, which would have among other things restricted picketing and abolished so-called hot cargo and secondary boycotts, brought out the labor vote. The Democratic candidates won decisive but not landslide victories over their Republican opponents.

Republican Governor Frank F. Merriam (1865–1955) on the campaign trail, 1938, appearing at an American Legion picnic at Lodi. (Courtesy of California State Library.)

These Democratic victories were all the more stunning since they marked the first time in forty years that the Democrats had gained control of the governorship and lieutenant-governorship. Downey's victory marked the first time in California's political history that a Democrat had won a United State Senate contest by a majority vote since the introduction of popular election of senators.

The Republicans had at least some good omens for the future in the elections of 1938. Earl Warren, District Attorney of Alameda County, had won his campaign for the attorney-generalship by winning both the Republican and Democratic primaries. Although one pro-Ham and Eggs opponent got some 400,000 write-in votes in the general election, Warren won overwhelmingly. In addition, the Republicans made gains in the number of congressional, state senate, and state assembly seats they won. Even Merriam had received more votes in 1938 than in 1934. Furthermore, the Ham and Eggs pension plan which had lost by 1,143,670 to 1,398,999 would be back again in a revised form in a special election in 1939, where it would be defeated again. It brought embarrassment to Olson and assisted in disrupting the coalition of voters who had elected him.

Expectations were undeservedly high among liberal Democratic circles when Culbert Olson took the oath of office on January 2, 1939. The circumstances in which the new Governor found himself were difficult. Nationally the high tide of New Deal reform had ebbed. In fact, the New Deal administration, which cut back Works Progress Administration projects significantly during the first two years of Olson's term, created for him his leading problems—increased relief rolls and financial needs. The majority of the California legislators, where party lines had minimum influence in the 1930's, were not reform-minded. Numerically the Democrats dominated the Assembly, holding forty-four of the eighty seats, and Republicans holding the remainder. The election of Assemblyman Paul Peek as Speaker was an early administrative victory. The Republicans controlled the Senate with twenty-two seats, the Democrats held seventeen, and there was one vacancy. The State Senate, when it met on January 2, took away the powers of the lieutenant governor to appoint committees and gave them to the Rules Committee headed by the new President Pro Tem, Jerrold L. Seawell, a Republican from Roseville. Olson would have difficulty in bringing the New Deal to California.

Complicating Olson's plans were a number of Democratic politicians whose aspirations created conflict within Democratic Party circles. Among these was Ellis Patterson who had not yet taken office when he declared his candidacy for the seat in the United States Senate held by Hiram Johnson. His support or opposition to Olson's legislative program was unpredictable. Robert Kenny, the newly elected State Senator from Los Angeles County was another individualist. A campaign worker for Olson, he had already embarrassed Olson by endorsing the candidacy of Earl Warren during the 1938 primary. Kenny's

289

aspirations for the governorship made full cooperation between the two men impossible. Assemblyman Samuel Yorty, a former left-winger from Los Angeles, began effective attacks upon and investigation of Communists in the State Relief Administration as preliminary to his candidacy for the United States Senate in 1940. These men made the building of a loyal Democratic organization impossible.[22]

Olson himself had personal limitations that contributed heavily to his difficulties during his administration. He was an intense partisan and deeply distrusted other Democratic politicians who did not measure up to his standard of party loyalty and regularity. This made it difficult for him to work with many Democrats both in his administration and in the Legislature. He had only a minimum of patronage at his disposal and much of that was in the State Emergency Relief Administration. His handling of appointments there, as disclosed during his administration, revealed that he was a practitioner of the spoils

Democratic Governor Culbert L. Olson (1876–1962), shortly before his physical collapse at the inaugural barbecue on the California State Fair grounds, January 7, 1939. (Courtesy of California State Library.)

system in the Jacksonian tradition that was out of keeping in a twentieth-century reform administration. Furthermore, he lacked both the experience and temperament necessary for the administrative aspects of his office. California, in replacing Merriam with Olson, had traded a mediocre conservative, whose major asset had been his long experience in politics, for a mediocre liberal, whose view of politics made him incapable of working within the loosely structued California political framework.[23]

Olson's administration opened with a dramatic act—the pardoning of convicted murderer Thomas J. Mooney, whom Olson and many others believed was innocent. He thus brought an end to the Mooney case, which had confronted each governor of California since the aftermath of the Preparedness Day bombing in San Francisco on July 22, 1916. This brought Olson international praise, particularly from labor circles, but also adverse comment from the McClatchy newspaper chain and other publishers in California.[24]

Olson, however, would not be able to enjoy the notice he received, for within a few hours, on January 7, 1939, he faltered from exhaustion while speaking before some 130,000 at a barbecue at the State Fairgrounds. His son Richard, whom he had appointed as his private secretary, not only took over the microphone at the barbecue but also the limelight as the administration's spokesman until February when Olson was able again to appear in public.

As Gladwin Hill remarked, after Mooney's pardon Olson's "administration became a doleful chronicle of frustrations and mistakes."[25] His first budget request which totalled $557,000,000 was accompanied by recommendations to increase current taxes and introduce new ones. The assembly Republicans and an emerging economy bloc of ten Democrats introduced cuts which stood in spite of administrative pressures. This marked the beginning of a deterioration of relations between the Governor and Legislature. The climax of these bad relations came in the Assembly in January, 1940, during a special session on relief funds and other proposals. The Assembly refused to retain the officers from the regular session by a vote of forty-three to thirty-three, and by the same vote selected Gordon Garland, an economy bloc Democrat from Woodlake, Tulare County, as Speaker to replace Paul Peek. Garland then took his place on the rostrum and ripped out the wires of a telephone which reportedly was connected with the Governor's office. The economy bloc Democrats believed they had both reversed the trend toward collectivism and saved constitutional government in California.

Olson proposed regulation of lobbyists, advanced the cause of public ownership of public power utilities, advocated compulsory health insurance, and introduced other reform measures but to no avail. He campaigned before the primary election of 1940 to purge the offending Democrats but had little success. The new legislative composition in 1941 was forty-two Democrats and thirty-eight Republicans in the Assembly and sixteen and twenty-four respectively in the State Senate.

The bright spot in his administration came in the Democratic presidential primary of 1940. Administrative pressures from Washington and the presence of Secretary Harold L. Ickes in March, 1940, brought agreement between the remnants of the McAdoo and Olson factions on an administration delegation but could not prevent the formation of either a left-wing slate headed by Patterson or an anti-third-term slate pledged to Vice President John Nance Garner. The Ham and Eggs pension movement entered a fourth slate pledged to Willis Allen, one of its leaders, for president. The Roosevelt slate, for which Olson campaigned vigorously, won a resounding victory with 723,782 out of a total of 977,431 ballots. Olson, the chairman of the delegation to the Democratic convention in Chicago, was chosen Democratic National Committeeman.

Meanwhile the California Republicans, who were still feeling the effects of the Merriam-Hatfield fight of 1938, devised a system by which delegates to the Philadelphia convention were selected by district and nominally pledged to State Senator Jerrold Seawell. The delegation, released to vote as it pleased, split its vote among the several candidates.

In the United States Senatorial primary Republican leaders united to back Hiram Johnson. This loner in California politics, whose support Roosevelt had sought as late as 1936, accepted the Republican endorsement with misgivings, but felt he needed the Republican support. Johnson, who had become one of the leading opponents in the Senate of Roosevelt's foreign policy and was against a third term, won handily. Antipathy among Republicans toward Roosevelt drew Republicans closer together than they had been since the opening of the progressive era. Johnson also crossfiled successfully on the Democratic ballot. Even though both Roosevelt and Olson spoke against him,[26] he led his nearest Democratic opponent by 300,000 votes. In the general election, the Republicans picked up an additional congressional and two assembly seats in spite of the fact that Roosevelt defeated Wendell Wilkie, the Republican nominee, in the state by more than a half million votes.

While the 1940 elections took place, defense measures began to replace depression issues even at the state level, particularly after the fall of France before Germany in June, 1940. After the President created a National Council of Defense, Governor Olson formed the California State Council of Defense in June to cooperate with the national effort. The antagonism between the executive and legislative branches delayed legislative backing until 1941. Likewise, the Legislature, meeting in an extraordinary session in December, 1940, delayed until the Spring of 1941 Olson's request to establish a state guard which was needed to replace the National Guard as it went into federal service. When Japan bombed Pearl Harbor on December 7, 1941, the state guard strength was some 15,000 and it was called to active duty. Olson called for its expansion and for an additional appropriation, but his opponents in the Assembly, fearful of the building of "Olson's army" held up legislation until they limited its size and cut its appropriation. The state guard became a leading issue in the 1942 elections.

Republican Attorney General Earl Warren, who believed Olson could not effectively lead the state during the war, announced his candidacy for the governorship after being assured of adequate support. In line with President Roosevelt's call for a cessation of "partisan domestic politics" during wartime, Warren announced he would run a nonpartisan campaign. He took the offensive, making political capital out of Olson's intense partisanship in defense matters and inability to work with the Legislature. He crossfiled on the Democratic ballot.[27]

That the Japanese evacuation did not become an issue in the campaign of 1942 is a commentary upon both wartime hysteria and the limitations of California (and American) political parties. The fact was that the major candidates were either in agreement on or fearful of the political consequences of making it an issue.

Table I
Sources of Foreign Born in California
Top Five Contributors in Each of Twelve Censuses 1850–1960

Number of times in top five			
1–3	4–6	7–9	10–12
France	Mexico	Ireland	Great Britain
	China		Germany
	Italy		
	Canada		
	Scandinavia		

Japan had never been a major contributor to the stream of immigrants to California. That honor belonged to western European nations, with the exception of China in the nineteenth century. Of the wartime enemies of the United States, there were relatively large numbers of Germans and German Americans and Italians and Italian Americans in California, but the Japanese and Japanese Americans composed only 1.4% (33,569 Japanese-born and 60,148 United States-born) of the California population. Unlike the Italian and German Americans, the Japanese Americans had neither risen in American political

293

life nor participated significantly in political parties. They were politically weak.

The "sneak attack" by the Japanese on Pearl Harbor had the effect of supporting anti-Oriental racist propaganda which had long circulated in California. In the nineteenth century, it had been directed against the Chinese and in the twentieth, against the Japanese. The anti-Japanese California Joint Immigration Committee, formed after World War I, although it had declined in importance after Japanese were excluded from further immigration to the United States in 1924, was still active.[28] It is not surprising that hate mongers and patriots by radio and press revived the issue and that minor politicians sought to make political capital out of the circumstances.

Their agitation supported the concurrent argument that relocation of the Japanese and Japanese Americans was a military necessity. Unwarranted fear of Japanese attack upon the mainland of the United States mounted after December 7. Americans had become particularly aware of "fifth column" dangers as a result of the success of the German military advance in Europe, and federal officials, particularly Secretary of the Navy Frank Knox in remarks made on December 15, 1941, and the Pearl Harbor investigating commission, headed by Supreme Court Justice Owen J. Roberts, in its report published on January 25, 1942, gave credence to rumors of fifth column work, espionage and sabotage in Hawaii. Although later proven incorrect, the Roberts Report had a telling effect in California and the nation. Olson, who had earlier led in pleas for tolerance of the Japanese and Japanese American, Attorney General Earl Warren, and others across the nation were persuaded of the necessity of Japanese removal. Olson supported removal with greater reluctance than did Warren.

Interestingly, Mexico, which did not have the anti-Japanese heritage of the United States and was not at war with Japan, ordered Japanese relocation from its Pacific Coast on December 8, 1941, on the grounds of military necessity.[29] President Roosevelt did not issue his executive order permitting relocation until Febraury 19, 1942. War hysteria captured the public and, thereby, the political parties. The political aspirant in California would have committed political suicide in 1942 if he had raised the Japanese relocation issue. Robert Kenny, who became Democratic candidate to succeed Warren as Attorney General, considered making it an issue but was advised against it. It would cost him votes.[30]

In the govenor's race, Warren won the Republican primary easily over nominal opposition and ran up a sizeable 404,778 votes to 514,144 for Olson in the Democratic primary. His huge primary vote confirmed his edge. The relatively low total vote cast, 47.2% as compared to 59.3% in 1934 and 59.9% in 1938 indicated relatively low interest in the campaign, particularly on the

WESTERN DEFENSE COMMAND AND FOURTH ARMY
WARTIME CIVIL CONTROL ADMINISTRATION
Presidio of San Francisco, California
April 24, 1942

INSTRUCTIONS
TO ALL PERSONS OF
JAPANESE
ANCESTRY
Living in the Following Area:

All of that portion of the City and County of San Francisco, State of California, bounded on the north by California Street, bounded on the east by Van Ness Avenue, bounded on the south by Sutter Street, and bounded on the west by Presidio Avenue.

Pursuant to the provisions of Civilian Exclusion Order No. 20, this Headquarters, dated April 24, 1942, all persons of Japanese ancestry, both alien and non-alien, will be evacuated from the above area by 12 o'clock noon, P. W. T., Friday, May 1, 1942.

No Japanese person living in the above area will be permitted to change residence after 12 o'clock noon, P. W. T., Friday, April 24, 1942, without obtaining special permission from the representative of the Commanding General, Northern California Sector, at the Civil Control Station located at:

Japanese American Citizens' League Auditorium,
2031 Bush Street,
San Francisco, California.

Such permits will only be granted for the purpose of uniting members of a family, or in cases of grave emergency.

The Civil Control Station is equipped to assist the Japanese population affected by this evacuation in the following ways:

1. Give advice and instructions on the evacuation.

2. Provide services with respect to the management, leasing, sale, storage or other disposition of most kinds of property, such as real estate, business and professional equipment, household goods, boats, automobiles and livestock.

3. Provide temporary residence elsewhere for all Japanese in family groups.

4. Transport persons and a limited amount of clothing and equipment to their new residence.

The Following Instructions Must Be Observed:

1. A responsible member of each family, preferably the head of the family, or the person in whose name most of the property is held, and each individual living alone, will report to the Civil Control Station to receive further instructions. This must be done between 8:00 A. M. and 5:00 P. M. on Saturday, April 25, 1942, or between 8:00 A. M. and 5:00 P. M. on Sunday, April 26, 1942.

2. Evacuees must carry with them on departure for the Assembly Center, the following property:

(a) Bedding and linens (no mattress) for each member of the family;
(b) Toilet articles for each member of the family;
(c) Extra clothing for each member of the family;
(d) Sufficient knives, forks, spoons, plates, bowls and cups for each member of the family;
(e) Essential personal effects for each member of the family.

All items carried will be securely packaged, tied and plainly marked with the name of the owner and numbered in accordance with instructions obtained at the Civil Control Station.

The size and number of packages is limited to that which can be carried by the individual or family group.

3. No pets of any kind will be permitted.

4. The United States Government through its agencies will provide for the storage at the sole risk of the owner of the more substantial household items, such as iceboxes, washing machines, pianos and other heavy furniture. Cooking utensils and other small items will be accepted for storage if crated, packed and plainly marked with the name and address of the owner. Only one name and address will be used by a given family.

5. Each family, and individual living alone, will be furnished transportation to the Assembly Center or will be authorized to travel by private automobile in a supervised group. All instructions pertaining to the movement will be obtained at the Civil Control Station.

Go to the Civil Control Station between the hours of 8:00 A. M. and 5:00 P. M., Saturday, April 25, 1942, or between the hours of 8:00 A. M. and 5:00 P. M., Sunday, April 26, 1942, to receive further instructions.

J. L. DeWITT
Lieutenant General, U. S. Army
Commanding

SEE CIVILIAN EXCLUSION ORDER NO. 20.

Japanese Evacuation order, with tape marks still showing, issued in San Francisco in 1942. (Courtesy of California State Library.)

part of organized labor. The war rather than politics held the center of attention. Olson attempted repeatedly and unsuccessfully to tie his administration to Roosevelt's and charged that Warren, with his nonpartisan leadership approach, was following the route of Adolph Hitler. In the general election the Republican candidate won by 1,275,287 to 932,995 votes. Plumas was the only county that gave Olson a majority. Other Democratic candidates for state-wide office ran ahead of Olson, perhaps because the Governor was so bitterly opposed by pension groups. Only Robert Kenny, who had run an independent campaign like Warren's, was victorious. The trend against the Democratic Party was national in scope and California was in harmony with the national mood.

The Great Depression and World War II were the major forces shaping California politics and politicians in the 1930's and early 1940's. A liberal Democratic Party faction tied to EPIC began to develop in the state in 1933. It gained partial control of the party in the election of 1934 and dominated it with Olson's victory. This coincided with the revolution in party registration, 1932–1942, by which California became nominally a Democratic state. However, political panaceas—products of widespread discontent—created avenues of sudden success for opportunistic politicians and disrupted the already weak political parties. The unsuccessful Olson administration confirmed to many the undesirability of intense partisanship. As long as many California voters continued to take party loyalty rather lightly, both tradition and expediency allowed politicians to follow the nonpartisan alternative.

FOOTNOTES

1 An American Association for State and Local History grant, 1964–1965, assisted the author in his research on this topic.

2 See: Jackson Keith Putnam, *The Influence of the Older Age Groups on California Politics, 1920–1940* (Unpublished Ph.D. dissertation, Stanford University, 1964), pp. 84–87; and Robert Joseph Pitchell, *Twentieth Century California Voting Behavior* (Unpublished Ph.D. dissertation, University of California, Berkeley, 1955), p. 60, on the nature of California political parties in the 1930's.

3 Upton Sinclair's EPIC plan is in his *I, Governor of California; And How I Ended Poverty: A True Story of the Future* (Los Angeles: Published by the Author, 1933), pp. 5–23. For Sinclair's most thorough record of the campaign, see his *I, Candidate for Governor; And How I Got Licked* (Pasadena: Published by the Author, 1934, 1935), 224 pp. Among the studies of the EPIC campaign are: Charles E. Larsen, "The Epic Campaign of 1934," *Pacific Historical Review* XXVII (May, 1958), 127–148; and, Clarence Fredric McIntosh, *Upton Sinclair and the EPIC Movement, 1933–1936* (Unpublished Ph.D. dissertation, Stanford University, 1955), 374 pp.

4 Richard S. Otto, past president of the End Poverty League, and Maynard Hamilton, past treasurer of the End Poverty League, personal interview with the author at Monte-

cito, California, May 22, 1965; Reuben W. Borough, past editor of the *EPIC News,* personal interview with the author at Los Angeles, California, May 21, 1965; and, Jerry Voorhis, *Confessions of a Congressman* (Garden City, N.Y.: Doubleday & Company, 1948), pp. 10–19.

5   E. M. Strangland to League for Independent Political Action, February 8, 1934, and, undated correspondence, 1934, Howard Y. Williams Papers, Minnesota Historical Society, St. Paul, Minnesota.

6   The negotiations between Sinclair and Downey, which were initiated by San Francisco Socialist Ernest Untermann, began around March 1 and were concluded around May 12, 1934. See: Sheridan Downey to Upton Sinclair, March 1, 1934, and Upton Sinclair to Ernest Untermann, May 12, 1934, Upton Sinclair Papers, Lilly Library, Indiana University, Bloomington, Indiana. On those with Olson, Culbert Olson to Upton Sinclair, June 18, 1934, and Richard S. Otto to Culbert Olson, July 19, 1934, Culbert Olson Papers, The Bancroft Library, University of California, Berkeley, California.

7   *EPIC News,* August 29, 1934, p. 8.

8   On Sinclair's private view of the interview with Roosevelt: Upton Sinclair to Franklin D. Roosevelt, October 5, 1934, and October 18, 1934, Roosevelt White House Papers, Franklin D. Roosevelt Memorial Library, Hyde Park, New York. On the pre-convention negotiations: W. E. Woodward to William Gibbs McAdoo, September 8, 1934, and, George Creel to McAdoo, September 23, 1934, William Gibbs McAdoo General Correspondence, Library of Congress, Washington D. C.; and Sheridan Downey to Upton Sinclair, September 3, 1934, William Gibbs McAdoo to Upton Sinclair, September 27, 1934, and George Creel to Upton Sinclair, November 27, 1934, Upton Sinclair Papers.

9   Putnam, *op. cit.,* pp. 246–258. The literature on the Townsend movement is summarized in Putnam's work and Abraham Holtzman, *The Townsend Movement: A Political Study* (New York: Bookman Associates, 1963), 256 pp.

10   Totten J. Anderson, "California: Enigmatic Eldorado of National Politics," *Politics in the American West,* Frank H. Jonas, ed. (Salt Lake City, Utah: University of Utah Press, 1969), p. 89.

11   The activities of Raymond Haight, whose ancestor was former California Governor Henry W. Haight, are best covered in: Bob Barger, "Raymond Haight and the Commonwealth Progressive Campaign of 1934," *California Historical Society Quarterly,* XLIII (June, 1964), 219–230. On Giannini's role, see: Russell M. Posner, "A. P. Giannini and the 1934 Campaign in California," *The Historical Society of Southern California Quarterly,* XXXIX (June, 1957), 190–201. For O'Connor's view see: J. F. T. O'Connor Diary, October 26–31, 1934, The Bancroft Library; and J. F. T. O'Connor to Marvin McIntyre, November 2, 1934, Roosevelt White House Papers.

12   Ronald Chinn, *Democratic Party Politics in California, 1920–1956* (Unpublished Ph.D. dissertation, University of California, Berkeley, 1958), pp. 105–110. This study was also consulted on the other elections of the era. Also; Royce Deems Delmatier, *The Rebirth of the Democratic Party in California, 1928–1938* (Unpublished Ph.D. dissertation, University of California, Berkeley, 1955), pp. 239–247. The analysis in Dewey Anderson and Percy E. Davidson, *Ballots and the Democratic Class Struggle; A Study in the*

Background of Political Education (Stanford, California: Stanford University Press, 1943), pp. 55–60, 263–267, 368–370, although limited to Santa Clara County, is very useful.

13   For background on Culbert Olson, see the excellent study: Robert E. Burke, *Olson's New Deal for California* (Berkeley: University of California Press, 1953), pp. 6–8. This work is authoritative on Olson's political career in California. Also useful are: Thomas W. Goodman, *Culbert L. Olson and California Politics, 1933–1943* (Unpublished M.A. thesis, University of California, Los Angeles, 1948), and the essay on Olson in H. Brett Melendy and Benjamin F. Gilbert, *The Governors of California: Peter H. Burnett to Edmund G. Brown* (Georgetown, California: The Talisman Press, 1965), pp. 395–408.

14   The observer on McAdoo was W. Y. Elliott, Chairman of the Department of Government, Harvard University. See: W. Y. Elliott to Franklin D. Roosevelt, September 21, 1935, Roosevelt White House Papers. On Olson's negotiations: Culbert Olson to Upton Sinclair, November 23, 1935; Upton Sinclair to Culbert Olson, December 27, 1935; Culbert Olson to George Dern (Secretary of War), February 26, 1936, and George Dern to Culbert Olson, March 6, 1936, Culbert Olson Papers.

15   Lloyd Ray Henderson, *Earl Warren and California Politics* (Unpublished Ph.D. dissertation, University of California, Berkeley, 1965), pp. 32–48, covers the California Republicans in 1936. For comments by a participant see: Philip Bancroft, *Politics, Farming and the Progressive Party in California* (Berkeley: Regional Oral History Office, The Bancroft Library, 1969. Interview conducted by Willa Klug Baum), p. 430, and Bancroft's letter in *Time* (April 27, 1936), pp. 4, 6.

16   Rodney Parker Carlisle, *The Political Ideas and Influence of William Randolph Hearst, 1928–1936* (Unpublished Ph.D. dissertation, University of California, Berkeley, 1965), pp. 175–177, 185–187.

17   Putnam, *op. cit.*, pp. 265–266. On Merriam, also see: Melendy and Gilbert, *op. cit.*, pp. 380–393; and Franklin Hichborn, "California Politics, 1891–1939" (Los Angeles: The Haynes Foundation, 1951), V, 2746–2750.

18   Hiram W. Johnson to Hiram W. Johnson, Jr., March 17, 1935, Hiram Johnson Papers, The Bancroft Library. For a selection of Hiram Johnson's political comment during his career as a United States Senator, see: Lawrence W. Levine, ed., "The 'Diary' of Hiram Johnson," *American Heritage*, XX (August, 1969), 64–76.

19   Putnam, *op. cit.*, p. 305. *Ham and Eggs for Californians* was the official newspaper of the movement.

20   In addition to the works related to Merriam cited above, see: Bancroft, *op. cit.*, pp. 397–405; and, Clarke A. Chambers, *California Farm Organizations: A Historical Study of the Grange, the Farm Bureau, and the Associated Farmers, 1929–1941* (Berkeley: University of California Press, 1952), pp. 190–192.

21   Putnam, *op. cit.*, pp. 325–333; and mimeographed transcript of radio broadcast by Governor Culbert L. Olson, CBS, Sunday Evening, December 3, 1939, California State Library. This speech was omitted from Culbert L. Olson, *State Papers and Addresses*. Selected by Stanley Mosk, Executive Secretary to the Governor (Sacramento: California State Printing Office, 1942), 501 pp. Burke, *op. cit.*, p. 16, takes a more charitable view of Olson's stand on the Ham and Eggs issue.

22   Chinn, *op. cit.*, pp. 124–129; and Edward L. Barrett, Jr., *The Tenney Committee: Legislative Investigation of Subversive Activities in California* (Ithaca, New York: Cornell University Press, 1951), pp. 1–28.

23   See: Chinn, *op. cit.*, p. 132, and Burke, *op. cit.*, pp. 231–232, on Olson's view of political parties.

24   Richard H. Frost, *The Mooney Case* (Stanford, California: Stanford University Press, 1968), pp. 374–402, 447–466, deals with the politics of the Mooney case in depth.

25   Gladwin Hill, *Dancing Bear, An Inside Look at California Politics* (Cleveland: The World Publishing Company, 1968), p. 89. Also: the observations of Herbert L. Phillips, *Big Wayward Girl: An Informal Political History of California* (Garden City, New York: Doubleday & Company, 1968), pp. 77–81, on relations between Olson and the Legislature

26   Hiram W. Johnson to Hiram W. Johnson, Jr., July 27, 1936, and February 14, 1940, Hiram Johnson Papers; *New York Times*, June 9, 1940, IV, p. 7; August 3, 1940, p. 13, and August 4, 1940, p. 1.

27   On the background of the disagreement between Olson and Warren, see: Henderson, *op. cit.*, pp. 108–135; Burke, *op. cit.*, pp. 194–199; and, John D. Weaver, *Warren, The Man, The Court, The Era* (Boston: Little Brown and Company, 1967), pp. 84–104.

28   The monograph by Roger Daniels, *The Politics of Prejudice: the Anti-Japanese Movement in California and the Struggle for Japanese Exclusion* (Berkeley: University of California Press, 1962), 165 pp., summarizes background research on the topic.

29   Michael Mathes, "The Two Californias During World War II," *California Historical Society Quarterly*, XLIV (December, 1965), 324–325.

30   Henderson, *op. cit.*, pp. 65–90, 103; and, Janet Stevenson, "Before the Colors Fade: The Return of the Exiles," *American Heritage*, XX (June, 1969), 22–25, 96–99, which is an interview with Robert Kenny on relocation and return of the Japanese and Japanese Americans. For different points of view, see: Morton Grodzins, *Americans Betrayed: Politics and the Japanese Evacuation* (Chicago: University of Chicago Press, 1949), 445 pp.; and, Leo Katcher, *Earl Warren: A Political Biography* (New York: McGraw-Hill Book Company, 1967), pp. 140–151.

The Era of
Earl Warren

California politics between 1942 and 1953 were dominated by one man, Earl Warren. Warren's role has been described in the following terms:

> Warren saw, as few others in state government did, the future growth of the state. He saw too, the human problems and misery that inhere in large populations: sickness, crime delinquency, deprivation, illness, ignorance; and his great objective was to prepare the state, both inside and outside government, to meet those problems. He saw the needs, he formulated the general plans to meet them, he pressed for legislative approval and implementation of the plans and when they had been approved he delegated to his department heads the responsibility for carrying them out. But in all this process, there was no party organization, no personal organization on which Warren relied.
>
> His kind of leadership required broad participation and this he was able to gain by personal stimulation, by gaining the confidence, and understanding of others, and by setting forth his goals simply and directly.[1]

The inauguration of Earl Warren as Governor of California on January 4, 1943, began an extraordinary period in the state's political history.

Warren's predecessor, Culbert Olson, was a partisan Governor whose election came during the latter part of the Great Depression. The bitter social and political issues of that depression had resulted in the reinstatement of party loyalty in California. Earl Warren was to be elected Governor of the state three times as a candidate who played down his Republican affiliation. The result was a

☞ James E. Gregg was primarily responsible for the original draft of Chapter 10.

The warmth of Earl Warren's (1891–   ) personality is evident in this photograph taken at his desk during his third term as Governor of California. (Courtesy of *Sacramento Bee*.)

return to nonpartisanship in California politics that was to last until 1959 when the practice of crossfiling was outlawed after the Democratic landslide of 1958.

Earl Warren as a man, and as a political leader, appeared to be infallible. His public and private image was one of absolute integrity. He was a man above party, a candidate without a machine, and a political leader and governor whose first loyalty was to pragmatic programs not party ideology. Throughout his career he either occupied public offices devoid of partisan ties, or at the state level he refused to play the role of a blind partisan while holding partisan office.[2] Elected with a sizeable mandate in 1942, Warren became one of the most popular governors in the history of California. He was re-elected in 1946 in the June primary, the only governor in the state's history to achieve such a victory. In the 1950 primary election he almost won both parties' nominations again and went on to win an overwhelming victory in the general election. His appointment as Chief Justice of the United States concluded his career as a state official, but his subsequent service on the Court has had great impact on both national and state government.

301

Warren was born in Los Angeles March 18, 1891. He was to become the thirtieth Governor of California, but only the fifth native son to hold the state's highest office. Of his twenty-nine predecessors and three successors only Pacheco, Pardee, Hiram Johnson, Rolph and Brown were native sons. His father was Norwegian and his mother Swedish. Warren's father, Methias, experienced poverty and poor health as repairman for the Southern Pacific. At the age of fourteen young Earl was working in the railway yards. When he was eighteen he entered the University of California at Berkeley where he completed his law degree and a bachelor's degree in political science. Prior to service in World War I, Warren worked for a private law firm for three years. He began his public career upon his discharge from the Army where he had earned a commission as a first lieutenant.

Following a short stint as clerk of the Judiciary Committee of the California Assembly in 1919, Warren was appointed a deputy city attorney in Oakland. For the next twenty-four years he was to serve in various law enforcement capacities at the city, county and state levels. By 1925 Warren was already District Attorney for Alameda County at the age of thirty-four. Having first been appointed to fill a vacancy, Warren ran for the office in 1926 and was elected. He was re-elected in 1930 and 1934. Good administration and vigorous prosecution of racketeers, bootleggers, corrupt investment and insurance schemes and graft in the sheriff's office earned Warren a national reputation.

Warren was challenged by public service. He proved to be an able administrator in his early career. He shunned private employment where he felt he would be subjected to too much direction. Later in his career one of his conservative critics was to note that Warren's lack of experience in private employment was probably responsible for his "socialistic" attitudes.

In 1938 Warren made a bid for the state attorney general post by crossfiling on the Republican, Democratic, and Progressive ballots. He won all three nominations and, therefore, did not face the task of running against an opponent on the ballot in the November general election.

Two concerns kept Warren in the public eye as Attorney General. First, were his attacks on gambling. Second, Warren and Governor Olson began a feud over civil defense prior to the beginning of World War II. The issue reached a climax with a direct conflict between Warren and Olson over the right of the governor to issue a proclamation naming officers to take charge of emergencies involving the war. Warren decided to challenge Olson for the governorship in 1942.

While Attorney General, Warren vigorously urged the promulgation of the executive order of President Roosevelt which resulted in the relocation of Japanese-Americans from California shortly after the start of the war. During his tenure as district attorney and as attorney general and during his early

302

years as governor, Warren was subjected to strong criticism by liberals in California. He earned the ire of labor when he vigorously prosecuted three union officials in 1936. His opposition to Olson's nomination of Max Radin, a University of California law professor, to the state's Supreme Court also stirred liberal opposition. As Governor and as Chief Justice of the United States, Warren has been a target of steady opposition from conservative and ultra-conservatives for his support of social programs and his court decisions concerning constitutional principles.

Warren was appointed to the United States Supreme Court by President Dwight Eisenhower on September 30, 1953. Just twenty-seven days before the appointment Warren had announced that he would not seek a fourth term as governor. Warren was only the third Californian to be appointed to the Supreme Court and the only native son ever appointed. He has been identified with the liberal wing of the court.

Warren's intended resignation from the court in 1968 sparked yet another controversy. His resignation submitted to President Lyndon Johnson was conditional upon the naming of his successor. In a bitter confirmation struggle in the United States Senate, Johnson's nominee, Justice Abe Fortas finally asked that his name be withdrawn. Warren then announced that he would retire at the conclusion of the term in the spring of 1969 clearing the way for President-elect Richard Nixon to appoint a Chief Justice. Warren had been accused of timing his retirement from the court to enable Johnson, rather than Nixon, to name his successor. The charge stemmed from a long time political coolness between Nixon and Warren which related to California and national politics. It was an ironic note to many observers of California politics that Chief Justice Warren was to swear into office his old political enemy President Richard M Nixon in January of 1969.

While Warren stressed nonpartisanship in all his campaigns and was considered to be a political "loner" throughout his elective career, he was an active participant in Republican politics at both the state and national levels. In 1928 he was an alternate delegate to the party's national convention. In 1932 he was a voting delegate. From 1934 to 1936 he was chairman of the Republican State Central Committee and was Republican National Committeeman from 1936 to 1938. In 1936 he headed a slate of delegates to the national convention as a "favorite son" having won the primary against a slate committed to Alf Landon who became party's presidential nominee that year. In 1944 Warren headed a favorite son ticket and was keynote speaker for the national convention.

California's growing influence in national politics has been reflected in the continuing temptation to California governors to try for the presidential or vice-presidential spots on both national tickets. Governors Warren, Brown, and Reagan were to be bitten by the "bug" in later years.

Warren with supporters on the campaign train to the 1948 Republican national convention. Robert Gordon Sproul, (1891–   ) (under Warren's hat) then president of the University of California, nominated Warren for President at the convention. (Courtesy of *Sacramento Bee*.)

Warren accepted the vice-presidential spot on the Republican ticket with Thomas Dewey in 1948. Only four other Californians have run for the vice-presidency. In 1912 Hiram Johnson was a candidate with Theodore Roosevelt on the Bull Moose ticket. In 1952 and 1956 Richard Nixon was elected as the Republican candidate. In 1956 Thomas H. Werdel was the running mate on a states rights ticket with T. Coleman Andrews of Virginia. In 1968 General Curtis LeMay was George Wallace's running mate in the unsuccessful third party effort of the American Independent Party.

Warren was available for the top of the Republican ticket in 1948 in the event of a Robert Taft–Harold Stassen–Thomas Dewey deadlock at the convention. Prior to the convention that year Warren was publicly critical of eastern Republicans who were calling for reduction of income taxes and removal of price controls. He criticized "meat ax" economies practiced by the House Appropriations Committee which threatened to cut the heart out of California's central valleys and other western irrigation and power projects.

In 1952 Warren was a more willing candidate for the presidential nomination of his party although he always had a somewhat politically naive idea that the presidency should seek the man, not the man seek the office. Again in 1952 Warren's chances for the presidential nomination depended entirely on a deadlock between front-running candidates. Just as in 1948, no such deadlock developed. The Eisenhower forces were able to put together a successful effort at the convention by challenging Taft delegates. California delegates stayed loyal to Warren despite efforts to break into their ranks by the Eisenhower people.

Some observers claim it was the events surrounding the 1952 convention that led to the political estrangement between Earl Warren and Richard Nixon. Two versions of what occurred have circulated in California political circles. Depending on whether one is a Warren man, or a Nixon man, either version seems plausible.[3] California's Republican delegation in 1952 was pledged to Earl Warren until released by him. Warren's appointee to the United States Senate, William Knowland, remained solidly behind the Governor in his abortive presidential bid. However, supporters of Richard Nixon, then the junior United States Senator from California, made soundings among the California delegates on behalf of General Dwight Eisenhower's candidacy. As the delegation train sped eastward, word of the Nixon soundings for Eisenhower reached Warren supporters who interpreted them as a "stab in the back." The fact that Nixon had an interview with Eisenhower prior to the train trip east, and then received the vice-presidential nomination at the convention fed fuel to the version which claims Nixon double-crossed Warren. Whether Richard Nixon made a deal to obtain the vice-presidential nomination, or not, Warren has remained cool to the young Californian whose rise on the national political scene was meteoric.

Warren supporters were charged with laying the groundwork for the "Nixon Fund" sensation that almost wrecked Nixon's political career in 1952. The two men had differing views on domestic issues; Nixon's were much more conservative than Warren's. Warren had spoken out as early as 1950 against the tactics of Wisconsin Senator Joseph McCarthy in his communist hunts, while Nixon had achieved his first national prominence as a result of the Alger Hiss case. Regardless of whatever the truth may be about Nixon's conduct as a member of the California delegation in 1952, Earl Warren interpreted it as untrustworthy conduct. Nixon supporters maintain there never was any "deal" with Eisenhower, and the entire incident was blown out of proportion. The Nixon version is a simple one. Nixon merely reported that he detected a swing to Eisenhower as a result of his conversations with party leaders. The California delegation remained firm behind Warren under Knowland's leadership, while Eisenhower went on to a first ballot victory over Taft and then picked Nixon as his running mate.

The Rumble of California Politics

Nixon served eight years as Vice President and ran for President in 1960 before returning to the California political scene in 1962 when he was defeated by Edmund G. Brown for the governorship. Warren, as noted previously, accepted the appointment of Eisenhower to the post of Chief Justice of the United States. By the time he was seventy-three Earl Warren was called upon to perform the most demanding task of his career. The nation's youthful, charismatic President, John F. Kennedy, had been assassinated in Dallas in November of 1963 and within a week Warren was asked to preside over the inquiry into the death of the president. Reluctant to accept the task, Warren was persuaded by President Lyndon Johnson. The commission which he chaired became known as The Warren Commission, and its report was known as "The Warren Report." The twenty-six volumes contained 17,000 pages and resulted in a unanimous report. The Warren imprints on the report were thoroughness of detail, sound administration, and an almost sentimental treatment of human motives and actions.

California politics during the Earl Warren era were dominated by the Republican Party despite Warren's nonpartisan technique. But the domination was a curious one. Democratic presidential candidates carried the state in 1944 and 1948. Yet Republican Earl Warren handily won the governorship in 1942, took both party nominations under crossfiling in 1946 and swamped his Democratic opponent in 1950. And these victories were accompanied by Republican control of the Legislature and most of the state-wide offices during the period. The oddity in the Republican domination which lasted until 1958 was that the party was always a minority party in the state.

Democrats accounted for 62.7% of the two party registration in 1942 at the time of Warren's first victory while the Republicans had only 37.3%. In 1946 when Warren won both nominations in the primary the Democrats had 60.8% of the two party registration while the Republicans had 39.2%. By 1950 when Warren ran for a third term, the Democratic registration had climbed to 61.2% yet the Republican governor won over his Democratic opponent with 64.9% of the two party vote.[4]

A variety of explanations has been advanced for this Republican domination. It has been suggested that the Republican victories were due to five factors:

1. The Republicans fielded well-known candidates and supported them well financially.
2. They had the advantages of being incumbents.
3. Crossfiling was in favor of Republicans who could hide their true political identities.
4. By controlling the Legislature the Republicans could gerrymander legislature districts to their advantage.
5. The vast majority of California newspapers supported Republicans.[5]

California's Democratic Party suffered from a number of handicaps during the Warren era. The party held the governorship from 1939–1943 and it carried the state for Democratic presidential candidates in 1944 and 1948. However, it was racked by factional splits in the 1930's which carried over into the Warren period. A pattern of bitter internal struggles between liberal and conservative Democratic candidates in primary elections led to crushing defeats in the general

This cartoon illustrates the typical internal bickering in the California Democratic Party during the 1940's. It also illustrates the newspaper's high regard for Earl Warren. (Courtesy of *Sacramento Bee*.)

307

election. Under crossfiling the Democrats suffered from the handicap of having Republican incumbents file at the top of the Democratic ballot without a party label after the incumbent's name.

The party held only one state wide constitutional office, the attorney-generalship, between 1942 and 1952. Robert Kenny gave up that office to campaign unsuccessfully for Governor in 1946. Edmund G. Brown reclaimed the office for the party in 1950. Democratic candidates usually found themselves opposed by a group of Democrats publicly supporting their Republican opponents. Party candidates often suffered from poor organization, a lack of funds and hostile treatment in the California press.

The Republican orientation of the California press had been demonstrated during the period 1948–1962. James E. Gregg concluded after an analysis of partisan editorial endorsements for president, governor and United States Senator that 80% of 125 California daily newspapers endorsed Republicans 75% or more of the time, 10% of the dailies endorsed Democrats 75% or more of the time and 10% of the newspapers were either independent or made no endorsements.[6] The extent to which the California press admired Earl Warren is shown by the fact that in 1950 not a single daily newspaper in the state endorsed his opponent, James Roosevelt.

Many observers of the California political scene have noted the relationship of the "Big Three" of California's newspapers, *The Los Angeles Times*, *The San Francisco Chronicle* and *The Oakland Tribune* to the Republican Party in the state. Some claim that Earl Warren was the political protégé of Joseph "Silk Hat Joe" Knowland, publisher of the *Oakland Tribune*. They point to Warren's appointment of young "Bill" Knowland, who was still in the Army, to the United States Senate in 1945 as being a "pay off" for the support from the elder Knowland during Warren's early political career in Alameda County. Regardless of other factors, Earl Warren and his attractive family made "good copy" for the state's press. His policy of holding unrestricted press conferences and his photogenic family made for favorable press treatment during his political career.

Warren's 1942 gubernatorial victory swept Republicans into all state-wide offices except the attorney-generalship that was held by Democrat Robert Kenny. While Democrats were not faring well in state-wide offices they did hold a slight 12-11 edge in the state's congressional delegation. And Democrat Sheridan Downey and Republican Hiram Johnson held the state's two United States Senate seats. Warren came into office with Republican majorities in both houses of the Legislature.

A state senate race in 1942 dramatically demonstrated the effects of crossfiling in California politics. A nominal Democrat who turned Republican, Jack Tenny, was elected in the primary over eleven Democrats and eight Republicans.

Tenny won both party nominations, having crossfiled on both parties' ballots, with 33% of the Republican vote and 29% of the Democrat vote. In a light voter turnout he was able to win election by garnering 9% of all registered voters in both parties in his district. Tenny became a symbol of irresponsible communist witch-hunting in California during the 1940's and early 1950's. The importance of the crossfiling device is demonstrated by the fact that during the 1940–1952 period 84% of the state senate races and 72% of the assembly races were won by candidates winning both party nominations in the primary elections. In 1943 Clair Engle first won election to Congress in a special election from the state's Second District. Engle would later win election to the United States Senate in 1958.

In 1944 Democrat Sheridan Downey handily defeated Republican Lieutenant Governor Frederick F. Houser for the United States Senate seat. (The Republican Lieutenant Governor should not be confused with Los Angeles District Attorney and later Republican Attorney General Fred N. Howser.) The state's congressional delegation switched to a 16–7 margin for the Democrats as a result of President Roosevelt's sweep of the state in 1944. The Democratic President won 56.8% of the two party vote in 1944 contrasted with Warren's 57.7% victory in 1942. Despite the national ticket sweep in California the Democrats were unable to wrest control of the Legislature from the Republicans in 1944. The Republicans held a 27–13 majority in the State Senate and a 43–37 edge in the Assembly which reflected only a one seat loss in the lower house despite the Democratic tide in 1944.

By the conclusion of his first term as governor, Warren was drawing some public criticism from conservatives in the Republican Party. In late 1945 Earl Lee Kelly, a former Director of Public Works under Governor Merriam from 1936 to 1939 indicated he might be a possible opponent to Warren for the Republican nomination for governor in 1946. Kelly said of Warren's nonpartisan and liberal stances that:

> If our party's chosen officials are too cagey or opportunistic to go into battle wearing the party's colors, then we must either get new leaders or get ready for receivership.

> If Governor Warren intends to ride into battle with one leg astride the Republican elephant and the other clinging affectionately to the Democratic donkey, I can't help but wonder if either animal will recognize him as master.[7]

In 1946 Earl Warren accomplished the unprecedented feat, now legally impossible in California, of winning the nomination of both parties for the governorship in the June primary.

The Rumble of California Politics

Warren succeeded in capturing the Democratic nomination despite an effort to put together a Democratic ticket known as the "package deal." Democratic Attorney General Robert Kenny campaigned with John Shelley, later a United States congressman and Mayor of San Francisco, as the party's lieutenant governor candidate. Also running as a part of the "package deal" were Edmund "Pat" Brown as the candidate for Attorney General and Mrs. Lucille Gleason, wife of movie actor Jimmie Gleason, as the party's candidate for Secretary of State. But 1946 was not to be a Democratic victory year, Instead, it was a disaster for the party. The head of the ticket, Kenny, conducted a colorless and apathetic campaign whose only pitch was an attempt to re-arouse partisanship in the state.

Warren conducted a nonpartisanship campaign based on the record of his first term. Stressing that he had no political machine Warren told the electorate: "No man should be permitted to be both Governor and a political boss. I repeat the promise I made four years ago—that whenever I leave the Governor's chair, I will return it to the people, unencumbered, and without any political strings around it."[8] Warren was content to run on his record, although he pondered making all-out attacks on the so-called "package deal" approach to state offices by the Democrats.

Kenny used the argument of party responsibility as a necessary part of successful government. He claimed that since California has a plural executive minor state-wide office holders should follow the leadership of the governor. His strategy, which backfired in an era of nonpartisanship in California politics, was to tie his campaign to other Democratic candidates.

Warren's response to Kenny and the many problems which faced California in 1946 was:

> their solution cannot be found in narrow partisanship any more than world problems can be solved through extreme nationalism. They only can be solved through independent, humane, forward-looking and financially sound government.

His opponent, Kenny, charged Warren with an administration that lacked planning for post-war problems. Kenny claimed that Warren's leadership in the Legislature had been ineffective and that key liberal aspects of Warren's programs had been voted down by Warren's own partisans in the Legislature. Warren responded by saying that he was opposed to a "disciplined" legislature and to "boss rule."

Warren concentrated on the positive accomplishments of his administration such as the establishment of the Department of Mental Hygiene, the reorganization of the Department of Public Health, increases in unemployment insurance and workmen's compensation, and fiscal responsibility which resulted in a budget surplus.

Warren in winning both the Democratic and Republican Party nominations for Governor ran up a victory total of 766,383 votes over Kenny on both party ballots. Also winning a double nomination under crossfiling in the 1946 Primary were Warren appointee Thomas Kuchel for Controller, Frank Jordon for Secretary of State, and Charles G. Johnson for State Treasurer. Kuchel defeated Harry E. Riley, a Republican who recently had turned Democrat and who was accused of attempting to trade on the name of the late Controller Harry B. Riley, It was a familiar pattern in the curious politics of California to see the voter confused with similarly named candidates running without party labels under crossfiling.

The Republicans completed their sweep in the general election of 1946. Another Warren appointee, United States Senator William Knowland, defeated Will Rogers, Jr. by almost 261,000 votes. In another familiar pattern in California politics, Rogers had beaten Democratic Congressman Ellis Patterson in a bitter primary before being defeated by Republican Knowland.

Rogers represented the liberal wing of the Democratic Party and had served in Congress prior to volunteering for the Army in World War II. His association with liberal causes and a liberal voting record in Congress led to some campaign charges against him in 1946. *Fortnight* magazine noted that to some Californians Rogers was "a Communist, fellow traveler and a crackpot."[9] Of Knowland the magazine said that Knowland had moved from a middle of the road record as a United States Senate appointee in 1945 to "the safe shelter of the right." It was a sweet victory for William Knowland's father, Joseph Russell Knowland, who was seventy-three in 1946 and had served as state assemblyman, state senator, and congressman and who lost his own bid for a United States Senate seat in 1914 to James D. Phelan.

Other Democratic survivors of the June primary who went down to defeat included John Shelley, loser to Goodwin Knight for the lieutenant-governorship, and Edmund G. "Pat" Brown who lost his race for the state attorney-generalship to Los Angeles District Attorney Fred N. Howser by over 300,000 votes. Despite the 1946 defeat, Pat Brown would be heard from again on the California political scene as a winning Attorney General and two-term Governor.

On the Republican ballot the names of Knight, Kuchel, Knowland and Richard M. Nixon were on the winning side in 1946. All were to play prominent roles in the future politics of the Golden State. Nixon had triumphed over ten year incumbent Congressman Jerry Voorhis who had been voted "best Congressman west of the Mississippi" by Washington correspondents. The campaign was a bitter one in which Voorhis was charged with being pro-communist. The campaign strategy of Nixon was to deflate his opponent and use public fear of communism as a major issue. Nixon cut his opponent to pieces in a series of five debates during the campaign, a technique which in the 1960 election for the presidency may have cost him victory. The 1946 campaign was the beginning of a long and bitter enmity between California Democrats and Richard Nixon.[10]

Fortnight magazine said that Goodwin Knight's victory in the 1946 landslide was "the sudden metamorphosis of a staid Los Angeles jurist who slithered out of his somber judicial robes to become California's potential butterfly." James Roosevelt, state chairman of the Democratic Party said of his party's defeat, "It is a vote of resentment against the inevitable irritations of reconversion from total war."

As a result of the outcome of the 1946 election the Republicans had a twenty-seven to thirteen majority in the State Senate and a forty-eight to thirty-two majority in the Assembly. Only fourteen Democratic candidates survived the 1946 primaries to run in the state's twenty-three congressional districts, while twenty Republicans were running. Democratic voters had given their party's nomination to Republicans in nine congressional districts, in ten state senatorial districts and in thirty-five assembly districts. The congressional delegation in 1946 contained fourteen Republicans and nine Democrats.

So the Democrats had little to be optimistic about in 1948 when Republican presidential hopeful Thomas Dewey running with California's popular Governor

Governor Thomas Dewey (1902 –), (left), fresh from his crucial 1948 Republican primary victory in Oregon is greeted by Earl Warren (right). Warren became Dewey's vice-presidential running mate on the national Republican ticket that year. (Courtesy of *Sacramento Bee*.)

Earl Warren as his vice-presidential running mate squared off against Democratic President Harry S. Truman.[11] But in that weird world of California politics Truman pulled one of the all-time upsets by winning the state as well as the national election. Truman's victory, however, was not reflected in the Legislature where the Democrats picked up only three seats in the Assembly and one in the Senate or in the House of Representatives where the Democrats gained only one seat.

Early in the 1948 campaign it appeared that the effort by the Independent Progressive Party would doom the Democratic ticket. The depth of the split was indicated by Robert Kenny's support of the third party. The public opinion polls in the state gave Truman only 43% (Gallup) and 39% (*Los Angeles Times*) of the projected vote. Truman won by a narrow margin of 18,000 votes in California. Support for the third party dwindled when it fielded opponents to popular liberals like Chet Holifield and Helen Gahagan Douglas for Congress. Hard work by the unions on behalf of Truman and a complacent "high level" campaign by the Republicans accounted for the outcome. Lack of legislative contests also hurt the Republicans as they won nine congressional seats, ten state senate seats and thirty-five assembly seats in the primary.

Governor Warren made a belated announcement of intention to seek a third term in 1950.[12] Earlier Lieutenant Governor Goodwin Knight had indicated an interest in the governorship. His ambitions in this regard had been frustrated by the failure of the national Republican ticket in 1948. Attorney General Fred Howser sought re-election despite the handicaps of public criticism leveled at his office over gambling scandals. Regular Republican support went to Howser's primary opponent, Edward Shattuck, who defeated the incumbent Attorney General in the primary. The Democrats nominated Edmund G. Brown who went on to win over Shattuck in the general election.

United States Senator Sheridan Downey did not run for re-election and threw his support to conservative Democrat Manchester Boddy, publisher of the *Los Angeles Daily News* in a primary contest with Congresswoman Helen Gahagan Douglas. After a bitter primary Mrs. Douglas faced Republican Congressman Richard M. Nixon in the general election.

An oddity of the 1950 primary was the more than 600,000 votes cast for a Communist candidate, Bernadette Doyle, who was defeated for the nonpartisan post, Superintendent of Public Instruction, by Roy Simpson.

The importance of the crossfiling device was demonstrated again in 1950 when eleven of twenty-three congressional races, sixteen of twenty state senate contests and fifty-eight of eighty assembly seats were won by candidates taking both parties' nominations.

The general election saw James Roosevelt challenge Warren in the gubernatorial race. Roosevelt attempted to win by campaigning for the partisan

Democratic vote. Warren campaigned for just one month in the fall and buried Roosevelt by over a million votes.

In the United States Senate race Richard Nixon defeated Mrs. Douglas by almost 700,000 votes. Nixon had the support of some prominent conservative Democrats and his campaign centered on the issue of domestic communism and Mrs. Douglas' "soft" attitude toward the political left. She was dubbed the "pink lady," and her voting record published on a "pink sheet." Nixon's campaign tactics infuriated Democrats, earned him additional ill will among his opponents in the state and marked him as a tough political in-fighter. Years later he was to remark that he was sorry about the episode, and that it happened when he was a very young man.

As a result of the 1950 elections the Republicans had control of all state-wide offices but one, and had margins of forty-seven to thirty-three in the Assembly, twenty-eight to twelve in the State Senate and thirteen to ten in the congressional delegation.

The degree to which the Republicans controlled the state is shown by the fact that Democrats outnumbered Republicans in sixty-five of eighty assembly districts and in all of the state senate seats up for election in 1952, yet the Democrats could elect only twenty-seven assemblymen and four senators. After the Eisenhower sweep of 1952 the Republicans increased their margins in the state Legislature to fifty-three to twenty-seven in the Assembly and twenty-nine to eleven in the State Senate. They also took nineteen of thirty seats in the House of Representatives.

The presidential primaries in California in 1952 saw challenges to both Republican and Democratic Party leadership by insurgent groups. Governor Warren's favorite son tactic came under fire from conservative Republicans led by Bakersfield congressman Thomas Werdel. The Werdel group campaigned with the slogan, "If You're for Taft, MacArthur, Eisenhower or Stassen, Vote the Free GOP Ticket with Werdel."[13] Warren defeated the Werdel slate handily by a two to one majority in the primary. Werdel was the only incumbent Republican congressman to go down to defeat in California in the general election despite a net gain of six Republican house seats in the state. It has long been speculated in state political circles that Warren supporters aided Werdel's opponent, Harlan Hagen, as a reprisal for the sniping at Warren by the reactionary wing of the California Republican Party.

President Truman's withdrawal left two contending Democratic slates in the primary. One slate pledged to Senator Estes Kefauver's candidacy was opposed by a hastily put together slate of regular Democrats headed by Attorney General Pat Brown. The Kefauver slate won in the primary, but then united behind Adlai Stevenson in the general election.

Two ballot propositions of political significance were voted on in 1952.

Grapes Of Wrath—'52 Version

WE LIKE TAFT BUT WE HATE WARREN MORE

GOP OLD GUARD

WERDEL SLATE OF PRESIDENTIAL DELEGATES

The anti-Warren slate in the 1952 presidential primary is lampooned in this cartoon. (Courtesy of *Sacramento Bee*.)

One would have abolished crossfiling. It lost by little more than 3,000 votes out of over four million. The second proposition, which passed, required candidates to list their party affiliation after their name, but allowed crossfiling to continue. The designation of party was to decrease greatly the number of candidates winning both party nominations before crossfiling was finally abolished in 1959. An unknown Democratic assembly candidate, Jess Unruh was victorious in 1954 after having been defeated in two previous campaigns.

Unruh was to become Speaker of the Assembly longer than any other man in California history after the Democrats took control of the Legislature in 1959.

The presidential campaign in California in 1952 was decided in Eisenhower's favor by over 700,000 votes. Nixon's rough campaign tactics as the vice-presidential nominee further earned him enmity among Democrats. Incumbent Republican United States Senator William Knowland retained his seat in the primaries with a crossfiling win. Governor Warren appointed Thomas Kuchel to the second United States Senate seat after it was vacated by Nixon's elevation to the vice-presidency.

Earl Warren became Governor of California during wartime in 1942 and as he left the office in 1953 the nation had just gone through the Korean War. Vast changes in the state resulted from the impact of World War II. Thousands of veterans, whose first exposure to California came while in uniform, migrated to the state after their discharge. And 850,000 California servicemen and women were to return to the state seeking employment, recreation, a high standard of living and educational opportunities. As a political pragmatist Earl Warren was determined that the state would meet the twin challenges of population growth and needed economic growth.

In his first inaugural address to the Legislature on January 4, 1943, Warren told the legislators:

> They (the people) sent you here as legislators and honored me with the Governorship for one reason alone—they expect us to work together and produce results. They rely upon our ability to fix our minds upon common objectives which are in their interests and reach achievement in goals through cooperative action.
>
> I am as you know a Republican. But I shall make no appeal to blind partisanship, or follow any other divisive tactics.

This was to be the Warren approach to the legislative branch during his eleven years as governor. He made no attempts to organize a working majority within the Legislature.

Yet long-time Warren critic, former Assemblyman Harold K. Levering said of the Governor's relationship with the Legislature: "Warren's fancied 'independence' of the Legislature was mere lip service—he was shrewd enough to put the screws on those few in his clique that he could."

Warren's relations with the Legislature were characterized by five factors:

1. He viewed the relationship as a working partnership.
2. He respected the independence of the Legislature as a co-equal branch of government with the executive and judicial branches.
3. He followed a policy of no interference in the legislative process and instructed his appointees not to "lobby" the Legislature.

4. He made no attempts at organizing a party group or a working majority in the Legislature.
5. He expressed no preferences on selection of legislative officers or committee chairmen.

One author said of Warren's relations with the Legislature that "in every way he complied with the spirit of the separation of powers."[15]

Warren's failure to actively build support for his programs and policies in the Legislature often meant that key committee chairmanships were filled by men who lacked sympathy for his programs, or even were hostile to them.

The growing amount of public business in California during the Warren era is reflected in the following table:

Table I
Growth of California State Government 1943–1954
Budget Expenditures and Receipts[14]

	Fiscal Year	
	1943–44	1953–54
State operations	$86,140,000	$346,907,000
Capital outlay	12,673,000	286,897,000
Local assistance	163,659,000	747,596,000
Total of above three items	262,472,000	1,381,400,000
State expenditures for Education[1]	95,798,000	509,017,000
State expenditure for highways[2]	23,725,000	255,261,000
Total state revenue	$394,745,000	$1,271,447,000

	Miscellaneous Data	
	1943	1953
Total population, July 1	8,506,000	12,190,000
Registered motor vehicles, December 31	2,944,572	5,922,726
Population of state institutions, June 30	36,185	57,089
State civil service employees, December 31	23,957	56,545

[1] Total of state operations, capital outlay and local assistance.
[2] Total of state operations and capital outlay.

Table II
Bills Handled by California Legislature and Governor[16]
1943–1953

General Session Year	Bills Introduced	Bills Passed	Bills Made Law	Bills Vetoed
1943	3,131	1,291	1,137	154
1945	3,540	1,604	1,527	113
1947	3,418	1,752	1,577	147
1949	4,701	1,713	1,603	110
1951	5,303	1,896	1,765	131
1953	5,522	2,088	1,895	195

Warren vetoed only 2% of bills passed by the Legislature. Governor's Brown and Knight were to veto less than 1% of the bills sent to them. On the average governors between 1923 and 1965 vetoed less than 2% of the bills passed by the legislatures. Only Governors Richardson, who vetoed 9% of the Legislature's bills in the 1923–1927 period and Olson, who vetoed 7% of the bills during his 1939–1943 term were at significant odds with the Legislature.[17]

It was not until 1945 that Warren requested state departments' recommendations on legislation to clear through his office. As with most governors' staffs, Warren's staff did not present legislation or testify in person before legislative committees. There was just one exception when Warren presented his ill-fated bills on pre-paid compulsory health insurance. His Executive Secretary William Sweigert presented this Warren legislation which was not backed by the medical profession and was not related to the operation of any of the state's medical departments. Warren lost his plan by one vote in the Assembly in 1945 and by larger margins in 1947, 1949 and 1950.

During his first two years in office Warren was successful in reducing taxes, increasing old age pensions, and widening coverage of unemployment insurance. In addition to proposing health insurance in 1945, Warren supported modernizing mental health care for Californians and further increases in old age assistance. During the 1945 session he suffered setbacks on proposals to again widen unemployment insurance and to create a commission to study minority problems in the state.

Warren succeeded in getting legislative enactment of a program he presented to a special session in 1946 dealing with the problems of returning veterans. He urged appropriations to implement an urban redevelopment act and extension of unemployment compensation to the sick.

The California Legislature's killing of Warren's compulsory health plan in 1945 promoted this cartoon. (Courtesy of *Sacramento Bee*.)

After his 1946 election Warren proposed legislative programs dealing with the growing state population that had increased by over two million since 1940. He again lost his bid for prepaid public health insurance, but won a bitter fight to increase highway user taxes to build new highways. He also won additional funds for hospitals and mental health care and labor legislation which outlawed jurisdictional strikes and improved mediation procedures in labor disputes. In 1949 he proposed construction programs for schools, prisons and hospitals and additional highways. Again he recommended health insurance, but was rebuffed.

319

In 1950 Warren warned that the days of state surpluses in the treasury were over and that economy was necessary. He called a special session of the Legislature to deal with social welfare, air pollution, gambling and lobbying. Warren had been extremely fortunate in his budgetary dealings with the Legislature during his first two terms. Few California governors have been fortunate enough to have budget surpluses and "rainy day funds," and Warren's good fortune prompted Carey McWilliams to say that even little Shirley Temple could have been a popular governor under such circumstances.

After his 1950 reelection Warren centered his attention on civil defense and extension of state veterans' benefits to Korean War veterans. He again recommended a state planning commission which he had been previously refused. He also recommended further improvements in social welfare benefits. In 1953, his last year as governor, he recommended measures to help California deal with its problems when it became the most populous state in the nation. He secured added highway construction, new mental hospitals and extension of educational benefits to Korean War veterans. He could not, however, get the Legislature to support his proposals to create a separate liquor control agency or to deal with problems of natural resources, human relations and governmental reorganization.

Warren (right) wishes his successor, Goodwin Knight (1896–1970), (left), well during Warren's last day as governor before leaving for Washington to become Chief Justice of the United States. (Courtesy of *Sacramento Bee*.)

320

Warren was most receptive to legislative proposals coming from the almost 200 boards and commissions in state government. For example, he always supported the recommendations of the State Personnel Board for salary increases for state employees even when such recommendation required a ten or fifteen million dollar appropriation or a tax increase.

A device which Earl Warren especially prized in the development of legislative recommendations was the governor's conference, or special committees, to study specific problems. During the Warren era over 15,000 Californians attended various governor's conferences paying their own traveling and living expenses. Warren saw such conferences as opportunities for the people of California to place themselves on record and for forums for reconciling divergent views on legislative recommendations on a wide diversity of problems facing the state.

Among the many topics on which citizen groups made recommendations through conferences and committees were employment, problems of the aging, mental health, water, traffic safety, sex crimes against children, educational television, industrial safety, care and treatment of senile patients, civil disturbances, unemployment insurance and agricultural labor.

While such conferences and committees came up with only a few specific solutions, their work did focus public attention on the problems. For example, Warren appointed a committee to investigate penal affairs in 1944 which resulted in an extraordinary session of the Legislature to enact major prison reforms. The Legislature had been informed of the inadequacy of California's prison system nine years before.

Warren's crime study commissions which studied adult correction and release procedures, juvenile justice, social and economic causes of crime and delinquency, and organized crime were especially effective. The Commission on Organized Crime uncovered shocking evidence of a state-wide system of racket protection for gambling, bookmaking, slot machines, punch boards, prostitution and narcotics. In addition, the Commission discovered evidence that staff of the office of Attorney General Fred N. Howser were involved.

The second report of the Governor's Commission on Organized Crime released March 7, 1949, shed considerable light on the feud which had developed between the Attorney General and Warren. Carey McWilliams described the feud as the "noisiest political brawl California has seen in many a day."[18] McWilliams noted that a violent battle had been shaping up for control of gambling and bookmaking in California and cited a series of gangland-type murders in the state. In a court struggle over use of Western Union wire services on horse racing Warren charged Attorney General Howser's office with leaking information to the interests under investigation.

The Commission report estimated that the gross take from slot machines in the state exceeded two billion dollars, 20% of which was used for protection payments to local law enforcement officials. Wiley Caddel, "Coordinator of Law Enforcement" in Howser's office, was shown to have an interest in a string of slot machines in Mendocino County. He was indicted and convicted on a charge of bribery. Warren's commission charged Attorney General Howser with keeping a staff of eleven investigators and stenographers at the scene of Caddel's trial which made matters difficult for the prosecution.

Howser was thought by many to have been put in office by "the secret boss of California," lobbyist Artie Samish.[19] When two "Samish men," Assemblyman Sam Collins and Fred Howser, both aspired to the state attorney-generalship, Samish settled the problem by having Howser run for the office and arranging to have Collins made Speaker of the Assembly. Samish noted that Howser's name was similar to incumbent Lieutenant Governor Fred Houser and said, "the people are likely to be confused between the familiar *Fred Houser* and my *Fred N. Howser*." And they were, and Samish's Howser won election to state office as Attorney General in 1946. Later he lost favor with Samish after scandal touched the attorney general's office and Howser could not even win his party's nomination for a second term. Samish was once described by a legislative investigation as "California's archlobbyist" who said, "I'm the Governor of the Legislature. To hell with the Governor of the state!" Writer Lester Velie, whose *Colliers* articles helped end Samish's control of the Legislature asked Earl Warren: "Who has more influence with the Legislature, you or Artie Samish?" The Governor replied: "On matters that affect his clients, Artie unquestionably has more power than the Governor."

Just as Earl Warren had become a governor without a party organization, so Artie Samish became a political boss in California without political organization of the traditional machine type. Described as "the only one of his kind," Samish became a political boss without a party who bossed Republicans and Democrats with equal impartiality. Samish parlayed his insight about the workings of the Legislature, money from his influential clients as a lobbyist, a well-developed political espionage system in Sacramento, control of the Board of Equalization which administered state liquor laws, control of key legislative committee members, and an almost unerring understanding of human character into what he described as "an endless chain of political strength."

Samish boasted that he could quickly tell if a man wanted "a baked potato, a girl, or money." His clients supplied him large amounts of campaign funds without requiring an accounting. The investigation of corruption in the state Legislature reported that between 1935 and 1938 Samish had received almost half a million dollars for his political activities.[20] He had access to almost all the state's billboards in a pretelevision era. His ability to pressure legislators stemmed from almost half a million persons affiliated with the trade associations he represented in Sacramento. His technique was to allow legislators beholden to him to vote as they wished on matters not affecting his clients. Thus, "Samish men" in the Legislature reflected liberal as well as conservative views.

Velie, in his *Colliers* exposé of Samish, said:

> The machine who "controls the state of California" falls into no easy identifying niche. He is neither labor boss, oil king, press lord, financial naboob, nor rabble rouser of the Huey Long type. You can't even neatly tag him as the Boss Pendergast or Crump or Hague of California.

Samish's clients included interests in beer, liquor, motor buses, railroads, tobacco, banks, building and loan companies, race tracks and chemicals. At his peak he was thought to have controlled a hard core of thirty of California's eighty assemblymen. By capturing the speakership and control of committees he could speed legislation or kill it to suit his clients. With his bloc of legislators Samish could make defensive or offensive alliances with other lobbyists. Said Velie of Samish, "so firm is his grip on the Legislature that other lobbyists, to be successful, follow a simple rule: They lobby Samish."

Samish recognized that the progressive reforms which had stripped California of political party responsibility made it necessary for political candidates to build their own bases of support. With senators and assemblymen being paid only $1,200, legislators were easy targets for "honest graft." The famous Philbrick legislative investigative report of 1938 said:

> Corruption is not necessarily bribery. The term is a general one suggesting loss of integrity—a taint. Instances of bribery encountered in the investigation were relatively few   . The principal source of corruption has been "money pressure." The principal methods of applying such pressure: fees paid to lawyer legislators and expenditures of lobbyists. The principal offender has been Arthur H. Samish. . . .

Of California's political reforms, former Attorney General Robert Kenny said, "We have reformed ourselves right into the hands of our executioners."

Samish's sense of humor helped bring about his eventual downfall, although it must be noted that it was a federal income tax evasion conviction that resulted in Samish's being jailed in 1953. Californians were outraged when Velie's *Colliers* articles gave nation-wide attention to Samish's role in their state Legislature. Samish's good humor got the best of him when he posed for photographs for the articles. He jokingly held on his knee a dummy dressed as a bum. Velie quoted Samish as saying, "That's the way I lobby," pointing to the dummy. "That's my Legislature. That's Mr. Legislature. How are you today, Mr. Legislature?" he inquired of the dummy.

'And How Are You Today, Mr. Legislature?'

What started as a joke by lobbyist Artie Samish (1897–   ) caused public outrage and led to the enactment of legislation requiring all lobbyists to register and report expenditures in California. This cartoon was taken from a photo in the *Collier's* articles about Samish. (Courtesy of *Sacramento Bee.*)

In an extraordinary session after the publication of the Velie articles the Legislature answered Samish by adopting the Collier Act which is still the foundation for lobby regulation in California. The Act requires lobbyists to register and report expenditures of funds during legislative sessions. Political candidates, however, still are not required to give detailed accounting of contributions so lobby contributions to campaigns are still largely unreported.

In addition to his role as lobbyist in the Legislature, Samish also influenced the outcome of various state-wide initiative and referendum ballot measures. Direct democracy was another reform from the progressive era which has allowed various interests to move into a political power vacuum. Just as Warren and Samish were the products of such a vacuum, so were an emerging group of public relations firms who became influential on the state's political scene during the Warren era.[21]

One such firm was Campaigns, Inc., founded in the 1930's by Clem Whitaker. In addition to handling candidate campaigns such as Earl Warren's in 1942 the firm, also known as Whitaker and Baxter, organized campaigns for or against ballot measures. Whitaker and Baxter were so successful in defeating Earl Warren's health insurance proposals that they were retained by the American Medical Association to defeat President Truman's national compulsory health insurance program.

Another type of firm which emerged on the California political scene was Robinson and Company of San Francisco which specialized in collecting signatures to qualify initiative and referendum measures. In 1948 it was necessary to collect at least 250,000 signatures to qualify an initiative measure. For a fee of $75,000 Robinson would guarantee to qualify a ballot measure. He also provided direct mail services for a cost of $180,000 to all five million voters in California in 1948. Robinson claimed to have put on the ballot 95% of all initiative and referendum measures on which Californians voted in thirty years. Robinson qualified Proposition 4 in 1948 which was pension promoter George McLain's successful effort to gain control of the state's welfare programs. In 1949 Robinson was hired by the California Council for the Blind to qualify a repealer of the McLain scheme which had even written into the state Constitution the name of Myrtle Williams as the interim director of state welfare programs.

During the Warren era California's population increased by over three million. On a multi-million dollar scale Earl Warren dedicated his administrations to meeting the needs generated by this tremendous growth. The needs of California citizens were for public services in education, highways, natural resource development, housing, mental health, recreation, prisons, and welfare. As one writer has put it, "The greatest testimonial to his efficacy was there was little subsequent regimes could point to that he had not done or tried to do."[22]

Warren's dedication to a philosophy of meeting the needs of people is best summed up in his own words:

> Happiness is best advanced where there is the greatest spirit of harmony, where opportunity in life is equal, where there is no squalor, where the health of all people is protected, and where the dignity of the human personality is recognized without regard to race or creed. None of these

325

things follow from mere numbers. They must be sought after, planned for and perfected as built-in segments of our social structure. I would urge every university, college, school, church, business and labor group, indeed every family to face squarely to the fact that we have the problem of providing for the happiness of more people than any state in the Union. And I would emphasize the fact that the millions to whose happiness we are dedicating ourselves are our children and their children. What better heritage could we leave them?[23]

FOOTNOTES

1   James R. Bell, *The Executive Office of the Governor Under Earl Warren, 1943–53* (Unpublished Ph.D. dissertation, University of California, Berkeley, 1956), p. 74. An excellent source of information on Warren's conduct of the duties of the office of governor. See also Richard B. Harvey, *Earl Warren: Governor of California* (New York: Exposition Press, 1969), 219 pp. Another excellent scholarly source on the Warren years.

2   Warren's gubernatorial papers in the state archives are not yet open. The definitive biography of Earl Warren remains to be written. Three journalistic, non-scholarly and sympathetic volumes lacking in interpretation, but filled with factual data about Warren's career are: Irving Stone, *Earl Warren, A Great American Story* (Englewood Cliffs, N.J.: Prentice-Hall, 1948), 176 pp.; Leo Katcher, *Earl Warren, a Political Biography* (New York: McGraw-Hill, 1967), 502 pp; and John D. Weaver, *Warren, the Man, the Court, the Era* (Boston: Little, Brown, 1967), 407 pp.

3   See Gladwin Hill, *Dancing Bear* (Cleveland, Ohio: The World Publishing Company, 1968), pp. 169–171, for an account sympathetic to the Warren view of the 1952 convention. See Earl Mazo, *Richard Nixon: A Political and Personal Portrait* (New York: Harpers, 1959), pp. 92–98, for an account sympathetic to the Nixon view of the 1952 convention.

4   See Eugene C. Lee, *California Votes 1928–1960* (Berkeley: Institute of Governmental Studies, University of California, 1963), for an excellent compendium and analysis of registration and voting in California during the period under discussion.

5   Henry A. Turner and John A. Vieg, *The Government and Politics of California* (3rd ed., New York: McGraw-Hill, 1967), pp. 46–48.

6   See James E. Gregg, "Newspaper Editorial Endorsements and California Elections," *Journalism Quarterly*, XXXXII (Autumn, 1965), 532–538; and *Newspaper Endorsements and Local Elections in California*, California Government Series, No. 12, May, 1966, Institute of Governmental Affairs, University of California, Davis, (monograph). Both publications are taken from an unpublished Ph.D. dissertation, University of California at Santa Barbara, 1964.

7   Harvey, *op. cit.*, pp. 165–166.

8   H. Brent Melendy and Benjamin F. Gilbert, *The Governors of California, Peter H. Burnett to Edmund G. Brown* (Georgetown, California: The Talisman Press, 1965), 482 pp.

9 *Fortnight*, November 4, 1946, pp. 18–21. *Fortnight* provides interesting insights into a variety of aspects of California life during late 1940's.

10 For an anti-Nixon version of the campaign see William Costello, "The Facts About Nixon—III, 1946—The First Campaign," *The New Republic*, October 12, 1959, pp. 9–14. For a view friendly to Nixon see Earl Mazo's political biography of Nixon previously cited.

11 Charles H. Titus and Charles R. Nixon, "The 1948 Election in California," *Western Political Quarterly*, II (March, 1949), 97–102.

12 Burton R. Brazil, "The 1950 Elections in California," *Western Political Quarterly*, IV (March, 1951), 67–71.

13 Ivan Hinderaker, "The 1952 Elections in California," *Western Political Quarterly*, VI (March, 1953), 102–110.

14 Bell, *op. cit.*, p. 10. Sources: California Department of Finance, Division of Budgets and Accounts, Financial Research Section, July, 1955; employee data from California State Personnel Board, July, 1955.

15 *Ibid.*, p. 55.

16 Table from Bell, *op. cit.*, p. 194.

17 Winston W. Crouch, *et. al.*, *California Government and Politics* (4th ed., Englewood Cliffs, N.J.: Prentice-Hall, 1967), p. 151.

18 Carey McWilliams, "Machines, Political and Slot," *The Nation*, May 28, 1949, pp. 608–610.

19 See Lester Velie, "The Secret Boss of California," *Colliers*, August 13, 1949, pp. 12–13, 71–73; August 20, 1949, pp. 12–13, 60–64, and Carey McWilliams, *California: The Great Exception* (New York: A. A. Wyn, 1949), pp. 199–205; Robert S. Allen, Ed., *Our Sovereign State*, "California: First Hundred Years," by Richard V. Hyer (New York: The Vanguard Press, Inc., 1949), pp. 373–413.

20 H. R. Philbrick, Legislative Investigative Report (Sacramento: State Printing Office, 1939).

21 See Robert J. Pitchell, "The Influence of Professional Campaign Management Firms in Partisan Elections in California," *Western Political Quarterly*, VII (December, 1954), 73–83.

22 Hill, *op. cit.*, p. 104.

23 As quoted in Eugene C. Lee (Ed.), *The California Governmental Process* (Boston: Little Brown and Co., 1966), p. 301.

The Rise and Fall of
Responsible Liberalism

The Warren era in California lasten ten years and nine months, from January 4, 1943 to October 5, 1953 when he was appointed Chief Justice of the United States. Earl Warren was the only man elected Governor of California three times. He was a good Governor and his non-partisanship had alienated a minimum of voters. He was succeeded by Lieutenant Governor Goodwin J. Knight. Rarely had one politician been so delighted at the advancement of another.

Many believed that Knight would represent a distinct break from the Warren era. Never had expectations been proven so wrong. Knight's early years in Republican politics had been dedicated to helping Hiram Johnson. In 1934, he campaigned for Frank Merriam for Governor and was rewarded the following year with a Superior Court judgeship in Los Angeles County. He had a reputation as a conservative but also as a good judge.

In 1946, he ran with Warren for Lieutenant Governor and won handily. The only excitement was provided by Knight himself when he openly disagreed with Warren over Fair Employment Practices and Health Insurance. In 1949, he could hardly hide his gubernatorial ambitions and he made sounds of running. It was a period of "snapping bitterness" between Knight and Warren. When he became Governor, Knight moved cautiously, retaining most of the Warren appointees and following the main lines of his program. He would continue the "honeymoon" until the 1954 election. But after that, some said, there will be deep trouble for the Republican liberals and the Warren appointees.

The Democratic Party was phlegmatic. State-wide, it could claim only the office of attorney general and Edmund G. "Pat" Brown was not anxious to

Frank A. Mesple was primarily responsible for the original draft of Chapter 11.

A quarter-century of California Governors: Earl Warren (center) was elected in 1942, reelected in 1946 and 1950. Goodwin J. Knight (left) succeeded to the Governorship when Warren was appointed Chief Justice of the U. S. Supreme Court in 1953. Knight was elected Governor in 1954. Edmund G. "Pat" Brown was elected in 1958 and 1962. The three Governors talk things over at a testimonial dinner for DeWitt "Swede" Nelson, retiring Director of Conservation and one of several appointees who served under all three Governors. (Courtesy of State of California Department of Water Resources.)

test Knight. Brown had previously announced he would not run against Earl Warren but was under increasing pressure when Warren first indicated he would not run and then was appointed Chief Justice. With Goodwin Knight sailing smoothly along and on the basis of an inconclusive poll, Brown declared for a second term as Attorney General in mid-December, 1953.

As Democratic Party leaders saw their best shot at the governorship disappear, they turned to Richard P. Graves, Executive Secretary of the League of California Cities, a political independent known as a "good government" type. Graves agreed, changed his registration to "Democratic" and filed.

Although the Democratic Party was shaking free from some of the geographical, philosophical and personality divisions that had plagued it, the job facing Graves was immense. There were only ten congressmen, eleven state senators and twenty-six assemblymen who were Democratic. Richard Graves would face the task of a gigantic buildup in the face of the warm Warren afterglow and Knight's incessant campaigning. "Goodie" Knight spread his smile and handshakes throughout the state. Herbert "Pete" Phillips of the *Sacramento Bee* counted eighty-four speeches in his first fifty-nine days as governor.

The California Republican Assembly met to endorse Knight without serious debate. The struggle over the lieutenant-governorship was another matter. Harold "Butch" Powers had succeeded to the post at the time Knight moved into the governorship. The former State Senator from Eagleville, popular, affable, and bipartisan, was challenged by James Silliman, Speaker of the Assembly, and Frederick F. Houser, Superior Court Judge from Los Angeles. Rumors were persistent that Vice President Nixon wanted Powers "dumped."[1] Silliman received the CRA endorsement but Powers vowed to stay in the race. There were increasing reports of Republican factionalism.[2] The view open to the public was relatively serene.

Artie Samish, reputed secret "Boss of California" had departed the Sacramento scene under indictment for income tax evasion and liquor scandals. He had been under investigation by a special legislative subcommittee under Assemblyman Casper Weinberger. Little could be made of the "scandals" to injure Knight on the Republican slate. Republican hopes were meager in one regard, however, as predictions of defeating Attorney General Brown were rare. Only the last minute entry of Frederick Napoleon Howser would provide a Republican candidate in the primary. Many predicted that Brown could win both nominations in June.

The biggest "break" in the campaign came with the stance of labor. Years before, when Knight had supported Merriam, had attacked Warren's social programs and had even joined in the ill-conceived attempt of conservative Republicans to fight Warren's leadership through the candidacy of Thomas Werdel, any thought of labor embracing Goodwin Knight would have been considered hallucinatory. Since assuming the governorship, Knight had dealt openly and favorably with labor, had kept appointees they favored, had expressed himself as favoring improved social insurance for the workers and had pledged to oppose "right to work" legislation, if introduced, and to veto it if it should ever reach his desk. Labor could hardly ask for anything more.

The primary confirmed the polls. Despite a Democratic registration edge of 763,592, Knight swamped Graves in total votes 1,917,591 to 973,756. He came within 150,000 of defeating Graves for the Democratic nomination. 718,695 Democrats voted for Knight, while only 112,919 Republicans favored Graves under the crossfiling permitted at that time.

A new law provided that candidates in the primary, although they might continue to crossfile, would be identified by party label, "Dem." or "Rep." This gave the Democrats their first complete "slate" for state-wide office in years and more importantly, provided for November runoffs for more seats than had ever occurred since crossfiling was adopted.

The Democrats could also point to another singular triumph. Edmund G. "Pat" Brown won reelection on both party ballots. He received 1,437,156 Democratic votes and prevailed over Frederick N. Howser in the Republican primary 685,873 to 408,169. He was the last state-wide candidate to crossfile and win the nomination of the two major parties, and the only state-wide Democratic candidate ever to do so.

Cornelius J. "Neil" Haggerty, Executive Secretary of the California Federation of Labor, announced its support for the Republican candidate. The billboards proclaimed "Knight is Right." Money came into the Republican campaign while the Democratic campaign workers had to scrounge for enough to meet a minimal payroll. Whitaker and Baxter, a political public relations firm, did a competent job.

There was a rumble of Republican division. The formal party was composed of vestigial organs left over from the massive surgery performed on the California political parties by Hiram Johnson. Yet these weak organs are often the corpse over which ambitious politicians fight. 1954 was the opening round for control of the Republican delegation to the national convention of 1956. After the election of Tom Caldecott as state chairman, a real "donnybrook" broke out over the vice-chairmanship. Knight wanted Howard Ahmanson, savings and loan executive from Los Angeles, and his campaign manager in previous years. Knowland and Kuchel supported Knight. Richard Nixon, through Congressman Pat Hillings, urged the candidacy of Ray Arbuthnot, Vice-Chairman of the Los Angeles County committee. Nixon was joined by Murray Chotiner, close associate of the Vice President. It got bitter. Knight met with the legislative members and laid down his law which was "support my guy or no patronage!" Arbuthnot pulled out. Hillings asked Knight to announce that Nixon was "not involved." The Governor refused and political observers sensed that there might be some more severe ruptures in the future.[3]

Knight won by 451,151. "Butch" Powers won the lieutenant-governorship to discredit the political acumen of the California Republican Assembly which endorsed Silliman and the *Los Angeles Times* which endorsed Judge Frederick F. Houser. Secretary of State Frank Jordan, Controller Robert Kirkwood, and Treasurer Charles G. Johnson continued the Republican incumbency in their offices.

The Democratics did pick up two state senate seats and seven in the Assembly. In one of the latter races, Thomas Rees defeated Charles W. Lyon, former Speaker of the Assembly, who was involved and subsequently sentenced in the liquor license scandals. In another race, Jess Unruh won election to the Assembly from the Sixty-Fifth District of Los Angeles.

1955 being an odd-numbered year, there was a legislative session to organize and lead. With the retirement of James Silliman, the assembly members began the tugging and hauling over the speakership. The Speaker of the Assembly

331

holds great power in California in his ability to name chairmen and appoint committees. Throughout November and December, Luther "Abe" Lincoln and H. Allen "Al" Smith sought supporters. After convening on January 3, 1955, "Abe" Lincoln was elected 41–38.[4] In the Senate, Santa Barbara's Clarence Ward was reelected President Pro Tempore. Knight's legislative message stressed the state's needs, while a later message recommended a variety of taxes, including liquor, beer, cigarettes, horse racing, and an increase in the higher brackets of the personal income tax.

1955 saw the diminution of one issue, liquor abuses, and the smoldering presence of a second more emotional issue in the name of Caryl Chessman.

The previous election had seen the adoption of Proposition 3 to take liquor enforcement away from the Board of Equalization and give it to a newly created Alcoholic Beverage Control Department. William G. Bonelli, member of the Board of Equalization from Los Angeles, had fought the proposition and lashed out at Knight, Brown, Weinberger and virtually everyone else involved in attempted reform. The proposition passed by a margin of two to one in 1954 and Bonelli was retired from the Board of Equalization by Robert E. McDavid—1,288,552 to 838,048. Although a life-long Republican, Bonelli had switched his registration to "Democratic" prior to the election. His subsequent demise led to continuing argument as to his partisan affiliation with each party offering him to the other. He had gone to his cattle ranch in Kingman, Arizona, and continued his criticisms of Proposition 3 and its supporters. He promised to come back "swinging" and dispel the vicious rumors about alleged malfeasance.

On March 4, 1955, there was a memorandum to the press from the Governor's office: "Governor Goodwin J. Knight today signed an extradition request addressed to the Governor of Arizona for the return of William G. Bonelli." Before the request could be effected, "Bill" Bonelli was in Hermosillo, Mexico. His biography had read like a success story; veteran of World War I, political science professor at Occidental College, Phi Beta Kappa, President of the Los Angeles City Council, State Assemblyman, Director of the State Department of Professional and Vocational Standards and, since 1938, member of the powerful Board of Equalization. Now the people had turned him down for reelection and he began the long self-imposed exile in Mexico. While others would still have to answer for the "liquor scandals," Bonelli's relations with the state amounted to occasional protestations of innocence and periodic demands that his retirement checks be sent to his Mexican address.

The second item in early 1955 was the ruling of Attorney General Brown that prison authorities could prohibit prisoners from submitting manuscripts to publishers. Caryl Chessman, the "Red Light Bandit," was to receive attention beyond prison officials. Within five years, his name would dominate the cause of abolition of capital punishment with profound impact throughout the world and with dramatic impact upon California politics. His books, smuggled out of San Quentin, would be widely read.

The legislative session ran its course. "The hour of midnight having arrived," the 1955 session of the Legislature adjourned *sine die*, Wednesday night, June 8. Although straight-up twelve o'clock was the mandatory closing time, on the assembly side the clock acted strangely—it slowed down just enough to allow some eulogies, confetti-throwing, song-singing and sentimental burying of hatchets. Goodwin Knight had survived his first regular legislative session since assuming the governorship in pretty good political condition.

Those "conservative" Republicans who saw bright hopes for their philosophies when Knight succeeded Warren, saw those hopes snuffed out as the Governor strengthened his liberal-moderate record and enjoyed the closest rapport with organized labor of any Republican governor in California state history.

The lid was bound to blow off. The *Los Angeles Times*, long the "bell-cow" of Republican conservatism, could not contain itself much longer. It began to voice conservative anti-labor concern that was to rise in pitch and intensity in the months and years ahead. On October 30, 1955, Kyle Palmer, Political Editor of *The Times*, discussed Knight's statement that "there are literally thousands of Republicans in the ranks of labor and it is our job to merit their support." Palmer replied that the "Governor could not have made a sounder statement of fact but he seems to have entirely missed the implication of his assertion." To Palmer and *The Times*, the way to merit labor support was to resist labor leaders. George Meany, President of the American Federation of Labor, added his capstone to the exchange by suggesting in San Diego that "America could use more Governor Knights."[5]

The deep-seated differences between Governor Knight and the conservative Republican press expressed by Kyle Palmer became increasingly evident as the debate was taken up by Republican leaders. The competing ambitions of Nixon, Knowland and Knight were increasingly exposed.

Eisenhower's announcement of candidacy brought the vice presidential spot into question. Knight began to put the delegation together and hired the political public relations firm of Whitaker and Baxter to assist. Throughout March and April, 1956, Goodwin Knight refrained from an endorsement of Vice President Richard Nixon for a second term.

A most revealing exchange came in late April. First, Nixon announced he would "gladly accept" the vice-presidential nomination. Then Eisenhower's Press Secretary, James Haggerty, quoted the President as being "delighted" with Nixon's decision. William Knowland said he would be glad to nominate Nixon again as he had done in 1952; Senator Tom Kuchel was "pleased" and

"Goodie" Knight who was described by the press as "cool," announced he would "support Nixon if Eisenhower approve[d]."[6]

The composition of the Republican delegation showed similar strains. While Knight retained the chairmanship, after numerous "harmony meetings" and "unity talks," it was decided to divide up the delegation equally between supporters of Nixon, Knowland and Knight with Tom Kuchel thrown in for ballast. This was hardly a promising sign for the days ahead. Despite the increasing strains upon the unity of California Republicans, the Democrats showed considerable hesitancy in taking on Senator Kuchel. The only proven state-wide vote-getter, Attorney General Brown, would have a "free ride" and national and state Democratic leaders urged him to run. Even the taunting of Sam Yorty, who accused Brown of a "political tease act" failed to budge him. Finally, in October, 1955, the Attorney General made it clear that he would not seek the nomination. Some Democrats were reported "disappointed" and even "bitter."[7]

Brown's withdrawal from consideration threw the senatorial nomination wide open. Sam Yorty was always ready and willing to run but the new State Senator from Los Angeles, Richard Richards, captured the imagination of the Democratic liberal activists and swept over Yorty at the California Democratic Council Convention. Yorty stayed in the race, denouncing the CDC and Richards daily, and running largely on his brand of anti-communism and against Red China.[8]

Brown was asked by Adlai Stevenson to head up his California campaign, as well as his delegation. The Stevenson vote was almost twice Kefauver's and "Pat" Brown added another argument to his own case for future political promotion.[9]

Richard Richards, who did not crossfile, handily defeated Sam Yorty in the Democratic primary.[10] Political columnists were quick to suggest that Samuel William Yorty might be politically "dead" after two successive defeats. As a member of the California Democratic delegation at the national convention in Chicago, Richards was to receive state-wide attention by television and radio for his impassioned plea for a strong civil rights plank in the party platform.

The general election came almost as an anti-climax. Despite the popularity of Adlai Stevenson among intellectuals and Democratic Party workers of the state, he was easily defeated by nationally popular Eisenhower.

Richards received labor endorsement but his inability to move Kuchel from the favored middle-of-the-road position proved decisive. Kuchel got 2,892,918 votes to Richards' 2,445,816.

The state legislative situation bears some attention. Throughout 1955 and 1956, there had been a series of resignations and deaths of legislators. When special elections were called, the Democrats showed increasing strength and narrowed the Republican margins.

The state senate races assumed more than usual interest. Before the election, the balance was twenty-two to eighteen and the Democrats entertained hopes of winning a majority. Hugh M. Burns, affable, nonpartisan Democrat from Fresno, had announced he would be a candidate for President Pro Tempore should the Democrats succeed. He had served as "acting" President following the death of Clarence Ward and prior to the election of Ben Hulse to that position in the final week of the 1955 Session. The result of the 1956 election was a twenty-twenty split with the expectation that the Lieutenant Governor, Republican "Butch" Powers, would break the tie and keep a Republican in control to succeed the retiring Hulse.

These expectations were not realized when the Senate convened in January, 1957, as two Republicans, Louis Sutton of Maxwell and Randolph Collier of Yreka, voted for Hugh Burns. The Senate had its first Democratic President Pro Tempore since 1891.[11]

No sooner had the dust settled from the 1956 campaign and the winning candidates assumed office than one of the most curious and unique episodes in California's unique and curious political history began to unfold. Goodwin Knight was proving himself a competent governor. His easy, gregarious, free-wheeling style may have been concern for some of his campaign aides but his wondrous collection of anecdotes and jokes charmed audiences up and down the state. Ralph Friedman described his broad gauge appeal: "His supporters range from progressive unionists such as Joe de Silva to Pro-America, the Yankee ghosts of Louis XIV; they include such assorted bedmates as AFL brass, the *Los Angeles Times*, the *Examiners of Los Angeles and San Francisco*, small town GOP papers, young intellectuals, and encrusted politicians, who go to the polls with the intention of voting for William McKinley."

Appropriate to such a diversified following, Knight's own philosophy—or lack of it—was summed up in a speech before the Sacramento Host Breakfast in 1955. "I suppose if I were to reduce my philosophy of government into a single phrase, I could do no better than to borrow the ancient saying: 'Moderation is best—avoid all extremes.' "[12]

The Democratic Party showed growing strength but Knight had handled himself well since assuming the governorship. He had put together a reasonably good general session in 1955 and came out of the 1956 session unscathed. Eisenhower was basking in nationwide adulation in the White House. Richard Nixon was at his side and expecting to inherit the presidency. William Knowland had served in the United States Senate since 1945 and had enjoyed the honor of leading the Republicans there.

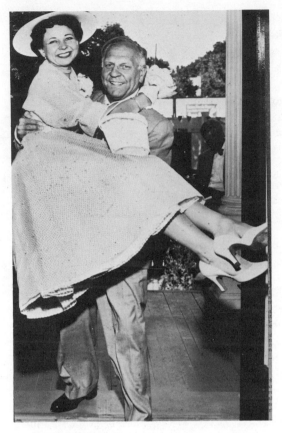

Governor Goodwin J. Knight carries his bride across the threshold at the Governor's Mansion in Sacramento. While in office, the widower Governor married the former Virginia Carlson, widow of World War II bombardier. (Courtesy of *Sacramento Bee*.)

Knight's marriage to Mrs. Virginia Carlson, thirty-six-year-old widow of a World War II bombardier, added a genuine romantic touch to a campaign manager's dream. But politics is full of ambitious men and, while the system is all the better for it, it can change the most idyllic and peaceful political scenes to total chaos.

William Fife Knowland was born and raised in politics. His father, Joseph R. Knowland, was a long-time Republican leader, a former congressman, and publisher of the *Oakland Tribune*. Young Knowland had served as an assemblyman, and as a state senator and was a Republican national committeeman in 1938 at the age of thirty. Three years later, he was chairman of that committee. In 1945, while overseas, he was summoned to Washington, D.C. by Governor Earl Warren to succeed the venerable Hiram Johnson, who had died in office after having served continuously since 1917.

On January 7, 1957, William Knowland surprised his colleagues in the

Senate, his political party nationally and locally, and his constituents, by announcing he would give up his senate seat at the close of his term in 1958. He had no problems with the voters. The announced reason, "in order to see more of my family," had a hollow ring. Kyle Palmer in the *Los Angeles Times* wrote: "My guess is that he will run for Governor" and "if a winner, then for the Republican nomination for President two years later."[13]

Just a few months earlier, Knight and Knowland had teamed up to gain control over the Republican State Central Committee. Why would he take on a popular incumbent of his own party? On April 28, 1957, Palmer interviewed Knowland in Washington but found him "mum as a clam."[14] The speculation of a possible move by Knowland to take on Knight grew. But why two years before the end of his term? Palmer, his ardent admirer, even found it hard to explain: "The Senator is one of the most self-contained, self-reliant and self-consulting figures in State and National politics."[15] Later, Palmer would write, "It can be said . . . that he is somewhat of a combination of political rhinoceros and sphinx. There is no manner of telling what he will do."[16]

Yet the *Los Angeles Times* should not have been so totally perplexed. That journal of anti-labor conservative Republicanism had steadily chastised Knight's romance with labor. In late 1955, the paper indicated that it "[might] very well support whoever opposed Knight because of his closeness to labor."

Knowland kept his own counsel but in August, 1957, he announced a tour of the state. He would divulge his future plans afterward. Meanwhile, Governor Knight rehired Whitaker and Baxter, announced that he was irrevocably in the race and undertook "a political fence-mending, hay-cutting, road-repairing, vote-cultivating drive seldom witnessed in California politics."[17] Knowland's announcement of his candidacy "produced one of the most acrimonious battles and amazing election upsets in California politics." What the California Republicans did to each other in 1958 was, from the standpoint of election year pragmatism, virtually unbelievable. "If California itself was aghast at the sudden intra-party carnage, the rest of the country found the goings-on utterly inexplicable."[18]

Knowland made it clear he would embrace a comprehensive set of conservative views in his campaign, topped off by his full endorsement of the anti-labor "right to work" initiative which would appear on the November, 1958, ballot as Proposition 18. Labor was aghast. Angry and defiant, Knight vowed that he had no intention of stepping aside and fired off a number of blasts at Knowland, many of which would be echoed by his Democratic opponent in the months ahead. His most telling accusation was the charge that Knowland merely wanted to "use" the California governorship as a "stepping-stone to the Presidency." Moderate and conservative Republicans, not to speak of the state's generally elated Democrats, promptly chose up sides for Armageddon.[19]

337

As Knight hung tough and took Knowland on, the early predictions by the polls of Knowland's invincibility began to weaken. The Republican state leadership began to show concern and the idea began to be widely expressed, in the *Los Angeles Times* and elsewhere, that Knight ought to reconsider. This only brought increased criticism from the Governor and the continued questioning of the Senator's tactics and motives.

Knowland claimed then and has consistently maintained that he had always believed in the "open" primary, that he expected Knight to stay in the race and that he had no personal part in the efforts to bring about Knight's withdrawal.

It began to become apparent that the campaign financing that Knight expected was slipping away. The Republican press throughout the state showed a preference for Knowland's brand of Republicanism. Another element was the Nixon supporters, who never quite forgave Knight for his reluctance in supporting the Vice President for renomination. When Whitaker and Baxter announced they were dropping the Knight "account," the Governor had little choice. After a few days of seclusion, the embattled Governor sought counsel in Washington. Richard Nixon became the principal negotiator in the effort to persuade Knight to withdraw from the gubernatorial race and run for the United States Senate. On November 5, 1957, after consultations with President Eisenhower and Nixon, Governor Knight emerged from the Vice President's office to read the announcement of his candidacy for the Senate. Nixon endorsed Knowland and Knight. There were some reports that Nixon would not seek 1960 delegates in California nor would Knowland campaign outside the State in 1960 but no confirmation of this kind of deal has ever been proved.[20]

The Democrats had a field day. They called it a "cynical deal," a "big switch" or the "big fix." Knight had been handed a "booby prize." Edmund G. Brown said that once again the Republican moneylenders had made a "package deal" and denied the party members a free and open choice. Knight described his own predicament: "I had no other choice. I was like a man in the middle of the ocean, standing on the deck of a burning ship."[21] This was by far the best thing that had happened to the Democratic Party in decades.

The Democratic ticket, as expected, was headed by Attorney General Brown. Twice elected District Attorney of San Francisco and twice elected Attorney General of California, he was pursuing a path remarkably similar to that of Earl Warren, whom he had served and for whom he had high personal regard. Although he had first run for the state Assembly as a Republican, he found the Democratic Party of Franklin Roosevelt more compatible to his views. He was considered a "middle-of-the-roader," refused to identify with either wing of the Democratic Party and claimed his intention of following the Hiram Johnson-Earl Warren traditions.

As Attorney General, he might anticipate relative political security. He had

338

sidestepped earlier pressures to run for Governor and United States Senator but after a meeting with the Democratic congressional delegation, he announced his candidacy on October 30, 1957, six days before Knight's decision to switch to the United States Senate race.[22]

Congressman Clair Engle proved an energetic and capable campaigner for the United States Senate seat vacated by Knowland and sought by Knight. Although Brown began the campaign by avoiding any "slate" approach, it soon developed into a unified and mutually cooperative campaign. When the California Democratic Council gave its unanimous approval to Brown, chose Engle, affirmed Stanley Mosk for Attorney General, Alan Cranston for Controller, and approved the rest of the slate, the Democrats enjoyed a primary campaign remarkably free from the internecine warfare that engulfed their Republican counterparts.

Collective bargaining distinguished the gubernatorial candidates more than any other issue. Knowland pressed his position relentlessly. It provoked labor to one of its most unified and effective political efforts.[23]

The candidacy of William Knowland, an "arch-conservative" in labor's book, at the expense of popular pro-labor Governor Knight, offered a logical rallying point for labor. Cornelius J. "Neil" Haggerty, Secretary-Treasurer of the State Federation of Labor, called upon the union members to get into the campaign—to walk precincts and distribute material.

While Democratic teamwork, augmented by labor, went on under capable professional campaign management, Republican bickering continued. Knight, hoping that other Republican candidates would drop out of the Senatorial race with the same sense of sacrifice he had felt would be disappointed by the continued candidacy of the Mayor of San Francisco, George Christopher.

Labor, totally committed to Brown and against "right to work," had to face an ironic dilemma with regard to Knight's Senatorial candidacy. Thoroughly pleased with their excellent relationship with Knight in Sacramento, labor had always had reservations about the effectiveness of liberal Republicans in Washington. Some felt that the only effective, practical course was to go down the line for the Democratic slate. Others felt this would be breaking faith with a man who had kept his promises to labor and also pointed out a vote of Engle's in support of the hated Taft–Hartley Act.

Labor's endorsing convention saw an Advisory Council vote 7-5 in favor of Engle, only to have the group's Executive Council vote 12-11 for Knight. Neil Haggerty commented: "Shall we help [Knight] on the way down to oblivion just when he has been made to sacrifice his office because of his friendship to labor?"[24] Haggerty said he would not "be able to sleep with himself" if labor abandoned Knight. A compromise was reached by recommending Engle to Democratic voters and Knight to Republican members.

Knowland continued to speak of "voluntary unionism" and of "right to work" as a classic American freedom. Yet the billboards with pictures of Nixon and Eisenhower proclaimed bipartisan support against Proposition 18. If the issue and the disunity of the Republican Party were not enough, the incoherence and excesses of the Knowland campaign left the "middle road" free to Brown and the Democrats.

Prior to the primary, Knowland remained in Washington "tending to his Senate business" and campaigned for only fourteen days. Mrs. Knowland and his two daughters traveled the state in an auto trailer, playing recorded speeches and distributing literature. Among the pieces handed out were five hundred copies of a pamphlet by Joseph Kamp, long identified as an extremist.[25] For once, the Republican candidate rather than the Democrat was accused of being outside the "respectable" political spectrum.

The primary election of June 3, 1958, resulted in obvious evidence of prospective Democratic successes in the general election. The gubernatorial race was a virtual popularity contest between Brown and Knowland. Both had crossfiled, the last time this could be done in a California primary. Traditionally, Republican voters were more "loyal" than Democrats who sometimes favored Republican candidates. June, 1958, was a dramatic exception: 313,385 Democrats voted for Knowland; 374,879 Republicans crossed party lines to vote for Brown. Roughly one in seven Democrats voted for Knowland, while more than one of five Republicans supported Brown. Knowland's task in the general election was indeed statistically formidable, if not insurmountable.

If things were bad for the primary, they got worse for the Republicans during the campaign for the general election. The script for prior elections had been thrown away. The time-tested Republican formula was a candidate who blurred party lines, monopolized the "middle-of-the-road" and forced the Democratic challenger into an allegedly left of center position. Totton Anderson observed, "The bemused electorate was offered, instead, a choice between a wealthy, arch-conservative, militantly partisan, austere Protestant Republican and a self-made, middle-of-the-road, relatively unpartisan, friendly Catholic Democrat."[26]

The Democrats held love feasts, while the Republicans continued to hack away at each other. Kuchel was aloof. Nixon made rather perfunctory and bland pronouncements on party unity. Knight refused to reciprocate Knowland's personal endorsement, accused the Senator of introducing an "Un-Republican issue," "right to work," into the campaign and tried to disassociate himself from the nominal head of the Republican ticket.

Mrs. Knowland sent a letter to 200 Republican leaders blasting "Big Labor" and accusing Knight of having a "macaroni spine." Her husband had to run to "prevent California from becoming another satellite of United Auto Workers President Walter Reuther's labor-political empire."[27] She did not leave much for

"Pat" Brown and Clair Engle to do or say.[28] Eisenhower was sent in to raise flagging spirits but aside from an enthusiastic personal reception, his presence did not do much good for the candidates.

Another unique development took place during the final week of the election campaign. The *Los Angeles Times*, the *San Francisco Chronicle*, and the *Oakland Tribune*, had always been considered an impregnable Republican journalistic triumvirate. On October 30, 1958, after supporting Knowland for the primary and during the campaign, the Editor of the *San Francisco Chronicle* stated: "We have been unfavorably impressed with the subsequent campaign." Without endorsing Brown, readers were urged to vote "for the candidate of their choice." The ultra-conservative *Long Beach Press Telegram* bitterly attacked Knowland and his wife, "the hatchet woman." The McClatchy papers supported the Attorney General, as did three of the four Hearst papers. Throughout the press, even from the friendly confines of the *Los Angeles Times*, came premonitions of Republican disaster. Only the proportions seemed to be in doubt. The results were beyond the fondest Democratic expectations. Brown crushed Knowland 3,140,076 to 2,110,911. Knowland carried only Alpine, Mono, Orange, and Santa Barbara counties.

It was a complete Republican debacle. Congressman Engle defeated Knight by 723,356. The Democratic successes moved down the ballot. All the Republican state constitutional officers were defeated but Secretary of State Frank Jordan.

The Assembly was in Democratic hands, forty-seven to thirty-three, while the State Senate was also Democratic, twenty-seven to thirteen. This was a far cry from those ancient times when Democratic state legislators were a novelty. Only thirty years before, the California Legislature boasted six Democratic assemblymen and three Democratic senators.

As Goodwin Knight was conceding that the Republican Party in California was in "its worst shape in a century," Brown began to set the legislative stage for his "responsible liberalism." He named an old associate, Republican businessman Bert Levit, to be his Director of Finance. He began to pull his staff together— Fred Dutton as Executive Secretary, Hale Champion from the *Chronicle* for Press Secretary and other bright young brain trusters like Warren Christopher and William Coblentz. On December 22, 1958, the Governor-elect promised an "aggressive and liberal administration," saying, "We want new blood, new ideas, and new ways of dealing with old problems."

Three days after his inauguration, the Governor introduced his Fair Employment Practices bill. It would bring effective reform. Knight had avoided the issue entirely and Warren had pushed for a "study" commission. The Governor personally proposed a measure to end the unique California tradition of cross-filing. This invention of Hiram Johnson which permitted a candidate to seek the nomination of his own party *and that of the opposition party as well*, had been the touchstone of incumbent governors and legislators but had been the special target on the issues oriented California Democratic Council which felt this practice blunted issues and platforms and encouraged incumbents to appeal to the broadest possible political spectrum.

Here Brown suffered his first break with a leading Democratic legislator. Hugh Burns, a Democrat, presided over a house where consensus was achieved with little regard for a member's party affiliation. In fact, only a few years previously, the Senate had approved a measure to make the Legislature legally "non-partisan."[29] Brown prevailed; crossfiling was killed.

The tax bill created bitter opposition. Organized labor resented "consumer" taxes on tobacco and beer. The well-organized and politically potent banks, insurance companies, corporations and race tracks instructed their lobbyists to resist the increase of their taxes, included in the tax "package." The relatively wealthy, many of whom had voted for Brown, looked askance at the increased personal income taxes affecting the upper brackets and the raise in the inheritance taxes. One of the best lobbied interests in Sacramento were the oil companies and their allies. The severance tax proposal brought out their big guns.

The more each interest group protested, the more it became apparent that the tax bill was relatively fair and equitable. Liberals like Philip Burton, assemblyman from San Francisco who would pale at the mention of cigarette or beer taxes' effect on the "workingman," voted for the bill as an equitable one. Many conservatives did likewise, under the pressure of "fiscal responsibility." The package nearly held together without change but cigars and oil eventually escaped taxation. Brown was particularly angry over the loss of the severance tax and blamed his defeat on the oil lobbyists.[30]

More and more bills came in with the notation, "Introduced at the request of the Governor." Ralph Brown, newly elected Speaker of the Assembly, worked quietly but effectively on the Governor's requests. Many of the assembly committee chairmen were sympathetic to the Governor's liberal program. Jess Unruh, Chairman of the powerful Ways and Means Committee, used his considerable talents and growing strength on the Governor's behalf. On the Senate side, a group of younger, liberal senators could be counted on for help. The veteran George Miller was invaluable in saving the Fair Employment Practices bill from crippling amendments and in salvaging the ban on crossfiling. Although Brown and Burns had philosophical differences, the Senator consulted with the Governor frequently and once he gave a commitment to help, he would deliver. Although he fought F.E.P. and anti-crossfiling bills and was unsympathetic to the minimum wage proposals, Hugh Burns proved an invaluable ally in the struggle to solve the water issue.

Brown, as Attorney General, had been personally involved in the legal issues surrounding water. He also knew the deep emotional feeling it aroused in the "counties of origin," in the heavily cultivated central valleys, in the delta, where many residents were fearful of salt water intrusion. He knew how vital the water issue was to Los Angeles and San Diego, both dependent upon the limited and litigation-wracked waters of Owens Valley and the Colorado River.

Yet with all these economic sensitivities, the immediate problem was political. Warren and Knight, despite their efforts and abilities, had failed. A northern dominated Senate and a southern dominated Assembly had to be brought together. A water plan had to be produced that could make long-range commitment to deliver and sell water. The north needed protection for its water rights and help from the devastating floods, like that of 1955.

The Democratic Party leaders in Sacramento decided to use Burns' Senate Bill 1106 as the main vehicle, and a Bond Act of $1,750,000,000 to be put before the people at the 1960 election.

Carley Porter, veteran Chairman of the Assembly Water Committee, shared in the decision-making and the strategy. The measure squeezed by the Senate with the bare minimum. Then the tactical decision was made to accept the senate version on the assembly side, thus avoiding a subsequent conference committee. Although it still had a long road to travel, this issue alone would go down as an accomplishment of historical proportions. The final legislative chapter would be the passage of the Bond Proposition in November, 1960, for which Brown campaigned up and down the state. Herbert Phillips would characterize Brown's 1959 legislative record "for volume and scope of enactments in a single session (as) comparing favorably . . . with that of Hiram Johnson in 1911." This record had been achieved with a minimum of damage to Brown's legislative relations. National newspapers and magazines took notice and proclaimed his "national stature." "Conservatives" were surprised at how easy Brown was to digest, the "moderates" felt it was an easy and profitable extension of the Warren era and the "liberals" were pleased at the programmatic commitment of the Governor.[31]

Nationally, the Twenty-second Amendment, pressed by Republicans in the wake of Franklin Roosevelt's four elections, made Eisenhower a constitutional "lame duck." While Governor Nelson Rockefeller of New York and Senator Barry Goldwater of Arizona had their followers, it became more and more apparent that the mantle of candidacy would fall on Richard Nixon.

The Democrats had no such front runner. Lyndon Johnson and Stuart Symington appealed to the conservatives, while Hubert Humphrey and Adlai Stevenson continued to hold the affection of the liberals. And a young, enthusiastic Bostonian named John F. Kennedy began to make inroads as he traveled the country from his political perch as Senator from Massachusetts.

TO GOVERNOR BROWN, "THE WINNER"— BASTian

The *San Francisco Chronicle* opposed the passage of the Water Bond Act (Proposition 1) of 1960. This post-election cartoon depicts Governor Brown lifting the "hand" of the winner, a leaky octupus entitled "The Water Plan." (Courtesy of *San Francisco Chronicle*.)

There were occasional suggestions of Brown's presidential potential. As head of the state-wide party, he had to avoid the clash of the national candidates which would leave the battlefield strewn with the dying and the wounded. Emissaries came and went. John Kennedy paid a "courtesy call" on the Governor at the Mansion. Brown made no secret of his personal desire that the candidates stay out of the California primary. In order to accomplish this, he decided to see that the delegation, while pledged to him as a "favorite son" would contain delegates favoring each of the national candidates. The results were disastrous to the Governor as national television carried the picture of a divided, antagonistic, feuding California delegation at the Los Angeles convention.

Another event in 1960 cut deeply into Brown's popularity with the public and strained his relations with many in the Legislature. Caryl Chessman had spent twelve years in Death Row at San Quentin. Legal and technical issues had occupied the attention of the courts throughout this time. His prior record of arrest and conviction, the violence and perversion of his crime, the fact the victim subsequently was sent to a mental institution and, most of all, Chessman's complete lack of contrition, made him an unlikely candidate for clemency in the public's mind. Yet his constant protestation of innocence and his skill in writing about himself and getting his story published and read, gave considerably impetus to the abolition of capital punishment movement. At the last minute, the Governor granted a sixty-day reprieve and announced that he would place the matter of the abolition of capital punishment on "special" call to be considered concurrently with the Budget Session in March, 1960.

The drama took place before the Judiciary Committee of the Senate. Senator Fred Farr presented his bill and supporters, many of them prominent national figures, appeared. Then came the opposition expressed primarily by law enforcement. The final vote was eight to seven against the bill.[32] Abolition of capital punishment was dead, and the special session restricted to this single "item" was adjourned. The senators went on to other chores. Chessman was put to death. Although some people gave Brown credit for his "convictions," his popularity suffered throughout the state. Many legislators felt he had thrown them a political "hot potato."

Yet his legislative record advanced. In 1960, Brown moved ahead with his Master Plan for Higher Education; in 1961, he successfully pushed through the Fisher bill on teacher credentialing over the strenuous and powerful opposition of the California Teachers Association. Senator Stan Arnold authored a measure to overhaul the Juvenile Court laws. Disability insurance was extended to agricultural workers. All attempts to alter the California Water Plan or restore crossfiling were beaten down.

In 1960 John F. Kennedy was elected President of the United States without California's help. Having carried the state himself by over a million two years before, Brown confidently predicted that Kennedy would do likewise. Early returns sounded good to the Democrats, but California's native son, Nixon, as the vote tally continued, was running a bit closer than the Democrats had reckoned possible. As the absentee votes were counted about a week later, Nixon could gain some solace in knowing that out of the more than 6.6 million votes cast in California, he had carried the state by 35,623. Richard Nixon's first political speech after his defeat was before the Republican State Central Committee on March 11, 1961. He said he had no intention of running for Governor in 1962. Seven months later, he announced his candidacy for that office.

On that night, September 28, 1961, Governor Brown was at his "summer residence" in Los Angeles. Sensing the public disapproval of his performance at the Democratic convention, even though he had sought support for the now popular Kennedy, and feeling also the sting of the Chessman case, he had spent considerable time reflecting upon his own political future. He had privately indicated to intimates that he was exhausted. The polls showed that his popular-

345

ity was at a low ebb, 17% behind Nixon. Any qualms he may have had were dispelled that night, as Nixon ripped into the Brown "record" and the "mess in Sacramento." Brown thought his record a good one. He decided to run against the man who was bound to activate a lot of dedicated Democratic workers.

But Nixon was not the only conservative seeking the governorship. Assemblyman Joe Shell, ex-U.S.C. athlete and assembly G.O.P. leader, was bound to stay in the race and seek the conservative vote. He accused his Republican contender of debasing the California governorship by seeking to use it as a stepping stone to the presidency. But Nixon had some good fortune. Former Governor "Goodie" Knight, still popular and wearing the mantle of Earl Warren's middle-of-the-road philosophy, was forced from the campaign on January 16, 1962, by a serious case of hepatitis. Former Lieutenant Governor Harold "Butch" Powers withdrew in March, 1962, when organizational and financial support failed to materialize.

Shell campaigned against Brown's "big government" and "spendthrift ways." As he flew his own plane across the state, "his attack upon Nixon was personal and lethal." Shell accused Nixon or his followers of disseminating "whispered lies" against Shell's family and of using "gutter tactics."[33] Nixon's opponents were quick to charge this to the "old Nixon." It helped to solidify the Democratic vote that remembered Nixon in the campaigns of 1946 and 1950. Nixon's innuendos of being beaten by possible election fraud by Kennedy in 1960 also began to sound like the sour grapes of a poor loser.[34]

The primary afforded few surprises but plenty of ammunition for future battles. Brown received 1,739,792 votes but Republicans were quick to point out that over 600,000 Democrats, roughly 25% of the party voters who had gone to the polls, failed to vote for the Governor. Minor candidates polled 294,313 votes; 250,000 people did not vote at all; 66,712 wrote in Joseph Shell and 35,833 wrote in Richard Nixon. On the other hand, Nixon had received 1,285,151 votes but Shell had gained 656,542, or one-third.

Brown went the party route by asking for the California Democratic Council pre-primary endorsement of his "ticket." Brown aides and supporters worked the convention to kill off any embarrassing resolutions that would be fodder for the Republicans. The stepping stone charges against Knowland were dusted off. Meanwhile, Senator Kuchel faced a right wing challenge. He too adopted a "good guy" stance against the warnings of impending socialism and sin by Loyd Wright and Howard Jarvis.

The nonpartisan contest for Superintendent of Public Instruction, in view of Roy Simpson's retirement, drew nine candidates. One million voters, perhaps intimidated by the multitude of candidates, did not even cast a vote for the office. Top man was Ralph Richardson, U.C.L.A. speech professor, President of the Los Angeles Board of Education and once staff secretary to Governor Brown. He was followed by Max L. Rafferty, school superintendent from La

Canada and advocate of Basic Education. Cecil Hardesty, the California Teachers Association candidate, was 15,000 votes behind Rafferty and was eliminated from the runoff to be held with the general election.

The campaign for governor dominated the political scene. Both sides presented a positive program for solving state problems but they got scant attention compared to the negative charges that were leveled. Brown charged Nixon with inexperience with state issues and keeping his eyes on the White House. Nixon claimed Brown played partisan politics, indulged in nepotism, and appointed incompetents to office. The loan by Howard Hughes to the Nixon family became an issue[35] while Nixon resurrected the charges of "soft on Communism." Fortunately for the voters, the Cuban crisis intervened and produced a temporary "moratorium" of the campaign. Both parties tried to reconstruct the crisis to suit their partisan aspirations.

The night before the elections, Nixon staged a televised, state-wide speech. Speaking with his wife and two daughters present in the sound stage set which simulated a living room, he attacked the "smears" and "campaign of lies" against him. Some said it was a re-run of the "Checkers" defense of the special fund during the 1952 presidential campaign. The Democrats followed with an hour long Hollywood variety show.

While the Nixon campaign spent heavily on television, the Democratic strategists put out considerable funds for a "get-out-the-vote" drive. Precinct workers were paid to assist in covering those precincts with both high Democratic registration and high "loyalty" factors. Jess Unruh joined with Don Bradley, the Brown campaign chairman, in working out the project. CDC volunteers, although decrying the "commercialization" of campaigning joined in walking the precincts.

At the final count, "California underwent another of its swift and mystifying reversals of sentiment."[36] Having given Nixon a narrow edge in 1960, it rejected him in 1962. Brown received 3,037,109; Nixon gathered in 2,740,351. Brown had accomplished what John Kennedy could not and was again being hailed as a "giant killer." Nixon, tired, shaken and unshaved, appeared before a press conference the next morning. He "retired" from politics and chastized the press (save Carl Greenberg of the *Los Angeles Times*) accusing them of "shafting" him and concluding with, "You won't have Dick Nixon to kick around any more." The political pundits all agreed that Richard Milhous Nixon was through in politics.

Senator Kuchel conducting one of the shortest campaigns in history, came to the state in mid-October to cite his good works. The Cuban crisis produced the "picture worth a million votes" of the Senator boarding an Air Force jet, complete in flying suit, to answer the President's call to the nation's Capitol. Richards lost to him 3,180,483 to 2,452,839.

In the Superintendent of Instruction race, Max Rafferty became the favorite of the conservatives who had supported Shell and Kuchel's opponents in the Republican primary, and of a lot of Californians who believed that "permissiveness" in public education was the reason for increasing social tensions. While Richardson was defending California's schools as among the best in the nation, Rafferty pressed his attack on them and advocated the return of the "Three R's" and the re-establishment of American traditions. Rafferty prevailed, 2,681,651 to 2,461,807.

Strains were beginning to tell in Brown's relations with the Legislature. Jess Unruh was elected Speaker of the Assembly in a unique post-session caucus in 1961 after Ralph Brown was appointed to the Court of Appeals. Unruh was to remain in this position until January, 1969, longer than any other man. Strong willed, able and articulate, Unruh felt the Legislature—or at least, his house—should assume greater initiative and innovation in the legislative process. With the support of his fellow assemblymen, he developed the best-staffed house of any in the United States. The friction between Unruh and Hale Champion, Press Secretary, then Executive Secretary, then Director of Finance for the Governor, became common knowledge to the press and around the State Capitol. Brown would try to work out a "rapprochement" with the Speaker but the two of them generally ended up in mutual recrimination. Their staffs would generally join in the fray.

Unruh used his platform as Speaker of the Assembly in the nation's largest state to become the best-known and most respected state legislator in the nation. He campaigned in other states as the prime exponent of state constitutional reform and legislative improvement. Some Unruh opponents argued that he used the ploy of improved legislative staffing to build up his own political organization for the future, but even they were quick to agree that the Speaker had done more to improve the California Legislature than any man in the state's history.

But Unruh was not content with these achievements. As Speaker, he defied the tradition that a presiding officer does not carry legislation and introduced—year after year—an enviable legislative program of his own. The Unruh Civil Rights Act, the Unruh Retail Installment Credit Act, the Unruh Pre-School Act and the Miller-Unruh Basic Reading Act of 1965 were only a few of his personal accomplishments.

The Unruh–Brown feud was apparently based upon a combination of factors, including the more or less typical legislative vs. executive wrangle, and a personal animosity based upon the political ambitions of each man. This added to the party split which was to cost Brown dearly in 1966.

California senators had their interests and priorities. *Baker v. Carr*, the first of the monumental reapportionment decisions, caused a general uneasiness throughout the Senate, which continued to district itself in accordance with the Federal plan initiated by the Farm Bureau in 1926. Under its provisions, no county could have more than a single senator nor could any more than three counties be combined into a single Senatorial District. For thirty-five years, the ten southern counties (now containing 62% of the population) had only ten senators, while the northern counties had thirty. Defenders of the Federal plan pointed out our own congressional model and the fact that the Assembly, proportionately divided, gave Los Angeles County thirty-one assemblymen.

Earl Warren had defended the Federal plan when he had been attorney general and governor of California. On two occasions, the people of the state had rejected abolition or change of the Federal plan. Yet, the more perceptive cast a wary eye at the court as its reapportionment cases spread beyond Tennessee to other states. To the senators, Brown's defense of their sacred Federal plan was imperative.

Before his assassination on November 22, 1963, President John F. Kennedy had called upon the people of the United States to fight discrimination. One area he called upon for remedy was housing. Governor Brown endorsed a Fair Housing proposal, asked for state-wide support together with Byron Rumford, the bill's author.

In the 1963 session the Fair Housing proposal did well in the Assembly but not in the Senate. Although controlled by the Democrats twenty-seven to thirteen, there were many in the senate leadership who felt the legislation was ill-advised. The California Real Estate Association made no secret of its opposition and began to raise the counter claim of sacred property rights.

The bill was sent to the Senate Governmental Efficiency Committee where for long days and weeks it rested in a state of somnambulism. President Pro Tempore Burns and Chairman Luther Gibson were known to have "grave reservations." Occasionally, the Chairman, Senator Gibson, would hold it up, look at it and return it "under submission." The Governor grew impatient, restive, and ultimately angry. His closest friends in the Senate urged him not to get personally involved in the struggle. The fight in the Senate ultimately reached epic proportions. The senate leadership, long able to avoid overt resistance to its authority, found a state of virtual revolution. Senators Edwin Regan, Joseph Rattigan and others took on Burns and Gibson.

Minority groups and liberals, together with a significant number of ministers, crowded the offices and corridors of the capitol building. Pickets blocking the Senate Chamber were physically removed. Resentment of the "sit-in" almost killed the bill. There was a last minute delaying tactic by Senator Clark Bradley of San Jose. Unruh applied pressure by withholding action on selected senate bills.[37] The Senate "lost its cool" and personal comments not usually said about gentlemen, much less of Senators, were expressed. At 11:45 p.m. of the final day, Assembly Bill 1240 received the necessary votes, was rushed to the Assembly for concurrence in senate amendments and on to the Governor.

The Rumford Act was not revolutionary legislation. It did not really move add Section 1419.5 to the Labor Code, relating to discrimination in housing.

Bill read third time.

Recommendation of the Governor

In accordance with Article IV, Section 34, of the Constitution, the Governor presented the following communication recommending the consideration of Assembly Bill No. 1240:

STATE OF CALIFORNIA, GOVERNOR'S OFFICE
SACRAMENTO, April 17, 1963

To the Honorable Members of the Assembly and Senate:

Assembly Bill No. 1240, "An act to repeal Part 5 (commencing with Section 35700) of Division 24 of, and to add Part 5 (commencing with Section 35700) to Division 24 of, the Health and Safety Code, and to add Section 1419.5 to the Labor Code, relating to discrimination in housing,"

in my opinion constitutes an emergency bill within the meaning of that term as used in Section 34 of Article IV of the Constitution of the State of California, the consideration of which should not await the final enactment of the Budget Bill.

I, therefore, recommend consideration of Assembly Bill No. 1240 as an emergency measure.

Respectfully submitted,

EDMUND G. BROWN, Governor

The question being on the passage of the bill.

Speaker Presiding

At 12.07 p.m., Hon. Jesse M. Unruh, Speaker of the Assembly, presiding.

Demand for Previous Question

Messrs. Bane, Cusanovich, Warren, Greene, and McMillan demanded the previous question. Demand sustained.

The question being on the passage of the bill.

Bill passed by the following vote:

AYES—Alquist, Bagley, Bane, Bee, Beilenson, Booth, Burton, Carrell, Casey, Crown, Danielson, Dills, Dymally, Elliott, Ferrell, Foran, Frew, Gaffney, Garrigus, Gonsalves, Greene, Henson, Johnson, Kennick, Knox, Marks, McMillan, Meyers, Mills, Moreno, Pattee, Petris, Powers, Quimby, Rumford, Song, Soto, Stanton, Thomas, Waite, Waldie, Warren, Williamson, Young, Z'berg, Zenovich, and Mr. Speaker—47.

NOES—Ashcraft, Badham, Barnes, Belotti, Britschgi, Burgener, Chapel, Collier, Cologne, Conrad, Cusanovich, Deukmejian, Donovan, Flournoy, Hinckley, Holmes, Lanterman, Milias, Monagan, Mulford, Stevens, Thelin, Veneman, Veysey, and Whetmore—25.

Bill ordered transmitted to the Senate.

Explanation of Vote on Assembly Bill No. 1240

DEAR MR. SPEAKER: Because of legislative business I could not be on the floor for the vote on Assembly Bill No. 1240. If I had been present, I would have voted "Aye."

LEO J. RYAN

Speaker pro Tempore Presiding

At 12.15 p.m., Hon. Carlos Bee, Speaker pro Tempore of the Assembly, presiding.

Name Placed Upon Roll Call on Assembly Bill No. 1240

Mr. Collier was granted unanimous consent that he be recorded as voting "No" on Assembly Bill No. 1240.

350

The three roll-call votes on the Rumford Fair Housing Act (Assembly Bill 1240). The Assembly vote (April 25, 1963) showed three Republicans among the forty-seven "aye" votes: Bagley, Marks, and Pattee, while all the "no" votes were Republican.

June 21, 1963]   SENATE JOURNAL   4799

The roll was called, and the bill passed by the following vote:

AYES—Senators Arnold, Begovich, Cameron, Cobey, Collier, Farr, Geddes, Holmdahl, McAteer, Nisbet, O'Sullivan, Petersen, Quick, Rattigan, Rees, Regan, Rodda, Short, Stiern, Teale, Weingand, and Williams—22.
NOES—Senators Backstrand, Bradley, Burns, Dolwig, Donnelly, Grunsky, McCarthy, Murdy, Pittman, Schrade, Sedgwick, Symons, and Way—13.

Bill ordered transmitted to the Assembly.

June 21, 1963]   ASSEMBLY JOURNAL   6289

The roll was called, and the Assembly concurred in Senate amendments to Assembly Bill No. 1240 by the following vote:

AYES—Allen, Alquist, Bagley, Bane, Bee, Beilenson, Belotti, Booth, Britschgi, Burton, Carrell, Casey, Cologne, Crown, Danielson, Davis, Dills, Donovan, Dymally, Elliott, Ferrell, Flournoy, Foran, Frew, Gaffney, Garrigus, Gonsalves, Greene, Henson, Hinckley, Johnson, Kennick, Knox, Lunardi, Marks, McMillan, Meyers, Milias, Mills, Monagan, Moreno, Mulford, Pattee, Petris, Powers, Quimby, Rumford, Ryan, Song, Soto, Stanton, Thelin, Veneman, Veysey, Waite, Waldie, Warren, Williamson, Winton, Young, Z'berg, Zenovich, and Mr. Speaker—63.
NOES—Ashcraft, Badham, Barnes, Chapel, Collier, Conrad, Deukmejian, Lanterman, and Whetmore—9.

Assembly Bill No. 1240 ordered enrolled.

The Senate vote taken only fifteen minutes before adjournment (June 21, 1963) showed all twenty-two "aye" votes from Democrats, while two, Burns and Donnelly, voted "no." The final Assembly vote was for concurrence with the Senate amendments.

many Negroes into middle class Caucasian neighborhoods. It did permit possible relief to overt discrimination and it was a pledge of good faith. It was bound, however, to cause the same sharp emotional cleavage among the people of California as it had among the members of the Senate. The Real Estate Association, rejecting Governor Brown's personal plea to "give it a chance" decided to push for an initiative. In its final form, the initiative did more than just repeal the Rumford Act. Proposition 14 would prohibit any infringement on the right to sell property.[38] This initiative measure became the overshadowing issue of the 1964 election.

There was another unforeseen development in 1964. Clair Engle was ill. In the course of his term as United States Senator, Engle had acquitted himself well and appeared certain of renomination and reelection. But in the fall of 1963, speculation began to be voiced about his health. Even the report just before Christmas that his medical advisor okayed his ambitions for reelection failed to stem the rumors. It was known that he had undergone brain surgery on August 24, 1963. On January 7, 1964, a forty-two second announcement of his candidacy for reelection went on the air. The four sentences and sixty-four words failed to convince anyone. "It solidified, rather than removed, doubts as to his ability to conduct a Statewide campaign."[39]

What followed was a political and personal tragedy. Mrs. Lucretia Engle gave repeated instructions not to release any medical information. Governor Brown, pledging his support, if Engle was able to campaign, requested more substantial evidence. The Senator had not been in his office since August. Twice he had appeared on the Senate floor, one arm in a sling, the other holding a cane, to cast key votes for the administration. Controller Alan Cranston, Congressman James Roosevelt and Attorney General Stanley Mosk expressed their desire to run if Engle was unable to.

The scene at the ensuing CDC Convention was dramatic. Roosevelt and Cranston were placed in nomination. Mosk withdrew. Engle said, "My work in the Senate makes it difficult for me to leave Washington," and phoned a plea for support. The voice, broadcast through the auditorium, seemed weak and unsteady. There was hushed silence, then a tremendous standing ovation, even though there also was the foregone conclusion the votes would go elsewhere. Tom Carvey, the president, then asked: "When will you be out to see us in California?" The reply, "Well, it's problematical, and a, and a"—then an agonizing pause—"it's, it's, it's, problematical."

Alan Cranston won the endorsement. Roosevelt congratulated him and withdrew. Clair Engle filed and called upon "old friends" to help him. He was to "withdraw" prior to the primary but his name, in accordance with the California Election Code, remained on the ballot.

Meanwhile, George Murphy, long-time Republican worker, former state chairman for the party, and actor who had danced with Shirley Temple years before, had filed for the Republican nomination. If a healthy Engle had run, Murphy would have been a sacrificial lamb doing his partisan duty. Now, it was a horse race—and Murphy was a stretch runner.

Not every Democrat was enamored by Cranston's candidacy. Brown had repeatedly declared for Cranston while denying that he, Brown, had "pressured" Stanley Mosk out of the race. Speaker Jess Unruh made no secret of his lack of enthusiasm for Cranston. With twenty-four hours yet to go before the closing of the filing deadline, Pierre Salinger flew into San Francisco. Flambuoyant, colorful, he had been Press Secretary to John F. Kennedy and Lyndon Johnson. Brushing aside the contention of some that he was legally disqualified from running,[40] he paid his $450 fee, took out his papers, acquired the necessary sixty-five signatures and joined the chase.

Jess Unruh said Salinger had consulted him but he "hadn't encouraged or discouraged [him]."[41] It was announced that Don Bradley, longtime campaign aide to Governor Brown, would manage the Salinger campaign. The Governor blew up at Bradley's decision, and carefully pointed out that it had nothing to do with his personal support for Cranston.

With all this, the campaign turned out to be almost anti-climactic. Murphy showed himself to be an excellent campaigner, drew the crowds, and avoided a commitment on Proposition 14, the misnamed Rumford repealer. Salinger got a lot of free publicity with a huge press conference in Governor Brown's office, billed as a "courtesy call" when "they reminisced about happier days." Smoking the ever-present cigar, with the aura of the assassinated President Kennedy still about him, Salinger pulled off a smashing victory over the studious, sober Cranston. Both managed to spend and commit money they did not have in their campaign treasuries.

Proposition 14 was the recurrent issue throughout the state. Although many Republican state legislators opposed it as ill-advised, and urged a "no" vote, Murphy said it was not a federal matter and was up to the voters. Salinger went down the line against it and it hurt his candidacy. Also the "carpetbagger" charge began to take its toll and the color and dash of his dramatic entry began to be used against him. After Engle died on July 30, 1964, Brown appointed Salinger to fill the unexpired term. Murphy criticized the appointment as "politics."

The Democrats called Murphy "just a song and dance man." But the voters did not hold his show business talents against him, liked his smile and pleasing personality, and, incidentally, his relatively conservative views. When the votes were counted, Murphy had 3,628,555 and Salinger 3,411,912. "Pete" Phillips suggested that "a new political day was dawning, for California at least, in which mass media exposure of agreeable personalities was to count much more heavily at the polling places than old-style vote hustlers were able to imagine."

"George Murphy's election walkover, marked by the inability of the California Democrats to hold their ranks intact, was a dress rehearsal of theatrical things to come."[42]

Proposition 14, which not only would strike down the Rumford Act but would limit the power of the Legislature to regulate the sale of property in the anti-discrimination field, was passed 4,526,460 to 2,395,747. Governor Brown, being interviewed by the press the morning after, was blunt and candid. He considered the vote on Proposition 14 a vote for bigotry. Many Californians, secure in their assumption that they really were just protecting their rights, resented the Governor's candor. Although the northern areas were less pronounced in their support of Proposition 14, it had a state-wide support. Only tiny Modoc County voted against it, 1,555 to 1,536.

353

Some might relate the passing of Proposition 14 to the six days of rioting in Los Angeles in the late, hot summer of 1965. The official report by the McCone Commission, the Governor's Commission on the Los Angeles riots, begins:

> In hindsight, the tinder-igniting incident is seen to have been the arrest of a drunken Negro youth about whose dangerous driving another Negro had complained to the Caucasian motorcycle officer, who made the arrest. The arrest occurred under rather ordinary circumstances, near but not in the district known as Watts, at seven o'clock on the evening of 11 August, a Wednesday. The crisis ended in the afternoon of 17 August, a Tuesday.
>
> When the spasm passed, thirty-four persons were dead, and the wounded and hurt numbered 1,032 more. Property damage was about $40,000,000. Arrested for one crime or another were 3,952 persons, women as well as men, including 500 youths under eighteen. The lawlessness in this one segment of the metropolitan area had terrified the entire county and its 6,000,000 people.[43]

Its political impact went far beyond the boundaries of Los Angeles County and lasted far after the afternoon of August 17. No matter how direct the causal relationship was, the Rumford Act, Proposition 14, and the Watts riots, spelled dynamite at the ballot box. Add the California Supreme Court's ruling that Proposition 14 was in conflict with the Federal Constitution and null and void.

Governor Edmund G. Brown cuts short a vacation in Europe to visit the riot area in South-Central Los Angeles. The arrow points to the Governor talking to residents of the area while surrounded by newsmen and National Guardsmen. (Courtesy of *Los Angeles Times*.)

Add the Hunter's Point riot, September, 1966, and you have political head-aches for Governor Brown, and all Democrats on the ticket in 1966.

Apportionment, the drawing of district lines, had always been considered a purely legislative function. Justice Brandeis had warned his colleagues not to get into this "political" thicket. But time upsets traditions. In 1962, the nation's highest court held that the malapportionment of the Tennessee State Legislature —the lines had not been changed for half a century—deprived that state's citizens of the "equal protection of the laws." The court said "one man—one vote." Even where a state's citizens said they preferred malapportionment, as in California, the court said it could not be done.

The Federal plan had been approved in 1926 and in effect since 1930. In 1948, the voters defeated Proposition 13 which would have given more state senate seats to southern California. In 1960, a north-south, 20-20 plan, Proposition 15, was also defeated. Since the Water Plan Bond issue of $1,750,000,000 was also on the ballot, Governor Brown, Mayor Norris Poulsen of Los Angeles, and many others argued against it as "divisive" at a time when north-south cooperation on the water issue was imperative. It lost. Brown appointed a "Blue Ribbon Commission" under Charles Wellman to study representation in the State Senate, and its recommendation to add senate seats to the more populous counties was submitted. Brown supported the plan, after promising to stay neutral, which angered a number of key senators, but Proposition 23 of 1962 lost, also, by 300,000 votes.[44]

The State Senate caucused and sent emissaries throughout the United States to seek support for a constitutional amendment to overturn the court's reapportion-ment ruling. Richard L. Carpenter, of the League of California Cities, testified before the Senate Judiciary Committee that reapportionment would be a blow to the state. Joseph Rattigan, Senator from Santa Rosa, gave chapter and verse on the Senate's fair and equitable treatment of urban interests.[45]

By the 1965 session, Governor Brown felt the court rulings left no alternative. Since only the Senate was affected, a deadlock developed over the disposition of the senate districts that would have to be created in Los Angeles. They were of more than passing interest to the thirty-one assemblymen from that county. When the constitutional deadline for the session passed, the Senate-Assembly deadlock was unbroken.

It remained for the State Supreme Court to add the final twist. Entertaining another case from the irrepressible Phill Silver, who had initiated the Senate case, the court added the Assembly to the court order, set a deadline and criteria and called upon the Governor to call a special session for the purpose of re-apportioning the state Legislature.

Brown complied. The Senate, grumbling about the court in general and Chief Justice Earl Warren in particular, went about its task of self-annihilation.

355

Senator Stephen Teale, Democrat from Rail Road Flat, was named chairman of a special eleven-man reapportionment committee. At least thirteen new districts would have to be carved out of Los Angeles. The Mother Lode and rural counties were grouped in huge districts. One stretched from the Oregon border down the crest of the Sierra to Calaveras County and then came down onto the Valley floor to pick up Stanislaus County and the necessary population. Another took in Merced, then went east to Madera and Mariposa, across the Sierra to Inyo and Mono, back west across the Sierra to take in Tulare and, for good measure, a finger of territory in southeastern Fresno County. With this maneuver, Burns made it difficult for Assemblyman Charles Garrigus to run for the State Senate. Many new districts contained all or parts of four and five old districts. Despite its mathematical logic, it wiped out a number of far-seeing and competent senators who had contributed a great deal toward meeting and solving the problems of an urbanized, industrialized state. The measure passed the Senate and twenty-two of the incumbents retired or were defeated. Only eighteen

Renault, Frontier

"Can't you see? It's all over between us."

One of the major concerns over reapportionment in northern California was its effect in swinging the majority in the State Senate to more populous southern California. (Courtesy of *Frontier Magazine*.)

veterans survived the reapportionment "purge." Fourteen of the new senators were ex-assemblymen. It was a traumatic experience for the Senate.

Speaker Unruh talked of running for the State Senate and sparked a bitter fight between Robert Crown and Carlos Bee for the right to succeed him. He later changed his mind and was returned to the Speaker's chair in 1967. The election of 1966 produced thirty-five new assemblymen. This was to be the largest turnover of legislators in the history of the state. On the senate side, the veterans retreated to the "heights" of leadership— the Rules Committee, the Finance Committee, the Revenue and Taxation Committee, and the Governmental Efficiency Committee. Seven senior senators formed an interlocking directorate.

California seems bound and determined not to have a calm, predictable campaign or election. Californians in 1966 were frustrated. They wanted simple solutions to complex problems. Water plans and master plans and a host of other "solutions" were insignificant compared to the disquiet caused by militant students, militant blacks and militant taxpayers.

"Pat" Brown had been in public office twenty-three years. For sixteen of these years, he was the "titular" head of the Democratic Party. Other ambitious Democrats were waiting in line. In addition to ambition, there had been an encyclopedic list of party fights and debilitating feuds. Old alliances had crumbled. Even the Mexican-Americans, caught up by the struggle of César Chavez, were mad at Brown's failure to meet their full list of demands and failure to welcome their "march" from Delano to Sacramento.

Mayor Sam Yorty of Los Angeles, "maverick" Democrat, blasted away at Brown. Speaker Unruh, once Brown's leading ally in the Legislature,[46] felt estranged and even though he couched his criticisms as a "natural conflict between the two branches," the newspapers were replete with Unruh quotes that the Brown administration "lacked imagination" or otherwise suffered from "tired blood." There was a sharp break with the Governor over the Petris–Unruh tax reform bill, Assembly Bill 2270 of the 1965 session.

Max Rafferty, never at a loss for words when it came to depicting Democratic difficulties, said, "The Governor and the Speaker have been going through the intricate movements of a vastly complex minuet, in which the two charmingly reluctant partners come together regularly to the soothing obligato of mutual compliments and flattery, and then move gracefully to a crescendo of heavy artillery fire and the whispering slither of long knives being eased from hidden scabbards."[47]

The Democrats had other conflicts open to public view. Carmen Warschaw, referred to as the "Dragon Lady" by her detractors, would do battle with Brown, Salinger, Cranston, or Assemblyman Charles Warren. In a bitter state convention, Warren defeated Mrs. Warschaw by the narrow margin of four

357

Two long-time leaders of the California State Legislature, President Pro Tempore Hugh M. Burns (Dem.-Fresno) and Speaker Jess M. Unruh (Dem.-Inglewood), shown during one of the "Hughie-Jess" television-press conferences held during the session in Sacramento. Burns was first elected to lead the Senate in 1957 and was replaced by Howard Way (Rep.-Exeter) in 1969 while Unruh was elected Speaker on September 30, 1961 and was succeeded by Robert Monagan (Rep.-Tracy) at the start of the 1969 legislative session. (Courtesy of *Sacramento Bee*, January 18, 1967.)

votes for state chairman. She was sure the Governor, or at least his "people" had led the fight against her. In truth, many of them had, although the Governor himself remained technically neutral.

Simon Casady, President of the CDC, had spoken out sharply against Vietnam policy and President Johnson. The Governor questioned Casady's judgment and propriety in heading up the party organization. The bloody fight, first over Casady's impeachment and then his removal at the convention, splintered the organization beyond any effective repairs for the 1966 campaign.

Meanwhile, the Republicans, still suffering from their chronic conservative-moderate split, kept most of their quarreling out of public view. The California Republican Assembly, United Republicans of California, and the Young Republicans were cheering sections for conservative candidates. Kuchel and some

"O Spirit of '58 and '62 — Are you there?"

The Democratic unity of 1958 and 1962 is lacking in 1966. The result was a Republican victory. (Courtesy of *Frontier Magazine*.)

liberal Republican state legislators warned about extremism and the prospective influence of the John Birch Society. Only the newly created California Republican League under William Grey advocated moderation and warned against "extremism."

The candidacy of Ronald Reagan was another first. "No other state, so far as anyone could remember, had previously entertained the notion, even briefly, of choosing a motion picture actor as a governor."[48] It was not a casual decision on Reagan's part. In the closing days of the 1964 Goldwater campaign, his televised appeal for support and funds received "rave" notices. For years, he had spoken to countless business and civic groups, espousing General Electric and conservative principles.

Through "seed money" provided by Henry Salvatori and other southern

California supporters, he had traveled the state, holding "give and take sessions" with local Republicans, acquainting himself with the issues that were bothering people and giving them his views. The reports back were impressive. He decided to run.

George Christopher, who had tried for state office unsuccessfully twice before, also decided to run. Remarkably like "Pat" Brown in his campaigning—and not very far removed in political philosophy—Christopher's strength would obviously rest with Republican moderates in the Warren–Knight tradition. With such a clear-cut differentiation, Democrats hoped for a Republican blood-bath. They were disappointed. Dr. Gaylord Parkinson, San Diego physician who had served as Republican State Vice Chairman, and who would move up to the chairmanship, urged the adoption of an "11th Commandment"— "No Republican shall speak evil of another Republican."

On the Democratic side, Brown, resentful of criticism, and buoyed by polls that showed he could be reelected, declared for a third term. Mayor Sam Yorty, blasting the "Brown Machine" and "arrogant power," followed suit. Through short, televised speeches released throughout the state, the Mayor articulated popular frustrations. His main targets were hippies, militants, disobedient children, university violences, and, as always, "Pat" Brown. His most telling criticisms were reserved for his southern California audiences: "I honestly don't believe 'Pat' Brown understands southern California and its problems."

The results of the June 8 Democratic primary showed Brown in deep trouble. He did not have a united party behind him. Yorty polled 981,088 votes, compared to 1,355,262 for Brown. The Mayor lost Los Angeles County by only 95,748 votes, carried conservative Orange County by 9,612, was particularly effective in the Central Valley, actually winning Kern County, and showed surprising strength in the Bay Area. "His showing proved that anti-Brown sentiment was both state-wide and preponderately conservative."[49]

The more sobering fact for the Democrats was the showing of Ronald Reagan in the Republican primary. Christopher cited Reagan's complete lack of political experience and questioned the influence of reactionary forces in his campaign. The more central issue was which candidate could defeat Brown. The State poll showed Christopher with a substantial margin on this issue in September, 1965. On May 3, 1966, the poll showed that Christopher would have beaten Brown by a greater margin than Reagan. Then, ten days later, came syndicated columnist Drew Pearson's "revelations" of a misdemeanor conviction Christopher had received involving his dairy business twenty-six years before. Most of the story had been revealed in Christopher's earlier campaigns. First, Christopher charged that the Reagan forces were out to "destroy" him. The campaign

After the June Primaries of 1966, Governor Brown and Mayor Sam Yorty of Los Angeles, his opponent in the Democratic Primary, held an "amity" meeting —The Mayor did not endorse either Brown or Ronald Reagan but continued his criticisms of the Democratic Governor. (Courtesy of *Sacramento Bee*.)

looked like a re-run of 1958. The Pearson "revelations" no doubt contributed to the reversal of the Christopher-Reagan trend. Knowledgable political writers contended that the Brown campaign had planted the story with Pearson, believing that Reagan would be the easier opponent for the Governor. The last poll before the primary gave Reagan a comfortable 17% margin over Christopher. Later, Christopher charged that the Democrats conspired to release the damaging material to Pearson. Liberal Republicans were resentful. Any hope of their support going to Brown was dashed.

But Reagan's appeal went far beyond the 50% of the registered Republicans who considered themselves conservatives. The results were: Reagan, 1,419,623; Christopher, 675,683. Only in the Bay Area was the Mayor able to obtain a majority. Democratic charges that Reagan was a dangerous reactionary were dismissed by an admiring public. Those Democratic dopesters who thought Reagan would be the easier to beat had their wish with a vengeance.

If the primary showed serious problems for the Democrats, the general election campaign confirmed them. There was a general rush for the Reagan bandwagon by Republican leaders and candidates. While Christopher did not personally endorse him, most of his campaign workers joined the Reagan staff.

Only Senator Thomas Kuchel remained aloof, a posture which was to cost him in his 1968 bid for renomination.

The platform bridged the "issue gap" between the wings of the party. "The extremism issue was met by the strategy of silence, and the racial-discrimination-in-housing issue, imbued with 'white backlash' implications, was handled by a demand for repeal or amendment of the Rumford Act."[50]

Reagan's "creative society" encompassed three major themes: morality, spending and taxes, and incumbency and politicians. With the competent campaign management of Spencer Roberts and Associates, Reagan gave smooth, articulate, set speeches. The "mess at Berkeley" became an extra bonus.

The Democrats had usually patched up their quarrels between the primary and the general elections. This pattern was shattered in 1966. Some Unruh people worked to get out the vote but the Speaker himself was out of the state until the last week of the campaign. Johnson had planned to come to California in conjunction with his trip to Manila in early November but he never appeared. His staying away was interpreted as reluctance to get involved in a losing effort. Senator Robert Kennedy made quick tours throughout the state, drew heavy and admiring crowds, but with little apparent advantage to the Governor.

The Brown organization itself sputtered. No issue seemed to grab hold. Like Nixon in 1962, the Governor tried a different issue a day, but without success. His "Old Reliable" was his record of eight years but no one got too excited about growth figures, legislative measures, or what national magazines said about the "good life" in California.

Although he never betrayed it to his campaign staff or his audiences, Brown knew he was behind. In Stockton, ten days before the election, he privately admitted he was lagging by 500,000 votes but hoped for a last-minute swing as people realized Reagan had no governmental experience and Brown had twenty-three years of it.

But Reagan played his "citizen politician" role admirably. Reviewing the problems besetting the state, he would always conclude "Maybe it's time the people get a non-politician to run the state."

The Brown forces kept hoping the merciless pace of campaigning would break Reagan's smooth performance. A couple of cracks had appeared: he had stormed out of a Republican National Negro Assembly meeting in Santa Monica, charging that his integrity had been questioned; and while touring northern California and answering newsmen's questions about the Water Plan, he had "misplaced" the Feather River and the Eel and had blown up at a reporter for "boring in." But, by and large, the Reagan campaign was masterful. The proposed solutions were simple but convincing.

The disorganized Brown campaign had a last-ditch hope. The Guggenheim firm had done a couple of superb jobs in the east in "human interest" political documentary biographies for television. Robert Kennedy had used them for image-building in his New York senatorial campaign. A large chunk of the Brown campaign treasury went into this effort. "Man vs. Actor" came out just a few days prior to the election. It did an excellent job of catching the qualities of "Pat" Brown; warm, affable, and compassionate. But in the course of the film— for less than ten seconds—Brown stops to talk to two young Negro children. "Do you know who I am?" "No," they reply and Brown laughs in good-natured embarrassment. "I'm Governor Brown and I'm running for reelection." Then he asks the wide-eyed children "And do you know who's running against me? An actor—and remember—it was an actor who shot Abraham Lincoln." The public reaction was hostile. "Pat" Brown, who had always campaigned and lived as the "man in the white hat" lost his image in those ten seconds. Indignant Republicans made political hay.

In the closing days, Reagan's margin seemed so safe he campaigned for his ticket which was Robert Finch for Lieutenant Governor, Houston I. Flournoy for Controller, Ivy Baker Priest for Treasurer, Spencer Williams for Attorney General, and incumbent Secretary of State Frank Jordan. The results were astounding. It was a smashing Reagan victory of nearly one million votes and a near Republican sweep. Robert Finch led the ticket by a margin of

While Democrats chided the Republicans for running actors for public office, George Murphy wins the United States senatorship in 1964 and Ronald Reagan wins the governorship two years later. They were old friends, professionally and politically. (Courtesy of *Frontier Magazine*, May, 1966.)

Renault, Frontier

Dancing Master

1,252,091 over Glenn Anderson who suffered from the criticism of the McCone report. His lead gave rise to speculation of Finch's future political prospects.

Flournoy and Priest won narrow victories that were not confirmed until the following day. Cranston's defeat coupled with his defeat of 1964 in the Democratic senatorial primary caused many to write his political obituary. Frank Jordan was reelected, as Californians had voted for Jordans for Secretary of State since 1910. Only Attorney General Lynch remained of the Democratic state-wide incumbents, defeating Spencer Williams by 473,454.

The Republican trend which swept the nation and the state sharply reduced Democratic margins in both houses of the state Legislature. Parkinson's "California Plan" for taking control of the Legislature before the critical reapportionment session of 1971 seemed right on schedule. Five Democratic assemblymen and five Democratic state senators were among the casualties, although Democrats retained slim control of the Senate and Assembly, assuring the reelection of President Pro Tempore Hugh Burns and Speaker Jess Unruh at the 1967 session.

A final note of political curiosity—the Committee for Responsible California Supreme Court was organized to unseat four Supreme Court Justices who were held responsible for invalidating Proposition 14. While unsuccessful, they achieved the highest vote ever cast against ratification of a Supreme Court Justice.

Just seconds after midnight on January 1, 1967, Ronald Reagan became the thirty-third Governor of California. A provocative but amiable governor who placed himself in the tradition of Hiram Johnson and Earl Warren had been replaced by a popular and articulate man who, although he had never before served in public office, had specific ideas of what Californians wanted their government to do. Yet deeply emotional issues, frustrations, and concerns were everywhere. The future showed promise and forebodings. In the words of Charles Dickens, "It was the best of times; it was the worst of times."

FOOTNOTES

1   This may be a major explanation of Powers' later role in supporting Brown over Nixon in 1962.

2   *Sacramento Bee*, "Politics in Review," March 22, 1954, pp. 1, 12. See also Thomas S. Barclay, "The 1954 Election in California," *Western Political Quarterly*, VII (December, 1954), 597–604.

3   Martin Hall, "A House Divided: California's G.O.P.," *Frontier Magazine* (October, 1954), pp. 5–6.

4   Dan Creedon (Rep., San Mateo), did not vote. He resigned immediately after the vote to become Legislative Advocate ("Lobbyist") for the Malt Beverage Industry.

5 Kyle Palmer, *Los Angeles Times*, October 30, 1955, II, p. 4.

6 *Los Angeles Times*, April 29, 1956, II, p. 4.

7 The *Sacramento Newsletter* had reported on July 8, 1955: "We know of no un-biased reporter who thinks Brown could unseat Knight."

8 Kyle Palmer, *Los Angeles Times*, June 3, 1956, II, p. 4: "Sam [Yorty] has been most resentful since his eclipse, but deprived of important support and lacking campaign finances, [he] has been able to do little more than bombard his successful party rival with critical letters and personal attacks."

9 Stevenson, 1,139,964; Kefauver, 680,722. *Statement of the Vote*, 1956, available from California Secretary of State.

10 On the Democratic ballot, Richards, 1,004,336; Yorty, 383,813. Yorty also received 62,913 in the Republican column, where Thomas Kuchel had 1,332,074. *Statement of the Vote*, 1956, available from California Secretary of State.

11 Sutton was reportedly angry over the failure of the party leaders to pay any attention to him. When he was passed over for the delegation to the national convention of 1956, some Democratic senatorial colleagues invited him along to theirs. He enjoyed it. Collier would subsequently re-register as a Democrat.

12 Ralph Friedman, "The Gay Beaver," *Frontier Magazine* (June, 1958), pp. 10–19. "Perhaps the frustration of Knight's opponents was best stated by Robert Kenny: 'He has such a wholesome insincerity.'"

13 Kyle Palmer, *Los Angeles Times*, January 13, 1957, II, p. 4.

14 *Ibid.*, April 28, 1957, II. p. 4. "I didn't even get a 'no comment' from him on all questions of future plans. (He) just looked right through me and suggested we have breakfast sometime next week."

15 Kyle Palmer, *loc. cit.*

16 Kyle Palmer, *op. cit.*, July 28, 1957, II, p. 4.

17 *Los Angeles Times*, July 7, 1957, II, p. 4.

18 Herbert Phillips, *Big Wayward Girl* (Garden City, New York: Doubleday & Company, 1968), p. 179.

19 *Ibid.*, p. 181.

20 Totton J. Anderson, "The 1958 Election in California," *Western Political Quarterly*, XII (March, 1959), 283. "The completeness of Knight's isolation was revealed in the release of Knowland's campaign organization, the evening *before* Knight's capitulation. In spite of the fact that Party officials are enjoined to remain neutral in a Party campaign, the list included both members of the Republican National Committee, the Presidents of the Young Republicans and the California Republican Assembly, and key county chairmen throughout the State. The degree of Nixon's commitment to Knowland was evident by the inclusion of several of the Vice President's closest friends and advisers. The sordid picture of partisan political mayhem being committed upon a popular, nonpartisan, reelectable Governor was undoubtedly a major factor in Knowland's defeat."

21 Knight maintained that the decision to switch was his own. *Los Angeles Times*,

November 6, 1957, I, pp. 1, 14; Richard Bergholz, *Los Angeles Mirror News*, August 24, 1956 p. 2; and Lawrence E. Davies, *New York Times*, January 13, 1957, I, p. 53.

22   Brown subsequently indicated he consented to run if one of the congressmen would join the ticket for the United States Senator. This Clair Engle agreed to do. Brown recounts that after a restless night, he phoned Engle to see if they might reconsider and possibly switch offices, with Engle running for Governor instead. This the congressman politely refused to consider.

23   Totton Anderson, *op. cit.*, p. 289.

24   William A. Park, "The AFL: Two-Headed Politics," *Frontier Magazine* (June, 1958), pp. 19–20. An interesting quote attributed to Haggerty: "Never in my years in Sacramento have I had a Governor, Republican or Democrat, call me into his office as Governor Knight and say: 'Neil, this is your bill—you write it; tell me what you want in it; I'll see that you get it.'"

25   W. H. Lawrence, *New York Times*, September 14, 1958, I, pp. 1, 76. "He had twice been cited for Contempt of Congress for refusing to supply information to Congressional investigators relating to contributions of his Constitutional Educational League."

26   Totton J. Anderson, *op. cit.*, p. 285.

27   *Ibid.*, p. 286.

28   Engle's problem was identification. Don Bradley, his Campaign Manager, said that a Lou Harris poll showed only 3.7% of Californians interviewed knew Clair Engle and of these, 23% thought he was a woman. Knight complained about the manly proportions of Engle on the billboards and charged his campaign of misleading the people. "He's really not a big man", said Knight. When asked about his size by Richard Bergholz of the *Los Angeles Times*, Engle replied: "Where I come from, you measure a man from the neck up."

29   Senate Bill 803 (1955 session). Passed Senate 24–9. It died in the Assembly.

30   This charge and others like it were made by Brown from time to time. It hurt his working relationship with some of his legislative supporters who resented the implication of "selling out" when they believed there were valid reasons to vote "no."

31   Their only reservations were that Brown had not used his influence to repeal the loyalty oath or the abolition of capital punishment—although he had said he would sign the former if it reached his desk and continued to support the latter, even though he did not include it as part of his "program." On the politics of the California Water Plan, see: Erwin Cooper, *Aqueduct Empire* (Glendale, California: The Arthur H. Clark Company, 1968), Chapter 13.

32   A verbatim report of the hearing has been published: *Hearing Report and Testimony on Senate Bill No. 1, 1960 Second Extraordinary Session*, March 9, 1960, which proposed to abolish the death penalty in California and substitute life imprisonment without possibility of parole.

33   Totton Anderson and Eugene Lee, "The 1962 Election in California," *Western Political Quarterly*, XVI (June, 1963), 402–403.

34   It is interesting that Earl Warren, Jr. openly supported Brown, as did ex-Lieutenant Governor Harold "Butch" Powers and Robert Eaton, son-in-law of Goodwin Knight.

35 One of the more comical aspects of the Hughes loan charges occurred at the Annual San Francisco Chinese New Year's celebration and parade when a Brown worker, Dick Tuck, prevailed upon a couple of gaily-clad Chinese to carry a huge banner behind the Republican candidate's car which asked the question, in Chinese: "Tell us about the Hughes loan, Mr. Nixon."

36 Phillips, *op. cit.*, p. 210.

37 Speaker Unruh was a master at applying tactical pressure. One month later, on July 30, 1963, during a special session, he was severely criticized for "locking up" the Republican assemblymen overnight.

38 The passage of the Rumford Act, together with its subsequent political impact, gave rise to some interesting conjecture. Could Brown have waited for the federal Civil Rights Act of 1964 which accomplished substantially the same purpose? Could he have avoided the political liability of his personal involvement? Would a two-year cutoff date, suggested by Speaker Unruh, have dissuaded the Real Estate Association from pushing the initiative?

39 Richard Rodda, *Sacramento Bee*, January 7, 1964, p. 1.

40 The California Supreme Court came to substantiate Salinger's position.

41 *Sacramento Bee*, March 20, 1964, p. A 10.

42 Phillips, *op. cit.*, pp. 219–220.

43 "Violence in the City—an End or a Beginning?" A report by the Governor's Commission on the Los Angeles Riots, December 2, 1965, pp. 1–2.

44 Don A. Allen, *Legislative Sourcebook* (Sacramento: Assembly of the State of California, 1965). This has an excellent resume and discussion of reapportionment.

45 Senator Rattigan established himself as a real authority on the subject. When State Senator Thomas Rees of Los Angeles resigned after winning a congressional seat, Rattigan handled the legislation affecting Los Angeles County. At the close of the session, he was invited to Los Angeles by the Board of Supervisors and presented a resolution as the County's "Outstanding Senator."

46 "California: The Politics of Confusion," *Frontier Magazine* (October, 1962), p. 6. Brown was quoted as saying: "Jess Unruh made his reputation on my program, and I made mine on the way he handled it."

47 Richard Bergholz, *Los Angeles Times*, December 21, 1965, II, p.2.

48 Phillips, *op. cit.*, p. 231.

49 Totton J. Anderson and Eugene Lee, "The 1966 Election in California," *Western Political Quarterly*, XX (June, 1967), 538.

50 *Ibid.*, p. 542.

Official and Unofficial
Party Organizations

The political parties within the state of California have been for the last hundred years among the least effective in the nation. There are numerous factors contributing to the relative ineffectiveness of political parties in the Golden State; among the most important are the voluminous laws and statutes governing their organization and operation. The weakness of political parties is partly due to the fact that the laws of the state are purposely designed to make them so.

To understand the cumbersome network of legal regulations woven around political parties in California, one must go back to the anti-railroad views of the nineteenth-century agrarians and Populists and of the twentieth-century progressives. Under the leadership of Hiram Johnson, the progressives emerged victorious in the election of 1910 and broke the Southern Pacific's hold on California.[1] In the process of smashing the Southern Pacific machine, which for so long managed to dominate both the Republican and Democratic parties, the progressives also poured discredit upon the parties themselves. Identifying the monopoly of control of the railroad with the parties, they set out to destroy as much as possible the organizational structure of the parties to the point of reducing them to virtual impotence.

The growing popularity and power of the Lincoln–Roosevelt League brought about the passage of the Direct Primary law in 1909, and took from the party convention the most important function of officially nominating candidates for public office. Two years later the Direct Primary law was amended to permit the electorate to express its preference for United States Senator; provision was made for a presidential primary election, and the party identification was removed from the ballot. Another blow was dealt to party organization when

☛ Leonard Rowe was primarily responsible for the original draft of Chapter 12.

partisanship was officially removed from contests for county, municipal, judicial and school offices throughout the state. Henceforth, the number of elective offices for which party contests could be waged was greatly reduced, lessening, if not altogether removing the need of politicians on the local level to be responsible to a political party.

The legal structure of political parties was changed to break the continuity of organization and representation, subject the parties to the domination of elected officeholders, and make the official party governing organs so large as to render them practically inoperative. A glance at the formal party structure, which remains essentially unchanged to the present day, will illustrate the point.

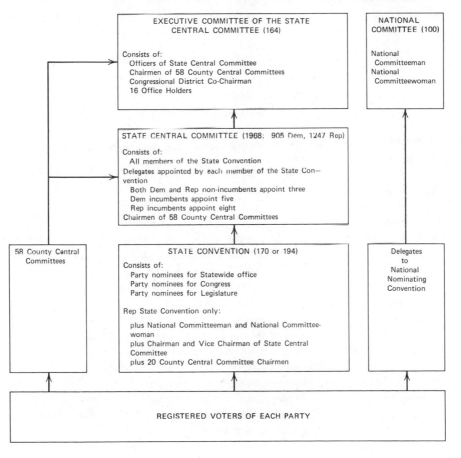

Official Party Organization in California.

The highest authority of the party is the State Convention, which consists of the party's nominees for elective state and federal offices and holdover incumbents. The convention, made up of at least 170 delegates, is required by law to meet in Sacramento every two years. The main function of the convention is to adopt the party's state platform, which is of limited significance. In presidential election years the convention also selects the party's presidential electors.

The State Central Committee is a huge and unwieldly body of more than 800 members. It is made up of all delegates to the party convention, each of whom appoints several additional members. The fifty-eight chairmen of the county central committees are also members of the State Central Committee. To insure equality of the sexes, the law requires that membership be equally divided between men and women. The composition of the State Convention and the State Central Committee clearly places these organs under the domination of the incumbent office-holders.

The functions of the State Central Committee are few. It meets once every two years in Sacramento, elects a party chairman, vice-chairman, executive committee, and other officers, and adjourns. Whatever formal powers the State Central Committee has are delegated for the most part to an executive committee which in turn exercises few functions. The party chairman and vice-chairman who alternate between the north and south every two years are charged with the actual management of party affairs.

Unlike the State Central Committee, the county central committees are popularly elected. While this affords, at least nominally, a greater voice to the electorate in selecting party leaders, in practice it has little meaning because the limited functions of these committees offer few inducements for able individuals to run for such office, and the relative obscurity of many of those who do makes popular selection less than meaningful. Furthermore, the different modes of selection of the State Central Committee and the county central committees makes these bodies virtually independent of one another, with only the county chairmen providing a formal link.

Elected every two years at the direct primary election and augmented by the party nominees for State Senate and state Assembly serving ex officio, the county central committees consist anywhere from twenty-one to thirty members, except in Los Angeles where committee membership exceeds 150. The functions of the committees are limited for the most part to the legally prescribed responsibility of conducting general election campaigns within the county. They are prevented by legal interpretation from endorsing candidates in a primary or conducting primary campaigns.

While in most counties the central committees have usually been dormant or moribund, those in the more populous counties have at times carried on

370

meaningful political activities, maintained permanent offices and even staff.
This has been particularly true during the upsurge of the GOP in the 1960's
when a conscious effort to revitalize the party structure on the county level,
particularly in Los Angeles and San Francisco, contributed to GOP electoral
victories.

The nature of California politics and of party structure has also been influenced by the diverse sectional character of the state. The rivalry between
the north, centered around San Francisco, and the south, centered around Los
Angeles, has left its mark on political organization. Even the official parties are
split between north and south, a division that is reflected in the manner of
selecting chairmen and vice-chairmen of the state central committees. The
chairmanship and vice-chairmanship rotate between north and south every
two years. If the chairman is from the north, the vice-chairman must be from
the south, and he traditionally succeeds to the chairmanship.

In addition to the cumbersome and restrictive official party structure other
conditions plague political parties in California. The spread of the civil service
system has clearly improved the quality of the public service, but at the same
time it has removed some of the oil that lubricates party machinery—patronage.
The approximately 4,500 appointive federal jobs within the state's borders
and the fewer than 600 state and local jobs of any significance available for
paid appointees offer limited inducement or reward for party work.

Fundamentally, a party structure is only as strong as its precinct organization. In California, party precinct organizations have been almost non-existent.
This is due not only to the lack of incentive and organizational effort, but also
to the mobility of the state's population. The movement of population into the
state and within the state has hampered the formation of permanent precinct
organizations. Also contributing to the weakness of party organization in
California was the practice of crossfiling. During the nearly half century of its
operation it reduced the nominating process to a farce.

The 1909 Direct Primary law contained a rigid party test under which a
candidate for public office had to declare under oath that he had supported
the party at the preceding general election and intended to vote for the party's
candidates in the ensuing election.[2] This did not quite satisfy the progressive
reformers, since it favored the regular partisan candidates and made it difficult
for those more independent to secure the nominations of the major parties.
The 1911 Legislature, firmly controlled by Hiram Johnson's progressives,
considerably weakened the party test for candidates by dropping the requirements of past partisan loyalty. The 1911 modification simply required candidates
to affirm that they intended to affiliate with the party whose nomination
they sought and that they would vote for a majority of its candidates.[3] Two
years later the pledge of future party support was dropped.

Richard L. Collins

George R. Reilly

Hugh M. Burns

Frank M. Jordan

Official and Unofficial Party Organizations

POLITICAL OFFICE RECORD HOLDERS

In all of California's history only twenty-four persons, thirteen Democrats and eleven Republicans, have either served in elective national and state office for thirty years or more or hold longevity records. Richard L. Collins (Rep.-Redding) (1873–1948) (upper left, courtesy of Miss Frances E. Tozier) is the overall record holder among the Republicans having served continuously in one office as a Member of the State Board of Equalization for forty years. Ulysses S. Webb (Rep.-San Francisco) (1864–1947) is the second longest holder of a single office having served as Attorney General for thirty-six years. Charles G. "Gus" Johnson (Rep.-Sacramento) (1880–1957) served thirty-four years as State Treasurer and is the third longest office holder in the Executive Branch holding a single office. George R. Reilly (Dem.-San Francisco) (1903–   ) (upper right, courtesy of George R. Reilly) is the longest Democratic holder of a single office in the Executive Branch having been elected as a Member of the State Board of Equalization in 1938 and serving continuously since. The record for Governor is Earl Warren (Rep.-Alameda) (1891–   ) with eleven years.

Herbert W. Slater (Dem.-Sonoma) (1874–1947) holds the record for service in the State Legislature with thirty-seven years and also the record for service in the State Senate having served thirty-three years at the time of his death. Hugh M. Burns (Dem.-Fresno) (1902–   ) (lower left, courtesy of Hugh M. Burns) is tied for second with legislative service with thirty-four years but holds the record for service as President Pro Tempore among the Democrats with twelve years. The overall record holder as President Pro Tempore is Arthur H. Breed (Rep.-Alameda) (1865–1953) with eighteen years but in those days the President Pro Tempore had no powers. While twenty Democrats have been Presidents Pro Tempore and only nineteen Republicans, Burns was the first and only Democrat to hold the post since 1891. Jess Unruh (Dem.-Los Angeles) (1922–   ) holds the record for Speaker of the Assembly with seven years. Vincent Thomas (Dem.-San Pedro) (1908–   ) has the all-time record for service in the Assembly having been elected in 1940 and serving continuously to date. Charles W. Lyon (Rep.-Los Angeles) (1887–1960) like Burns coupled Assembly and Senate service for a total of thirty-four years. Randolph Collier (Dem.-Yreka) (1902–   ) has served thirty two years in the State Senate, having been elected in 1938 and serving continuously to date in that body. Two others have been elected to the State Legislature for thirty-two years. Hugh P. Donnelly (Dem.-Turlock) (1890–1969) and Thomas A. Maloney (Rep.-San Francisco) (1889–   ) both served in the Assembly and the Senate, although their service was reversed, Maloney going from the Senate to the Assembly, and Donnelly going from the Assembly to the Senate. Harry L. Parkman (Rep.-San Mateo) (1879–1966) coupled Assembly and Senate service for a total of thirty years. Clarence F. Lea (Dem.-Sonoma) (1874–1964) holds the record for service in the House of Representatives with thirty-two years. Coupled with his ten years service as District Attorney of Sonoma County, Lea is the overall record holder among the Democrats with forty-two years. Harry R. Sheppard (Dem.-San Bernardino) (1885–1969) served thirty years in Congress. The record for service in the United States Senate is twenty-nine years held by Hiram W. Johnson (Rep.-San Francisco) (1866–1945). Put together with his six years as Governor, Johnson served the people of the State of California for thirty-five years.

Besides Johnson, six others have put together various combinations of service that put them at the three decade mark. Augustus F. Hawkins (Dem.-Los Angeles) (1907–   ) and Cecil R. King (Dem.-Los Angeles) (1898–   ) combined service in the Assembly and the House of Representatives to total thirty-six years. Hawkins continues to serve in the latter body. Thomas H. Kuchel (Rep.-Anaheim) (1910–   ) served in the Assembly and the Senate and then as State Controller and United States Senator for a total of thirty-two years. George C. Perkins (Rep.-Oroville) (1839–1923) coupled service as State Senator and Governor and United States Senator to total thirty-one years. George P. Miller (Dem.-Alameda) (1891–   ) coupled his Assembly service with Congress where he still serves for thirty years. Clair Engle (Dem.-Red Bluff) (1911–1964) also totaled thirty years service as District Attorney of Tehama County, State Senator, Congressman, and United States Senator.

Besides these twenty-four individuals, five families have put together family spans of office holding for more than three decades. Frank C. Jordan (father) (Rep.-Sacramento) (1860–1940) and Frank M. Jordan (son) (Rep.-Sacramento) (1888–1970) (lower right, courtesy of Frank M. Jordan) together won every election to the Secretary of State post from 1910 to 1970, serving between them for fifty-six years. The elder Jordan died in office in 1940 and was succeeded by Paul Peek on a gubernatorial appointment, but Peek lost to the younger Jordan in 1942, who died in office in 1970. Another father and son combination, Arthur H. Breed (Rep.-Alameda) (1865–1953) and Arthur H. Breed, Jr. (Rep.-Alameda) (1903–   ) held an Alameda County State Senate seat for forty-six years with the exception of one four year period when the younger Breed was in the State Assembly and William F. Knowland occupied the seat. The Coombs family of Napa County put together forty-four years of service in the Assembly and State Senate and Congress with Nathan Coombs (Dem.-Napa) (1826–1877), Frank L. Coombs (Rep.-Napa) (1853–1934), and Nathan F. Coombs (Rep.-Napa) (1881–   ), spanning a period of 106 years to 1961. The Knowlands of Alameda County put together thirty-five years of service, with the father Joseph R. Knowland (Rep.-Alameda) (1873–1966) putting together sixteen years in the Assembly and State Senate and Congress beginning in 1899, and the son William F. Knowland (Rep.-Alameda) (1908–   ) contributing nineteen years ending in 1959. Father Franklin J. Powers (Rep.-Modoc) (1867–1937) and son Harold J. "Butch" Powers (Rep.-Modoc) (1900–   ) put in thirty-two years in the Assembly and State Senate with the latter finally winning the Lieutenant Governorship.

But of great significance to the future political life of California was a little-discussed, almost unnoticed amendment which the Senate Elections Committee attached to the Progressives' 1913 primary bill. The added provision read: "Nothing in this act contained shall be construed to limit the right of any person to become the candidate of more than one political party for the same office upon complying with the requirements of this act."[4] Crossfiling was born.[5]

Crossfiling maintained the closed primary for the voters, but in effect established an open primary for the candidates. Used with caution at first, the practice spread to the point where practically all serious candidates ran in the primary for the nomination of the opposition party as well as their own. By the 1950's more than 80% of the candidates for all partisan offices crossfiled in the primary election. Many candidates were successful in winning the nomination of both major parties, and thereby the election, the rate of success being at times little short of phenomenal. Between 1940 and 1952, 68% of all partisan offices in California were won by crossfiling with a peak of 72% in 1952. During the same period, 40% of the contests for the United States Senate, 47% for the House of Representatives, 71% for the California State Assembly, and 83% for the State Senate were won by successful crossfiling in the primary.[6] Peaks in successful crossfiling were reached in the Assembly with 80% in 1944, and in the State Senate with 90% in 1944 and 1952. Dramatic illustrations of the effect of crossfiling for the top state-wide offices came when Hiram Johnson in 1934 and 1940 and William F. Knowland in 1952 won election to the United States Senate by capturing the Democratic as well as the Republican nominations, and when Earl Warren achieved the same feat in his election as governor in 1946. In these, as well as in the less dramatic contests, whenever a candidate captured the nomination of both major parties in the primary, the voter was left without a choice in the final election.

Crossfiling was particularly advantageous for incumbents. From the mid-thirties through the forties well over 80% of all candidates who won final election by successfully crossfiling in the primary were incumbents, and by 1950 the figure rose to over 90%.[7] Incumbents normally enjoy a campaign advantage over their challengers. In California, however, their success was also aided in no small measure by the fact that their names appeared first on the ballot and—until 1954—without indication of their party affiliation. One of the consequences for the political parties was an increase in power exercised by the officeholders and their supremacy over other elements within the party.

But perhaps the most serious effect of crossfiling on political parties in California was the loss of party control over nominations. With many Democrats capturing Republican nominations, and with even more Republicans capturing Democratic nominations (during the period 1914 through 1956, 68.8% of all successful crossfilers were Republicans),[8] the effect could only be a further weakening and frustration of political parties. For when a political party cannot win its own nominations, it loses much of the purpose for its existence.

The effect of crossfiling on party nominations must be considered perhaps the the single most important stimulus which led party leaders and organizations to seek unity in the primary. Nominations were lost when intraparty competition in the primary divided the party vote and made it possible for the candidate from the other party to gain a plurality. In order to prevent such loss of nominations, it was obviously necessary for each party to eliminate as much internal competition in the primary as possible. Party endorsement of candidates in the primary, and preprimary conventions to unite behind single candidates for each office, were therefore in large part a natural outgrowth of crossfiling.

Caught up in the pressures of the press, lobbies and intraparty rivalries, party leaders were torn by factionalism and frequently could reach no agreement among themselves on nominations. Systematic party action to unite on nominations had to await an infusion of new blood and organizational vitality. Handicapped by the unwieldy, legally prescribed official party structure, rejuvenation of the parties could only come through the formation of extra-legal, unofficial, party organizations, unemcumbered by the detailed provisions of the Elections Code. Consequently, the Republicans in 1934 formed the California Republican Assembly. The Democrats followed nearly twenty years later with the California Democratic Council.

The early 1930's were difficult years for California Republicans. Franklin D. Roosevelt's presidential victory in 1932 was accompanied by corresponding Democratic gains and Republican losses on the state level. To stem the Democratic tide, Republicans needed new blood, new leadership, and organization.

Initiative for a revitalization came from a group of insurgent younger leaders and party workers who felt the need to strengthen public confidence in the Republican Party, to free the party from domination by conservative, if not reactionary, leadership and to formulate new programs. Following defeat in the 1932 election, these insurgents started forming grass-roots volunteer organizations. In 1934 they organized the California Republican Assembly.

Membership in the Assembly is open to any registered Republican paying small annual dues. The basic structure of the organization has remained unchanged throughout the years. The state-wide governing body is a board of directors, consisting of the president, immediate past president, eleven vice-presidents, several other officers, one director from each congressional district, and additional regional directors as may be appointed by the president and approved by the board of directors. Local assemblies in counties and cities are chartered by the state-wide board of directors.

While not a mass organization (membership has never reached much above 10,000) the power and influence of the California Republican Assembly in the Republican party has been great, at least until 1964. With local assemblies operating in most of the state's fifty-eight counties, it has served as a precinct organization for the Republican Party. It has also served as a training ground for political leaders and public officials. But the Assembly's most significant function has been the formal endorsement of Republican candidates in the primaries —state-wide and local.[9]

The first opportunity to make endorsements for state-wide offices came in 1938, but it was frustrated by a threatened split in the California Republican Assembly. There were two Republican candidates in the race for governor— Governor Frank Merriam and Lieutenant Governor George J. Hatfield—and both wanted the California Republican Assembly endorsement in the primary. Faced with a clash between two forces of nearly equal strength, and trying to avoid a split within the California Republican Assembly, the 1938 convention delegates voted against making any endorsement. Merriam won the nomination in the primary, but it was widely felt that the Merriam–Hatfield split contributed greatly to the subsequent general election victory of Democratic gubernatorial candidate Culbert L. Olson.

A full year before the 1942 primary, the president of the California Republican Assembly named a committee of twenty-nine to consider and recommend candidates for state-wide office. The committee, which included representatives from each of the state's congressional districts, set the pattern for future endorsement procedures, and became the prototype of the candidates and fact-finding committees.

Having considered a number of possible candidates, and aiming at avoiding a party fight in the primary, the committee made its recommendations to the 1942 annual convention. Earl Warren, then Attorney General, was recommended for Governor, Harry B. Riley for Controller, and Charles G. Johnson for Treasurer. There were others in the running, especially for Governor. The convention's endorsement followed the committee's recommendation. This was done in spite of threats from other candidates that they would run in the primary regardless of a Warren endorsement. Nevertheless, the CRA-endorsed slate won in the primary and general election.

The series of relatively uneventful conventions that followed was livened up by some drama in 1950—the repudiation of an incumbent, and the overruling of the CRA's own subcommittee. The repudiated incumbent was Attorney General Frederick N. Howser. The overruling of the subcommittee involved the endorsement of Richard M. Nixon.

Attorney General Howser's administration had been criticized publicly for alleged ties with gambling interests, and shortly before the 1950 convention, testimony before a Sonoma County Grand Jury revealed that "the punchboard monopoly put $50,000 into Howser's 1946 campaign as the purchase price for immunity from interference by his office."[10] There had also been open hostility between Howser and Governor Warren, and the Warren organization was preparing to replace the Republican Attorney General. The California Republican Assembly Candidates and Fact Finding Committee therefore recommended the endorsement of Edward Shattuck, then Republican State Chairman and a friend of the Governor. Although Howser denied all allegations against him and "made an almost tearful plea" to make no endorsement for Attorney General,[11] it was to no avail. The delegates condemned Howser's administration as having allowed the "vicious growth and development of organized crime and rackets in California."[12] Shattuck received the unanimous endorsement.

The other unusual event in 1950 involved the endorsement of the Republican candidate for the United States Senate. Senator Sheridan Downey's announced intention to retire resulted in two candidates seeking the California Republican Assembly endorsement—Judge Frederick F. Houser and Congressman Richard M. Nixon. The special subcommittee on senatorial candidates recommended, by

377

Edward S. Shattuck (1901–1965), one of the organizers of the California Republican Assembly and its president, 1936–1937. He became a delegate to the Republican National Conventions of 1936, 1948, and 1956, and served as a Republican National Committeeman, 1956 –1960. (Courtesy of *Sacramento Bee*.)

a vote of six to three, that Judge Houser be endorsed. But the full Candidates and Fact Finding Committee, by a secret ballot of thirteen to twelve reversed its subcommittee's recommendation. Nixon then received the endorsement.

The first reversal for the California Republican Assembly came four years later. With all state-wide offices up for election in 1954, the California Republican Assembly endorsed all Republican incumbents, none of whom faced significant intraparty opposition. By then Goodwin J. Knight was already Governor, having succeeded Earl Warren upon his appointment as Chief Justice of the United States. Thomas H. Kuchel had been appointed United States Senator to fill the unexpired term of by then Vice-President Nixon and Robert Kirkwood had moved up to Controller—the post vacated by Kuchel. Only the offices of lieutenant governor and attorney general presented the possibility of an endorsement contest.

The two leading Republican contenders for lieutenant governor were Harold J. Powers, who had become the incumbent by moving up from President Pro Tempore of the Senate when Knight became Governor, and James W. Silliman, Speaker of the Assembly. It was no easy choice for the California Republican Assembly. Silliman had strong support in the Candidates and Fact Finding Committee, which recommended his endorsement. Although there was considerable sentiment for Powers among the delegates, the convention narrowly upheld the committee's recommendation. The California Republican Assembly endorsement, however, was reversed decisively in the primary by the Republican voters, who favored Powers by a margin of nearly seven to one.

There was no CRA endorsement for the office of attorney general in 1954, the GOP failing to put forward a strong candidate. The Republican nomination was subsequently won by Democratic Attorney General Edmund G. Brown, who drew more votes than the two Republican candidates combined. However, the 1954 election saw the beginning of the end of crossfiling; none of the state-wide Republican incumbents were able to capture the Democratic nomination. All won in the general election, however.

1958 was an important year for the CRA. As usual, the CRA endorsement went to the uncontested incumbents: Lieutenant Governor Harold J. Powers, Controller Robert C. Kirkwood, Treasurer A. Ronald Button, Secretary of State Frank M. Jordan. However, the candidacies for Governor, United States Senator, and Attorney General were steeped in bitter conflicts. Long before the Assembly's 1958 convention, Senator William F. Knowland announced his intention not to run for reelection. When he finally announced his candidacy for the office of governor, a bitter primary battle appeared in the making. It was averted, however, when Governor Knight, faced with the threat of dried-up campaign funds and press support, agreed to run for Knowland's seat in the Senate instead.

While the Governor's switch averted one primary contest, it clashed with the political ambitions of San Francisco's Mayor George Christopher and gave rise to another conflict. Assured by Knight that he would fight to remain Governor, Christopher made known his plans to succeed Knowland in the Senate. Knight's subsequent change of heart, therefore, created another intraparty conflict. Unlike Knight, Christopher did not withdraw and decided to fight for the nomination in the primary election.

The CRA's role in both conflicts was not an easy one. In the Knowland–Knight controversy it took unusually fast, although perhaps uneasy, action. With both men still publicly in the race, the seven-member fact-finding subcommittee for the office of governor urged a full four months prior to the endorsing convention "unqualified endorsement of our great United States Senator William F. Knowland as the gubernatorial candidate for the Republican Party in the State of California."[13] It was, of course, unnecessary for the convention to decide between Knowland and Knight. By the time the convention met, the decision had already been made largely by other men and events, and Knowland was the only Republican gubernatorial candidate.

This, however, was not the case in the races for United States Senator and for Attorney General. Both Knight and Christopher wanted the endorsement for the Senate. But Knight deserved special support in return for his action in providing a clear field for Knowland. Thus the subcommittee for that office reported:

> The qualifications of Mayor Christopher were considered to be outstanding and it was recognized that he is a candidate of great integrity and capability. Governor Knight due to his splendid record as governor of the State of California, highest personal qualifications and electability was recommended by the sub-committee for endorsement.[14]

Though not unanimously—the full Candidates and Fact Finding Committee and the delegates divided nearly two to one—the recommendation carried.

The race for attorney general was a different situation still. Democrat Edmund G. Brown's candidacy for Governor left the contest for Attorney General wide open. Two Republicans, Caspar W. Weinberger and Patrick J. Hillings, aspired for the office. Weinberger, an assemblyman from San Francisco, had an outstanding record of legislative service in Sacramento. Very active in civic and party affairs, he was one of the most popular Republican leaders in northern California. Hillings, a conservative congressman from Whittier and a close friend of Vice President Nixon, had strong southern California support for his candidacy. He did not officially seek the CRA endorsement, but he was nevertheless considered by the Fact Finding Committee, whose mandate was to evaluate all announced candidates.

Fully aware that Hillings' support in the more populous southern part of the state might well be decisive in the primary, the CRA convention nevertheless overwhelmingly endorsed Weinberger. Hillings won the primary, and for the second time in its history a CRA-endorsed candidate for state-wide office failed to win the Republican nomination. This reversal was dwarfed by the size of Republican losses in the 1958 general election. The succeeding elections were no kinder to the Republicans. The Democrats maintained control through 1964 when their power began to crumble from internal dissention.

The same general factors which gave rise to the California Republican Assembly also gave birth to the California Democratic Council—a series of defeats at the polls, crossfiling and the desire to prevent its disastrous effects in the loss of nominations, the ineffectiveness of the statutory party organizations and the need for new party blood and leadership.[15] In addition, however, there was the Stevenson presidential campaign of 1952.

The elections of 1950 and 1952 were once again low points in the history of the Democratic Party of California. Democratic losses mounted during the 1940's,

380

culminating in the defeat of 1952. The deepest humiliation came when Senator William F. Knowland won the Democratic nomination for the United States Senate by successfully crossfiling in the primary. And all this took place with the Democrats maintaining a nearly three to two registration majority!

Clearly some new action and direction was needed to strengthen the party. While Stevenson lost to Eisenhower in 1952, his presidential campaign in California gave rise to an instrument for Democratic salvation. Stimulated by the

Both Adlai Stevenson (1900–1965) and Estes Kefauver (1903–1963) used the California Democratic Council convention in Fresno as a kick-off point for their California primary campaigns. Here Stevenson attends a birthday party in his honor. (Courtesy of George Ballis.)

enthusiasm of the Stevenson campaign, a grass-roots movement began taking shape. Neighborhood clubs sprung up in nearly every part of the state. Democratic clubs have appeared in California from time to time, but have never shown any signs of permanency or growth. The Stevenson candidacy, however, brought out a new type of political activist—men and women of education whose political enthusiasm stemmed from ideas and ideals. Disappointed, but undismayed by Stevenson's defeat, many of these clubs survived to provide a new basis of political expression and action. Some leaders recognized the potential of the movement and set out to shape it into an effective auxiliary organization which could give new life to California's Democratic Party.

Rejuvenation began with a soul-searching workshop conference at Asilomar in January 1953. Any and all California Democrats were invited. Most of the regular party leaders came; so did hundreds of club members and party workers. The general theme of the conference was the question uppermost in the minds of many Democrats: "What's Wrong with the Democratic Party in California?" The 500 persons attending broke up into a number of panel sessions trying to search out answers and solutions. The most significant solution lay in the adoption of a plan for preprimary conventions for the purpose of selecting and endorsing a full slate of candidates.

State Chairman Senator George Miller and Alan Cranston, a newcomer to party politics who distinguished himself at Asilomar, led the successful efforts to translate the plans into organizational reality—the development of county and congressional district Democratic councils, composed of delegates from the chartered clubs, including women's clubs, Young Democrats, and all other recognized groups, and from county central committees. The major function of the councils was to endorse single Democratic candidates in the primaries and work for their nomination and election.

The California Democratic Council was officially born at the November 1953 convention in Fresno. The main purpose of the organization would be ". . . to conduct a preprimary convention every two years to endorse the best possible Democratic candidates for statewide partisan office and to build party unity behind them." The same would be done on the assembly district, congressional district, and county levels. Organizationally and structurally, individual clubs were coordinated into assembly district and congressional district councils. A formal tie-in with the statutory party organization was achieved by the provision that local clubs be chartered by the county central committees of the party. The assembly district and congressional district councils were chartered by the state organization with its board of directors largely made up of one representative from each congressional district.

With CDC officially established, there was little time to be lost for the primary was only six months away. The test would simply be whether or not the

Democrats would be able to maintain unity in the primary and win their own nominations. But first they would have to make the endorsements, and for that purpose another convention was called early in February, 1954.

If an open convention can be defined as one in which there are genuine contests among candidates and a minimum of pre-arranged results, that convention was wide-open indeed. Although considerable pre-convention campaign activity had taken place, there was no doubt that the real decisions would be made by the nearly 1,500 delegates. There were spirited contests for most of the endorsements, and sometimes, as in the case of the endorsements for governor and United States Senator, spirits ran very high.

There were four men in the race for the gubernatorial endorsement, but only two of them were considered as serious contenders—Richard P. Graves, who had recently resigned his post as Executive Director of the League of California Cities, and Berkeley Mayor Laurance L. Cross. Having announced their candidacies well in advance of the convention, both agreed to abide by the decision of the convention and not run in the primary against the endorsed candidate. Graves was a newcomer to the Democratic Party, having been a registered Republican until very shortly before he filed for candidacy. However, his Republican background, his friendship with former Governor Earl Warren, and his connections through the League of California Cities, were considered by many to be assets in California's nonpartisan tradition. Opposition came largely from certain elements of organized labor.

The Graves–Cross contest was quite fiery, with Cross supporters describing their candidate as "not a 40-day Democrat, but a 40-year Democrat," and the Graves people referring to their candidate as "electable." Supported by most of the Democratic Party officials, Graves won the endorsement by a vote of 957 to 519.[16]

The endorsement of the United States senatorial candidate engendered a different kind of contest, caused in part by the belief that there was a fair chance of defeating the Republican incumbent Thomas H. Kuchel.[17] Well before the convention, several prominent Californians had been approached about running, but for various reasons they had declined. When the convention met there was only one candidate—Congressman Samuel W. Yorty of Los Angeles.

Yorty had promises of substantial financial support and impressive labor backing, and many Democratic Party officials were behind him. Still, his candidacy caught no fire among most of the delegates in Fresno. There were strong feelings and charges of "red-baiting" against Yorty, stemming largely from his record while in the Assembly and his role as first Chairman of the state's Un-American Activities Committee. Suspicion of Yorty was not allayed by his rather liberal voting record while in Congress; when some Yorty managers at the convention began labeling those who resisted his candidacy as "red" and

383

"left-wing," an open "stop-Yorty drive" developed. This movement focused on the person of Peter Odegard, Chairman of the Political Science Department at the University of California at Berkeley. Having come to the convention as a delegate without any thought of becoming a candidate, he complied with requests to discuss political issues and problems before various caucuses; and suddenly he found himself about to be drafted, but he declined.

The results of the 1954 endorsing convention were heartening to California Democrats. For the first time in more than a decade the Democrats presented a complete slate of candidates for all state-wide offices. For the first time since the beginning of crossfiling there was only one Democratic candidate for each office except governor, where there was only one other token Democratic entry. Thus there were no serious primary fights among state-wide Democratic candidates, and for the first time in many years there was a new force in the Democratic Party. Equally important, all endorsed candidates won in the primary against crossfiling Republicans. With the exception of Attorney General Brown, however, they did not win in the general election. The 1954 Democratic primary election achievements on the state level were accompanied by a similar performance on the local level. For the first time in many years, California Democrats succeeded in winning the great majority of their own party nominations, and in the general election the voters had a choice between candidates of the two major parties for nearly every office.

To ascribe all of these results to the CDC preprimary endorsements would be misleading. As much, if not more, credit must go to a change in the ballot which was passed by the voters in 1952 and became effective with the 1954 primary. For the first time since the adoption of crossfiling the candidates' party affiliation was indicated on the ballot next to their names,[18] and voters showed a remarkable tendency to vote for candidates of their own party. Whatever credit is given the party designation on the ballot, the value of the CDC endorsements and the organizational effort behind them cannot be underestimated. The first challenge of a CDC-endorsed statewide candidate came in 1956 and involved the nomination for the United States Senate.

Having won the endorsement and primary in 1954, but having lost the election, Yorty decided to try again in 1956. This time, however, there was another candidate, State Senator Richard Richards from Los Angeles, in the running and the lingering anti-Yorty sentiment had leadership and direction. Both men came to Fresno to win the CDC endorsement, but it was immediately apparent that Richards had the majority of the delegates. Sensing imminent defeat, Yorty took the rostrum, angrily charged that the convention was "rigged, wired, and stacked" and withdrew his name announcing that he would defy the verdict of the delegates and run for the Democratic nomination in the primary.

When Yorty in fact did file in the primary, the California Democratic Council faced its first major crisis. The CDC, by then nearly 40,000 strong, met the crisis with an all-out campaign for Richards. The result was a vindication for the CDC when Richards defeated Yorty by a vote of nearly three to one. The prestige of the organization, and especially the value of its endorsement, was reaffirmed.

When the nearly 2,000 delegates and almost as many alternates and observers met in Fresno in January, 1958, to endorse candidates for the 1958 primary, there were contests for several of the state offices. The liveliest contest was centered once more around the candidacy for the United States Senate. Attorney General Brown and most of the influential party leaders had decided upon Congressman Clair Engle as their candidate. Engle, an effective campaigner from Red Bluff, had made a name for himself as chairman of the important House Interior and Insular Affairs Committee. With the aid of the official party organization and a paid professional staff, Engle set out to campaign throughout the state. In the absence of any other candidate in the field, it appeared that Engle would win the CDC endorsement by default.

However, in the late fall of 1957, Los Angeles Supervisor Kenneth Hahn threw his hat into the ring, and two months prior to the convention Professor

Michigan Governor G. Mennen (Soapy) Williams (1911–   ) keynotes the historic 1958 California Democratic Council convention. (Courtesy of *CDC Observer.*)

Peter Odegard announced his intention to seek the CDC endorsement for the United States Senate. Hahn was not considered a serious candidate, but it was different with Odegard. In the brief period of time before the convention, he managed to appear before delegate caucuses in nearly half of the state's thirty congressional districts. Had he entered the race in October instead of December, he might well have won at Fresno. But Engle's careful preconvention preparations throughout the state, and the support of most party officials before and during the convention, had their effect.[19] A change in the convention rules prior to the balloting to require a 50% vote for endorsement instead of the 60% previously adopted by the Board of Directors also helped. When the first ballot was over Engle had won by 54% of the vote while Odegard received 36% and Hahn the rest. Partly in recognition of Odegard's popular appeal, the party professionals offered him the endorsement for Lieutenant Governor, but Odegard declined. Attorney General Brown received the uncontested endorsement for Governor and Judge Stanley Mosk of Los Angeles was similarly endorsed for Attorney General.

In the primary that followed the CDC faced its second serious challenge. Democratic State Senator Robert I. McCarthy of San Francisco had announced his candidacy for Attorney General but refused to submit his name to the CDC convention. In fact, he expressed strong criticism of the CDC preprimary endorsements, at one time referring to "the phony so-called endorsing antics of the hot-rod set of the Democratic party."[20] CDC supporters countered that the real reason for McCarthy's refusal to be considered by the convention was Judge Mosk's strength.

With Senator McCarthy running against Judge Mosk in the Democratic primary, the CDC once more mustered all its strength to uphold the principle and the value of its endorsements. It was a very close contest, but again the endorsed candidate won. Although full credit must be given to CDC's efforts in the campaign, it is clear that geography and population were on the side of the clubs. With very few exceptions CDC-endorsed candiates won in the primaries, but this time success at the primary carried over into the general election. The Knowland–Knight switch of candidacies and the rift within the Republican party, the highly controversial right to work issue which Knowland espoused, and other factors worked in the Democrats' favor. But the preprimary endorsements and the CDC were important elements contributing to Democratic unity in that campaign and to the sweeping victory of 1958.

The 1958 Democratic victory and the subsequent abolition of crossfiling were in part the product of CDC's success with preprimary endorsements. But success carries within itself the seeds of danger. From the very beginning the movement was not without opposition within the party, primarily from some "old pros" who regarded CDC's role in nominations as undesirable, potentially irresponsible and dangerous. Some believed that with the repeal of crossfiling there was no longer the danger of losing the nomination to a candidate of another party and, therefore, no reason why the nomination should not be decided in the primary without prior endorsement. A number of Democratic politicians resented the potential challenge posed by the CDC. On occasion, the CDC has been criticized for being too "issue oriented" and for endorsing "idealist" candidates without too much concern for "electability," thereby showing some lack of political "realism." There is no question about the CDC's orientation. For example, the 1964 annual conference adopted resolutions favoring United States trade with Communist China; withdrawal of American troops from South Vietnam; abolition of the House Committee on Un-American Activities; the end of foreign travel restrictions by United States citizens; the right of public school teachers to strike; abolition of capital punishment; legalizing abortions where there is substantial risk of grave impairment of the health of the mother or child; a two dollar an hour minimum wage; and extension of unemployment insurance and child labor laws to agriculture.[21] Republicans have campaigned against CDC-endorsed candidates by hanging the "albatross" of one or another CDC resolution around the Democrat's neck. In spite of these problems, the CDC remained the most vital element within the Democratic Party for a few more years.

In the early 1960's the political pendulum in California began to swing in the other direction. The Republicans, with virtually nowhere to go but up, won the coveted governorship in 1966 as well as almost all of the constitutional offices. By 1969 they had captured control over both houses of the Legislature, and the Democratic Party was left in shambles. Both parties became transformed in the process of Republican resurgence and these transformations had serious effects upon the CRA and the CDC. The CRA was captured by right wing forces; the CDC deteriorated to near impotence.

The transformation of both organizations can be traced in the 1964 election.[22] The seriousness of the conservative onslaught became evident in 1962 when the conservative wing of the GOP made a bid for the gubernatorial and United States senatorial nominations. Not victorious, but with an impressive demonstration of strength, the conservatives launched a program to take over the official and unofficial party organs. Their formula of success lay in a four-pronged approach: to take over the volunteer party organizations; to endorse and support only those candidates who adhered to conservative principles; to defeat moderate Republican elected officials; and to capture control of the Republican State Central Committee.

The conservative take-over of the volunteer auxiliary party organizations came shortly after the 1962 election and Nixon's defeat by Democratic incumbent Governor Brown. First to succumb to the conservative assault were

Edmund G. (Pat) Brown (1905–   ) accepts the endorsement of the California Democratic Council in 1958, the year of the Democratic sweep. (Courtesy of *CDC Observer*.)

the Young Republicans when, at their state convention in February 1963, a conservative won the presidency. The California Republican Assembly followed the same road one year later when at its convention in March 1964 the militant conservatives wrested the leadership away from the moderates. There was no need to take over the United Republicans of California (UROC). That organization was founded by conservative Republicans in April 1963, and one year later it reportedly had 10,000 members organized in 290 units throughout the state.[23] The endorsement of Goldwater by all three groups came as a matter of course. The Goldwater forces prevailed in the June primary, which brought out a record 80% of the Republican voters, defeating the Nelson Rockefeller backers by some 68,000 votes. Unfortunately for Rockefeller, the birth of a child to his second wife a few days before the primary had recalled to many voters the circumstances of his divorce and remarriage.

Equally successful was the conservative candidate endorsement policy. Endorsements were denied a number of Republican incumbents because they failed to meet the standards of conservatism as defined by the endorsing organizations. Since lack of endorsement also meant denial of organizational and financial support, the cost to moderate Republicans in the subsequent primary and general election was considerable. As for the California Republican

Official and Unofficial Party Organizations

Assembly, its capture by conservative forces marked the beginning of its road to virtual extinction as a vital force in California Republicanism.

For the Democrats, and particularly for the California Democratic Council, 1964 marked a significant turning point. The string of CDC successes in winning nominations in the primaries for its endorsed statewide candidates was broken, and with it a United States senatorial seat was lost. Looking ahead toward 1964, the Democrats had no apparent reason for alarm. There seemed to be little danger of losing control in the State Legislature, and there was every expectation that Clair Engle, the popular Democratic Senator, would be re-elected for another term. However, in August 1963 brain surgery left the Senator partially paralyzed and virtually unable to speak. A number of individuals began to cast longing glances toward Washington, and at least three in addition to Senator Engle were considered to be serious contenders—State Controller Alan Cranston, Attorney General Stanley Mosk, and Congressman James Roosevelt.

The endorsing convention of the California Democratic Council on February 22 with more than 2,000 delegates and as many alternatives present, became the arena for the competition for support. With the value of a CDC endorsement clearly established, the jockeying for position became increasingly bitter. When it became clear to the Mosk forces that Cranston had the upper hand, Mosk decided to withhold his name from formal consideration by the convention.

In what was clearly a holding action aimed at blocking a Cranston endorsement, Speaker Jess Unruh urged continued support of Senator Engle. This attempt, however, suffered an irreparable blow when a live telephone message from Engle to the assembled delegates came through as little more than incoherent stammering.

Cranston had little difficulty in winning a decisive victory on the first ballot with 1,197 votes against Roosevelt's 727 and Engle's 281. Living up to his promise, Roosevelt withdrew from the race and announced his support for Cranston. Mosk's plans remained unclear for a while, but he withdrew from the race in early March 1964. Governor Brown subsequently appointed him a Justice of the California Supreme Court. Senator Engle's candidacy remained alive until his second hospitalization in the latter part of April made it impossible to continue the pretense and he finally withdrew from the race.[24]

Senator Engle's withdrawal meant clear sailing ahead for Cranston as far as the Democratic Senatorial nomination was concerned—or so it seemed for a while. That situation changed drastically when Pierre Salinger entered the race on March 19, beating the filing deadline by a matter of hours and the internecine struggle that many Democrats tried so hard to avoid broke out in full fury.

In the end Cranston lost to Salinger by a close vote of 1,177,517 to 1,037,748, with Salinger's margin of victory assured by his 165,000 plurality in Los Angeles County. But Pierre Salinger lost the election to his Republican opponent by a margin of 216,643. Elected to the United States Senate from California was George Murphy, the dancing actor from Hollywood, who had gained national political attention first when he and actress Irene Dunne had led the "We Want Warren" chant from the podium of the Republican National Nominating Convention in 1948.

Thus 1964 marked a turning point for both major parties and some of their unofficial organizations. The GOP took a turn to the right and developed successful formulae for subsequent electoral victories. Democrats subjected themselves to bloodletting, internecine struggle leading to a series of defeats and the subsequent loss of political control of the state. Other developments accelerated these trends. The Republicans succeeded in revitalizing their formal party organizations on the state and county levels as well as developing a more professional, business-like approach to politics. The Democrats virtually fell apart, fractured by the war in Vietnam as was the country, with the CDC

United States Senator George L. Murphy (1902–   ) discussing his views on the bracero program in 1965. (Courtesy of *San Francisco Examiner*.)

leading the rebellion against President Lyndon B. Johnson, but falling victim in the process. These developments must be analyzed, however briefly, in order to understand better the politics of California during the latter part of the 1960's.

The resurgence of the GOP in California in the 1960's was caused in part by application of rational planning to politics and development of party organizations on all levels. While the significance of volunteer organizations has declined, there has been a strengthening and activation of the state and county committees as well as the all-important Republican Associates.

Perhaps one of the most remarkable developments in recent years has been the transformation of the Republican State Central Committee. Presently it employs a very competent staff of nearly twenty who could best be characterized as "IBM types"—professional, efficient, ideologically detached, and young. The policy it professes to follow is "studied neutrality" among the various ideological factions of the party. This neutrality applies only when there is a significant contest for nominations; otherwise, the committee works very closely with and for a party leader. Apparently there is no particular problem with funds for organizational needs. In 1967–68 the State Central Committee expended approximately one million dollars for staff, rent, publications, and other expenses exclusive of actual campaign costs. The availability of funds makes it possible to employ public relations firms to direct the work of the Committee. Spencer–Roberts has been performing this function in recent years and has been consulting on campaigns under contract with the State Central Committee as well.

The major Republican county committees such as Los Angeles and San Francisco have also increased and improved their professional staff and activities. The Los Angeles County Committee developed the effective "Los Angeles County Plan" which was subsequently adopted throughout most of California. The plan involves essentially an all-out effort on election day through the organization of "victory squads." On election day of 1968 the Los Angeles County Committee was able to get out some 2,200 volunteers, supplied largely by Republican Associates through business firms. Computerization and data processing are employed to good advantage with names, skills and other information about volunteers recorded on IBM cards and tapes and mailer cards processed by computers sent out to approximately 10,000 Republican volunteers. Furthermore, there has been an activation of precinct organization, especially in Los Angeles County, and an effort is made to keep precinct organizations alive not only during campaigns but also between campaigns to keep up with the shifting population.

Important as improved organization, professionalization, and functions of the Republican organizations have been, political control of California would

391

not have been attained as speedily without the California Plan. The brainchild of Republican State Chairman Dr. Gaylord Parkinson prior to the 1964 campaign, the California Plan (also referred to as the Parkinson Plan) provided a blueprint for gaining GOP control of the State Legislature by 1970. Employing a "rifle shot" approach to winning elections, the plan involved five steps:

1. In-depth analysis of the top ten marginal assembly districts;
2. The establishment of priority "target districts"—the five most vulnerable for Republicans to "recapture" in 1964;
3. Enlistment of all elements of the party in regions surrounding the target districts;
4. Hiring of paid specialists to assist Republican candidates chosen in key districts;
5. Winning of five districts at each of the four elections between 1964 and 1970.[25]

The success of the California Plan is now history. 1964 brought Republican victories in four out of the five target districts, and the Republicans exceeded their own target date by gaining control over both houses of the Legislature before 1970.

In addition to the professionalization and upsurge of activity of the official party organs and the California Plan, credit for the impressive Republican victories in recent years is due to at least one of the informal, volunteer organizations, the Republican Associates. Founded in Los Angeles in 1951, it remains strongest in that county with a membership approaching 3,500 and a professional staff of ten. San Diego, Fresno, Orange, and Sacramento counties are reported to have memberships of over 1,000 each. The San Francisco Bay area organization, the Bay Area Alliance, claims approximately 500 members.

While most Republican organizations are largely oriented toward business, none is more so than Republican Associates. Membership lists read like a business *Who's Who*, and it operates as close to a business enterprise as any political organization could. They work closely with, and through, corporations, especially in the recruitment of "victory squads," election day precinct workers who come largely from among corporation staffs and employees.

The functions of the organization consist mainly of political research, education, candidate development, campaign clinics, publication of campaign manuals, precinct work, and similar activities. The organization prides itself in its professionalism and research activities, and the Los Angeles organization claims to have the largest Republican political research facilities west of Chicago. Ideologically it is non-partisan within the Republican Party, and according to the organization's Statement of Purpose, it "studiously avoids becoming involved in philosophical struggles within the Republican Party."

This neutrality makes it possible to serve as a safe platform for Republican speakers and candidates of all ideological and other factions, thereby acting as a unifying force within the GOP.

A note must be added about Republican volunteer party organizations in addition to the California Republican Assembly and Republican Associates, that have been active on the California scene with varying degrees of effectiveness. United Republicans of California, slightly to the right of the rightist-dominated CRA has a membership approaching that of the CRA (well under 10,000) but wields less influence. The Young Republicans, with a membership of less than 5,000 is hardly an effective political force. The California Republican League was formed by a group of moderate leaders following the take-over of the CRA by the extreme right and the subsequent Goldwater disaster, but with a membership of little more than 1,000 its influence has hardly been felt. The Federation of Republican Women, however, with more than 30,000 members has been of considerable importance, primarily in mobilizing women for the Republican cause. Finally, mention must be made of the United Republican Finance Committee. As the principal fund-raising organ for the GOP and its candidates, its role in electoral success of the party, although not publicized, must never be underestimated.

The impressive Republican gains in the latter part of the 1960's produced corresponding Democratic losses. Not only did the Democrats lose control of the governorship and state Legislature, but their most vigorous volunteer organization, the California Democratic Council, was decimated.

We have seen how the CDC suffered its first state-wide defeat in 1964 when its endorsed candidate, Alan Cranston, lost the United States senatorial nomination in the primary to Pierre Salinger. This in itself was not a crippling blow. Neither was the appearance of a rival volunteer organization, Democratic Volunteers in California, a serious threat to the CDC. Instigated by Democratic Speaker Jess Unruh in 1964, the DVC was to provide campaign muscle for Democratic Party candidates without making preprimary endorsements or becoming involved in policy questions and issues. One of the unique features of the CDC was its issue orientation. Far from being a handmaiden, the CDC often acted as an independent force within the Democratic Party. This resulted at times in embarrassment to and friction with some Democratic incumbents who welcomed the muscle of the CDC but not the ideas. The DVC was oriented toward party work rather than public issues, but it never really got off the ground. The little effect it had hardly extended beyond southern California.

The first storm over Vietnam within the California Democratic Party and the CDC, the Casady affair, broke out early in 1966. Simon Casady, a colorful former newspaper publisher from El Cajon, was elected president of CDC in March 1965. Ironically, he was suggested for that post and promoted initially by the State Controller and first president of the CDC, Alan Cranston, as well as incumbent Governor Brown. Within a year Casady was ousted from that post in a pressure campaign led primarily by the same two men. The controversy over Casady started brewing shortly after his election and soon developed into a full-fledged storm and an organizational schism. In September 1965 Governor Brown's request that Casady resign met with Casady's refusal. Finally, Casady was deposed in a bitter, divisive, convention in February 1966 by a delegate vote of 1,001 to 895. Two charges had been advanced against Casady—administrative incompetence, and intemperate attacks against President Johnson over the Vietnam war. Although apparently there were grounds for dissatisfaction with Casady's organizational abilities and efforts, the major reasons for the ouster apparently lay somewhere else. Like many Americans, Casady became increasingly critical of the Johnson administration's war policy in Vietnam, and soon became a leading voice calling for a cessation of United States bombing and a genuine turn toward peace. Understandably, his views became troublesome, not only to the Johnson administration, but also to a number of Democratic incumbents and to Governor Brown who was concerned about his forthcoming campaign for re-election. With Ronald Reagan as his probable Republican opponent, Brown's strategy was to portray Reagan as ultra-conservative, even extremist, and claim the politics of moderation for himself. However, this bid was seriously impaired by the Governor's identification with and support from an organization headed by a president whose criticisms of the war many considered radical and intemperate. Casady was a liability to Brown's re-election bid.

The administration forces won, but it was a Pyrrhic victory. Not only did the bitter struggle shatter the CDC, but the same convention that deposed its leader also adopted a resolution condemning the Johnson administration's policy in Vietnam and calling for direct negotiations with the National Liberation Front to end the war. And in the end Governor Brown, while receiving the half-hearted endorsement of a crippled CDC, went down to defeat in 1966 at the hands of Ronald Reagan.

A seriously wounded CDC still had a role to play in the years that followed and primarily in the bitter struggle over the Democratic presidential nomination of 1968. With growing popular protest over the Vietnam war, the CDC intensified its efforts to seek a change in the Johnson administration's policy toward peace in Vietnam. Its efforts frustrated, the CDC then provided much of the impetus of the "dump LBJ" movement within the Democratic Party.

In the aftermath of the 1968 election, the CDC was shattered and largely impotent. The activities and membership of what was only a few years ago the largest and most vital voluntary Democratic Party organization in the country had declined sharply. Its future was uncertain.

FOOTNOTES

1 *Supra*, Chapters 4, 5, and 6.

2 California Statutes (1909), 694.

3 California Statutes (1911), 774.

4 State of California, *Journal of the Senate* (1913), 2710; California Statutes (1913), 1389.

5 A considerable literature has grown up on crossfiling in California, but only a few items can be suggested here: Dean E. McHenry, "Cross-Filing of Political Candidates in California," *The Annals*, CCIIL (November, 1946), 226–231; Dean E. McHenry, "Invitation to the Masquerade," *National Municipal Review*, XXXIX (May, 1950), 228–232; Evelyn Hazen, *Cross-Filing in Primary Elections* (Berkeley: Bureau of Public Administration, University of California, 1951); Robert J. Pitchell, "The Electoral System and Voting Behavior: The Case of California's Cross-Filing," *Western Political Quarterly*, XII (June, 1959), 459–484; and, James C. Findley, "Cross-Filing and the Progressive Movement in California Politics," *Western Political Quarterly*, XII (September, 1959), 699–711.

6 Robert J. Pitchell, *op. cit.*, p. 464–465.

7 *Ibid.*, p. 471.

8 *Ibid.*, p. 467–468.

9 A detailed history of preprimary endorsements of the California Republican Assembly may be found in Leonard Rowe, *Preprimary Endorsements in California Politics* (Berkeley: Bureau of Public Administration, University of California, 1961). The account that follows is drawn largely from that study.

10 *San Francisco Chronicle*, March 26, 1950, p. 1.

11 *Ibid.*, p. 1.

12 *Ibid.*, March 27, 1950, p. 1.

13 California Republican Assembly, Candidates and Fact Finding Committee, *1958 Report*, submitted to the annual California Republican Assembly Convention meeting in San Jose, March 15 and 16, 1958, Appendix I.

14 *Ibid.*, Appendix II.

15 The following account is drawn primarily from Leonard Rowe, *Preprimary Endorsements in California Politics* (Berkeley: Bureau of Public Administration, University of California, 1961). Other studies of the California Democratic Council include: Francis Carney, *The Rise of the Democratic Clubs in California*, Eagleton Foundation Case Study in Practical Politics (New York: Henry Holt, 1958); and, James Q. Wilson, *The Amateur Democrat* (Chicago: The University of Chicago Press, 1962).

16 *San Francisco Chronicle*, February 7, 1954, p. 1.

17 Kuchel, formerly State Controller, had been appointed to the Senate to complete the term of Vice President Richard M. Nixon.

18 An initiative was placed on the ballot in 1952 to repeal crossfiling. Those who wanted to save crossfiling put on the ballot an alternative measure retaining crossfiling

but providing that a candidate's party affiliation be printed on the ballot next to his name. A defensive step to head off the repeal of crossfiling, the measure was adopted. Crossfiling itself narrowly missed being repealed by less than 4,000 votes, and was abolished by the Legislature in 1959.

19 The *Fresno Bee*, January 12, 1958, p. 1, reported: ". . . the Odegard forces put up a fight which caused important Democratic Party leaders to move in as effective vote recruiters for the northern congressman."

20 *San Francisco Chronicle*, February 20, 1958, p. 10.

21 Edmond Constantini, *The Democratic Leadership Corps in California* (Davis: Institute of Governmental Affairs, University of California, 1967), p. 130.

22 An excellent account and analysis of the 1964 campaign is given in Totton J. Anderson and Eugene C. Lee, "The 1964 Election in California," *Western Political Quarterly*, XVIII (June, 1965), 451–474. Another intriguing facet of that campaign is reported in John R. Owens, *Money and Politics in California: Democratic Senatorial Primary, 1964* (Princeton: Citizens' Research Foundation, 1966).

23 Anderson and Lee, *op. cit.*, 457.

24 The withdrawal came too late for his name to be removed from the ballot, and Engle received 119,967 votes in the primary.

25 The California Plan, Annual Report (1965).

California and National Politics

Shortly after high noon on January 6, 1961 the President of the United States Senate banged down his gavel and declared that the junior Senator from Massachusetts was to become the next President of the United States of America. Richard M. Nixon had become the second Vice President in history to officiate over the election of a rival; John C. Breckenridge had done the same for Abraham Lincoln one hundred years earlier. Eight years later Hubert H. Humphrey would have performed the same duty for Nixon, but his assignment by President Lyndon Johnson as the United States representative in Oslo to the funeral of Trygve Lie, the first Secretary-General of the United Nations, relieved him of this onerous task.

Table I

Marginal Presidential Victories in the United States

Elections	Voted for Loser	Winning Margin	Total Votes Cast	Percent
1960		113,057	68,832,778	0.17
1884		23,005	10,052,706	0.22
1968		517,777	73,359,762	0.71
1888	Cleveland	100,476	11,381,032	0.88

There have been four presidential elections in the United States where the winning margin was less-than 1% of the total vote cast—two in the 1880's in which Cleveland was involved and two in the 1960's in which Nixon was involved.

 Royce D. Delmatier and Earl G. Waters were primarily responsible for the original draft of Chapter 13.

The Kennedy–Nixon contest had been the closest presidential election ever held. The margin of difference, a mere 113,057 votes, was .17 of 1%. Only two previous elections had found fewer votes separating the candidates but the percentages were greater since the total votes cast was less. In 1884 Cleveland won by 23,005 votes over Blaine but the percentage was .22 of 1%. In 1888 Cleveland and Harrison were separated by 100,476 votes and the differential was .88 of 1%. Until the 1968 election these had been the only three in which a decision was made by less than 1% of the voters. The Nixon–Humphrey race added the fourth when Nixon polled only 517,777 votes more than Humphrey out of the total 73,359,762 cast. The percentage this time was .71 of 1 %.

Nixon's vote represented only 43.3% of the total popular vote, the lowest since Woodrow Wilson won with 41.8% in a three way race in 1912, and the third lowest in history. While the 73 million votes cast in 1968 set a record in numbers of votes, the percentage of the 120 million Americans of voting age was only 60.8%, the lowest since the 60.5% voted in 1956 when Eisenhower was chosen for his second term.[1]

In the 1968 three-way presidential race third party candidate George C. Wallace, with his running mate General Curtis E. LeMay, rolled up 9,898,543 popular votes for 13.5% of the total cast. This was the highest third party popular vote since Robert M. La Follette received nearly 17% in 1924 and the largest popular vote in history for a third party candidate. It was the fifth time in the present century that a substantial number of electoral votes had gone to a third party candidate. In the 1912 campaign Theodore Roosevelt led his Bull Moose Party to win the largest bloc of electoral votes, eighty-eight, ever received by a minor party. In 1924 La Follette polled more popular votes than any minor party candidate until 1968 but won only the thirteen electoral votes of his home state of Wisconsin. In 1948 J. Strom Thurmond received the thirty-eight electoral votes of Alabama, Louisiana, Mississippi, and South Carolina plus one from Tennessee, and in 1960 Harry F. Byrd of Virginia received fifteen electoral votes despite the fact he was not even a candidate. Wallace gathered the votes of Alabama, Arkansas, Georgia, Louisiana, and Mississippi plus one from North Carolina for an aggregate of forty-six electoral votes.

Thurmond in picking up the lone Tennessee vote cast by presidential elector Preston Parks became the first candidate since 1820 to receive an electoral vote not cast in accordance with the wishes of his state. In that year James Monroe received all of the electoral college votes excepting that of William Plumer, a former New Hampshire governor. It has been said that Plumer cast his vote for John Quincy Adams for the sentimental reason that George Washington should remain the only president ever to receive a unanimous vote. But Plumer was personally hostile to Monroe, and it is more likely that he dissented

'Would You Mind Raising The Winner's Hand?'

(Courtesy of *Sacramento Bee*.)

more in disapproval of Monroe's first administration than as a tribute to the first president.[2]

When Thurmond received his lone vote, political scientists argued that the attempts then being made by Dixiecrats to persuade electors to cast their votes contrary to popular choice overmagnified the dangers of such efforts ever

399

being successful. But it has happened three times since. In 1956 an obscure Alabama state judge, Walter B. Jones, received an Alabama elector vote by W. F. Turner intended for Adlai Stevenson. In 1960 Henry D. Irwin of Oklahoma voted for Harry F. Byrd instead of Nixon. Irwin had worked with R. Lea Harris of Montgomery, Alabama, between the November 8 general election and the meeting of the college of electors on December 19 to induce Republican electors to elect a Byrd–Goldwater coalition. And in 1968, Dr. Lloyd W. Bailey, a Rocky Mount, N. C. opthalmologist, defected and cast his vote for Wallace even though Nixon won the popular vote in North Carolina.

The closeness of elections in 1948 and 1960 and 1968 has brought a growing demand for the abolishment, or at least the modification, of the electoral college. In 1950 the Lodge–Gossett amendment, approved by the Senate but lost in the House, proposed dividing the states' electoral votes in the exact ratio to popular votes cast. Had such a plan been operative in 1896 William Jennings Bryan would have been president. In 1953 the Mundt–Coudert resolution called for electors to be selected by congressional and senatorial seats. Such a plan would have given Nixon 280 electoral votes and the presidency in 1960. Neither of these plans would correct the possibility of a candidate becoming president while receiving fewer votes than his opponent.[3]

The stark possibility of a third party candidate tying up the electoral college and forcing the decision to Congress which presented itself in 1948 and 1960 and 1968 has stimulated the demand for reform.

Those who defend the present system argue that a direct vote would encourage candidates to concentrate their campaigns and their administrations on the large metropolitan areas to the detriment of the sparsely settled regions, that it would make unlikely the selection of a candidate from a small state and, that it would lead to the establishment of national voter standards.

But the direct vote would seem the only way to assure that the man with the most votes does become president. And the proponents of the direct vote gained considerable headway when on April 29, 1969, the House Judiciary Committee approved a constitutional amendment by an overwhelming 28 to 6 vote to junk the electoral college in favor of the direct vote.

The emergence of California as a dominant factor in national politics was, until November 1968, more fantasy than fact. Despite its geographical size and more importantly its large population, California had not achieved the political strength in the national scene. The simple explanation for this failure to assert the power represented by numbers would be the ineptness of some of its political leaders. Currently, California has displayed all of the aspects of a big overgrown puppy being constantly outmaneuvered by smaller but more agile dogs. The astute political minds of the older, more sophisticated state governments have continued to play the key roles in the nation's political selections and elections.

'You're Through, Bub, I'll Take It From Here!'

(Courtesy of *Sacramento Bee*.)

But there are more cogent reasons for the Golden State's failures on the national scene. Its very bigness coupled with its comparative newness as a heavily populated state lead to an incohesive situation. The economic interests of its population are many because of the multitude of industries. Regional needs further divide its people while the splits in social and political philosophies due to the different origins of its populace make the state enigmatic to all who seek leadership through unification of supporters. While the Democrats have maintained a majority of the registered voters since 1934, each election demonstrates once more that California voters lack party loyalty and can always be depended upon to vote for a candidate as an individual regardless of his party affiliation.

With the 1916 snub of Governor Hiram Johnson by Charles Evans Hughes, with its disastrous results for Hughes and the Republicans, each presidential candidate has wooed California voters with increasing vigor. Although California delegates had played a prominent role in the 1932 nomination of Franklin D. Roosevelt, it was only in 1916 and later with Nixon's 1968 victory that the courting had had any dramatic effect on a national election. As California has grown it has witnessed each succeeding presidential candidate fighting harder and harder to win California support. In fact, the necessity of seeking California's vote emerged crystal clear since it was this state's forty electoral votes which gave Nixon the required majority. Nixon's electoral vote total of 301 would have been nine short had he not received the votes of California, although it is true that he added four more Southern and Border states—North Carolina, South Carolina, Missouri and Delaware—to his 1960 total.

Nixon's victory has been described by the *Sacramento Bee* and others as "the most remarkable comeback in political history." Defeated by Kennedy in 1960 and automatically eliminated from an elective national office as a base of operations, Nixon sought to rebuild by unseating California's Governor "Pat" Brown in 1962. Bitterly disappointed in this attempt he angrily renounced politics and shortly thereafter left the state to take up residence in New York. In so doing he reversed the trend of more than 100 years during which politicians had been moving West to further their ambitions. His departure from his native state was undoubtedly predicated solely on the fact that he had nearly lost the state to Kennedy in 1960 winning by only 35,623 out of 6.6 million votes, and on the thumping he had just received at the hands of "Pat" Brown. For until then Nixon had ridden the pinnacles of success starting with his win over Congressman Jerry Voorhis in 1946 and his election to the United States Senate in 1950. His rise had become meteoric with his selection as a running mate by Dwight D. Eisenhower in 1952. Only six years had then elapsed since he had been an unknown entering politics for the first time. Still, when he was nominated as the Republican candidate for President in 1968 he had not won an election in his own right for eighteen years. Once again it seemed that California voters were unpredictable: they rejected a man running for Governor, then supported him for President; they voted in Nixon, a Republican, and at the same time and in the same polling places they rejected the Republican Party's nominee for United States Senator, Max Rafferty, and elected instead a

Democratic candidate, Alan Cranston, whom they had rejected for the same office only four years before.

Nixon's razor-thin win in California in 1960, was a cliffhanger which was not definite until the tabulation of the 243,000 absentee ballots had been completed two weeks following the election. But that year Kennedy had already sufficient electoral votes without California. Still, at 6:00 a.m. the day following the election, Kennedy was leading, and on the second day after the election when the unofficial tally was completed, Kennedy was still ahead by 32,136 votes. While the ultimate outcome of California's election would not have changed the situation nationally it did center attention momentarily. This was due to the efforts being made by Republicans to switch the results in other states, principally Illinois, Missouri, New Jersey and Texas. Had these Republicans been able to change these states then California would have swung the election.[4]

In 1968 with more voting machines and the supposedly more perfected computer operations by the networks, California polls closed with the promise of another photo finish, this time with the state destined to end up being the deciding vote. Closeness in national and state elections was nothing new in California voting patterns—this marked the ninth presidential election out of the thirty in California history where the winning candidate had taken the state by less than 1% of the total vote.

An analysis of the 1960 and 1968 elections makes clear that both Kennedy

Table II

Marginal Presidential Victories in California

Elections	Voted for Loser	Winning Margin	Total Votes Cast	Percent
1912	Roosevelt	174	673,527	0.03
1880	Hancock	78	164,244	0.05
1892		290	269,098	0.11
1916		3,420	1,045,858	0.38
1948		17,865	4,021,537	0.44
1868		502	108,670	0.46
1960	Nixon	35,623	6,592,591	0.54
1896		1,987	320,421	0.60
1860		734	118,920	0.62

There have been nine presidential elections in California where the winning margin was less than 1% of the total vote cast.

and Humphrey lost by failing to win heavily in those areas generally favoring Democratic candidates. The San Joaquin Valley, the East Bay and San Francisco normally can be relied upon to support Democrats. In the Kennedy election all but two of the twenty-six counties which favored him were in northern California; Los Angeles and Ventura were the two southern counties.[5] Kennedy actually lost the election in California in the San Joaquin Valley where his winning margin was not sufficient to overcome Nixon's edge in the normal Republican areas of the state. The valley must be carried strongly in any close election for a Democrat to win. It was this vote which gave Harry Truman his majority in 1948, and it was this area which voted for Adlai E. Stevenson while he was losing in all other areas in 1956.

Nixon's margin in the eight traditionally Republican counties of Orange, Riverside, San Bernardino, San Diego, Santa Barbara, Marin, Santa Clara and Santa Cruz was 36,590 over Kennedy's plurality in the three Democratic areas. In order to win Kennedy needed 56.24% of the San Joaquin Valley to offset the lead and fell short gaining only 51.75%. Nixon captured four of the key and usually safe Democratic counties of Kern, Tulare, Stanislaus and San Joaquin. Truman's winning margin in the San Joaquin Valley was 55.03%. These results in the San Joaquin Valley were further highlighted by the fact that Nixon lost his home county of Los Angeles by 21,157 votes and would have proven to be his first defeat in California had Kennedy pulled the votes generally expected in the San Joaquin Valley. Also of interest is the fact that Kennedy bettered Stevenson's vote in the staunchly Republican San Diego County by 8.74%. These figures point up the excellent organizational job done by Democratic leader Jess Unruh, the Kennedy–Johnson southern California campaign manager. And this, in spite of the fact that Kennedy ran 200,000 votes behind the local Democratic Party candidates for the state Assembly, in part because the citizen elements of the Democratic Party were embittered by his local alliances.[6] It also perhaps indicates the lack of leadership in southern California in the subsequent losing elections of "Pat" Brown in his bid for re-election in 1966 and Humphrey in 1968 when Unruh did not provide strong support and Democratic leadership faltered.

Humphrey's defeat in California was greater than Kennedy's but can be attributed to the same basic failure, falling far short of the necessary pluralities in areas which generally supported Democrats. He lost three of the same four San Joaquin Valley counties that Kennedy lost, saving only Stanislaus. Even so he came out of the nine San Joaquin Valley counties with only a 16,000 vote edge. The Bay Area, excluding Marin and Sonoma counties, did much better for Humphrey with the counties of Alameda, Napa, San Francisco, San Mateo, Santa Clara, Contra Costa and Solano all going against Nixon. But the 165,000 margin given Humphrey by these nine counties was wiped out by Orange

County alone which gave Nixon 166,000 votes more than Humphrey so that even had he won the same plurality in Los Angeles that Kennedy achieved, his loss in the San Joaquin Valley would have defeated him for Nixon had picked up another 94,000 lead in San Diego County and, of course, Humphrey lost Los Angeles County by 43,000. Since 1950 the majority of the population in the United States has resided in the metropolitan areas of the country. But whereas in 1960 the majority of the metropolitan area population resided in the central cities, by 1968 the majority of the metropolitan area population was residing in the suburbs. Of the metropolitan areas where more than one million votes were cast, only Los Angeles was carried by Nixon in 1968. And whereas Humphrey had carried Los Angeles City by 160,000, he lost the suburbs by 203,000.

In the Kennedy election a study of voter distribution by religious preference may suggest an answer to the San Joaquin Valley results. The "Catholic vote" undoubtedly aided Kennedy in some of the larger states that he needed to win. Still a strong and not altogether "Protestant vote" cut into the Senator's margin of victory in those states as well as nationwide. Within the San Joaquin Valley the religious issue probably figured more importantly than other parts of the state. A survey made by Facts Consolidated, an independent research firm, showed that of the normally Democratic voters who in 1960 went Republican, 77.5% were Protestants. Only 13.7% of the Catholic Democrats made such a switch. While religious prejudice in voting did not sweep the state, it could be spotted in certain sections. The San Joaquin Valley with its transplanted Oklahomans, Texans, Tennesseans and Arkansans is noted for its strong fundamentalist tendencies, especially in the four counties which Kennedy lost. Recognition of the religious factor becomes unavoidable when the Kennedy vote is compared with the fact that of sixteen congressional and legislative seats at stake in the valley in 1960, fifteen were won by Democrats and that these candidates received 57.28% of the total votes cast, which was 5.53% greater than their party's standard bearer.[7]

Humphrey's campaign of course was not affected by any religious factors, but it was marked from the beginning with the dissatisfaction which had grown against the Johnson administration because of urban riots, campus disorders and more especially the Vietnam war. But the San Joaquin Valley had developed its own local problem and this, more than those other issues which were occupying the voters' minds nationally, was the reason Humphrey did so poorly in that region. For the San Joaquin Valley is the center of highly developed "agri-business" and its hub, Fresno County, is the leading agricultural county in the nation. Dominating the farming throughout this end of the valley are the gigantic operations of large landholders who have historically profited through the use of cheap labor. Over one million Mexican-Americans or Chicanos as they refer to themselves provide much of the "stoop labor." From

1942 to 1964 this labor force was supplemented through the importation of Mexican nationals known as "braceros." During the Johnson administration and even before, labor leaders had commenced the organization of farm workers and were opposed to the continued use of "braceros." This strife has continued to grow and the controversy between the landowners, strongly supported by the business community, and the farm workers figured prominently in the campaign of Pierre Salinger and George Murphy for United States Senator in 1964, "Pat" Brown and Ronald Reagan for Governor in 1966 and in the Humphrey–Nixon 1968 elections. In each instance the Democratic candidate suffered heavy losses in the San Joaquin Valley by reason of his support of the farm workers.[8]

Perhaps no one has made a more searching analysis of why Nixon, the popular Eisenhower's heir-apparent and dominant figure on the national scene for fourteen years, lost to the not so well-known junior Senator from Massachusetts than Nixon himself. Stewart Alsop, probably at the time not realizing it, pointed to the real reason some weeks before the election with his penetrating analysis "Campaigning With Nixon." In this he discussed Nixon's problem in attempting to attract the large numbers of uncommitted voters so successfully won by "Ike" in his two great victories. In both the 1952 and 1956 elections over 61 million votes were cast. In the 1960 election the total was 68.8 and in 1968 it was 73.3 million. The non-presidential elections of 1954 and 1958 by contrast attracted only 42 million. Eisenhower twice grabbed off a majority of the 20 million "lazy" voters who only bother to vote in presidential election years.

Nixon obviously realized that his only chance of becoming the thirty-fifth President was in duplicating the feat performed by "Ike", and so Nixon's basic speech, made at stop after stop and parts of which were repeated in the television debates, was deliberately and expertly tailored to appeal to the great bloc of politically unsophisticated voters. Its theme was an over-simplified, anti-communist, pro-American approach geared to the magic word "Peace". It left many thoughtful independents wondering if Nixon really understood the basic issues facing the country.

The strategy had worked well for Nixon in 1946 when in his maiden political campaign he defeated the veteran New Deal Congressman Jerry Voorhis by effectively branding him a "fellow traveler" in his speeches, mailings and telephone calls. One 1946 campaign leaflet asserted that "a vote for Nixon is a vote against Communist principles." In 1950 when running against Helen Gahagan Douglas for the United States Senate his campaign issued the notorious "pink sheet" which drew sinister implications from House roll calls which found Mrs. Douglas' votes similar to "Communist Party lining" Representative Vito Marcantonio of New York in 354 issues over a six year period.[9]

Yet it was during this same period of Nixon's triumphs that the nation saw the beginning of what Samuel Lubell labeled the *Revolt of the Moderates*, the post World War II period's equivalent of Harding's "Return to Normalcy." After every great war, the public becomes fed up with the foreign crises and longs to return to the relative simplicities of internal affairs. The need for solutions to domestic problems which have been shunted aside because of international events becomes manifest. New ideas and new men to advance them are needed. The 1960 election was to prove that that time had arrived. Nixon's strategy failed to recognize this demand and thereby failed to attract a victor's share of the twenty million part-time voters.[10]

Kennedy became the youngest president ever to be elected by scoring where it counted most. He went after the bigger states losing only Indiana, Ohio and California. New York, Pennsylvania and Michigan fell into the Democratic column for the first time since 1944. Kennedy put together three key blocs of states. He carried six of the nine industrial states, eleven of the seventeen southern and border states, and three of the six New England states. Of the small states outside of these three blocs he won only four, Hawaii, Nevada, Minnesota and New Mexico. The FDR–JFK coalition of Big Cities and the Democratic South has been said to be as unmanageable as Hubert Humphrey and James Eastland on the one hand and Nelson Rockefeller and Barry Goldwater on the other.

In his 1968 comeback Nixon demonstrated he had studied well and profited greatly by his losing experiences in 1960 and 1962. From the start his 1968 campaign was a well-calculated program aimed at appealing to the voters' basic desire for peace at home as well as abroad. He promised to end the war in Vietnam, he spoke out for an end to urban riots and campus disorders, and he stood foursquare for law and order and an end to crime. He would not disclose his end-the-war-in-Vietnam plan and did not attempt to spell out his solutions to the other problems, so that he gained support without risking a loss of support from voters who might have disagreed with his specific methods of resolving the complex domestic issues. He again stuck with a stereotyped speech carefully written to create the image of a new Nixon and this time avoided any unrehearsed confrontations. The image makers' efforts to create a "new Nixon" were largely successful despite the *Newport Argus Champion* and others who commented "There is no new Nixon. What we have here is the old Nixon, a little older." Especially did he dodge a repetition of the nationwide television debates. And this time he did not waste his effort campaigning in every state but sought out centers of population winding up his campaign with a gigantic and well-rehearsed rally in Los Angeles which was televised throughout the nation.

His extreme caution almost led to a mistake but events proved it not to matter. This was his selection of Spiro T. Agnew as his running mate. Nixon offered to make Lieutenant Governor Robert Finch of California his running mate the morning after Nixon won the Republican presidential nomination, but Finch declined, and within hours Nixon decided on Agnew as his second choice. As Governor of Maryland, Agnew was totally unknown to the nation. Agnew's ineptness on the national scene quickly became apparent with some unguarded references to ethnic groups, such as "Polacks" for the Polish and "Fat Japs" for the Japanese. While these were embarassing to Nixon, fortunately for him they had little or no effect on the election.

Humphrey, on the other hand, was forced to throw caution to the winds and indulge in a free-swinging, fighting campaign, striking directly at issues and offering specific solutions. He, too, concentrated on the heavily settled areas, and the closeness of the 1968 election will leave forever unsettled the contention that had he been an earlier starter in the presidential sweepstakes the outcome would have proven different.

A popular axiom in American political history has been, "As Maine goes, so goes the Nation." What validity this phrase has had has never really been determined. At best it can be said that Maine voted in September and the rest of the nation in November. Since Maine's election law was altered in 1958, this September date is no longer true as the presidential and state elections are now combined. An analysis of key presidential elections of the past would indicate that it would be far more meaningful to say, "As the 'Big Six' go, so goes the Nation." The six states referred to—New York, California, Pennsylvania, Illinois, Ohio, and Michigan—each have over twenty electoral votes at the present time. Texas, which has twenty-five electoral votes is omitted from a potential "Big Seven" because as a southern state, it has not for the past 100 years presented a true two-party picture.

In sixteen of the last thirty-one presidential elections the winning candidate has carried all of the "Big Six" states. In only nine elections has the victor lost more than one of them. And in only three elections of the last thirty-one— 1848, 1884, and 1916—has the winner lost more than three of these key states. Over this same period, these six states taken individually have failed to be on the winning side only thirty-four times out of 186.

Political analysts have thought it significant that in the forty-six presidential elections in our nation's history, the victorious candidate has lost New York State but five times—1856, 1868, 1876, 1916, and 1948. The 1968 election adds one more time. Significant as this statistic undoubtedly is, it certainly carries far more weight in an historical analysis of the nineteenth-century political past than in any attempted prognostication of the twentieth-century political future. In all three of the elections in the present century where New York voted for the loser, California in each instance voted for the winner.

Prior to 1916, of course, this certainly was not true; one needs only to cite

'*For you, Spiro, we'll work on the image of silent wisdom.*''

(Courtesy of *San Francisco Examiner*.)

the elections of 1848 and 1884, two of the three instances in which the winning candidate lost more than three of the "Big Six" states. In each case, his capture of New York's bloc of electoral votes was sufficient to offset what might have been a ruinous loss. An equally noteworthy but completely different example of New York's decisive role in the national politics of the nineteenth century is to

409

be found in the election of 1888. A Cleveland victory in New York in that year would have deprived Benjamin Harrison of his electoral majority despite the latter's capture of all but two of the other northern and western states.

The election of 1848 is of interest for several reasons. Tuesday, November 7, 1848, marked the first time all the states had observed a uniform election day. This election also was one of only three in which the party capturing the White House failed to secure control of either house of Congress. When the Republican Party registered the second such failure in 1956, despite the avalanche of votes favoring a second Eisenhower term of office, political commentators sought to draw parallels with the earlier contest because in each case a popular war hero had won the presidency. However, the picture presented by the 1848 election was a considerably more complex one.

In that year the race for the presidency was a three-way one, between General Zachary Taylor, the crusty old hero of the Mexican War; Lewis Cass of Michigan; and former President Martin Van Buren. Taylor and Cass were the major party candidates, having been nominated by the Whigs and the Democrats respectively. Van Buren was making his third bid for the Presidency, this time on a third-party ticket, the Free Soilers. The latter candidacy was to be of negative significance for while Van Buren received no electoral votes, he polled 291,263 popular votes. Of this total, 120,510 were garnered in New York. This was enough to remove the state from the Democratic column and place it behind the Whig Party. Thus, had it not been for Van Buren and his Free Soil supporters in New York, Cass would have defeated Taylor by a margin of thirty-six electoral votes. As it was, Cass and Van Buren jointly received 52.64% of the total popular vote cast in the country.[11]

A second instance where a shift of the New York electoral delegation would have changed the results of a presidential election was in the contest of 1884. This election presents the only case where a candidate has lost five of the "Big Six" states and still defeated his opponent. New York was the only one of the six states carried by Grover Cleveland, but this was enough to give him the victory. The famous "foot-in-mouth" statement of the Reverend Mr. Burchard concerning the Democratic Party's affinity for "rum, Romanism, and rebellion" undoubtedly accounts for the decisive, last-minute shift of New York's Catholic vote which delivered the state to Cleveland. The margin by which James G. Blaine, the "Plumed Knight" of the Republicans, lost New York and with it his hopes of extending his party's long tenure in Washington was a scant 1,149 votes.[12]

Cleveland's fate in 1888 was the very opposite of what it had been four years earlier. Benjamin Harrison, grandson of former President William Henry Harrison, carried every one of the "Big Six" states. Once more the popular vote margin between the rival candidates in New York State was a narrow one

—13,002 out of a statewide total of 1,315,373. This time, however, the edge was to the Republicans. If Cleveland, instead of Harrison, had received the New York bloc of electoral votes, he would have had a majority in the Electoral College and been re-elected as had happened four years earlier. Cleveland was to have his revenge in 1892, however, when he decisively turned back Harrison's try for a second term.[13]

In all three of the presidential elections which Cleveland entered—1884, 1888, and 1892—he won a majority of the popular vote. Thus, in 1888, the eccentricities of our Electoral College system gave the United States a minority president for the third and last time to date. Also, it may be noted that in no election since 1888 could a shift of the electoral votes of just New York State alone have altered the outcome of a presidential race.

The makeweight role so fatefully played by New York on occasion in the nineteenth century seems to have been passed across the continent to California in the twentieth. Certainly the three elections in this century where the winning candidate did not carry a majority of the "Big Six" states—1916 and 1948 and 1968—would lend firm support to this contention. It was during the first of these elections that Charles Evans Hughes, the Republican candidate, went to bed on election night thinking he had turned back Woodrow Wilson's second-term attempt; while it was during the second that Thomas E. Dewey sat through the long election night watching Harry Truman do the impossible. Although from 1916 on, California voters became increasingly important to presidential candidates, their choice was not to decide another election until fifty-two years later when in 1968 California put Nixon over the required 270 electoral college votes. For although Truman in 1948 carried California by the narrowest of margins, he would have been elected without this state. A different, but equally determining, role was played by California in the preliminaries of the 1932 campaign.

Hughes' seemingly over-confident mood had, perhaps, been justified at the time he retired, since the returns from the eastern section of the country had been most encouraging, and, during the night, extras came off the New York presses conceding the election to Hughes. However, by the next morning, it had become apparent that California, by the slim margin of 3,420 popular votes, had returned Wilson to the White House. If California's electoral votes had gone to Hughes, he would have been the winner in the Electoral College by one vote. This final outcome in 1916 was all the more stunning, since in this very state where the Republican Party's national hopes had been foiled, California's popular Republican Governor Hiram Johnson had won a United States Senate seat by some 300,000 votes.[14]

This strange contrast was not altogether coincidental. Hughes had failed to master the intricacies of California's intraparty politics. More out of political naiveté than from firm political convictions, he had allowed himself to fall into the arms of the state's moribund Republican Old Guard. Under the not disinterested guidance of this ultra-conservative group, Hughes ignored the progressive Johnson, the first man to win a second gubernatorial term in sixty-one years. The latter, who had also shown his strength with California voters in 1912 when as Teddy Roosevelt's running mate he had helped carry the state for the Bull Moose ticket, later gave limited and indifferent support to Hughes' candidacy. Hughes, one might say, helped to beat himself by his inept alignment with the wrong group at the wrong time.

The astute New York congressman, John W. Dwight, remarked that Hughes could have been elected for a dollar if a man of good sense, with a dollar, would have invited Hughes and Johnson to his room when they both were in the Virginia Hotel on that pleasant Sunday morning in Long Beach. He would have ordered three Scotch whiskies, which would have been seventy-five cents, and that would have left a tip of twenty-five cents for the waiter. That little Scotch would have brought those men together; there would have been mutual understanding and respect; and Hughes would have carried California and been elected.

Thirty-two years later, California, in conjunction with Ohio, again played a leading role in capping a national election with a startling result. President Truman's tremendous victory in 1948 is probably the most baffling in all of American political history. No candidate has ever had to face up to more gloomy portents. The Republicans had won the mid-term elections in 1946. The left-wing elements of the Democratic Party had departed the ranks with Henry A. Wallace, even as had the right-wingers with Strom Thurmond. The big city Democratic leaders were looking out the window as Truman heroically carried on his whistle-stop campaign. The Republicans had again nominated Thomas E. Dewey of New York who had waged a futile campaign against FDR's fourth term bid. Roosevelt, in the middle of the world's most fearsome war, scarcely gave a thought to his re-election. His most formidable champion within the Cabinet family, the old curmudgeon, Interior Secretary Harold L. Ickes, dismissed Dewey as "the little man on the wedding cake," a skillful ridicule of the mustached Dewey's dapper appearance. But the Dewey backers explained away this defeat with the perhaps valid reasoning that he had been given an impossible assignment in being pitted against the invincible FDR, particularly in the middle of a war. Now, the Republicans had the taste of victory already in their mouths. And this confidence was not without foundation. Every pollster in the country was predicting Dewey's victory. As the results poured in on election night, it soon became evident that New York, Pennsylvania, and Michigan all had fallen to Dewey, and the *Chicago Daily Tribune* headlined "Dewey Defeats Truman."[15]

Yet in the final analysis, Truman had the voters on his side. The final tally

The famous news photo showing gleeful President Harry S. Truman (1884–   ) holding aloft the *Chicago Daily Tribune* with its premature headline that he had been defeated by Dewey. (Wide World Photos.)

showed this election to have been one of the closest on record. If just 8,933 voters in California had voted for Dewey instead of Truman, and if just 3,554 voters in Ohio had voted for Dewey instead of Truman, a total of fifty electoral votes (twenty-five in each state) would have been lost from the Democratic column. The 253 electoral votes left to Truman would have been thirteen short of the requisite majority. Since the Dixiecrats' Thurmond had received thirty-nine of the Deep South's electoral votes, however, Dewey would have had only 239 even with the change suggested above. As in 1800 and in 1824, the election would have been thrown into the House of Representatives. Hence, it is not unjustified to say that Truman's phenomenal victory was dependent on the fewer than 25,000 popular votes, out of a nationwide total of 48,836,579, which represented his winning margin in California and Ohio.

There was nothing so narrow about the Democratic victories in California during the era of Franklin D. Roosevelt. Four times running, F. D. R. scored

413

smashing triumphs in the nation and in the state—a fact political commentators are not likely to forget. An aura of invincibility came later to surround Roosevelt. In achieving his unprecedented series of victories, he not only became the first Democratic candidate since Pierce in 1852 to receive a majority of the popular vote, but also performed this feat four consecutive times. In none of the other eight successful Democratic bids for the presidency (Buchanan, Cleveland, Wilson, Truman, and Kennedy) did the candidate receive a popular majority.

Political commentators are not so likely to remember the key role played by California in Roosevelt's nomination. In 1932, the Democrats still followed the two-thirds rule in their nominating conventions. The potential divisive effect of this outmoded device had been amply illustrated eight years before at what still remains the longest political convention in the nation's history. The delegates to the 1924 Democratic Convention had had to endure through 103 ballots in the sweltering heat of Madison Square Garden before picking John W. Davis as the party standard-bearer. Party leaders such as House Speaker John Nance Garner, one of Roosevelt's leading rivals for the nomination, began to fear that such a marathon might be repeated in 1932 when by the end of the third ballot Roosevelt had a simple majority, but was still short of the necessary two-thirds. William Gibbs McAdoo, President Wilson's son-in-law, and William Randolph Hearst, "Lord of San Simeon," took the initiative in dealing with the problem. Together with Jesse W. Carter, later to be a distinguished Associate Justice of the California State Supreme Court, they proceeded therefore to engineer a switch of the California delegation from Garner to Roosevelt. With the presidential nomination thus secured for F. D. R., second spot on the ticket was handed to "Cactus Jack" as a consolation prize.[16]

In less than forty years, then, California filled a strategic role in two hairbreadth presidential decisions. Both in stunning the nation in 1916 and in helping Harry S. Truman stun the nation in 1948, the California electorate caused the seemingly impossible to happen. In addition, California helped return to the national scene the most dominant American political figure of the first half of the twentieth century. It was no longer New York that changed election results as had been the case in the nineteenth century. Ironically, in 1916, 1948 and 1968, New York voted for the loser. California, until the election of 1960, had voted for the winner in every election but one since 1884. Only in the three-way contest of 1912 had she backed the defeated candidate, giving eleven of her thirteen electoral votes to Theodore Roosevelt.

Since the Mexican War and California's admission to the Union, California has voted Democratic in presidential election years eleven times. Only New York and Illinois among the other "Big Six" states have done so a greater number of times. Ohio comes close to this with a record of supporting the Democratic nominee nine times, while Pennsylvania and Michigan voted similarly eight times. Texas, on the other hand, has only voted for two Republican candidates for President, Hoover and Eisenhower, in its entire history. Furthermore, in belatedly swinging to Nixon, California lined up with the loser for just the fourth time in her 122 year history under American rule. Only Illinois can make that same claim during this same period of time.

The night-long uncertainty of 1960's election night was deepened by the ambiguous electoral situation in Alabama, Georgia and Mississippi. In the latter two states unpledged slates had been elected, while in Alabama six of the eleven electors chosen by the seldom-used congressional district method had indicated their unwillingness to vote for Senator Kennedy. There was a possibility, although doubtless a slim one, that this situation coupled with a near-even split between Kennedy and Nixon electoral votes in the other states would throw the election into the House of Representatives. An unqualified claim of victory on the national level was not made by the Kennedy forces until Minnesota's eleven electoral votes were finally nailed down.

Discontent in the South in 1960 with the national Democratic leadership encouraged the Republicans to make great efforts throughout this area. Arizona's arch-conservative Republican Senator, Barry M. Goldwater, criss-crossed the region seeking to convince southerners of the benefits to be derived from closer ties between Republicans from the North and Democrats from the South.

If the nation should witness the development of a true two-party system in the South, then a nationwide realignment within the two parties would inevitably take place. In such a realignment the Far West would hold the key to the future, for already the balance of power in the Democratic delegation in Congress has started to move westward. California, naturally, will have the major role in this shift of power. Of the sixty-nine congressmen assigned to the thirteen far western states, thirty-eight belong to California. Forty of the ninety-five electoral votes of this region are Californian. The importance of this latter point will become more and more evident as the once-solid South slowly breaks up. Formerly, the Democratic Party could count confidently upon the 128 electoral votes of the eleven southern states, reasonably hope to add to this the fifty electoral votes of the six border states, and thus be only ninety-two electoral votes short of the necessary winning majority. Now, more and more, southern and border-state defections will have to be made good from the far western bloc. Following the 1970 census, the far western states will receive seven additional congressmen with California getting six. The electoral votes of the region will then total 102, with California having forty-six. The southern states will only have a net gain of one. California, it may be safely concluded, will play a role of ever-increasing importance upon the national political scene as the United States moves on into the future.

The 1968 campaign year has been called "A year of political surprises." It

415

certainly was one of surprise, disappointment, and tragedy. Actually the campaigning had started long before the dawn of the new year. Nixon had been working ceaselessly, almost from the time he left California in a huff to take up residence in New York, towards the fulfillment of his ambition which had received such drastic setbacks in 1960 and the gubernatorial campaign of 1962. As Senator Everett M. Dirksen of Illinois summed it up at the end of Nixon's victorious campaign, "He wanted to be president hard enough to pay the price in toil, sweat, and tears, and tears were not the least part of it." Throughout these dark years Nixon had been tireless in his efforts to stay before the public as a Republican national leader. Globe-trotting constantly to maintain his posture as a spokesman on international policy, he also made himself available throughout the nation to speak at Republican affairs and in behalf of Republican candidates at all levels. He worked diligently to maintain the strong ties with party leaders and to assure himself of having the necessary votes at the Republican National Convention when the time came.

Other prominent Republican hopefuls were also working. Nelson Rockefeller, while publicly disclaiming interest in again seeking the nomination after his defeat by Goldwater in 1964, maintained his public base as New York's Governor and quietly worked toward the day when opportunity would again present itself. Michigan's governor, George Romney, was an early avowed candidate—perhaps too early, for as an open candidate his actions received harsher judgment than those of others. In an effort to present himself as one equally knowledgeable on foreign affairs as Nixon appeared to be, he visited Vietnam and endorsed the Johnson policies. When he later detected a change in public opinion he sought to disclaim this endorsement with his now famous statement that he had been "brainwashed." It was this blunder which undoubtedly lost him support and caused his ultimate failure. On this point Senator Eugene McCarthy, when asked if Romney's brainwashed statement had killed his chances, said, "Not really. Anyway I think in that case a light rinse would have been sufficient." Ronald Reagan, riding high from his 1966 victory over "Pat" Brown, the man who had defeated both Knowland and Nixon, had been stricken with an acute case of "Potomac fever," and although he constantly denied any interest in becoming a presidential candidate, those close to the scene were witnesses to his behind-the-stage build-up which belied his words. Nixon, in the face of Reagan's coyness, remarked, "The Governor appears to be becoming a more active non-candidate." By the time Rockefeller and Reagan finally admitted to being candidates it was too late. Nixon had by then more than enough delegates solidly committed.[17]

On the Democratic side campaigning prior to 1968 had also started. Senator Robert F. Kennedy had left his job as United States Attorney General shortly after Johnson succeeded Kennedy's assassinated brother and jumped successfully into the race for United States Senator from New York. Political observers saw this as a move to disassociate from the Johnson administration so that he could later seek the presidency himself. And Senator Eugene McCarthy of Minnesota had announced as a candidate for the presidency in November, 1967. McCarthy's candidacy was based upon his disagreement with the administration over Vietnam. He became the leader of the "doves" and as such appealed tremendously to the young people. This, of course, was essentially the same group from which the Kennedys received such strong emotional allegiance. So identical were the groups from which McCarthy and Kennedy elicited almost fanatic support that Governor John B. Connelly of Texas accused McCarthy of being a "stalking horse" for Kennedy. Meanwhile, former Governor George C. Wallace of Alabama had unofficially launched his third party drive appealing to the Deep South and the right wingers, the same groups for which Barry Goldwater had been such an attraction in 1964.

Officially the 1968 campaign commenced with Nixon's not unexpected declaration on February 1 of candidacy in the New Hampshire primary. On February 8, Wallace formally announced his third party drive declaring he would keep peace on the streets if it took "30,000 troops . . . with two foot long bayonets" and that he would change the "so-called civil rights laws," which he said were in reality "an attack on property rights, free enterprise and local government."

Although it was expected that President Johnson would seek a second full term, on February 10 the Americans for Democratic Action's national board endorsed, by a vote of sixty-five to forty-seven, the candidacy of McCarthy. It was the first time in twenty years that the organization did not support an incumbent Democratic president.

On February 28, just twelve days before the New Hampshire primary, Romney made a startling announcement in Washington. He was withdrawing from the race because he had failed to obtain broad-based Republican support. Political observers attributed his withdrawal to the fact that private polls had shown he would do poorly in New Hampshire and also that Rockefeller, one of his main supporters, had shortly before made a statement indicating his availability.

In the New Hampshire primaries on March 12, Nixon won 79% of the Republican vote with Rockefeller receiving 11% on a write-in. This was hailed as a great victory for Nixon because it showed that he had not lost his voter appeal. Actually this was like most of the rest of Nixon's primary campaigning, merely shadowboxing. He chalked up a string of victories without opposition from Lindsey, Rockefeller, Romney, Percy or Reagan. He was not only like his campaign slogan, "Nixon's the One," he was the only one. McCarthy polled, what to many was a surprising 42% of the Democratic vote against a 48%

417

organized write-in vote for the President. This success was not lost upon Kennedy who four days later officially announced his candidacy. Only a few months before Kennedy had stated he would support President Johnson and that he could not see himself as a candidate under any circumstances. But Kennedy had been under increasingly strong pressure by party leaders from various parts of the country to declare himself a candidate. Former Governor of Ohio Mike DiSalle had privately and publicly urged the Senator to run, as the only candidate who could unify badly shattered Democratic Party forces. In California, Assembly Speaker Jess Unruh, the state's most influential Democrat after the defeat of Governor "Pat" Brown in 1966, held numerous private conversations over the telephone and in person with Kennedy. Unruh has written:

> I told Senator Kennedy that if he was still reluctant to enter the Presidential race because he felt it would ruin the Democratic Party (a concern he had expressed several times to me privately) that he could forget it. In California, the party was already in a shambles. With only two days left before the deadline for filing of candidacy papers, fully half the Republican assemblymen in the California Legislature (19 of 38) had no Democratic challenger.
>
> We chatted briefly and hung up. But I felt sure I had touched the one thing that provided the biggest drag on a Kennedy candidacy—his fear of being accused of wrecking the Democratic Party. It may well have been the only thing on which Robert Francis Kennedy was afraid.[18]

In the end, Kennedy took the advice of Democratic officeholders such as Di Salle and Unruh while rejecting the advice of most of his staff members and ad hoc members of the "Kennedy clan," and declared himself a candidate for President of the United States.

The next big surprise occurred on March 21 when Governor Rockefeller announced, at a press conference which everyone believed had been called to formally declare his candidacy, that he would not run. This was followed ten days later by the year's biggest surprise when President Johnson, in a nationwide television speech called to discuss Vietnam and announce the unilateral cessation of bombing, dropped his own bombshell. At the end of a forty-minute speech in what almost seemed to be an afterthought, he made an announcement. It was made in such a low tone of voice in such a quiet and calm manner that many listeners missed or almost missed it and could hardly believe their ears. "I shall not seek," he said, "and I will not accept, the nomination of my party for another term as your president." Just four years previously Johnson had received the largest popular vote majority and the greatest percentage of the total vote cast ever won by a presidential candidate—61.1%, stamping out the records of Jackson, Harding, Roosevelt and Eisenhower.

On April 2, McCarthy captured fifty-two of Wisconsin's sixty Democratic delegates with 57.6% of the vote and 35.4% going to the delegation entered for President Johnson. Nixon, unopposed, won 81.3% of the Republican vote and all thirty of the state's delegates.

On April 23, McCarthy, the only presidential candidate of either party entered in the Pennsylvania primary received 76.5% of his party's vote while Nixon on a write-in carried off 76.3% of the Republican vote. Four days later Hubert H. Humphrey declared his candidacy saying that while he would run on the record of the Johnson administration, "I am my own man."

The following week, April 30, Rockefeller gave the public another surprise by reversing his earlier stand and formally announcing his entry, saying that people of all political persuasions had urged him to reconsider and he had been moved to change his position by the "gravity of the crisis we face as a people."

On May 28 in Oregon, Kennedy received a setback so unexpected to him that he all but withdrew stating that McCarthy's victory of 45% of the Democratic vote over his own 39% was a crushing defeat and had eliminated him from contention. The setback was the first Kennedy family defeat in a string of twenty-seven victories. On May 21 at the San Francisco Press Club Kennedy had said "I think that if I get beaten in any primary I am not a very viable candidate." Nixon meantime had picked up 73% of the Republican vote against a heavily financed and well organized write-in campaign for Reagan who polled only 23%. Rockefeller, also a write-in, received only 4%. Jess Unruh, Kennedy's California campaign chairman, has said he believes the Oregon defeat provided the first real impetus to the Kennedy candidacy. "People began to regard Bob Kennedy as a real human being, not some kind of a super-human politician who could do no wrong." As a result, in the week before the California primary, the heretofore lackadaisical California campaign began to come together. In the California primary campaigning had started off listlessly. Reagan had effectively fended off the entrance of any of the Republican hopefuls declaring that while he himself was not a candidate he would head up a "favorite son" delegation in order to give California a position of strength at the Republican convention. Events proved this to be an entirely false premise since by the time Reagan arrived at Miami and openly launched his candidacy, Nixon had things all wrapped up, and the California delegation had nothing left to bargain for. When Reagan did announce his candidacy, Governor David Cargo of New Mexico quipped, "It's like a woman eight and a half months pregnant announcing she's going to have a baby."

By the time Johnson announced his withdrawal and Humphrey had declared his candidacy, California Democrats had been lined up in either the Johnson delegation or the McCarthy and Kennedy camps. There ensued a mad scramble by many to jump off the bandwagons they were on and climb aboard with Humphrey. Tom Lynch, a weak and colorless Democrat, whom "Pat" Brown had appointed Attorney General more out of loyalty to an old friend than in recognition of him as a leader, put together a slate of delegates pledged to Humphrey from which most of the strong Democratic leaders of the state were notable by their absence.

Meanwhile, the dissidents were whooping it up and attracting considerable attention from the press. Wallace, sensing an opportunity, and obviously mislead by the amount of news coverage being given to those expressing dissatisfaction with the announced candidates of either major party, spent a disproportionate amount of time and money campaigning in California. But neither his American Independent Party nor the Peace and Freedom Party, another newly formed party, was successful in making any substantial inroads in either of the state's major parties. When it was all over the American Independent Party had registered 1.1% of the voters while the Peace and Freedom Party had registered 0.7%. Between the two, however, they had succeeded in entering candidates in forty-seven assembly, twenty-five congressional and fourteen senate districts and the Peace and Freedom Party had also qualified a candidate for the United States Senate. None of these candidates came close to victory. Probably the American Independent Party failure to file a candidate for the United States Senate was due to their affection for Republican Max Rafferty who was challenging veteran Senator Thomas H. Kuchel.

The Kuchel–Rafferty contest for the Republican nomination for the United States Senate then became the only primary contest in the state of any great interest. For, even after Johnson's withdrawal and Humphrey's entry, the three-way race between Humphrey, McCarthy and Kennedy did not generate the usual interest of a presidential campaign. The presidential primary took on some last minute spirited interest following Kennedy's defeat by McCarthy in Oregon the week before. McCarthy had been working hard in California even before Kennedy entered the campaign. After the Kennedy entry Democratic Speaker Unruh, who had performed so splendidly as southern California campaign manager for John F. Kennedy, undertook to manage the campaign again, this time for Robert Kennedy. The Humphrey campaign was a disorganized, underfinanced and badly managed effort. When the voting was over Kennedy was beside himself with joy over his comeback after Oregon. He had topped McCarthy 1,472,166 to 1,329,301. It was a remarkable recovery and again a demonstration of the organizational ability of Unruh. It is a terrible conclusion that the election night must go down as a great blot on California's political history. When Sirhan Sirhan shot Robert F. Kennedy that evening, it became the only successful assassination of a presidential candidate in the nation's history. The Lynch slate failed to get even a respectable vote, securing only 380,286 Democrats. George McLain, the senior citizen advocate, had polled substantially more votes than that, 646,387, in 1960 when he headed a presidential delegation in opposition to Governor Brown's favorite son delegation.

Many believed the California presidential primary was only an exercise and that Humphrey would get the nomination at the national convention regardless of the outcome in this state. Unruh did not share this belief. As one of the instigators of the Kennedy candidacy nationally, he was convinced that the Senator's personal magn,ism plus the Unruh political organization could win the state in November as well as in June. Events at the Chicago Democratic convention, and the apparent paper-thin degree of delegate support for Vice President Humphrey when a Ted Kennedy campaign balloon was launched there, at least make it possible that Robert Kennedy might have won the Democratic nomination had the tragic events of election night in California not occurred.

The role of the huge California delegation to the tumultuous Democratic National Convention in Chicago in 1968 was also noteworthy. The Californians, chaired by Unruh, were technically uncommitted, having been elected to vote for Robert Kennedy only hours before his death in Los Angeles. In the two months after that tragedy and preceeding the convention, Unruh skillfully filled delegate vacancies with McCarthy supporters, so that the unit that went to Chicago in August, 1968, was actually a coalition of anti-administration Democrats. Humphrey never made a real attempt to tie down any of the California delegates, and when the votes were counted, the Vice President had received less from the delegation than any other candidate, including Black Democratic leader Channing Phillips from the District of Columbia.

Denied an opportunity to participate meaningfully in the nomination process, especially after the unequivocal withdrawal of Senator Ted Kennedy as a possible presidential candidate, Unruh nevertheless made the California delegation a focal point. From his headquarters in Chicago's La Salle Hotel, Unruh engineered the only live, televised confrontation before any delegation of the three major presidential contenders, Humphrey, McCarthy and South Dakota Senator George McGovern. He established the almost unheard-of policy of having all delegation caucuses open to the press, and of holding the final meeting—when the 174 delegates cast their votes for the presidential nominees —before live television cameras.

The Unruh delegation in Chicago also was the largest single delegation to vote consistently in floor debates for those issues vigorously opposed by the Johnson–Humphrey strategists who ran the convention from the rostrum: the minority Vietnam plan, abolition of the unit rule from future conventions, to name two of them. Political observers conjectured that the television and press coverage Unruh received as a result of his convention leadership was more valuable to him in a future state-wide campaign than anything he had ever done before in California. But it was also clear that he had forged a coalition of the young, the liberals and the minorities to be reckoned with in future California politics.

Jess Unruh (1922–   ), Speaker of the California Assembly in 1968 and chairman of the Robert Kennedy presidential campaign in California, led the 174-vote California delegation to the 1968 Democratic convention in what many observers agreed was the most convincing public performance of his political career. (Courtesy of Jess Unruh.)

Racial groups seeking equality wish to be judged on their own merits, and people generally are loath to view themselves as less important than abstract generalities. No state is more likely to take note of such issues than California with its polyglot population. To its initial Spanish and Mexican people have been added people from most every nation and religion of the world. Each of these ethnic groups, while proud of their American heritage and proud of being Californians, still wear with pride their ancestral origins. They have formed their own separate lodges, clubs, neighborhoods, and even cities. As the United States is the melting pot of the world, California is the melting pot of the nation.

From the first mention of its name in the fifteenth century Montalvo novel *Las Sergas de Esplandian* to the middle decades of the twentieth century, California has signified a land of golden opportunity to the peoples of the world. Wave after wave of migration has crossed the Rockies and the Sierra Nevada, rounded the Horn and crossed the Isthmus. They have come by sailing vessel, prairie schooner and tin lizzie. And yet in the period since the great migration of the "Okies" escaping the dust bowls of the thirties, the flood of new arrivals has become greater and greater. On July 1, 1969 California's population reached 20,155,000, the first state to reach this magic figure. California's net gain in the last twenty-nine years is some 13,248,000 or nearly double its 1940 population of 6,907,000. This growth alone exceeds the total 1960 population of any state excepting New York, and is greater than the total population of such

422

countries as Australia, Ceylon and the Netherlands. Almost twice—7,949,000—as many people have moved to California since 1940 as lived in the entire thirteen far western states in the year 1900. These states, California, Washington, Oregon, Colorado, Arizona, New Mexico, Utah, Montana, Idaho, Hawaii, Wyoming, Nevada and Alaska, had a combined population of 4,330,000 at the end of the so-called great westward movement of the nineteenth century. Yet this number is small by comparison with the great westward movement into California alone during the last twenty-nine years. This latter migration is a swarm of humanity greater in magnitude than the number of all those who moved to the Golden State in the hundred years after the first overland party left Missouri in 1841. It has become the greatest mass migration in the history of mankind.

The growth of California's black population was slow from the mid 1870's

(Courtesy of the San Francisco *Chronicle*)

423

to 1940. Between 1850 and 1860 California's black population increased from about 1,000 to over 4,000 and constituted about 1% of the total population. Between 1860 and 1910, the black population increased to 21,645 but it constituted less than 1% of the total population. Beginning in the decade of 1910–1920, Blacks began to desert the South but this migration did not greatly affect the West. However, between 1920 and 1940, the black population of California soared from 21,645 to 124,306, with slightly more than one-half of the Black Californians concentrated in the Los Angeles area. It was during this time that Frederick M. Roberts was elected to the state Assembly from Los Angeles in 1918.

Since 1940 almost 1,300,000 Black people have sought homes in California and have located themselves generally in the areas of Los Angeles, San Jose, San Francisco and Oakland. Because of their numbers and the ever-increasing awareness that a voice in government is vital to their interest, they—in the last decade—succeeded in electing several Black men to political office.

Augustus F. Hawkins, Dem.-Los Angeles, served as state assemblyman from 1934 to 1962. He beat Roberts for the seat. In 1961 he introduced a bill, A.B. 801, which would have banned discrimination in all private housing offered for sale, lease, or rental by any person except the owner of a single-unit residence occupied by him as his residence. It was passed by the Assembly but failed in the Senate. He was elected as the first Black from California to the United States House of Representatives in 1962.

William Byron Rumford, Dem.-Berkeley, was first elected to the Assembly in 1948. In 1963 he proposed a new Fair Housing bill. The bill, A.B. 1240, would have banned discrimination in the sale or rental of all publicly assisted housing and all privately financed housing other than dwellings with four or fewer units. The Rumford Act was passed in the last frantic hour of the last day of the 1963 session and California became the twelfth state to enact a fair housing law. However, the Governor's signature had hardly dried when an effort got under way to qualify a referendum aimed at the law's repeal. But the repeal effort failed and the act became operative. The California Real Estate Association, however, launched a campaign to amend the Constitution so as to nullify the principal provisions of the Rumford Act, and by law, February 1964, the required number of signatures was obtained and the issue was certified for submission to the voters as Proposition 14. It was adopted by an almost 2-1 vote, only to be held unconstitutional, first by the California and finally by the United States Supreme Court.

John J. Miller, Dem.-Berkeley, was elected in 1966 to the seat being vacated by Rumford when the latter ran for the State Senate from Alameda County. Rumford was defeated, by 801 votes, and in 1968 when he ran again for his old assembly seat, Miller prevailed in the primary. In March, 1970 Miller was elected as Assembly minority leader when Unruh resigned the post to run for governor. This was the highest position of legislative leadership that a Black had attained. A three-way stalemate had developed between Joe A. Gonsalves of La Mirada with fourteen votes, Willie L. Brown, Jr. of San Francisco with thirteen votes, and Robert W. Crown of Alameda with seven votes, with twenty votes needed for election. Crown and Brown dropped their bids for the post to unite behind Miller, and Miller defeated Gonsalves, twenty to seventeen. Two assemblymen were absent, and on the earlier ballot, there had been three abstentions.

Mervyn M. Dymally, Dem.-Los Angeles, who was born in Trinidad, British West Indies, was elected to the Assembly in 1962 and became the first foreign-born Negro to serve in the California Legislature, and in 1966 the first Negro in California's history to be elected to the State Senate. Dymally represented the United States Department of State as a goodwill ambassador in 1964 when he toured seven East and Central African countries and in 1965, when he toured the Caribbean and British Guiana. In 1963 he was voted the Outstanding Freshman Legislator by Women for Legislative Action.

Five other Black people have held California state government posts. Reverend F. Douglas Ferrell, Dem.-Los Angeles, served two terms in the Assembly from 1962 to 1966. Willie L. Brown, Jr., Dem.-San Francisco, a successful attorney, was first elected to the Assembly in 1964. In February, 1969, he became the first Afro-American in state history to be elected to a legislative leadership position by being unanimously elected as state Assembly Democratic Whip. Yvonne W. Brathwaite, Dem.-Los Angeles, a vigorous civil rights attorney, was elected in 1966 to the state Assembly. Bill Greene, Dem.-Los Angeles, who had been the legislative advocate for the Building Service Employees International Union, Local 347, was elected in 1966 to be the assemblyman from the Fifty-third Assembly District. Greene was the first Negro to serve as an assistant Clerk of the Assembly and as a consultant to Assembly Speaker Jess Unruh. He was also legislative assistant to Dymally. Leon Ralph, Dem.-Los Angeles, a former administrative assistant to Assembly Speaker Jess Unruh, was elected in 1966 to be the assemblyman from the south-central Los Angeles Fifty-fifth District.

In 1962 Alfred H. Song, Dem.-Monterey Park, became the first Korean American to be elected to the state Assembly, and in 1966 won election to the State Senate. In 1966 March K. Fong, Dem.-Oakland, became the first Chinese American to be elected to the state Assembly. She was joined by the second Chinese American in the state Assembly in 1968—Tom Hom, Rep.-San Diego. Of these thirteen Black and Oriental Americans elected to the state Legislature in California, only Roberts and Hom have been Republicans, and eight of the thirteen have been from Los Angeles County.

In addition, Blacks have succeeded in being elected to school boards and

425

Willie L. Brown, Jr. (1934–   ) has long been interested in providing equal educational opportunities for all, and in 1969 authored a bill setting aside January 14, the birthday of Martin Luther King, as Black American Day in California's public schools. (Courtesy of Willie L. Brown, Jr.)

city councils. On May 27, 1969, a record-smashing turnout of 80% of the voting populace of Los Angeles, numbering over one million—15% of whom are Black—went to the polls and almost elected the liberal Black City Councilman Thomas Bradley over the incumbent Samuel Yorty as Mayor. Bradley, a former police lieutenant but now a successful attorney described as a soft-spoken non-mud-slinger, was defeated by only 55,000 votes by Yorty whose eight-year administration was said to be riddled with graft and corruption. The voters of the nation's third largest city were still not ready to elect a Black as their mayor.

The year 1958 had proved to be a bumper year for California Democrats. In the majority since the 1930's they had only succeeded in electing a governor for one term and gaining control of the Assembly briefly and intermittently during those years. But in 1958 they won every state executive office with one exception and, for the first time since 1880, control of both houses of the

426

Tom Bradley (1918–   ), Los Angeles City Councilman, got a ringing endorsement in his race for Mayor from Senator Edward M. Kennedy (Dem.-Mass.) Bradley was born on a Texas cotton plantation, the second of six children. (Courtesy of United Press International.)

Legislature. Behind the scenes had been the hard work of State Senator George Miller, Jr. of Contra Costa County and his aide and part-time secretary of the Democratic State Central Committee, Don L. Bradley. As chairman of the Democratic State Central Committee from 1952 to 1954 Miller had employed Bradley primarily to put together an organization aimed chiefly at picking up seats in the State Senate. Miller's theory was to gain control of the Senate first and then worry about the governorship. His strategy worked remarkably well. After 1951 the Democrats won every special election for the State Senate through 1958, six in all, for a net gain of four seats since two of the vacancies filled were already in Democratic hands.

Miller had come to the Legislature in 1947 when every state-wide elective office and both houses of the Legislature were in firm control of the Republicans. The following year he was elected to the State Senate in the primary by winning both party nominations. At the time he entered the Senate the Democrats were outnumbered twenty-six to fourteen. By 1956 they had achieved an even status with both parties counting twenty votes, and the 1958 elections gave the Democrats an overwhelming twenty-six to thirteen which soon became twenty-eight to twelve with the filling of the existing vacancy and the switch of veteran Senator Randolph Collier of Yreka from Republican to Democrat. In the Assembly the 1958 elections gave the Democrats forty-seven to thirty-three, and they had a majority of the congressional seats from California. So the Democratic landslide of 1958 had resulted in victories beyond Miller's hopes and the success he sought in capturing the Senate had culminated in a complete and devastating rout of the Republicans. By 1961 the Democrats had reached their

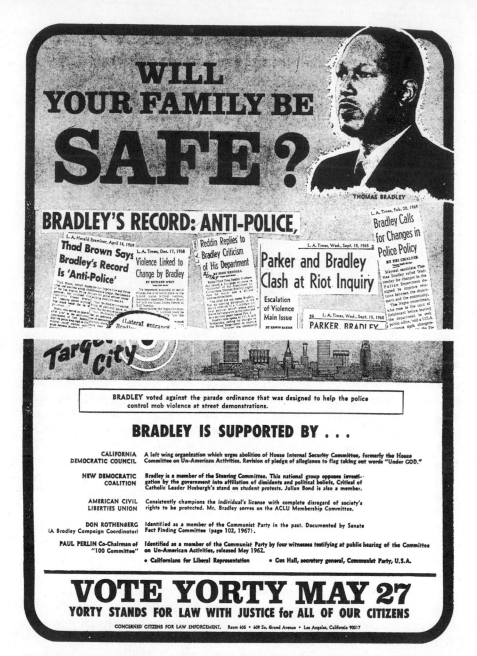

The Los Angeles mayoralty race became one of the bitterest political fights in all of
California history. Bradley outdrew Yorty by more than 100,000 votes in the fourteen
candidate primary, but Yorty used racial appeals and smear tactics to narrow the gap
and win in the general election. (Courtesy of *Los Angeles Times*.)

peak in the Senate with the Republicans left with twelve lonely votes. From that point on, the decline, which often follows an overabundance of strength, set in partly due to intraparty squabbling. Ironically, Miller's untimely death on New Year's Day 1969 restored to the Republicans the majority vote which they had lost the decade before. His death also marked the end of an era. The Democrats had lost a strong and colorful leader who, as much as any other single individual, had sparked the party to its position of control.

Thomas H. Kuchel, a native Californian and scion of a prominent pioneer Orange County publishing family, was elected by an Orange County district to the Assembly in 1936 at the age of twenty-six. He was elected to the State Senate in 1940. Appointed by Governor Warren to the office of State Controller upon the death of Harry B. Riley in 1946 he easily won election to that post the same year, and re-election in 1950. On the election of Nixon as Vice President in 1952, Warren appointed him United States Senator and in 1954 he was elected to complete the unexpired term, and re-elected in 1956 and 1962. Initially a conservative, Kuchel's long experience coupled with the hard facts of California and national politics had taught him moderation. In this he was in tune with his Republican colleagues in the United States Senate and was so well regarded by them that they elected him Assistant Republican Leader.

But Kuchel's moderate posture did not set so well with California's right wing. In 1962 right wing groups challenged his candidacy with Lloyd Wright. Another Republican challenger was Howard Jarvis. Kuchel withstood these primary efforts handily polling 1,357,975 Republican votes against Wright's 247,300 and Jarvis' 180,768. In the general election Kuchel faced Richard Richards, the Democratic State Senator from Los Angeles who had sacrificed his state senate seat to make the run. In this race Kuchel was again an easy winner with 3,180,483 votes against Richards' 2,452,839. Kuchel had received more votes than Democratic Governor Brown who was defeating Nixon. Only veteran Republican, Secretary of State Frank M. Jordan, opposed by a Democratic unknown, and incumbent Democratic State Controller Alan Cranston being challenged by a little-known right-wing Republican assemblyman, received more votes than Kuchel.

The 1962 election had shown that Kuchel's moderate position, while causing him some losses in the Republican ranks, was helping him maintain political power in the state because of his appeal to the Democrats. Undoubtedly because of his moderate position, as well as the fact that he was rankled by the efforts of the right wing to unseat him, he refused to endorse the candidacies of Barry Goldwater for President and George Murphy for United States Senator in 1964, and in 1966 he backed the former San Francisco Mayor George Christopher, gubernatorial candidate, in the Republican primary against Ronald Reagan, and refused to endorse Reagan in the general election.

429

By the time the 1968 election rolled around California Republicans were irate in their feelings about Kuchel. Disregarding the fact that Kuchel had twice been elected to the Assembly and twice to the State Senate from Orange County, and five times to state-wide office (State Controller twice and United States Senator three times) and had never been defeated, they set out to beat him. It was a clearcut case of spite overruling reason. For Kuchel had not only achieved a position of leadership in the United States Senate but his service in that body starting with 1954 had given him fourteen years of seniority, something badly needed by California to offset the usual domination which seniority had given to the southern states.

To many Republicans, however, party discipline was a far greater consideration than the welfare of their state in terms of maintaining a representative in the United States Senate whose seniority assured the state of a strong voice in that body. To effect this discipline they rallied behind the banner of Max Rafferty. Rafferty, a native of New Orleans, was a local school administrator until he popped into state-wide prominence in a hectic scramble in 1962 for the non-partisan office of State Superintendent of Public Instruction to succeed the retiring Roy Simpson. He ran second in a field of nine in the primaries, thus qualifying for a run-off at the general election. Espousing a return to the "Three R's" he quickly became the darling of the right wingers and won the November election by 200,000 votes out of a total of over five million cast, defeating Ralph Richardson who had been the leader in the primary. The message in this election was lost upon Kuchel who had so easily staved off the right wing challenge in his own race the same year.

The subsequent messages of the rise of the right wing, assisted by the militant and dissident actions on the city streets and college campuses, contained in the defeat of Nelson Rockefeller by Barry Goldwater in the 1964 California primary and the election of George Murphy to the United States Senate that same year, and also apparent in the defeat of Christopher by Reagan in the 1966 primary, in Reagan's election and in Rafferty's re-election that same year also escaped Kuchel. However, these signals were not lost on some of Kuchel's strong supporters. Sensing the possibility of Kuchel losing the primary and believing he could win the general against all comers if he could get his own party nomination, veteran labor leader Bryan Deavers, president of the State Building Trades Council, led a movement to switch Democrats into the Republican ranks before the primary. This effort to assure Kuchel of the Republican nomination had some success but fell far short of the necessary numbers. Kuchel himself apparently never appreciated the depth of his own troubles for he continued to devote his attentions to his senatorial duties and spent little time in California. He failed to rally such strong Republican leaders as Senator Everett Dirksen who undoubtedly could have swung a substantial number of Republican voters had he ventured to California to support Kuchel's campaign. His campaigning was far short of the Herculean efforts which were necessary for victory. When the votes were in, Rafferty had polled 1,112,947 against Kuchel's 1,043,315, a difference of 69,632 votes. Ironically, it was Kuchel's native County of Orange that had defeated him. Rafferty received 44,199 more votes in that county than Kuchel. If the county had given that plurality to Kuchel he would no doubt have gone on to victory in November. Many shocked Republicans said they only wanted to scare Kuchel, not defeat him, but the die was cast.

The Republicans' petulant "disciplining" of Senator Kuchel was all that kept their party from a smashing victory in the California general election of 1968. Kuchel's primary defeat had thrown the Senate race into a contest between Rafferty and ex-State Controller Alan Cranston, a former track star at Stanford, where he was a forty-nine flat quartermiler in 1936.

Elected to office for the first time in 1958, Cranston had been re-elected Controller in 1962 rolling up the highest total vote cast for any candidate in that election. Flushed with victory he jumped into the race for the United States Senate when it appeared the ailing popular Democratic Senator Clair Engle would be unable to stand for re-election. But Engle's friends were standing by him and resented Cranston's bumptious entry, despite Cranston's backing by Governor Brown. As it became more apparent that Engle could not in fact make the campaign effort believed necessary, Attorney General Stanley Mosk, who had received more votes in 1958 than any other candidate and was easily re-elected in 1962, toyed with the idea of making the run. When Mosk decided against this venture, Assembly Speaker Unruh, together with Mosk, prevailed upon Pierre Salinger to enter the contest. Salinger had been President Kennedy's press secretary, and had stayed on with President Johnson. His wide exposure to television news audiences by reason of his White House position had made him a public figure. Resigning his post, Salinger made a dramatic jet dash for California to file his candidacy just before the deadline. In a whirlwind campaign he swamped the lustreless Cranston in the primary only to lose to Murphy in November. Many reasons have been put forth by observers to account for Salinger's "snatching of defeat from the jaws of victory." There were many factors, including the bracero problem of the San Joaquin Valley which attributed to his losing, but his brash entry into the race was as much resented by many Californians as was Knowland's in 1958 and, of course, Cranston's supporters were bitter about Salinger having squashed their candidate.

In the 1968 general election party fortunes were reversed. Cranston had entered the race against Kuchel in the role of sacrificial lamb. His only serious primary opposition was State Senator Anthony C. Beilenson of Los Angeles who, with his supporters, quickly aligned with Cranston against Rafferty. The personal bitterness this time was within the Republican ranks where deep

431

resentments were held against Rafferty by Republicans angered by his defeat of Kuchel. Then, too, the many Democrats who had always supported Kuchel not only were appalled by Rafferty's extremism but were furious at him for costing the state a senior senator. The Cranston–Rafferty campaign became the hottest issue in the state drawing more attention than the Nixon–Humphrey race.

What really tore it for Rafferty was the disclosure by the *Long Beach Press Telegram* that Rafferty, who was conducting a hawkish campaign on the Vietnam issue even advocating the use of nuclear weapons, had dodged military service in World War II by reason of physical fitness despite the fact he was then employed as a physical education instructor. The stories, carried by the press throughout the state, revealed that he had walked with the aid of a cane all during the war years and dramatically thrown it away on VJ Day. When the votes were counted Cranston received 3,680,352 against Rafferty's 3,329,148, a margin of 351,000 votes. California voters had once again demonstrated their unpredictability and their willingness to consider the individual candidate over the party. The unbaring of Rafferty's willingness to fight as long as somebody else did it for him was without question the single factor of his defeat. With California being the home of the greatest number of veterans of any state, 2,783,000 of them, any story suggesting draft dodging or other military shortcomings is bound to do serious damage to a candidate. In this instance, many of his right-wing supporters, themselves war veterans, became disenchanted with Rafferty's candidacy following the exposé.[19]

With this exception the Republicans enjoyed their best year since the decline and fall of their party following the Warren and Eisenhower successes. They had won the United States Senate seat from the Democrats in 1964 and all other offices excepting Attorney General in 1966. They had reversed the trend of special elections from the days when the Miller-Bradley team were handily picking off legislative seats, and they were rapidly approaching control of both houses of the Legislature. Going into the 1968 elections the Senate stood evenly divided 20-20 while the Assembly remained under the control of Speaker Unruh with forty-two Democrats to thirty-eight Republicans. But the November elections turned the table and the Republicans with forty-one Assembly seats had won the speakership. This coveted chair went to Republican moderate Robert T. Monagan of Tracy, an able legislator with a decided independence from the Reagan administration policies. Unruh became minority leader, viewed by some as a stronger and more independent base from which to launch his anticipated 1970 campaign against Reagan.

Despite their overall gains the Republicans failed to improve their position in the Senate where all incumbents were returned leaving the count at 20-20. When the Republicans had achieved this status in 1966 they had held hopes of

1945   1968

RAFFERTY

"THE MAN WHO THREW AWAY HIS CANE ON VJ DAY."

GRAYSMITH

Boomerang

(Courtesy of *San Francisco Chronicle*.)

unseating the Democratic President Pro Tempore of the Senate, the veteran Fresno Senator Hugh M. Burns. They had based these hopes on the fact that the Lieutenant Governor, as President of the Senate, is permitted to vote in the case of ties. This in fact is his only function in the Senate over the pro forma handling of the gavel at the sufferance of the Senate. The real power has been vested in the President Pro Tempore since 1938, when outgoing Republican Lieutenant Governor George J. Hatfield, one of the most astute politicians of the century, pushed through rule changes stripping the Lieutenant Governor of authority in a maneuver to prevent his Democratic successor, Ellis E. Patterson, from having any real voice over the then Republican Senate. Successive senates have shown no desire to restore any power to the Lieutenant Governor even when he was of the majority party.

The genial Burns had been first elected to the Assembly in 1936 and after three terms was elected to the Senate in 1942. In 1957 he was elected President

Pro Tempore in a 20-20 senate with Republican Harold J. "Butch" Powers serving as Lieutenant Governor. Burns, by then a skillful politician, avoided embarassing his good friend Powers with a tie vote situation by securing two votes from Republican senators.

Now, ten years later, the Senate again evenly divided, the Republicans disdained the idea of recruiting votes from the Democratic senators, believing they could present Lieutenant Governor Robert H. Finch, elected by more votes than Reagan, with twenty solid votes and he would cast the twenty-first and tie-breaking vote. But Republican failure to agree on any candidate among themselves made their efforts abortive.

The untimely death of Senator George Miller, Jr. on New Years Day 1969, again raised Republican hopes and with the election of Republican John A. Nejedly to replace Miller, giving them an edge of twenty-one to nineteen, they made another try. Once again Republican failure to line up behind a single candidate and their rejection of a Democratic coalition left the popular Burns unscathed. This condition continued through the session until May when, annoyed by the actions of some of the freshmen and liberal Democrats in the Senate and the persistent efforts of Tulare County Republican Howard Way to strong-arm Republicans into electing him, Burns suddenly demanded a caucus of the entire Senate "to settle this question for once and for all so that we can get down to the business of legislation."

Most observers believed that Burns, the "old Pro," was moving with the certainty of a solid count, but the results proved disastrous when eight Democrats joined in a coalition and elected Way despite the fact that he still had failed to solidify the Republicans. One Republican supporter of Burns, Senator John G. Schmitz of Orange County, an avowed member of the John Birch Society, remarked: "It is perhaps more than accidental that so many of the swing votes which overthrew Burns came from former members of the Assembly, both Democrats and Republicans who were first elected to the Senate after reapportionment in 1966 . . . the consequences of his election by so curious a coalition may well come back to haunt him."

Two hundred and seventy-four days after Republican Senator Howard Way of Exeter became President Pro Tempore of the California Senate when a bipartisan coalition ousted Senator Hugh M. Burns of Fresno, Way himself was removed from the leadership position by a bipartisan group of senators dissatisfied with his leadership. He was replaced by Senator Jack Schrade, a San Diego Republican.

Six of the twenty-three votes Schrade received in a February 10, 1970, floor vote were crucial to Way's removal. They were crucial because each of the six senators had voted for Way on May 14, 1969, in his successful ouster of Burns. Switching their support from Way in 1969 to Schrade in 1970 were three

Democrats (George E. Danielson of Los Angeles, Mervyn M. Dymally of Los Angeles and Tom Carrell of San Fernando) and three Republicans (Fred W. Marler Jr. of Redding, John A. Nejedly of Walnut Creek and H. L. Richardson of Arcadia). It should be noted here that Schrade was reportedly elected President Pro Tempore in a caucus vote by a bare majority of twenty-one senators, and that two senators (Danielson and Nejedly) switched their support for Way in the caucus to support for Schrade on the floor.

The ouster of a Republican President Pro Tempore by another Republican in an election year and the subsequent revelation that the new President Pro Tempore had in 1969 accepted a major campaign contribution from a firm that would benefit from a bill being reviewed by a committee of which Schrade was a member overshadowed nearly all matters before the Senate.[20]

With the 1968 election California's role as a dominant figure on the national scene was established. Not only did the Golden State place, for the first time, one of their own natives in the White House, but it had been the key state in promoting his candidacy. Many Californians have reached positions of prominence nationally in this century, starting with Franklin K. Lane, Secretary of the Interior in the Wilson administration and the second Californian to achieve cabinet status. Herbert Hoover, although an Iowan by birth, claimed California residence. William F. Knowland held the post of majority leader of the United States Senate and Thomas H. Kuchel held an equally important position as Assistant Republican leader. Earl Warren became the Chief Justice while Richard Nixon served two terms as Vice President.

Commencing with Earl Warren, each succeeding California governor has been given serious attention by the press as a potential presidential candidate. Knowland thought the chances of a California governor obtaining the nation's highest office so likely that he forsook his lofty Senate position to seek the governorship. Knight, Brown and Reagan have all looked longingly at the White House.

With the actual capture of the presidency by a Californian it was only natural that some of his top selections would come from his home state. Lieutenant Governor Robert H. Finch became Secretary of Health, Education and Welfare. Other prominent Californians were quickly chosen to assist the new President including Herbert Klein, Virginia Savelle and Murray Chotiner. From the Assembly he selected the well-liked John G. Veneman, a moderate Republican from Modesto, thus reducing the Republican majority to forty to thirty-nine which shortly thereafter became an even thirty-nine to thirty-nine with the tragic and untimely death of the popular and respected Alan G. Pattee of Monterey. The Republicans made a fast recovery from this temporary setback by capturing both special elections and restoring their majority of 41–39 with Clare L. Berryhill replacing Veneman and Robert G. "Bob" Wood taking

435

Pattee's seat. Wood was dramatically sworn in only hours before his vote was needed to pass the budget bill.

Richard Milhous Nixon, in achieving his long and elusive objective of becoming President, established three firsts in the nation's history. He was the first President to come from one of the thirteen far western states and the first to come from California. He was also the first presidential candidate to run and lose, and run again and win since presidential electors began to be elected by popular vote in 1828. Finally, he was the first vice president in 132 years to be elected directly to the presidency. Other vice presidents had taken office as a result of a President's death and had then won a term in their own right.

California has voted Democratic in six out of the last ten presidential elections; it voted Republican twice for Eisenhower and twice for Nixon. With the rebirth of the Democratic Party in 1932, there have been nineteen general elections for the offices of governor or president out of which the Republicans have won ten. California has been notoriously independent over the state's entire political history. The past record of party defections on both sides has led observers to believe California more individualistic and volatile than any other key state.

Despite California's emergence as a new and lusty political giant, it is still experiencing growing pains. While the nation is just waking to the significance of California's rise to a position of commanding influence on national elections, the state is far from achieving the full power which normally would be held by the state with the greatest population. This, in part, is caused by its unpredictability. The experienced politicians of the older and more stable states of the East and North are wary of a state which time after time demonstrates its maverick tendencies. The South never has trusted California with its conglomerate populace and wavering philosophical positions. And even now with its capture of the administration, and its forthcoming new position in the House with what will be the largest delegation of any state following 1971, California still will not enjoy the strength of a political giant because the voters of California seem to be enchanted with the old political saw of "it's time for a change." They have not learned that under the seniority system which governs congressional power, mere numbers does not give strength. The southern states long ago recognized political realities and returned their congressmen term after term. Because of their seniority southern congressmen have a lock on most of the important committee chairmanships. California elected a new United States Senator in 1964 and another in 1968; yet it takes a minimum of two terms for a senator to achieve any position of power in that august body. Seniority in the House takes just as long and freshmen congressmen are a dime a dozen and have little more voice in the nation's affairs than the page boys. It takes years for a Representative to gain any authority on a committee, let alone become chairman. Until Californians recognize the importance of seniority in Congress the state will not fulfill its true status as a political power in national government.

The one thing about California which can safely be forecast is that in any election in the forseeable future the nation can look to the Golden State for surprises. Having swung back and forth like a pendulum throughout the twentieth century between conservatism and progressivism, between liberalism and reactionism, and between Republican and Democratic parties, its unpredictability is predictable. California's recent swing farther and farther to the right has even astounded the right wingers. As Nixon perhaps more readily than many others grasped the political make-up of the nation in 1968, the majority of people are "the unyoung, the unblack and the unpoor." The antics of militant segments of ethnic minority groups, coupled with what some call the fuzzy thinking of college professors, and student dissidents and radicals, have combined to bring about a period of reaction which has favored the election of conservatives. But there is always a high mark beyond which extremism, whether it be right or left, cannot go. Despite the thinking of those like George Wallace who contended that "there's more of us than there is of them," California demonstrated by the defeat of Rafferty that it is only willing to react up to a point. Whether the high level mark has been reached in the Bear Flag State cannot yet be ascertained, but it can be predicted that the peak will be reached in this decade, and the movement back to the middle and perhaps even a little to the left will take place, indubitably to be followed in time with another swing back to the right and so on. The astute politicians must then only be able to figure out precisely when such shifts will take place.

As dawn breaks on a new decade and California swings into its thirty-fifth gubernatorial election in the year 1970 the future of the Republican Party fairly glistens. Having recaptured both houses of the Legislature and all of the state's top political offices excepting the attorney generalship and one United States senatorship, the GOP looks forward to even greater domination of the political scene. Not since the early 1950's have they enjoyed such a hold on the state.

For the Democrats the curtain rises on a bleak scene. Time and dissension which seem to go hand in hand with the majority party have taken their toll. The political stars who led them to their victories have faded. It would seem they must now wait for the Republicans to falter and for the development of new personalities within the Democratic ranks before they can recover from the setbacks of the sixties. Whatever hopes they may have entertained to produce some attractive new candidates at the start of the new year received a dousing when two prospective candidates for Governor or United States Senator announced they would not seek office. These were Mayor Joseph Alioto and Dr. S. I. Hayakawa, both of San Francisco, both having risen to prominence

Governor Ronald Reagan (1911–) answers questions of the printed and electronic media at once a week press conferences during the legislative session at Sacramento. The Governor also makes frequent use of television and radio to report to the people of California. (Courtesy of Ronald Reagan.)

in the late sixties. And if they had hoped to retain the one state-wide office in Democratic hands, an office which had proved to be the stepping stone to the governorship for Earl Warren and "Pat" Brown, the announcement by Attorney General Thomas Lynch that he would retire opened the way.

As the year opened, the Democratic Party had only two avowed candidates for top state offices. Former Assembly Speaker Jess Unruh looked out upon a virtually deserted field for either Governor or United States Senator and declared himself for Governor. Of course he had been jockeying for just such a situation for the past eight years. Now he had not only gained an apparently clear field for the coveted office but found himself in the position of being the strongest leader in the Democratic Party. This latter status is somewhat ironical to members of the party organizations since it was Unruh who personally was responsible for much of the cleavage in the Democratic ranks. It was he who denounced the CDC, and it was he who had much to do with the injection of Salinger into the race against Cranston, and it was he who encouraged the maverick Democrat Mayor Sam Yorty's opposition of Governor Brown, and it was he who supported the Kennedys against Johnson and Humphrey.

Despite his somewhat rule-or-ruin machinations, Unruh's declaration for Governor immediately brought some surprising commitments of support even before any other potentials had an opportunity to come forth. Among these early surprise endorsements was that of Senator Cranston who might well have been in the United States Senate four years sooner had it not been for Unruh's maneuvering. Unsurprising was Yorty's skittish withholding of support for

Jess Unruh, (1922–   ) elected Speaker of the California Assembly in 1961, held that powerful office until January 1969 when Republicans regained control of the lower house. Unruh's tenure was longer than that of any other man in California history, and was marked by major improvements in California's legislative process. (Courtesy of Jess Unruh.)

Unruh, his former ally, accompanied by his not unusual maverick denouncing of Unruh, and the projection of himself as a candidate for governor.[21]

For United States Senator the young Congressman John V. Tunney of Riverside, scion of former heavyweight champion Gene Tunney, found himself in the position he had been seeking the previous year of being the only declared candidate. In the wings was Congressman George E. Brown, Jr. of Monterey Park, about to declare in the contest to unseat the song and dance Senator, George Murphy. And by the time that filing had closed, Supervisor Kenneth Hahn of Los Angeles County had become the third Democrat in the race for the United States Senate seat. As filing closed on Friday, March 20, for the primary election, the real surprise in the United States Senate race was the filing during the last hour in the Republican primary by Norton Simon, multi-millionaire industrialist and moderate Republican, who had earlier attempted to entice Robert H. Finch into the race.

The absence of many Democratic candidates for other top state-wide offices seemed to underline the self-proclaimed invincibility of the Republicans in the forthcoming general elections. Apparently encouraged by the belief that any Republican nominated in the primary was sure to be victorious in the November elections, the GOP girded for a knockdown dragout primary for the office of attorney general even before Lynch's withdrawal. Two State Senators, John L. Harmer and George Deukmejian, from Glendale and Long Beach, had declared themselves before the campaign year opened. Spencer Williams, the party's 1966 candidate and former Santa Clara County Counsel, resigned his post in the Reagan administration to make another attempt. With these three formally announced, Los Angeles District Attorney Evelle J. Younger who had been steadily preparing for the past four years, declared himself in, and many

Table III

Democrat	Office	Republican
Jess Unruh Former Speaker of the Assembly Inglewood	Governor	Ronald Reagan Incumbent Pacific Palisades
John V. Tunney United States Congressman Riverside	United States Senator	George Murphy Incumbent Beverly Hills
Alfred E. Alquist State Senator San Jose	Lieutenant Governor	Ed Reinecke Incumbent Tujunga
Charles A. O'Brien Chief Deputy Attorney General Danville	Attorney General	Evelle J. Younger District Attorney Los Angeles
Ronald Brooks Cameron Former United States Congressman Whittier	Controller	Houston I. Flournoy Incumbent Claremont
Edmund G. Brown, Jr. Attorney at Law Los Angeles	Secretary of State	James L. Flournoy Attorney at Law Los Angeles
Milton G. Gordon Former Real Estate Commissioner Los Angeles	Treasurer	Ivy Baker Priest Incumbent Los Angeles
George R. Reilly Incumbent San Francisco	State Board of Equalization First District	Leo Bagdonas State Board Auditor Santa Cruz

Democrat	Office	Republican
John W. Lynch Incumbent Tulare	State Board of Equalization Second District	Ann Root Corneille Accountant Oakland
William M. Bennett Former Public Utilities Commissioner Kentfield	State Board of Equalization Third District	Ernest N. Kettenhofen Agri-Businessman San Anselmo
Richard Nevins Incumbent Pasadena	State Board of Equalization Fourth District	Howard Jarvis Tax Reduction Expert Los Angeles
Wilson C. Riles Deputy State Superintendent Sacramento	Superintendent of Public Instruction Non Partisan	Max L. Rafferty Incumbent La Canada

observers said he would be the one to beat. The lone Democratic entry into the race was Charles A. O'Brien, the Chief Deputy Attorney General under Lynch, who had been itching to get into the race for some time.

The Democrats' apparent disregard of the importance of the office of lieutenant governor was proving to be an enigma to astute observers. Occupied by a Republican untested in a state-wide race who came into that office demonstrating an Agnew tendency to foot-in-mouth utterances, the lieutenant governorship seemed to be the best long shot of the campaign year for Democratic hopefuls. And since that office inherits the governorship in the event of a vacancy, veteran political watchers saw it as a possible Achilles' heel for the Republicans.

As the primary election on Tuesday, June 2, was concluded, and the votes were counted and tallied, the Republicans had nominated nine candidates for state office from Los Angeles County. Only in the three State Board of Equalization districts, where it was legally impossible to do so, had they not chosen candidates from the state's most populous county. In the race for the nomination for Attorney General, Younger had easily out-distanced his three rivals, polling more votes than all his opponents combined. In the Secretary of State's race, James L. Flournoy, a Black Attorney at Law, thoroughly surprised both the frontrunners, George W. Milias, Assemblyman from Gilroy and former chairman of the Republican State Central Committee, and Mrs. Alberta Jordan, widow of the late Secretary of State, who was attempting to continue the Jordans' hold on the office that extended back to 1910.

On the Democratic side Unruh buried Yorty under an avalanche of votes. Yorty told the television audience on election night that he was proud of his crusade to save the Democratic Party from the radicals. The crushing defeat of the Los Angeles Mayor should have proved to him that the Democratic voters of the state were finally getting tired of his constant criticism of Democratic Party candidates before coming out in support of those representing the opposing party. However, San Francisco Mayor Alioto immediately pledged his support to Unruh, and said that he would undertake any assignment that Unruh wished him to in the campaign. Tunney nosed out Brown, a battle of two anti-war doves, to earn the right to oppose Murphy, a pro Nixon hawk, in the general election. Edmund G. Brown, Jr., son of the former Governor, was to face Flournoy in the race for Secretary of State. He had decisively defeated Hugh M. Burns of Fresno, former President Pro Tem of the State Senate, who was trying for Slater's Democratic record of thirty-seven years in office. One more term would have done it. Now left with a chance in this decade to break the records of Lea, Collins or Slater were Hawkins, Reilly or Collier.

There was some evidence that the Republican Party also might not be completely unified. Henry Salvatori, southern California oil magnate and one of Reagan's close financial contributors, had openly attempted to defeat Paul N. "Pete" McCloskey, Jr., popular San Mateo County Congressman and former Marine war hero, for not supporting Nixon on Vietnam. McCloskey had won the primary easily. Simon, when capitulating to Murphy, repeated that Salvatori and his boys would have to be taken on. During the campaign Simon had also criticized Murphy for his $20,000 consulting contract with Technicolor, Inc. Rafferty, the outspoken state school superintendent, had barely failed to get a majority in the primary as he had done four years before, and would face Wilson C. Riles, his Black deputy state superintendent, in the finals.

For the 150 offices up in the 1970 elections, there could be at least twenty new faces in the coming year. There were four retirements, four deaths, and eleven running for other offices: three for Congress, two for United States Senator, two for Secretary of State, two for State Senate, one for Governor, and one for Lieutenant Governor. Of the eleven seeking other office, eight were successful, and only three were not: Brown, Burns, and Milias. Of the 134 seeking renomination, only one was not successful when he was beaten in his own party primary: Congressman Jeffrey Cohelan, twelve year veteran liberal, by Berkeley City Councilman Ronald V. Dellums, Black and able and militant.

With the general election ahead, an alleged secret plan held by the Republican

442

backers of Reagan was either really closely guarded or was not being given credence by the Democrats. Admittedly, the supposed plot seemed ridiculous at first blush but the logic advanced by those who claimed to know it to be true made it seem more plausible on reflection. The scenario to be unfolded had Reagan forsaking the governorship after the 1970 election to occupy the seat held in the United States Senate by his fellow movie actor Murphy. Of course, for this to work would require not only both Murphy's and Reagan's re-election but also the re-election of Reagan's Lieutenant Governor.

The reasoning for the musical chairs was based upon Reagan's and his backers' ambitions for his future. Enamored by his strong support for the presidential nomination in 1968, both he and his backers became inflamed with Potomac fever. Being realistic they knew that Reagan had to stay politically alive until 1976 since he could not run against Nixon who most certainly would seek a second term. As Senator, where he would not be as directly responsible for events which transpire as a governor is, the almost certain loss of popularity which is experienced by any two-term governor of California could be avoided. Further, the office of United States Senator offers a much better opportunity to travel around the country making campaign speeches for Republicans and endear himself to the party. Pointing out how "Pat" Brown defeated the veteran Senator William F. Knowland in the race for Governor by more than a million votes, and eight years later suffered a defeat of the same magnitude by a political novice, they argue that federal office is the only possible objective for Reagan to seek.

As further proof that the plan is not imaginary the studied efforts of the Reagan backers to keep former Lieutenant Governor Finch, whose moderate stands gained him more votes than Reagan in 1966, out of the 1970 Senate race are recited along with the claim that Reagan had declared he would run for the Senate if Finch entered the field. And to cinch it Reagan backers point out that Murphy would not be a candidate excepting for this plan of Reagan's backers who are also Murphy's backers.

But, as Robert Burns wrote, "The best laid schemes of mice and men Gang aft agley" so could the hopes of the Republicans for continuing victories and domination of the state's political affairs slip away because of an arrogance of success or a reversal of the bountiful economy or some other pitfall of political life. As for the opportunity of the Republicans to capitalize on reapportionment of the Legislature to insure continued power in the state, it would be well to recall that Republicans lost their power in the fifties after having control over the redistricting and that, with the Democrats dictating 1961 redistricting amidst irate charges of gerrymandering to insure their hold on the Legislature, the tables turned to benefit the Republicans. What those who have controlled the redistricting have apparently missed is the very phenomena which constantly puzzles the rest of the nation: California's population and its moods are in such constant flux that its course can only be charted from the stern for it can only see where it has been and not where it is going.

FOOTNOTES

1   The 1968 election figures are taken from Republican National Committee Research Division, *The 1968 Elections: A Summary Report With Supporting Tables* (Washington, D. C.: Republican National Committee, 1969), 269 pp.

2   Lynn W. Turner, "The Electoral Vote Against Monroe in 1820—An American Legend," *The Mississippi Valley Historical Review*, XLII (September, 1955), 250–273.

3   Ruth C. Silva, "The Lodge–Gossett Resolution: A Critical Analysis," *The American Political Science Review*, XLIV (March, 1950) 86–99.

4   "Will Kennedy's Lead Stand Up?" *U. S. News and World Report*, XLIX (December 5, 1960), 41–43.

5   State of California, *Statement of Vote: General Election, November 8, 1960.* Compiled by Frank M. Jordan, Secretary of State (Sacramento: State Printing Office, 1960).

6   Theodore H. White, *The Making of the President: 1960* (New York: Atheneum Publishers, 1961), p. 363.

7   The inept handling by Brown of the California delegation in 1960 is discussed in John H. Bunzel and Eugene C. Lee, "The California Democratic Delegation in 1960" in Edwin A. Bock and Alan K. Campbell, eds. *Case Studies in American Government* (Englewood Cliffs, N. J., Prentice-Hall, Inc., 1962), pp. 133–174. See also Eugene C. Lee and William Buchanan, "The 1960 Election in California," *Western Political Quarterly*, XIV (March, 1961), 309–326.

8   See the articles in Manuel Servin, *The Mexican-Americans: An Awakening Minority* (Beverly Hills, California: Glencoe Press, 1970), pp. 160–199.

9   William Costello, *The Facts About Nixon: An Unauthorized Biography* (New York: The Viking Press, 1960), pp. 64–67.

10   (New York: Harper and Brothers, 1956), Chapters 4 and 5.

11   Stefan Lorant, *The Presidency: A Pictorial History of Presidential Elections from Washington to Truman* (New York: The Macmillan Company, 1952), Chapter 16. While Lorant does a splendid job on presidential elections, another book vividly describes the national nominating conventions: Edwin P. Hoyt, Jr., *Jumbos and Jackasses: A Popular History of the Political Wars* (Garden City: Doubleday and Company, Inc., 1960), 505 pp.

12   *Ibid.*, Chapter 25.

13   *Ibid.*, Chapter 26.

14   *Ibid.*, Chapter 33.

15   *Ibid.*, Chapter 41.

16   *Supra*, Chapter 8.

17   Reagan's image of "the good guy in the white suit" was tarnished a bit the previous year with his circumlocutions regarding some homosexual activity in the Governor's office while he was away at the Republican National Governors' Conference. "Spots on Mr. Clean," *Newsweek*, November 13, 1967, 34–35.

18   Jess Unruh, "RFK: A Victim of the Image Makers", *Long Beach Press-Telegram*, June 9, 1969 p. B3.

19   A. J. Laugguth, "Would You Believe Senator Max Rafferty, R. Calif.?" *The Saturday Evening Post*, (October 19, 1968), pp. 60–67. See also Frank H. Jonas and John L. Harmer, "The 1968 Election in California," *Western Political Quarterly*, XXII (September, 1969), 468–474.

20   The material on the President Pro Tempore of the California State Senate in Chapter 13 and in the Appendix was taken in part from Douglas G. Detling, "The 1970 Leadership Change in the California Senate" (Unpublished Seminar Paper, Chico State College, 1970), pp. 1–2.

21   An excellent volume discussing the two gubernatorial rivals in the 1970 election is: Lou Cannon, *Ronnie and Jesse, A Political Odyssey* (Garden City, New York: Doubleday & Company, Inc., 1969), 340 pp.

APPENDIX

Governors of the State of California

NO.	NAME	DATE	PARTY	HOME TOWN
1.	Peter H. Burnett	December, 1849	Democrat	San Jose
2.	John McDougal	January, 1851	Democrat	Sacramento
3.	John Bigler	January, 1852	Democrat	Sacramento
4.	John Neely Johnson	January, 1856	American	Sacramento
5.	John B. Weller	January, 1858	Democrat	San Francisco
6.	Milton S. Latham	January, 1860	Democrat	San Francisco
7.	John G. Downey	January, 1860	Democrat	Los Angeles
8.	Leland Stanford	January, 1862	Republican	Sacramento
9.	Frederick F. Low	December, 1863	Republican	San Francisco
10.	Henry H. Haight	December, 1867	Democrat	San Francisco
11.	Newton Booth	December, 1871	Republican	Sacramento
12.	Romualdo Pacheco, Jr.	February, 1875	Republican	Santa Barbara
13.	William Irwin	December, 1875	Democrat	Yreka
14.	George C. Perkins	January, 1880	Republican	Oroville
15.	George Stoneman	January, 1883	Democrat	San Gabriel
16.	Washington Bartlett	January, 1887	Democrat	San Francisco
17.	Robert W. Waterman	September, 1887	Republican	San Bernardino
18.	Henry H. Markham	January, 1891	Republican	Pasadena
19.	James H. Budd	January, 1895	Democrat	Stockton
20.	Henry T. Gage	January, 1899	Republican	Los Angeles
21.	George C. Pardee	January, 1903	Republican	Oakland
22.	James N. Gillett	January, 1907	Republican	Eureka
23.	Hiram W. Johnson	January, 1911	Republican	San Francisco
24.	William D. Stephens	March, 1917	Republican	Los Angeles
25.	Friend William Richardson	January, 1923	Republican	Berkeley
26.	Clement C. Young	January, 1927	Republican	Berkeley
27.	James Rolph, Jr.	January, 1931	Republican	San Francisco
28.	Frank F. Merriam	June, 1934	Republican	Long Beach
29.	Culbert L. Olson	January, 1939	Democrat	Los Angeles
30.	Earl Warren	January, 1943	Republican	Oakland
31.	Goodwin J. Knight	October, 1953	Republican	Los Angeles
32.	Edmund G. "Pat" Brown	January, 1959	Democrat	San Francisco
33.	Ronald Reagan	January, 1967	Republican	Pacific Palisades

449

United States Senators
from the State of
California (Seat "A")

NO.	NAME	DATE	PARTY	HOME TOWN
1.	John C. Fremont	December, 1849	Free Soiler	San Francisco
2.	John B. Weller	January, 1852	Democrat	San Francisco
3.	David C. Broderick	January, 1857	Democrat	San Francisco
4.	Henry P. Haun	October, 1859[1]	Democrat	Marysville
5.	Milton S. Latham	January, 1860	Democrat	San Francisco
6.	John Conness	February, 1863	Democrat	Sacramento
7.	Eugene Casserly	December, 1867	Democrat	San Francisco
8.	John S. Hager	December, 1873	Democrat	San Francisco
9.	Newton Booth	December, 1873	Republican	Sacramento
10.	John F. Miller	January, 1881	Republican	Napa
11.	George Hearst	March, 1886[1]	Democrat	San Francisco
12.	Abram Pease Williams	August, 1886	Republican	San Francisco
11.	George Hearst	January, 1887	Democrat	San Francisco
13.	Charles N. Felton	March, 1891	Republican	San Francisco
14.	Stephen M. White	January, 1893	Democrat	Los Angeles
15.	Thomas R. Bard	January, 1900	Republican	Hueneme
16.	Frank P. Flint	January, 1905	Republican	Los Angeles
17.	John D. Works	January, 1911	Republican	Los Angeles
18.	Hiram W. Johnson	November, 1916	Republican	San Francisco
19.	William F. Knowland	August, 1945[1]	Republican	Oakland
20.	Clair Engle	November, 1958	Democrat	Red Bluff
21.	Pierre Salinger	August, 1964[1]	Democrat	San Francisco
22.	George Murphy	November, 1964	Republican	Beverly Hills

·Date of appointment by the Governor of the State of California. Other dates for the United States Senators indicate month and year of election. United States Senators were elected by the Legislature, 1849–1913, and were elected directly by the voters thereafter.

United States Senators from the State of California (Seat "B")

NO.	NAME	DATE	PARTY	HOME TOWN
1.	William M. Gwin	December, 1849	Democrat	San Francisco
2.	James A. McDougall	March, 1861	Democrat	San Francisco
3.	Cornelius C. Cole	December, 1865	Republican	Sacramento
4.	Aaron A. Sargent	December, 1871	Republican	Nevada City
5.	James T. Farley	December, 1877	Democrat	Jackson
6.	Leland Stanford	January, 1885	Republican	Sacramento
7.	George C. Perkins	July, 1893[1]	Republican	Oroville
8.	James D. Phelan	November, 1914	Democrat	San Francisco
9.	Samuel M. Shortridge	November, 1920	Republican	Menlo Park
10.	William Gibbs McAdoo	November, 1932	Democrat	Los Angeles
11.	Thomas M. Storke	November, 1938[1]	Democrat	Santa Barbara
12.	Sheridan Downey	November, 1938	Democrat	Atherton
13.	Richard M. Nixon	November, 1950	Republican	Whittier
14.	Thomas Kuchel	December, 1952[1]	Republican	Anaheim
15.	Alan Cranston	November, 1968	Democrat	Los Altos

[1]Date of appointment by the Governor of the State of California. Other dates for the United States Senators indicate month and year of election. United States Senators were elected by the Legislature, 1849–1913, and were elected directly by the voters thereafter.

Presidents Pro Tempore
of the State Senate

NO.	NAME	DATE	PARTY	HOME COUNTY
1.	E. Kirby Chamberlin	December, 1849	Democrat	San Diego
2.	David C. Broderick[1]	January, 1851	Democrat	San Francisco
3.	Elcan Heydenfeldt[1]	January, 1851	Whig	San Francisco
4.	Benjamin F. Keene	February, 1852	Democrat	El Dorado
5.	Royal T. Sprague	January, 1855	Democrat	Shasta
6.	Delos R. Ashley	January, 1856	American	Monterey
7.	Samuel H. Dosh	January, 1857	Democrat	Shasta
8.	Samuel A. Merritt	January, 1858	Democrat	Mariposa
9.	William B. Dickinson	January, 1859	Democrat	El Dorado
10.	Isaac N. Quinn[2]	January, 1860	Democrat	Tuolumne
11.	Charles J. Lansing[2]	January, 1860	Democrat	Nevada
12.	Pablo de la Guerra[3]	January, 1861	Democrat	Santa Barbara
13.	Richard Irwin[3]	January, 1861	Democrat	Plumas
14.	James McM. Shafter	January, 1862	Republican	San Francisco
15.	A. M. Crane	January, 1863	Union	Alameda
16.	R. Burnell	December, 1864	Union	Amador
17.	Stephen P. Wright	December, 1865	Union	Del Norte
18.	Lansing B. Mizner	December, 1867	Union	Solano
19.	Edward J. Lewis	December, 1869	Democrat	Tehama
20.	James T. Farley	December, 1871	Democrat	Amador
21.	William Irwin[4]	December, 1873	Democrat	Siskiyou
22.	Benjamin F. Tuttle	December, 1875	Democrat	Sonoma
23.	Edward J. Lewis	December, 1877	Democrat	Tehama
24.	George F. Baker	January, 1880	Republican	Santa Clara
25.	William Johnston	January, 1881	Republican	Sacramento
26.	Reginaldo Del Valle	January, 1883	Democrat	Los Angeles
27.	Benjamin Knight, Jr.	January, 1885	Democrat	Santa Cruz
28.	Stephen M. White	January, 1887	Democrat	Los Angeles
29.	Thomas Fraser	January, 1891	Republican	El Dorado
30.	R. B. Carpenter	January, 1893	Republican	Los Angeles
31.	Thomas Flint, Jr.	January, 1895	Republican	San Benito
32.	Edward I. Wolfe	January, 1905	Republican	San Francisco
33.	Albert E. Boynton	January, 1911	Republican	Butte
34.	Newton W. Thompson	January, 1915	Republican	Los Angeles
35.	Arthur H. Breed	January, 1917	Republican	Alameda

NO.	NAME	DATE	PARTY	HOME COUNTY
36.	William P. Rich	January, 1935	Republican	Yuba
37.	Jerrold L. Seawell	January, 1939	Republican	Placer
38.	William P. Rich	January, 1941	Republican	Yuba
39.	Jerrold L. Seawell	January, 1943	Republican	Placer
40.	Harold J. "Butch" Powers	January, 1947	Republican	Modoc
41.	Clarence C. Ward	March, 1954	Republican	Santa Barbara
42.	Ben Hulse	June, 1955	Republican	Imperial
43.	Hugh M. Burns	January, 1957	Democrat	Fresno
44.	Howard Way	May, 1969	Republican	Tulare
45.	Jack Schrade	February, 1970	Republican	San Diego

[1]In January of 1851, when John McDougal became Governor, David C. Broderick was elected President of the Senate. Elcan Heydenfeldt was elected President Pro Tempore of the Senate.

[2]In January of 1860, when John G. Downey became Governor, Isaac N. Quinn was elected President of the Senate. Charles J. Lansing was elected President Pro Tempore of the Senate.

[3]In January of 1861, the second year of John G. Downey's term, Pablo de la Guerra was elected President of the Senate. Richard Irwin was elected President Pro Tempore of the Senate.

[4]In February of 1875, when Romualdo Pacheco, Jr. became Governor, the Legislature was not in session, and no President of the Senate was elected. William Irwin continued as President Pro Tempore of the Senate until his inauguration as Governor in December of 1875.

Presidents Pro Tempore, 1849–1970, by section and political party:

North	36
South	9
Republican	19
Democrat	20
Union	4
American	1
Whig	1

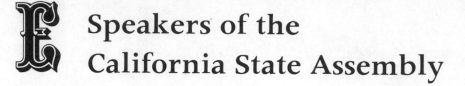

Speakers of the
California State Assembly

NO.	NAME	DATE	PARTY	HOME COUNTY
1.	Thomas J. White	December, 1849	Democrat	Sacramento
2.	John Bigler	February, 1850	Democrat	Sacramento
3.	Richard P. Hammond	January, 1852	Democrat	San Joaquin
4.	Isaac B. Wall	January, 1853	Democrat	San Francisco
5.	Charles S. Fairfax	January, 1854	Democrat	Yuba
6.	William W. Stow	January, 1855	Whig	Santa Cruz
7.	James T. Farley	January, 1856	American	Amador
8.	Elwood T. Beatty	January, 1857	Democrat	Calaveras
9.	N. E. Whitesides	January, 1858	Democrat	Yuba
10.	William C. Stratton	January, 1859	Democrat	Placer
11.	Philip Moore	January, 1860	Democrat	Nevada
12.	R. Burnell	January, 1861	Democrat	Amador
13.	George Barstow	January, 1862	Republican	San Francisco
14.	Timothy N. Machin	January, 1863	Union	Mono
15.	William H. Sears	December, 1863	Union	Nevada
16.	John Yule	December, 1865	Union	Placer
17.	Caias T. Ryland	December, 1867	Democrat	Santa Clara
18.	George H. Rogers	December, 1869	Democrat	San Francisco
19.	Thomas B. Shannon	December, 1871	Republican	San Francisco
20.	Morris M. Estee	December, 1873	Republican	San Francisco
21.	G. J. Carpenter	December, 1875	Democrat	El Dorado
22.	Campbell P. Berry	December, 1877	Democrat	Sutter
23.	Jabez F. Cowdery	January, 1880	Republican	San Francisco
24.	William H. Parks	January, 1881	Republican	Yuba
25.	Hugh M. La Rue	January, 1883	Democrat	Sacramento
26.	William H. Parks	January, 1885	Republican	Yuba
27.	William H. Jordan	January, 1887	Republican	Alameda
28.	Robert Howe	January, 1889	Democrat	Sonoma
29.	Frank L. Coombs	January, 1891	Republican	Napa
30.	Frank H. Gould	January, 1893	Democrat	Merced
31.	John C. Lynch	January, 1895	Republican	San Bernardino
32.	Frank L. Coombs	January, 1897	Republican	Napa
33.	Howard E. Wright	January, 1899	Republican	Alameda
34.	Alden Anderson	January, 1899	Republican	Solano
35.	Cornelius W. Pendleton	January, 1901	Republican	Los Angeles

NO.	NAME	DATE	PARTY	HOME COUNTY
36.	Arthur G. Fisk	January, 1903	Republican	San Francisco
37.	Frank C. Prescott	January, 1905	Republican	San Bernardino
38.	Robert L. Beardslee	January, 1907	Republican	San Joaquin
39.	Philip A. Stanton	January, 1909	Republican	Los Angeles
40.	A. H. Hewitt	January, 1911	Republican	Yuba
41.	C. C. Young	January, 1913	Republican	Alameda
42.	Henry W. Wright	January, 1919	Republican	Los Angeles
43.	Frank F. Merriam	January, 1923	Republican	Los Angeles
44.	Edgar C. Levey	January, 1927	Republican	San Francisco
45.	Walter J. Little	January, 1933	Republican	Los Angeles
46.	F. C. Clowdsley	September, 1934	Democrat	San Joaquin
47.	Edward Craig	January, 1935	Republican	Orange
48.	William Moseley Jones	January, 1937	Democrat	Los Angeles
49.	Paul Peek	January, 1939	Democrat	Los Angeles
50.	Gordon H. Garland	January, 1940	Democrat	Tulare
51.	Charles W. Lyon	January, 1943	Republican	Los Angeles
52.	Sam L. Collins	January, 1947	Republican	Orange
53.	James W. Silliman	January, 1953	Republican	Monterey
54.	Luther H. Lincoln	January, 1955	Republican	Alameda
55.	Ralph M. Brown	January, 1959	Democrat	Stanislaus
56.	Jess Unruh	September, 1961	Democrat	Los Angeles
57.	Robert T. Monagan	January, 1969	Republican	San Joaquin

Speakers, 1849–1970, by section and political party:

North	44
South	13
Republican	29
Democrat	23
Union	3
American	1
Whig	1

Tom Bradley's Acceptance Speech

Tom Bradley never gave this speech because he was defeated in the 1969 Los Angeles mayoralty race by incumbent Mayor Yorty.

Tonight we have won a great victory. It is a victory not of a man, but of an idea. It is a victory not of partisanship, but of principle. And it is a victory not of the few, but of the many. To all of you who made this possible by voting for me and working in my campaign, my deep thanks. Tens of thousands of men and women, young people and children of all faiths, black and white, worked together to fashion our victory. You did a magnificent job. To all of you who did not vote for me, let me say this: The election is behind us. The problem of governing our city is ahead of us. To make our system work, all of us must pull together. I ask you to join me in this effort. Let all of us here tonight pledge an end to the bitterness and divisiveness that often marked the campaign. If our campaign proved anything it is the idea that our democratic system *is* capable of peaceful change, that it is open to all and that people do not live by fear but by hope, not by hate but by love. I have believed that all my life. And I have lived by that belief. I shall try to govern Los Angeles guided by that belief. I want all of you to help me achieve that objective. Thank you again. You were wonderful, all of you.

~INDEX~

457

Index

Barry, James H.: opponent of Haskell, 101; supports Cator, 102; in 1896 campaign, 120
Barry, John, 109
Bartleson, John, 8
Bartlett, Washington: died while Governor, 12, 92; elected Mayor of San Francisco, 92; elected Governor (1886), 92
Baruch, Bernard M., 206
Bay Area Alliance, Republican volunteer organization, 392
Bean, Walton, historian, on Mooney trial, 184
Bear Flag, 4
Bee, Carlos, 357
Beek, Joseph A., 168
Beerstecher, Charles J., at Constitutional Convention of 1878–1879, 86; New Constitution Party supporter, 88; on Railroad Commission, 89
Beesemyer, Gilbert H., 223–224
Beilenson, Anthony C., 431
Belcher, Isaac S., 86
Bell, Theodore A.: gubernatorial candidate (1906), 149; gubernatorial candidate (1910), 159–160; Democratic leader, 193; gubernatorial candidate (1918), 195–196
Bellamy, Edward, 100
Belshaw, C. M.: anti-Southern Pacific Republican, 146; introduction of primary measure, 155; as potential gubernatorial candidate (1910), 158
Benham, Calhoun, 30
Bennett, Nathaniel, 88
Berman, Jacob (Jack Bennett), 222–223
Berryhill, Clare L., 435
Betts, Bert, 236
Bidwell, John: journey to California, 8; role in National Conventions of 1860 and 1864, 30; declines nomination (1867), 33, 56–57; gubernatorial candidate (1875), 34, 64–65
"Bifurcated session", 170
Bigler, John: reelected Governor, 12; becomes Governor, 15

"Big Six" states, 408–415
Billings, Warren, 184
Blacks: role in early California, 5–6; discrimination against, 6–7; begin to gain rights, 7; nineteenth century leaders, 7; first Black legislator, 196; Channing Phillips as political leader, 421; population growth of, 422–423; in California politics, 423–428
Blaine, James G., 410
Blake, George H., 42
Blake, Maurice C., 91
Bledsoe, A. J., 115
"Blue Ribbon Commission" on reapportionment, 355
Board of Equalization, 332
Boddy, Manchester: liberal Democrat, 241; Democratic primary candidate for U.S. Senator, 313
Bonelli, William G., 332
Bones, John W., 83
Booth, Newton: resigned while Governor, 12; "Long-hair" state senatorial candidate (1865), 56; becomes Governor, 60; becomes U.S. Senator, 34, 62–64; opposition to Hayes' appointment, 91
Booth, Willis H., 187
Boroughs, Reuben, 274
Bowers, W. W., 109
"Braceros," 405–406
Bradley, Don L.: role in election of 1962, 347; Salinger campaign manager, 353; as Democratic Party official, 427–429
Bradley, Thomas, 426
Brathwaite, Yvonne W., 425
Breckenridge Democrats: election of 1861, 25; defeat in 1861, 52
Breckenridge, John, 25
Bretz, Arnold, 110
Broderick, David C.: sketch of early career, 15–17; achieves control of Democratic Party, 19; feud with Gwin, 19–23; as Anti-Lecompton Democrat, 20–21; duel with Terry, 21; dies while U.S. Senator, 24; Republican Party leanings, 49–50

458

Index

California Democratic Council: endorses Richard Richards, 334; endorsements in election of 1958, 339; opposition to crossfiling, 342; endorsement of Brown, 1962, 346; convention of 1964, 352; in 1966 election, 358; origins, organization, and function, 380–382; purpose, 382; endorsements in 1954, 382–384; results in 1954, 384; endorsements in 1956, 384–385; endorsements in 1958, 385–386; criticism of, 387; turning point in 1964, 389; controversy over Casady, 393–394; aftermath of 1968 election, 394

California in national politics: weakness of, 400–402; increasing importance of, 402; role in 1932 Democratic National Convention, 413–414; in recent presidential elections, 415–416; national office holders and appointees, 435; California in national politics, cause of lack of influence, 436–437

California Plan, 391–392

California political parties. *See* Political parties, (California)

California Real Estate Association: opposed to Rumford Act, 349; proposes Proposition 14, 351; campaign to repeal Rumford Act, 424

California Republican Assembly: 1954 endorsements, 330; origins and purposes, 376; endorsements in 1942, 377–378; endorsements in 1950, 377–378; endorsements in 1954, 378–379; endorsements in 1958, 379–380; role in Knowland–Knight fight, 379–380; take-over by conservatives, 388–389

California Republican League: organization, 359; influence, 393

California Water Plan: bond issue, 343; passage of Bond Proposition, 343; in 1960, 345

California Weekly: Lincoln–Roosevelt League journal, 156; on Legislature of 1909, 158

Californios: role in politics, 4; and the Republican Party, 45–46

Cameron, George T., 201

Caminetti, Anthony, 170

Campaigns, Inc. *See* Whitaker and Baxter

Campbell, Alexander, 88

Cannon, Marion: on political role of Farmers' Alliance, 103; Democratic endorsement of, 108; elected Assemblyman in 1892, 109; support of White's candidacy, 110; expulsion from Populist Party, 110–112

Capital punishment issue, 332–333, 344–345

Carlson, Mrs. Virginia, 336

Carnahan, H. L., 192–193

Carpenter, Richard L., 355

Carrillo, Jose Antonio, 4

Carson, Kit, 8

Carter, Jesse W.: as La Follette supporter, 208; Garner supporter, 239; on switch to Roosevelt in 1932, 249; role at 1932 Democratic National convention, 413–414

Casady, Simon: as President of California Democratic Council, 358; as critic of Vietnam policy, 393–394

Cass, Lewis, 410

Casserly, Eugene: resigned while U.S. Senator, 24, 34; elected U.S. Senator in 1868, 34; at Constitutional Convention of 1878–1879, 86

Castle, Curtis H.: Populist nominee (1896), 120; elected to Congress in 1896, 121

Cator, Thomas V.: role at Nationalist Convention, 102; runs as reform candidate, 102; as Populist leader, 107; Maguire–Cator feud, 108–109; role in Populist Party (1893–1898), 112; on free silver, 112–114, 117; Bryan supporter in 1896, 119; role in Democratic Populist fusion, 120; joins Republicans, 122

CDC. *See* California Democratic Council

Central Pacific Railroad: as a political issue, 60, 77; discharges workers, 70

461

Index

Cox, James M., 197
CRA. *See* California Republican Assembly
Crail, Joe, 230–231
Cranston, Alan: elected Controller, 236, 251; election of 1958, 339; in election of 1964, 352–353; organization of CDC, 382; in election of 1964, 389; in 1968 election, 403; sketch of political career, 431; in election of 1962, 431–432
"Creative society", Reagan campaign slogan, 362
Creel, George: as McAdoo supporter, 205; as Garner supporter, 238; and Democratic patronage, 265; as gubernatorial candidate in 1934, 266–267; in primary campaign in 1934, 273; repudiation of Sinclair, 276
Crime study under Warren, 321–322
Crocker, Charles: early Republican, 44; "spite" fence, 77
Crocker, Edwin B., 44
Crocker, William H.: as conservative Republican, 177, 198; in election of 1916, 186–188; as Republican National Committeeman, 210; as Hoover delegate in 1932, 237
Cross, Laurance L., 383
Crossfiling: effect on Democratic Party, 177; origins and significance, 171, 374; definition of, 193; modifications of, 193; effect in 1932, 252; and Earl Warren, 302; during Warren era, 306, 308–309; importance of 1940–1952, 308–309; in 1946 election, 311; importance in 1950 election, 313; issue on ballot in 1952, 314–315; effect of mandatory party identification, 330, 384; in 1958 primary, 340; abolition, 341–342; influence on party organization, 371, 374–375; survey of use and results, 374–375; incumbent advantage, 375; effect on party control of nominations, 375
Crown, Robert, 357

Curry, Charles F., 159
Curry, John, 50
Curtin, John B.: unsuccessful gubernatorial candidate in 1914, 174; gubernatorial candidate against Hiram Johnson in 1916, 178
Curtis, Charles, 210
Cutter, W. M., 141
Cutting, Bronson, 246

Darrow, Clarence, 181–182
Davis, John W., 207
Davis, W. H., 158
Day, John G.: Workingmen's Party officer, 77; addresses workingmen's groups, 77–78
Dayton, William L., 26
Debs, Eugene: organizer of Socialist Party of America, 122; presidential candidate, 179
Deavers, Bryan, 430
de la Guerra, Pablo, 4
Dellum, Ronald V., 442
Democratic Party: early organization, 14–15; dominance in state politics to 1879, 15; state convention (1854), 19; Lecompton faction in Legislature (1860), 24; early intraparty bickering, 26; tenure of Governors and U.S. Senators, 28–29; national convention (1864), 30; during Civil War, 30–31; supports "short-hair" policies, 33; split in 1860, 50; "fusion" with Populist Party, 108, 119–120; strength in 1880's and 1890's, 109; on free silver, 116–117; election of 1896, 117–120, 130; state convention (1906), 149; state convention (1908), 157; state convention (1910), 159–160; during Progressive years, 177–179, 193; election of 1918, 195–196; election of 1920, 196–197; weak role (1894–1934), 202–204; centers of strength in 1920's, 202–204; national convention (1924), 205–207; factionalism during 1920's,

Index

Dutton, Fred, 341
Dymally, Mervyn M., 425

Earl, E. T.: as publisher of *Los Angeles Express*, 155; TR backer, 172; and other Progressives, 173
Edgerton, Henry, 91
Edson, E. B., 140
Edson, Katherine Philips, 169
Eisenhower, Dwight D.: picks Nixon as running mate (1952), 305; victory in California (1952), 316; in election of 1956, 333–334; role in election of 1958, 341
Election: of 1848, 410; of 1849, 9–10; of 1856, 26, 46–49; of 1857, 49–50; of 1859, 50; of 1860, 25, 30, 50–52; of 1861, 52; of 1863, 25, 30, 54; of 1864, 30, 54; of 1867, 33–34, 56–59; of 1868, 34; of 1871, 60; of 1875, 34–35, 64–66; of Constitutional delegates (1878), 84; of 1879, 88–89; of 1880, 91; of 1884, 92, 410; of 1886, 92; of 1888, 410–411; of 1890, 101–102; of 1892, 107–110; of 1894, 112–116; of 1896, 116–122, 128, 130; of 1898, 133, 137; of 1900, 137–139; of 1902, 139–143; of 1904, 143, 146; of 1906, 146, 148–149; of 1908, 156–157; of 1910, 158–160; of 1912, 172–173; of 1914, 174–175; of 1916, 186–189, 402, 411–412; of 1918, 193–196; of 1924, 207–208; of 1926, 208; of 1928, 208–210; of 1930, 217–218; of 1932, 230–264, 413–414; of 1934, 272–281; of 1936, 281–283; of 1938, 287–289; of 1940, 291–292; of 1944, 309; of 1946, 309–312; of 1948, 312–313, 412–413; of 1950, 313–314; of 1952, 314–316; of 1954, 328–331; of 1956, 333–334; of 1958, 337–341, role of CDS endorsements, 386–387; of 1960, 343–345, 397–398, 402–407, 415; of 1962, 345–348, 429; of 1964, 388–390; of 1966, 357–364; of 1968, 394, analysis of, 402,

Election (*continued*)
415–422, 430–432; of 1970 (primary), 438–442
Electoral college, 400
Elevator, The, 56
Ellery, Nathaniel, 159
Elliott, John B.: McAdoo supporter at 1920 Democratic National Convention, 197; as McAdoo supporter (1924), 205; as Garner supporter, 239; predicts Garner victory, 243–244; opposes Sharkey oil bill, 244
Employers Council (San Francisco, 1901), 131
End Poverty in California. *See* EPIC Movement
End Poverty League: as EPIC organization, 273–274; campaign finances, 274; on presidential delegation (1936), 282
Engle, Clair: from nonmetropolitan area, 28; election of 1958, 236, 251, 339–341; elected to Congress, 309; endorsed by CDC, 385–386; illness and election of 1964, 351–352, 389, 431; death while U.S. Senator, 24, 353
Engelbright, Harry, 258
EPIC Movement: spread of, 266–267; impact on Democratic registration, 267; plan, 273; basis for rapid growth, 274; End Poverty League ticket (1934), 274–275; results of primary (1934), 275–276
Eshleman, John M.: sketch of, 169; as Lt. Governor, 192
Espee. *See* Southern Pacific Company
Estee, Morris M.: at Constitutional Convention, 1878–1879, 86; defeat in 1882, 91; gubernatorial candidate in 1894, 113
Ewing, Calvin, 115

Fair Employment Practices Act, 341–342
Fair Housing. *See* Rumford Act
Farley, James A.: as FDR supporter, 239, 241; role at 1932 Democratic national convention, 247–250; in campaign of 1934, 280

464

Index

Garrigus, Charles, 356

Geary, John W., 15

George, Henry: author of *Progress and Poverty*, 71; on Denis Kearney, 75; refuses Workingmen's Party nomination, 84; on Constitution of 1879, 88

Giannini, A. P.: role in California banking, 213–215; opposition to Governor Richardson, 214; and J. F. T. O'Connor, 265; and election of 1934, 280

Gibson, Luther, 349

Gillett, James N.: from nonmetropolitan area, 28; supporter of Flint, 139; gubernatorial candidate in 1906, 146, 148–149

Gleason, Mrs. Lucille, 310

Glenn, Hugh J., 89

Gold discovery, 9

Goldwater, Barry: presidential aspirant in 1960, 343; endorsement by unofficial party organizations, 388; seeks southern votes, 415

Good Government Fund, 131

Good Government League (GGL), 131

Gorham, George C.: Union Party gubernatorial candidate (1867), 33, 56–58; opposes Chinese immigration, 33

Governor, office of: length of term, 11–12; power in early years, 28, 30

Governors: party affiliations, 12; survey of, 12–13; also as U.S. Senators, 12–13; in diplomatic posts, 13; on California state budgets, 200–201; use of veto power, 318; as potential presidential candidates, 435

Governor's conferences, 321

Graves, Richard P.: gubernatorial aspirant (1954), 328–329; endorsement by CDC, 383

Gray, William, 359

Great Depression: effect in California, 215; effect on California agriculture, 215–217; effect on 1932 election, 236–237, 262

Greenback Labor Party, 91–92

Greene, Bill, 425

Gregg, A. J., 113

Gregg, James E., 308

Grenner, Gustav, 177

Gwin, William M.: selected as U.S. Senator (1849), 10–11; early life and career, 17; feud with Broderick, 19–23; as Chivalry Democrat, 20–21; joins the Confederate Army, 22; imprisonment, 25

Hagan, Harlan, 314

Hager, John S.: appointed U.S. Senator, 24, 34; resolution to 1866 Legislature, 32; at Constitutional Convention of 1878–1879, 86

Haggerty, Cornelius, 339

Hahn, Kenneth: not endorsed by CDC, 385–386; in 1970 election, 439–442

Haight, Henry H.: becomes Governor, 33–34; opposition to Fifteenth Amendment, 34; becomes Governor, 57–58; defeated in 1871, 60

Haight, Raymond L.: defeated in primary in 1934, 267; gubernatorial candidate in 1934, 272, 278, 280; and Upton Sinclair, 278, 280

Hale, Marshall: as Hoover supporter in 1928, 209; as Hoover delegate in 1932, 237; on results of presidential primary of 1932, 244–246

Ham and Eggs: pension plan, 285–286; opposed by Republicans, 287; Olson position in 1938, 289

Hancock, Winfield S., 91

Hardesty, Cecil, 347

Harding, Warren G., 198

Hargreaves, Mrs. Grace, 239

Harmer, John L. 439–442

Harriman, E. H., 143, 156

Harriman, Job, 179–180

Harrison, Benjamin, 410–411

Harrison, Maurice F.: elected Democratic State Chairman in 1932, 210, 258; and Democratic patronage, 265

Harrison, Pat, 248

Haskell, Burnett, 101–102

Index

Johnson, Hiram W. (*continued*)
Republican League, 172; the
election of 1912, 172–173; disagreement with Heney, 174; re-
elected as Governor (1914), 174;
and unionism, 181; investigation
of San Diego "free speech" fight,
182–183; and Wheatland Riot,
183; anti-Japanese sentiment, 185;
Alien Land Law, 185–186; endorsement of Hughes in 1916,
186–187; Virginia Hotel incident,
188; Governorship at an end, 189;
resignation as Governor, 192; and
Direct Primary Law of 1909, 193;
opposition to William Stephens,
193; and Immigration Act of
1924, 204; reelection as U.S.
Senator (1928), 209–210; Republican antagonists in 1920's,
210; opposition to Hoover, 214;
progressive dilemma in 1932,
246; supports FDR in 1932, 259;
reelection by crossfiling, 268;
opinion on Republicans and
Townsend Plan, 285; reelection
in 1940, 292; vice presidential
candidate (1912), 304; use of
crossfiling, 375; in 1916 election,
402, 411–412
Johnson, J. A., 107
Johnson, James, 32
Johnson, John F., 214
Johnson, John Neely: becomes American
Party Governor in 1855, 11, 26
Johnson, Lyndon B., 418
Joint Special Committee of Congress to
Investigate Chinese Immigration,
72–73
Jones, John P., 58
Jordan, Mrs. Alberta, 442
Jordan, Frank C., 195
Jordan, Frank M.: elected Sec. of State
(1946), 311; reelected (1954), 331;
reelected in 1958, 341; reelected
(1966), 363–364; in election of
1962, 429
Julian, Chauncey C., 221–223
Julian Petroleum Corporation, 221–223

"July Riots" of 1877, 73–74

Kalloch, Isaac S.: feud with Charles de
Young, 89; attempts to impeach,
89–90; defeat as San Francisco
Mayor, 91
Kalloch, Milton, 89
Kamp, Joseph, 340
Kansas-Nebraska Act, 40
Kearney, Denis: early career and beliefs,
75; becomes anti-Chinese, 75;
Workingmen's Party officer, 77;
addresses workingmen's groups,
77–79; arrests, 79; at San Jose,
81–82; with Benjamin F. Butler,
84–85; support of Constitution of
1879, 88; president of Working-
men's Party, 88–89; alliance with
Isaac Kalloch, 89; later career, 93
Keesling, Francis V.: as Republican vice
chairman, 177; role in 1916
election, 188
Kefauver, Estes, 314
Kelly, Earl Lee, 309
Kennedy, John F.: loses Calif. to Nixon,
345; election of 1960, 397–398,
402–407; religious factor in 1960
election, 405
Kennedy, Joseph P., 249
Kennedy, Robert F.: role in campaign
of 1966, 362; in election of 1968,
416–420; assassination, 420
Kenny, Bernard F., 86
Kenny, John J., 86
Kenny, Robert W.: and election of 1930,
218; campaign of 1932, 231;
political ambitions, 289–290; on
Japanese relocation, 294; elected
Attorney General, 236, 296, 308;
1946 gubernatorial campaign, 308,
310–311; supports Independent
Progressive Party, 313; on California political reforms, 323
Kent, William: as LaFollette supporter,
172; role in Progressive Party,
173; U.S. Senate candidate, 198
Kerns, Thomas J.: Populist candidate for
Assembly, 108; "Big Eight" episode, 110

Index

Index

Index

Nixon, Richard M. (*continued*)
1968, 402, 407–408, 416–422, 430–432; sets political record, 436
"Nixon Fund", 305
Non-Partisan City Central Committee of One Hundred (Los Angeles), 131
Nonpartisan elections: introduction, 171; impact on political parties, 368–369
Nonpartisan offices, 193
Nonpartisans (1878–1879): organized, 84; control of Constitutional Convention of 1878–1879, 84–85
Nonpartisanship: in election of 1942, 294, 296; and Earl Warren, 301
Norris, George, 246
The North Californian (Oroville), 48–49
Nunes, Joseph A.: as early Republican leader, 43; slavery opponent, 46
Nye, Gerald, 246

Oakland Tribune: in Republican newspaper triumvirate, 176, 201; support of Friend Richardson, 200
O'Brien, Charles A., 440–442
O'Connor, James F. T.: as McAdoo supporter, 205; as FDR southern California campaign manager, 242; becomes U.S. Comptroller of Currency, 265; sketch of political career, 266; refusal to run for Governor, 266; role in election of 1934, 280
Odegard, Peter: at CDC convention (1954), 384; seeks CDC endorsement (1958), 385–386
O'Donnell, Charles C.: Chinese investigation witness, 73; addresses Workingmen's groups, 78; makes address, 81
Oil industry: role in Calif., 212; effect on Great Depression, 215; speculation, 221; Sharkey oil bill, 244; opposes severance tax, 342
Older, Fremont: role in Progressive Party, 173; critic of Mooney trial, 184; as liberal Democrat, 241
Olin, Spencer, Jr.: characterization of

Olin, Spencer, Jr. (*continued*)
Hiram Johnson, 167; on election of 1914, 174
Olson, Culbert L.: Democratic Governor, 12, 236; as La Follette supporter, 208; as liberal Democrat, 241; EPIC endorsement, 275; becomes Democratic State Chairman, 276; sketch of career, 281; as legislator, 281; conflict with McAdoo, 281–282; opponent of Townsend plan, 285; in election of 1938, 287–288; administration, 289–292; personal limitations, 290–291; pardon of Mooney, 291; illness, 291; and reform proposals, 291; relations with Legislature, 291, 293; role in Democratic presidential primary in 1940, 292; becomes Democratic National Committeeman, 292; and defense measures, 292–293; and Japanese evacuation, 294; defeat, 294, 296; as partisan, 300; feud with Warren, 302–303; use of veto, 318
Omaha Platform of Populist Party (1892), 112–113, 117
Otis, Harrison Gray: publisher of *Los Angeles Times,* 139, 201; as Flint supporter, 139; at Republican convention of 1904, 143; at Republican convention of 1908, 156–157; characterized by Hiram Johnson, 167–168; and *Los Angeles Times* bombing, 181; anti-IWW speech, 182–183
Otto, Richard, 274

Pacheco, Romualdo, Jr.: becomes Governor, 12, 34–35; elective and appointive offices held, 13; as Governor, 28, 64; sketch of later career, 35; candidate for Lt. Governor, 64
Pacific Outlook, 156
Pacific Railroad: as political issue, 44–45; legislation of 1865, 54
Pacific Union, 102
"Package deal" (1946), 310

474

Index

Index

Richardson, Friend W. (*continued*)
election of 1930, 217–218; as
Superintendent of Banks, 283; use
of veto, 318
Richardson, Ralph, 346–348
Richfield Oil Company, 224–225
Riles, Wilson C., 442
Riley, Bennett: calls Constitutional Convention of 1849, 9; appointment of
Burnett, 13
Riley, Harry B., 377
Riley, Harry E., 311
Roach, Philip A., 76
Roberts, Frederick M., 196, 424
Roberts, Owen J., 294
Roberts Report, 294
Robinson, Henry M., 223
Robinson, Joseph, 210
Robinson and Company, 325
Rockefeller, Nelson: presidential aspirant
in 1960, 343; 1964 defeat, 398; in
election of 1968, 416–422
Rodda, Albert S., 34
Rogers, Will: comments on Democratic
Party, 202; on McAdoo supporters,
205–206
Rogers, Will, Jr., 311
Rolph, James, Jr.: Governor, 12; as
gubernatorial candidate (1918),
193–196; at 1928 Republican
national convention, 209; elected
Governor, 210, 217–218; as Governor, 219–220; as leader of
Hoover delegation, 237; death of,
265
Romney, George, 416–422
Roney, Frank: as Workingmen's Party
officer, 83; as Kearney adversary,
83–84
Roosevelt, Franklin Delano (FDR): as vice
presidential nominee, 197; nomination of A. E. Smith, 210; in election of 1932, 241, 258–259; and
Hiram Johnson, 268; conference
with Sinclair, 276; supports McAdoo in 1938, 287; and Democratic presidential primary of 1940,
292; and Japanese relocation, 294;
Calif. strength in 1944, 309; Cali-

Roosevelt, Franklin Delano (FDR) (*con't*)
fornia's role in 1932 nomination of,
413–414
Roosevelt, James: comment on 1946
election, 312; as gubernatorial candidate, 313–314; as U.S. senatorial
aspirant, 352, 389
Roosevelt, Theodore (TR): in election of
1904, 139, 146; 1911 political tour,
172; and the election of 1912, 172–
173, 398, 414; rejects nomination
in 1916, 186
"Rotten Eggs Campaign", 47
Rowell, Chester H.: editor of *Fresno
Morning Republican*, 132; as
officer in Lincoln-Roosevelt
League, 155–156; on Harrison
Gray Otis, 157; role in selecting
Hiram Johnson, 158; as TR supporter, 172; as senatorial candidate, 174; anti-Japanese sentiment,
185; plan to unite Progressives and
Republicans, 186; as chairman of
Republican State Central Committee, 188; and Johnson's plans for
his gubernatorial candidacy, 193;
in Calif. Anti-Saloon League, 194;
in Progressive Voters League, 198;
as supporter of Phelan, 199; at
1928 Republican national convention, 209
Rowell, Dr. Chester: sketch of, 133; as
Bard supporter, 137
Ruef, Abe: on Republican Executive
Committee, 129; as political boss,
132; in 1902 Republican convention, 140; alliance with Hayes
brothers, 143–146; in 1906 Republican convention, 148; grand
jury indictment of, 149, 155
Rumford, William Byron, 349, 424
Rumford Act: passes Legislature, 350–
357, 424; initiative to repeal, 351
Runyon, Damon, 249

Sacramento Union: 1865 description of
Democratic Party, 30–31; supports
Newton Booth, 62
Salinger, Pierre: appointed to U.S. Senate,

478

Index

Index

Wood, Robert G., 435
Workingmen's Clubs, 77
Workingmen's Party (California): origins, 70; Kearney as leader, 75; organization and platform, 77; parade, 79–81; intraparty dissension, 81; San Jose meeting, 81–82; branches, 82; first state convention, 82; early election victories, 82–83; nomination conventions, 84; role at Constitutional Convention, 85–87; zenith of power, 88; on Constitution of 1879, 88–89; decline of, 89; significance, 93–94
Workingmen's Party of the United States, 73–74
Workingmen's Protective Association, 72
Workingmen's Trade and Labor Union, 75–76
Works, John Downey: U.S. Senatorial candidate, 158–159; on recall of judges, 171; as regular Republican, 176
Wozencraft, Oliver M., 88
Wright, Lloyd, 429

Yorty, Samuel W.: investigation of Communists in state government, 290; Democratic U.S. Senatorial aspirant in 1956, 334; in election of

Yorty, Samuel W. (continued)
1966, 357–360; and the CDC, 383–385; in 1969 Los Angeles election, 426; in 1970 election, 438–442
Young, C. C.: as Speaker of the Assembly, 170; author of crossfiling measure, 171; as candidate for Lt. Governor in 1918, 194; favors Prohibition Amendment, 196; progressive Republican nominee of 1926, 198; submits first complete budget, 200–201; and election of 1926, 208; as Hoover supporter in 1928, 209; support of A. P. Giannini, 214; and election of 1930, 217–218; defeated in primary election in 1934, 267
Young, John P.: on Constitution of 1879, 88; supporter of Silver Convention, 116
Young, Milton K.: as gubernatorial candidate in 1930, 210; defeat by Rolph, 218; as Garner supporter, 239; as gubernatorial candidate in 1934, 267
Young Republicans: 1963 take-over by conservatives, 387–388; effectiveness, 393
Younger, Evelle, 439–442